SERIES IN HEALTH,
PHYSICAL EDUCATION,
PHYSICAL THERAPY,
AND RECREATION

Charles A. Bucher, Editor

MOVEMENT EXPERIENCES
FOR
CHILDREN

MOVEMENT EXPERIENCES FOR CHILDREN: CURRICULUM AND METHODS FOR ELEMENTARY SCHOOL PHYSICAL EDUCATION

Evolyn L. Schurr
The University of Illinois

NEW YORK

APPLETON-CENTURY-CROFTS

EDUCATIONAL DIVISION

MEREDITH CORPORATION

DEDICATED TO MY FATHER AND MOTHER

PREFACE

This book has been written for teachers of physical education in order to further their understanding of movement and to help them gain confidence in their work with children. Knowledge gained from teaching elementary school children and prospective teachers, supervising student teachers, and working with teachers on the job has been drawn upon in the formulation of the ideas and in the selection of the materials presented in this book.

Movement Experiences for Children is intended to serve as a comprehensive guide to the planning and implementing of a developmental physical education program for children from kindergarten through eighth grade. Although its primary use will be in methods classes for majors in physical education and general elementary school education, this book will also benefit teachers in the field who may refer to it for information about current trends methods, references, and activities. Much of the material is designed to contribute to the teacher's understanding of movement and of the wide movement experiences proposed for today's elementary school child. Along with the content suggestions for each grade's activity areas are discussions of methods and considerations in content selection.

The book is divided into four major sections. Part I provides an overview of elementary school physical education, of the child, and of the curriculum. Part II concerns the teaching process itself: principles of motor learning and methods to implement them, practical suggestions for organizing content and class presentation, and the process of evaluation. Part III serves as a source of information concerning the foundations of all movement skills. Included in Part IV are the experiences, or the activity content, through which the broader skills, concepts, and understandings are developed and reinforced.

Often, physical education books written for use by elementary school classroom teachers have neglected topics central to the proper execution of movement skills, yet professional physical educators base their teaching on these ideas. In Part III, information is presented which I hope will be a valuable addition to the limited source material available in this area. Chapter VII is designed to show the teacher the relationship between the body mechanism and the efficiency and effectiveness of motor skill performance. The mechanical principles of movement, the actions of muscles and body joints, fundamentals of exercise and principles of relaxation are presented in this chapter. Chapter IX is devoted to an analysis of basic movement. This includes a discussion of Movement Education and a structure for studying movement. The fundamental skills common to all physical education activities are also treated. The detailed descriptions of the skills are intended to aid the many teachers and students who have expressed the need for such information in order to understand more fully how a skill is performed. Key teaching phrases, as well as suggestions for study and exploration of each skill, accompany the descriptions. Each skill and its use is discussed in relation to other skills. Part III also includes an explanation of movement terms which are of current interest to elementary school physical educators in order to facilitate the practical use of the material concerning movement skills. Methods of teaching movement are treated extensively in Chapter IV.

I hope that prospective and practicing teachers will find this book helpful as they encourage children to improve skills and to understand what their bodies are capable of doing. The teacher should feel confident in his field and place an emphasis on the quality of the students' performance. There is no greater need in the field of physical education than for well-prepared teachers at the elementary school level.

Special gratitude is given to the following companies that have contributed photographs used as the basis for many of the drawings appearing in the book: Program Aids Company, Mount Vernon, New York; Salsich Recreation Equipment Company, St. Louis, Missouri.

I wish to thank the many teachers and students who have shared their ideas and evaluated the materials that have been used in this book. Most of all, I appreciate the help of the children with whom I have worked; from them I have gained a valuable understanding of their needs and interests.

E. L. S.

CONTENTS

Part I
OVERVIEW

Chapter I

PHYSICAL EDUCATION IN THE ELEMENTARY SCHOOL

Historical aspects of physical education in the school curriculum

Purposes of physical education in the elementary school

Values of physical education to the elementary school child

What is physical education in the elementary school?

The teacher of physical education in the elementary school

Physical education deals with the education of an individual in terms of his body—how he moves in relation to his immediate environment, and how he appears to others. Eleanor Metheny, a contemporary philosopher of physical education, describes a physically educated person as "one who has fully developed the ability to utilize constructively all of his potential capacities for movement as a way of expressing, exploring, developing and interpreting himself and his relationship to the world in which he lives." [1]

In order to become physically educated, one must receive guidance

[1] Eleanor Metheny, "The Third Dimension in Physical Education," *Journal of Health, Physical Education and Recreation* (March, 1954), p. 27.

and encounter the experiences which will contribute to his development at a time when habits and patterns of movement are being formed. Thus, a daily instructional program of physical education is essential in all of the elementary grades.

Metheny's description implies that in the daily physical education lesson a child learns much more than the skills and rules of activities. Therefore, the prospective teacher must be familiar with more than a list of activities to teach. He needs to learn what kinds of skills, activities, experiences, and interactions a child should encounter in his formative years in order to become a physically educated person. He also needs to learn *how* to encourage a child to use his abilities productively.

The concept of physical education as stated in the first paragraph is quite different from that of the past. As with all educational disciplines, years of study and research have resulted in many changes in the philosophy, content, and method of preparing children to move and live effectively in the complex, modern world.

HISTORICAL ASPECTS OF PHYSICAL EDUCATION IN THE SCHOOL CURRICULUM

The spontaneous play of children and the more organized efforts of adults in various forms of games, sports, exercises, and dance are an important part of all civilizations. Early in the history of American education, leaders recognized that physical exercise is specifically valuable to health and welfare. Many colleges, universities, and public school systems introduced instruction in health and physical exercises after programs were initiated at the Round Hill School, Northampton, Massachusetts, in 1825 and at Harvard University in 1826. The state of California passed legislation in 1866 regarding programs of physical education that would increase the health and vigor of the mind and body. Since that time, most states have enacted laws which make physical education a vital part of the public school curriculum.

Physical education in the curricula of the 1800's was primarily corrective in nature, with an emphasis on formal exercises. Various systems of physical education were borrowed from European and Scandinavian countries and adapted for use in American classrooms and gymnasia.

As our society expanded and changed economically, politically, and culturally, so did the nature of education and physical education. Educational curricula began to reflect the values and needs of the democratic system. The nature of physical education became preventive and broad rather than corrective and primarily one of formal exercises. Content emphasis has changed periodically along with the changes in education attendant to major political and economic forces of the time.

In recent years American education has been based on a developmental concept with the ultimate goal being growth of the individual to his fullest capacity. Most educators recognize the importance of including physical education as an integral part of the elementary school curriculum in order to reach this goal. In 1937, Mabel Lee, a prominent leader in the physical education profession, stressed that "the most effective program of physical education should be that of the elementary school since it not only deals with children at the most plastic age but reaches the greatest number to be reached." [2] Today's leaders expand Miss Lee's reasoning with a vast knowledge of the values derived from a well planned physical education program in the elementary school based on evidence from research in the fields of child development, medicine, psychology, education, and physical education.

PURPOSES OF PHYSICAL EDUCATION IN THE ELEMENTARY SCHOOL

Physical education, as a subject in the elementary school curriculum, is widely interpreted and applied. For some educators the primary purpose of physical education is to help children develop good motor skill patterns and to acquire sport skills which will serve as a basis for active leisure time activities. For some, it is a time for exploration of basic movement skills with little structured learning. For others, the primary purpose is to promote good health and well-being or physical fitness. Many educators see the greatest contribution of organized physical education as a laboratory for development in the area of social and emotional growth. For some teachers, it is a period during which children may "blow off steam." For most children, however, physical education means play and fun!

To say that physical education is "play and fun" is an oversimplification; however, sometimes it is important for us to approach things the way children most often do—in terms of the results. What do educators want as their end product? How can we encourage the development of a complex, many-sided person operating in a complex world? Logically, the contributions of physical education to the development of this ideal product cannot be single in purpose but comprehensive in nature.

Although there appears to be a divergence of opinion as to the pri-

2 Mabel Lee, *The Conduct of Physical Education* (New York, Barnes, 1937), p. 27.

mary purpose of physical education and its subsequent contributions to the school child, all physical educators have a common goal in mind. It is to develop fully each child's capacities enabling him to function as a responsible citizen.

The attainment of this goal is highly dependent upon the development of motor or movement skills. In their book *Success Through Play* Kephart and Radler wrote, "Whether covert or overt, motor activity of some kind underlies all behavior including higher thought processes. In fact any behavior in which you indulge can function no better than do the basic motor abilities upon which it is based." [3]

Theory and the results of research indicate that physical education in the elementary school curriculum contributes to individual development in physical, social, emotional, and intellectual areas. Consequently, the purpose of physical education is to provide a developmental program of physical activities which contributes to the *optimum* physical, social, emotional, and intellectual growth of each child.

VALUES OF PHYSICAL EDUCATION TO THE ELEMENTARY SCHOOL CHILD

All subject areas in the elementary school curriculum contribute to the child's social, emotional, and intellectual growth. Physical education is primarily concerned with contributions to his physical growth and development. More than five-sixths of the child's school day is spent in developing and acquiring intellectual skills. Less than one-sixth of his day may be spent in learning about himself, how and why he moves, and understanding the reaction of other people to his movements. In this brief period of time, teachers must help each child develop his skills and understanding of movement in order for him to function successfully in the other five-sixths of the day. The physical area contains aspects of physical growth and fitness as well as acquisition of motor skills.

Physical growth

Heredity determines physique or basic body build. Intrinsic factors and environment control growth. Physical exercise stimulates growth of body tissues, organs, and bones; and it is essential for optimum physical development.

[3] D. H. Radler with Newell C. Kephart, *Success Through Play* (New York, Harper & Row, 1960), p. 29.

The physiological law of use and disuse implies that exercise promotes growth, and a cessation of exercise or disuse results in atrophy or retardation of growth. Muscle tissues are especially influenced by this law. Much evidence has been gathered from research to indicate that muscles increase in size and strength as a result of repeated exercise; however, the reverse is true if exercise is discontinued or withdrawn. Mineralization of bone tissues increases as greater stress due to exercise is placed upon bones. Exercise affects the lateral growth of bones but does not affect the length. Lack of function, as is evidenced by paralysis of some nature, causes bones to remain small and undeveloped.

Healthy, normal growth of the organs of the respiratory and circulatory systems also is stimulated by vigorous exercise. The demands of exercise require the heart to pump more blood to supply more oxygen to the working muscles. Consequently, the breathing mechanism is accelerated, and the lungs must increase in capacity to provide greater amounts of oxygen. The ability to do this work depends upon the strength of the musculature of the organs. Thus, the law of use and disuse is applicable as well to the condition of the organic muscles and the efficiency of the systems they control. Flabby skeletal muscles in children are an indication of a poorly developed cardiorespiratory system. Anna Espenschade summarizes a comprehensive review of research on the contribution of physical activity to growth with the following statement:

Desirable changes in bones, connective tissues, fat, and musculature occur as a result of exercise. These changes are not necessarily permanent but are dependent upon continued activity. More lasting changes in structure almost certainly result from long continued specialization. Exercise, then, stimulates growth of body and makes the individual stronger and more capable of efficient function.[4]

The human body has an inherent urge and need for activity. Gardner Murphy stated that "Activity needs are indeed as fundamental as the nutritive need. We are provided with a set of complex organic equipment and if it is not allowed to function something happens to us, just as in using it we find joy."[5] Children satisfy this need in play. Adults satisfy much of it in work. In many instances the "American way of life" has inhibited the opportunity for fulfillment of the urge for activity. Most adults once met activity needs through the demands of their vocation, but many jobs today are sedentary. The working day is short, and many recreational pursuits are also sedentary. Urbanization, and the apartment living which results, curtails space in which children may play. Congested traffic makes it hazardous for small children to walk to and from school. The consolidation of schools often requires long bus rides for even very young children. The necessity of going directly home and waiting inside

4 Anna S. Espenschade, "The Contributions of Physical Activity to Growth," *Research Quarterly*, Vol. 31, No. 2, Pt. II (May, 1960), p. 360.
5 Gardner Murphy, *Human Potentialities* (New York, Basic Books Inc., 1958), p. 339.

for one or both working parents to come home certainly restricts vigorous play after school. Lawrence Rarick states: that "Observations of pre-adolescent school age children indicate that they need four to five hours of physical activity each day; adolescents need a minimum of one and one-half to two hours each day." [6] Therefore, one can easily understand that children's natural activity must be supplemented in order to satisfy their normal urge and need for activity. A good physical education program will partially fulfill this need. It will also improve motor skills and promote a good attitude toward the necessity for and the enjoyment of physical activities in future leisure time.

Physical fitness

A child is able to function in his environment according to the level of physical fitness which he possesses. Physical fitness is the condition of the body necessary in order for a person to carry out his daily tasks without undue fatigue, yet have enough energy to pursue leisure activities and meet emergency situations requiring additional exertion. This definition implies that a person must develop and maintain muscle strength, endurance, and cardiovascular efficiency; he must be free from disease, make compensations (adjustments) for chronic physical handicaps, and maintain optimum weight. Of course, all of these factors are interrelated and are all dependent upon physical exercise.

Prompted by the fact that children of other countries surpassed American children on some tests of physical fitness, much has been written recently about physical fitness. Nationwide concern and subsequent action regarding the physical fitness of children and adults was promoted by Dwight D. Eisenhower, John F. Kennedy, and Lyndon B. Johnson during their terms as President. Much study and research has been undertaken to expand our knowledge of the effects of a poor fitness level, the importance of physical fitness, the development of fitness, and the values of physical education to physical fitness.

Hein and Ryan [7] analyzed and assessed over one hundred clinical and research studies concerning the contributions of physical activity to physical health. They cite the following points as the values of physical exercise:

1. Maintenance of desirable weight, thereby indirectly reducing the possibility of degenerative diseases and a shorter life span associated with overweight
2. Improvement of health and the cardiovascular system

[6] Lawrence Rarick, "Research Evidence on the Values of Physical Education," *Theory Into Practice*, Vol. III, No. 3, The Ohio State University (June, 1964), p. 109.
[7] Fred V. Hein and Allan J. Ryan, "The Contributions of Physical Activity to Physical Health," *Research Quarterly*, Vol. 31, No. 2, Pt. II (May, 1960).

3. Preservation of the physical characteristics of youth and the accompanying psychological effects which exert a favorable influence on prolonging life
4. Enablement of the individual to meet emergencies more effectively and thus help to preserve health and to avoid disabilities. The habits of exercise if developed in childhood will lead to the enjoyment of these benefits, valuable at any age.

Overweight or obesity in children has increased a great deal in the last decade. The inactive habits of many children combined with an availability of rich foods are the major reasons for this situation. Most overweight youngsters encounter social and emotional problems in school, and most are antagonistic toward exercise. The teacher needs to work with these individuals and their parents in an attempt to promote exercise in addition to that in the regular program.

Although one seldom sees oneself in a state of emergency where an optimum level of physical fitness would be important to survival, it is important to be aware of the dangerous situations anyone might encounter. Hein and Ryan [8] have compiled a comprehensive list of possible emergency situations which are described here in summary form.

1. A short run at maximum speed from a standing start to escape an oncoming vehicle, to catch a public conveyance, in pursuit, or pursued
2. A fall into water in heavy clothing, perhaps with an associated injury, or a struggle with another in the water or in a flood
3. A fall from a height under conditions precluding immediate rescue, as in an isolated place, a shaftway or a well, and with associated injury
4. Entrapment or entombment in a burning house, in a collapsed dwelling, or under the earth
5. Exposure in wilderness areas, without protective clothing, equipment, or adequate shelter
6. Injury and containment in a motor vehicle, train, or airplane, and delayed rescue
7. Unusually heavy and prolonged physical activity such as might be required by the circumstances resulting from a natural catastrophe

In addition to the physical condition of the body affecting one's ability to survive these situations, the quality of neuromuscular skill is also important. Adaptation of movements to unusual situations, reaction to other objects and subsequent fast movement, and coordination of various parts of the body are all benefits of a well-planned physical education program. A creative teacher can simulate problems comparable to the above, eliminating the psychological impact of the danger, and encourage the children to solve them through movement.

It is obvious that physical exercise benefits organic vigor at all ages.

[8] *Ibid.*, p. 276.

The values to children are long-range as well as immediate for they will acquire the techniques of and the interest in maintaining physical fitness throughout their lives. If children are identified as physically unfit, a well-designed program can be undertaken to develop acceptable standards of fitness in a short time.

The latter is shown by the results of a series of physical fitness tests developed by the American Association for Health, Physical Education and Recreation, a department of the National Education Association. The tests were given to 9200 boys and girls of ages ten through seventeen, in forty-nine states. The results show that every age group performed better on every test item than their older brothers and sisters had on similar tests given during the 1957–58 school year.[9] The administration of the first series of tests was made in conjunction with the previously mentioned inquiry into the fitness of the youth of the country.

In announcing the results of the most recent tests, Carl A. Troester, Jr., A.A.H.P.E.R. Executive Secretary, stated that the improvement in scores reflects several factors:

Nearly half of the states have strengthened their physical education requirements in the last few years—with an increasing emphasis on physical education for elementary school children. In addition, parents, school administrators, and medical personnel are becoming increasingly aware that children need daily physical education.[10]

Acquisition of motor skills

As discussed earlier, all behavior is based on motor skills. The child begins to develop motor skills in the prenatal stages, and consequent skill development follows a sequential pattern. Children have acquired patterns of performance in the basic locomotor and nonlocomotor skills prior to their entering school. As these basic skills form the foundations of the everyday work tasks and play skills of children, it is important that an instructional program is started in the first grade to ensure proper acquisition and refinement of the more difficult skill patterns. Unfortunately, many children enter first grade with a very low level of locomotive and manipulative skills. Although maturation provides them with the equipment or readiness to learn, they must have opportunities to practice and refine their skills. It is true that some progress can be made through the trial and error process; however, constant analysis of errors and suggestions for correction can reduce the number of repeated failures.

[9] Paul Hunsicker and Guy Reiff, *A Survey and Comparison of Youth Fitness—1958–1965*, Cooperative Research Project No. 2418 (University of Michigan, 1965).
[10] Carl Troester Jr., "N.E.A. Department Test Notes Gains in Youth Fitness," *N.E.A. Reporter* (December, 1965), p. 3.

Many studies have supported the hypothesis that specific instruction in skill will result in learning. Repeated practice is the essential element in acquiring proficiency, and greater retention of skills is promoted by overlearning. However, in the primary grades maturation may exert a greater influence on new skills than does learning. Opportunity for general practice through game play, and exploration with certain skills, will prove more productive at this stage than emphasis on extended practice and direct skill teaching.

Sports are an important element of the American culture today, and they exert influences on the populace in many ways. The acquisition of a certain level of proficiency in traditional American sports is beneficial to both girls and boys, and a knowledge of the conduct of sports is also valuable, whether one participates as a spectator or as a player. Since most adults tend to select leisure time activities in which they had formerly achieved skill, guided practice in learning sports skills is essential so that people will have a variety of sports activities to enjoy.

Sport skills are combinations of various fundamental (basic) movement patterns adapted to specific sports implements, boundaries, rules, and strategies. Consequently, a good foundation can be established for sport skills in the instruction and generalized practice which takes place in the primary grades.

Motor skills also provide avenues of expression for creative and aesthetic efforts. Only by learning through experience what the body can do can the child explore this mode of self-expression. The learning and practice of motor skills is essential in order for a child to acquire the tools to achieve desirable goals of physical fitness, recreation skills, scholastic achievement, and social efficiency.

Intellectual development

Physical education is valuable in the intellectual development of the school child, usually measured by scholastic achievement. The child's level of achievement is primarily dependent upon his intellectual capacity, but whether or not his potential is realized depends a great deal upon his physical development.

Throughout history, philosophers and educators have stressed the importance of a sound body and good health as a framework for optimum mental effectiveness. As physical exercise contributes to the physical fitness level and the social and emotional adjustments as previously described, it is setting the stage for the child to learn well academically. If a child is well adjusted socially and emotionally, he will have a good self concept, be self-assured, and will desire to work well in school.

Recently, results of research and study on the relation of motor skills and academic achievement have indicated that the type of movement experiences a young child has may influence his academic achievement. Both Godfrey [11] and Kephart [12] worked with low achievers and discovered that perceptual skill deficiencies were prominent factors in poor academic work. It appeared that programs of motor therapy aided these children in developing their symbolic-perceptual systems, and thereby improved their academic achievement.

Most children develop the ability to monitor propioceptually through their play experiences before beginning school, but for those who do not, primary programs stressing work with the fundamental skills in an exploratory setting increase orientation of the body in space and development of the muscle-sensory system.

Cowell and Ismail [13] studied the results of motor aptitude tests and academic success and IQ and found that measures of coordination and balance were good predictors of academic achievement. Much experience in activities including many balance and coordination items should therefore promote a better chance for academic success for children.

The motor learning process itself is, in part, an intellectual one. Successful performance is dependent on a knowledge of the component parts of the skill, an understanding of how the skill is to be utilized, and insight into actions and results. As the skill is performed repeatedly, the physical action must be accompanied by reflective thinking in terms of what the student has observed from demonstrations or observations of other's actions, directions, and his own past trials.

Children are gaining a knowledge of how the body operates and what it is capable of doing when they are exposed to good teaching in physical education, a program which stresses a problem-solving approach and emphasizes acquiring good basic movement skills at the primary level. An understanding of the cause-and-effect relationship of exercise and fitness is essential to the maintenance of fitness throughout life and the selection of fitness activities as an adult.

Efficiency of movement is the ultimate goal in all play and work skills. The mechanical principles of movement are learned by children, and the concepts are applied to the learning of new play or work skills. Prior to the complete understanding of principles and identification by definition, concepts or generalized applications of them can be made in the exploration and problem-solving phases with basic movement skills in the primary grades. As the student matures intellectually, and physical laws and principles are introduced in the classroom, direct analogies can be made as to how the body operates like a machine.

[11] Barbara S. Godfrey, "Motor Therapy and School Achievement," *Journal of Health, Physical Education and Recreation* (May, 1964), p. 28.
[12] Radler and Kephart, *op. cit.*
[13] Charles Cowell, A. H. Ismail, and Newell Kephart, *Utilization of Motor Aptitude Tests in Prediction of Academic Achievement* (Purdue University, 1963).

Social and emotional growth and development

Physical education contributes to the child's social growth and development, since it provides an opportunity for the acquisition of social skills and moral values. Quite frequently, physical education is referred to as a laboratory for children to experience social interactions. The many varied activities provide excellent opportunities for children to interact with individuals, small groups, large groups, and authority figures. Concepts of courtesy, modesty, cooperation, honesty, dependability, respect for authority and rules can all be developed through active participation in realistic, demanding situations.

The mere experiences of social interactions do not insure the development of social skills and moral values. The skills must be taught. The teacher must plan situations where children have responsibilities—friendly rivalries, where cooperation of each group member is important to success—and where there is the chance to make decisions involving honesty. The teacher must make the most of the "teachable moments" when problems arise, and he must guide the children in their value judgments and social behavior.

Most of a child's social contacts are in a motor skill setting. Therefore, good play skills are of major importance in the social life of a child. In writing about the movement experiences of young children, Gutteridge states:

Skill in bodily activity has deep rooted social significance. It is to be ranked first among factors that lead to a child's acceptance among his peers. Approval raises for him the value of an activity and leads him to put forth to reach acceptable standards and to compete successfully with others.[14]

Among the developmental tasks which Havighurst [15] lists for middle childhood (ages six to twelve) is that of learning physical skills necessary for ordinary games highly valued in childhood. The psychological basis for this is the fact that the peer group rewards a child for his successes, and punishes him by indifference or disdain for failure. The cultural influence suggests that girls are expected to learn these skills to a lesser degree than boys. Girls can do rather poorly in game skills and still hold status in the group, while boys who do poorly lose status.

In a longitudinal study of social recognition at the elementary school

[14] Mary Gutteridge, "A Child's Experiences in Bodily Activity," *46th Yearbook*, Part II (National Society for Study of Education, 1947), p. 108.
[15] Robert J. Havighurst, *Developmental Tasks and Education* (New York, Longmans 1953), p. 54.

age, Hardy [16] found that the best-liked students were superior in athletic ability to the unpopular students. She concluded that the most popular children were, on the whole, usually proficient in the type of playground activities commonly engaged in by boys and girls of elementary age.

In a study of third graders of high, average, and low ability in motor performance, Rarick and McKee [17] found that the individual who was highly skilled in motor activities was also more popular, of higher intelligence, and better adjusted in school than the student exhibiting less skill. Reiman [18] investigated the relationship between motor performance, scholastic achievement, and the peer status of fourth grade children. The results showed positive relationships between peer status, motor achievement, and scholastic achievement. Again, physical skill appeared to be more important in peer status for boys than girls. These and many more studies indicate that a good level of motor skill is important to a child's relationships and status in his peer group. The individual who is "accepted" has fewer emotional tensions and thus will function more efficiently both physically and mentally. It is apparent that the child who enters school with poor motor skills and little previous opportunity to learn games is at a serious disadvantage if he receives no instruction or the opportunity to improve his situation at school.

Activity releases built-up tensions and pressures acquired from a prolonged period of concentration on academics. The physical education period which is scheduled at an appropriate time following sessions in the demanding subjects of math or science can reduce stress. Results of several studies indicate that students concentrate and/or perform better in the classroom after a period of vigorous activity.

Physical education contributes to the development of emotional control, since play periods are filled with emotionally charged situations. Games are demanding whether or not there is an emphasis on competition. Dance and gymnastic performances are exciting in themselves. Anxieties build up. Both losing and winning produces anger, disappointment, elation, or joy. Learning to control these emotions can only come about through experiences and guidance. Team competition teaches the discipline of accepting failure. Children can adjust better to a defeat when they share this defeat with teammates.

---

[16] Martha Hardy, "Social Recognition at the Elementary School Age," *Journal of Social Psychology*, Vol. 8 (May, 1937), p. 365.

[17] Lawrence Rarick and Robert McKee, "A Study of Twenty Third Grade Children Exhibiting Extreme Levels of Achievement on Tests of Motor Proficiency," *Research Quarterly*, Vol. 20 (May, 1949), p. 143.

[18] Fred Reiman, *Observation of Certain Factors Associated with Peer Status of a Group of Fourth Grade Children* (Unpublished Master's Thesis, University of Wisconsin, 1958).

In discussing the development of self-control Breckenridge and Vincent state:

To the psychologist, control of one's own body means the beginning of self-control in general. In bringing his own body under control the child brings under control the most ever present piece of his environment. Having controlled this most obvious part of himself, the child finds it easier to bring his temper and other emotions under control.[19]

This only emphasizes the need for many movement experiences for the primary grade child.

A child's successes and failures provide him with a self-concept which, in turn, influences his personality development and his approach to new tasks and experiences. As children grow in size and age, they begin to make judgments and comparisons of other children and relate their perceptions to their own body images. Prescott states:

The child continually uses his own body in interacting with objects, persons, and processes in his own environment. Gradually he gains a measure of control over his body and learns its potentialities and limitations. Experiences with others also lead children to compare themselves with each other and to rate themselves as stronger or weaker, more skilled or less skilled, fully equipped or handicapped, attractive or ugly in comparison with others.[20]

Play skills and games are common activities to all children and, as such, success in them is highly prized. A child recognizes that success in skills comes only through his own repeated efforts to achieve his goal. When the goal is initially too difficult for the individual, the attendant failures reduce his enthusiasm and confidence in approaching other new experiences. If in the primary grades, the physical education program is conducted on a developmental basis and the teacher utilizes an approach where each child can experience a sense of achievement in control of his body over his environment, the child's appreciation of his ability to approach new tasks will help establish a positive self concept.

WHAT IS PHYSICAL EDUCATION IN THE ELEMENTARY SCHOOL?

It has seemed to the author more effective to present the answer to this question first, rather than to offer a description of physical education and a list of objectives. The purpose was defined, and the values that can be

[19] Marion E. Breckenridge and E. Lee Vincent, *Child Development* (New York, Saunders, 1960), p. 309.
[20] Daniel A. Prescott, *The Child in the Educative Process* (New York, McGraw-Hill, 1958), p. 388.

gained by children from a well-planned developmental program of physical education were discussed. For the most part, results from research in the fields of psychology, education, physiology, medicine, and anthropology are offered as evidence of these values.

It should be obvious to the reader that physical education is more than exercise or movement alone. The many and varied activities are tools through which a child learns about himself; what he is capable of doing; how he can control his body; how he can adapt to the forces about him (whether these forces be space, inanimate objects, or other people); and how he can maintain his state of well-being. Proficiency in a wide variety of movement skills gives him personal and social mobility in his work and play experiences and sets a foundation for future success. Movement is the key to the means of reaching the values previously stated. Command of movement skills helps a child to function efficiently in all of his life experiences.

The primary aim in the elementary school should be to help each child develop proficiency in movement skills in a wide variety of activities. The emphasis is not on extremely high degrees of skill but on efficient performance in many skills. From the joy and satisfaction of confident movement and the physical benefits of the efforts and exercise necessary to reach efficient performance, a foundation is laid for a desire to maintain a healthy body, to be involved in active participation, and to develop a high degree of skill.

Specific aims of physical education in the elementary school are:
1. To promote the optimum physical development of each child
2. To develop the motor skill ability of each child in terms of performance, adaptability, ingenuity, and efficiency in coping with new and varied situations
3. To develop physical and mental coordination
4. To provide situations where each child can feel a sense of achievement through his own efforts and perseverence
5. To provide opportunities for as wide an experience as possible in all types of movement activities
6. To provide situations where each child must learn to work alone, to cooperate and compete with himself and others, and to cooperate and compete at the same time
7. To provide situations where each child must exert inquiry, expression, creativity, and self-control in movement experiences

Underlying all of these aims is the emphasis on the individual child. Obviously, organization and method are as important in the realization of these aims as is content selection. Variety in all these areas is essential, and regardless of the technique utilized, concern for the individual is essential. Basic principles of movement must be correct, but the style and form of performance may be varied in accordance with individual ability and interpretation. Therefore, teachers must not demand uniform performances, nor should they accept every kind of solution to a movement problem.

Physical education, then, is the subject in the elementary school curriculum in which learning of neuromuscular skills and understandings, intellectual skills and understandings, social skills and understandings, and value systems are taught through the medium of movement. It must be remembered that it is the only subject in the curriculum which is solely responsible for the child's physical development, and, as such, its greatest contribution and concentration is in this area.

THE TEACHER OF PHYSICAL EDUCATION IN THE ELEMENTARY SCHOOL

How well an individual learns anything depends upon the extent of practice and guidance involved. It is true that children acquire most of the basic movement patterns without direct teaching, but the refinement of the skills and the efficient use of the skills in relation to specific goals require a broader understanding and development of them than the child can acquire through trial and error alone. Early detection of errors in performance, and suggestions for improvement by a teacher can forestall a fixation of the error and avoid a great deal of frustration.

The primary functions of the teacher of physical education are to provide the appropriate learning situations and an adequate understanding of the concepts to be learned which relate to physical action. In order to do both of these well, the teacher must have a good understanding and knowledge of child growth and development factors, physiological principles, a wide variety of physical activities, and of basic movement skills. In addition to these knowledges and understandings, the teacher must have an interest in the total development of children, an attitude that physical education is a vital part of the curriculum, a good sense of humor, and a willingness to study new materials and ideas in the field of elementary school physical education.

As teachers who have taken an undergraduate major in physical education have the most extensive formal education in the majority of the aforementioned areas, it is most desirable to have this type of specialist teaching physical education at all grade levels. However, many elementary school administrators believe that it is better to have self-contained classrooms in the primary grades. The rationale for this is that usually the classroom teacher knows the children best, and that the children are more secure with only one teacher rather than several special area teachers.

Although the specialist may be best qualified through the virtue of training to help children realize the many values of physical education, a great number of classroom teachers must teach physical education. Due to a shortage of specialists and the financial inability of many school boards to hire specialists, the classroom teacher must implement the program in many schools.

Recently, Caskey [21] studied the status of elementary school physical education in forty-six states and the District of Columbia. The results indicated that in 47,015 elementary schools in thirty-six states, eighty-two percent of the schools have classroom teachers teaching physical education. Many school systems have a consultant who assists the classroom teacher with demonstrations, planning, curriculum guides, and in-service training. Many states retain consultants to help teachers in areas where local consultative services are not available.

There is a trend toward the inclusion of a resource area in under-graduate elementary education programs. A student elects several courses in a special area of his choice. Thereafter, as a teacher, he may serve as the resource person in his school and give other teachers assistance in this area. Frequently where this is true, teachers share their specialties, and one may teach the physical education for two or three classes, another may handle the music, another the art, and so forth. In some schools, teachers concentrate on developing techniques and a background of knowledge in specific activity areas. Hence, a team-teaching plan is evolved where each teacher concentrates on teaching the activity in which he feels most confident and competent.

State certification requirements usually require that elementary school teachers have courses in methods and materials of elementary school physical education, child growth and development, basic sciences, health, and educational psychology. With this background in content, an under-standing of the need for a good developmental physical education pro-gram, some consultative services, reference books, and most of all, a desire to do well in all of his teaching, almost any teacher can provide children with desirable learning in motor skill activities.

Summary

The materials in this chapter should convince the classroom teacher of the contributions of physical education to the child's welfare and of the necessity of a developmental program for everyone. Subsequent chap-

[21] Sheila Caskey, *The Status of Elementary School Physical Education in the United States* (Unpublished Study, Southeast Missouri State College, 1965).

ters will review and present learning principles and teaching methods and techniques to enlarge the teacher's background. Actual activity content for each grade is presented in a progressive fashion.

Throughout the book, primary refers to kindergarten, first and second grades; intermediate, to third and fourth grades; and upper, to fifth, sixth, seventh, and eighth grades. Specialists are usually found in the seventh and eighth grades; however, as little material is available to either the specialist or the classroom teacher who must teach in these two grades, suggestions are made in this book for carrying on progressions in them.

The teacher must bear in mind that presentation of activities alone will not meet student needs. The method of presentation, the child's understanding of what he is doing in terms of action, and the teacher's guidance and insistance on quality of performance according to each child's abilities are vital in this fulfillment. Most leaders in physical education and elementary school administration have confidence that, given guidance and the proper tools, the classroom teacher can handle the most important assignment in physical education—that of helping each child to act more confidently in his environment by acquiring good movement skills.

SUGGESTED REFERENCES FOR FURTHER STUDY

American Association for Health, Physical Education and Recreation, *This Is Physical Education* (Washington, D.C., The Association, 1965).

Espenschade, Anna S., "The Contributions of Physical Activity to Growth," *Research Quarterly,* Vol. 31, No. 2, Pt. II (May, 1960), p. 360.

Hein, Fred V., and Allan J. Ryan, "The Contributions of Physical Activity to Physical Health," *Research Quarterly,* Vol. 31, No. 2, Part II (May, 1960).

Chapter II

UNDERSTANDING AND FULFILLING THE NEEDS OF CHILDREN

Growth and development factors

The exceptional child

The slow learner

Children come to school in various states of readiness; with different backgrounds, different abilities, different interests; and many other dissimilarities. In order to face the challenge of helping each child develop to his fullest potential, the teacher must know as much as possible about the characteristics of all children. Studying the natural and man-made factors that either inhibit or promote the child's ability to learn should help the teacher plan his method and program as well as enable him to understand the child with whom he is working.

Although all children are basically very much alike and follow much the same sequence of growth and development, the time schedule of this sequence varies slightly for many individuals. Due to environment, accident, or other causes, some children do not follow the typical sequence; therefore, we find many exceptional children in our schools. Materials in this discussion provide a background of how children grow and develop, what implications growth and development have for physical education, and how and what to provide for the needs of all types of children.

GROWTH AND
DEVELOPMENT FACTORS

The developmental factors related to different age groups are vital in regard to the child's ability to learn motor skills and activities. An extensive review of research by Bayley and Espenschade [1] indicates that the development of motor ability is a function of maturation, and the acquisition of skill is influenced a great deal by the extent of practice. Therefore, when a basic growth stage has been reached, carefully planned learning experiences will influence the quality of the skill pattern.

There are many good sources which describe in detail the characteristics of growth and development of children in terms of physical, social, emotional, and intellectual factors. It would be wise for the teacher to refer to these sources before teaching physical education to a particular age group, and to recognize the implications of them. The specific characteristics will not be repeated here; however, reference will be made to a few pertinent generalities referring to the process of maturation.

The acquisition of motor skill patterns is dependent upon an orderly progression of development from simple gross movements to more complex movement patterns. Many researchers who have studied the development of motor patterns from the fetal period to that of adulthood have compiled ideas on the order of skill progressions. Most of the basic movement patterns have been established by the time a child is five years old. The function of the teacher of elementary school physical education is to help the child refine skills into a mature pattern and to introduce variations and combinations of the basic movement skills.

The quality of the performance of skills is dependent upon the child's physical abilities of strength, endurance, flexibility, agility, coordination, and balance. All of these are related to age. It must be remembered that children of the same chronological age mature at slightly different rates; however, growth is sequential, and a general pattern may be anticipated for all.

Physical and motor
development

Children continue to grow in strength from the first grade on. Boys at all ages have a slight advantage in this respect over girls. This difference

[1] Nancy Bayley and Anna Espenschade, "Motor Development and Decline," *Review of Educational Research,* Vol. 20 (1950), p. 367.

increases markedly at puberty and increases for both sexes after the post-pubescent stages. At puberty the shoulder width of boys continues to grow in size, and likewise the throwing ability becomes greater. Hip width increases just before puberty, much more so for girls than boys. This greater width may produce some mechanical inhibition in the run of the girl as she matures. Boys have a greater energy level than girls at all ages. The arm length of boys is greater than that of girls from the age of two on. Although these differences between boys and girls are slight prior to puberty, achievement in skill performance is greater at all grade levels for boys in most skills except in stunts requiring balance.[2]

Generally, girls enter puberty in the fifth, sixth, or seventh grades and boys enter approximately two years later. A period of rapid growth and changes in the body system characterize the pubescent age. Since boys generally begin to mature later than girls, there will be considerable differences in their stature, interests, emotions, and needs during the upper grade years. Due to greater muscular strength, cardiovascular endurance, and cultural factors among others, boys tend to be superior in skill level and achievement. In this respect, the gap between the two sexes widens in the upper grades. Boys play more vigorously and enjoy contact activities. There is a need to separate the sexes for some activities.

The body build of a child helps determine his success in motor performance. One's basic body build is established approximately between the ages of six and seven. As early as first grade, variations in physique among both boys and girls are noticeable. Some will be tall and slender, with small bones and light musculature (ectomorphs); some will be stocky and muscular (mesomorphs); and others will have a tendency to be round, flabby, and accumulate fat easily (endomorphs). These characteristics change very little throughout life.

Mesomorphs will usually be stronger and excel in activities requiring gross strength and stability. Ectomorphs may move more quickly, and be better at games requiring running and jumping. Endomorphs usually display less muscular strength and have a more passive attitude toward activity. Naturally, there are gradations and combinations of these three types of basic body builds. Recent studies indicate that the type of body build does play an important part in determining the nature of motor activities in which a child will have most success. From the descriptions given, it is obvious that the endomorphs can not be expected to do as well in most activities as the others and that a child with this type of body build must be encouraged to be active.

Normal, healthy children abound with energy during all of the elementary grades. Some teachers have an unfounded concern that too much

2 Lulu M. Jenkins, *A Comparative Study of Motor Achievement of Children of Five, Six and Seven Years of Age* (New York, Bureau of Publications, Teachers College, Columbia University, 1930); and Robert D. Johnson, "Measurement of Achievement in Fundamental Skills of Elementary School Children," *Research Quarterly*, Vol. 33, No. 1 (March, 1962), p. 94.

vigorous activity will cause children to become fatigued and will be harmful. Most young children will rest or change their activity when they become tired. They recuperate quickly. Children in the middle and upper grades may have to be watched for signs of fatigue or overexertion because the development of a highly competitive spirit may allow them to push beyond the point of fatigue.

In reality, repeated exercise results in improved organic development of both the heart and respiratory system. Too often the physical education period does not require enough strenuous exercise. Recent studies show that the young child's tolerance for exercise is greater than was once thought to be true.

Elementary school children continue to grow increasingly long-legged; therefore, the ability to run and jump increases with each year of growth. Balance improves rapidly in the primary years. At the third grade level most children can control balance reasonably well; however, practice in this area will improve the development of this quality measurably. This is evidenced by better body control, which can be expected in games and activities requiring quick changes of direction and sudden stops and starts in the middle and upper grades.

Changes in vision also take place in the process of growth. Great accuracy cannot be expected in primary grades. Activities requiring much fine hand-eye coordination should not be stressed before late second or third grade. Any activities involving accuracy in the primary grades should utilize a large stationary target. Throwing at moving targets may be introduced in the late second grade. Obviously, this should involve large objects. Practice will help the development of sensori-motor coordination necessary for accuracy, but expectations by the teacher should be geared to the level of maturity of the individual child.

Reaction time improves progressively with age. Intermediate grade children can be expected to react to movements of other objects, people, and signals much more quickly than those in the primary grades. At both levels there is great variability in reaction time between individuals; therefore, a great number of speed or timed events should not be stressed. Opportunities for practice in activities requiring quick reactions and movement in relation to others help a child move more easily and time his actions better so that he develops more control and coordination.

Sport skills involving combinations of movement patterns must be introduced in a progressive fashion commensurate with the growth pattern of children. Children in the upper grades are capable of learning highly complex motor skills. Paul Hunsicker [3] states that research shows that "children by 10 years of age have the neuromuscular potential to master the skills required in practically any physical education course offered at

3 Paul Hunsicker, Physical Fitness, *What Research Says to the Teacher,* #26 (Washington, D.C., Department of Classroom Teachers, National Education Association, 1963), p. 25.

the college level." This does not mean that an elementary school child could pass the college courses, since he might not have the strength or size. However, he does have the potential of mastering the neuromuscular skills. Often sport skills and activities are not introduced until high school because of the mistaken assumption that they are too difficult for elementary school children to learn. It is the size of the equipment and the complexity of the rules of the official games which are too difficult for children, not the skills. Lead-up games are available in which the skills can be used and practiced until the child is physically and socially mature enough to play the official sports.

Social and emotional growth

The drive to be active is characteristic of most children in the first two grades. Due to this, their attention span is short. Most of them would prefer to play by themselves or in small groups. They are not really ready to play in groups that involve great cooperation, nor are they ready to do any one thing for long periods of time. Long practice periods on specific skills are impractical. Working on skills with complex patterns or with equipment which is too small or too large to handle creates frustration and disinterest for young children.

Although young children want to be "first," little stress should be placed on competition or on being first. In the primary grades children are discovering themselves and what they can do, so they have little competence to compete. The push to win coupled with their natural desire to be first may lead to poor social habits of cheating, lying, and alibiing.

Children in grades three and four become increasingly interested in becoming proficient in skills, and they will work hard and long to improve these. Their interest in games with more concrete rules grows. They can work with a greater number of people at one time in a more cooperative manner, and interest in group success becomes more important. Simple team games appeal to them, as there is a chance to use skills in exciting ways and an opportunity to use strategy. They are capable of understanding more complex rules and resent games which are too simple. When activities are not challenging they become bored quickly, and behavior problems often arise.

Due to increased social maturity as well as physical maturity, the organization of the class may change somewhat, and more group-work may be undertaken. Self-control is improved to the extent that many small groups may be working independently. Focus may be put on one major lead-up game for the unit, since interest is sustained longer when the team spirit is stronger.

Intermediate grade children are ready to compete and need challenges, but the challenges must be reasonable and attainable. Competition is motivating only as long as there is a chance to win. The child's experiences of winning and losing must be balanced with a slight overbalance on the winning. According to Hilgard,[4] "tolerance for failure is best taught through providing a backlog of success that compensates for experienced failure." However, there is a danger in tailor-making experiences in such a way that a child will always encounter success. At some point he needs to learn the values of working hard to achieve success. Achievement without any effort encourages an unrealistic attitude toward accomplishments.

In the upper grades children continue to grow in all respects. Their ability to concentrate improves; consequently, they are interested in longer practice periods. Interest in team play is high due to the "gang" spirit. Also, their ability to learn more complicated rules and to understand and use simple strategy expands.

Cultural factors play a large role in the interest and success in skills of boys and girls at this age. Proficiency in skills and games is important for both sexes, and social acceptance is often related to this factor. However, boys are expected to be well skilled to maintain status in the peer group, but girls may maintain status even though their skill level remains the same or even regresses. As boys are stronger and more intensely interested in activity than girls are, it is important that the teacher not use an organization which permits boys to dominate game play and exclude girls. There are many activities in which boys and girls can play together harmoniously and on even terms, but boys and girls should be separated for some sports activities because of the differences in their interests in vigorous participation.

Physiological factors
affecting behavior

Since the biological constitution of a child determines his physiological behavior pattern, the teacher should be aware of a few of the physiological variances which have been found to influence behavior and performance of children. The autonomic nervous system influences the personality and behavior of the child. It has been found that emotional inhibition, excitability, fatigue, aggressiveness, neatness, and activity levels are variables which cannot be controlled at will by all children. Some cannot be quiet for a long period of time; some cannot be neat and precise; some display great excitability at the least provocation; some appear to have a low tolerance for excessive activity.

[4] Ernest R. Hilgard, *Theories of Learning*, 2nd ed. (New York, Appleton-Century-Crofts, 1948), p. 407.

When a teacher encounters a youngster who cannot control himself in one of the areas mentioned, he should consider the effect the child's biological constitution may have on his behavior before declaring him uncooperative or a discipline problem. The school personnel responsible for pupil health records and referrals would have to be consulted in cases such as these. A better understanding of the child's problems may produce different methods and expectations. The teacher who expects performance and behavior of the whole class to be uniform is in error.

Growth and development characteristics and the implications of these for the physical education program are summarized here (in chart form) by grade groups. Although some of this material may be repetitious of items discussed, the chart will help the prospective teacher to understand better the pattern as a whole.

It is impossible to designate the grade when these characteristics will appear for each child. Due to individual differences in rate of growth there will always be overlap from grade to grade. The grades have been grouped together in periods of time where the characteristics and needs will most likely first appear and be resolved before changing into another stage.

THE EXCEPTIONAL CHILD

Current estimates are that approximately one out of every ten children deviates from the average in some aspect of physical, mental, social, and emotional development and behavior. Generally, a child deviates or is in exception to the average in only one of these aspects and has the normal needs, desires, and abilities in the others. Consequently, he must learn and engage in the same type of comprehensive school program as his peer group. Naturally, some of his learning experiences must be adapted to his limitations. Frequently, if a child does not have the opportunity to participate in the typical activities of his peer group, his problems and limitations grow, and he becomes handicapped in more than one area.

It is very likely that in each classroom there will be exceptional children of some type. The present educational practice is to integrate them into regular classrooms and activities as much as possible. In many school districts there is not a sufficient number of exceptional children to make the setting up of special classes feasible, and often there is not enough money to provide special education for children with specific handicaps. In some instances, districts cooperate and share the services of specialists.

Even where children do have special remedial or adapted academic programs, the children are integrated into art, music, and physical educa-

Table 2-1. Summary Chart of Growth and Development Characteristics and Implications for Physical Education Program Content

KINDERGARTEN, GRADES 1 AND 2

Characteristics	Needs	Types of Experiences
1. Spurt of growth of muscle mass	1. Vigorous exercise requiring use of large muscles	1. Running, chasing, fleeing type games; hanging, climbing, supportive type exercises
2. Gross movement skills becoming more refined	2. Exploration and variations of gross motor skills; opportunities to refine skills	2. Self-testing activities of all types; dance activities
3. Manipulative skills still unrefined, but improving; will catch balls with body and arms more so than hands	3. Opportunities to manipulate large or medium size objects; throw small balls	3. Ball-handling activities; work with beanbags, wands, hoops, progressing from large to smaller objects
4. Imaginative, imitative curious	4. Opportunities for expression of ideas and use of body	4. Creative dance, story plays, creative stunt and floor work; exploration with all basic skills and small equipment
5. Very active, great deal of energy	5. Ample opportunities for vigorous play, particularly at the onset of the physical education period, recess needed in other half of day	5. Running, games, stunts, large apparatus; more locomotor work than nonlocomotor activities
6. Short attention span	6. Activities which take short explanation and to which some finish can be reached quickly; frequent change in activities or tasks	6. Simple games, simple class organization so activities can be changed quickly; conversations in movement
7. Individualistic or egocentric	7. Needs experiences to learn to share or become interested in others; engage in parallel play alongside of other children rather than with them	7. Much small group work, self-testing activities, exploration of movement factors

Table 2-1. Continued

GRADES 3 AND 4

Characteristics	Needs	Types of Experiences
1. Gross motor patterns more refined and graceful	1. Use of skill for specific purposes	1. Introduction to specific sport skills in grades 3 and 4; expressive style skill utilized in dance; traditional dance steps
2. Hand-eye coordination improved; growth in manipulative skills	2. Opportunities to handle smaller objects; more importance placed on accuracy; throw at moving targets	2. Ball-handling activities, use of bats, paddles, target games
3. Sees need to practice skills for improvement of skill and to gain social status	3. Guided practice sessions, self-testing problem situations	3. Drills, skill drill games, self-testing practice situations
4. Balance more highly developed; better body control	4. Opportunities to work on higher beams, bars; more activities requiring static balance	4. Large apparatus work, tumbling, stunts
5. Increased attention span	5. Activities with continuity, more complex rules and understandings	5. Lead-up games to sports, low organized games with more complex rules and strategy
6. More socially mature, interested in welfare of group	6. Make a contribution to a large or small group, remain with one group for a longer period of time, help make and accept decisions with a group	6. Team activities, dance compositions with small groups
7. Greater sex differences in skills; some antagonism toward opposite sex (4)	7. Ability grouping and separation by sex for some team games	7. Tag football for boys; separate softball games for boys; combative type stunts; folk dance; after-school activities for grade 4
8. Great interest in proficiency and competitive spirit (particularly boys) may drive to fatigue	8. Recognition of symptoms of fatigue and place of rest, relaxation, and moderation in competition	8. Self-testing activities; relaxation techniques; interval training with developmental exercises
9. Spirit of adventure high	9. Activities requiring courage, adventure, initiative; recognition of safety factors	9. Self-testing activities of all types; use of large apparatus; low organized games demanding courage; creative dance compositions

Table 2-1. Continued

GRADES 3 AND 4

Characteristics	Needs	Types of Experiences
10. Tendency toward poor posture	10. Understanding of body mechanics, development of endurance and strength	10. Developmental exercises, vigorous running games, large apparatus, and fitness activities; individually planned program for those below average in posture and fitness
11. Intellectually curious	11. Learn mechanical principles of movement, similarities of movement patterns, and physiological principles	11. Self-testing activities of all types; problem-solving method used in analyzing own skill patterns; creative dance; developmental exercise programs

GRADES 5 AND 6

Characteristics	Needs	Types of Experiences
1. Coordination highly developed, keen interest in proficiency in skills	1. Need to learn more difficult skills; more coaching on refinement of skills; use of skills in games, routines, and compositions	1. Lead-up games to sports in season; instruction and practice in sport skills; more advanced dance step patterns and folk dances; track and field; apparatus routines; intramurals
2. Greater sex differences in skills, interests; most prefer to play and compete with own sex; boys play more vigorously and rougher than girls	2. Separation of sexes in classes or within classes for many activities	2. Co-educational dance; swimming, gymnastics, activities, recreational games; sexes separate in team sports and fitness activities; intramurals for each sex
3. Good skills and physique important to social acceptance, particularly for boys	3. Instruction and practice sessions in skills, understanding of fitness elements, understanding of changes in growth and abilities due to puberty	3. Fitness tests; developmental exercises; work with apparatus; classroom discussions and movies about puberty (may be done in cooperation with nurse or parents)

Table 2-1. Continued

GRADES 5 AND 6

Characteristics	*Needs*	*Types of Experiences*
4. Group or gang spirit is high, allegiance to group is strong	4. Need to belong to a group with some stability; make rules, decisions, and abide by group decision; longer term of membership on a squad or team	4. Team games, tournaments, group dance compositions, gymnastic squads with student leaders, gymnastic meets, track and field meets
5. Social consciousness of need for rules and abiding by rules; can assume greater responsibility	5. Participate in setting rules, opportunities for squad captains or or leaders	5. Student officials; plan and conduct tournaments in class and after school; students plan own strategy, line-ups, etc.
6. Flexibility decreasing	6. To maintain flexibility within structural limitations	6. Stunts, tumbling, apparatus, developmental exercises
7. Muscle growth of boys increasing; most girls in puberty	7. Interest in maintaining good posture, fitness level; build good attitudes toward activity and proficiency for girls; knowledge of methods of increasing strength and endurance for boys	7. Apparatus, developmental activities, track and field, more individual and dual activities, intramurals

GRADES 7 AND 8

Characteristics	*Needs*	*Types of Experiences*
1. Coordination very highly developed; skill level increasing more rapidly for boys than girls; skill level for girls reaches a plateau	1. Learning more advanced sport skills; opportunities for refinement and use of skills in sports, routines, compositions	1. Modified team and individual sports, more demanding dance skills and composition work, intramurals for both sexes and individual
2. Sexes differ in skills and interests; boys' muscle strength much more than girls'	2. Separation of sexes in classes if possible; male teacher for boys; sexes brought together for some activities	2. Team sports for both; recreation in individual sports, volleyball, gymnastics, social, folk, and square dances
3. Most girls in puberty and some in grade 8 reaching full stature, some boys starting puberty, less sex antagonism, boys' interest in opposite sex increases	3. Understanding of changes due to puberty, better understanding of body mechanism	3. Fitness activities, body mechanics

Table 2-1. Continued

GRADES 7 AND 8

Characteristics	Needs	Types of Experiences
4. Prestige associated with good skills for boys; lack of interest in activity for girls due to cultural influences	4. Many opportunities for individual coaching and practice of skills; girls need to be encouraged to maintain fitness and an interest in activity	4. Much game play and individual coaching in class and in intramurals; interest clubs
5. Intellectually very capable and knowledgable, ability to deal with the abstract	5. Opportunities for logical reasoning and creative thinking	5. More emphasis placed on strategy in game play; creative dance composition work; more involved routines in gymnastics
6. Feeling of insecurity, unsure of self in group (particularly seventh graders); great desire to be a part of a group	6. Need to have feeling of acceptance by teacher and other members of class; great understanding and patience needed by teacher (especially in grade 7); children need recognition	6. Involved in selecting teammates; work in small groups; expected to produce in group work projects; involved planning special events and after school tournaments and playdays

tion with children of their own age range, so each may experience as many typical situations with his peer group as possible. After all, as an adult he will live and work surrounded by people without handicaps. He must learn to view his handicap in a positive and realistic manner and adjust to the world about him.

Participation in a well-planned physical education program is the prerogative of every child. For those with handicaps the regular program must be adapted to meet their needs. Adapted physical education in the elementary school is not a corrective program. If a child's particular handicap requires therapy or correction, this must be conducted by a specialist trained in corrective procedures working under the prescriptive advice of the child's physician.

Childen for whom activities might have to be adapted varies from those who have been absent for a few days to those who have a temporary physical handicap, a permanent physical handicap, a heart condition, impaired hearing, impaired vision, impaired speech, epilepsy, an allergy, low or exceptionally high mentality, emotional maladjustment, or social maladjustments. Emotional and social maladjustments are the most difficult to recognize; therefore they are the least frequently diagnosed as handicaps until they become severe. The teacher must remember that a child who has been ill only a day or two will suffer a loss of strength and endurance. Therefore, his adjustment to a typical work and play schedule

---

_____ School

Pupil   _____   Date _____

Dear Dr. _____

    Our school curriculum includes a daily half-hour period of guided physical education. The program includes a balanced variety of activities which are adapted to meet the needs of every child in the class. Below is a list of these activities.

    Will you please indicate the nature of _____ condition and state the type of activity he needs most and what is definitely contraindicated. Please check the activities in which he can participate with modifications for his condition.

Nature of condition _____

Needs most _____

_____

Contraindicated _____

_____

Quiet Games	PIU* _____			
Basic Movement Skills	PI _____	Track and Field	IU	_____
Creative Dance	PIU _____	Basketball	IU	_____
Folk Dance	PIU _____	Volleyball	IU	_____
Active Low Organized	PIU _____	Softball	IU	_____
Games	PIU _____	Soccer	IU	_____
Apparatus Work	PIU _____	Tag Football	U	_____
Stunts, Tumbling	PIU _____	Track and Field	IU	_____
Ball Skills	PIU _____	Paddle Tennis	U	_____
Rope Jumping	_____			_____

* P = Kdg, 1, 2   I = 3, 4   U = 5, 6, 7, 8

What is the approximate length of time for which you recommend the modified program? _____

                        Thank you very much,

                        _____ Principal

Figure 2-1. Physician's Form Letter for Adaptive Activities.

must be gradual while his strength and endurance are being regained.

    It is not within the realm of this book to discuss each handicap and problems associated with them. Rather, guidelines will be offered for the teacher of physical education to follow when he needs to plan for modifications.

In order to know how to adapt the physical education program, the teacher must know as much as he can about the individual for whom he is making the adjustments. The special teacher of a class of children with the same handicaps should be knowledgeable as to the problems, needs, and hazards concerned; and it is necessary for the classroom teacher or the physical education specialist to learn all he can about the specific handicap of an exceptional child who enters his classroom.

Primarily, however, it is the responsibility of the school administration to work with teachers in planning work with exceptional children. If there is a school nurse, the teacher should work very closely with her. The teacher's first responsibility might well be that of screening the children and identifying those with handicaps. He must refer the child to the appropriate personnel in the school and make the parents aware of the child's problem.

When a child enters school with a handicap, information about his condition and limitations must be secured from his physician as well as from his parents. The physician should be sent a form letter regarding activities included in the regular program that can be adapted for the handicapped. The physician should indicate the child's limitations and nature of his handicap. He may make suggestions for special activities or check the ones that the child needs and can perform if they are adapted to his abilities. A sample is presented in Figure 2-1.

After receiving this information from the physician, the teacher should talk with the parents. He can explain the objectives of the program, the types of activities, and their modifications. Some parents, overprotective of handicapped children, are prone to discourage activity, and they make the child fearful of it. In the conference the teacher can reassure the parents, and he will learn more about the child and understand better how he might react to activity.

Objectives to be emphasized in adaptive program

In addition to the general objectives of physical education for all children, there are a few major objectives that need to be emphasized for the exceptional child. The child must develop a positive and realistic attitude toward his capabilities, limitations, and potentialities in physical activities. He must learn how to be self-directive in regulating the extent of his participation in physical activities. He must acquire a knowledge of and skill in a variety of games and activities in which he can participate alone and with other children in his leisure time.[5]

[5] Edna Engberg, *Physical Education Activities for the Physically Handicapped* (Springfield, Ill., Office of the Superintendent of Public Instruction, 1963).

General suggestions for
adapting activities

Some modifications can be made in the majority of the regular activities despite a child's handicap. However, there may be situations in which this cannot be done logically, and both the student and the teacher must accept this. The adaptation can not be so great that it will interfere with the normal progress of the majority of the children in the class.

Frequently, a handicapped youngster may not have sufficient strength to master a particular skill, or must work longer on his adapted pattern than the normal children do to learn a new skill. In either of these instances the handicapped youngster may have to work longer individually within the class or at home in order to use his new skill successfully in a group.

All of the other children in the class must understand a child's handicap to a certain extent. If they do, they will be eager to help modify rules and skills and be much more accepting of his limitations. Everyone must know the special rules and modifications that are set for the child in the game. The handicapped youngster will learn that if he tries hard and does his best within the limits of his capabilities, other children will accept and support him physically and socially.

Adaptive physical education does not mean letting the youngster keep score or pass out the pinnies. It means adapting for participation in activity. When a great deal of individual work or self-testing activities are included in a program, adaptation is not too difficult. The child and teacher can work out adaptations just as every other child is working individually. Modifications of rules and how skills are used in large group, team games, and dances are a little more challenging. Some general modifications are:

1. When locomotion is a problem, a child can do the specific skills of a game which do not require mobility. For example: he can bat in softball and someone else can run for him. In volleyball, he can rotate into the game to serve. Support in the standing position may be necessary or the child may sit. If mobility is possible but greatly inhibited, the style of locomotion may be changed and/or distances altered. For example: if a youngster can not walk but can crawl, anyone who is chasing him may be required to crawl also. In a relay race it may be just as great a challenge for the handicapped child to go half the distance as it is for the others to go all the way, so that the race would be equal if the distance were modified for the handicapped child.

2. When vision is a problem, targets must be larger, balls thrown slower, names called when it is one's turn to catch, and suggestions given for adjusting direction for better accuracy. Some children may be able to throw, but not catch and vice versa. In either case, another child may do one of the tasks for the handicapped child.

3. When hearing is a problem, a partner might be assigned to give the child with impaired hearing manual signals and to reinforce directions by a demonstration.

4. When mentally retarded children are in a class, it must be remembered that they do not think as fast or make decisions as quickly as normal children. They are most like normal children in the physical area and can usually learn to do most motor skills tasks fairly well with instruction. However, they often get confused in games which require application of a large number of rules and when there are many changes in possession of the ball. They should be placed in positions which do not demand too many quick decisions until they are comfortable in and confident of the conduct of the game.

5. When the regular activity cannot be modified to fit the needs of a handicapped youngster, he may practice a skill or play another type of game in which he can play alone; for example, he may play a target toss game or table games; throw and catch against the wall; or perform strength or endurance exercises.

Ingenuity is the key to successful adaptive programs. The teacher will find that in working on modifications, both he and the class members will benefit greatly from analyzing activities in order to modify them. Anxiety and enthusiasm to do what normal children are doing should not foster an overindulgence on the part of the handicapped youngster and create a problem rather than a solution. Should he need more help, the reader is referred to the books written about adaptive physical education which are listed in the references at the end of the chapter.

THE SLOW LEARNER

There is a growing awareness of the significance of the level of perceptual-motor development in the academic achievement of children. Results of research indicate that many youngsters, who in their preschool years did not experience play and movement activities which enabled them to develop adequate spatial concepts of size, shape, and direction; control of balance; and a variety of body movements, frequently encounter problems in learning to read, write, spell, and do arithmetic problems. Their inability to keep up with their classmates often leads to frustration, failure, and social problems. Complete diagnosis and treatment of children with these problems takes more training and more information than can be presented here; however, the teacher should be aware of what type of motor behavior to look for if he suspects a child is suffering from poor perceptual-motor development.

Radler and Kephart in their book *Success Through Play* [6] point out that when children come to school they are expected to have reached a

6 D. H. Radler with Newell Kephart, *Success Through Play* (New York, Harper & Row, 1960).

certain level of readiness in skills in four areas of behavior: motor, symbolic, social, and numerical. All of these presuppose that a child has mastered certain major and minor muscle movements and combinations of such movements that enable him to coordinate eye-hand movements, have a sense of laterality and directionality, perceive forms correctly, and make temporal-spatial translations. These expectations give an indication of areas of motor activities in which a child will exhibit poor control and performance if he has not reached the readiness level to learn academic skills and understandings typical of his age group.

If a slow learner has difficulty in solving movement problems which require balance, hand-eye coordination, rhythm, awareness of space in regard to his own body, directionality, laterality, and gross motor coordination, the teacher will be aware that retardation in motor development might underlie his lack of success in academic work. Of course, the teacher must compare the child's motor performance with that typical of his age group. Included here are a few suggestions of specific behaviors which indicate poor perceptual-motor skills. The teacher may use them as a screening device. If he finds deficiencies that need to be investigated further, he should report his findings to the proper school authorities so that a complete diagnosis may be made and plans for improvement be undertaken. *Success Through Play* and *The Slow Learner in the Classroom* (see Suggested References for Further Study) provide sources for better understanding of this problem and specific instructions for remedial work.

A few words or terms must be defined to help the reader understand the discussion better. *Laterality* is an awareness of right and left within one's own body and the ability to control the two sides of the body simultaneously or separately. *Directionality* is an awareness of right, left, up, down, front, and back in space. This external awareness of direction develops from the internal sense described as laterality. The *mid-line* of the body refers to the vertical center of the body. *Spatial orientation* or *awareness* is the concept of the relationship between the body and the body parts with objects in space. *Posture control* is the ability to maintain balance in a static position or in a moving position. *Posture flexibility* is the ability to regain posture control after changing positions.

Screening activities to study perceptual-motor development

PROBLEMS IN BALANCE

ACTIVITIES: Walk on a line painted on the floor. Walk forward, backward, and sideward on a low balance beam. Stand on one foot for ten seconds. Stand on a rocker board.

SUSPICIOUS BEHAVIOR: Failure to maintain balance at all. Failure to use arms to catch balance. Consistent use of only one arm or one side to regulate body weight or consistent use of arms in symmetrical fashion. Need to run or walk very fast to maintain balance. Hesitancy or need to look backward to maintain balance. Hesitancy and trouble in shifting directions. Hesitancy in sideward walking. Attempts to cross over with trailing foot in sideward walking, rather than always leading with the right foot when going to right or left foot when going to the left.

Behavior such as this indicates a general lack of postural control and and flexibility, lack of sense of laterality, and poor spatial orientation.

PROBLEMS IN LATERALITY AND RHYTHM

ACTIVITIES: Jump on one foot; jump, alternating feet. Hop on one foot; alternate feet. Skip. Hop in a pattern of right-right-left, left-left-right, left-left-right-right.

SUSPICIOUS BEHAVIOR: Inability to shift weight to maintain balance when jumping or hopping on one foot. Difficulty in using feet alternately. Difficulty in maintaining rhythm or flow of pattern in hopping.

Behavior such as this indicates a general lack of body control and co-ordination, poor sense of laterality, or inability to alternate movements across the mid-line, and/or poor control of rhythm or flow of movement.

PROBLEMS OF BODY IMAGE

ACTIVITIES: Play Simon Says (p. 374) where leader indicates to the group to touch different parts of body or to use various parts of body to do something. Play mirror game where leader moves various limbs and in various combinations but gives no verbal command. Followers must imitate or duplicate the movements of the leader.

SUSPICIOUS BEHAVIOR: Errors or slowness in response to touching and using the correct body parts. Hesitancy in movements. Confusion in matching the leader's movements. Use of wrong limbs or matching behavior of opposite limbs. Reverses patterns of leader.

Behavior such as this indicates a lack of awareness of location of body parts, a lack of coordination and control of body parts, a poor sense of laterality, and a poor idea of body image.

PROBLEMS IN EYE CONTROL, HAND-EYE, FOOT-EYE COORDINATION

ACTIVITIES: Using a tether ball, or simply a ball attached to the end of a rope suspended from the ceiling, child should follow the ball with his eyes as it swings across in front of him, backward and forward, and as it swings around in a circle. He should reach out and touch ball; hit ball with hand; hit ball with large paddle; catch objects of various sizes from varying distances; kick a stationary ball, a moving ball. Set up a pattern of squares painted on floor or newspapers arranged on floor in an irregular pattern so that the child must use varying lengths of steps and alternate feet to step on squares as he progresses around the room.

SUSPICIOUS BEHAVIOR: Difficulty in keeping eyes on ball as it crosses midline of body; moves head instead of eyes. Inability to touch or hit ball as it moves. Difficulty in catching ball. Reaching out for ball and moving head back. Closing eyes as ball reaches him. Hesitancy in deciding which foot to use to step on square. Always trying to use the same foot. Trouble adjusting length of step to varying distances between squares.

Behavior such as this may indicate a malfunction of the muscular system of the eye or a lack of coordination with perception and motor action. The former must be treated by a physician. If the latter is true, a lack of sense of laterality, directionality, and spatial orientation is indicated.

PROBLEMS IN SPATIAL ORIENTATION

ACTIVITIES: Set up a low hurdle or use a low table (or another person on hands and knees). Have child go over and under the obstacle; pass between two objects placed close together. Tell the child to throw to and at a large stationary object; throw at and to a moving object; run and throw a ball up in the air and catch it.

SUSPICIOUS BEHAVIOR: Inability or difficulty in estimating height of obstacle and size of step needed to clear it. Difficulty in judging amount of space and necessary body adaptations needed to go under the obstacle or through a narrow space. Difficulty in judging distance target is from self. Difficulty in judging how far ahead of person ball must be thrown so ball and person meet. (This is a difficult task for a young child.) Difficulty in judging where ball is in space while one is moving.

Behavior such as this indicates that a child has problems of awareness of his body parts in space and of his body in relation to other objects in space.

The suggested activities are but a few in which observations of children's behavior in tasks which are basic to good perceptual-motor development may be made. These are activities which are usually conducted within the regular physical education program. If all of the children in the class do these tasks, the teacher will get a reference point as to what good control is. He may quickly screen children whose behaviors do not appear similar to those of the majority. Later he may make more specific observations of those that appear to deviate from the majority.

It must be remembered that within one class few children will exhibit gross deficiencies in these areas. These few will benefit from an individualized remedial program of perceptual-motor activities. Ideally, a specialist should be available to work with the slow learner at school and to help orient his parents as to activities he can do at home to "catch up." When a specialist is not available, the classroom teacher may study a child's area of deficiency and plan activities to help him. Activities similar to those used in screening provide good practice devices. However, it will be necessary in most cases to start with simpler concepts and tasks of balance, direction, and movement in space and eventually work up to these. More detailed and lengthy suggestions may be found in Kephart's book *The Slow Learner in the Classroom.*[7] Keep in mind that this discussion concerns the child who entered school with subnormal control of perceptual motor skills. A well planned physical education program in the primary grades. as proposed in this book, will include the study of the factors affecting basic movement skills and much variety and variability in the exploration of skills and movement in space. These experiences will enrich a normal youngster's perceptual-motor skills and certainly improve those of children who are slightly underdeveloped in this area before they encounter great academic difficulties.

Summary

Although all children follow a sequential order of growth and development, they are not on the same timetable as to the time and degree of completeness of development. The teacher has to be flexible when selecting activities and methods to account for the individuals within his class.

The discussion of differences between boys and girls should help the teacher understand that boys on the average can perform skills, particularly those requiring strength and endurance, better than girls. In the upper grades, boys and girls should be separated for vigorous activities which require strength and endurance where there is any competition between individuals and/or groups.

The development of motor skill patterns is a matter of maturation and is sequential. Therefore, the physical education curriculum must be sequential with the emphasis in the primary grades upon developing variability, adaptability, flexibility, and variety in the use of basic motor skill

---

[7] Newell Kephart, *The Slow Learner in the Classroom* (Columbus, Merrill, 1960).

patterns—changing to the development and refinement of specific skills in a variety of increasingly complex games, dance, and gymnastic activities in the upper grades. Emotional and social control develops sequentially also; therefore, activities and organization should be geared to the evolvement from self interest to group interest.

Experiences should be structured to allow children to be successful the majority of the time. Many self-testing situations should be planned so that steps in progress can be realistic and attainable with some effort. Ability grouping will enhance realistic competition between individuals and/or groups. Expectations of performance can be judged in part on individual physical maturity, body build, and body structure.

Children who are handicapped by structural or functional limitations must be given special consideration. Activities and experiences within the regular class must be adapted to their capabilities. Children who have had little opportunity for experiences to promote the development of perceptual-motor skills prior to entering school, need special help and activities to acquire physical and academic skills characteristic of their age group.

In addition to the instructional program, opportunities for free choices of play activities, enrichment of motor skill learning, and use of skills and knowledge in a less teacher-directed situation must be provided. Here again, variety is important due to individual differences in interests and abilities.

SUGGESTED REFERENCES
FOR FURTHER STUDY

Breckenridge, Marion E., and E. Lee Vincent, *Child Development* (Philadelphia, Saunders, 1960).

Espenschade, Anna, *Physical Education in the Elementary Schools. What Research Says to the Teacher,* #27 (Washington, D.C., Department of Classroom Teachers, National Education Association, 1963).

Espenschade, Anna, "Motor Development" in *Science and Medicine of Exercise and Sports* (New York, Harper & Row, 1960).

Fait, Hollis F., *Special Physical Education* (Philadelphia, Saunders, 1966).

Hunsicker, Paul, *Physical Fitness, What Research Says to the Teacher,* #26 (Washington, D.C., Department of Classroom Teachers, National Education Association, 1963).

Journal of Health, Physical Education and Recreation (April, 1966). Nine feature articles on physical education for the mentally retarded.

Kephart, Newell C., *The Slow Learner in the Classroom* (Columbus, Merrill, 1960).

Radler, D. H., with Newell C. Kephart, *Success Through Play* (New York, Harper & Row, 1960).

Rarick, G. Lawrence, *Motor Development During Infancy and Childhood* (Madison, Wisconsin, College Printing and Typing Co., 1961).

Chapter III

THE CURRICULUM

Considerations in curriculum planning

Basic movement skills

Activity areas

Total curriculum content

Extraclass program

The curriculum in elementary school physical education is a sequence of experiences designed to help the child gain skills and concepts which will allow him to function efficiently and effectively in all of his life experiences, whether they be social, mental, or emotional. Experiences which teach skills, concepts, and understandings in the following areas form the curriculum of physical education.

1. The neuromuscular skills of movement and the factors of space, time, force, level, energy, intensity, and relationships with people and inanimate objects which affect the performance of the skills
2. The development and maintenance of physical fitness
3. The social behavior skills needed for good interpersonal relations and individual adjustment

The many and varied activities of physical education serve as the tools through which these broader skills, concepts, and understandings are reinforced and developed.

The actual subject matter of the physical education curriculum revolves around four major activity areas—Gymnastics, Games and Sports, Dance, and Aquatics. Within each of these there is a progressive order of acquisition and refinement of skills and knowledges in different forms of the activities throughout the child's school years. Each grade, class, and individual varies in readiness to learn specific things in regard to maturation, time allotted to instruction, competence of the teachers, facilities, and equipment. It is difficult to say at exactly what age or grade level each skill, game, dance, or other activity should be introduced. However, in this chapter suggestions are made for the nature of the activities and amount of time spent on each under the assumption that an instructional program is offered beginning in first grade. A separate chapter is devoted to each activity area with a suggested progression of content for each grade. The latter is offered as an aid to the inexperienced teacher. Guidelines are given to help the teacher select specific experiences within each activity, as no progression can fit every class. There is a growing trend toward ungraded classrooms in the intermediate and upper grades as well as the traditional ungraded first two years. It is hoped that by applying the guidelines, teachers will learn how to select suitable activities rather than rely on a suggested progression.

CONSIDERATIONS IN CURRICULUM PLANNING

The primary consideration that must be followed when planning the curriculum is the developmental level of the children involved. Around the needs, capabilities, and interests of the children are planned the nature of the activities, the percentage of time devoted to each, the sequence of activities, the emphasis within the activity, and the duration of the units. Secondary to the developmental level of the children, and sometimes more confining, are the practical considerations of time, facilities, equipment, materials, and teachers.

Most schools do not have ideal facilities, unlimited budgets, or physical education specialists; however, a well-balanced developmental program can be conducted with careful selection of activities based on the following five criteria.

1. Select activities which are suitable to the maturation level in terms of physical, mental, social growth. Remember to provide for individual differences within the group.
2. Select activities which reflect a progression of difficulty and increasingly more challenging tasks.
3. Select activities which reflect a balanced program. Balance should be considered in terms of use and development of all parts of the body, mental applications, emotional controls, and social interactions.
4. Select activities which provide maximum activity and participation for everyone in the class.
5. Select activities which provide for invention, self-discovery, and self-direction.

In this chapter each activity area and the forms of activities within them are discussed. Table 3-1 presents this material in outline form.

BASIC MOVEMENT
SKILLS

In studying the curriculum of physical education in the elementary school, consider all of the child's activity experiences as a wheel or circle where all of the experiences contribute to the optimum development of the whole child. Each activity area offers unique media through which general and specific objectives are best realized. The *hub* of the wheel is basic movement skills which are indigenous of all of the activities (Figure 3-1). All other specific sport, dance, gymnastic, and aquatic skills are but combinations of these movement skills. Therefore, a good foundation of skill and understanding must be laid in the primary and intermediate grades. Acquisition of skill cannot be left to chance. Many opportunities for practicing skills in varied situations must be provided, and they must be accompanied by good instruction and coaching of individuals.

As has been mentioned previously, children come to school having encountered or experienced most of the fundamental motor skills. This is not to say they know how to perform all of the skills proficiently or in various combinations. They have done the many natural movements of childhood in their first five years of life in proportion to the freedom and opportunities they have enjoyed in their home or neighborhood environment. Most of their skill patterns were acquired by necessity, by curiosity in exploration, by trial and error, and by imitation of other people's movements.

The extent of each child's experiences is dependent on the encouragement, the freedom, and the space available to move and explore. It is

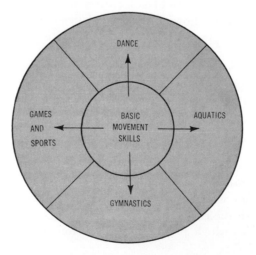

Figure 3-1. Relationship of Basic Movement Skills to All Activities.

reasonable to think that a child raised in a small apartment in a crowded neighborhood will have less movement experiences than one from a home with a yard; unless parents and/or the community make provisions for play space. Parents may limit a child's movement experiences by an overprotective attitude, oversolicitation, or disdain for noise and laughter.

The primary grades may be considered as the introductory period in relation to instructional work with skills. In the first two grades the greatest percentage of time of the total physical education program is devoted to exploration and refinement of basic movement skills. It is in this phase of the program that a child improves his skills and coordination through varied experiences as he matures physically, mentally, and socially. He learns what factors affect movement and how to use his body in relation to them. With guidance and instruction from the teacher he learns to adapt his movements to many new factors: space about him, number of people, different speeds or tempos, different levels, and variations of force and intensity. Thus a child gains confidence in movement, familiarity with sports objects and implements, large and small pieces of apparatus, and an understanding of his body potential. A good understanding and acquisition of the basic movement skills and factors that affect them also provide the child with the bases of creativity and self-expression.

The basic skills are developed, studied, and used in two kinds of

Table 3-1. Activity Areas and Forms Within Each

Activity Areas	Forms of Activities
Gymnastics	Basic Movement Skills
	Developmental Exercises
	Stunts
	Tumbling
	Small Equipment
	Large Apparatus
Games and Sports	Low Organized Games
	Relays
	Quiet and Classroom Games
	Individual and Dual Games
	Sport Skills
	Lead-Up Games to Individual Sports
	Lead-Up Games to Team Sports
Dance	Dance Fundamentals
	Creative Dance
	Folk Dance
	Recreational Dance
Aquatics	Swimming
	Diving
	Boating
	Water Games

styles: (1) *expressive* style, where movement skills are used to respond to various stimuli and to express ideas and emotions as required for dance and dramatic activities; (2) *objective* style, where movement skills are used to do specific tasks required for games, sports, gymnastics, and work.

In the primary grades most of the instructional time is spent on basic movement skills and the various factors that affect how the skills are performed. The emphasis is on developing variability, adaptability, flexibility, and variety in use of the skills. The same skills and factors are studied in the three settings of dance, gymnastics, and games. Each of these settings provide unique opportunities for exploring and experimenting in different relationships with people and inanimate objects.

Very frequently today, the basic movement skill work in the primary and intermediate grades is referred to as Movement Exploration or Movement Education. In reality, this is an approach or a method of presenting and developing skills and understandings of use of the body in relation to all aspects of movement. It is very difficult to isolate any movement learning as a subject or activity area in itself, since what is taught or done in Movement Education is vital to every activity area. Exploratory work with movement skills can precede or be an integral part of every lesson, regardless of the nature of the activity or the grade level. Best learning will result if the exploratory type of method is characteristic of the instruction in all activity areas, as this method requires the student to develop his powers of perception in relation to his movement activities.

Both the use of the exploratory method and the stress on the study of basic movement skills and factors that affect them are consistent with recent emphasis in child development and in the kindergarten and primary education curricula. The theories of Delacato [1], who bases his rationale on the premise that there are significant developmental stages of neurological organization which cannot be bypassed, and of Kephart [2], who emphasizes a developmental sequence of learning based on a systematic relationship motorwise to environment, provide much of the bases of the current expansion of basic skill work in the kindergarten and primary grades. The theories of Gesell and Piaget serve as the bases for problem solving, exploration, and experimentation as the means of developing all of the child's functions (motor, auditory, visual, emotional, conceptual) in the preschool and primary years.

As children grow older and more skillful, less time is spent on direct instruction with basic movement skills. Instruction and practice become more specific to the activity area in which skills are needed. In the intermediate grades, this is evidenced in beginning work with sport implements, larger pieces of apparatus, specific dance steps, patterns, and

[1] Carl Delacato, *The Treatment and Prevention of Reading Problems* (Springfield, Illinois, Charles C Thomas, 1964).
[2] Newell C. Kephart, *The Slow Learner in the Classroom* (Columbus, Merrill, 1964).

compositions. In the upper grades, skill instruction becomes very specific to sports and applications to specific pieces of apparatus and dance techniques. At this point, care must be taken that adequate time is allotted to specific instruction and practice of these skills. Standards of good performance should be upheld rather than acceptance of any quality of movement in game, apparatus, or dance activities.

Although the importance of physical activity to neural development and perceptual formations has been recognized and a concentration on activities to enhance this development has become the focal point of many kindergarten and primary physical education programs, it would be a mistake to conclude that acquisition of specific activity skills is not important. Methods may have changed, but the development of good skill in sports, dance, and gymnastic activities is not out-of-date. It is in the process of acquiring these skills that most of the primary purposes of physical education are served and the associated and concomitant values of physical education are gained.

ACTIVITY AREAS

Gymnastics

This area of activities is broad and inclusive. Most of the activities are of a self-testing nature, which implies an opportunity for a child to test himself, to prove himself, to discover his abilities, and to achieve success by his own efforts. The challenge of success is individual in regard to each child's body build and skill. The forms of gymnastic activities are:
1. Basic movement skills
2. Developmental exercises
3. Stunts
4. Tumbling
5. Activities using small equipment
6. Activities on large apparatus

Guided developmental experiences in all of these forms provide for development of large muscle groups, strength, muscle endurance, agility, balance, flexibility, and coordination. Work in this area affords excellent opportunities for the development of perseverance, courage, initiative, resourcefulness, and understanding of individual differences.

Developmental exercises
For the most part, developmental exercises call for combinations of basic movement that may require use of isolated parts of the body or gross

body movement. This type of exercise lends itself to work with the whole group where the teacher may pose challenges to be met, ask for original or creative exercises, or introduce new concepts in a more direct manner. Many basic maneuvers used on apparatus may be practiced first on the floor—such as landing techniques, balance stunts, weight bearing, and others. What are sometimes referred to as "fitness activities" fall into this category. Exercises that help develop strength—such as, push-ups, sit-ups—those that help develop endurance—such as jumping jacks, running in place—and many others are developmental. This form of gymnastic activity may be used profitably in all grade levels and may very well be utilized at the beginning of every lesson for loosening-up purposes, introductory activities, or for a whole lesson.

Stunts

There is some overlap with stunt activities and developmental exercises. Traditional stunts are usually set feats that require certain elements of flexibility, strength, balance, agility, or combinations of these. Original stunts may be created by children at all ages. When one cannot perform a stunt on the first try, he is challenged and motivated to work until he masters it. A series of stunts as a challenge to be accomplished over a period of time provides valuable opportunities for social growth as well as physical growth.

Tumbling

Tumbling activities include rolling, balancing, supporting one's weight when inverted, and springing. The elements of agility, flexibility, strength, balance, and coordination are developed through tumbling activities. As with stunts, there is always the element of challenge involved in trying to develop good form as well as accomplishing the initial tasks. Most tumbling activities build one upon another, so a definite progression must be followed whether tumbling activities are initiated in the second grade or in the seventh grade.

Small equipment

In the primary grades exploratory work with small objects and equipment of all types is stressed. The child develops his manipulative ability, hand-eye coordination, and foot-eye coordination. He experiments with a variety of shapes, sizes, and weights of small equipment-balls, bean bags, hoops, wands, jumping ropes, stilts, rings, paddles, bats, and others. In this way he gains a familiarity and confidence in using his body in a variety of relationships which each object demands. He also may experiment and invent many different ways to use equipment without regard to a prescribed manner.

In the intermediate grades work with sport implements and balls is directly related to the basic skills of the specific sports. It is important that the size of the equipment be appropriate to the size of the children.

Apparatus

Work on apparatus is largely exploratory in the primary and intermediate grades. The emphasis is on learning how to get on, over, and off objects, and learning the application of basic principles of mechanics and movement to many different apparatus situations. Confidence and familiarity with various pieces of apparatus are developed before formal set patterns of specific exercises or routines on apparatus are initiated. The former is accomplished in the primary grades in combination with exploratory work in adapting basic movement skills to apparatus. The latter type of work is begun in the upper grades. As with all of the other forms of gymnastic activities, strength, balance, coordination, and flexibility can be developed through apparatus work. Developing shoulder girdle strength is one of the major values of apparatus work. The hanging and supporting opportunities are more numerous than in any other activity area.

Games and sports

Games and sports have been an important part of most cultures from the beginning of civilization. Children and adults play games for fun and for the satisfaction they provide. Most afterschool and leisure time activity of both children and adults is drawn from the game and sports activity area. In the physical education program there is a type of evolution process from games of simple organization to official sports. This evolution may be likened to a pyramid where the basic movement skills serve as the base and official team and individual sports as the apex of the pyramid (Figure 3-2).

At the same time that work in basic movement skills is underway, in the primary grades, games of low organization in which the skills are used in a variety of ways are introduced. In this way the child begins to recognize the purposes and values of good skills. The more confining game situation demands a cognitive process in the use of skills as well as physical prowess. Most games provide vigorous activity; however, there are games designed for inactive relaxation and confined spaces.

The value of games in promoting good social development cannot be overemphasized. Games may be selected for the primary child which help promote good habits of taking turns, following directions, recognizing boundaries, working together, being a leader, and many others. There are a variety of forms of games, each of which can make a contribution to the development of a specific type of social behavior.

Although it is recommended that only twenty-five percent of the program time in the primary grades be devoted to games, there is still danger that a teacher may include too many games or not select games for specific outcomes. To the children the game may be played just for fun, but to the teacher every game which is played should be a means of producing definite developmental outcomes. Each game presented should reveal a progression of difficulty in use of skills, rules, and strategy. The various forms of games and specific learning experiences for each are presented in Chapter XI.

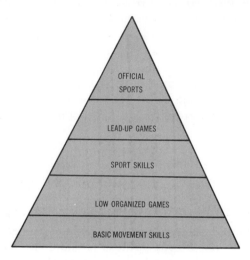

Figure 3-2. Evolution of Games and Sports in the Elementary School.

Starting in third grade, special attention is given to exploration with balls and implements specific to team and individual sports. At this point the primary purpose is to help children develop competence in the basic skills which serve as the foundation for specific sport skills. Basic mechanical principles are stressed as new combinations of movements are introduced for use with different sizes of balls, implements, and the particulars of each sport. These skills are then used in lead-up games.

Depending on the sport, lead-up games are introduced as early as third grade. A lead-up game may be defined as a game within itself; however, it must include one or more skills, similar rules and simple strategy of an official sport. Lead-up games range from one of utmost simplicity to an increasingly complex game which is almost identical to that of the official sport.

Through careful selection from grade to grade, a definite progression can be developed while the sport skills, rules, and strategy are learned accumulatively to a point where those of the official parent game can be learned with ease. Therefore, children can enjoy games which are planned for their level of skill, size, understanding, and interest, from the middle elementary years to high school when they become ready for the official rules of each sport.

The social values gained from team games or sports are many. In these games there are great opportunities for teaching valuable social responses through both competition and cooperation. All of our democratic traits are brought to the fore with the need of team work and personal sacrifices in the pursuance of team play. The satisfaction that the child derives from his small contribution to the part of a winning team will help build unselfish adults. The understanding of the inevitability of having to lose at times can forestall the development of a "sore loser" and encourage the recognition of the need for improvement in the next quest.

As children mature, they naturally become more interested in group activities, vigorous activity, and improvement in skills. The percentage of time spent in low organized games decreases proportionately until in the upper grades practically no amount of time is assigned to them. It must be remembered that children at these ages still like to play simple games for the sheer enjoyment of it, but not too long nor too often. In the upper grades, beginning skills and lead-up games related to individual sports are given more attention. It is this type of games that will be utilized most by the individual for leisure time activities.

Dance activities

People have danced for pleasure and purpose throughout the recorded history of mankind. Dance can serve as a means of communication of ideas and expression, creativity, and as a recreative activity.

Dance activities is an inclusive term, as there are several forms of dance. In the elementary school four major aspects of dance are studied: fundamentals, creative, folk, and recreational. All dance activity is based on movement affected by the elements of space, force, and rhythm. The fundamentals include basic locomotor and nonlocomotor movement skills, rhythm skills, and space elements.

Actually, the movement skills are the same as those taught and explored as basic movement skills; however, in dance the expressive form of the skills is stressed. More emphasis is given to the coordination of the movements and rhythmic elements. It is difficult to separate the two activities as far as attention to fundamental skill work is concerned. The basic difference is in the application of skills.

In the primary grades work with dance fundamentals is usually associated with a dramatic purpose and has some type of rhythmic accompaniment. The creative area takes the form of portraying incidents or telling a story in movement, or pretending to be an object or animal within the childrens' realm of experience. Primary children enjoy singing games and very simple folk dances. Since today in many schools the latter two forms are taught in conjunction with the music lessons, the classroom teacher has an opportunity to integrate the music and dance lessons quite productively.

Once children have explored the fundamental skills of locomotion and rhythm, they are ready to learn the traditional dance steps which are combinations of various basic locomotor movements. These are then the basic steps for the various folk dances which are learned throughout the school years and form the basis of most of the recreational dance forms.

Creative work is continued in all the grades. As children grow older, their experiences and interests expand, and consequently their need and desire to express themselves grow. Making one's own dance is extremely vital and exciting to children of all ages. The complexity of the dance, the refinement of the skills involved, and the length of time for the preparation of the dances increases proportionately by grades.

The introduction of social dance skills and etiquette is dependent on the social needs of children in their respective communities. Most frequently there are school or community parties or dances that require some dance skills by eighth grade. As boys particularly may not be interested in this phase of dance unless they have a real tangible need to learn, it is foolish to force social dance on groups before they can use their skills in a social situation.

Aquatics

Although swimming and water sports are an integral part of the American people's recreation and pose many safety hazards, a minority of children learn how to swim. The cost of building and maintaining pool facilities is prohibitive for most school systems. The majority of pools are found in the secondary schools.

When community pools are available, the school personnel should seek a way to include swimming instruction for children starting in the third grade. Children quite rapidly learn to swim at that age. Fear of the water appears to be overcome more quickly by younger children than by older ones.

If swimming is included in the elementary school program, usually qualified swimming instructors are hired rather than the classroom teacher being responsible for the instruction. Content for an aquatic program is not included here; however, source books are recommended for

Table 3-2. Percentage of Time Devoted to Each Activity Area

ACTIVITIES	GRADE								
	Kdg.	1	2	3	4	5	6	7	8
Dance	25%	25%	25%	20%	20%	20%	20%	15%	15%
Gymnastics	60	50	50	40	40	35	35	30	30
Games and Sports	15	25	50	40	40	45	45	55	55
Aquatics (if possible)				10	10	10	10	10	10
				(Delete time equally from others)					

reference if one is teaching swimming to young children. No time is allotted to aquatics in the suggested time divisions; however, if it is included in the program, no more than ten percent of the total time should be devoted to it. The ten percent should then be deducted equally from the other activity areas.

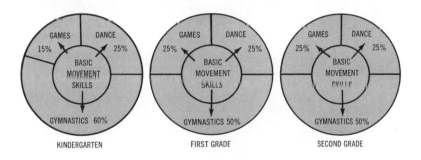

Figure 3-3. Suggested Division of Time for Activities for Kindergarten, First and Second Grades.

TOTAL CURRICULUM CONTENT

One can see that each activity has specific applications for contributing to the various phases of the development of the child. As the goal is one of a well-balanced individual, the content must be well balanced. The description of the forms of activities within each area has indicated the implications of the various stages of growth and development as related to emphasis and time spent at the different grade levels. Tables 3-2 to 3-4 portray a suggested percentage of time to be planned for each activity in summary form. Study the changes from grade to grade with the information about child growth and development in mind (Figures 3-3 to 3-6).

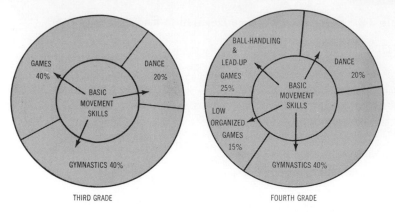

Figure 3-4. Suggested Division of Time for Activities for Third and Fourth Grades.

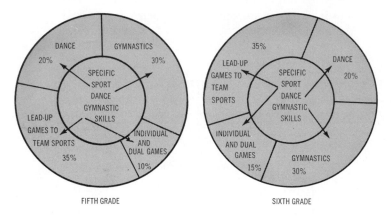

Figure 3-5. Suggested Division of Time for Activities for Fifth and Sixth Grades.

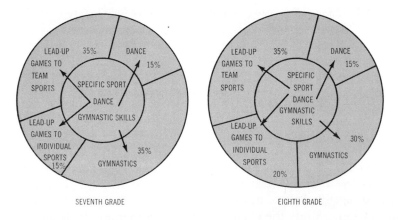

Figure 3-6. Suggested Division of Time for Activities for Seventh and Eighth Grades.

Table 3-3. Seasonal Activity Units

FALL

Kindergarten	*Grade 1*	*Grade 2*
Basic Movement Skills	Low Organized Games	Low Organized Games
Ball Skills	Basic Movement Skills	Basic Movement Skills
Playground Apparatus	Ball Skills	Ball Skills
Low Organized Games	Playground Apparatus	Playground Apparatus
	Rope Jumping	Rope Jumping
	Hoops, Wands, etc.	Hoops, Wands, etc.

WINTER

Kindergarten	*Grade 1*	*Grade 2*
Basic Movement Skills	Apparatus	Apparatus
Dance	Dance	Ball Skills and Games
Creative	Creative	Basic Skills
Fundamentals	Folk	Dance
Ball Skills	Fundamentals	Creative
Ropes	Ball Skills	Folk
Wands	Basic Movement Skills	Fundamentals
Low Organized Games	Rope Jumping	Rope Jumping
	Stunts	Stunts
	Tumbling	Tumbling
	Hoops, Wands, etc.	

SPRING

Kindergarten	*Grade 1*	*Grade 2*
Basic Movement Skills	Ball Skills and Games	Ball Skills and Games
Ball Skills	Basic Movement Skills	Basic Movement Skills
Small Equipment	Low Organized Games	Low Organized Games
Low Organized Games	Playground Apparatus	Rope Jumping, Hoops,
Playground Apparatus	Rope Jumping, Hoops,	Beanbags, etc.
	Wands, Beanbags, etc.	

FALL

Grade 3	*Grade 4*
Basic Movement Skills	Basic Movement Skills
Low Organized Games	Low Organized Games
Soccer Skills and Lead-Up Games	Soccer Skills and Lead-Up Games
	Developmental Exercises

WINTER

Grade 3	*Grade 4*
Large Apparatus	Apparatus
Ball Skills and Games	Basketball Skills and Lead-Up
Low Organized Games	Games
Net Games	Low Organized Games

Table 3-3. Continued

WINTER

Grade 3

Dance
  Creative
  Folk
Stunts and Tumbling
Small Equipment

Grade 4

Dance
  Creative
  Folk
Stunts and Tumbling
Volleyball Skills and Lead-Up
  Games

SPRING

Grade 3

Basic Skills of Track and Field
Ball Skills and Games
Low Organized Games

Grade 4

Low Organized Games
Softball Skills and Lead-Up Games
Track and Field

FALL

Grade 5

Soccer Skills Lead-Up Games
Developmental Skills
Individual and Dual Games

Grade 6

Soccer Skills and Lead-Up Games
Individual and Dual Games
Developmental Exercises

WINTER

Grade 5

Apparatus
  Parallel Bars, Horizontal Bar,
  Climbing Ropes, Balance Beam
  (36 in.), Vaulting Bench
Basketball Skills and Lead-Up
  Games
Low Organized Games
  Co-recreational games
Dance
  Creative
  Folk
Stunts and Tumbling
Volleyball Lead-Up Games

Grade 6

Apparatus
  Parallel Bars, Horizontal Bar,
  Climbing Ropes, Balance Beam
  (36 in.), Vaulting Box
Basketball Skills and Lead-Up
  Games
Dance
  Creative
  Folk
  Recreational
Modified Volleyball (6 ft. 6 in. net)
Stunts and Tumbling

SPRING

Grade 5

Softball Skills and Lead-Up Games
Track and Field
Developmental Exercises

Grade 6

Softball
Track and Field
Wall Paddle Tennis

Table 3-3. Continued

FALL

Grade 7	*Grade 8*
Modified Soccer	Flag Football (Boys)
Track and Field	Regulation Soccer
Individual and Dual Games	Individual and Dual Games
Flag Football (Boys)	Developmental Exercises

WINTER

Grade 7	*Grade 8*
Apparatus	Apparatus
Parallel Bars, Balance Beam (40 in.)	Climbing Ropes, Vaulting, Parallel
Horizontal Bars, Vaulting Box	Bars, Horizontal Bar, Balance
Dance	Beam (48 in.)
Creative	Dance
Folk	Folk'
Round, Square, Social	Round, Square, Social
Regulation Basketball	Regulation Basketball
Regulation Volleybull	Stunts
Stunts	Tumbling
Tumbling	Paddle Badminton
Paddle Badminton	

SPRING

Grade 7	*Grade 8*
Modified Softball	Paddle Tennis
Track, Field	Softball
Puddle Tennis	Track, Field

EXTRACLASS PROGRAM

Extraclass activities are a vital part of the physical educational curriculum. They are an extension of the physical education instructional program and serve various purposes and needs of children. They provide an enrichment service for all. Children need more activity than the half hour or forty-five minutes the scheduled class period provides. There are athletically gifted youngsters, just as there are intellectually gifted youngsters, who desire and need more time and opportunity than class time to refine skills. Game play in student directed activities and competitive situations is the proving ground for using skills and working together. As extraclass activities are less teacher-directed than class instruction, opportunities for social development abound in the more informal setting. Extraclass activities take several forms: intramurals, noon hour activity, recess, extramural or interscholastic sports, playdays, field days, and clubs.

Intramurals

Supervised play periods after school where everyone who wishes to may attend are usually called intramurals. In some schools they are called recreation hour. The nature of the program may be varied. Most frequently seasonal sports are played and teams are organized among those who attend. A tournament usually follows several nights of free play. Sometimes this is an enrichment of the instructional program where more advanced skills are taught to those who are interested and capable of learning more than time permits in the regular class. It may be a free play period where equipment and space are available for several activities and children do what they choose.

    Whatever the format, intramurals should be an outgrowth of the instructional program. Everyone who is interested should be able to play.

Schedule

Certain afternoons are usually scheduled for specific grade groups depending on the organization of the school and the availability of facilities. Most often intramurals are offered starting in the fourth grade. Where play facilities are limited in neighborhoods and where many mothers work, free play periods are held for children in the primary grades also. Following are two typical intramural schedules (Table 3-4).

    If there are several sections of each grade, interclass tournaments might climax several weeks of mixed free play. The emphasis should be on participation and recreation for all, not on intense competition. Teams are frequently formed on the basis of size or ability in order to equalize competition.

Table 3-4. Two Typical Intramural Schedules

FALL

Monday:	*Tuesday:*	*Wednesday:*	*Thursday:*	*Friday:* Grade 4, Boys and Girls
Grade 6, Boys	Grade 6, Girls	Grade 5, Boys	Grade 5, Girls	
Flag Football	Soccer	Soccer	Soccer	Alley Soccer
Paddle Tennis	Paddle Tennis	Flag Football	Kickball	Four Square

WINTER

Basketball	Basketball	Basketball	Basketball	Net Games
Volleyball	Volleyball	Volleyball	Volleyball	Basketball Lead-Up
Gymnastics	Gymnastics	Gymnastics	Gymnastics	Games
Co-Rec Dance	Co-Rec Dance			Dodgeball games

SPRING

Softball	Track and Field	Softball	Kickball	Kickball
Track and Field	Softball	Track and Field	Track and Field	Track and Field
		Tether Ball	Tether Ball	Tether Ball

FALL

Monday: Grades 5 and 6, Boys	*Tuesday:* Grades 5 and 6, Girls	*Wednesday:* Grades 5 and 6, Boys	*Thursday:* Grades 5 and 6, Girls	*Friday: Co-Rec* Grades 5 and 6, Co-Rec
Flag Football	Soccer	Flag Football	Kickball	Paddle Tennis Four Square Tether Ball

WINTER

Basketball	Basketball	Basketball	Basketball	Dance
Volleyball	Volleyball	Volleyball	Volleyball	
Gymnastics	Gymnastics	Gymnastics	Gymnastics	Volleyball
				Paddle
				Badminton Table Tennis Shuffleboard

SPRING

Track and Field	Track and Field	Track and Field	Track and Field	Paddle Tennis
Softball	Softball	Softball	Kickball	Tether Ball Softball

Supervision

If a specialist is available, the after school program should be assigned to him as part of his teaching load. Sometimes classroom teachers are assigned on a monthly or weekly basis. The school principal should be alert to scheduling so that after-school supervision does not become a burden to the teacher. Frequently rotation plans are worked out where supervision of the playground before school, during recess periods, during lunch hour and after school are shared by all on an equal time basis. Teachers who supervise intramurals should receive additional compensation if the assignments cannot be shared by all on an equal time basis.

Children play a vital role in planning and implementing the intramural program. The activities are those in which students profess an interest and/or desire to learn more. This may include activities in which everyone is not interested or for which there is not enough equipment for everyone to use long enough in class to gain great proficiency. For example, some of the more mature boys in sixth grade may profess an interest in weight lifting or body conditioning. It may not be prudent or practical to include this in the regular instructional period but it might be offered after school as an interest club.

Students may also help draw up teams for tournaments. How to draw up tournaments is described on page 105. Responsibilities for managing teams, scoring, helping with equipment, and some of the officiating should be assigned or made voluntary tasks. Fifth and sixth graders should not be expected to assume too great of the share of the responsibility. The teacher's influence should be discreetly obvious in that things are well organized and function smoothly.

Information sheets concerning the time schedule and the nature of the activities offered in the intramural program should be sent home to parents. A slip granting permission for their children to participate should be required. This also assures the school personnel that parents have been informed of the time that children are expected home from school. Figure 3-7 is a sample form including pertinent information to parents.

Noon hour activities

Many children do not go home at noon, but stay at school and eat lunch. There usually is free time between the eating period and the start of afternoon classes. Provision should be made for active play, semi-active play, and quiet activities. This is not an instructional period. Most often the physical education specialist is assigned to this responsibility, or shares it with classroom teachers on a rotational basis. Some schools hire adult teacher's aids for this responsibility in order to free teachers at the noon hour. Where children come to school by bus, a before-school play period with supervision may also be a necessity.

_____ School

Date _____

Dear Parent:

In order to satisfy the activity needs and interests of the children of _____ School, we are conducting a supervised after school intramural play program. The activities will be an outgrowth of those regularly taught in the physical education classes. Activity will end promptly at 4:45. If you wish your child to participate, will you please sign the permission slip and have your child return it to his room teacher?

I hope you will have an opportunity to visit the school sometime during the intramural period. Any suggestions you may have for making this program more worthwhile will be greatly appreciated.

Thank you,

_____, Principal

Schedule
3:30 to 4:30

Mon.	Tues.	Wed.	Thurs.
Boys	Girls	Co-Rec	4th
5–6	5–6	5–6	grade

_____

Tear here

Date _____

(Pupil's Name)

_____ has my permission to stay after school when his class may play in the intramural program.

_____ Parent

Address _____

Phone _____ _____

Figure 3-7. Intramural Permission Slip.

The playground supervisor's duties are mainly those of observation to foster both safety in play and the sharing of play space and equipment. Children should be free to select the type of activity they wish; however, some may need encouragement to participate or to join a group that is already playing.

The activities should be those that children can organize and conduct themselves. For the most part, there should be free play. Much equipment and play space should be available. Generally, it is necessary to designate the areas of the playground in which certain types of activity may be played. If only one part of the grounds is suitable for games requiring a large play space, the use of this part may have to be shared between boys and girls or grade levels on a rotational basis. If not, the oldest boys may dominate the use of it. Areas for primary grades and upper grades are usually designated so that small children do not run into playing areas unaware of balls and receive injuries.

Safety rules should be established for all playground areas and equipment. The student council may take a part in formulating the rules and even in maintaining them. Room representatives can relay safety information to students. An organization plan for issuing and returning equipment should be worked out at the start of the year in order to relieve the supervisor from constant responsibility for equipment and to prevent undue loss of equipment.

Recess

Children need an active free-play time after periods of concentration and inactivity. Usually a period of ten minutes is set aside in the middle of the half day in which the physical education period is not scheduled. The same type of activities and supervision followed at noontime is suitable for recess periods. Some exercises and games may be played in the classroom if and when activity is needed and when no time or space is allotted for recess.

Extramural or interscholastic activities

Extramural activities are those in which play occurs between students from two schools. Interscholastic competition, where teams or individuals play a regular schedule of games with other schools, is not recommended for children under twelve years of age in statements issued by various professional physical education and medical associations.[3] There has been a great deal of controversy on this subject.

Most of the criticism concerns the emotional demands put upon children when competition and the need to win are unduly stressed. Since children under twelve are prone to bone-and-joint injury because the growing ends of the long bones are not yet completely calcified, contact sports like tackle football, wrestling, and boxing are definitely not recommended. Investigation has not revealed any great proportion of physical harm from interscholastic competition. However, it has been found that the boys who are the most successful athletes before twelve are the boys who are the most physically mature.

[3] American Academy of Pediatrics Committee on School Health, "Statement of Policy on Competitive Athletics," *Pediatrics* (October, 1956), p. 672; and American Association for Health, Physical Education and Recreation, *Desirable Athletic Competition for Children* (Washington, D.C., The Association, 1952).

It is common to find interscholastic athletics for boys in the seventh and eighth grades and, more infrequently, in the fifth and sixth grades. The decision of whether or not to have a program of this type is not always that of the classroom teacher or even of the principal. It is usually decided by the administration of the school system, but, of course, each teacher and principal does have some influence in the long run, and they should be aware of the dangers inherent in an overemphasis on competition and winning.

Occasionally, extramural events stem from the intramural program, and a city tournament is held with winners in intramural programs representing each school. If there is such a program scheduled, the teachers and principal should make sure that it is conducted with neither an undue emphasis on winning nor on subsidiaries such as cheerleading exhibitions, booster clubs, fancy uniforms, awards, and admission fees. If an event of this type is planned, medical exams prior to the season, parental permission, adequate physical conditioning, and short practice periods should be required.

Play days

Play days are special events where students from several schools participate together in selected activities. The emphasis is on each child playing several activities with other children, not on competing on a school team against another school team. Several activities are conducted at one time. The day, or half day, is climaxed by a large group activity, such as singing or dancing. Refreshments may or may not be served.

Some school systems have city play days once a year when children from selected grades meet at one school and participate in several activities. The idea and the arrangements are much like those of a one school play day. Little recognition is given to individual winners, but good fun in trying to do one's best is encouraged. Much is gained from the social interactions of meeting and playing with and against children from other schools.

Field days

Many schools devote one afternoon in the spring to an all school or intermediate and upper grade field day when classes may be dismissed for a few hours. Each child may be on the blue team or the gold team and compete for his color team. Activities are those which are learned in physical education classes. Typical activities may be: running races, broad jumps, target throws, distance throws, dodgeball games, softball, volleyball, kickball, and others. Teachers may serve as judges, timers, and scorers so that all students may play. Naturally, an event such as this must be well planned so that everyone is able to participate. Scheduling in terms of space, participants, and officials must be carefully decided in ·advance so that everyone is aware of his responsibilities.

SUGGESTED REFERENCES
FOR FURTHER STUDY

American Academy of Pediatrics Committee on School Health, Statement of Policy on Competitive Athletics, *Pediatrics* (October, 1956), p. 672.

American Association for Health, Physical Education and Recreation, *After-School Games and Sports, Grades 4, 5, 6* (Washington, D.C., 1964).

American Association for Health, Physical Education and Recreation, *Desirable Athletic Competition for Children* (Washington, D.C., 1966).

American Association for Health, Physical Education and Recreation, *This Is Physical Education* (Washington, D.C., 1966).

American Red Cross, *Swimming and Diving*, rev. ed. (Washington, D.C., 1962).

American Red Cross, *Water Safety Instructor's Manual* (Washington, D.C., 1962).

Delacato, Carl, *The Treatment and Prevention of Reading Problems* (Springfield, Ill., Charles C Thomas, 1964).

Division of Girls' and Women's Sports, "Guidelines for Interscholastic Athletics for Junior High School Girls," *Journal of Health, Physical Education and Recreation* (September, 1966, p. 36).

Kauffman, Carolyn, *How To Teach Children To Swim* (New York, Putnam, 1960).

Kephart, Newell C., *The Slow Learner in the Classroom* (Columbus, Ohio, Merrill, 1964).

Kleindienst, Viola K., and Arthur Weston, *Intramural and Recreation Programs for Schools and Colleges* (New York, Appleton-Century-Crofts, 1964).

Shaffer, Thomas E., "Athletics for Elementary School Youth, A Medical Viewpoint," *Theory Into Practice,* Vol. III, No. 3 (The Ohio State University, June, 1964).

Part II
THE TEACHING
PROCESS

Chapter IV

MOTOR LEARNING AND METHODS TO ENHANCE LEARNING

Learning is usually defined as a permanent change in behavior brought about through experiences. Motor learning is defined by Cratty [1] as "the rather permanent change in motor performance as observable, voluntary, goal-centered movement." There are a number of learning theories which attempt to explain the various factors which enable learning to take place. Space does not permit discussion of these theories; however, information about them can be gained from reading the books [2] recommended in the footnotes and bibliography. The reader has undoubtedly studied learning theories in basic educational psychology courses.

Usually, learning is discussed in terms of the specific nature of the type of learning to be accomplished, i.e., cognitive, verbal, perceptual, or motor. Of course, the latter is of predominant interest to the teacher of physical education; however, it should be remembered that all are, to a certain degree, interdependent.

Quite recently the contribution of play activities to the development

[1] Bryant J. Cratty, *Movement Behavior and Motor Learning* (Philadelphia, Lea and Febiger, 1964), p. 26.
[2] *Ibid.*, Chapter 11.

and improvement of perceptual skills has been emphasized. Activities in the primary grades where body actions are studied in relation to the factors of space, relationships, and qualities of movement further develop perceptual skills which are vital to a child's skill in reading, writing, and understanding. Participating in perceptual-motor activities helps a child form concepts that enhance his learning in all areas.

MOTOR SKILL LEARNING

The selection of methods and techniques of teaching should be based on how children learn motor skills. Our knowledge of how one learns is based on theories both empirically and experimentally derived. There is no one simple explanation of how one best learns motor skills. Many variables operate to enhance or inhibit optimum motor learning.

Educators have formulated principles of learning as a result of extensive research and experimentation. Some of these principles with specific implications and applications to the teaching of physical education are presented in the next few pages. Incorporated in these are the latest results of research in regard to conditions of learning motor skills and motor performance. These should serve as criteria for the selection of content, method, procedure, and evaluative processes.

Principles of learning

Readiness to learn

very important

The activities presented to a child should be appropriate to his maturation level. The learner should have achieved the strength, endurance, and coordination necessary to perform a skill. He must be intellectually able to understand the purpose of the activity and the relationship of movements. If the activity involves other people, his social maturity must be consistent with the interpersonal relationships which the activity demands. The teacher must select content in terms of a planned progression for children in his situation. Details such as size of areas, equipment, and length of playing time must be adapted to meet the physical size and ability of the group.

Goal-centered learning

The learner should know the goal toward which he is working. The goal should be reasonable and within the attainment of the learner. In all instances the teacher must present a clear picture of what the student is to learn. This may be done in a variety of ways—through challenges, problems to be solved, discussions, opportunities for observation of a good demonstration, film strips, movies, loop films, posters, diagrams, exhibition games, and others. The presentation of the goal will vary with the maturational level of the learner.

Interest in learning

The student learns fastest and best when he has a purpose and interest in learning. The teacher must help students identify purposes in learning specific activities—for example, in relating practice of skill to improvement of game play. Student's interests should be considered in program planning; however, instruction should develop interests and new motives as a product of learning. Children often desire to repeat what they know or do well, as they feel confident and comfortable in a familiar situation. New interests and purposes can be formulated as an outgrowth of new experiences.

Generalized pattern of learning a new skill

When learning a new skill, the learner first produces a pattern which is his concept of what the skill is. This concept is gained from demonstrations, explanations, associations, or combinations of these. The first attempt is usually rough, but this trial serves as a basis for the learner to reflect on his efforts and match his conception of what it should be. Repeated trials by the learner produce an improvement in quality. The teacher should help by directing his attention to the basis of errors in the essential parts of the skill. This "directing" should not concern details or be in the form of detailed explanations. Additional models or demonstrations should be provided, for a beginner should see a demonstration several times so that he has an opportunity to gain a good perception of the general pattern, goals, and purposes of the skill. He evaluates and compares his performance on the basis of these demonstrations, and he again practices the skill after reflecting on what he saw in the demonstration or what he learned from the teacher's cues. As learning progresses, the teacher can talk in more detailed terms as the stage of refinement demands it. This process as described may take several practice sessions. How refined one's skill becomes depends on the learner's opportunity for practice, needs, and interest in a high degree of skill.

Form of skill

There is no one best form of a skill that a person must acquire. Each person develops his own characteristic form or style of movement. An individual's best form occurs after he has refined his pattern by making adjustments to his own structural and physiological limitations and when he utilizes the correct mechanical principles which make his performance efficient and allow him to reach his goal.

Involvement in the learning process

Learning is an active process—this principle implies that the learner must perform skills repeatedly. At the same time he actually repeats the skills, he must be doing some reflective thinking in terms of what he is doing and how well he is doing. With younger children, as well as adults, the teacher can guide in this process by providing questions to the learner which stimulate his thinking and understanding. Involving the learner both in finding the basic causes of his lack of success in reaching a goal and in discovering ways of correcting faults can be done by structuring experiences which lead him to gain insight into the problems.

Individualization of learning

Learning is an individual process. While most instruction is given in a group situation, the amount of learning which takes place varies with each child. Each student is unique in terms of physical size, motor ability, physiological constitution, social development, interests, motives, and intellectual capacity. The teacher's planning and methods should provide for these differences by involving exploration, problem-solving, many self-testing activities, and individual coaching. This principle is very significant in ascertaining the evaluative process to be utilized and in forming expectations for each student.

Learning cues

Individuals vary greatly in terms of the type of learning cues that are most meaningful to them. Some respond best to verbal cues, some to visual cues, some to manual guidance. Individuals also vary as to which combination of cues work best—manual-visual, verbal-visual, manual-verbal, or manual-verbal-visual. At later stages of learning one combination has been found to be more effective than that used at the initial stage. These differences dictate that all of these in various combinations must be used in teaching, if each child is to benefit from cues.

Correction of errors

Prompt correction of errors is necessary in order to avoid a fixation of the errors. This must be done early in the learning process, but only after the child can comprehend the place of the error in the total pattern. For example, how one is using the arms in skipping isn't significant until the step pattern is correct, nor are detailed corrections for accuracy in archery if the student is unable to release the arrow from the bow.

Transfer of learning

Speed of learning new skills is somewhat dependent on how well one adapts and applies previous skill learnings to the new task. This transfer of learning is not automatic, as research shows that skill learning is specific. Similarities in patterns and activities must be pointed out to the learner by the teacher. References to mechanical principles and likeness of patterns should be a part of the presentation of any new skill. For example, the volleyball serve is much like an underhand throw; in order to throw the ball farther, the trunk must rotate; in order to hit the ball farther, the trunk must rotate.

Whole-part learning

Children usually learn skills and activities better and faster when they are presented in a whole-part manner. Early learning should be concerned with complete, meaningful units. Detailed instruction on any one part of a skill should not be stressed until children have a concept of a skill pattern and an opportunity to reproduce it. The child must first get the idea of the skill as a whole. As a child repeats the pattern, he usually modifies it to be more similar to the correct one. It may be necessary to isolate a certain part of the skill if trouble is encountered; however, a return to practicing the whole skill should follow immediately.

Dances, sports, and games consist of many skills which are wholes in themselves. The teacher should introduce the whole game and then teach specific skills. Many skills are learned as wholes long before they are put in the game or a dance; however, the nature of the game or dance dictates a new way in which the skill is utilized.

For example, traditional dance steps are learned in an exploratory fashion. The step pattern is evolved through experimentation, then studied in relation to other movement factors such as different tempos, various directions, a partner, combinations of steps, and others. Later, folk dances are introduced in which how the step is used will vary with each dance.

Retention

The best retention of learning a skill results from good initial learning and, thereafter, from overlearning. The teacher should provide many opportunities for using skills in game and dance situations. Practice drills should simulate the game situation as much as possible. Mastery of a skill, however, is not a prerequisite for using the skill in a game or a dance. The motivation for subsequent practice is an outgrowth of game play.

Knowledge of results

Motivation can be maintained only when the goal of any activity is understood and progress toward the attainment of it is known. The teacher should select measurement devices for appraising progress in terms of appropriateness for the activity and the level of the learner. These may range from day-by-day verbal comments to highly structured achievement tests. Whatever evaluative device is utilized, it should be understood by the students and the results reported to them immediately. Suggestions for improvement should be given at the same time the results are presented. Self-testing activities allow for immediate feedback of improvement or lack of improvement.

Progression in learning

For efficient learning, instruction should be planned that the activities and experiences of the learner are continuously related and interrelated into larger, more meaningful, more inclusive hierarchies of understanding. The need for long-term as well as daily planning, so that there is an ordered progression from simple to complex, cannot be overstressed. A teacher should consider previous learnings of his class and of the individuals within it as the primary focus in his planning. It is true that the exploratory method will evoke many spontaneous learning situations and may channel the planned lesson into a more meaningful direction; however, the teacher must not lose sight of his original objectives. If lessons take this direction every day, progression will be lost, and good learning cannot be promoted.

Quality of experiences and environment

The learning experience is a process of interaction between the learner and his environment. The quality of learning is determined by the quality of the experience. In order to have valuable, satisfying learning experiences, the child must be provided with a rich environment. This demands a wide variety of content, materials, ample equipment for each child, many opportunities for practice, and turns in the use of equipment. The teacher should use a flexible organization and techniques which allow pupils to interact with other children. Opportunities for individual and small group work should be provided in order that the students work together in making decisions and experimenting with methods of doing things without teacher direction. A democratic atmosphere enhances sharing of ideas and promotes a feeling of freedom to ask for and receive help.

Scheduling

Many research studies have shown that skill learning is best at the beginning level when practice periods are short and frequent. An entire class period should not be devoted exclusively to the practice of one skill. The teacher should not plan to teach a different activity every day of the week. For elementary children units should be planned for twice weekly or three times a week for a number of weeks. Activities which contain skills that are very similar should not be taught in the same season.

EXAMPLE:	*Mon.*	*Tues.*	*Wed.*	*Thurs.*	*Fri.*
	Dance	Dance	Games	Small Equipment	Small Equipment
			rather than		
	Dance	Games	Ball Skills	Stunts	Rope Jumping

Accuracy and speed

Most research findings indicate that accuracy developed at a slow speed is lost when the speed of the movement is increased. Therefore, in teaching activities which require a combination of speed and accuracy for maximum quality of performance, the teacher should not teach a skill at a decreased tempo in order to emphasize the development of accuracy.

Accuracy and speed should be stressed at the same time. If the skill involves a long sequence of movements, the learner could go through the movement slowly for a few times, but repeated practice at a modified speed is impractical. Demonstrations should not be conducted at a tempo slower than that necessary for the learned skill.

Leadership

A well-qualified leader has a great influence on the amount of learning that is accomplished. The personality of the teacher and his interest in the students is as important as is his knowledge of his field. Children are quick to respond to a teacher who expects them to learn and is actively interested in helping them. When a teacher participates in the games, gives individual attention, dresses appropriately, and demonstrates well what he expects, he will motivate his pupils to do their best. Although teacher demonstration is not an essential technique in working with young children, students enjoy and benefit from seeing the teacher occasionally perform the skills they are learning.

METHODS

Teaching methods in any particular subject area are usually dependent upon the general philosophy of education prevalent in a culture or country. Within this general framework or philosophy, an individual teacher's methods are then related to the philosophy of the administration in his teaching situation. Fortunately, in America there is some flexibility within most school systems for individuality in choice of methods. Most educators currently follow a pragmatic type of philosophy which encourages a variety of methods with the ultimate goal being the development of the whole child. Since the trend in elementary school education is to emphasize the growth and development of the individual, the teacher must know and use a variety of teaching methods in any subject.

Actually, a child learns within the framework of his own abilities and capacities. The teacher provides the setting, the opportunities, the experiences, and the inspiration for each child to succeed within his own limitations. There are a variety of ways in which a teacher can make these provisions. Good teaching methods depend on both artistry and scientific applications. All children do not respond equally well to all methods. One method may lend itself to the teaching of certain activities better than another. Therefore, a teacher must be ready to change methods rapidly and productively when the situation demands a change. Whatever the method a teacher employs, he must understand how a child learns motor skills and also apply the principles of learning to his chosen method.

Traditional method

The following pattern describes what has come to be known as the traditional method of presenting a new motor skill. The teacher briefly describes the skill and its use and then shows the class what the skill looks like in the context in which it is used. These two processes may be reversed. The verbal description should be extremely brief. The students then try to do the skill several times before any errors are pointed out or more explanations or directions are given. This step is then followed by more demonstrations and, if necessary, verbal explanation to enhance the student's observation. Then more time is given for practice. The teacher gives coaching hints to individuals who are in need, by pointing out and correcting errors. If the skill involves an object or an implement, demonstration, and/or explanation should be preceded by an opportunity for the students to become familiar with the object or implement to be utilized. Usually, a drill formation is set up for students to practice the skill in a prescribed manner. Before completion of the first learning session, some provision should be made for using the skill in a situation as close as possible to that expected when the skill is mastered.

A similar pattern may be followed in the presentation of games, dances, rules, and concepts, whether it be to a large group or to one student.

This method can be effective or ineffective depending on the teacher's cognizance of the learning principles previously presented. The distinguishing feature of this method is that it is direct in nature. The teacher tells and shows the students how the skill is to be performed. He presents a very clear goal for the student. However, there are advantages and disadvantages to this method as there are in everything. The greatest disadvantage is that this method does not allow for as much inventiveness and creativity on the part of the students. The goal rather than the learning process is the most important aspect of this method. At the elementary school level where rate of maturation is so varied, methods should also be used which allow for diversity of performance.

This method is best employed when one particular skill is being learned rather than many general knowledges in relation to a skill. The direct method provides security for the beginning teacher, since children are working on the same aspect of a skill or an activity and are thereby easier to control and study as a group. It is also easier for a beginning teacher to establish a good progression from one aspect of a skill to the next. Some children also respond better to the security of knowing exactly what they are to do and where they are going. This gives a sound starting point from which to learn.

At some stages of skill and movement learning children do not understand how or what is to be done. Then the direct method is the most expedient way to help them. It aids some teachers who may, at times, have difficulty phrasing problems or questions that will lead to correct application of principles for safe and efficient performance.

Children need and sometimes want more organized activity than an indirect method allows. The direct method is most often more economical in terms of the time available for learning essential facets of a skill or an activity. It should be obvious that a good teacher will recognize that there can be modifications and combinations of any particular method. Good practices in relation to demonstrations, observation, explanation, and evaluation within the lesson are discussed later.

Problem-solving method

The problem-solving method of teaching skills and activities is far from new; however, in recent years it has gained favor and publicity in all subject areas. When used with young children and particularly when studying basic movement factors rather than one new skill, it most often is called the exploratory method or approach. Although the two terms are used interchangeably by some people, there are a few differences. Exploration as a method for teaching movement factors will be discussed separately.

The basic pattern of teaching a new skill is as follows. The skill is introduced by the teacher who presents the problem in terms of what has to be accomplished by the skill. The class then experiments with solving the problem. After experimenting, the class and teacher observe classmates' performances, and discuss the progress. This provides a basis for evaluating one's own performance. Everyone practices in order to refine his skill while the teacher circulates and gives individual coaching.

The observation phase may vary according to the skill and the age level of the students. There is no reason that a movie or a demonstration by someone with previous knowledge of the skill cannot be utilized in a problem-solving approach. The important factor is that it be shown *after* the students have experimented with the skill and can therefore study the performance in reference to their own concepts and problems. The demonstration may be as provocative a stimulator as the teacher's questions.

While the class is experimenting with the skill, the teacher structures a series of experimental experiences wherein the students will proceed to learn in the same manner as described earlier. Students are encouraged to discover the correct way for them to accomplish the goal and solve the problems rather than be given the solution. The teacher makes suggestions in questions and in comparisons gained from doing things in a variety of ways. Observation of others aids each child in evaluating his own performance and provides a basis for improvement or refinement of his skill.

The greatest advantage of this method is that it encourages reflective thinking, association, and self-direction. It is an indirect method by nature, since the teacher is a catalyst in concerning the student with the learning process. This method calls for creativity in the learner and the teacher. The teacher must be able to structure problems and situations that will encourage the student to apply basic principles and his own capabilities to achieving the goal.

Problem-solving permits more individualization of learning as well as allows the teacher to know each child better. The freedom evoked by experimentation demands self-control, and the children must be encouraged to develop this.

Exploratory method

As previously stated, the use of exploration as a method for teaching basic movement factors is popular in work with young children. In these circumstances, specific skills are not studied as much as movement tasks. A problem-solving approach is utilized, but the goal or problem is usually not so narrowly defined, and the answers in movement tasks may be quite varied. The teacher is more interested in the learning process than in one common answer to a problem, and since young children have varied movement backgrounds and are at various stages of maturation, their interpretation of tasks may be quite dissimilar.

Exploration as a method takes advantage of the intrinsic interest in exploring and experimenting. The curiosity, joy, and involvement in self-discovery lead a child into learning concepts and understanding himself and his environment. It also encourages freedom of expression and creativity.

No demonstration is given prior to experimenting with the skills. All demonstrations are those of class members who have evolved their solution to the problems within the same working period. Therein lies the major differences between the traditional and exploratory approach. In the former, each step of learning as well as the expected goal in the lesson is set by the teacher. In the latter, the teacher sets the initial problem and then accepts a number of different responses as the answer. Every solution in movement is accepted as correct. He then may take one or more of these answers and use it as a channel for another problem.

This may lead a beginning teacher to think that a lesson utilizing exploration needs only to be introduced and it will take its own course. This is far from true, for a movement study lesson needs to be carefully planned, and the teacher must have definite objectives or goals to be accomplished for each lesson. Each lesson must be planned within the framework of a broader unit or yearly progression.

The general pattern of the exploratory method is the following. The teacher sets the problem or task; he then allows the class to explore and experiment to solve the problem or task. After a period of time, a demonstration by a class member or members permits observation and evaluation of progress; students then continue to practice and refine their problem or tasks. Meanwhile, the teacher circulates among the students giving individual help by probing, asking questions, and challenging.

There is no doubt that children will develop self-direction in learning through exploration if the teacher affords the proper structure and guidance in the learning experiences. "Learning how to learn" in a child's early school years, should provide him with the tools and insight to approach new problems of movement skills in later years.

This approach can be used productively at any age level whenever new concepts or skills are introduced; however, techniques may vary somewhat because of the background of the students. The idea that a child's own solution to each problem is *always* correct is more logical with younger children than older children, and more so in introductory stages than at later stages of learning.

The content of movement study cannot vary much from year to year, but the quality and complexity of the movement patterns should be progressively difficult due to greater powers of understanding, coordination, and strength. These things must be taken into consideration in implementing all phases of the exploratory method. After several years of study one would expect children to have a sound understanding of the factors affecting movement and be able to make associations and applications quickly and in a more independent manner.

Implementing the exploratory method in studying basic movement factors

The terms "explore" and "experiment" denote that one might expect a great deal of independent and diverse approaches and solutions to movement problems. This is exactly what the teacher who uses the exploratory method must expect.

In planning a lesson the teacher selects the major movement factor or factors to be studied (Chapter IX, p. 225). Depending on the stage of development of the factors, he should study the course of learning that is desirable for the lesson and the expected goal. He then formulates the initial problem. This may take a rather broad form where much variety in responses may be expected. The term problem is used here but the term task is equally appropriate. Completing the task is the problem for the students.

The teacher then anticipates some of the responses and formulates possible questions which will lead to the refinement of the problem. The students may all answer the question by trying their own answer in movement or the teacher may elicit verbal responses. Everyone can then apply the responses appropriate to their needs.

After more experimentation by the class, a few members may be asked to demonstrate what they have worked out. The teacher may direct the others to watch certain phases of the demonstration. He plans to make his own observation while the children are working so that he can select children who are doing things which he thinks will stimulate ideas or allow opportunities for comparisons. He may ask the observers what characteristics of the demonstrator's patterns make them good, or different, or fulfill the objective of the problem. After he has carefully guided their thinking, he will allow time for each child to apply what he has learned by refining and practicing the solution. If particular concepts are to be learned, these may be reinforced with verbal summary or guided observation at the end of the class period. Most frequently, what has been studied can be further tested or reinforced in a specific game, dance, or gymnastic activity. Following is an outline of the means of implementing the exploratory method when studying basic movement factors. The chart outlining basic movement factors on page 225 may serve as the content basis for the progression. The descriptions and examples of each factor as presented in Chapter II indicate the relative level of difficulty of each factor. Generally, the progression of study should follow this order.

1. Development of basic knowledge, understanding of and ability to use all of the factors through exploration
2. Development of use of logical combinations of the factors as they affect movement skills through experimentation and exploration
3. Use of movement factors in solving problems structured by the teacher (small problems will also be used as stimulators for experimenting and exploring for development of knowledges and skills in steps 1 and 2)
4. Use of movement factors in solving problems and creation of patterns, sequences, and compositions; use of patterns and skills in organized games, dances, and gymnastic activities
5. Application of factors to learning new skills and activities with progressively less guidance from the teacher

Practical suggestions

The teacher may encounter some problems when he first employs the exploratory method, for one cannot easily anticipate responses to problems or questions until he has worked with children over a period of time. Even then he will be amazed at the variety of reactions. In order to anticipate responses, he must consider: How should it be done? What are the logical errors? What is the hardest part of it? What principles are involved that everyone should know and follow? From these questions one can anticipate possible subproblems.

The degree of restriction of exploration should be varied. If all problems that are posed are too unstructured and allow complete freedom of response, it is possible that quality of performance and variety in use of skills may be ignored. It may please the teacher that everyone is busy, but without direction and without progression toward a goal, a child may actually just be repeating what he enjoys. The astute quick thinker particularly will suffer if the teacher allows aimless exploration to dominate each lesson.

The teacher should know the basic mechanics of each skill and the principles that control them. If the major factors being studied are changes in direction and level, a child may choose to run while he does this. If his run is such that he runs with his weight on the heels, this becomes a new problem which must also be approached. Each child's answer may be his own, but if within it he has violated good mechanics and basic principles, it is not really acceptable. This is the challenge for the teacher—should he structure a new problem and still retain an indirect method or change to a direct method? The latter may be preferable if the diversion will detract significantly from the original problem, or if the time taken proves to be more distracting to the rest of the class.

Frequently, a change to a direct approach is desirable when a safety factor is being ignored. For example, when exploring curling and rolling, young children may be doing rolls where they take the weight on their heads. More expedient and safer would be an explanation to the whole class of where the weight should be taken.

While children are working and experimenting, the teacher should be circulating in the class and observing the progress made and problems encountered. While he gives assistance to individuals and notes the general achievement of the class, he formulates specific questions or poses the next problem in his own mind.

The approach used in giving verbal direction should be varied. Questions may be asked; challenges may be given or problems set for the whole class while they are actively working; the class may stop and listen; a verbal discussion may take place and then activity resumed; a demonstration may be observed and followed by discussion and reclarification of the problem; a demonstration may be observed, followed by activity with no discussion; or there may be individual verbal encouragement. None of these should be used exclusively.

There is a hazard in too much verbalization. Some teachers look upon the problem-solving technique as intellectualizing activity, and thus spend more time in discussion than in activity. Discussion should take place, but a significant part of it should be the students' response in movement rather than in words.

Some lessons involving work with small movements may not be very vigorous. This may occur when the nonlocomotor skills are being explored. It is important to include some provision for large-muscle activity and a variety of movement in every lesson. Work with small movements should be followed with activity involving large movements.

Success with the exploratory method is achieved through experience, trial, and ingenuity. The teacher as well as the students must be imaginative in his approach.

EXAMPLES OF IMPLEMENTING METHODS

In order for the reader to better understand some of the suggestions applying the indirect approach in teaching basic skills and movement factors, a few examples have been developed. Specific suggestions for teaching methods in specific activities are contained in the respective activity chapters. General suggestions pertaining to planning, organization, and techniques are discussed in Chapter V.

EXAMPLE 1

MAJOR FACTOR TO BE STUDIED: Quality of movement—running fast and stopping quickly.

MAJOR CONCEPTS OR PRINCIPLES TO BE LEARNED OR REINFORCED: Acceleration and maintenance of balance.

PROCEDURE:

1. *Initial problem:* "Run anywhere in the room and stop when you hear the drum." (Allow several experiences of this.)
2. *Possible responses in movement:* Many children will take several steps forward before coming to a full stop; some will lose balance and fall; some will fall forward onto hands; some will shuffle feet to keep balance; some will use arms and body sway to keep balance; some will start slowly and anticipate beat of drum; some will have picked up speed just as drum sounds.
3. *Possible questions by teacher:* "What is our problem in stopping?" or more directly, "We seem to have a problem in coming to a full stop without taking some extra steps? What can we do about that?"
4. *Anticipated responses:* Bring weight back, lean back, keep feet under body, use arms to help, etc. Here the teacher may tell everyone to try some of these suggestions; or rephrase a few of the suggestions and

tell everyone to try these; or be somewhat more direct and ask "Can you stop with one foot ahead of the other? Can you bring your weight directly over your feet? Can you keep the upper part of your body erect?" Class then experiments with these suggestions. Some of the more direct questions might be asked only of those who indicated a need for them.

5. *Demonstration:* Select a few children who are stopping quickly with good balance. While others are observing, direct their attention to the position of the feet and the bent knees.
6. *More experimentation by children*
7. *New problem:* "You want to get to the other side of the gym as quickly as possible, but you must stop every time the drum beats."
8. *Experimentation*
9. *Teacher's questions:* "How can you get started more quickly? Will taking small quick steps and pushing hard against the floor help you start to run faster? Try it."
10. *More experimenting and demonstration if necessary*
11. *Summary of concepts about starting and stopping drawn from the children*
12. *Introduction of game: Red Light* (p. 330)

It is obvious that before the lesson the teacher must analyze the two actions of stopping and starting as well as the skill of running. He must know what principles control the actions and be able to summarize concepts of starting and stopping, if he expects to help children learn to control this aspect of movement and learn the concepts of acceleration and balance.

EXAMPLE 2

MAJOR FACTOR TO BE STUDIED: Space—changes in level.
PROCEDURE:
1. *Initial problem:* "In what way can you move across the room and be very close to the floor? . . . Try a different way to move."
2. *Possible responses in movement:* Crawling, wriggling on stomach or back, rolling.
3. *Further challenges:* "This time see how close to the ground you can move with only two parts of your body supporting you. . . . Can you change levels and using the same body movement be as far from the ground as possible? . . . Can you change from high to low or to middle as you move? . . . Change on the accent of the drum. . . . Is it hard to change levels without stopping your movement?"
4. *Demonstration and discussion:* Of varieties in levels and how to keep balance.
5. *New problem:* "Move at a low level like some animal who always

moves close to the ground. . . . Move like some animal who always is at a high level. . . . Move like an animal who seems to move at a medium level."
6. *Experimentation*
7. *New problem:* "Can you move like a machine which moves at a low level? . . . at a high level? . . . Can you move like a machine that changes levels as it operates?"
8. *Demonstration and observation:* Of various machines at work.
9. *Discussion:* Of what is involved most often in quick changes of level (bending, stretching, balance).

This example may be expanded in the area of the animal imagery or machine imagery depending on the level and interests of the children. Young children have difficulty in changing to a low level and moving there unless they use a broad base. Throughout the lesson the teacher should encourage changes in level.

EXAMPLE 3

MAJOR FACTOR TO BE STUDIED: Development of the jump for height.

MAJOR CONCEPTS OR PRINCIPLES TO BE LEARNED OR REINFORCED: Landing on balls of feet to absorb shock, bending knees as you start the jump so that you can push off harder against the floor, a swinging upward with the arms to help you gain height (example of teacher making suggestions with questions and challenges to the whole class to be answered in movement).

PROCEDURE:
1. *Teacher's questions and challenges:* "Bounce up and down . . . lightly. . . . Point your toes as you go up. On what part of your feet do you land? . . . Jump up and land on your heels . . . now on the balls of your feet. . . . Which was the most comfortable? Do you bend your knees before you jump? Try it. . . . Did you go higher? Try again. . . . Do you bend your knees when you land? How does that help? How can you use your arms to help go higher? . . . Swing arms down and up! Does it help if your arms go high? How high? Stretch. . . . Does it help if you look at your hands high above your head? . . . Jump and reach as high as you can. . . ."
2. *Discussion:* Summary of concepts that help increase height in jump, and absorbing force in landing.

The teacher may make references to the principles throughout this session through his questions and challenges. There need be no discourse between the teacher and the students except through movement. Carefully planned challenges, questions, and observations are required in order to correct errors in the use of force and direction.

EXAMPLE 4

MAJOR FACTOR TO BE STUDIED: Development of a jumping-rope routine with music (use a march recording).

PROCEDURE:

1. *Initial problem:* "Everyone listen to the music then jump the rope trying to stay with the music. . . . Everyone jump with two feet together . . . moving forward. . . . Jump with alternate feet moving forward. . . . This time try going backward. . . . Can you go to the side and keep jumping in time with the music? Sit and rest. Let's listen to the music and listen for the changes of phrases. Clap when the phrase changes. . . . This time jump, and when you hear the phrase change your jump in a different direction. . . . Can you change level while you are jumping? This is pretty hard, but try it. . . ."
2. *Demonstration and observation:* Watch Joe, Jane, and Jerry change level as the phrase changes.
3. *Setting of problem for individual routine:* "Everyone must make up his own routine. You must jump rope and include changes in direction, style of jump, and at least one change of level in your routine. You can work out and practice your routine for four minutes, then we'll watch the routines."
4. *Work period*
5. *Presentation of routines:* Three or four at a time.
6. *Discussion and evaluation:* Were all factors included? Did changes occur as phrases changed? What routines were particularly interesting, why?

    The preliminary work should have given children ideas for changes in direction, in level, and style of jump as well as the idea of changing as phrases change. Often it is helpful to give everyone the challenge of the same short routine prior to the assignment of individual routines. This gives them an understanding of the format of a routine. Rope jumping is quite exhausting, so discussion should be held frequently to allow a rest period.

EXAMPLE 5

MAJOR FACTORS TO BE STUDIED: Body actions, changes in body shapes—curling and stretching.

PROCEDURE:

1. *Initial problem:* Show a stretched position with your body. . . . Show a different stretched position. . . . Can you use another part of your body to support you in a stretched position?
2. *New problem:* Curl up your whole body. . . . Can you curl just one part of your body? . . . Change from one curled position to another

. . . quickly. . . . Change your point of support and curl up again.

3. *New problem:* Curl up your whole body, change to a fully stretched position. . . . Continue to change from a curled to a stretched position. . . . Try to make a quick stretch and a slow curl.

4. *Demonstration and observation*

5. *Evaluation:* Discuss changes from curl to stretch. Possibilities that extension or stretched position may be only that part of body from point of support, depending on point. Discuss possibility of next problem of moving when making the curled position.

6. *Refinement of problems:* Work on quick stretch and slow curl, moving into a different position on curl.

7. *Evaluation and possible demonstration of new moves with curl*

8. *New problem:* Using a short rope, throw your rope on the floor. . . . Travel along your rope using a curled position. . . . Change the design of your rope and combine stretches and curls.

9. *Demonstration and observation:* Show various designs.

10. *Evaluation*

Guidelines for explanation and/or discussion

Regardless of the method utilized, there is some verbalization in every lesson; however, it should be kept to a minimum. The explanation sets the stage for the kinesthetic concept of the particular skill or activity to be taught. A few considerations concerning length, use, and timing of directions are discussed here.

Be sure that everyone is listening before proceeding. A definite signal should be established which signifies, "Stop, look, and listen!" This may be the use of: command such as "freeze" or "statues"; a beat on a drum; a chord on the piano; or a whistle. The use of the latter is discouraged, since the whistle is also used for starting signals and indication of infractions in games. Do not expect children to be absolutely quiet immediately. It takes a few seconds to complete a sentence, to catch one's breath, and to sit down. Beginning teachers might practice counting to twenty before beginning to speak.

The teacher should stand in a position so that everyone can see and hear him and so that he can see every student. The teacher should use a vocabulary that is meaningful to the students, without "talking down" to them.

Be familiar with what is to be said, so it is not necessary to repeat or say something another way in order to be sure everything is included. Summarize and repeat only key phrases or words that children need to use and remember in the skill. Be sure to do this after getting responses from children, since frequently they do not speak loudly and clearly enough for the others to hear.

The initial introduction to a skill or activity should be brief but inclusive enough so that it is preparation for what is to come. Detailed explanations or directions before a student has tried a skill are useless, as he has no reference point for understanding. Include only the key words or actions that are essential to starting the activity. A demonstration may accompany a few words of explanation. Other visual aids may also be helpful, such as diagrams of foot positions or of step patterns.

Watch and analyze the initial experimentation with the skill or task. If a large percentage of the class is having problems with the same things, ask a question or make a suggestion that will help everyone. If problems seem to be of an individual nature, help those children to analyze the sources of their errors.

When asking for questions from the class, encourage specific questions. This will not only eliminate unnecessary general questions, but will also cause the students to think about particulars and thereby review what has been said. For example, rather than asking, "Are there any questions?" ask "Are there any questions about the grip? Are there any questions about the stance?"

Guidelines for demonstrations

A demonstration may take various forms and be essential at various times. The major difference between the traditional and the problem-solving approach is the placement of initial demonstration. In the former it precedes the student experiments and in the latter it follows these. The demonstration used in the exploration method must be that contributed by the class, not by the teacher. There is no such qualification in a true problem-solving approach.

A demonstration is used for a variety of reasons:
1. It may serve as a model from which a student gets his original conception of what is to be done.
2. It may be used to illustrate the use of the skill in a game, dance, or routine.
3. It may serve as a motivating factor.
4. It may be used to compare similarities of skill patterns,
5. To portray varying forms or styles,
6. To show what has been learned, and
7. To self-evaluate and make comparisons.
Demonstrations may come from a variety of sources including:
1. The teacher

2. A student or several students in the class
3. A highly skilled performer
4. Someone in the process of being taught a skill or stunt if no one is able to do it before the instruction takes place
5. A group or squad showing how skills are used to advantage in specific situations, such as games, dances, etc.
6. Movies, loop films, film strips, pictures, posters, and diagrams

Emphasis should be placed on the technique involved rather than the results of the skill, unless the purpose is to see the results. For example, if demonstrating a throwing pattern, throw the ball to the wall so students will not become more interested in how far the ball goes rather than how it is thrown.

Since each child will notice something different in the demonstration, it should be done several times, and immediately after the demonstration, opportunities for practice and participation should be provided, unless the demonstration was that of learned material and is a culminating event of the class session.

There is no advantage in having a highly skilled person demonstrate for those who are learning a skill for the first time, since their concept of the skill will be quite general. However, the demonstrator must be adept enough to employ the correct mechanics, and the skill must be performed at the tempo normally used. When children are asked to demonstrate, do not ask the same ones to perform repeatedly.

Guidelines for observations

Both teachers and students must learn to observe the performance of others accurately and fairly. The teacher's observation throughout the lesson permits him to evaluate the work on current problems, and the general progress of the class, and helps him in setting up new problems and planning for future tasks.

Keen observation is based on prior knowledge of what is valued in performance. The teacher must have a standard established which concerns quality and variety. He may recognize potential problems in the way a skill is performed or by the fact that certain necessary steps are omitted from the performance.

Since demonstrations are designed to improve understanding of skills and movement patterns, children need guidance in their observations. Specific factors to be aware of may be stated before the demonstration and then discussed afterward, or the demonstration may precede the questions, and in this way observational powers may be checked. As the demonstration is underway, the teacher may ask questions or give cues to focus attention on specific phases of performance.

Following the observation, a short discussion may be held, or children may immediately practice what they have learned from the observation. Comparisons of styles and quality may be made. Discussion of the latter must be discretely guided.

Observation of others may give the shy or slower youngster a springboard for action. A new variation of a task may stimulate further exploration or experimentation by the rest of the class.

Guidelines for evaluation within the lesson

Evaluation within the daily lesson is a vital part of the teaching-learning process. The teacher's role is to involve individuals in self-analysis, and the students in a critical analysis of the status and progress of the class as a whole.

The evaluation need not be long or involved. The critical aspects are timing and the teacher's ability to focus attention on the most important facets of the matter. Most frequently, the last few minutes of the lesson are reserved for evaluation. This also serves as a culmination of the lesson, a period to relax, a group-unifying process, and a planning period for the next lesson.

The teacher may prepare for the evaluation by making a comment as to the purposes of the lesson or emphasizing what was to be accomplished in the working period. He may ask a pertinent question, or his comments may provoke leading questions from the students. Through class discussion based on personal participation and observation of others during the working period, the class can appraise their progress or lack of it, and agree on what must be done to improve.

As stated, a demonstration may precede or accompany the evaluation. It is possible that no discussion is necessary when self-evaluation is the primary purpose of the demonstration. The teacher may offer a few pertinent questions or remarks to guide individuals in making comparisons of various performances. Afterward, pupils should be free to put their analyses to work in improving their own tasks.

Immediately following the lesson, the teacher should make his own evaluation of the lesson. Following are a few questions he may ask himself.

1. Were the objectives of the lesson accomplished? If not, why?
2. Were all of the students actively involved in the lesson?
3. What resulted from the lesson and the student's evaluation that should be incorporated in the next lesson?

4. Was there any particular behavior or improvement in an individual of which I should make special note?

In Chapter VI are more detailed discussions concerning evaluations of lessons and teaching techniques.

SUGGESTED REFERENCES
FOR FURTHER STUDY

Barrett, Kate Ross, *Exploration, A Method for Teaching Movement* (Madison, Wis., College Printing and Typing Co., 1965).

Bilbrough, A., and P. Jones, *Physical Education in the Primary School* (London, University of London Press, 1963).

Cratty, Bryant J., *Movement Behavior and Motor Learning* (Philadelphia, Lea and Febiger, 1964).

Diem, Liselott, *Who Can* (Frankfort, Germany, William Limpert, 1955).

Halsey, Elizabeth, and Lorena Porter, *Physical Education for Children* (New York, Holt, Rinehart & Winston, 1963), Chapter 9.

Lemen, Mildred, "Implications of the Problem Solving Method for Physical Educators," *Journal of Health, Physical Education and Recreation* (March, 1966), p. 28.

London County Council, *Educational Gymnastics a Guide for Teachers* (London, London County Council, 1963).

Ragsdale, Clarence, "How Children Learn the Motor Types of Activities," *Learning and Instruction, 49th Yearbook,* Part 1, National Society for the Study of Education (Chicago, University of Chicago Press, 1950).

Ulrich, Celeste, "The Tomorrow Mind," *Journal of Health, Physical Education and Recreation* (October, 1964), p. 17.

Chapter V

ORGANIZATION OF CONTENT AND CLASSES

Planning units of instruction

Place of practice drills, skill games, and lead-up games

Effective use of equipment and space

Grouping within the class

Physical education for boys and girls in the upper grades

Tournaments

Facilities, equipment, and supplies

Organization is one of the keys to success in teaching any activity. Long before the teacher actually presents a lesson to his class, he must consider many factors which are essential to favorable results. These are areas which often cause difficulty for the inexperienced teacher. The better he plans and organizes, the more confidently he will approach the lesson and the more valuable the experience will be to the students. Included in this chapter are practical suggestions and discussions of several factors vital to good organization in all types of physical education lessons.

PLANNING UNITS
OF INSTRUCTION

Many teachers fail to see the importance of planning activities in well-organized units of instruction. Most units are seasonal and fall into six or eight weeks of instruction in an activity meeting two or three days a week (p. 57). Prior to the starting date of the unit, the teacher needs to appraise the unit as a whole and select the specific concepts, principles, skills, knowledges, rules, dances, games, etc., to be included in light of what he expects his students to learn. He should also plan the type of procedures to be followed in evaluating the progress of the students. Finally, he needs to plot a calendar for a logical order of progression of lessons. This initial planning will insure that the learning is progressive, sequential, and inclusive. The calendar must be flexible due to irregularities in scheduling and in the learning process.

The following items must be considered before planning begins:
1. Grade or classification of the pupils involved
2. Number of pupils in the class
3. Facilities available for use
4. Length of class period and number of times a week it meets
5. Equipment available for use
6. Amount of previous instruction or previous experience that the pupils have had in the activity
7. Estimated range of ability or skill level of pupils

The teacher can then follow this suggested outline when actually planning the unit.

UNIT PLAN OUTLINE

    I. Objectives of the unit in terms of the learner
        A. General objectives
           These are broad general objectives that are unique to physical education and can be accomplished best through the specific unit of activity. Learning in physical, social, emotional, and intellectual areas are to be considered.
        B. Specific objectives
           These concern what is to be accomplished with the specific activity. These should be related directly to the general objectives. Practicality in terms of the available time is important.

    II. Development of the activity
        1. List of skills or techniques to be taught or reviewed in progressive order

    2. Lead-up games or dances
    3. List of knowledges that should be gained
       Examples:
       a. Basic concepts or principles
       b. Rules of the game
       c. Use of specific skills
       d. Team play and strategy
       e. Dance formations

  III. Plans for class organization
Decision of how class will be divided for small group work, skill drills, and team play. Possible plans might be: ability grouping, division by sexes, sizes. Rotation plans for station work in gymnastics, and method by which students are assigned to groups are established.

  IV. Equipment needed

   V. Health and safety precautions
    1. List of safety rules for students
    2. Precautions to be taken by teacher

  VI. Motivation devices
    Examples:
    1. Audio-visual materials
       a. Movies, film strips—date to be ordered and used
       b. Posters
       c. Diagrams
    2. Tournaments, track meets, gymnastic meets
    3. Special events
       a. Demonstrations by specialists
       b. Assembly program
       c. Parents' visit
       d. Demonstration for another class

  VII. Evaluation of results of teaching (in reference to the objectives of the unit)
    1. Skill performance
       a. Choice of skill tests to be used
       b. Subjective rating of performance
    2. Knowledge
    3. Social responsibility or citizenship

  VIII. Block plan
    1. Timetable of what will be taught in each daily lesson of the unit

IX. Reference list
1. Sources of information for teacher
2. Books or materials available for student use

The daily lesson plan grows out of the unit plan. The actual activities to be taught each day are taken from the unit block plan. The daily plan cannot be made too far in advance, as each day's accomplishments are the basis for the next lesson. However, the general outline of the plan should be made sometime well in advance of when the lesson is taught. The nature of the activity and the time it comes in the unit dictate how much time is allotted to each phase of the lesson. More time must be devoted to learning and practicing skills in drills or skill games or self-testing situations in the initial lessons of the unit. As the unit progresses, the time spent on drills decreases, and the amount of time planned for playing the game, working on compositions, or routines, increases.

As he is making the lesson plan, the teacher should ask himself these three questions.
1. *Why* do I teach this lesson? (State objectives.)
2. *What* materials or activities are to be used to attain the objectives of this lesson?
3. *How* shall I plan to present these activities to the pupils?
Each teacher will develop his own style of daily lesson planning. Included here is a suggested outline.

OUTLINE OF DAILY LESSON PLAN

I. Objectives of lesson
The teacher should focus his attention on a few specific points that he intends the students to learn in the lesson. The objectives are not that the children will learn a game, but what they will learn through playing the game. A teacher should be able to verbalize what he expects the students to learn.

II. Equipment needed
Number and kind of balls, sticks, records, play space, pinnies, lines, *et al.*

III. Procedure to be followed
1. How class will be organized
2. How teams or groups will be formed
3. What will be explained; how long will this take?
4. What will be demonstrated, who will demonstrate—time this will take

    5. Formation for drills; time for drills
    6. Length of time for compositions, routines, games

IV. Major coaching or teaching points
    1. Rules to be emphasized during game
    2. Cue words or coaching phrases (for skills) which will be repeated
    3. Reinforcement of basic concepts to be learned

 V. How class will be concluded
    1. Evaluation with pupils
    2. "Show off" time of skills learned
    3. Plans for next lesson

VI. Self-evaluation of lesson and teacher

PLACE OF PRACTICE
DRILLS, SKILL GAMES,
AND LEAD-UP GAMES

The instructional unit may be approached by teaching the skills first, followed by the game, or by introducing the focal game first and then the skills. Proponents of the latter approach feel that initially children are interested only in playing the game. A need and desire to improve skills grows from action in the game itself. Other teachers feel that the logical progression is to teach skills first, since playing without skill leads to frustration and subsequent disinterest in the game. Obviously, both of these methods have their advantages and disadvantages.

If children have acquired a rich background of fundamental skills in the lower grades, and the teacher has provided them with opportunities to develop beginning sport skills, they can easily begin to play games suited to their ability level with just a cursory introduction to the skills involved. The danger in teaching skills first is an overemphasis on skill for skill's sake resulting in a lack of opportunity for children to see the relationship of the skill and its use in a game situation. Practice of skills is *essential;* however, practice drills and games can be selected which children will enjoy while still developing and perfecting techniques. The danger of placing the major emphasis on the game might result in the pupils' lack of understanding of the need for good skills. It is evident that proficiency in skill performance depends on practice which will enable individuals of all levels of ability to improve.

Practice drills are organized activities which involve a repetition of a specific skill or combination of skills but involve no elements of game rules or team scoring. In their simplest form, practice drills may consist of individual work with the teacher setting a task with provisions for individual stages of progress. When a child achieves a relative degree of competency and confidence, the instructor designs drills which are as nearly like the game situation as possible. Too often drills are static, slow, and unrealistic; consequently, the transition from drill to game is frustrating, and the drills prove to be valueless.

Practice drills must be progressive as games. Just as in the developmental progression of games, the teacher must allow time and practice at each stage of drill for the students to gain confidence and proficiency in skills. As an example of how this can be done, a progression of skill drills for the acquisition of offensive and, to a lesser extent, defensive tactics for soccer-type games is described in the following paragraphs.[1] The basic skill involved is passing. Each specific phase of the drill should be used when it is needed for the lead-up game being taught. The whole progression should be developed over a period of years or could be utilized as a review when the emphasis is on offensive passing in seventh or eighth grade. This same drill can be utilized with the skill of passing for basketball, speedball, hockey, lacrosse, and football.

As the drills become more complex, the student gains ability and confidence in passing. The additional tasks involved and the number of teammates and opponents dictate that the student adapt the skill to the new situations. Timing and accuracy of the pass are of primary importance. The principle of drill progression, like that of games, involves increasing the complexity in an ordered fashion.

The first step is to provide a situation in which the technique of passing can be acquired without any stress. The initial drill can simply involve one player practicing a pass, on the move in a specified direction and then to a particular spot. The next drill involves alternate passing between partners while they are running down the field. This demands greater accuracy in passing because of the judgment that must be made as to the speed of the teammate and the distance to be covered.

After a reasonable degree of skill is acquired in the latter situation, one stationary defense player is added to the drill. He takes a position opposite the player with the ball (Figure 5-1a). This person simulates a defense player in a game situation; however, initially he remains stationary and may not tackle or intercept. When the passer adjusts to timing the pass just out-of-reach of his opponent, the defense player is permitted to reach with one leg. The importance of the correct judgment of timing of the pass is further increased when later the defense player is permitted to move in any direction.

A more advanced drill follows with an equal number of attack and defense players (Figure 5-1b). Here again the additional player is station-

[1] Evelyn L. Schurr, "Theory of Progression in Soccer Games and Skill Drills," *Soccer Speedball Guide 1964–1966* (Washington, D.C., Division of Girls' and Women's Sports, American Association for Health, Physical Education and Recreation, 1964), p. 23. Reprinted by permission.

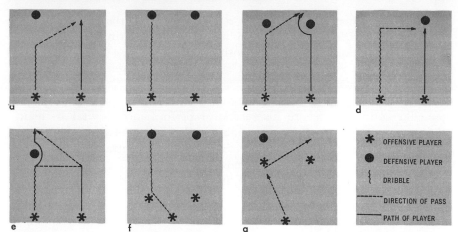

Figure 5-1. (a) One Stationary Defense Player. (b) Two Stationary Defense Players. (c) Defense Player Marks; a Through Pass Is Executed. (d) Defense Player Covers; a Flat Pass Is Executed. (e) Triangular Pass. (f) Defense Player Covering. (g) Defense Player Marking.

ary until greater passing accuracy is attained and the receiver learns to cut in to take the pass. Then the defense player is allowed to reach and move freely in the order prescribed above. The greater difficulty of this drill is due to the placement of the pass in relation to the position of the receiver's opponent. The passer must observe whether the opponent is in a marking or covering position. If he is marking, a through pass is executed behind the defense player (Figure 5-1c). Should he be covering, a flat pass is made as seen in Figure 5-1d.

The latter drill, with the defense player covering, provides an excellent progression into the more advanced concept of a triangular pass. In essence this is a dodge or means of evading an opponent in which the receiver of the flat pass immediately sends a through pass back to the original passer (Figure 5-1e).

Though the emphasis is placed on offensive play, indirectly, defensive concepts are developed simultaneously. As the freedom of the defense player is expanded (from stationary to reaching to moving freely) he begins to develop judgment in respect to timing a tackle, attempting an interception or permitting the forward to play the ball unmolested.

More advanced drills can be constructed by adding an equal number of defensive and offensive players. Additional stress may be exerted upon the original passer by the necessity of receiving a pass from a fellow defense player behind him. This drill is more complex due to the new task of fielding the ball and detection of whether or not his opponent is marking or covering. If the defensive player is covering, the attack player simply fields the ball and continues play depending on the subsequent action of his opponent. If the defensive player is marking, the attack player must cut back and field the ball, keep it under control, and pass immediately. Then he might be in a position for a triangular pass. In this series of drills, the defensive player is in a covering position first (Figure 5-1f), next in a marking position (Figure 5-1g), and finally the position is left to the discretion of the defensive player where he may either cover or mark.

As the student experiences these sequential drills, he is exposed to gamelike conditions where his successful performance is vital to team attainment of success. When providing ordered progression of lead-up games and skill drills, the teacher simply follows central psychological principles of learning. One of the most basic and evident of these being, learning should proceed from the simple to the complex.

Group drill formations

As an aid to the teacher a few group drill formations are diagramed. Most of these are quite versatile and may be modified to fit specific needs. Often game directions state to have the class take one of these formations. These also provide good formations for relays of various types. Children can learn the formations by name and get into action quickly.

1. Mass or Group (Figure 5-2a)
   This drill is useful for individual work in which directions or demonstrations are given by a leader. Pupils should make a quarter turn to face teacher so that all will have an unobstructed view of him.
2. Single Circle (Figure 5-2b)
   The object may be passed around or across the circle. If ball is passed around, pivoting may also be practiced. When giving directions the teacher should break the circle. He should never stand in the center when addressing the whole group.
3. Circle and Leader (Figure 5-2c)
   This formation may be used for a stationary drill where the leader throws the ball to circle players, and they throw it back. In a moving drill, a player may follow the ball back and forth, changing with the leader. A player may move around the circle catching or throwing the ball from gaps between other players.
4. Leader and Class (Figure 5-2d)
   The squad is spread in a semi-circle with the leader centered in front of them.
5. Zigzag (Figure 5-2e)
   This drill provides practice of throwing, catching, and kicking from

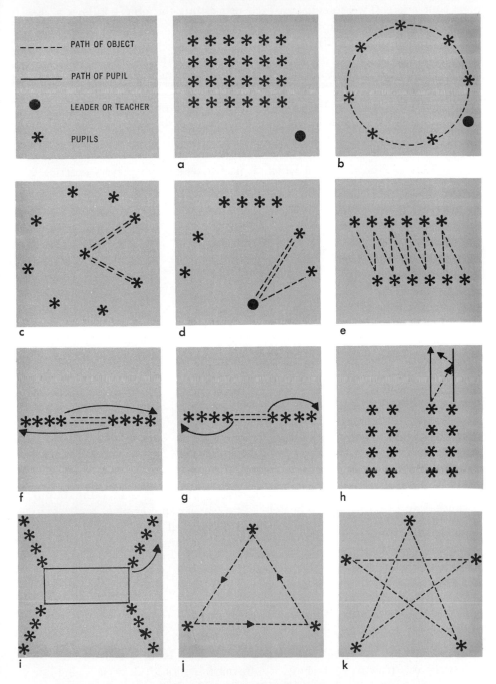

Figure 5-2. Group Drill Formations.

an angle. Two squads face each other, but the object follows a zig
zag pattern. A pupil may follow the object.

6. Shuttle (Figure 5-2f)

   This is a moving drill where the first person in one line throws,
   kicks, or dribbles to the other line and then takes a new place at the
   end of the opposite line.

7. Shuttle and Turn Back (Figure 5-2g)

   The object is passed back and forth, but person moves to the end of
   his own line when his turn is over.

8. Double Columns (Figure 5-2h)

   This is a moving drill which is useful when two players practice a
   skill where they pass an object back and forth as they move down the
   field. Another column may be added if multiple play is demanded,
   as in forward line play in soccer, hockey, lacrosse, etc.

9. Square or Corner (Figure 5-2i)

   This drill can be used with players who are running, dribbling, or
   carrying an object around the square, then returning to the end of
   their own line. It may be a stationary drill with the object going
   around the square and players moving to the end of their own line.
   The player may move to another line. The object may also be passed
   across the square.

10. Triangular (Figure 5-2j)

    This drill is similar to the square or corner formation. However, it
    is used better for small group practice. The object may go in any
    direction.

11. Star (Figure 5-2k)

    This drill is much like that of the triangular formation but is more
    effective in the practice of deceptive passing where no set pattern is
    required. The pupil may move with the object and exchange places
    with someone else.

In presenting drills to the class it is imperative that the pupils
understand well what is to be done. The teacher should place the class in
the formation to be utilized in the drill and tell everyone to sit down.
He should use one couple or unit of the formation as a demonstration
group and have them proceed with the drill until the pattern is clearly
understood by all. If the class is being conducted outside or in an extremely large indoor setting, only the demonstration group is put into
formation so all members of the class can see and hear the directions
and subsequently get into the drill formation and get activity underway quickly.

If the skills being presented are new and involve control and accuracy in throwing or kicking, the formation should allow for adequate
space between people or groups. When small hard objects such as
softballs are being used, more space than usual is needed for safety reasons. Groups should not be placed back to back for practice drills.

Once the class is in a drill formation, sufficient number of trials should be provided for each child, as one learns through repeated practice. If only two or three trials are to be permitted, the time taken for getting into the formation is unwarranted. While the drills are in progress, the teacher should circulate and give individual help. This proves valuable only if the child can follow up the suggestions with more opportunities for practice.

Skill games are games which principally involve the use and practice of one or two skills. A game element of competition is involved, but the rules are simple and the game can be started and completed very quickly. This is a means of giving children an extensive opportunity to use the skill currently being stressed under game conditions. An example of this would be the game of Keep Away (p. 412) where the skills of passing and intercepting are practiced much as they are used in the game of basketball.

A lead-up game is a game which is utilized as an instrument to teach skills, rules, knowledges, appreciation, and strategies of an official sport. It must include at least one skill, rule, and simple team strategy that can be identified with the parent game. Its organization must be such that it offers an opportunity for a team or individual climatic effort such as scoring a goal, or preventing a goal, and redirecting effort to counteract the other team's achievements. These skills, rules, and strategies become more complex as children progress in physical maturity and skill. At the point when children are physically and mentally mature enough to handle official sport rules, the lead-up game they are playing should be almost identical with the parent game, so that the transition will be simple and smooth. One lead-up game is the focal point of each unit. Playing several games within a unit is sometimes distracting and leads to confusion. Success and enjoyment of a game at the end of a unit builds enthusiasm for learning a new and more complicated game the following year.

EFFECTIVE USE OF
EQUIPMENT AND SPACE

The values of practice drills or games are somewhat dependent on the effective use of equipment and space. How much time is spent on skill practice is subject to how many opportunities each child has to execute the skill. If there is a ball for every two children rather than one ball for many, the time allotted to skill practice may be less. Of course, the same amount of time may be spent but greater results in terms of improvement in skill would be expected. Often teachers organize drills by squads and fail to see opportunities to break into smaller units in order to utilize all of the available equipment.

The teacher should not overlook the values of a wall as a teaching aid. Much time can be saved with younger children in throwing and catching activities by using the wall as a target or rebound object. Younger children have a difficult time catching small balls; consequently, when throwing is practiced, much time is spent on chasing the ball. This is especially true when work on the overhand throw is started. Children can concentrate on the throwing pattern and need not be concerned about catching a hard thrown ball. As the ball rebounds off the wall, it loses some of its force. Everyone may start relatively close to the wall, and as an individual's skill improves, he may move farther away.

The wall is extremely helpful when teaching beginning volleyball skills. Beginners can hit the ball thrown up in the air by themselves easier than they can hit a ball which has been volleyed by someone else. The ball should be caught as it rebounds from the wall and then thrown up again. Repeated volleys returned off the wall do not simulate a beginning volleyball game; however, strength can be developed in this manner. Much time can be saved when learning the serve if the ball is hit into the wall rather than across the net. This enables the pupil to concentrate on the skill pattern rather than on where the ball goes.

Children can learn the skill pattern of batting earlier than they can learn to pitch accurately. The use of a batting tee enables them to practice batting or to play a game utilizing batting without waiting for a good pitch to cross the plate.

When practicing ball-handling skills, there is no need to use the exact type of ball specified for the game at hand. For example; in a basketball unit, soccer balls, volleyballs, and playground balls may be used for practicing shooting, dribbling, and passing. If a limited number of balls and baskets are available, one group of children can be practicing a skill requiring one type of equipment and another group a skill which requires different equipment or no equipment at all.

Balls and implements which are related to the size of the children involved are essential to their success. When purchasing equipment, intermediate size footballs, basketballs, bats, protective devices, and goals should be ordered. Playground balls of various sizes are inexpensive and can be used as substitutes for many official types of balls.

GROUPING WITHIN
THE CLASS

Grouping students into small working units aids both the students and the teacher in many ways. Although the units may be termed squads, groups, teams, or units, they will be referred to as squads in this discussion. The major value of using squads to the teacher is organizational. They allow him to get activity underway quickly and to make smooth transitions from one type of activity to another.

Values of squads

Whenever small-group work is to be done, use of squads is invaluable. Track and field and gymnastic activities demand small working groups, since several work stations are needed due to the nature of the equipment and space, and periodic rotation is required from one type of event to another. Good use of space and equipment for many self-testing activities and practice drills is more possible if squad work is utilized. Teams can easily be formed by combining squads, and games and relays requiring small teams may be started quickly by utilizing existing squads.

Assignments of responsibilities for equipment and student planning can be given to squads. The teacher can spot some social behaviors more quickly as a child reacts to an intact group for a period of time. Evaluating progress and analyzing errors is easier if one watches a small group work, rather than watching a large scattered group.

Squads offer children stability and a close working relationship with a group. They learn to work and plan together. In many instances, they must share responsibilities. If one child in the squad is given leadership responsibilities, each of the others learns how to follow a peer member. Squad membership develops teamwork and group spirit.

Forming squads

There are a number of ways in which squads may be formed. The nature of the activity and objectives of the unit usually determine the method. Children may be grouped according to abilities, characteristics, or at random. If the former is to be true, results of skill tests, fitness tests, sociometric tests; height, weight, body build; observation of skill and social behavior may serve as the basis for assignment to squads.

There are advantages and disadvantages to homogenous grouping on the basis of ability. Whenever progress on the part of either the highly skilled or the low skilled is likely to be retarded, the two levels should be homogenously grouped. This is more likely to be true when equipment is used and the activity is highly progressive. For example, in high jumping the bar is usually raised after each successive jump. If one or two pupils cannot jump sixteen inches, they certainly are doomed to defeat each time the bar goes up an inch. Unless the bar is raised and lowered for each person, the poor jumper has little chance to improve. Raising and lowering the bar takes a great deal of time. In game play the highly skilled need the challenge of playing against others of comparable ability. For example, the good hitter needs to hit against good pitching; he needs the challenge of having to beat out a hit, rather than getting a free trip around the bases because the fielders are not capable of fielding the ball and throwing it accurately to the baseman.

Some poorly skilled youngsters are easily discouraged as they watch those who are consistently successful. However, they need to watch others in order to get a concept of how skills are done well and how skills are used in a game or dance situation. The teacher can forestall discouragement on the part of the poorly skilled by using a variety of organizations, by having better skilled youngsters in a squad help those who are not well skilled, by giving guidance during the observation of demonstrations, and making provisions for many self-testing activities.

There should be opportunities for team play and small group dance compositions where groups are heterogenous in nature. When boys and girls are separated for some activities, there should be provision for some mixed activities also. Cooperation among team members should be stressed.

Squads should remain intact long enough to accomplish the purposes of stability of membership. Usually squads are reformed with the change of units of activity. There is little value in changing frequently. Some activities such as dance do not lend themselves to squad organization. Squads do not have to be used each time a small group is formed. In sports and games, teams may be formed with combinations of different squads. When a tournament culminates a unit, new teams may be formed.

The number of children in a squad is dictated by the organization of the unit and the amount of equipment and space available. For example, if six stations are to be used in apparatus, six squads should be formed. In volleyball there are six members on a team; therefore, squads should have six members. In softball there are nine members on a team; therefore, two squads of five each could be combined to form one team with two players becoming rotating umpires. Some of the values of squad organization are lost if more than six or eight members are in a squad. An even number of squads is most desirable in order to combine them for teams. Following are suggestions for organizing squads.

I. Teacher-assigned groups on the basis of:
   a. Homogenous ability, size, fitness qualities
   b. Heterogenous with each group having equal number of students of low and high ability, size, fitness qualities
   c. Sociometric questionnaires
   d. Social behavior
   e. Random selection from class list
   f. Counting off within the class

II. Pupil participation in selecting squads:
  a. Electing four leaders, leaders choose members. (The selection of members should be done in a cooperative closed session of leaders and teacher.)
  b. Electing leaders, student goes to leader of his choice. (Maximum number of squad members must be stated.)
  c. Participation in sociometric questionnaire
  d. Drawing numbers, colors, or places
  e. Pupils' ideas, solicited and followed

PHYSICAL EDUCATION FOR BOYS AND GIRLS IN THE UPPER GRADES

Many physical educators recommend that boys and girls be separated for physical education activities beginning in the fifth grade. There is not unanimous agreement on this recommendation; however, it is justifiable in terms of the physiological, physical, and psychological differences of the sexes which increase at the start of puberty. This is particularly true in activities which require strength and vigorous activity.

In spite of opinion on this subject, many elementary schools are not in a position to separate into boys' and girls' classes due to a lack of facilities, physical education specialists, school organization, and combinations of same. Any teacher will recognize the differences between boys and girls in skill, strength, and interest in activities starting as early as fourth grade and increasing in the fifth and sixth grades. Boys frequently dominate play; consequently, girls' skills and interest become retarded when they remain together for all activities in the upper grades. The wise teacher can avoid this problem by heeding the following suggestions.

There is no problem, as stated above, when a dance unit is held, and there should be few problems during a gymnastics unit, as everyone can proceed at his own pace. Boys will be more interested in combative type stunts and may do better in activities requiring shoulder strength. Girls will be more inclined toward balance type activities and will probably do better than boys in them. There is no reason why boys and girls must be required to do all of the same stunts within a unit. Although official rules for most team sports differ somewhat for boys and girls, the skills, knowledges, and strategies involved are much the same. While children are learning these things there are a number of lead-up games in which they can participate together without harm or inequalities.

This author suggests ability groupings for work on skills and game play for the most part. Undoubtedly, there will be a few highly skilled girls and a few poorly skilled boys in each class. These children would derive no benefit where the division is by sex. Skill practice in ability groupings facilitates individual or small group remedial work with the poorer students and enables the better skilled to learn new and more challenging tasks. However, all game play should not be by ability, or the children with a low level of skill would not have the opportunity to be motivated by playing with those who are skilled. Frequently, games and drills should be planned where heterogenous grouping is used but teams are of equal ability.

In games where single opponents are pitted directly against one another in a defensive-offensive situation, the teacher can organize the positions on teams where boys will oppose boys and girls oppose girls. An example of this would be the line up for Toss-Up Basketball (p. 415), where every other person in line would be a girl on both teams. Therefore, one girl would emerge from each line to be the runner and the two pit their skills against each other.

There is no reason why boys and girls cannot be separated within a class for separate games at times. An obvious example of this would be for the tag football unit for boys. In the sixth grade many boys play in leagues or groups outside of school where modified official boys' rules are used in basketball and baseball. Thus games of lesser challenge should not be imposed upon them for whole units of time in the school situation. Boys often play a vigorous, more demanding style of soccer, basketball, volleyball when girls are not involved. Of course, vigorous play is what should be promoted. Occasionally, they may be brought together for game play with equal numbers on both teams. Girls can learn a great deal from the more highly skilled boys if the teacher encourages teamwork and assistance, rather than permitting domination or ridicule of the girls by the boys.

TOURNAMENTS

Sports units should be climaxed by a tournament of some sort. This not only has great motivational value but also gives the students an opportunity to put their newly acquired skills, knowledges, and strategies to use in a student-directed activity. Teams should be charged with planning their strategy and teamwork without direct supervision of the teacher. This also gives the teacher an opportunity to evaluate the students' application of what they have learned during the unit. The three most suitable types of tournaments for class use are described in the following pages. Directions for constructing each are included.

Round robin tournament

The best type of tournament for class use is a round robin where each team or each individual plays every other team or individual. In this way no one is eliminated, and the participation may be enjoyed by all. This is also a good type of tournament for intramural activities, the only disadvantage being that if there are a large number of teams, it takes excessive time to complete all of the rounds.

In order to plan for the amount of time required to complete the tournament one can determine the number of games to be played by applying the following formula:

(N = number of teams)

$$\frac{N(N-1)}{2}$$

EXAMPLE: 6 teams $\frac{6(6-1)}{2} = \frac{6 \times 5}{2} \quad \frac{30}{2}$ 15 games to be scheduled

The procedure for constructing the schedule of games for an even number of teams is as follows:

1. Number the teams.
2. Number the teams in sequence down the first column and up the second. Number one remains stationary, and the other teams rotate in a counter-clockwise direction.
3. There will always be one less round than the number of teams or individuals in the tournament.

Six team tournament

Round 1	Round 2	Round 3	Round 4	Round 5
1 vs. 6	1 vs. 5	1 vs. 4	1 vs. 3	1 vs. 2
2 vs. 5	6 vs. 4	5 vs. 3	4 vs. 2	3 vs. 6
3 vs. 4	2 vs. 3	6 vs. 2	5 vs. 6	4 vs. 5

If there is an uneven number of teams to schedule, a bye (no play) is given to one team each round. The bye becomes the stationary point.

The procedure for constructing the schedule of games for an uneven number of teams is as follows:

1. Number the teams.
2. Place the word "bye" at the top of the first column of each round. List the number of the teams in sequence down the first column and up the second. The bye remains the stationary point, and all of the numbers rotate counter-clockwise one place in each round.
3. There will always be the same number of rounds in the tournament as there are number of teams.

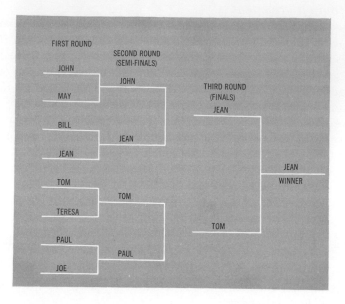

Figure 5-3. Elimination Tournament with Eight Players.

Five team tournament

Round 1	Round 2	Round 3	Round 4	Round 5
Bye 5	Bye 4	Bye 3	Bye 2	Bye 1
1 vs. 4	5 vs. 3	4 vs. 2	3 vs. 1	2 vs. 5
2 vs. 3	1 vs. 2	5 vs. 1	4 vs. 5	3 vs. 4

A team is given two points for each win, one point for a tie, and no points for a loss. The winner of the tournament is the team with the most points. The winner may also be determined by the percentage of games won after the tournament is over. The percentage is found by dividing the games won by a team by the number of games the team played.

The teacher may wish to have a tournament to determine the winning squad, but may find that squads have too few players to form a whole team for certain games. In this case he can combine squads for teams, using a different combination for each game. The round robin procedure is used to determine the combination of squads for each game. Both squads on the winning team receive points for the victory. At the end of the tournament the squad with the most points is the champion.

EXAMPLE:

Round 1	Round 2	Round 3
Squads 1 & 2 vs. 3 & 4	1 & 3 vs. 2 & 4	1 & 4 vs. 2 & 3

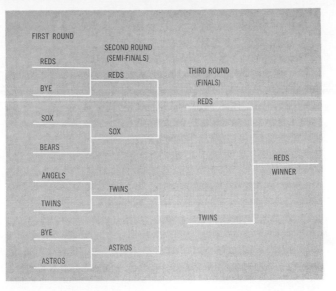

Figure 5-4. Elimination Tournament with Six Teams.

Elimination tournament

If an individual or team champion is to be determined in a very short period of time, an elimination tournament is desirable. Since each time a team plays and loses, it is eliminated, the tournament may include a great number of teams and be concluded rather quickly. However, the feature of elimination does not provide much activity for everyone. This type of tournament may climax a long season of round robin play, or it may conclude a unit on the final day.

The teacher determines the number of games which must be scheduled by subtracting one from the total number of teams in the tournament. (N — 1 = Number of games to be scheduled.) The procedure for constructing the schedule of games for a number of teams which is a power of 2 (4, 8, 16, 32, 64, etc.) is as follows:

1. Number or name the teams.
2. Draw the same number of lines as there are teams. Each two in ascending order are coupled together (Figure 5-3). Fill in the lines by drawing the numbers of the teams at random or whichever way is desired. Those coupled together play each other in the first round. Those who win move out into the second round and play the team coupled with them. The losing team is eliminated from the tournament. Successive rounds are played until one winner emerges. Figure 5-3 is an example of a tournament with eight teams.

The procedure for constructing the schedule of games for a number of teams which is not a power of two is as follows:

1. Number or name the teams.

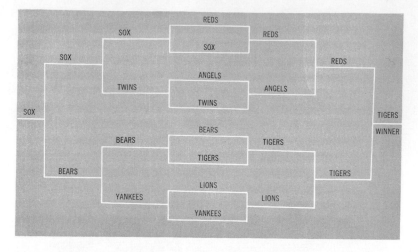

Figure 5-5. Consolation Tournament with Eight Teams.

2. A system of byes (no play) is used in the first round. To determine the number of byes needed, subtract the number of teams from the next highest power of two. For example; if six teams are playing, $8 - 6 = 2$ byes. Draw eight lines for the first round. The byes are placed near the top and near the bottom of the first round. If there are more than two byes, they should be equally distributed. Sometimes the strongest teams in the tournament are given the byes so that they do not meet in the first round and they will not eliminate the weaker teams in the first round. Team names may be drawn at random and put into the first round in order of drawing.

3. The teams who drew byes are automatically put over into the second round. Other first round games are played, and the winners advance to the second round. The losers are eliminated from the tournament.

Play continues until one team is left. Figure 5-4 shows the pairings for a tournament of six teams.

Consolation tournament

When there is time, it is desirable to have a consolation tournament. Each team which loses in the first round gets to play at least one more time by moving into a new tournament of the losers. There may or may not be a final game between the winners of the winners and the winners of the original losers. Figure 5-5 shows the format for a consolation tournament of eight teams.

Ladder tournament

Ladder tournaments are a good means of conducting a continuous tournament during part of each period. They are particularly suited to individual activities or sports and in classes where there are not a large number of students. The objective is to climb to the top of the ladder and remain there until the tournament is declared over.

Participants are placed on a ladder and may challenge players above them. As they win they move up the ladder. This type of tournament is challenging, motivating, and encourages initiative. As children can continue the tournament without the teacher's help, it works well for noon hours, recess, and/or after school activities.

The procedure for constructing a ladder tournament is as follows (see Figure 5-6):

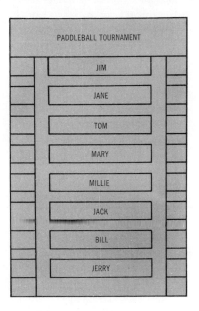

Figure 5-6. Ladder Tournament.

1. Use a board with hooks placed in ladder style, or a chart with movable nametags arranged one above the other.
2. Make a tag for each contestant and place one on each rung of the ladder. It is sometimes wise to place the better players near the bottom of the ladder so they have to work their way up to the top.
3. Set a date for completion of the tournament. The person whose name is at the top on that date will be the winner.
4. Post a set of rules for the tournament next to the ladder. Suggested set of rules:
   a. A player may challenge people one or two rungs above him.
   b. Winner changes places on the ladder with the person whom he defeated, if he were the challenger.

    c. If challenger loses, he must play at least one other player before he may rechallenge the winner.

    d. Challenges must be met within a specified period (depending upon how frequently the opportunities for play arise).

    e. Established rules are used for specific types of tournament (rules for game, what score constitutes game, set, match, etc.).

Pyramid tournament

A pyramid tournament is much like that of a ladder tournament only it affords more opportunities for challenges. A player may challenge anyone on the level above him (Figure 5-7). The final winner is the one who reaches the top of the pyramid at the close of the tournament.

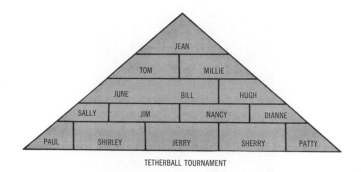

TETHERBALL TOURNAMENT

Figure 5-7. Pyramid Tournament.

FACILITIES, EQUIPMENT, AND SUPPLIES

The quality and effectiveness of any physical education program depends to a great extent upon the facilities and equipment available with which to conduct the program. Facilities are the permanent structures within and on which the program takes place, such as the gymnasium and playgrounds. Equipment includes items which are usually movable and rather durable, but must be replaced periodically. Items such as apparatus, mats, net standards, basketball baskets, record player, etc., are considered equipment. Items which are less expensive and expendable within a few years time are usually called supplies. Balls, bats, wands, records, etc., fall into the supply category.

    Few teachers have an opportunity to plan facilities or make many changes in existing ones; however, they do need to know how to make the best use of what is available. Occasionally when new buildings are

planned, teachers are asked to make recommendations to a building committee. Sources of information pertaining to recommended specifications
are available for those planning the construction.[1]

Most teachers have an opportunity to make recommendations for the
purchase of new equipment and supplies. All should be aware of minimum needs and the approximate price of most items.

Facilities

Outdoor space

The National Council on Schoolhouse Construction [2] has recommended
that an elementary school provide a 10-acre site with an additional acre
for every 100 pupils, for play space. The junior high school should provide a minimum site of twenty acres, plus an additional acre for every
100 pupils of predicted ultimate enrollment. Many older schools have
less space than this and where open space is at a premium some newly
built schools do not meet these requirements.

Where streets run adjacent to the play space, a fence should be constructed for reasons of safety. A portion of the play space should be hard
surfaced so play may be held in inclement weather, and games may be
played where a good bounce on the ball is desirable. It is preferable to
have this area adjacent to a windowless wall of the building so that balls
may be safely hit or thrown against the wall. Lines forming boundaries
for popular games should be permanently painted on the hard top surface. Suggested line markings are:

> Paddle tennis courts
> Four square courts
> Bases, 30 feet apart
> Tether ball courts
> Safety line, 6 feet from edge of entire area
> Rectangular area with center line for low organized games
> Hopscotch courts
> Circles

The majority of the area should be well turfed, free from holes and
rocks, and suitable for field games and track and field activities. A back
stop should be available for softball. One or two jumping pits filled with
sand or tanbark should be to one side.

---

1 Athletic Institute, *Planning Areas and Facilities for Health, Physical Education, and
  Recreation* (Washington, D.C., American Association for Health, Physical Education
  and Recreation, 1965); and National Council on Schoolhouse Construction, *Guide for
  Planning School Plants* (East Lansing, Michigan, The Council, Michigan State University, 1964).
2 *Ibid.*

A separate area for placement of apparatus should be set aside. A soft surface of sand, tanbark, or wood shavings should be under and around the apparatus. Listed below are some developmental pieces of equipment which should be permanently installed in this area.

Climbing structures
Horizontal bars, multiple sizes
Horizontal ladder
Parallel bar
Monkey rings
Climbing poles
Turning bar
Old tree trunks laid horizontally on ground
Rails or beams
Creative equipment as available

Traditional playground equipment such as swings, teeters, slides, and merry-go-rounds are being replaced by creative and developmental equipment. The latter provides opportunities for children to develop strength, balance, skills, and to be imaginative in the use of their skills.

A separate play area may be designated for preschool and primary grade children so that no balls from older children's games are hit or thrown into an unaware group. If space and finances permit, separate apparatus areas may also be set up.

Portable equipment for outdoor use should include:

Standards for net games
Tether ball poles and balls
Jumping standards
Bamboo crossbars
Portable basketball goals
Hurdles
Bases
Goal stands
Field markers

Indoor space

Available indoor play space varies in every school. A gymnasium 50 feet by 75 feet with a 20-foot ceiling is recommended. The floor should be wooden and treated with a nonskid wax. Windows and lights should be covered with protective screening. There should be no sharp edges protruding from the walls or objects along the walls. The latter   must be carefully checked if there is an all-purpose room rather than a separate gymnasium.

An equipment storage room should be located off the gymnasium. Ideally, locker rooms for changing clothes and showering should be available for children in and above the fifth grade.

As much wall space as possible should be left free and clear for target games and skill practice. There should be several electrical outlets on each wall. Provision must be made for attachment of nets to the wall and climbing ropes to the ceiling. Basketball backboards which may be adjusted for height should be installed at both ends of the floor.

Permanent lines which will serve many games should be painted on the floor. A safety line painted 6 feet from the wall all around the play area may also serve as the outside boundary for many games. Two parallel lines painted one foot apart in the center of the floor can serve to divide the room into two play spaces, and also provide a buffer space for games where each team or side occupies one half the court. Large circles may be painted on both halves of the floor. When temporary lines are needed, poster paint serves well, as it will not rub off immediately but can easily be removed with a wet cloth.

When an all-purpose room serves as the cafeteria, auditorium, meeting room, community room, and gymnasium or any combination of these, careful scheduling must be supervised by the administrator, with priority given to physical education classes. If classes are interrupted or cancelled frequently when other groups wish to use the room, a good physical education program cannot be ensured. It is imperative that careful attention is given to the proper cleaning of the floor, if the room is used for many purposes other than classes.

Frequently, the only indoor play space available is the classroom. Many activities with the exception of running and throwing games can be conducted in a satisfactory manner in the classroom, if necessary. This calls for ingenuity and good organizational techniques on the part of the teacher. Moveable furniture is essential if anything but quiet or semiactive games are to be played. Most dance activities can be conducted if the floor is cleared. If mats and small equipment can be moved into the classroom, all gymnastic activities with the exception of those requiring large apparatus can take place. Doorway gym bars, heavy library tables, sturdy boxes, and small-sized vaulting boxes can be moved from room to room.

Equipment

Recommended equipment and supplies for an elementary school with an average class size of twenty-eight pupils are listed in Table 5-1. Although the prices are approximate, they may help the teacher recognize the need for teaching pupils to take care of equipment. It is most economical to have all equipment stored in a central storage room and shared by all classes. Adequate containers, shelves, and hooks should be placed in the room so that children can learn to replace equipment neatly and safely. A plan for care and distribution must be worked out

Table 5-1. Suggested Equipment and Supply List for an Elementary School (K-8)

Item	Number	Approximate Cost Per Item	Can Be Improvised
Blackboard			
First aid kit	1	$10.00	
Instant cold pack	6	4.00	
Instant heat pack	6	4.00	
Ball inflator	1	6.00	
Color bands (4 colors)	30	1.00	X
Bags to carry balls	4		X
Gymnastics			
Mats 4 by 6 feet	6	52.00	
Balance beams (6-inch)	2	40.00	X
(30 by 36 inches)	1	70.00	
Horizontal bar	1	45.00	
Doorway bars	2	4.00	
Folding all-purpose unit, (horizontal bars, rings, ropes, chinning bars)	1	236.00	
Vaulting bench or box	1	70.00	X
Parallel bars	1	70.00	
All-purpose climber	1	180.00	X
Hanging rope	2	25.00	
Games and Sports			
Supersoft softballs	10	$1.95	
Softball bats	6	2.00	
Face masks	2	4.95	
Chest protectors	2	5.00	
Bases (indoor)	4	7.00	X
Bases (outdoor)	6	2.00	X
Batting tee	2	9.80	
Volleyballs (leather)	4	14.45	
Volleyball nets	2	13.50	X
Volleyball standards	2	63.95/pr.	X
Basketballs (intermediate size)	4	11.85	
Footballs (intermediate size)	4	11.25	
Kicking tee	1	2.00	
Belts for flag football	24	15.00/doz.	X
Soccer balls (rubber)	4	12.95	
Tetherball poles	2	9.25	X
Tether balls	2	10.15	
Paddle tennis paddles	12	3.20	
Paddle tennis balls	12	.35	
Aerial tennis paddles	12	3.00	X
Aerial tennis birds	6	1.00	
Deck tennis rings	6	1.25	
Playground balls (5-inch)	12	1.45	
(8½-inch)	12	2.70	
(10-inch)	2	3.50	
(13-inch)	2	3.75	

Table 5-1. Continued

Item	Number	Approximate Cost Per Item	Can Be Improvised
Small Equipment			
Jumping ropes (16-lb.			
sash cord) short	24	$.20	X
Long	10	.50	X
Elastic rope	1	3.00	
Duck 'n Indian clubs	10	1.00	X
Wands	10	.50	X
Hoops	10	1.50	
Beanbags	30		X
Plastic fun balls	4	1.00	
Fleece balls	10	2.25	
Tennis balls	10	.80	
High jump standards—bars	1 set	35.00	X
Dance			
Dance record player	1	125.00	
Dance drum	1	13.95	X
Econ. castanet	4	1.00	X
Tambourine	2	2.50	X
Maracas	2	3.00	X
Cluster bells	3	1.25	X
Adequate record supply			
General Supplies			
Whistles	2	.75	
Whistle lanyard	2	.75	X
100-foot measuring tape	1	5.45	
Stop watch	1	11.95	
Lime marker	1	4.49	

with all school personnel so that it may be used to the best advantage. Equipment should be inspected frequently to see that it is in good repair. It should be cleaned periodically.

In some schools each room has its own equipment and supplies, and they are stored in the classroom. This may be more convenient, but it frequently limits the variety and number of pieces available at one time. Frequently, each room has a few balls which are used at recess time so that no items need be wanted by more than one group at the same time. Equipment for quiet games in the classroom is usually purchased out of the classroom supply budget.

It is wise to purchase high quality equipment. Usually, it will last longer and will be safer. When balls are to be used outside, they should be rubber rather than leather. Rubber balls, cheaper and easier to care for, frequently last longer than leather balls.

Many items may be improvised. School shops, maintenance departments, fathers of pupils and/or P.T.A. groups can often make or install some large apparatus equipment at cost less than that purchased and installed commercially.[3] A few suggestions for improvising equipment are listed below.

OUTDOOR APPARATUS:

1. Turning bars, horizontal bars, parallel bars, climbing poles—made from used pipe and set in concrete
2. Tree trunks set horizontally or supported on an angle; used for vaulting, balancing, climbing
3. Railroad tracks and ties; used for balancing
4. Concrete culverts, large cement blocks, large packing boxes (painted and any protruding nails removed), ladders set between two sturdy supports; used for exploratory climbing, crawling, and jumping

SMALL EQUIPMENT AND SUPPLIES:

1. Color identification bands, made from pieces of muslin
2. Bowling pins acquired from bowling alley proprietors
3. Old bicycle and automobile tires and tubes from service stations
4. Pins or boundary markers made from large plastic bottles filled with sand
5. Bases made from potato sacks filled with grass or straw
6. Batting tee made from pipe covered by garden hose
7. Standard for nets and tether ball made from pipe set in a tire filled with cement
8. Jumping ropes made from 16-pound sash cord cut into varying lengths with ends dipped in paint
9. Wands made from broom handles or one-inch dowels
10. Paddles of various type made in shop from three-quarter inch plywood
11. Beanbags made from old denim and filled with corn or beans
12. Medicine ball made from an old basketball filled with sand
13. Jumping boxes, vaulting benches, made from sturdy old tables or boxes

Most equipment and supply items can be purchased from a local sporting goods store or through sporting goods company representative, who may deal with the school principal or purchasing agent. A few supply houses are listed below. Sources for records are listed in Chapter X.

SUPPLY HOUSES

Cosom Sports Co.   6030 Wayzata
Plastic Play Equipment   Minneapolis, Minnesota

[3] Joel Carter, *How to Make Athletic Equipment* (New York, Ronald, 1960).

Kwik Kold
Hot and Cold First Aid Packs
Box 638
Moberly, Missouri

Rawlings Sporting Goods
2300 Delmer Blvd.
St. Louis, Missouri

Child Craft Equipment, Inc.
155 E. 23rd St.
New York, New York

Physical Education Supply Associates
Specializing in Foreign Books and
Equipment
P.O. Box 292
Trumbull, Connecticut

Program Aids Company
550 Garden Avenue
Mount Vernon, New York
W. J. Voit Rubber Co.
160 Varick St.
New York, New York

Wolverine Sports
3666 S. State St.
Ann Arbor, Michigan

Oregon Worsted Co.
(Fleece Balls)
Portland, Oregon

Nissen Corp.
Gymnastics Equipment
930 27th Ave., S.W.
Cedar Rapids, Iowa

Porter Athletic Equip.
9555 Irvine Park Rd.
Schiller, Park, Illinois

Salsich Recreation Co.
Elementary School Apparatus
11023 Manchester
Kirkwood, Missouri

SUGGESTED REFERENCES
FOR FURTHER STUDY

Aaron, D., and B. Winawer, *Child's Play* (New York, Harper & Row, 1965).

Athletic Institute, *Planning Areas and Facilities for Health, Physical Education and Recreation* (Washington, D.C., American Association for Health, Physical Education and Recreation, 1965).

Athletic Institute, *Equipment and Supplies for Health, Physical Education and Recreation* (Chicago, Athletic Institute, 1960).

Carter, Joel, *How to Make Athletic Equipment* (New York, Ronald, 1960).

Kleindiest, Viola K., and Arthur Weston, *Intramurals and Recreation Programs for Schools and Colleges* (New York, Appleton-Century-Crofts, 1964).

National Council on Schoolhouse Construction, *Guide for Planning School Plants* (East Lansing, Michigan, The Council, Michigan State University, 1964).

Chapter VI

EVALUATION OF THE PRODUCT AND THE PROCESS

Interpretation of
the results of tests

Use of the
results of tests

Evaluation of
the child

Evaluation of
the program

Evaluation of
facilities and
equipment

Evaluation of
the teacher

Evaluation of
the lesson

Evaluation is a constant procedure of determining where an individual, a group, a program, or a process is in relation to established values or goals, and the subsequent use of this information in redirecting efforts to reach the values or goals. In simple terms, the teacher utilizes evaluation to see if he has accomplished what he has set out to do, and if he has not, how he can in his future efforts.

Evaluation in physical education involves measurement of the progress and status of the child, facilities, equipment, program, teacher, and daily lesson. The measurement process involves many techniques and types of tests and can be both quantitative and qualitative. The value of the results of measurement lies in the completion of the evaluative process where the results are studied and plans made to implement the findings in the future. The process and the interpretation of results involves the teacher, student, and parents.

The tools of evaluation are many. The most widely used, reliable, and valid are the objective written and performance achievement tests. As some desirable qualities of performances cannot be measured by objective tests and must be measured subjectively, careful observation of performance and behavior must be made and recorded in the form of rating scales, performance charts, anecdotal records, check lists, and questionnaires. Group and individual discussions, conversations, and conferences are also tools of measurement.

As the child is the focal point of the educative process, most of the evaluation centers about him. His status and progress must be evaluated in terms of the primary goal of physical education; that is, for each child to develop into his fullest capacity to function as a good citizen (Chapter I, p. 6). The specific goals involve development and growth in the physical, mental, social, and emotional areas (Chapter I, p. 6). These goals suggest that both subjective and objective measurements must be made of status and achievement in the areas of physical development, skill performance, knowledge, and social behavior. Specific tests yield information that should enhance learning and teaching in each of the areas. When results of specific tests are analyzed and interpreted in relation to other test results, a broad evaluation can be made of the child and the contribution of the program to him.

INTERPRETATION OF THE RESULTS OF TESTS

The results of tests may be interpreted in two general ways. Individual scores may be compared to those of a larger group or to previous scores. The former may be a class, all the children of a comparable age or grade in the city, state, or country as determined by a normative scale. In order to make a valid comparison of an individual score with that of a norm, the child's background and abilities must be comparable to that of the population upon which the norm is based.

Since there are such great differences between individual children in maturity, size, and background, it is not always wise to use norms, even within a class. The greatest value of norms is that the teacher has a general idea of high and low level of performance of a group. If this information is tempered by the recognition of individual differences, the teacher has some reference to what is typical for an age group.

The most valuable and meaningful interpretation of test results is in terms of improvement of the individual or the group. Therefore, if standardized tests are to be given, they should be utilized more than once. It is much more important to know that a child's fitness level improved from October to May and remained the same or improved by the following October than to know that in May he was at the fifty-fifth percentile.

It is better to know that in the fourth week of the unit John could jump four inches farther than he could the first week, than to know he could jump 68 inches at the end of the unit.

USE OF THE RESULTS
OF TESTS

The results of tests may be used to motivate; to give guidance to a child, to diagnose weaknesses and strengths of the individual and the program, and to make reports to parents.

Motivation

Children are motivated to varying degrees and in various ways by testing. Almost all children want to do their best, and when their best is measured in an objective manner they will work hard to achieve. How frequently they are tested and how the test results are used will determine the values of testing in terms of positive motivation. If where one stands in relation to the group is always stressed and a youngster is always at the bottom, the tests may prove to be more frustrating than motivating. If the emphasis is on self-improvement and the goals are in small enough steps so that improvement is possible, then testing is a positive motivating factor.

Informal testing in the primary and intermediate grades is an important part of the learning and teaching process. The evaluation that follows and/or accompanies the observation of performance should be structured so that children will assess their own performance and then try to improve it in the subsequent time allowed for practice.

Many self-testing activity situations should be set up where there is a sliding scale of evaluation of performance. Following is an example of a self-directed activity where a child works at his own rate and progresses to the next stage of achievement after he has mastered the first stage.

THE PROBLEM (AS STATED TO THE CHILD): Using an overhand pattern, throw the ball against the wall, and catch it as it bounces back. When you can do this fifteen times without dropping the ball, move back to the next line. Each time you can do this successfully at one line, you may move back to the next line.

GENERAL SET-UP: Lines would be drawn at varying distances from the wall to designate different stations. Each student would be free to go to the space which fits his stage of throwing proficiency and to move to the next space consistent with his progress.

Guidance

A down-to-earth approach should be used when explaining expectations of improvement and success in skill performance. Children should be told and helped to understand that some children will always do better than others in some skill tests. When long jumping, they should know that people with longer legs usually will be able to jump farther than those with short legs. Those who are taller and stronger probably will be able to throw a ball farther if they throw it correctly. In some instances, children who have had instruction and experiences outside of school will score higher than those who are learning skills for the first time.

In items where equal levels of performance may be gained, they should be informed how to improve scores. For example, if strength is a key ingredient to success in a skill, they should learn how strength is gained. They should learn that practice is the indispensable element for improvement of skills. Many times children want to know if they will be credited for their effort even if their scores are not high. They should learn that true effort is revealed by the comparison of the results of several administrations of the test. The important thing to the child should not be how well he performs in comparison to another, but how much he improves.

Reporting progress to parents

Parents deserve to know how their children are doing. Measures of status and achievement in three basic areas should form the basis of the report in the primary grades. The first is whether the child's status in learning and refining basic motor skill patterns is characteristic of his age group and whether or not his skills and use of them is improving steadily. Secondly, the report should include some indication of general fitness level. Thirdly, an indication should be made of his social behavior as it affects his relationship with others in the physical education setting. The report should be cumulative so that progress or decline will be evident from one reporting period to the next.

The procedure of reporting progress to parents varies considerably. Now in many schools all reporting occurs in conferences between parent and teacher. Often a written descriptive report of general progress in all areas is made. Seldom is the single letter grade used for assessment in the elementary grades. Physical education is often recorded as satisfactory or unsatisfactory in play skills, or a check list of excellent, fair, poor is utilized. One report form usually serves all subject areas in a school system.

Descriptive comments should accompany reports that utilize a check list or S or U in order to explain the check or to define strengths or weaknesses. A child may be satisfactory in one area and unsatisfactory in another. A child's progress in a subject with as much diversity of content as physical education can hardly be assessed in such a dichotomous way as S or U. Report forms for the intermediate and upper grades should in-

Table 6-1. Progress Report in Physical Education for Primary Grades

MIDTOWN ELEMENTARY SCHOOL
PROGRESS REPORT IN PHYSICAL EDUCATION

Name_____ Grade_____

Period 1 Date_____ Period 2 Date_____

Areas	Report Period 1	Comments	Report Period 2	Comments
Motor Skill Typical of Age Group				
Fitness Level				
Social Behavior				

Key

1- Excellent.

2- Better than average for age level.

3- Typical of age level.

4- Slightly below that expected for age level.

5- Atypical of age level. *Must* improve.

Teacher's Signature_____

Parent's Signature_____

Comments:

clude the same basic information as those for primary grades, but progress in specific types of activity should also be indicated. See Tables 6-1 and 6-2 for suggested forms.

Ideally, the physical education program should be discussed at a parents' meeting early in the year. The evaluation plan should be described and explained so that parents will understand the report.

Table 6-2. Progress Report in Physical Education for Grades Four Through Eight.

MIDTOWN ELEMENTARY SCHOOL
PROGRESS REPORT IN PHYSICAL EDUCATION

Name_____ Grade_____

Period 1 Date_____ Period 2 Date_____

Achievement in Activities	Report Period 1	Comments	Report Period 2	Comments
1._____				
2._____				
3._____				
4._____				
5._____				
6._____				
7._____				
8._____				
9._____				
10				
Fitness Level				
Social Behaviors				

Key

1- Excellent for age level.

2- Better than average for age level.

3- Typical of age level.

4- Slightly below that expected for age level.

5- Atypical of age level. *Must* improve.

Teacher's Signature_____

Parent's Signature_____

Comments:

Diagnosing strengths and weaknesses

Studying the results of tests can serve as a diagnostic tool for assessing the needs of individuals and of the group. There are standardized tests of fundamental skills which include test items of the basic skills of running, throwing, catching, jumping, kicking, as well as of general coordination.

Usually norms have been established on a large group of children and reported in percentile scores or T-scores.

These tests, or a teacher-constructed battery of selected items, can be administered at the start of the year. The teacher may study the group results in comparison to other similar groups and therefore assess program emphasis needs. He may study individual scores within the group and identify low achievers and high achievers. This may serve as one basis for grouping for class work. Results of fitness tests may be utilized in the same way. Some of the same test items are found in both fitness and achievement test batteries. A follow-up test may be given at the end of the year to assess progress. Perhaps only the items that indicated great weaknesses may need to be tested the second time. Unless specific practice and instruction is done with the skills in question, a great deal of progress cannot be expected.

An individual teacher can construct his own norms if he collects scores for two or three years. He may revise them periodically thereafter. In this way he can objectively assess comparisons of children, his program, and his teaching from year to year.

EVALUATION OF THE CHILD

Physical measurements

As the unique contribution of physical education is in helping the child through the medium of motor activity, most measurement is involved with assessing his motor performance and the physical factors which affect his level of performance. The status of the physical qualities of health, posture, nutrition, and the specific elements of physical fitness is directly related to how efficiently and effectively a child can function in motor skills. Periodic testing in these areas must be done before expectations or standards of performance can be set or comparisons of achievement are made.

Health
An evaluation of the child's health status must be made periodically by a physician. The results and implications should be made known to the teacher of physical education so that he is aware of the child's limitations and needs of exercise. This information is usually disseminated to the teacher by the school nurse. Schools vary in their requirements of medical examinations before entrance to school and at specified grade levels.

The teacher should develop a daily practice of observing children for minor deviations in appearance, habits, and energy level. Suspicious signs of inflamed eyes, flushed face, grey color, sneezing, coughing, listlessness, rashes, itching, fatigue, restlessness, complaints of headaches, sensitive reactions to criticism all bear investigation and referral to the school nurse or the parent.

Posture

Poor posture and poor physical and mental health are interrelated. Observation of posture habits and periodic posture exams are important to forestalling undesirable posture habits which become increasingly difficult to overcome if neglected. A simple posture test is suggested in Chapter VIII, p. 183.

Height and weight

Usually the classroom teacher or the physical education teacher must weigh and measure children two or three times a year. These records not only give an indication of a normal or abnormal growth pattern, but also can serve as a rough basis for classification or grouping in the physical education class.

Height, weight, and age have a relationship to performance in physical education. As a child grows older he gains in height and weight. These gains are generally accompanied by growth in strength, power, and coordination. If one assumes that gains in height and weight are related to physiological maturity, then the child who is taller and heavier can be expected to be more mature and therefore have added advantages in the accompanying elements of strength, power, and coordination. Expectations of performance level for the short, light child then would be different than for the heavy, tall child. Thus, these measures may be a criteria for grouping for activities.

Physical fitness

The components of physical fitness and tests to measure status in physical fitness are discussed at great length in Chapter VIII. Assessment of fitness is important at the beginning of any school year so that the teacher knows in what areas his class as a whole is weak, and he can plan his program in order to best correct weaknesses. He needs to identify individuals with low fitness scores in order to help a child understand his weaknesses and to plan for correction with the child. Parents should be notified of their child's fitness status early in the year so they can help him at home.

The greatest value of fitness testing comes in a retest in the middle of the year and/or at the end of the year so that changes in status can be measured. Once again the results should be useful in planning programs, helping the child understand his status, motivating the child, and reporting to parents and administrators.

Skill performance

Since the majority of the time spent in physical education involves learning and improving skills, it is only logical that improvement in skill performance would be the best measure of the results of instruction in physical and motor skills. Just as the teacher constructs or uses standardized written achievement tests to measure attainment or improvement in academic subjects, so should he use performance tests as objective evidence of achievement in skill learning.

As the emphasis in the primary grades is on work with basic skill patterns to increase adaptability, variability, flexibility, and variety in the use of them, few objective skill tests are used in the evaluation of skill improvement. Most evaluation is done through observation; however, the teacher should make a systematic observation of each basic skill pattern and record a child's progress in his adaptability, variability, flexibility, and variety in their use. Too often the teacher is unaware of progress and status of the individual since he does not critically analyze the child's solution to movement problems.

In the intermediate and upper grades skill tests should be given, and the results recorded. Some standardized tests constructed for the basic sport skills may be used, or the teacher may construct his own. Stunts usually can be evaluated on the basis of whether one cannot or can do them; gymnastics and dance skills can only be judged subjectively. In addition to giving individual skill performance tests, the teacher should also plan to assess the use of the skills in game play, in a dance, or in a gymnastic routine. Learning the basic concepts of how to use skills properly is as important as learning how to do them.

Motor ability and motor achievement

Tests which measure a child's achievement in the basic or fundamental movement skills are often referred to as motor ability tests. Measures of throwing, jumping, striking, catching, and running both for speed and in a style which entails a shift of weight and changes of direction, are made for the purpose of classification, or grouping, and guidance of children. These tests measure the child's achievement in the skills which form the basis of children's play activities. There are a number of these tests, but few have been developed for the elementary school grades. The Johnson Fundamental Skills Test is described here in detail. A few others are described briefly, together with the sources which contain detailed directions and norms for the tests.

CARPENTER GENERAL MOTOR CAPACITY TESTS: The purpose of these tests is to measure general motor capacity in the first three grades. The results can be used for a general prediction of achievement, grouping, and guidance. Various jumping skills and stunts are tested. Source: Aileen Carpenter, "Measuring General Motor Capacity and General Motor Achievement in the First Three Grades," *Research Quarterly* (December, 1942), p. 444.

CARPENTER GENERAL MOTOR ACHIEVEMENT TEST. The purpose of this test is to measure general motor achievement in the first three grades. The directions contain a method of arriving at an achievement quota for each child. Test items include a broad jump, shot put, and weight-lifting. Source: Aileen Carpenter, "Measuring General Motor Capacity and General Motor Achievement in the First Three Grades," *Research Quarterly* (December, 1942), p. 444.

HANSON MOTOR PERFORMANCE TESTS OF ELEMENTARY GRADE CHILDREN: Hanson established the reliability and constructed percentile norms by sex and grade level for approximately four hundred children in grades one through six in the state of Minnesota for sixteen fitness and skill tests. Test items include a throw for distance, wall pass, soccer punt for distance, soccer wall volley, volleyball serve, pitching accuracy, potato race, pull-ups, jump-reach, rope skip, sit-ups, Hanson shoulder test, Bass balance test, 50 yard dash, broad jump, and 600 yard walk-run. These items test a wide variety of skills taught in the elementary grades and could be used as a measure of achievement in specific sports or as a general measure of achievement for grouping, guidance, and diagnostic purposes. Source: Margie Hanson, *Motor Performance Testing of Elementary School Age Children,* unpublished Ph.D. dissertation (University of Washington, 1965).

LATCHAW MOTOR ACHIEVEMENT TEST: Latchaw constructed seven tests to measure general motor achievement for boys and girls in grades four, five, and six. She determined the reliability for each and constructed achievement scales using T-scores. The tests are basketball wall pass, volleyball wall volley, vertical jump, standing broad jump, shuttle run, soccer wall volley, and softball repeated throws. The results of the tests can be used to measure status, and/or progress in the specific sport skills. Source: Marjorie Latchaw, "Measuring Selected Motor Skills in Fourth, Fifth and Sixth Grades," *Research Quarterly,* 25 (December, 1954), p. 439. Also, Marjorie Latchaw and Camile Brown, *The Evaluation Process in Health, Education, Physical Education, and Recreation* (Englewood Cliffs, N.J., Prentice-Hall, 1962), p. 83.

PEACOCK ACHIEVEMENT SCALES IN PHYSICAL EDUCATION ACTIVITIES FOR BOYS AND GIRLS: The purpose of this test is to measure the proficiency of children in performing the gross motor activities of softball throw for distance, soccer punt for distance, 40 yard run, standing broad jump, side-stepping, grip strength. Achievement scales using T scales for boys and girls ages seven through fifteen are presented. The results of these tests can be used to determine status and progress in the specific skills to aid in grouping students and diagnosing strengths and weaknesses. Source: Harold Barrow and Rosemary McGee, *Measurement in Physical Education* (Philadelphia, Lea and Febiger, 1964), p. 173.

JOHNSON FUNDAMENTAL SKILLS TEST: Johnson developed tests of fundamental skills for boys and girls in grades one through six. He established the validity and reliability for each test. He administered the tests to 2,545 boys and 2,195 girls in seven sites of southern Minnesota. From these scores he constructed the percentile norms which appear in Figures 6-3 through 6-8. The directions for the tests of kicking, pass and catch, jump and reach, and zigzag run follow. A batting test was included in the original battery, but since it requires a commercial device to deliver the balls it will not be described here.

Directions for
administering tests [1]

ZIGZAG TESTS

EQUIPMENT: Four folding chairs and one stop watch.

MARKINGS: Four folding chairs are placed 6 feet apart on a gymnasium floor, between a starting line and an X placed on the wall of the gymnasium. The first chair is placed 6 feet from the starting line, and the last chair is placed 6 feet from the wall. The X, 6 inches in size, is 4 feet from the floor and placed on the wall. The length of the starting line is 1 foot. There should be an area 20 feet long behind the starting line that is free from obstruction.

DIRECTIONS FOR PERFORMANCE: The subject is instructed to stand behind the middle of the starting line and, on the command "Go," to run either to the right or to the left of the first chair, to zigzag around the three remaining chairs, to touch the X, to return in the same manner, and to touch the starting line with his foot.

SCORING: Time to the nearest tenth of a second required for running the course. Three trials are given, with the shortest time being the score. For any of the following fouls the subject is required to run the course again: having any part of the forward foot over the starting line when the command is given; not zigzagging around the chairs in the prescribed manner; and not touching the X on the wall before returning toward the starting line.

---

[1] With permission of Robert D. Johnson and the American Association for Health, Physical Education and Recreation, publishers of the *Research Quarterly*.

Table 6-3. Percentile Norms for Johnson Fundamental Skill Test (Grade 1)

Percentile	Kick (pts.)		Pass-and-Catch (pts.)		Jump-and-Reach (in.)		Zigzag Run (sec.)	
	B	G	B	G	B	G	B	G
100	34	30	34	29	11-5	10-5	8.0	8.8
95	28	27	26	23	9-0	8-5	9.2	9.4
90	27	26	24	21			9.4	9.9
85	26	25	23	20	8-5	8-0	9.8	10.0
80			22	19			9.9	10.4
75	25	24	21	18	8-0	7-5	10.0	10.8
70			20	17	7-5	7-0	10.2	10.9
65	24	23	19			6-5	10.4	11.0
60		22	18	16	7-0		10.6	11.4
55	23			15		6-0	10.8	11.5
50			17		6-5		10.9	11.6
45	22	21		14		5-5		11.8
40			16	13	6-0		11.0	
35	21		15	12		5-0	11.2	
30	20	20	14	11	5-5		11.4	12.0
25		19	13	10		4-5	11.6	12.2
20	19	18	12		5-0	4-0	11.8	12.4
15	18	16	11	9	4-5		12.0	12.6
10	17	14	10	8	4-0	3-5	12.2	12.8
5	14	10	9	5	3-5	3-0	12.8	13.4
0	12	8	6	3	3-0	2-5	13.0	13.6

JUMP-AND-REACH

EQUIPMENT: Chalk dust, and one piece of construction paper, 6 inches wide and 3 feet high, ruled off in half inches.

MARKINGS: Horizontal lines are drawn on the construction paper one-half inch apart. The paper is fastened to the wall at such a height that the 0 line on the chart is just below the point that represents the standing reach of the shortest performer.

DIRECTIONS FOR PERFORMANCE: The subject stands with one side of his body parallel with the wall chart. He dips his forefinger in chalk, reaches as high as possible, and makes a chalk mark on the chart. He then jumps upward as far as possible and makes a mark on the wall at the peak of his jump.

SCORING: The score is the inches (to the nearest half inch) between the two chalk marks. The subject is given five jumps, with the highest jump recorded as his score. The subject is not allowed to make any preliminary steps forward before the jump.

Table 6-4. Percentile Norms for Johnson Fundamental Skill Test (Grade 2)

Percentile	Kick (pts.)		Pass-and-Catch (pts.)		Jump-and-Reach (in.)		Zigzag Run (sec.)	
	B	G	B	G	B	G	B	G
100	36	35	39	35	12-5	11-0	7.6	7.8
95	33	33	38	31	10.0	9-5	8.0	8.2
90	31	31	34	28	9-5	9-0	8.4	8.6
85	30	30	32	27			8.8	8.8
80	28	29	31	26	9-0	8-5	8.9	9.0
75		28	30	25	8-5		9.0	9.4
70	27	27	29	24		8-0	9.2	9.5
65		26	28	23			9.4	9.6
60	26		27	22	8-0	7-5	9.5	9.8
55		25	26	21			9.6	
50	25	24	25		7-5		9.8	9.9
45			24	20		7-0		
40	24	23		19			9.9	10.0
35	23	22	23	18	7-0	6-0		10.2
30	21	20	22	17	6-5		10.0	10.4
25	20		21	16	6-0		10.1	10.8
20	19	19	20	15		5-5	10.2	
15	18	18	19	14	5-5	5-0	10.6	11.0
10	17	16	17	12	5-0	4-5	10.9	11.2
5	14	14	13	10	4-5	4-0	11.2	11.8
0	10	12	8	7	4-0	3-5	11.4	12.0

KICKING TEST

EQUIPMENT: One soccer ball.

MARKINGS: On a flat wall space, a target area 5 feet high and 10 feet wide is marked with one-half inch tape. This area is divided into five equal rectangles placed perpendicular to the floor. The number 5 is taped in the center rectangle of the target, number 3 is taped in the rectangles adjacent to the center rectangle, number 1 is taped on the two remaining rectangles. On the floor three lines 3 feet long are marked: one is 10 feet from the wall; one, 20 feet; and one, 30 feet from the wall.

DIRECTIONS FOR PERFORMANCE: The subject places the soccer ball behind the 10-foot line marked on the floor. From that position he attempts to kick the ball in such a manner that it may hit the wall target. The subject kicks three times from each of the lines marked on the floor. Two practice kicks are made at each line before the three kicks for the record are made.

SCORING: The subject receives the number of points indicated on the target area into which the ball is kicked. If the ball is kicked on a line

Table 6-5. Percentile Norms for Johnson Fundamental Skill Test (Grade 3)

Percentile	Kick (pts.)		Pass-and-Catch (pts.)		Jump-and-Reach (in.)		Zigzag Run (sec.)	
	B	G	B	G	B	G	B	G
100	40	36	41	38	13-0	12-0	7.4	7.4
95	37	34	40	34	11-5	10-0	7.8	8.0
90	36	32	39	33	11-0	9-5	8.0	8.2
85	34	31	38	32	10-0	9-0	8.2	8.4
80	33	30	37	30			8.4	8.8
75			36	29	9-5	8-5	8.6	8.9
70	32	29	35	28			8.7	9.1
65	31	28	34		9-0	8-0	8.8	9.2
60	30	27	33	27			9.0	9.3
55		26		26	8-5			9.4
50	29	25	32	25		7-5		9.5
45		24	31				9.2	9.6
40	28		30	24	8-0	7-0	9.3	9.8
35	27	23		23			9.4	
30		22	29	22			9.6	
25	26	21		21	7-5	6-5	9.8	10.0
20	25	20	28	20	7-0	6-0	10.0	10.4
15	23	19	27	19	6-5		10.2	10.6
10	22	18	25	18	6-0	5-5	10.4	10.8
5	20	17	21	10	5-0	5-0	10.6	11.0
0	16	16	17	13	4-5	4-5	10.8	11.2

between two areas, the score is that for the area with the large number. A ball kicked from in front of the restraining floor line counts zero, and another trial is given.

THROW-AND-CATCH TEST

EQUIPMENT: One 8½-inch playground ball (grades 1, 2, and 3) and a regulation-sized volleyball (grades 4, 5, and 6).

MARKINGS: A 3-foot square is placed on a flat wall with one-half inch tape. Its bottom line is 4 feet from the floor. An inner square, 10 inches in from all four sides, is placed on the wall target. Starting 3 feet from the wall, and in line with the wall target, there are placed five 2 foot squares, each 1 foot behind the other.

DIRECTIONS FOR PERFORMANCE: With both feet inside the first square the subject stands facing the wall target and throws the ball at the wall target; keeping both feet inside the square he attempts to catch the ball in the air when it rebounds from the wall. The throw should be made with an underhand motion. After two practice trials the sub-

Table 6-6. Percentile Norms for Johnson Fundamental Skill Test (Grade 4)

Percentile	Kick (pts.)		Pass-and-Catch (pts.)		Jump-and-Reach (in.)		Zigzag Run (sec.)	
	B	G	B	G	B	G	B	G
100	42	39	50	43	15-0	14-0	7.0	7.2
95	38	37	47	40	13-0	11-0	7.6	7.8
90	37	35	45	39	12-0	10-5	7.8	8.0
85	36	34	43	38	11-5	10-0	8.0	8.4
80	35	33	42	37	11-0		8.2	8.6
75		32	41	36	10-5	9-5	8.4	8.8
70	34	31	40	35	10-0		8.5	9.0
65				34		9-0	8.6	9.1
60	33	30	39				8.7	9.2
55			38	33	9-5	8-5	8.8	9.4
50	32	29		32			9.0	9.5
45	31		37		9-0	8-0	9.1	9.6
40		36	31				9.2	9.7
35	30	28	35	30		7-5	9.3	9.8
30	29	27	34	29	8-5	7-0	9.4	10.0
25		26	33	28	8-0		9.6	10.2
20	28	25	32	27		6-5	9.8	10.4
15	27	24	31	26	7-5	6-0	10.0	10.6
10	25	22	30	24	7-0	5-5	10.2	10.8
5	23	20	27	21	6-5	5-0	10.6	11.2
0	19	16	23	16	6-0	4-5	10.8	11.4

ject is given three trials for record when he is in each of the five squares.

SCORING: Two points for successfully throwing a ball in or on the inner wall target square; two points for successfully catching the rebounding ball in the air while standing in the floor square; one point for successfully throwing a ball in or on the outer wall target square; one point for successfully catching the rebounding ball in the air, on or outside the floor square. The subject's score is the total points scored from all five squares. If the subject steps out of the square while throwing, the throw is nullified and another trial is given.

Specific sports skill tests

Few tests to measure achievement in the specific sports skills have been designed for the elementary grades. Recently, the Research Council of the American Association for Health, Physical Education, and Recreation conducted a project of developing and establishing skill tests and norms for all sports taught in schools to help teachers effectively evaluate the skill performance of boys and girls ten to eighteen years of age. A manual containing the directions for the skill tests, directions for admin-

Table 6-7. Percentile Norms for Johnson Fundamental Skill Test (Grade 5)

Percentile	Kick (pts.)		Pass-and-Catch (pts.)		Jump-and-Reach (in.)		Zigzag Run (sec.)	
	B	G	B	G	B	G	B	G
100	43	40	57	53	16-0	15-0	6.6	6.8
95	40	38	54	50	14-0	13-0	7.0	7.2
90	39	36	52	45	13-0	12-0	7.2	7.4
85	38	35	50	44	12-5		7.3	7.8
80	37	34	48	43	12-0	11-5	7.4	
75	36	33	47	42		11-0	7.5	
70	35		46	41	11-5	10-5	7.6	8.0
65		32	45	40	11-0		7.8	8.1
60	34	31	44		10-5	10-0		8.2
55				39				8.3
50	33		43	38	10-0	9-5	8.0	8.4
45		30	42	37			8.1	8.5
40	32		41		9-5	9-0	8.2	8.6
35		29	40	36			8.3	8.8
30	31	28	39	35	9-0	8-5	9.4	8.9
25		27	38	34		8-0	8.5	9.0
20	30	26	37	33	8-5	7-5	8.6	9.2
15	29	25	36	32	8-0	7-0	8.8	9.4
10	28	23	34	31	7-5	6-5	9.0	9.8
5	26	20	33	29	7-0	6-0	9.2	10.0
0	23	14	29	24	6-5	5-5	9.4	10.2

istration of the tests, norms for ages ten to eighteen, suggestions for interpreting results, and suggestions for the use of the results, is available for each sport from the A.A.H.P.E.R., 1201 16th St., N.W., Washington, D.C. for seventy-five cents. Each school library should contain a copy of the skill tests manual for the sports which are conducted in its physical education program. If these manuals are not available nor can the teacher find a skill test to suit the needs or ages of his class, he may modify an existing test or design his own test.

Selecting skill tests

There are a few criteria which should be observed when selecting, modifying, or constructing a sport skill test.
1. The test should measure as accurately as possible what it is supposed to be measuring, that is, the ability to perform a skill basic to the sport.
2. The test should yield dependable and consistent scores.
3. Only skills basic and important to the sport should be tested.

Table 6-8. Percentile Norms for Johnson Fundamental Skill Test (Grade 6)

Percentile	Kick (pts.)		Pass-and-Catch (pts.)		Jump-and-Reach (in.)		Zigzag Run (sec.)	
	B	G	B	G	B	G	B	G
100	44	42	59	55	17.5	16-0	6.0	6.6
95	41	40	56	51	16-0	14-0	6.8	7.0
90	40	38	54	49	15-0	13-0	7.0	7.2
85	39	36	53	47	14-0	12-0	7.2	7.4
80	37	35	52	46	13-5		7.6	7.5
75		34	51	45	13-0	11-5	7.4	7.6
70	36		50	44	12-5		7.5	7.7
65	35	33	49	43	12-0	11-0	7.6	7.8
60			48				7.8	7.9
55		32	47	42	11-5	10-5		8.0
50	34		46	41		10-0	7.9	8.1
45		31		40	11-0			8.2
40	33		45				8.0	8.3
35	32	30	44	39	10-5		8.1	8.4
30			43	38		9-5	8.2	8.6
25	31	29	42	37	10-0		8.4	8.8
20	30	28	41	36		9-0	8.5	9.0
15	29	27	40	35	9-5	8-5	8.6	9.2
10	28	25	39	33	9-5	8-0	8.8	9.6
5	26	20	37	31	8-5	7-0	9.2	10.0
0	23	15	34	28	8-0	6-5	9.0	10.5

4. The test should simulate how the skill is used in the sport.
5. The test should be of suitable difficulty for the group taking it. If distances are too far and no one experiences success, it will not be motivating or educationally sound.
6. It should be possible to score the test objectively.
7. The administration of the test should be simple; require few complicated directions, require no elaborate or expensive equipment, require a minimum amount of space and time, require as few people as possible to administer it.
8. Only one person should be involved in a test at one time. For example, when testing batting ability, if one relies on a person to pitch the ball so it may be hit, reliability of the test will be reduced, as the speed, height, and accuracy of the throw may vary with each pitch.
9. Scores on the test should be variable enough so that skill level can be differentiated.

In an attempt to obtain objective achievement scores, many teachers spend proportionately more time on testing than teaching. The length of a unit and the amount of time spent on learning the skill are factors to consider in selecting tests. The inclusion of a test of a skill which was introduced and practiced only once would be unfair to children and at the same time would be of little assistance in assessing pupil progress or the teaching process. Plans for evaluating both the student and the unit should be made in the initial planning stages. In that way, testing will be done with a purpose and will be a vital part of the teaching-learning process. Skill tests, as a rule, are good practice drills also. Specific suggestions for skills that should be tested are included in each activity chapter.

Administration of tests

Good organization and preplanning for the administration of performance tests are essential if time is not to be wasted. A list of general suggestions for the preparation and actual administration of most all skill and fitness tests follows.

I. Before the testing session:
   1. Select the test on the basis of its value to the student and the intended use of the results.
   2. Learn the directions for the tests.
   3. Plan how the tests can be given in the space available. Sketch out a plan so that best use of space is made, and a flow of traffic from testing station to testing station can be maintained without interference. If some tests in a battery are timed and enough stations are available, half the class can be tested at once with the other half scoring. Try to select tests that may take place within the same time limit.
   4. Check on equipment to see that everything is available and in working order. Have all equipment in place before testing is ready to start.
   5. Select and train those who will help administer tests. These might be older students or squad leaders from the class. It is preferable to have students who do not have to take the tests themselves and therefore can stay at each testing station for the entire testing session.
   6. Plan organization of class for the tests by squads, by individuals moving at their own rate from station to station, or whatever way best suits the situation. Designate one person per group as the official in charge of scoring.
   7. Prepare score cards. If groups move together, one score card per group will suffice. If individuals move independently, each will need a score card and a pencil.
II. Administering the test:
   1. Allow for a warm-up period before the tests. This may be a light exercise series or practice of the tests.
   2. Organize groups.

3. Explain the tests, the test procedure, the rotation system, the purpose of the test, and the use of the results. Try to motivate the students to do their best.
4. Demonstrate each test just as it is to be done and to be scored.
5. Administer the tests. Keep things moving, spot-check each test to see that scoring is being done correctly. When a time test is given, have a central timer who maintains a regular rhythm of "ready, go." Blow a whistle at the end of the test, and announce that the next person should be ready. Allow only a few seconds between trials, and the students will quickly adjust to being ready. When several trials of a test are given for each person, be sure that there is a rest period between trials to offset fatigue. Where visual motivation from trial to trial is important, such as in the long jump or throw for distance, the trials should be taken consecutively.

III. After the testing:
1. Collect score cards.
2. Tally scores onto a master score sheet. Convert scores into a form that will be used to interpret scores. If norms are available, a simple comparison of raw score and standard score may be made. If no norms are available, standard scores may be computed for the particular test.
3. Record scores in form they will be studied and interpreted for the students. Individual and group profile charts provide a visual diagnostic tool, if several test items have been given or the test has been given before. Comparisons of gain or loss may be made easily in this manner.
4. Report and interpret results to students as soon after the test as possible. Interpret scores in terms of status, progress, strengths, and weaknesses. Suggest possible ways to improve skills. If possible, results should be discussed with individuals. If time does not permit this with all students, the teacher should make an effort to talk with those who have extremely low scores.
5. The test results should be used in a broader evaluation of the student, program, and teacher. If the testing was a pretest, time should be allowed for practice of the test, and individual help may be given to those with low scores before the final test is given.

Subjective rating of skills

When a skill is evaluated as to its use in a game situation or a skill does not lend itself to an objective test, observation must serve as the measurement tool. The skills of dancing, swimming, and gymnastics fall into this category. Attitudes and social behavior must be measured by observation techniques also.

Naturally, observations are very subjective and are based on opinion and personal judgments. Both teachers and students can and should learn how to make observations as objective as possible so that they will be valuable evaluation tools.

Students must have criteria on which to base their observations. The teacher should make suggestions that the students watch for certain things. Children in the primary grades need guidance to look for a few particulars and then a follow-up of their observations with questions and summaries that will reinforce them. In this way their powers of observation are developed.

Table 6-9. Rating Scale for the Overhead Volley

| PHASE OF SKILL | SQUAD_____ | | | | | | | |
| | Student | | | | | | | |
	1	2	3	4	5	6	7	8
1. Judges flight of ball accurately, is in line with ball.								
2. Flexes knees, shoulders, wrists in preparation for hit.								
3. Contacts ball with fingers and thumbs.								
4. Extends hips, knees, ankles which results in forward, upward motion of body.								
TOTAL POINTS								

Directions: Observe each student's performance and place number of category which best describes the performance of the student in each phase of the skill.

Key

0- Failed to execute skill at all.

1- Poorly executed, inadequate performance, results of hit poor.

2- Acceptably executed, adequate results of hit, inconsistent pattern.

3- Well executed, good results of hit, confident movements, consistent pattern.

4- Outstandingly well executed, effective results of hit, smooth consistent pattern, little room for improvement.

When rating students the teacher needs a rating scale or check list in order to guide his observation. A few suggestions for making and using a rating scale follow. A sample rating scale is shown in Table 6-9.

1. Plan for the rating in the original unit plan. Decide upon the purpose of the rating. This may determine the form of the scale, the time necessary to rate, and the discrimination power of the scale. If teams are to be made from the ratings, the discrimination will not have to be as fine as if grades are to be based on the rating.

2. The skill or trait to be rated must be decided upon. Then the quali-

ties or factors of the skill or trait should be broken down into just what will be rated. Frequently, teachers try to rate too much. Break the skill down into the most important elements.

3. Decide on the number and type of categories to be used, i.e., descriptive words, letter scale, point scale or whatever. Each category should be defined so that the rater looks for the same trait with the same standards in mind. This is particularly important if more than one person is rating. For instance, the term "average" may be interpreted diversely if it is not defined clearly.

4. Rate each student under the same conditions. It is best to make observations during activity, but all must have the same opportunity to

Table 6-10. Check List for Overhead Volley

PHASE OF SKILL	SQUAD_____						
	Student						
	1	2	3	4	5	6	7
1. Judges flight of ball accurately, is in line with ball.							
2. Flexes knees, shoulders, wrists, in preparation for hit.							
3. Contacts ball with fingers and thumbs.							
4. Extends hips, knees, ankles which results in forward, upward motion of body.							

Directions: Observe performance and check those phases of the overhand volley which the student performs correctly.

perform under similar conditions. For instance, if passing is to be rated in soccer, each child must have an opportunity to play a position where he will have a comparable chance to pass. The forward line affords more opportunity to pass than would the goalkeeper's position, so all positions must be rotated periodically.

5. Equalize competition when ratings depend upon two people or a team in a competitive situation. In couple stunts and balances, equal abilities and sizes must be assured. In a couple dance, one partner's performance may influence the appearance of the other's performance.

6. Rate everyone on the same quality at one time, rather than rating one person on all qualities and then rating the next person on all qualities.

7. Don't make rating scales too long or too complicated or the process will be too time consuming.

Check lists (Table 6-10) help to objectify observations by providing the observer with a list of items to be aware of as the observation is made. They do not provide for an estimate of quality, but usually are checked as "yes" or "no" in regard to presence. An incidence chart (Table 6-11),

Table 6-11. Volleyball Incidence Chart

Date_____ Team Name_____

Fouls		Skills	Successful	Unsuccessful
Pushing		Serve		
Holding		Receive serve and set		
Catching		Key set		
Net		Spike		
Line		Block		
Foot Fault		Recover from net		
		Dig		
TOTALS				

Place tally (1) mark beside type of foul which is called against team.
Place tally in proper column each time a skill is executed.

on which the number of times an incident occurred or a skill was used is recorded, serves much the same purpose as the check list in organizing observation. Check lists and incidence charts are frequently used in studying social behavior and attitudes.

Knowledge testing

Since the acquisition of specific knowledges and understandings is one of the objectives of every unit of instruction in physical education, measurement of the child must also be made in this area. Starting in the third or fourth grade, teachers should construct tests to measure learning of what was stressed as a specific concept, rule, procedure, or principle. Classroom teachers may integrate measures of spelling and vocabulary with words and terms learned in the classroom and in the gymnasium.

As with skill tests, the time taken for written tests must be in balance with the time spent on instruction. Provision for the test should be made when the unit is planned so that it is an integral part of the teaching-learning process. Rules, scoring procedures, terms, basic principles, strategies, and understanding lend themselves to written tests.

Evaluation of social behavior

Each activity affords the opportunity for the development of certain social and emotional traits. Provisions for providing learning experiences in the area of social behavior should be made when the unit is planned. Development of some particular traits is a major objective of certain units, whereas development of other traits is a constant objective, and equally possible through the majority of activities. In the case of the former, a special evaluation may be made of the trait as a youngster manifests it throughout play or work in the unit. Periodically, the teacher may wish to make a check list of traits so that he will be aware of the social behavior of each child. If he has a difficult time determining whether or not a certain child behaves in a way which is consistently good, bad, or indifferent, he should make a systematic study of the child's behavior in order to assess the overall progress. Various forms for measuring behavior may be utilized, and they usually take the form of a rating scale or check list. Children may fill out some forms in a self-evaluation.

Suggested here are some of the social behavior items that may be evaluated regarding expected behavior (as indicated by child growth and development factors) as a child participates in physical education activities.

1. Does he share equipment readily?
2. Does he take turns in order?
3. Does he make contributions of ideas in group problem-solving?
4. Does he accept suggestions and criticism from his peers?
5. Are his ideas his own, or does he tend to voice ideas that are similar to those of someone else?
6. Does he accept suggestions and criticism from adults?
7. Does he accept decisions of others when they are officials or leaders?
8. Does he exaggerate, cheat, or alibi in order to be first or to win?
9. Does he abide by the rules even if no one is watching him?
10. Does he appear tense or anxious when practicing or playing?
11. Does he appear happy or confident?
12. Does he work to improve skills or learn new ones?
13. Does he carry out assigned responsibilities?
14. Does he show leadership ability?
15. Does he help others?

EVALUATION OF THE
PROGRAM

The program is measured against the specific objectives of physical education in general, those of the particular school, those of the physical education curriculum, and those of the teacher, through a study of the results of measurements of the items listed below. Some of the measurements may involve statistical evidence, some subjective judgments, some are made by the student, teacher, parent, and the administrator. All of these are discussed, results are synthesized, and the program as a whole is evaluated. Future plans for improvement should be made and implemented in order to complete the evaluation process. Suggested below are some of the items which may be considered in the evaluation of the program.

1. Objectives of program clearly defined, and sequential experiences outlined for the year
2. Physical fitness status of the children
3. Achievement in skills by children
4. Knowledge gained by children
5. Social behavior of children
6. Daily class period allotted to physical education
7. Activities suited to maturation level of children and provision made for individual differences
8. Variety of activities offered in the program
9. Adequacy of facilities and equipment
10. Utilization of existing facilities and equipment to best advantage
11. Adequate after-school activity program
12. Adaptive measures for exceptional children
13. Integration of physical education with other subjects in the curriculum

Many state departments of education, state universities and colleges, and professional organizations assist local schools in evaluation of programs. A specialist or team of specialists may facilitate evaluations by means of visitations, provision of evaluative forms, and/or follow-up consultative service to interpret the results of the evaluation. Materials for evaluating the physical education program may be obtained from several sources which are listed in the bibliography.[2]

EVALUATION OF FACILITIES AND EQUIPMENT

Facilities and equipment are evaluated in terms of safety, adequacy, appropriateness, and efficiency. A yearly evaluation in all of these aspects serves as the basis for budget requests for the entire program. When requests for annual budget monies or additional funds are made, a well-organized, precise statement of conditions, needs, and requests is much more impressive and workable than a vague request for a certain sum of money or number of items. The teacher's report furnishes the principal with tangible evidence of need when he requests money from the school board.

[2] See first, third, and sixth items in Suggested References for Further Study at the end of the chapter.

EVALUATION OF THE TEACHER

The teacher is generally evaluated by the supervisor, the principal, the students, and himself. The supervisor and principal usually evaluate the teacher on the basis of observation of one or more lessons. This procedure varies from school system to school system. Formal evaluation of the teacher by the students most often is reserved for older students, and informal evaluation is evidenced by the general atmosphere and attitude of the class itself.

The most important evaluation of the teacher is his own. After leaving the student-teaching situation, few teachers encounter the opportunity to discuss their lessons, planning, and techniques with anyone. This may seem like a relief, temporarily; however, it soon leaves a void in the teacher's growth. Periodically, the teacher must evaluate his practices in working with students, the experiences which he provides for his class, the growth of his class, and his own professional growth. The daily lesson evaluation with the class should provide a measure of planning and efficiency. In discussions, the type of responses and participation of the class will indicate the degree of involvement in the learning process. The students' understanding or lack of it will also be revealed.

Evidence of good teaching practices, accomplishment of objectives, and degree of student progress seen in careful consideration of each lesson must be further studied by a consideration of broader aspects. Listed here are a number of questions which the teacher can ask himself periodically.

1. Can I verbalize what I intend for my students to learn each day?
2. Do I plan units of work?
3. Do I plan each lesson carefully? Is it a contributing part of the whole unit?
4. Do I consider each child and his abilities in my planning and teaching?
5. Am I democratic in my organization and conduct of the class?
6. Do I help individuals learn to identify their own problems and guide them into solving them, or do I just tell them what to do?
7. Are the experiences that I plan challenging?
8. Do I evaluate student progress fairly and consistently?
9. Do I build lessons upon the evaluation of the previous lessons?
10. Do I consider relating and integrating learning experiences of the students from other areas of the curriculum?
11. Do I allow for student expression and evaluation?
12. Do I make the best use of facilities and equipment?
13. Is there a good learning atmosphere in my class?

14. Do I cooperate with other teachers and the administration in respecting time schedules, care of equipment, and proper use of space assigned?
15. Do I enjoy teaching each class?
16. Do I improve my knowledge and skills of teaching physical education through reading current literature, attending meetings, or taking part in in-service training when it is available?
17. Do I ask for help from the supervisor, consultant, principal, or other teachers when I need it?

EVALUATION OF THE LESSON

The daily lesson is the basic unit of the physical education program. The teacher must evaluate each preceding lesson before he plans for the next one. The following questions synthesize information that has been discussed in preceding chapters about teaching methods, learning principles, organization, individual differences, discussion, and demonstration into practical terms as one evaluates and plans a lesson. These are questions that a supervisor or supervising teacher may ask as he reads a lesson plan or observes a lesson.

1. Do the activities meet the objectives of the lesson?
2. Are the activities within the range of ability and interests of the pupils?
3. Does the selection of activities show progress from the last lesson?
4. Does the selection of material show a recognition of need of review and clarification, as revealed in the evaluation of the last lesson?
5. Do the activities provide a balance of big-muscle activity with lighter activity?
6. Does the selection of activities provide for maximum participation of the entire class?
7. Is some provision made for those not actively participating to have an active part and interest in the lesson?
8. Are there plans for a good system of the distribution and collection of equipment? Is there an awareness of the proper type and number of pieces of equipment needed for this lesson?
9. Are there any plans to utilize student leadership?
10. Is there a clear understanding of the points the demonstration should stress?
11. Are the explanations and directions clear, concise, and to the point?
12. Are questions that are to be asked the class formulated well?
13. Are questions from the class anticipated? Are weaknesses and coaching hints anticipated?

14. Are any provisions made for individual differences within this particular class?
15. Does the organization ensure safe play?
16. Are any provisions made for continuous teaching during game play, individual, and small group work periods?
17. Are any provisions made for class evaluation?

SUGGESTED REFERENCES
FOR FURTHER STUDY

American Association for Health, Physical Education and Recreation, *Evaluation Schedules in Physical Education* (Washington, D.C., The Association).

Barrow, Harold, "The A.B.C.'s of Testing," *Journal of Health, Physical Education and Recreation,* Vol. 33 (May, June, 1962).

California State Department of Education, *Criteria for Evaluating the Physical Education Program, Kindergarten, Grades One Through Six* (Sacramento, State Department of Education, 1960).

California State Department of Education, *Evaluating Pupil Progress* (Sacramento, State Department of Education, 1960).

Cassidy, Rosalind, *Counseling in the Physical Education Program* (Bureau of Publications, Teachers College, Columbia University, 1959).

Neilson, N. P., and Glen Warnett, *A Score Card for Use in Evaluating Physical Education Programs in Elementary Schools* (Salt Lake City, Utah, University of Utah Press, 1955).

Scott, M. Gladys, and Esther French, *Measurement and Evaluation in Physical Education* (Dubuque, Iowa, Wm. C. Brown Co., 1959).

Part III
FOUNDATIONS OF MOVEMENT

Chapter VII

UNDERSTANDING THE BODY MECHANISM

Mechanical principles

Actions of the body joints

Muscle action

Fundamentals of exercise

Relaxation

In previous discussions of the purposes, aims, and values of physical education in the elementary school, repeated references were made to movement skills as the medium through which physical education contributes to the optimum development of the child. Therefore, an acquisition of good movement skills is essential to each child. The teacher's responsibility is to help each child understand and learn a wide variety of skills. In discussing the importance of motor performance as an avenue to other learning, M. Gladys Scott states in her book, *Analysis of Human Motion:*

The physical education teacher must have thorough knowledge of, and ability to analyze, that performance. Only in this way can the teacher become the guide toward the most effective learning and provide the greatest benefit to the physical organism, and perhaps even avoid making mistakes that will be injurious to the organism.[1]

In order to analyze performance, the teacher must know and understand how skills are executed. Mechanical principles regulate all movement and dictate how the body moves most efficiently and effectively.

[1] M. Gladys Scott, *Analysis of Human Motion, 2nd ed.* (New York, Appleton-Century-Crofts, 1963), p. 7.

These principles are basic to the effective performance of all skills, play or utilitarian. If the teacher understands how the physical or mechanical laws relate to human movement, he will be able to apply them to all skills and be better able to recognize and correct errors. All skills have common elements, and the ability to perceive these will help the teacher plan skill-learning experiences for children which involve transfer of learning to related skills.

There are other factors which determine how effectively a child can utilize these principles and knowledges. These include physical limitations of body build, strength, endurance, and flexibility. The teacher should know the basic principles of improving and maintaining the physical components that are necessary in varying degrees to perform certain tasks. External and internal factors of the child's environment also affect efficient movement. The mental and emotional factors which are a prerequisite to good skill-learning were discussed in Chapter IV.

Through trial and error and incorporation of concepts gained from observation of others, most children have learned to utilize movement principles in their skills at an early age. For instance, when a child is learning to walk, his biggest problem is maintaining balance. In his initial attempts he immediately sits down at the first indication that he is losing his balance. He walks on the full sole of his foot with his feet widely separated, and he takes small steps to maintain a wide base of support. He also raises his arms to a position where they can be helpful in maintaining balance. He is actually applying the mechanical principles of stability or balance by widening his base of support and keeping his weight low.

As he grows, he continues to learn concepts of principles. However, some children have difficulty in making observations, and few see the relationships between principles and various movement patterns. Fewer make applications when learning new skills unless the teacher directs their attention to them.

The teacher must make an effort to teach children the basic principles of movement and supply meaningful situations where the children can understand and see the application of them in a variety of forms. When introducing new skills, he should relate similarities in patterns and principles to those that children already know. A problem-solving approach lends itself to the discovery and application of the principles by the child himself. Attention can be drawn to the way they are utilized even before children can understand the principles or name them. Observance of the principles should be demanded in all movement experiences.

All of these principles are studied in science units at some time in the elementary grades; however, they are not always related to the body, and some children have difficulty understanding them. A child is surrounded by examples of how they work. What better teaching method could there be than to relate them to the working of the child's own

Figure 7-1. Changes of the Location of Center of Gravity as Body Position Changes.

body in play activities?

In the following pages essential principles of stability, motion, force, and leverage as they affect movement skills are presented. One section discusses how they specifically apply to sports skills where objects are handled. An attempt has been made to present them in a way that will be meaningful to the student or teacher who has not had the advantage of a course in kiniesiology (the science of bodily movement). For the student who has had such a course, this should serve as review or summary.

The laws or principles are explained, and examples given which are found in the play experiences of children. Suggestions are given for movement activities which will help children understand certain principles better. The ideas alone are stated, for the teacher can implement them through any method he wishes. Basic concepts that children should gain are summarized.

MECHANICAL PRINCIPLES

Gravity

Everything on earth is subject to one or more forces which affects the

motion or equilibrium of the body. A push or pull exerted against an object is called a force. Forces are man-made or natural. Gravity is a natural
force which pulls everything toward the center of the earth. Gravity always pulls through the center of weight or mass of an object. Therefore,
the center of weight of the body is known as the center of gravity, or the
point about which all of the body parts exactly balance. The center of
gravity of balls or cubes is in the exact center of the object. Depending
upon body structure and distribution of weight, this point in the human
body usually lies near the top of the hips, and a little to the rear, between
the front and the back of a person's trunk. This point changes as the
position of the arms and legs changes, or an external weight is added to
any one part of the body (Figure 7-1). The line passing vertically downward through the center of gravity to the center of the earth is the line
of gravity.

Stability

Stability is an important factor in all movement skills. Depending on the
action involved, one may wish to maintain balance, upset balance in
order to move quickly, or regain balance. A stable position is also important for the production of force. When all the forces acting upon a
body are equalized, the body is in a state of equilibrium. When the
center of gravity is directly over the base of support, a body is balanced.
    The base of support is that part of a body which is in contact with
the supporting surface which is holding the body in vertical equilibrium
against the force of gravity. Whenever there are two or more points of
contact, the base also includes all the space between the contact points.
Although the usual base is the feet, activities present themselves where
various body parts become the base. In a headstand there is a three-point
base, the head and the two hands. When lying flat on the back, the whole
area of the body which is touching the floor is the base.
    *The nearer to the center of the base of support the center of gravity
is, the more stable the body.* Therefore, the body weight should be in
the center of the stance. This is why many directions for skills say to dis-
tribute the weight evenly. If the purpose of the skill is to make a quick
move in a predetermined direction it would say—"weight back or weight
forward," so the body could be thrown off balance quickly.
ACTIVITY: Working in partners, partner A straddles a line with weight
    centered over base of support. Partner B tries to push A over the
    line by pushing shoulder against shoulder. Still straddling the line,
    A shifts weight to the left foot. B tries to push A over the line by
    pushing against his right shoulder. After doing this, the students can
    contrast how much harder it is to dislodge someone from a position
    if his body weight is centered over the base of support rather than
    if it is at the edge of the base.

The larger the base of support, the more stable the body. A wider base allows more room for movement before the center of gravity moves outside the base.

ACTIVITY: Working in partners, A stands on one foot on a line. B tries to push him across the line by pushing shoulder against shoulder. A stands with feet close together with weight on both feet on the line. B tries to push him off the line in the same manner. A stands with feet about sixteen inches apart on the line. B tries to push him over the line. The students then can contrast the ease of pushing one off balance with the size of the base.

A foot position which allows for a larger base in the direction of the movement gives added stability. When one is running and must come to a stop, the feet should be in a forward stride position with the weight centered over both feet. This position allows room for more forward movement before the center of gravity passes outside the base of support. When receiving a force, or a fast-moving object, the base should be spread in the direction of the oncoming force for the same reason.

ACTIVITY: Partner A stands in a side stride position (feet side by side but apart) on a line. B tries to push A forward across the line. Then A stands with line between the feet. B tries to push A forward or backward across the line. When they contrast foot positions and stability, they should see that the forward stride position was the most stable.

The closer the center of gravity is to the base of support, the greater will be the stability. A position with knees bent lowers the center of gravity; consequently, in many activities when a force is to be received, the directions state to bend the knees.

ACTIVITIES: Partner A gets into a position on all fours. B should try to displace him from that position by pushing shoulder against shoulder or hip against hip. A stands up tall, and B tries to displace A from his position. They should contrast the feeling of stability from the low to high positions.

Sensory control of stability

There are sensory organs which control stability also. The sensory control center of balance is located in the inner ear where the semi-circular canals are the mechanism of equilibrium while the body is in motion, and the otoliths are the mechanism of stability while the body is static. Proprioceptive endings are found in muscles, tendons, and ligaments. They contribute to the development of a kinesthetic sense, or what is commonly referred to as the feel of correct body position.

Visual perception also plays a part in maintaining balance. With the eyes focused upon an object to help determine relative position of the body, an individual can usually control his position better than if the eyes are closed or allowed to wander with the movement.

In general, the eyes should be focused in the direction of the intended movement. Actually, the head tends to move or assume a position in the direction in which the eyes are looking. If the eyes look downward, the head will undoubtedly move forward and downward, thus changing the center of gravity and throwing the body off balance. It is especially important to focus on a spot twenty feet straight ahead in walking on the balance beam or when on a trampoline, unless, of course, one wishes to change position.

Basic concepts about stability which children should learn

1. For greatest stability, the center of weight should be directly over the base of support.
2. When receiving a fast moving object or a heavy force, widen the base of support in the direction from which the force is coming.
3. When applying a force, widen the base in the direction it is to be applied.
4. To stop quickly, bend the knees (drops weight closer to base of support) and place feet in a forward stride position.
5. When falling or leaning to one side, raise and lower arms or legs or some other body part on the side opposite the direction of the fall or lean.
6. When carrying or lifting a heavy object, keep object close to body.
7. When moving in a rotary manner, keep eyes focused on one spot straight ahead.

Motion

Motion implies movement. The body may move as a whole, some parts or one part of the body may move, or the body may move some other object. Everything that moves is governed by the laws of motion which were formulated by Sir Issac Newton. The laws describe under what condition and how things move.

NEWTON'S LAWS OF MOTION, LAW 1. *An object at rest will remain at rest, and an object in motion will remain in motion at the same speed and in the same direction unless acted upon by a force.* The tendency for an object to remain at rest or continue in motion is called inertia. Force can be the pull of muscles or the force caused by gravity, air resistance, or friction. This simply means that a ball will remain stationary until it is kicked or pushed, and it will continue to move in a straight line at the same speed until a wall, or someone's body stops it. If nothing gets in its way, the force of gravity, friction, and/or air resistance will cause it to cease moving.

Once a body movement is begun, the inertia of the body is overcome by the work of the muscles. If the movement is continued, the effect of inertia is overcome. Therefore, in performance where repeated body actions are required, much less energy is expanded if the movement is continued rather than if the body comes to a dead stop and inertia must be completely overcome again. For example, when doing sit-ups it is much easier if the up-and-down motion is continuous, than if the body comes to a complete stop in the down position and inertia must be overcome again when the upward motion is made.

ACTIVITIES:

1. Children can place a soccer ball in front of them and see that it will not move until a force is applied to it. When they apply a force as they kick it, it moves. If they kick it toward a wall, the direction of the ball will change as it hits the wall.
2. Children can experiment with sit-ups or pull-ups as described in the example above. They can contrast the amount of work or energy expended if the movement is continuous or if they stop between each sit-up.

LAW 2. *The amount of acceleration (change in speed and/or direction) of an object is directly proportional to the force acting on it and inversely proportional to the mass. If unequal forces are applied to objects of equal mass, the greatest force will cause the greatest acceleration; if equal forces are applied to objects of unequal mass, the greatest mass will have the smallest acceleration.* Given a certain box to move, a child must push to make it move and push harder to make the box go faster, but if two heavy weights are put into the box, he must push even harder to make the box move as fast. The greater the force applied to an object, the greater the change of speed and direction will be. The greater the mass (weight), the greater the force must be to reach a certain change of speed.

ACTIVITY: Children can throw balls toward a wall from increasingly farther distances and contrast the amount of force and strength needed to throw from the farthest distance as opposed to the shortest distance. Balls of extremely different weights can be used to contrast the differences in the amount of force needed in relation to greater mass. A soccer ball and a plastic ball would afford a contrast. Perhaps a bowling ball could be brought into the gym for use in a demonstration.

LAW 3. *For every action there is an equal and opposite reaction (counter-force).* When a foot pushes against the ground, the ground pushes back, and the body is propelled forward. When swimming, the arms push back against the water, and the body is driven forward.

ACTIVITY: Jump and reach. Relate bending knees and pushing down hard on the floor to the distance that one can jump and reach. The harder one pushes against the floor, the higher one goes in the air. If scooters are available, relate pushing against the floor with one foot while rest of weight is on the scooter to discovering that the floor pushes back against the foot and makes the scooter go.

Basic concepts about motion that children should learn

1. Anything that is standing still will stay still until someone or something exerts a force against it.
2. Things that are moved or are moving will keep on moving unless a force stops them.
3. Whenever one object moves, another object moves too. When you push on something, it pushes back. When you pull on something, it pulls back.
4. The greater the force against an object the faster it moves.
5. The heavier an object, the greater the force has to be to move it.

Factors that affect motion

Mass is an important factor that affects motion. Mass is the measure of quantity of matter (anything that occupies space) in an object. Although some people think of mass as weight, this is not true, since weight is the gravitational pull on the mass of an object. For example, objects here on earth have the same mass as they do when they are in outer space, but they are weightless in space as there is no pull exerted by gravity in space. Some balls are much the same size, such as a soccer ball and a volleyball, but one has greater mass than the other and appears to be heavier. A balloon may be much larger but have less mass than a tennis ball. Mass may be the same, but shape may be different. A football has approximately the same mass as a basketball. *The mass of an object affects an object's motion.* The greater the mass, the more difficult it is to move an object.

ACTIVITY: Children may push a bowling ball and a volleyball with one finger and contrast the force needed to push each. They should try to stop each ball with the palm of the hand and decide which ball is harder to stop. Any two balls with considerable differences in weight but similar size may be used. The children can see that the shape of a football and a basketball are different, but the mass is similar. By throwing them, they will realize it takes the same amount of force to throw each.

Basic concepts about mass that children should learn
1. Mass is the quantity of matter in an object.
2. Two objects may be the same size but have different masses.
3. Two objects may have different shapes but have the same mass.
4. More force is needed to move objects with greater mass.

Momentum is the quantity of motion. It is a measure of both speed and mass. The greater the speed of a body, the greater the momentum. The greater the mass of a body, the greater the momentum. If two balls have the same mass the one with the most speed will go the farthest. If one object has greater mass than another the same size and they are propelled at the same speed, the one with the greater mass will go farthest. The more momentum an object has, the longer it will remain in motion. When jumping for distance, a person runs very fast before he takes off so he will build up momentum in order to go farther horizontally in the air before gravity pulls the body down to the ground.

When a moving body hits a stationary body or object, the one which is moving may stop and transfer its momentum to the other object, or both objects may move. The total momentum of the two bodies before impact equals the total momentum after impact.

ACTIVITY:
1. Through playing the game of Stop and Go (p. 330), running and stopping on signal, children may contrast how much longer the body will remain in motion after the stop signal when they run at different speeds.
2. Children can roll one ball at a stationary ball and see the reaction as they meet. In the game Poison Ball (p. 346) this factor may be further studied.

Basic concepts about momentum that children should learn
1. Momentum is affected by both speed and mass.
2. The greater the speed of an object, the greater the momentum.
3. The greater the mass of an object, the greater the momentum.
4. Momentum may be transferred from one object to another.
5. The total momentum remains constant when one object strikes another.

A push or pull exerted against an object is called a *force*. Everything one does is subject to one or more forces which affect the motion or equilibrium of the body.

Gravity is a natural force which was explained earlier as it affects the body in relation to balance. Gravity will be discussed in greater detail in relation to how it affects projectiles.

Air resistance is a force which is always present and slows the fall of moving bodies. The effects of air resistance on bodies or objects is dependent upon their size, shape, and form which determines the air flow around them.

The velocity at which an object is moving also is a factor in amount of air resistance. A light object with a large surface area falls more slowly than a small object with great mass. This is why a badminton shuttle and a tennis ball when dropped from a height do not fall to the earth at the same rate of speed. They also have a different flight pattern when they are hit. Contrast, too, the fall of a balloon and a golf ball.

Acceleration is the rate of change of velocity (speed). This may mean going slower or faster, not necessarily just the latter. A reduction in velocity is usually spoken of as deceleration. The higher one wishes to jump vertically, the greater the vertical acceleration has to be before the downward acceleration, due to gravitational force, becomes greater than upward acceleration.

Friction is the resistance to the forward motion of one surface or object moving over another. The force resulting from the friction between two surfaces depends upon the type of surfaces and the force pushing them together.

There must be friction if there is to be motion. There must be some friction between the surface of shoes and the surface on which one walks or there would be no traction. Traction is the adhesive friction and is the reason why tennis shoes are worn on gym floors and cleated shoes are worn on grassy surfaces. In some instances it is desirable to reduce the amount of friction. Sharpening ice skate blades reduces friction between the blade and the ice.

There are three forms of friction; starting, sliding, and rolling friction. Starting friction is that present between the instant that force is applied and the object starts to move. This type causes the greatest resistance to motion and is the hardest to overcome. When one body slides or is dragged across another it is called sliding friction, and when a wheel rolls across a surface it is rolling friction. The latter is the easiest to overcome. Therefore, any heavy object which can be put on wheels will be easier to move than if it is resting flat on the floor.

The force that results from friction slows or stops the forward motion. This opposition to movement is called a frictional force. The amount of the frictional force that opposes the motion of an object is dependent on its shape. The less surface area in contact with another object the easier it is to move. Frictional forces opposing the motion of rough surfaces are greater than those opposing the motion of smooth surfaces.

Activity: Using a partially deflated soccer ball and a normally inflated one, let children kick each ball alternately and help them contrast the difference in the roll of the ball and the amount of force needed to kick each ball the same distance. If a ball can be kicked or rolled in grass that needs cutting and then kicked or rolled in a swath that has just been cut, children will see the effect of friction in regard to surfaces. They will see the need to kick the ball harder on a rough surface as opposed to a smooth one. In softball the need to run up to field a ground ball in the outfield should be apparent to them as they see how the speed of the ball diminishes as it rolls through the grass as opposed to the smoother surface of the infield.

The heavier an object, the more friction there is to be overcome. If an additional downward force is added to the object; such as pushing down on something, friction is increased. Therefore, if anything heavy is to be moved, the push should be made horizontal to and a little below the center of weight of the object.

Centripetal force is the name given to any force directed toward the center of a circular path of motion. There is an opposing force which works against this inward pull. For example, an object which is moving in a circular motion must have this inward pull to keep it going in a straight line; if a ball is attached to the end of a rope and the rope is swung around the head, one can feel a great force pulling outward. This is *centrifugal force*. Centrifugal force is the inertia tendency of a body in motion to travel in a straight line and is the reaction to centripetal force.

ACTIVITY:

1. Using the game **Jump the Shot** *(p. 344)*, relate the principles of centripetal and centrifugal force as the children learn how to turn the rope around the circle. In this game a strong rope with a ball or a deck tennis ring tied to the end may be used. The leader stands in the center and turns the rope so the "shot" swings around the circle just under the feet of the people standing in the circle. The circle players must jump as the rope passes under them. If they touch it, they are eliminated from the game. Children often have trouble getting the rope to swing out and maintain a steady swing. They should understand, by actually trying to swing the rope, that it takes a few turns before the shot will travel in a complete circle above the ground, as inertia must be overcome (Newton's 1st law). As they pull the rope toward the center and feel the outward pull, relate the force needed to keep the ball from flying off into the air to centripetal force. As they feel the ball pulling away from their hand, relate this to centrifugal force which is the reaction of the inward pull exerted by the child to keep the ball from going off in a straight line. After the game, one child may demonstrate turning the rope and then letting go of it. As the shot flies straight out and down from the point of release, relate the principle of inertia that the ball will tend to move forward in a straight line. The friction of the air and gravity will cause it to drop down to the ground.

2. If the children have good body control, a game of Crack the Whip may

be played on the grass. In this game everyone stands in a line and holds hands and runs. When everyone is running, the leader turns quickly and stops. Everyone else should stop but it will be evident that those closest to the leader will stop first and those out toward the end of the line will circle around the leader and as momentum picks up, the line will probably break as the "whip is cracked." Those on the end will continue running in the same direction as they were going when the line breaks or the "whip was cracked." Children can relate their flight to centrifugal force.

Basic concepts about forces that children should learn
  1. A force is a push or a pull.
  2. Gravity pulls downward.
  3. Acceleration is the rate of change of speed.
  4. The greater acceleration that is desired, the greater the force must be.
  5. Air resistance pushes against an object and slows down its flight through air.
  6. The larger the surface area of an object the more air resistance will affect its movement.
  7. Friction is the resistance to the forward motion of one surface or object moving over another.
  8. The amount of friction depends upon the surface area in contact between two bodies.
  9. Friction must be overcome to move an object.
  10. There must be some friction between the surface one walks on, runs on, or pushes against.
  11. Rolling friction is the easiest to overcome.
  12. An object that moves in a circle has a force on it that pushes the object to the outside of the circle; therefore, it must have an inward pull against it to keep it from flying off on a tangent.
  13. If an object that is moving in a circular path is released it will go off in a straight line from the point where it was released.

Types of motion

Motion is of two types, *linear* and *rotary*. Linear motion is that which is in a straight line. In linear motion the body as a whole moves the same distance, in the same direction, at a constant rate of speed. The body is usually carried by another object such as a sled, skis, car, or bus. The body acquires the same motion as the object which carries it. An object, such as a ball, when carried by the hand acquires the same motion and speed as the hand. After it is released, it continues to move at the same speed until it is acted upon by another force.

Rotary motion consists of movement of a body around a center of rotation or an axis. Most human movement is a combination of rotary and linear motion. Most movement patterns involve rotary movement to a point where the rotary speed is converted into linear speed to propel the body or object into a linear path or forward movement. The resultant linear force is dependent upon the weight of the object and speed and the length of the radius of the circle of rotation (the distance between the center of gravity and the axis of the rotation). In a forward roll this would be from the center of gravity to a point near the knees. Throwing patterns are examples of this combination of linear and rotary motion. A ball that is thrown takes the direction of a straight line tangent to the arc in which it was moving when it was released.

In rotary motion the shorter the radius of the circle of rotation, the greater will be the rotary speed, and conversely the longer the radius, the lesser the speed. When turning around in a circle, the closer the arms and legs are to the body in a tucked position, the quicker the turn can be made. As an ice skater twirls around he draws his arms in toward the body as speed is built up. When he wishes to slow down, he extends his arms away from the body. If great linear speed is desired the radius should be lengthened. In throwing and striking activities where speed is desired, the arm should be fully extended at the moment of release or impact; therefore, the ball will travel at a faster rate of speed than if the elbow were bent.

ACTIVITY: When working on rolling and tucking, help children contrast how much faster they can roll if their body is all tucked in a tight ball than if their arms and legs are out to the side or if their body is straight. They can observe how other children straighten their body in order to stop rolling.

Leverage

Body movements are possible through a system of levers. A lever is a mechanical device to produce turning about an axis. It is used to gain a mechanical advantage for speed or so that less effort is necessary to accomplish work. A lever has a fulcrum which is the axis or center point, a force arm, which is the distance from the fulcrum to the point of application of the force, and a resistance arm, which is the distance from the fulcrum to the resistance upon which the force is acting.

The bones of the body are levers. The force to move the levers is produced by muscles and the fulcrum is the joint where a specific movement takes place. The resistance is the center of gravity of the part of the body part to be moved plus the weight of any object held or placed on the body.

There are three types of levers, and each is classified by the relative

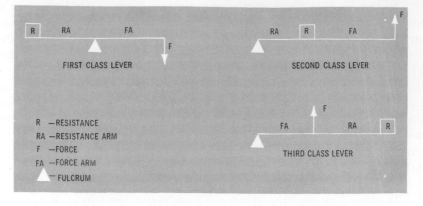

Figure 7-2. The Three Different Classes of Levers.

position of the fulcrum, force, and resistance (Figure 7-2). In a first class lever the fulcrum is located between the resistance and the force. A second class lever has the resistance between the fulcrum and the force. It is a third class lever, when the force is between the fulcrum and the weight (resistance).

The mechanical advantages of the lever are either in producing speed or strength. The first class lever may do either or both. Second class levers favor force, and the third, speed. The decision of advantage is in terms of the ratio of the length of the force arm to the resistance arm. If one wants to exert great force, the force arm should be as long as possible. If one wants to create great speed, the force arm should be as short as possible and the resistance arm as long as possible.

Most movements of the body are made through third class levers

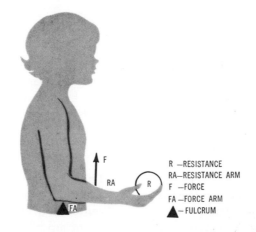

Figure 7-3. Utilization of a Third Class Lever in the Body.

(Figure 7-3). Note that in the third class lever the force arm is short in relation to the longer resistance arm. The force arm of the body's levers are short due to structure, as the muscles insert close to the joint and most of the weight is far from the joint. Therefore the body can do tasks which require speed or handling of light weight objects better than heavy tasks. Usually some type of machine must be utilized for the heavy tasks.

Most sports movements usually require the action of many levers. When it is desired to give speed to an object to be thrown or hit, or if the speed is transferred by an instrument held in the hand, many levers function in sequential order so there is a build up of force and speed. Implements held in the hand such as racquets, bats, and paddles are an extension of the body and lengthen the body's levers. Applications of this can be seen in the discussion on production of force.

Basic concepts about levers which children should learn
1. Levers are used to gain a mechanical advantage for speed or so that less effort is necessary to accomplish work.
2. The mechanical advantage of a lever is the ratio of the length of the force arm to the resistance arm. (The distance between the effort and the fulcrum and the distance between the fulcrum and the weight or object to be moved.)
3. The longer the force arm the greater the force produced.
4. The longer the resistance arm at the time of release the faster the action can be. In throwing, the straighter the arm the faster the ball may be thrown. A racquet, bat, or paddle adds to the length of the lever, and therefore the object can be propelled faster.

The body's force

It is obvious that force and motion are closely associated, since it is only through force that motion is initiated. Therefore, it is important that the teacher understand how force is developed and how it is used. The source of force in the human body is strength derived from a muscle or a combination of muscles. Force is needed to move the body itself, or to move another body or object with one's own body. The factors concerned with force will be discussed in terms of production of force, application of force, and receiving and absorption of force.

Production of force
The amount of force which needs to be produced depends upon the purpose of the movement. Since the muscles supply force one should recognize certain facts about them and their operation in order to efficiently use them for specific purposes.

Naturally strong muscles will exert more force than weak ones. The muscles of the legs, hips, and thighs are larger and stronger than those of the arms, and back. Several muscles or muscle groups working together will supply more force. If a heavy object is to be moved, force should be exerted directly on the object by all of the large muscles of the legs, hips, thighs, shoulders, and arms simultaneously. Muscles exert more force when they are extended or stretched before they contract. This is why a windup is used before pitching a ball or a backswing is taken before throwing any ball.

The most effective total force is developed when the force from each contributing part of the body is applied in a single direction in a sequential order. The greater the mass of the muscles or number of muscles supplying the force and the longer it is applied to an object the greater the force will be. Therefore, the greater the length and the number of levers that are brought into action in successive fashion, the greater the amount of time will be provided for force to develop.

There is a summation of forces as each body part contributes its share until momentum reaches its maximum at the point of application of the force or the release of an object. The momentum developed is imparted to the object which is hit or propelled.

If the momentum is stopped immediately after release of an object or at impact, a jerking motion results, the arc of the movement is shortened, and the speed of the hand is slowed before the object actually leaves the hand. A follow-through motion insures that the center of the arc of the throwing movement is at the point of release, and the maximum speed or force generated is transferred to the object. The follow-through is also a safety factor in terms of reducing possible strain of the shoulder and arm if momentum were stopped immediately.

Production of maximum force can be seen in the proper mechanics of an overhand throw. A forward stride position enables the thrower to rotate the body over the back foot in order to have a great number of muscles contribute to the subsequent forward motion. The ball is brought back to a position well behind the body by a full extension of the arm and hand. In this manner the lever is the whole body and allows a greater distance over which momentum may be developed in the forward motion. As the ball is carried forward, the full weight of the body is behind the forward movement. Each contributing muscle and body part is brought into action in a sequential manner. All of this force is then transferred to the ball, and it acquires the same rate of speed at which the hand is moving at the time of release.

Application of force

The force should be applied to an object as directly as possible in the direction it is to go. To move the body upward, the body must be erect

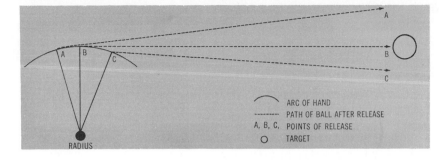

Figure 7-4. Path of Ball After Different Points of Release.

and all the force directed upward. To move an object forward, the force should be applied through the center of the weight of the object in the desired direction. If force is applied away from the center of weight, a rotary motion will result. Any force applied in a direction other than that which an object is to go is a hindrance and waste of effort. For example, in running, if the arms are swung from side to side the forward motion is retarded.

The direction a body or object takes is a line tangent to that which the arm or implement is moving at the point of release or impact. This means that an object can be released or hit only at the point where the arc is tangent to the desired target, if accuracy is to be achieved (Figure 7-4). The follow-through movements after the object is released do not change or alter the direction of the object.

Absorption of force

When it is necessary to absorb or receive the force of a thrown object, as in catching a ball, a fall, another body, or a kick, there should be a gradual reduction of force. The shock should be spread over as large an area as possible and over as long a distance as possible. When landing from a jump the bending at the hips, knees, and ankles gives more time for momentum to dissipate. A softball glove helps disperse the impact of a ball over a large area of the hand, as well as lengthening the time it takes for the ball to slow down. If when falling or sliding, one tries to land on a large portion of the body, the force of the impact will be absorbed more gradually and there will be less chance for injury.

Since a force applied anywhere other than through the center of weight sets up rotary motion, balance or stability becomes a problem in receiving or absorbing force. Hence, one should get in line with the oncoming force and assume a balanced position with the body weight low and over the base of support.

Basic concepts about the body's force
that children should know

1. To push or pull heavy objects, big muscles of the legs, hips, and thighs should be used. All of the muscles should be used at the same time.
2. Push should be applied to the center of the weight of the object and in the direction the object is to go.
3. As more muscles are used, more force is produced.
4. As the muscles act faster, more force is produced.
5. As a greater number of body levers or parts are used, the amount of time available to build force becomes greater.
6. Each body part should act in order. The throwing pattern follows the order of: trunk rotation, upper arm, lower arm, hand, fingers, release.
7. In kicking, the order is: upper leg, lower leg, foot, contact.
8. The more fully each working muscle is stretched, the more force it can supply.
9. As large an area as possible should be used in order to absorb force.
10. Each joint should give when landing from a jump, or when catching a ball.
11. A follow-through in all hitting and throwing activities ensures maximum application of force and allows time for gradual reduction of momentum.

Principles related to projectiles

Since many physical education activities require projection of the body or objects of some type into the air, a few mechanical principles will be related directly to projectiles. A projectile is any object that is sent into motion into space. The body is a projectile as it moves through space in a jump, dive, or a rebound in trampolining. Of course any ball, ring, or shuttle as it is thrown or hit becomes a projectile. The flight a projectile travels in space is affected by gravity, air resistance, angle of release (or angle at which it was struck), spin, and the degree of initial force that launched it.

Initial force

How the force to project an object is generated in the body was discussed earlier in the chapter and is related to specific skill patterns of throwing, striking, and jumping in Chapter IX. The amount of force imparted to

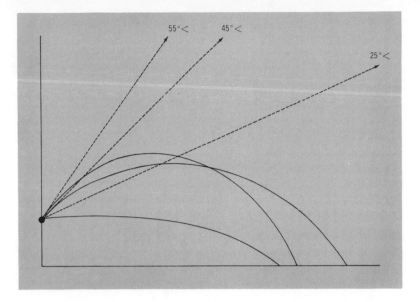

Figure 7-5. Path of Objects Projected at Various Angles.

an object is dependent on the mass of the object and the distance and speed necessary for the purpose of the flight

It is important to remember that whenever an implement is used, it actually becomes an addition to the arm as a longer resistance arm. The longer the resistance arm, the greater the resulting momentum. The momentum acquired from the shift of weight, and rotation of the body all are transferred to the implement which in turn transfers it to the ball or other object.

When the implement or lever is longer, greater velocity can be achieved, but a long lever is often difficult to control. Weight and size of implements such as bats, rackets, and clubs should be determined by the size and weight of the person using them. For this reason, when children first learn tennis and badminton skills, use of short paddles rather than regular rackets is recommended.

Gravity

Gravity will exert a downward pull on an object. In the absence of any air resistance or any upward force, any objects dropped from a height will fall to the ground at a standard rate of speed (32 ft./sec./sec.) If an object is thrown horizontally with no upward force and at the same speed it will fall to the ground in the same amount of time and will land a slight distance from the thrower. If the same object is thrown straight up (ninety degree angle) its speed will gradually diminish until the up-

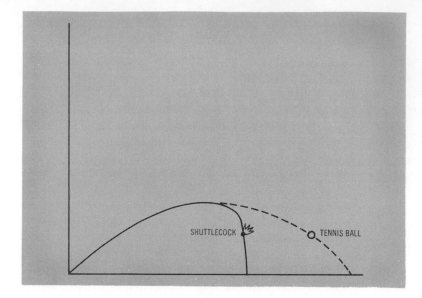

Figure 7-6. Path of a Shuttlecock as Compared to a Tennis Ball Projected at the
Same Angle.

ward force and the force of gravity are in equilibrium, then it will fall
to earth. When it reaches the point at which it was initially projected it
will be traveling at the same speed with which it was projected.

If a ball is given a diagonally upward force, the vertical force is
decelerated by gravity until the two are in equilibrium, then it starts its
downward path. It takes the same amount of time for the object to reach
the height from which it was projected as it did to reach its high point.

The distance an object travels depends upon the initial speed and
angle at which it was released. As the angle is lower, the horizontal
component is greater and the resistance to gravity is less; therefore, the
ball does not stay in the air long enough to go very far. If the angle is
large, the object will be in the air longer but will go only a short distance.
Usually, the greatest distance is obtained when the object is projected approximately at a forty-five degree angle (Figure 7-5).

Air resistance
Air resistance has little effect on the type of activities usually engaged
in by the elementary school child. However, shuttlecocks may be used and
their flight will be affected by air resistance. The pattern of flight will be
that of almost a vertical descent after the shuttle has reached the top of
its ascent (Figure 7-6). The teacher should remember that larger and

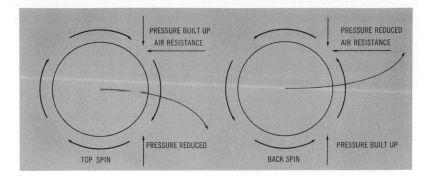

Figure 7-7. Effect of Spin on Path of Ball.

lighter objects are most affected by air resistance. The influence would be a slight decrease in height and distance that larger and lighter balls would travel.

If a ball has spin on it there will be an effect on the flight by air resistance. If a ball has no spin the air resistance is the same on the surface that meets the wall of air through which the ball must pass. When it is spinning, the side which is turning into the wall of air meets greater resistance. The resistance on the opposite side which is turning away from the original direction of the ball is diminished. The ball then tends to move where there is less resistance and the direction of the ball changes. It will curve in the direction of the least resistance. When the ball has a right spin, the flight will curve to the right, and the ball will bounce to the right. When it has a left spin, the flight will curve to the left, and the ball will bounce to the left when it hits the ground.

If there is spin on the top (forward spin), the ball tends to drop faster, as the least resistance is on the bottom of the ball. This type has a long and low bounce. If there is back spin, the resistance is greater on the back, so the ball tends to rise and remain in the air longer. This type has a shorter, higher bounce (Figure 7-7).

Accuracy
The most important factor in accuracy is the point of release or the point of impact on the object. This must be that point in the arc of the arm or implement at which the ball is tangent to the target. Since the throwing and striking movements are rotary, the arm is moving in an arc; however, it is slightly flattened just before release or impact on the object. This requires timing, concentration, and practice. The trunk should be rotated forward only as far as necessary to allow the arm to remain in a straight line toward the target. The hand or implement should travel in a straight

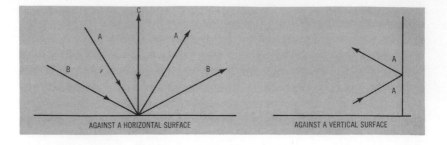

Figure 7-8. Angle of Rebound.

a line as possible toward the target on the backswing and on the follow-through. Focusing on the target until the ball is in flight helps retain concentration on the straight line.

Angle of rebound

Usually a ball will rebound at an angle equal to that which it strikes a surface (Figure 7-8). Spin, elasticity of the ball, and the firmness of the surface affect the angle of rebound. Spin was discussed previously. All balls are flattened somewhat by the force of the impact against a hard surface. A hard or properly inflated ball is restored to its original shape very quickly, and the angle of rebound affected very little. A soft or old ball allows some of the force to be absorbed, and the rebound is lower. The same is true if the striking surface is not firm. If the striking implement is not held firmly or is allowed to "give" when it contacts the ball, the rebound or projecting force is considerably less, and the direction of the rebound may also be changed.

Basic concepts about projectiles that children should learn

1. A projectile is anything that is sent into space by some force.
2. A sport implement (bat, racket, paddle) becomes a part of the body.
3. A ball which is projected at a large angle at the time of release will travel high in the air a short distance and be in the air longer than a ball released at a small angle.
4. To throw the ball as far as possible the ball should be released at approximately a forty-five degree angle.
5. To project the body into the air and to have it go the greatest forward distance, the take-off from the ground should be at a forty-five degree angle.
6. If a ball spins to the left, the path of the ball will curve to the left, and the ball will bounce to the left.

7. If a ball spins to the right, the path of the ball will curve to the right, and the ball will bounce to the right.
8. A ball with top spin will drop faster and have a long and low bounce.
9. A ball with back spin will rise in the air and travel farther and it will have a high and short bounce.
10. A ball must be released at a point when the hand is tangent to the target.
11. Eyes should be focused on the target.
12. The throwing arm should be brought straight back and straight forward in the throw.
13. A ball will bounce back from the floor, wall, racket, bat, or paddle at the same angle at which it hit.
14. A bat, racket, or paddle must be held firmly when contact with the ball is made.

The mechanical principles presented here are those which are most essential to basic skills. When working with highly skilled individuals, the teacher may wish to refer to more detailed resource material. The fundamental skill patterns are analyzed in Chapter IX. The basic mechanical principles relative to the understanding of the different factors involved in each movement pattern are described. The reader will find that the material in this chapter is the background for Chapter IX.

The teacher should help children understand the principles of force, balance, motion, and direction as each skill is introduced. Naturally, the vocabulary and depth of detail should be commensurate with the maturity level of the students. First graders can learn *how* to use the body to gain more force and *how* to retain balance. Concepts about levers and force are usually introduced in the third grade science curriculum. Thereafter, additional information about work and machines is presented in subsequent years. It would be wise for the teacher to relate body movement and the physical principles as the concepts are learned in the classroom.

ACTIONS OF THE
BODY JOINTS

Movement of the body actually starts from specific joints, which are where two or more bones join or come together. Joints are classified by their potential for mobility. A few joints are immovable. The greatest number are classified as freely movable, and these are the ones involved with body actions. Within these are varying degrees of movement due to limitations imposed by the muscles, tendons, and ligaments which hold the joints together.

Children should be aware of the joints and their fullest range of movement which can be achieved. The degree to which one can use joints throughout their fullest range is called degree of flexibility. The way to increase and maintain flexibility is to use the joints and stretch the connective tissues within the muscles.

Joint movements

There are a few terms which describe the movements of body parts due to action within the joints. As many body actions are described in these terms, both the teacher and the students should include them in their vocabulary.

Flexion takes place when adjacent bones of two body parts are brought together and the angle between the two diminishes. With young children the terms "bend," "shorten," and "make small" are often used.

Extension takes place when the adjacent body parts are returned to their original position or when they are in a standing position. With young children the terms "straighten," "stretch," "reach," and "make tall" are often used.

Hyperextension refers to a continuation of movement beyond the original or standing position. Most commonly, and in this book, the term "extension" is used in reference to body action even though the action moves beyond the original position into hyperextension.

Rotation refers to a movement of a segment around its own longitudinal axis. The body part may be turned inward or outward (medial or lateral rotation, respectively). With children this usually is referred to as "twisting."

Circumduction refers to a movement where the end of a segment or body part as a whole describes a circular pattern. The shape of this movement is similar to that of an ice cream cone; the point is the joint where the action takes place, and the wide end of the cone is the area where the circle is made. With children this is usually referred to as "turning."

Abduction is a sideward movement away from the midline of the body.

Adduction is a sideward movement inward toward the midline of the body.

The major joints and their actions are summarized below.

1. *Spine* (as a whole): flexion, extension, adduction, abduction, rotation and circumduction
2. *Head and neck:* flexion, extension, abduction, rotation, circumduction
3. *Shoulder:* flexion, extension, abduction, rotation, circumduction
4. *Elbow:* flexion, extension; no hyperextension, circumduction, or rota-

tion (except at radio-ulnar joint)

5. *Wrist:* flexion, extension, abduction, adduction, circumduction, rotation

6. *Hip:* flexion, extension, abduction, adduction, circumduction, rotation; little hyperextension

7. *Knee:* flexion, extension; slight rotation in free standing position; no hyperextension

8. *Ankle:* flexion (dorsal), extension (plantar), hyperextension, circumduction; no abduction, adduction or rotation

9. *Foot:* flexion, extension, abduction (pronation), adduction (supination)

It should be remembered that this is a very general description of joint movements and that within each of these there are varying degrees of movement. There is an interrelation of all of these joint actions as the body parts move. Children should be encouraged to experiment with the range of motion. They will learn to appreciate the varying ranges and uses of the body parts. They should note the greater mobility and range of the shoulder, arms, and hands than that of the spine, hips, knees, ankles, and feet. At the same time, they should realize the strength and the stability for supporting the body weight which the latter afford. Suggested movement experiences to explore these actions are given in Chapter IX.

With younger children the common terms of bend, stretch, sideward, twist, and turn may be used, but the terms should be associated with the feelings and actions of the joint. As children study and learn about the structure and functions of the body in health classes, the terms and movements should be related to action in the physical education classes.

MUSCLE ACTION

Man's ability to move is dependent upon the action of muscles and their control by the nervous system. Through a complex coordination of the nervous system and sensory devices, messages concerning various external stimuli and needs for muscle action and movement are coordinated. The development of the nervous system determines the efficiency and quality with which the muscle system is controlled.

As there is a continuous relay of impulses from the nervous system to the muscles, the muscles are in a constant state of partial contraction which is called tonus. When a muscle is not used due to neglect or immobilization of some type, there is less nerve supply to a muscle and it loses its tonus. Muscles with good tonus are firm and smooth; those which are flabby and weak have poor tonus. Muscles must be exercised to retain shape and strength.

When a muscle is stimulated by the nervous system, tension is developed and movement is produced. When activated muscles pull or contract, the muscle shortens. Muscles are arranged in pairs and counterbalance the joint which they cross. As one muscle contracts, the paired muscle relaxes. Efficient movement is hampered sometimes by the inability of the paired muscles to contract and relax in a coordinated manner. Movement is then jerky and wasteful. This problem can be eliminated through learning the techniques of relaxation and through much practice of movements in order to coordinate the actions.

The sources of energy for the muscle to contract are oxygen and other substances which are brought to the muscle by the blood supply. There is a ready supply of these in the muscle, but if action is sustained for any length of time, the muscle becomes fatigued unless the blood supply is supplemented and maintained. Certain biproducts of action are produced and must also be removed by the blood supply.

Whether or not there is an adequate supply of oxygen and blood to the muscles depends upon an individual's state of endurance. There are two types of endurance, cardio-vascular and muscular. The latter is related to the individual muscle which enables the muscle to contract over a period of time. Physiologically, the recovery rate of the muscle is increased due to a greater number of functioning capillaries in the muscle. This increase comes about through use and exercise.

Cardio-vascular endurance is related to work or contractions of large muscle groups over a long period of time. Stress is placed on the respiratory and circulatory systems of the body as they must supply adequate blood and oxygen to the muscles when they are called upon to work over a period of time.

FUNDAMENTALS OF EXERCISE

The condition of a muscle is dependent on the amount of exercise it gets. When a muscle is not used, it atrophies or deteriorates, strength decreases, capillary function decreases, size decreases, and it becomes limp. If the muscle is used regularly, hypertrophy will result. In this event, all of the conditions just mentioned will increase rather than decrease. This is the law of use and disuse. However, it is possible to increase the strength of a muscle three times or more without a proportional increase in size. Girls or women need not worry that exercise will produce bulky, masculine-looking muscles, for the normal amount of exercises will produce firm and well-toned muscles.

In order to maintain the desired amount of strength, regular exercise is essential. It is a physiological fact that a muscle will increase in strength only if it is called upon to increase its workload beyond what is ordinarily required of it. This is called the principle of overload.

Providing an overload can be done in two ways, increasing the duration of an activity and increasing the intensity of it. This simply means that a pupil must lift something heavier or do something over a longer period of time than he usually does it. Obviously the term is relative to the individual. Asking a pupil who can do only one sit-up to do three more would be a heavy overload and would, therefore, be unrealistic. Asking one who can do thirty-five to do two more would be a small overload and probably not a difficult undertaking.

The development of strength is specific to the muscle or muscles involved in a particular exercise or activity. Therefore, in order to maintain or build strength in general, a school program must include a wide variety of activities which necessitate use of all muscle groups. Specific exercises are available which will aid strength-building in isolated muscles or muscle groups.

There are two types of exercise, *isotonic* and *isometric*. In isometric exercises the muscle contracts against a resistance which is greater than the force the muscle can produce. There is no actual work done, no shortening of the muscle, no movement, but within the muscle itself tension is created and values gained from the increased tension. Pushing against an immovable object and holding the contraction for a few seconds provides a simple isometric exercise. The values of isometric exercises are that little time is needed for them, as few contractions at any one time are necessary, and little space or equipment are necessary.

In isotonic exercises the muscle contracts against a resistance less than the force in the contraction, and the body part to which the muscle attaches moves. The tension within the muscle is constant throughout the period of contraction. Lifting a weight, which may be a brick, a book, or the body weight itself, is an isotonic exercise. Most exercises for children are isotonic, since there is always joint movement involved. These exercises can be made more interesting than the isometrics, and greater endurance is developed through isotonics.

There are three basic points to remember when plans are made to build strength.
1. There must be an overload on a muscle. The resistance must increase as the capacity of the muscle increases. The overload may be an increase in degree repetition, duration, speed, and intensity of contraction of the muscle.
2. There must be regular practice.
3. Muscle strength is specific. Exercises or activities should be planned to localize effort in order to build up weak areas.

Muscular endurance is highly related to strength. The more a muscle is used, the more functioning capillaries there will be. Building muscle endurance is dependent on the overload principle. Continued contractions of the muscle beyond the point of apparent fatigue will enhance both the development of endurance and strength of the muscle.

In building general cardio-vascular endurance, large muscle activities have to be extended over a long period of time during which the respiratory and circulatory systems can build a tolerance for more work. It is difficult to build endurance if an activity or exercise is used in which a child has little skill, because there is a great deal of wasted effort in his uncoordinated movements. One must build skill first, then endurance. As with strength, the development of cardio-vascular endurance is dependent upon the overload principle.

Running is an excellent activity through which to develop endurance. The distance run must be increased gradually and regularly. After increasing the distance, the overload may be applied in terms of speed in which the distance must be covered.

Each child starts out with a different tolerance level for exercise, and each should have a varying degree of intensity and duration added daily or periodically. There are four basic points to remember when plans are made to build endurance.

1. Build skill first.
2. All work should be done near one's limit.
3. Increase work load first in terms of duration of time, then tempo.
4. Practice should be regular.
5. Endurance activities should be individualized and gradated.

RELAXATION

Teaching the techniques of relaxation to elementary school children is extremely important from two standpoints. Relaxation of muscles is essential in all movements due to the paired nature of muscle arrangement, where the antagonistic muscles relax while the opposing muscles are contracting. Clumsy, awkward, inefficient skills are a result of an imbalance between relaxation and contraction. The ability to relax is an important asset to maintaining good physical and mental health. There are many pressures, real or imaginary, in our society today which lead to frustration, tension, fatigue, and ultimately to poor health. The ability to relax at will can relieve some of those tensions and prevent possible illnesses or breakdowns.

Relaxation is the release of tension in a specific muscle, or more generally, a number of muscles. It is a motor skill and must be learned. The basis of learning it is a recognition of a state of feeling of tension or tonus in the muscle. One must be able to differentiate between the feeling of tension and relaxation.

In addition to teaching the techniques of relaxation, the teacher should create an atmosphere in the classroom and the gymnasium in which pressures and resulting tension will be at a minimum. Undue emphasis on competition for grades and academic success should be avoided. The teacher should help parents understand realistic goals for children in terms of their ability. Both the academic program and the physical education program should be geared to individual abilities. Schedules should be planned so that the most demanding academic subjects do not follow one another. Planning should allow enough flexibility so that short activity breaks may be taken when needed.

Teaching the techniques of relaxation

In order to differentiate between contraction and relaxation, children must experiment with the feel of the two as they use their muscles. When children are sitting down, suggest that they make their arm like a baseball bat, then like a piece of loose rope. They should contrast the feeling of the muscles within that arm and also the feel of it as they touch it with the opposite hand. The terms contract and relax should be continually associated with the action and the feel. The terms tense and tension should also be related to contract and contraction.

Suggest extending the arm and contracting the upper part and the lower part of it at the same time. As they do this, ask if they can move the arm. They will find that if muscles in both parts are contracting with the same amount of force there will be no movement. This is an isometric contraction. Suggest relaxing the bottom part some and contracting the top. It will be apparent that there will be movement toward the muscle that is pulling the hardest.

Further exploration such as this with various body parts may be pursued. Experiences which help them to control relaxation of muscles in each body part, or one part of a part, or one leg and the opposite arm, or a hand or a foot, or one side of the body, etc., should be structured. Some of these should take place when the child is in a standing position or when he is moving; for example, he should be asked to "walk with the legs stiff and the arms limp."

Most of the suggestions have been related to differential relaxation of specific parts of the body. Experiences should be provided for general relaxation where one tries to relax the whole body. This is usually done in a reclining position and involves relaxation in breathing also. The expiratory phase may be passive as the air is let out. At first this may be accompanied by a loud sigh or noise. Gradually there will be a slower rate of respiration due to passive expiration.

Imagery may be utilized as a technique to acquire a relaxed state.

Following are a few suggestions that can be made to the class to encourage general relaxation.

1. Melt like an ice cream cone on a hot day.
2. Be a rag doll.
3. Be a balloon that has burst.
4. Be squashy.
5. Be a soft fluffy cloud.
6. *Contrast:* Be a tin soldier, then a rag doll.
7. *Contrast:* Be a piece of steel, then a feather pillow.

Similar ideas may be used to induce differential relaxation.

1. Be a mast on a sailboat and let your arms be sails in a stiff wind. What happens to the sails when the wind stops blowing?
2. Let your body be a tulip stalk and your head be a tulip flower that has been snapped partially off the stem.
3. Be a bird that has one wing broken.

Relaxation must also be taught in relation to specific skills. Once children recognize the contrast between contraction and relaxation and its relation to movement, they must apply this in their skill performance. The teacher must be alert to opportunities to point out the need for relaxation in specific skills. He should watch for tenseness in individuals as they perform, and encourage free swinging movements, particularly in striking events. The feel of correct position and tension of body parts during movement should be stressed as new skills are learned.

Summary

The information in this chapter should provide the teacher or prospective teacher with a better understanding of how the body operates in relation to movement. The majority of the material has been presented to the teacher as information about the mechanical laws that structure movement, the movement possibilities of the body, and the fundamentals of exercise. The teacher in turn must teach this information to children through body movement. He must use this information in order to understand why, what, and how he can utilize the activities presented in the latter part of this book to help children successfully realize the movement potentials of their bodies.

SUGGESTED REFERENCES
FOR FURTHER STUDY

Broer, Marion, *Efficiency of Human Movement* (Philadelphia, Saunders, 1966).

Bunn, John W., *Scientific Principles of Coaching* (Englewood Cliffs, N.J., Prentice-Hall, 1962).

Dunn, Lois, *Motion, Vol. 4, Investigating Science with Children* (Darien, Connecticut, Teacher's Publishing Co., 1964).

Scott, M. Gladys, *Analysis of Human Motion*, 2nd ed. (New York, Appleton-Century-Crofts, 1963).

Souder, Marjorie, and Phyllis Hill, *Basic Movement* (New York, Ronald, 1963).

Ubell, Earl, and Arline Strong, *The World of Push and Pull* (New York, Atheneum, 1964).

Wallis, Earl L., and Gene Logan, *Exercise for Children* (Englewood Cliffs, N.J., Prentice-Hall, 1966).

Chapter VIII

PHYSICAL FITNESS

Factors of physical fitness

Assessing physical fitness

Improving physical fitness

In recent years there has been much attention and concern about the fitness status of the children and adults of America. Most of this concern was touched off by the discovery that children of some foreign countries scored higher on certain fitness tests than American children. A review of history indicates that there have been periods of concern over fitness whenever America has been exposed to the threat of war. The combination of the need for military preparedness during the "cold war" period and the revelation of the low fitness level of American children in 1956 sparked a national interest in improving the fitness level of all Americans.

Dwight D. Eisenhower originated a committee on the fitness of youth in 1956. John F. Kennedy supported the cause for fitness and enlarged the original committee to the President's Council on Youth Fitness. This council sought cooperation from professional physical educators, medical and health groups. With further encouragement from President Johnson, this council has continued to supply information, materials, and guidance in promoting fitness testing, standards, programs, and interest throughout the country. Almost every magazine, newspaper, and television station carried an advertisement or story stressing fitness during the years of 1960–1967.

The profession of physical education has long accepted the responsibility for development of physical fitness of school children as one of its prime objectives. When many studies showed that America's youth were inferior to that of other nations, the profession took up the challenge and opportunity to study and promote programs designed to improve the fitness level of all children and adults.

One hundred delegates at an American Association for Health, Physical Education and Recreation Fitness Conference in Washington in 1956 agreed to the following definition of fitness.

Fitness is that state which characterizes the degree to which the person is able to function. Fitness is an individual matter. It implies that ability of each person to live most effectively with his potential. Ability to function depends upon the physical, mental, emotional, social and spiritual components of fitness, all of which are related to each other and are mutually interdependent.

Obviously, this is a broad definition of fitness and refers to an individual's ability to function well in his environment. A careful study of it reveals the development of the same abilities and qualities as those to which the purposes and objectives of education in general and physical education are directed. It follows then that physical education can make a contribution in terms of preparedness in all areas; however, its unique contribution is in the development and maintenance of *physical* fitness. In a well-balanced physical education program the development of physical fitness should be stressed, and the qualities of social, emotional, intellectual, and spiritual well-being should be developed concurrently and concommitantly

Physical fitness involves the development of the physical qualities needed so that an individual can function efficiently and effectively in his environment. This would involve provisions for guidance in posture, nutritional status, health habits, strength, endurance, flexibility, power, agility, balance, and motor skills.

Contrary to the opinion that the only job of physical educators is to provide and structure exercise and activities to develop fitness, they must also encourage a positive attitude toward the importance of fitness. The child should understand the values, the need for, and the skills related to acquiring and maintaining physical fitness. Thereafter, the provision of opportunities for exercise will be of more long-lasting value. All attitudes are developed and/or acquired through knowledges, experiences, and insights into particular learnings. The more positive and rewarding the experiences in the physical education program are, the more appreciative of physical fitness the individual will become, and his habits and expectations of good physical fitness will be more positive. The development of these attitudes is reserved not just for the gymnasium. Parents and teachers must relate knowledge and appreciation to total fitness.

A good attitude toward the necessity of acquiring and maintaining good physical fitness can be gained best through a good developmental physical education program. Starting in the primary grades children should be taught not only the skills of fitness but an understanding of the qualities of physical fitness. They should discover that vigorous activities are fun. Some realization of fitness should be inherent in every activity presented in the daily lesson. Provided with a program planned for maximum participation for all, most children in the elementary school should have few deficiencies in fitness qualities.

The President's Council of Youth Fitness, in cooperation with nineteen leading national education and medical organizations, has developed a plan of action for a basic physical fitness program and makes the following recommendation to school administrators.[1]

1. Pupils who have a low level of muscular strength, agility, and flexibility should be identified by a screening test as part of the health appraisal. Pupils so identified should be required to participate in a program of developmental exercises and activities designed to raise their physical performance to desirable levels.
2. At least fifteen minutes of vigorous exercises and developmental activities should be included in the daily physical education program.
3. Objective valid tests of physical achievement should be used to determine pupil status, measure progress, and motivate pupils to achieve increasingly higher levels of physical fitness.
4. While giving priority to the three basic recommendations above, the school should strive to provide a comprehensive program of health education and physical education for all pupils.

The reader should pay particular attention to the last recommendation. Although the Council is primarily interested in the development of fitness, it recognizes that exercises for fitness are not physical education. The development of fitness can take place through a good comprehensive physical education program; however, for those pupils who have not had a good program, or who are below minimal levels of fitness, special activities must be planned. The recommended fifteen minutes is minimal and is not intended to suffice for the entire physical education period. However, each period should involve at least fifteen minutes of vigorous activity of some nature. This excludes time for organization, discussion, planning, relaxation, and less vigorous activities.

Many factors contribute to the development of physical fitness. A child must have the basic equipment in terms of health, energy, body structure, and opportunity before the activities of physical education can be very effective. Everyone has some degree of fitness, and all can improve upon his present status. The teacher must know how to determine and interpret status before he can set expectations of ultimate attainment.

FACTORS OF PHYSICAL FITNESS

The areas of physical fitness which are of greatest concern to the elementary school teacher will be described and suggestions will be given for

[1] President's Council on Youth Fitness, *Youth Physical Fitness* (Washington, D.C., Superintendent of Documents, 1960), p. 14.

development and maintenance in the four areas of health, posture, nutritional status, and components of physical fitness.

Health

The health status of the child provides the limits or extent of the minimum fitness level that one can expect of him. Expecting a child with health problems to achieve a high level of physical fitness is as unrealistic as expecting a racing car to win a race without fuel. The classroom and the physical education teacher have two major responsibilities in regard to the health status of each pupil. One is to identify pupils whose health level or habits appear to be below normal and then refer them to the proper authorities for examination and treatment. The authorities may vary in any one school system from a school nurse, physician, principal, or parents. Teachers are in a good position to notice deviations from the norm in appearance, behavior, or energy level of children. Listlessness, fatigue early in a game, poor color, hypersensitivity to reactions of other children in give-and-take situations, inability to see approaching balls quickly enough to catch them, and lack of interest in activities all indicate a need for further investigation.

The second responsibility is to be acquainted with and understand the health status of each child. This also includes an understanding of the limitations and fitness needs of children who have physical defects which are not remediable such as, structural malformations, deafness, partial loss of sight, and heart conditions. Modifications of exercise and activities may have to be developed for a child with a particular handicap. Children returning to school from absences due to prolonged illnesses will have suffered from a loss of physical fitness and will have to rebuild muscle strength and endurance. The inactivity induced by even a brief confinement to bed results in a depreciation of strength and endurance.

The school administration has the responsibility for requiring or providing periodic medical examinations for each child. The classroom teacher may be expected to assist with some phases of this examination, such as screening of visual and hearing defects, and weighing and measuring. The administration also has the responsibility for providing a healthful environment for children. Naturally, the teacher plays a vital part in daily routine provisions of a healthy environment through attention to proper ventilation, rest periods, seating, and others.

Posture

It is extremely difficult to ascertain the cause and effect relationship of good or poor posture to fitness, health, nutritional status or psychological factors. There is no one ideal posture. In the course of a day a child is in

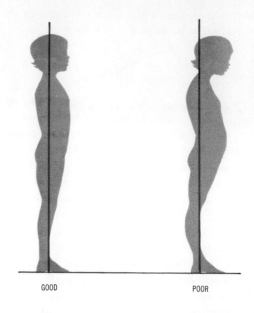

GOOD   POOR

Figure 8-1. Examples of Good and Poor Body Alignment.

many postures—sitting, running, standing, and walking. Generally, good
posture is judged when one is in a standing position and the body is in
good alignment with the body segments which are well balanced over the
base of support. The body line should be vertical with a nearly vertical
line running from a point just in front of the ankle joint, through the
middle of the kneecap, the middle of the hip joint, the edge of the shoulder, and up through the middle of the ear (Figure 8-1).

When maintaining this position, the body is constantly fighting the
downward force of gravity. The anti-gravity muscles must have enough
strength and endurance to hold this position. If poor posture is prolonged
over a long period of time, muscles adapt both in length and function to
the faulty position, and it becomes increasingly difficult to correct the
fault. The teacher should remember that the physical environment of the
classroom contributes to posture defects. As children grow, the size of
their desks needs to be increased. Also, adjustments to see the blackboard
from an awkward position or due to inadequate lighting can cause poor
habits of sitting posture which may be hard to remedy.

Although there is little evidence from research to substantiate the belief, it is a common belief that there is a relationship between posture
and health. When the body segments are out of line, vital internal organs
are possibly pushed out of the proper position, pressure is placed upon
them, and as a result, proper growth and functioning is impaired.

Improper diet and fatigue affect the amount of energy that one has to exert upon good posture. Emotional stresses or depression affect the mental attitude toward a good self-image. An alert teacher will notice a sudden change in posture and should then look for any deviations in the child's habits or attitudes. A child with a slight hearing loss may strike a posture which enables him to lean closer to what he is trying to hear. In this and similar cases one can easily see the interrelation between poor health and poor posture.

Assessing posture

Usually, the teacher's responsibility for assessing posture is limited to observation for minor and/or major deviations from the normal. There are posture tests available from different sources; however, the teacher may devise his own check list and look for the signs of good posture which are listed below [2]

STANDING:

1. Feet parallel and about six inches apart.
2. Head high, as if balancing a book on the head.
3. Chest out.
4. Stomach and hips firm.
5. Abdomen and back as flat as possible.
6. Knees very slightly flexed—not locked.
7. Weight evenly distributed on each foot. Most of the body weight on balls of feet.

SITTING:

1. Sit back in the chair, so that hips touch the back of the chair.
2. Sit tall.
3. Keep chest out and neck in line with upper back.
4. When writing, lean forward from the hips. Keep head and shoulders in line.

WALKING:

1. Knees and ankles limber and toes pointed straight ahead.
2. Swing legs directly forward from the hip joints.
3. Lift feet off the ground; don't shuffle.
4. Shoulders and arms swing free and easy—no pulling or tension.
5. Head and chest high.
6. The heel touches the ground first in each step.

In this list no mention is made of symmetry. It is important that the hips and shoulders appear level as one observes from the front or back of the child. The terms used in this list may also be used for cue words when making suggestions for good posture. Observation of standing posture is enhanced if a long mirror is utilized. A piece of tape running down the mirror will help aid the teacher in checking body alignment

[2] *Ibid.,* p. 94.

as the child stands in front of the mirror. A plumb line or string with a weight on one end can be hung in a doorway and used to check body alignment as the child stands next to the line. See Figure 8-1 for proper alignment. The most common faults of posture are forward head, round shoulders, sway back, protruding shoulder blades, hollow back, protruding abdomen, ankle pronation (weight on inside of foot), and imbalance of shoulders and hips. Many young children will exhibit a protruding abdomen, a slight hollow in the back, and protruding shoulder blades but not have marked posture deviations. These are signs of immaturity and naturally resolve themselves into a more mature contour in later grades if proper activities are provided for natural growth of strength.

When marked deviations are found, the child should be referred to the proper authorities and the parents. Corrective exercises must be given by the physical education specialist under the prescription of the doctor. Exercises to maintain good posture and improve some poor posture habits of a minor nature due to a lack of muscle strength and control are found in Chapter XIV under *Developmental exercises*. Provision for many climbing, hanging, and swinging activities will help build good posture. Most running games and dance activities do not provide enough vigorous use of the upper trunk, shoulder, and arms.

Nutritional status

Physiologically, nutrition is defined by Webster as the sum of the processes by which an animal or plant absorbs or takes in and utilizes food substances. This is evident in the human body in terms of growth, development, maintenance, and repair of body tissues and bones.

Growth in children follows a steady progressive pattern. Any sudden change in the pattern may indicate a nutritional deficiency which may be manifested in a sudden loss of weight, excessive gains in weight, cessation of growth, or excessive fatigue. The teacher can subsequently screen children who exhibit any of these characteristics through periodic simple observation techniques.

Screening may be accomplished objectively through a periodic measurement of height and weight. The danger in this is that often the teacher weighs and measures children several times a year but no one ever studies the results. Unless a growth record is kept and studied, time is wasted in weighing and measuring. Another danger is that all children may be compared in terms of height, weight, and age without due regard to body build.

There is a growing trend in elementary schools toward the use of growth charts. Heights and weights are plotted on these charts in channels which represent a pattern of growth of a typical child in a youngster's age group. The theory is that a child will maintain a regular pattern of growth typical for his age and body build. If at some time his growth pattern slips out of the channel, there is cause for investigation of contributing causes. The Meredith Physical Growth Record Chart and directions for its use and interpretation are included here (Figures 8-2 & 8-3). Copies of the chart may be obtained from the American Medical Association, 435 N. Dearborn St., Chicago, Illinois. Directions for use of the Meredith Physical Growth Chart:

DETERMINING WEIGHT: Obtain the weight of each pupil in September, January, and May. Wherever possible use beam-type platform scales. Before each weighing period check the scales; if they do not balance correctly, adjust them. Have the girl remove her shoes and as much other clothing as practicable (the weight measures used in developing the chart were taken on girls wearing undergarments only). With the pupil standing near the center of the platform of the scales, her hands hanging free, determine weight to the nearest one-half pound.

DETERMINING HEIGHT: Use a metric measure fixed in the upright position, and a wood headpiece. The measure may be a yardstick, metal tape, or paper scale; it should be fastened firmly to an upright board or to a smooth wall with no wainscoting. A satisfactory headpiece is easily made in the school workshop by joining at right angles the shorter edges of two pieces of seasoned wood seven inches by five inches, and mounting within the ninety degree angle a triangular wood brace having an opening for insertion of the fingers.

MEASURING HEIGHT WITH SHOES REMOVED: Have the pupil stand with heels, buttocks, and upper part of back in contact with the wall or board; feet almost together but not touching each other; arms hanging at the sides; heels in firm contact with the floor; head facing straight forward; and chin lifted but not tilted up. When he is positioned, place one face of the headpiece against the upright scale and bring the other face down, keeping it horizontal, until it crushes the hair and makes contact with the top of head. Take two separate measurements and record height to the nearest one-fourth inch.

REGISTERING HEIGHT AND WEIGHT STATUS: Assume you have determined the height and weight of May Atkin. May weighs 48 pounds, is 45 inches in height, and will have her fifth birthday tomorrow. Find age 5 below the height portion of the chart and 45 inches along its left-hand margin. Plot a point above 5 years and opposite 45 inches. Below this dot on the height portion of the chart write "45.0." Next, find age 5 years below the weight portion of the chart and 48 pounds along its left-hand margin. Plot a point above 5 years and opposite 48 pounds. Above this mark in the weight portion of the chart write "48.0." With the completion of these directions, the

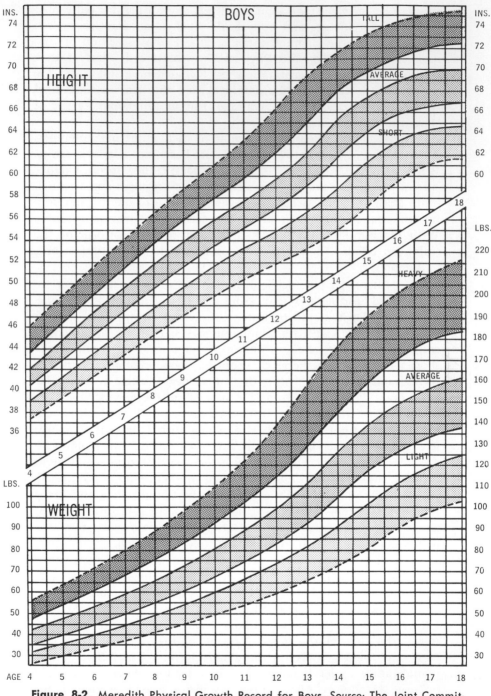

Figure 8-2. Meredith Physical Growth Record for Boys. *Source:* The Joint Committee on Health Problems in Education of the National Education Association and the American Medical Association. Reprinted by permission.

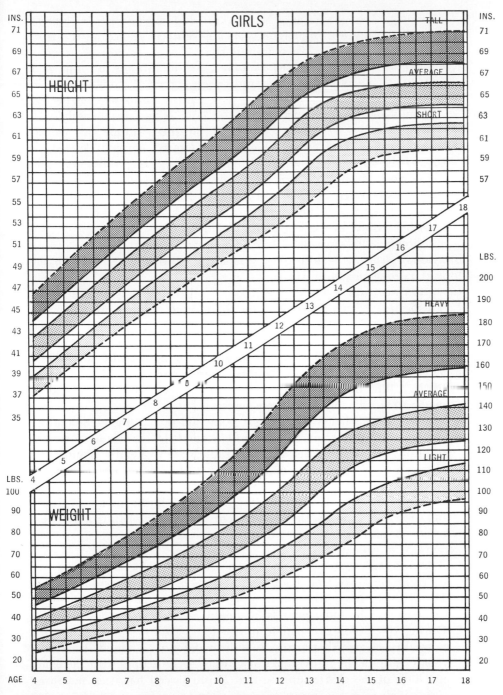

Figure 8-3. Meredith Physical Growth Record for Girls. *Source:* The Joint Committee on Health Problems in Education of the National Education Association and the American Medical Association. Reprinted by permission.

height and weight status of May Atkin at age five years is fully registered. At any age from four years to eighteen years, the status of other girls can be registered similarly.

REGISTERING HEIGHT AND WEIGHT PROGRESS: Assume May is now one year older. At age five years four months she weighed 50 pounds and had a height of 46 inches, at age five years eight months she weighed 52 pounds and was 46.5 inches tall, and now at age six she weighs 55 pounds and is 47.5 inches in height. Further, assume that points representing these records have been plotted correctly on May's chart. Having status records at more than one age, it becomes possible to draw individual growth curves, or lines of progress. May's progress between ages five and six years can be depicted by drawing lines connecting (a) her points in the height part of the chart and (b) her points in the weight part of the chart.

Following the same procedure, height and weight progress of any individual girl may be portrayed over part or all of the period from age four years to age eighteen years.

INTERPRETING STATUS:

1. The figures written above or below the plotted points readily describe each pupil's overall body size at the age or ages measures have been obtained.

2. The channels in which a pupil's height and weight points for a given age are located indicate her standings with reference to schoolmates of like age. The illustrative values given at age six years show May to be moderately tall and moderately heavy.

3. When a pupil's height and weight points do not lie in corresponding channels, the discrepancy may denote normal slenderness of stockiness of build, or it may reflect an undesirable state of health. Assume the chart shows a new pupil to be "average" in height and "light" in weight. He should be screened for medical study to determine whether he is a "satisfactorily healthy" boy of slender build, or a "medically unsatisfactory" boy with an incipient infection, a nutritional deficiency, or an unsuitable activity program.

INTERPRETING PROGRESS:

1. The difference between a girl's recorded heights (or weights) at two different ages gives the amount of change in the intervening period. For example, May Atkin between five and six years of age gained 2.5 inches in height and 7 pounds in weight.

2. During the childhood span from age four years to age eleven years, normality of growth progress is indicated by approximately parallel relationship of the individual's height and weight lines with the channel lines of the chart. Suppose that Ruth Tweed has been measured successively from age five years to age eight years. Her height lines runs along the middle of the "average" height channel, while her weight

line runs fairly close to the middle of the average weight channel until age seven years then takes a steep turn upward. Ruth should be screened for medical investigation—her disproportionate gain in weight may reflect the need for a prescribed diet, a change in daily regimen, or drug therapy.

3. Interpretations of growth progress after age nine years are made on the same basis as earlier except that allowance must be made for individual differences in age of the circumpuberal "spurt" in height and weight. Suppose (a) Harriet and Elise are nearly alike in height and weight at each age from five to nine years, and (b) the time of rapid adolescent growth in these measures begins before ten years for Harriet and after twelve years for Elise. For boys it would be thirteen years and fifteen years. In the early teens when Elise is continuing to grow in height and weight at childhood rates, this growth should not be appraised as "unsatisfactory."

ABOUT THE CHART: The height and weight measurements for constructing the chart were collected in 1961–1963 on Caucasian girls and boys attending public and private schools in Iowa City, Iowa. To obtain the channels, age distributions for height and weight were subdivided as follows: top 10 percent (tall, heavy), next 20 percent, middle 40 percent (average), next 20 percent and lowest 10 percent (short, light).

Without the proper development a child cannot attain the strength to maintain a good physical fitness level nor the skills to maintain good social status. Without a sound body the child will find it difficult to fulfill his total educational potential.

Components of physical fitness

There are a number of components which contribute to the attainment of efficient work habits. Actually, these components are basic to all good movement. Some of these contribute more than others to physical fitness. One may possess a high degree of one and not of another. The most fit person attains a high degree in most of the components.

Most basic to physical fitness are strength, muscular endurance, cardio-vascular endurance, and a high degree of power, flexibility, agility, speed, balance, and coordination. Every teacher should know what these are and how each is affected by exercise.

Strength

One of the most basic components to success in all movement is strength. Muscular strength is defined as the amount of force that can be exerted by a particular muscle. The strength of a muscle is dependent on its size and quality. Muscles grow in size in relation to general growth, nutrition, and amount of exercise. Varying degrees of strength needed in muscles is dependent upon the type of work or activity which is to be done beyond the ordinary daily needs.

Physiologically, the muscle will increase in strength only if it is called upon to increase its workload beyond what is ordinarily required of it. This is called the principle of overload. Muscle strength is just maintained, not increased, if no additional effort or intensity is added to exercises or activities.

The development of strength is specific to the muscle or muscles involved in a particular exercise or activity. Consequently, the teacher must plan a variety of activities which will necessitate use of all of the muscle groups. Many of our popular games and sports require the use of the muscles of the legs, lower back, arms and hands, but not much use of the upper back and shoulder girdle muscles. Opportunities should be provided for hanging and inverted activities where shoulder area muscles must help support the weight of the body.

Endurance

There are two types of endurance, cardio-vascular and muscular. The latter is related to the individual muscle which enables the muscle to continue to contract over a longer period of time. This is highly related to strength.

Cardio-vascular endurance is related to work or contractions of large muscle groups over a long period of time. Stress is placed on the heart and the respiratory and circulatory systems of the body when they must supply adequate blood and oxygen to the muscles. Certain adjustments are made in these systems as the use of the overload principle demands them. Generally children will not over-exert themselves. In order to develop both types of endurance and strength they must be pushed to do a little more or try a little harder than they did the time before. The amount of extra effort needed will vary for each child in relation to his present status.

Agility

Agility is the ability of a person to change direction or body position quickly and regain poise or control to proceed with another movement. Agility is highly dependent upon or interrelated with speed, strength, balance, and coordination. It is developed through practice and confidence in movement. The acquisition of agility is not only important to success in games and sports requiring quick changes of direction and dodging of objects or other people, but also to safety outside of the play situation. Instruction and opportunities to participate in activities requiring fast starts, stops, and changes of direction should be included in the daily program.

Flexibility

Flexibility is the range of movement in a joint. The degree of flexibility determines the extent of extension and flexion of a joint and consequent body action in terms of bending, reaching, twisting, and turning. The degree of flexibility is first determined by the nature of the joint itself and then by the ligaments and muscles related to the joint. Flexibility is very specific to each joint. One may be quite flexible in one area but not another. Within the limitations of the bone structure and the condition of the ligaments, range of movement can be expanded through exercises of stretching the muscle.

A high degree of flexibility not only enables a child to perform some activities more efficiently, it also provides a safety factor in terms of absorbing sudden shocks or blows around vulnerable joint areas. The knee and ankle joints are prone to sudden jolts in everyday activities.

Power

Power is the capacity of the body to release maximum force or muscle contraction in the shortest possible time. Power denotes explosive movements, a release of maximum force at maximum speed. Obviously, power is highly dependent upon the elements of speed and strength. Power is important to success in performance of jumping, kicking for distance, throwing for distance, charging an object or opponent, starting a run with a fast takeoff or sudden bursts of speed, or pulling away from an assailant. It can be improved through gains in strength and practice of the activities just mentioned.

Speed

Speed is the rapidity with which one repeats successive movements of the same pattern. Great speed in muscle contraction is not always conducive to the greatest efficiency of movement. It seems that there is an optimum speed at which muscles contract with the greatest conservation of energy for the amount of work done.

Success in some activities is highly dependent upon how fast one can move body parts or the whole body from one place to another. This need is also inherent in some occupations or in the face of imminent dangers. Speed of movement can be improved through practice for good technique and efficiency of movement.

Balance

Balance is the ability to maintain a desired position of the body whether in a static or held position or in a dynamic or moving state. It denotes a degree of stability and ease in control of the body in a specific position.

Balance is an important factor in most games, sports, and dance and gymnastic activities. Most life and work activities require good balance in order to prevent falls and accidents. The balance of children can be improved through exposure to and practice of balance activities.

Coordination

Coordination is the ability to integrate muscle movements into an efficient pattern of movement. Coordination makes the difference between good performance and poor performance. The efficiency of skill patterns depends upon the interrelation of speed, agility, balance, and muscle movements into a well-coordinated pattern. The child must understand the movement to be performed and see the relationships of each movement to the total pattern. Development of kinesthetic perception usually allows movements to become rhythmical and efficient.

Good coordination is not only essential to good performance in sport and game skills, but it is also vital to all daily and vocational tasks where efficient movement and conservation of energy are important. Only a great deal of guided practice of specific skills will produce well-coordinated movements.

ASSESSING PHYSICAL FITNESS

As the components of physical fitness are specific and not necessarily interrelated, the teacher must select a variety of tests to determine specific areas of weakness in individuals. The selection must be prudent as the administration of a great number of tests can be very time-consuming. The results of the tests may be used to diagnose the physical status of each child, to identify those needing special help, to measure achievement, and to aid in program-planning of activities.

Primary grades

In the first and second grades, children do not always exert maximum effort in performance, and it is difficult to assess fitness status. Their attention is easily diverted, and often they become curious about the test itself, the measuring instruments used, and the tester, and therefore, they do not concentrate on their performance.

Most children at third grade level become extremely interested in testing. Typically they develop a desire to best their own performance. It is productive in terms of reliability and validity to begin some assessment of fitness at this level. Tests of strength, speed, power, and endurance will help to identify the underachievers and will also prove highly motivating.

There are very few physical fitness test batteries which are recommended for use with children below the fourth grade. Some of those which are available and have norms are listed on page 197. A few tests which may be administered to primary grade children are described. The teacher may select one or all of them to use as a screening device to identify the underachievers. Minimum levels of achievement are suggested for both boys and girls in grades one through three. If a child scores below these levels, a concentrated effort should be made to plan a remedial or special exercise program for the individual.

Tests for grades one, two, and three

SIT-UP

PURPOSE: To measure abdominal strength, endurance, and speed.
DIRECTIONS: Page 201.

STANDING BROAD JUMP

PURPOSE. To measure leg strength and power.
DIRECTIONS: Page 202.

THROW FOR DISTANCE

PURPOSE: To measure power.
DIRECTIONS: Page 203.

30-YARD DASH

PURPOSE: To measure speed.
DIRECTIONS: Page 203. Reduce the distance to 30 yards for the first three grades.

SEAL CRAWL

PURPOSE: To measure arm and shoulder girdle strength, endurance, speed.
DIRECTIONS: Mark two lines 20 feet apart. Child starts behind starting line with weight held on hands on the floor with elbows straight, legs out behind and dragged along the floor (Seal Crawl, p. 523). On the signal "Go," he moves forward and to the finish line 20 feet

away as fast as he can. If he falters, he should assume the starting position and continue until he crosses the line. While he is moving, the knees may not touch the floor, and the subject may not push with the feet. To do either of these constitutes a mistrial, and the test must be repeated.

SCORING: The time is taken from the signal "Go" until the hands cross the finish line. Score is recorded to nearest tenth of a second.

Table 8-1. Minimum Levels of Performance

Grade	Sit-Ups (no.)		Broad Jump (in.)		Throw (ft.)		Dash (sec.)		Seal Crawl (sec.)	
	B	G	B	G	B	G	B	G	B	G
1	3	3	36	32	30	15	9	9	20	26
2	5	5	40	36	40	20	8.5	8.6	18	20
3	8	7	42	38	55	28	7	7.5	13	17

Intermediate and upper grades

Children in grades four and above become quite interested in measurement of their skills and their fitness level. They are capable of producing an all-out effort when tested. Boys are particularly interested in acquiring strength and prowess. As social status for boys at fourth grade level becomes quite dependent upon motor skill achievement, it is extremely important that the boy with a low fitness level be identified and helped. Although a few girls at this age become slightly disinterested in physical education activities due to cultural influences, the majority of them are as interested as the boys but not quite so intent.

The President's Council recommends that a screening test be given to all children. This will help identify the very lowest children in a very short time. This test may be administered quickly at the start of the year, or it may be used as the only fitness test if it is not feasible to administer a whole series of tests. The test consists of three items:

1. Pull-ups (arm and shoulder strength)
2. Sit-ups (flexibility and abdominal strength)
3. Squat thrusts (agility)

Instructions for the screening test

PULL-UP (BOYS)

DIRECTIONS: Page 198.
To PASS: Boys must complete one pull-up.

MODIFIED PULL-UP (GIRLS)

EQUIPMENT: Any bar adjustable in height and comfortable to grip. A piece of pipe, placed between two stepladders and held securely, may be used.

STARTING POSITION: Adjust height of bar to chest level. Grasp bar with palms facing out. Extend the legs under the bar, keeping the body and knees straight. The heels are on the floor. Fully extend the arms so they form an angle of 90 degrees with a body line. The partner braces the pupil's heels to prevent slipping.

ACTION:
1. Pull body up with the arms until the chest touches the bar.
2. Lower body until elbows are fully extended.
3. Repeat the exercise the required number of times.

RULES:
1. The body must be kept straight.
2. The chest must touch the bar and the arms must then be fully extended.
3. No resting is permitted.
4. One pull-up is counted each time the chest touches the bar.

TO PASS: Ages ten to seventeen must complete eight modified pull-ups.

SIT-UP (BOYS AND GIRLS)

DIRECTIONS: See page 201.
TO PASS: Boys (ages ten to seventeen) must complete fourteen sit-ups. Girls (ages ten to seventeen) must complete ten sit-ups.

SQUAT THRUST (BOYS AND GIRLS)

EQUIPMENT: A stopwatch, or a watch with a sweep-second hand.
STARTING POSITION: Pupil stands at attention.
ACTION:
1. Bend knees and place hands on the floor in front of the feet. Arms may be between, outside or in front of the bent knees.
2. Thrust the legs back far enough so that the body is perfectly straight from shoulders to feet (the push-up position).
3. Return to squat position.
4. Return to erect position.

SCORING: The teacher carefully instructs the pupils how to do correct squat thrusts. The teacher tells the pupil to do as many correct squat thrusts as possible within a 10 second time limit. The teacher gives the starting signal, "Ready! Go!" On "Go" the pupil begins. The

Table 8-2. Fitness Tests for Elementary School Children

Name of Test	Grade or Age Level	Test Items	Source
A.A.H.P.E.R. Youth Fitness Test	Grade 5 to College	Pull-ups Sit-ups Shuttle run Standing broad jump 50-yard dash Softball throw 600-yard run-walk	AAHPER, Washington, D.C.
New York State Physical Fitness Test	Grades 4 to 12	Posture test Target throw Modified push-up Side-step 50-yard dash Squat stand Treadmill	New York State Education Dept. Albany, N.Y.
North Carolina Fitness Test	Grades 4 to 12 (Ages 9 to 18)	Sit-ups Sidestepping Standing broad jump Pull-ups Squat thrust	Dept. of Public Instruction, Raleigh, N.C.
State of Washington, Physical Fitness Tests for Elementary School Children	Ages 6 to 12	Standing broad jump Bench push-ups Curl-ups Squat-jump 30-yard dash	State Office of Public Instruction, Olympia, Wash.
Tulsa Elementary Physical Fitness Test	Grades 4 to 6	25-50-yard dash Pull-ups Zigzag run Sit and reach Sit-ups Standing broad jump Softball throw for distance Side-step 300-600 yard run-walk	Mrs. Beatrice Love, Supervisor of Elementary Education, Public Schools, Tulsa, Okla.
Glover Physical Fitness Items	Ages 6 to 9	Seal walk Shuttle run Standing broad jump Sit-ups	Barrow, Harold, and McGee Rosemary, *Measurement in Physical Education* (Lea & Fegiber, 1964).

Table 8-2. Continued

Name of Test	Grade or Age Level	Test Items	Source
Oregon Motor Fitness Test	Grades 4 to 6	Push-ups (boys) Knee touch sit-ups (boys) Hanging flexed-arm position (girls) Crossed-arm curl-ups (girls) Standing broad jump	Supervisor of Physical Education, State Dept. of Education, Salem, Ore.
Amateur Athletic Union Physical Fitness and Proficiency Test	Grades 1 to 12 (ages 6-18)	Sprints, walk-run Sit-ups Pull-ups Push-ups Standing broad jump Baseball throw Continuous hike for distance Running high jump	AAU, 231 West 58th St., New York, N.Y.

partner counts each squat thrust. At the end of 10 seconds, the teacher says, "Stop."

To Pass: Girls (ages ten to seventeen) must complete three squat thrusts in 10 seconds. Boys (ages ten to seventeen) must complete four squat thrusts in 10 seconds.

There are a number of physical fitness test batteries designed for boys and girls in grade four through high school, and, for that matter, for adults also. Many states and organizations have combined specific tests of fitness elements and developed norms for their respective populations. The most widely utilized battery is that of the American Association for Health, Physical Education, and Recreation which was designed for use by teachers all over the country. The test was planned to be comprehensive in nature, to be easy to administer, to require little equipment, and to yield norms based on a sampling of children from all parts of the United States.

Included here is a list of names of test batteries, test items in the batteries, age levels for which the test is suitable, and addresses of sources of the various tests. Many of these may be secured free of charge or for a small fee. Manuals describing the tests, directions for administering them, and norms are usually provided.

Directions for the AAHPER youth fitness test [3]

PULL-UP (BOYS)

EQUIPMENT: A metal or wooden bar approximately 1½ inches in diameter is preferred. A doorway gym bar can be used, and if no regular equipment is available, a piece of pipe or even the rungs of a ladder can also serve the purpose (Figure 8-4).

Figure 8-4. Improvised Equipment for Pull-Up—Doorway Gym Bar in Background, Ladder in Foreground.

Figure 8-5. Starting Position for Pull-Up.

DESCRIPTION: The bar should be high enough so that the pupil can hang with his arms and legs fully extended and his feet free of the floor. He should use the overhand grasp (Figure 8-5). After assuming the hanging position, the pupil raises his body by his arms until his chin can be placed over the bar and then lowers his body to a full hang as in the starting position. The exercise is repeated as many times as possible.

RULES:

1. Allow one trial unless it is obvious that the pupil has not had a fair chance.

[3] With permission of the American Association for Health, Physical Education and Recreation, 1201 Sixteenth St., N.W., Washington, D.C.

2. The body must not swing during the execution of the movement. The pull must in no way be a snap movement. If the pupil starts swinging, check this by holding your extended arm across the front of the thighs.
3. The knees must not be raised and kicking of the legs is not permitted.

SCORING: Record the number of completed pull-ups to the nearest whole number.

FLEXED-ARM HANG (GIRLS)

EQUIPMENT: A horizontal bar approximately 1½ inches in diameter is preferred. A doorway gym bar can be used; if no regular equipment is available, a piece of pipe can serve the purpose. A stopwatch is needed.

Figure 8-6. Starting Position for Flexed-Arm Hang.

DESCRIPTION: The height of the bar should be adjusted so it is approximately equal to the pupil's standing height. The pupil should use an overhand grasp (Figure 8-6). With the assistance of two spotters, one in front and one in back of pupil, the pupil raises her body off the floor to a position where the chin is above the bar, the elbows are flexed, and the chest is close to the bar (Figure 8-7). The pupil holds this position as long as possible.

RULES:
1. The stopwatch is started as soon as the subject takes the hanging position.

2. The watch is stopped when (a) pupil's chin touches the bar, (b) pupil's head tilts backwards to keep chin above the bar, (c) pupil's chin falls below the level of the bar.

SCORING: Record in seconds to the nearest second the length of time the subject holds the hanging position.

SIT-UP

EQUIPMENT: Mat or floor

DESCRIPTION: The pupil lies on his back, either on the floor or on a mat, with legs extended and feet about 2 feet apart. His hands are placed on the back of the neck with the fingers interlaced. Elbows

Figure 8-7. Flexed-Arm Hang.

are retracted. A partner holds the ankles down, the heels being in contact with the mat or floor at all times (Figure 8-8). The pupil sits up, turning the trunk to the left and touching the right elbow to the left knee, returns to starting position, then sits up turning the trunk to the right and touching the left elbow to the right knee. The exercise is repeated, alternating sides (Figure 8-9).

RULES:

1. The fingers must remain in contact behind the neck throughout the exercise.

2. The knees must be on the floor during the sit-up but may be slightly bent when touching elbow to knee.
3. The back should be rounded and the head and elbows brought forward when sitting up as a "curl" up.
4. When returning to starting position, elbows must be flat on the mat before sitting up again.

SCORING: One point is given for each complete movement of touching elbow to knee. No score should be counted if the fingertips do not maintain contact behind the head, if knees are bent when the pupil lies on his back or when he begins to sit up, or if the pupil pushes up off the floor from an elbow. The maximum limit in terms of number of sit-ups shall be: 50 sit-ups for girls, 100 sit-ups for boys.

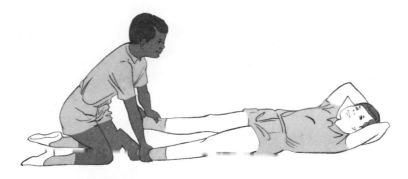

Figure 8-8. Starting Position for Sit-Up.

SHUTTLE RUN

EQUIPMENT: Two blocks of wood, 2 inches by 2 inches by 4 inches, and stopwatch. Pupils should wear sneakers or run barefooted.

DESCRIPTION: Two parallel lines are marked on the floor 30 feet apart. The width of a regulation volleyball court serves as a suitable area. Place the blocks of wood behind one of the lines as indicated in (Figure 8-10). The pupil starts from behind the other line. On the signal "Ready? Go!" the pupil runs to the blocks, picks one up, runs back to the starting line, and *places* the block behind the line; he then runs back and picks up the second block, which he carries back across the starting line. If the scorer has two stopwatches or one with a split-second timer, it is preferable to have two pupils running at the same time. To eliminate the necessity of returning the blocks after each race, start the races alternately, first from behind one line and then from behind the other.

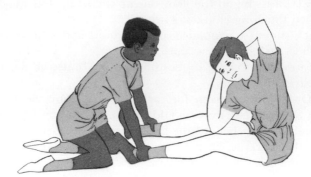

Figure 8-9. Sit-Up.

Figure 8-10. Starting the Shuttle Run.

RULES: Allow two trials with some rest between.

SCORING: Record the time of the better of the two trials to the nearest tenth of a second.

STANDING BROAD JUMP

EQUIPMENT: Mat, floor, or outdoor jumping pit, and tape measure.

DESCRIPTION: Pupils stands as indicated in Figure 8-11, with the feet several inches apart and the toes just behind the take-off line. Preparatory to jumping, the pupil swings the arms backward and bends the knees. The jump is accomplished by simultaneously extending the knees and swinging forward the arms.

RULES:

1. Allow three trials.

Figure 8-11. Measuring the Standing Broad Jump.

2. Measure from the take-off line to the heel or other part of the body that touches the floor nearest the take-off line (Figure 8-11).
3. When the test is given indoors, it is convenient to tape the tape measure to the floor at right angles to the take-off line and have the pupils jump along the tape. The scorer stands to the side and observes the mark to the nearest inch.

SCORING: Record the best of the three trials in feet and inches to the nearest inch.

50-YARD DASH

EQUIPMENT: Two stopwatches or one with a split-second timer.

DESCRIPTION: It is preferable to administer this test to two pupils at a time. Have both take positions behind the starting line. The starter will use the commands "Are you ready?" and "Go!" The latter will be accompanied by a downward sweep of the starter's arm to give a visual signal to the timer, who stands at the finish line (Figure 8-12).

RULES: The score is the amount of time between the starter's signal and the instant the pupil crosses the finish line.

SCORING: Record in seconds to the nearest tenth of a second.

SOFTBALL THROW FOR DISTANCE

EQUIPMENT: Softball (12-inch), small metal or wooden stakes, and tape measure.

DESCRIPTION: A football field marked in conventional fashion (5-yard

Figure 8-12. Starting the 50-Yard Dash.

intervals) makes an ideal area for this test. If this is not available, it is suggested that lines be drawn parallel to the restraining line, five yards apart. The pupil throws the ball while remaining within two parallel lines, 6 feet apart (Figure 8-13). Mark the point of landing with one of the small stakes. If his second or third throw is farther, move the stake accordingly so that, after three throws, the stake is at the point of the pupil's best throw. It was found expedient to have the pupil jog out to his stake and stand there; and then, after five pupils have completed their throws, the measurements were taken. By having the pupil at his particular stake, there is little danger of recording the wrong score.

RULES:
1. Only an overhand throw may be used.
2. Three throws are allowed.

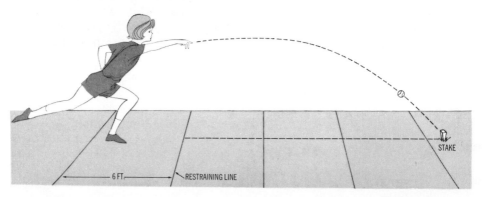

Figure 8-13. Measuring the Softball Throw for Distance. Wherever Ball Lands, Measure Distance Perpendicular to Starting Line.

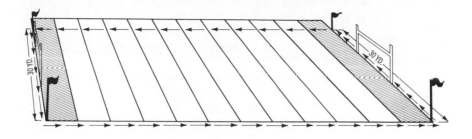

Figure 8-14. Using Football Field for 600-Yard Run-Walk.

3. The distance recorded is the distance measured at right angles from
   the point of landing to the restraining line (Figure 8-13).
SCORING: Record the best of the three trials to the nearest foot.

600-YARD RUN-WALK

EQUIPMENT: Track or area marked according to Figures 8-14 to 8-16, and
   stopwatch.
DESCRIPTION: Pupil uses a standing start. At the signal "Ready? Go!" the
   pupil starts running the 600-yard distance. The running may be in-
   terspersed with walking. It is possible to have a dozen pupils run at

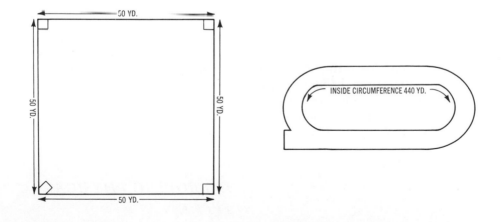

Figure 8-15. Using Any Open Area for 600-Yard
Run-Walk.

Figure 8-16. Using Inside Track for
600-Yard Run-Walk.

Table 8-3. Flexed Arm-Hang for Girls (Percentile Scores Based on Age, Test Scores in Seconds)

Percentile	Age								Percentile
	10	11	12	13	14	15	16	17	
100th	66	79	64	80	60	74	74	76	100th
95th	31	35	30	30	30	33	37	31	95th
90th	24	25	23	21	22	22	26	25	90th
85th	21	20	19	18	19	18	19	19	85th
80th	18	17	15	15	16	16	16	16	80th
75th	15	16	13	13	13	14	14	14	75th
70th	13	13	11	12	11	13	12	12	70th
65th	11	11	10	10	10	11	10	11	65th
60th	10	10	8	9	9	10	9	10	60th
55th	9	9	8	8	8	8	8	9	55th
50th	7	8	6	7	7	8	7	8	50th
45th	6	6	6	6	6	6	6	7	45th
40th	6	5	5	5	5	6	5	6	40th
35th	5	4	4	4	4	4	4	4	35th
30th	4	4	3	3	3	3	3	4	30th
25th	3	3	2	2	2	2	2	3	25th
20th	2	2	1	2	1	1	1	2	20th
15th	2	1	0	1	1	0	1	0	15th
10th	1	0	0	0	0	0	0	0	10th
5th	0	0	0	0	0	0	0	0	5th
0	0	0	0	0	0	0	0	0	0

one time by having the pupils pair off before the start of the event. Then each pupil listens for and remembers his partner's time as the latter crosses the finish. The timer merely calls out the times as the pupils cross the finish.

RULES: Walking is permitted, but the object is to cover the distance in the shortest possible time.

SCORING: Record in minutes and seconds.

IMPROVING PHYSICAL FITNESS

After tests have been given they must be analyzed. The teacher must study them in terms of group and individual status and achievement. He

Table 8-4. Sit-Up for Girls (Percentile Scores Based on Age, Test Scores in Number of Sit-Ups)

Percentile	Age								Percentile
	10	11	12	13	14	15	16	17	
100th	50	50	50	50	50	50	50	50	100th
95th	50	50	50	50	50	50	50	50	95th
90th	50	50	50	50	50	50	50	50	90th
85th	50	50	50	50	50	50	50	50	85th
80th	50	50	50	50	49	42	41	45	80th
75th	50	50	50	50	42	39	38	40	75th
70th	50	50	50	45	37	35	34	35	70th
65th	42	40	40	40	35	31	31	32	65th
60th	39	37	39	38	34	30	30	30	60th
55th	33	34	35	35	31	29	28	29	55th
50th	31	30	32	31	30	26	26	27	50th
45th	30	29	30	30	27	25	25	25	45th
40th	26	26	26	27	25	24	24	23	40th
35th	24	25	25	25	23	21	22	21	35th
30th	21	22	22	22	21	20	20	20	30th
25th	20	20	20	20	20	19	18	18	25th
20th	16	19	18	19	18	16	16	16	20th
15th	14	16	16	15	16	14	14	15	15th
10th	11	12	13	12	13	11	11	12	10th
5th	8	10	7	10	10	8	7	9	5th
0	0	0	0	0	0	0	0	0	

With permission of the American Association for Health, Physical Education and Recreation, 1201 Sixteenth St. N.W., Washington, D.C.

can ascertain which of the components of fitness were not adequately developed through the activities presented in the regular program. In the case of a few individuals who failed to meet minimum levels, he needs to talk with each child and make plans for individual improvement. The child needs to know that expectations for him are realistic. He should not be expected to catch up immediately with the rest of the class.

If a child is unable to achieve much success in tests, it is logical to assume that his attitude toward plunging into a strenuous exercise program may be apprehensive or negative. It is possible that the major reason for his poor level of fitness is just a poor attitude toward exercise or even a poor attitude which was fostered by his parents. Motivating the child toward a desire for a high fitness level is essential before any progress can be made.

First of all, the student must have some understanding of the factors

Table 8-5. Shuttle Run for Girls (Percentile Scores Based on Age, Test Scores in Seconds and Tenths)

Percentile	Age								Percentile
	10	11	12	113	14	15	16	17	
100th	8.5	8.8	9.0	8.3	9.0	8.0	8.3	9.0	100th
95th	10.0	10.0	10.0	10.0	10.0	10.0	10.0	10.0	95th
90th	10.5	10.2	10.2	10.2	10.3	10.3	10.2	10.3	90th
85th	10.8	10.6	10.5	10.5	10.4	10.5	10.4	10.4	85th
80th	11.0	10.9	10.8	10.6	10.5	10.7	10.6	10.5	80th
75th	11.0	11.0	10.9	10.8	10.6	10.9	10.8	10.6	75th
70th	11.1	11.0	11.0	11.0	10.8	11.0	10.9	10.8	70th
65th	11.4	11.2	11.2	11.0	10.9	11.0	11.0	11.0	65th
60th	11.5	11.4	11.3	11.1	11.0	11.1	11.0	11.0	60th
55th	11.8	11.6	11.5	11.3	11.1	11.2	11.2	11.1	55th
50th	11.9	11.7	11.6	11.4	11.3	11.3	11.2	11.2	50th
45th	12.0	11.8	11.8	11.6	11.4	11.5	11.4	11.4	45th
40th	12.0	12.0	11.9	11.8	11.5	11.6	11.5	11.5	40th
35th	12.1	12.0	12.0	12.0	11.7	11.8	11.8	11.6	35th
30th	12.4	12.1	12.1	12.0	12.0	11.9	12.0	11.8	30th
25th	12.6	12.4	12.3	12.2	12.0	12.0	12.0	12.0	25th
20th	12.8	12.6	12.5	12.5	12.3	12.3	12.2	12.0	20th
15th	13.0	13.0	12.9	13.0	12.6	12.5	12.5	12.3	15th
10th	13.1	13.4	13.2	13.3	13.1	13.0	13.0	13.0	10th
5th	14.0	14.1	13.9	14.0	13.9	13.5	13.9	13.8	5th
0	16.6	18.5	19.8	18.5	17.6	16.0	17.6	20.0	0

With permission of the American Association for Health, Physical Education and Recreation, 1201 Sixteenth St. N.W., Washington, D.C.

involved in fitness. A few children's books which describe fitness factors and the importance of fitness in the child's vocabulary are included in the bibliography. It would be wise for each elementary school to have copies of these books in the library. The teacher should encourage students to read books of this type, and they are excellent reference books for use in health instruction.

Many teachers fail to realize that most parents are very interested in their children becoming fit and will respond to helping their children at home if they understand the problem. Presentation of objective evidence of poor test results is quite convincing to those who may resist a general statement that their child is unfit. Together the child, the parents, and the teacher may set up a plan for specific types of exercises to be done at home as a supplement to the regular activities at school. If the child's physical condition is below par, and the program at school is

Table 8-6. Standing Broad Jump for Girls (Percentile Scores Based on Age, Test Scores in Feet and Inches)

Percen-Tile	10	11	12	Age 13	14	15	16	17	Percen-tile
100th	7' 0"	7'10"	8' 2"	7' 6"	7' 4"	7' 8"	7' 5"	7' 8"	100th
95th	5' 8"	6' 2"	6' 3"	6' 3"	6' 4"	6' 6"	6' 7"	6' 8"	95th
90th	5' 6"	5'10"	6' 0"	6' 0"	6' 2"	6' 3"	6' 4"	6' 4"	90th
85th	5' 4"	5' 8"	5' 9"	5'10"	6' 0"	6' 1"	6' 2"	6' 2"	85th
80th	5' 2"	5' 6"	5' 8"	5' 8"	5'10"	6' 0"	6' 0"	6' 0"	80th
75th	5' 1"	5' 4"	5' 6"	5' 6"	5' 9"	5'10"	5'10"	5'11"	75th
70th	5' 0"	5' 3"	5' 5"	5' 5"	5' 7"	5' 9"	5' 8"	5'10"	70th
65th	5' 0"	5' 2"	5' 4"	5' 4"	5' 6"	5' 7"	5' 7"	5' 9"	65th
60th	4'10"	5' 0"	5' 2"	5' 3"	5' 5"	5' 6"	5' 6"	5' 7"	60th
55th	4' 9"	5' 0"	5' 1"	5' 2"	5' 4"	5' 5"	5' 5"	5' 6"	55th
50th	4' 7"	4'10"	5' 0"	5' 0"	5' 3"	5' 4"	5' 4"	5' 5"	50th
45th	4' 6"	4' 9"	4'11"	5' 0"	5' 1"	5' 3"	5' 3"	5' 3"	45th
40th	4' 5"	4' 8"	4' 9"	4'10"	5' 0"	5' 1"	5' 2"	5' 2"	40th
35th	4' 4"	4' 7"	4' 8"	4' 8"	5' 0"	5' 0"	5' 0"	5' 0"	35th
30th	4' 3"	4' 6"	4' 7"	4' 6"	4' 9"	4'10"	4'11"	5' 0"	30th
25th	4' 2"	4' 4"	4' 5"	4' 6"	4' 8"	4' 8"	4'10"	4'10"	25th
20th	4' 0"	4' 3"	4' 4"	4' 4"	4' 6"	4' 7"	4' 8"	4' 9"	20th
15th	3'11"	4' 1"	4' 2"	4' 2"	4' 3"	4' 6"	4' 6"	4' 7"	15th
10th	3' 9"	3'11"	4' 0"	4' 0"	4' 1"	4' 4"	4' 4"	4' 5"	10th
5th	3' 6"	3' 9"	3' 8"	3' 9"	3'10"	4' 0"	4' 0"	4' 2"	5th
0	2' 8"	2'11"	2'11"	2'11"	3' 0"	2'11"	3' 2"	3' 0"	0

adequate, it stands to reason that the child's problem is unique and that he needs special attention to help solve his problem.

Explanation of physical fitness tests and guidelines for interpretation of the results may be made to parents at a P.T.A. or parents' room meeting early in the year. Thereafter, if a profile chart of each pupil's scores is sent home periodically, the parents will be much more interested and aware of the meaning of specific scores. If it is found that scores of many children are lower than those of national or state norms, it may be wise to prepare group profiles and present these to the parents. It may be that facilities, equipment, time allowed for physical education or preparation of the teachers are inadequate. After the parents become aware of and interested in the problems, they may exert their influence toward the improvement of the deficiencies.

Prerequisite to a fit school population of course is the opportunity

Table 8-7. 50-Yard Dash for Girls (Percentile Scores Based on Age, Test Scores in Seconds and Tenths)

Percentile	Age								Percentile
	10	11	12	13	14	15	16	17	
100th	6.0	6.0	5.9	6.0	6.0	6.4	6.0	6.4	100th
95th	7.0	7.0	7.0	7.0	7.0	7.1	7.0	7.1	95th
90th	7.3	7.4	7.3	7.3	7.2	7.3	7.3	7.3	90th
85th	7.5	7.6	7.5	7.5	7.4	7.5	7.5	7.5	85th
80th	7.7	7.7	7.6	7.6	7.5	7.6	7.5	7.6	80th
75th	7.9	7.9	7.8	7.7	7.6	7.7	7.7	7.8	75th
70th	8.0	8.0	7.9	7.8	7.7	7.8	7.9	7.9	70th
65th	8.1	8.0	8.0	7.9	7.8	7.9	8.0	8.0	65th
60th	8.2	8.1	8.0	8.0	7.9	8.0	8.0	8.0	60th
55th	8.4	8.2	8.1	8.0	8.0	8.0	8.1	8.1	55th
50th	8.5	8.4	8.2	8.1	8.0	8.1	8.3	8.2	50th
45th	8.6	8.5	8.3	8.2	8.2	8.2	8.4	8.3	45th
40th	8.8	8.5	8.4	8.4	8.3	8.3	8.5	8.5	40th
35th	8.9	8.6	8.5	8.5	8.5	8.4	8.6	8.6	35th
30th	9.0	8.8	8.7	8.6	8.6	8.6	8.8	8.8	30th
25th	9.0	9.0	8.9	8.8	8.9	8.8	9.0	9.0	25th
20th	9.2	9.0	9.0	9.0	9.0	9.0	9.0	9.0	20th
15th	9.4	9.2	9.2	9.2	9.2	9.0	9.2	9.1	15th
10th	9.6	9.6	9.5	9.5	9.5	9.5	9.9	9.5	10th
5th	10.0	10.0	10.0	10.2	10.4	10.0	10.5	10.4	5th
0	14.0	13.0	13.0	15.7	16.0	18.0	17.0	12.0	0

With permission of the American Association for Health, Physical Education and Recreation, 1201 Sixteenth St. N.W., Washington, D.C.

for children to exercise. A daily instructional physical education period of adequate length should be a part of the total school organizational plan. Thirty minutes for grades one through four, and forty-five minutes for grades five through eight should be allotted to instructional programs. This should be supplemented with provision for after-school activities. Special interest groups or remedial groups provide opportunities for improving fitness. Children who need special help may feel better pursuing remedial work with others with similar problems.

Isolated exercises are not the only means of building physical fitness. In fact, isolating a specific part of the lesson as fitness exercise time may be more harmful than helpful. Children should recognize that the play activities they enjoy contribute to development of physical fitness. Apparatus work, basic movement skill work, stunts and tumbling, active games, work with small equipment, and dance activities can be planned in a progression and sequence where all muscle groups of the body are

Table 8-8. Softball Throw for Girls (Percentile Scores Based on Age, Test Scores in Feet)

Percen-tile				Age					Percen-tile
	10	11	12	13	14	15	16	17	
100th	16/	141	159	150	156	165	175	183	100th
95th	84	95	103	111	114	120	123	120	95th
90th	76	86	96	102	103	110	113	108	90th
85th	71	81	90	94	100	105	104	102	85th
80th	69	77	85	90	95	100	98	98	80th
75th	65	74	80	86	90	95	92	93	75th
70th	60	71	76	82	87	90	89	90	70th
65th	57	66	74	79	84	87	85	87	65th
60th	54	64	70	75	80	84	81	82	60th
55th	52	62	67	73	78	82	78	80	55th
50th	50	59	64	70	75	78	75	75	50th
45th	48	57	61	68	72	75	74	74	45th
40th	46	55	59	65	70	73	71	71	40th
35th	45	52	57	63	68	69	69	69	35th
30th	42	50	54	60	65	66	66	66	30th
25th	40	46	50	57	61	64	63	62	25th
20th	37	44	48	53	59	60	60	58	20th
15th	34	40	45	49	54	58	55	52	15th
10th	30	37	41	45	50	51	50	48	10th
5th	21	32	37	36	45	45	45	40	5th
0	8	13	20	20	25	12	8	20	0

With permission of the American Association for Health, Physical Education and Recreation, 1201 Sixteenth St. N.W., Washington, D.C.

challenged and the tempo and intensity of them are stepped up to a challenging point for everyone according to his needs. In terms of endurance there is hardly a more challenging activity than a vigorous folk dance.

Exercises for fitness

Although the author does not propose an elaborate program of exercises for developing fitness in the elementary school, there may be a need for such in some situations due to lack of time, facilities, and equipment for a well-rounded program. There may be a need to build up children who have had no previous opportunity for activity which develops fitness qualities. Learning how to do a number of exercises is valuable to children from several viewpoints:

Table 8-9. 600-Yard Run-Walk for Girls (Percentile Scores Based on Age, Test Scores in Minutes and Seconds)

Percen- tile	10	11	12	Age 13	14	15	16	17	Percen- tile
100th	1'42"	1'40"	1'39"	1'40"	1'45"	1'40"	1'50"	1'54"	100th
95th	2' 5"	2'13"	2'14"	2'12"	2' 9"	2' 9"	2'10"	2'11"	95th
90th	2'15"	2'19"	2'20"	2'19"	2'18"	2'18"	2'17"	2'22"	90th
85th	2'20"	2'24"	2'24"	2'25"	2'22"	2'23"	2'23"	2'27"	85th
80th	2'26"	2'28"	2'27"	2'29"	2'25"	2'26"	2'26"	2'31"	80th
75th	2'30"	2'32"	2'31"	2'33"	2'30"	2'28"	2'31"	2'34"	75th
70th	2'34"	2'36"	2'35"	2'37"	2'34"	2'34"	2'36"	2'37"	70th
65th	2'37"	2'39"	2'39"	2'40"	2'37"	2'36"	2'39"	2'42"	65th
60th	2'41"	2'43"	2'42"	2'44"	2'41"	2'40"	2'42"	2'46"	60th
55th	2'45"	2'47"	2'45"	2'47"	2'44"	2'43"	2'45"	2'49"	55th
50th	2'48"	2'49"	2'49"	2'52"	2'46"	2' 46"	2'49"	2'51"	50th
45th	2'50"	2'53"	2'55"	2'56"	2'51"	2'49"	2'53"	2'57"	45th
40th	2'55"	2'59"	2'58"	3' 0"	2'55"	2'52"	2'56"	3' 0"	40th
35th	2'59"	3' 4"	3' 3"	3' 3"	3' 0"	2'56"	2'59"	3' 5"	35th
30th	3' 3"	3'10"	3' 7"	3' 9"	3' 6"	3' 0"	3' 1"	3'10"	30th
25th	3' 8"	3'15"	3'11"	3'15"	3'12"	3' 5"	3' 7"	3'16"	25th
20th	3'13"	3'22"	3'18"	3'20"	3'19"	3'10"	3'12"	3'22"	20th
15th	3'18"	3'30"	3'24"	3'30"	3'30"	3'18"	3'19"	3'29"	15th
10th	3'27"	3'41"	3'40"	3'49"	3'48"	3'28"	3'30"	3'41"	10th
5th	3'45"	3'59"	4' 0"	4'11"	4' 8"	3'56"	3'45"	3'56"	5th
0	4'47"	4'53"	5'10"	5'10"	5'50"	5'10"	5'52"	6'40"	0

With permission of the American Association for Health, Physical Education and Recreation, 1201 Sixteenth St. N.W., Washington, D.C.

1. An understanding of the need for a warm-up period before strenuous exercise may be developed. Learning the progression of starting from slow, rhythmical stretching and swinging movements to faster, more vigorous movements can be accomplished through a guided exercise series.
2. A brief exercise or calisthenic routine at the start of the period should provide exercise for all muscle groups, since the activity done in the rest of the period may not provide this opportunity.
3. If exercises are learned correctly, benefit will be gained from them.
4. One should build a repertoire of exercises that one may do on his own when it is not possible to do more vigorous big muscle activity due to time, space, weather. It is hoped that this will be carried into adulthood and even that a child will teach his parents the exercise habit.

Table 8-10. Pull-Up for Boys (Percentile Scores Based on Age, Test Scores in Number of Pull-Ups)

Percentile				Age					Percentile
	10	11	12	13	14	15	16	17	
100th	16	20	15	24	20	25	25	32	100th
95th	8	8	9	10	12	13	14	16	95th
90th	7	7	7	9	10	11	13	14	90th
85th	6	6	6	8	10	10	12	12	85th
80th	5	5	5	7	8	10	11	12	80th
75th	4	4	5	6	8	9	10	10	75th
70th	4	4	4	5	7	8	10	10	70th
65th	3	3	3	5	6	7	9	10	65th
60th	3	3	3	4	6	7	9	9	60th
55th	3	2	3	4	5	6	8	8	55th
50th	2	2	2	3	5	6	7	8	50th
45th	2	2	2	3	4	5	6	7	45th
40th	1	1	1	2	4	5	6	7	40th
35th	1	1	1	2	3	4	5	6	35th
30th	1	1	1	1	3	4	5	5	30th
25th	0	0	0	1	2	3	4	5	25th
20th	0	0	0	0	2	3	4	4	20th
15th	0	0	0	0	1	2	3	4	15th
10th	0	0	0	0	0	1	2	2	10th
5th	0	0	0	0	0	0	0	1	5th
0	0	0	0	0	0	0	0	0	0

With permission of the American Association for Health, Physical Education and Recreation, 1201 Sixteenth St. N.W., Washington, D.C.

In order that exercises are valuable, certain principles of exercise should be heeded.

1. Exercise must be done consistently and regularly. If practice ceases, strength and endurance are lost almost as quickly as they are gained.
2. To increase strength or endurance the overload principle must be employed. The number of times an exercise is done must be increased, the tempo at which it is done must be increased, and the resistance which is offered must be increased if gains are to be made.
3. Exercises must be strenuous and vigorous. They must be done with purposeful movement. A child must be encouraged to make a genuine effort; he must not quit when he feels the first signs of being tired.
4. A child must be motivated to do exercises well. Acquisition of skill is important here too, since speed cannot precede control, and lack of success does not contribute to the desire to work harder and longer.

Table 8-11. Sit-Up for Boys (Percentile Scores Based on Age, Test Scores in Number of Sit-Ups)

Percentile	Age								Percentile
	10	11	12	13	14	15	16	17	
100th	100	100	100	100	100	100	100	100	100th
95th	100	100	100	100	100	100	100	100	95th
90th	100	100	100	100	100	100	100	100	90th
85th	100	100	100	100	100	100	100	100	85th
80th	76	89	100	100	100	100	100	100	80th
75th	65	73	93	100	100	100	100	100	75th
70th	57	60	75	99	100	100	100	100	70th
65th	51	55	70	90	99	100	99	99	65th
60th	50	50	59	75	99	99	99	85	60th
55th	49	50	52	70	77	90	85	77	55th
50th	41	46	50	60	70	80	76	70	50th
45th	37	40	49	53	62	70	70	62	45th
40th	34	35	42	50	60	61	63	57	40th
35th	30	31	40	50	52	54	56	51	35th
30th	28	30	35	41	50	50	50	50	30th
25th	25	26	30	38	45	49	50	45	25th
20th	23	23	28	35	40	42	42	40	20th
15th	20	20	25	30	36	39	38	35	15th
10th	15	17	20	25	30	33	34	30	10th
5th	11	12	15	20	24	27	28	23	5th
0	1	0	0	1	6	5	10	8	00

With permission of the American Association for Health, Physical Education and Recreation, 1201 Sixteenth St. N.W., Washington, D.C.

Skillful movements save energy. Knowledge that his efforts are being productive is also motivating. Retests should be given frequently enough for a child to realize what gains he has made from his efforts.

5. Exercise periods should be reasonable in length and allow for individual differences in tolerance for exercise. Feeling stiff and uncomfortable after exercises will not prove very motivating for future sessions.

Presenting exercises

Exercises may be presented formally or informally. If a series is to be done by the group or by the individual at the start of each lesson, it is wise to build a routine by making a formal presentation until children can conduct exercises by themselves. A few guidelines are offered here:

1. Build awareness of space needed for exercises. If a leader is respon-

Table 8-12. Shuttle Run for Boys (Percentile Scores Based on Age, Test Scores in Seconds and Tenths)

Percentile	10	11	12	13	14	15	16	17	Percentile
					Age				
100th	9.0	9.0	8.5	8.0	8.3	8.0	8.1	8.0	100th
95th	10.0	10.0	9.8	9.5	9.3	9.1	9.0	8.9	95th
90th	10.2	10.1	10.0	9.8	9.5	9.3	9.1	9.0	90th
85th	10.4	10.3	10.0	9.9	9.6	9.4	9.2	9.1	85th
80th	10.5	10.4	10.2	10.0	9.8	9.5	9.3	9.2	80th
75th	10.7	10.5	10.3	10.1	9.9	9.6	9.5	9.3	75th
70th	10.8	10.7	10.5	10.2	9.9	9.7	9.5	9.4	70th
65th	10.9	10.8	10.6	10.3	10.0	9.8	9.6	9.5	65th
60th	11.0	10.9	10.7	10.4	10.0	9.8	9.7	9.6	60th
55th	11.0	11.0	10.9	10.5	10.2	9.9	9.8	9.7	55th
50th	11.2	11.1	11.0	10.6	10.2	10.0	9.9	9.8	50th
45th	11.4	11.2	11.0	10.8	10.3	10.0	10.0	9.9	45th
40th	11.5	11.3	11.1	10.9	10.5	10.1	10.0	10.0	40th
35th	11.6	11.4	11.3	11.0	10.5	10.2	10.1	10.0	35th
30th	11.8	11.6	11.5	11.1	10.7	10.3	10.2	10.1	30th
25th	12.0	11.8	11.6	11.3	10.9	10.5	10.4	10.4	25th
20th	12.0	12.0	11.9	11.5	11.0	10.6	10.5	10.6	20th
15th	12.2	12.1	12.0	11.8	11.2	10.9	10.8	10.9	15th
10th	12.6	12.4	12.4	12.0	11.3	11.1	11.1	11.2	10th
5th	13.1	13.0	13.0	12.5	12.0	11.7	11.5	11.7	5th
0	15.0	20.0	22.0	16.0	16.0	16.6	16.7	14.0	0

With permission of the American Association for Health, Physical Education and Recreation, 1201 Sixteenth St. N.W., Washington, D.C.

sible for directing exercises, a formation should be set up that allows everyone to see the leader. It is best to use a scattered formation in which everyone makes a quarter turn and faces the leader. Once the formation is learned, children can quickly assume it, and little time is wasted starting the class.

2. The teacher should establish a routine that student leaders may follow.
   a. Announce name of exercise.
   b. Assume starting position for exercise. (If exercise is new demonstrate it several times.)
   c. Give signal "Ready and one, two. . . ." First move starts on "one."
   d. Count cadence loudly. Most exercises are done to a two-beat count, or a four-beat count. Words may be substituted in rhythm, such as "Down, up; down, up."

Table 8-13. Standing Broad Jump for Boys (Percentile Scores Based on Age, Test Scores in Feet and Inches)

Percentile	Age								Percentile
	10	11	12	13	14	15	16	17	
100th	6' 8"	10' 0"	7'10"	8' 9"	8'11"	9' 2"	9' 1"	9' 8"	100th
95th	6' 1"	6' 3"	6' 6"	7' 2"	7' 9"	8' 0"	8' 5"	8' 6"	95th
90th	5'10"	6' 0"	6' 4"	6'11"	7' 5"	7' 9"	8' 1"	8' 3"	90th
85th	5' 8"	5'10"	6' 2"	6' 9"	7' 3"	7' 6"	7'11"	8' 1"	85th
80th	5' 7"	5' 9"	6' 1"	6' 7"	7' 0"	7' 6"	7' 9"	8' 0"	80th
75th	5' 6"	5' 7"	6' 0"	6' 5"	6'11"	7' 4"	7' 7"	7'10"	75th
70th	5' 5"	5' 6"	5'11"	6' 3"	6' 9"	7' 2"	7' 6"	7' 8"	70th
65th	5' 4"	5' 6"	5' 9"	6' 1"	6' 8"	7' 1"	7' 5"	7' 7"	65th
60th	5' 2"	5' 4"	5' 8"	6' 0"	6' 7"	7' 0"	7' 4"	7' 6"	60th
55th	5' 1"	5' 3"	5' 7"	5'11"	6' 6"	6'11"	7' 3"	7' 5"	55th
50th	5' 0"	5' 2"	5' 6"	5'10"	6' 4"	6' 9"	7' 1"	7' 3"	50th
45th	5' 0"	5' 1"	5' 5"	5' 9"	6' 3"	6' 8"	7' 0"	7' 2"	45th
40th	4'10"	5' 0"	5' 4"	5' 7"	6' 1"	6' 6"	6'11"	7' 0"	40th
35th	4'10"	4'11"	5' 2"	5' 6"	6' 0"	6' 6"	6' 9"	6'11"	35th
30th	4' 8"	4'10"	5' 1"	5' 5"	5'10"	6' 4"	6' 7"	6'10"	30th
25th	4' 6"	4' 8"	5' 0"	5' 3"	5' 8"	6' 3"	6' 6"	6' 8"	25th
20th	4' 5"	4' 7"	4'10"	5' 2"	5' 6"	6' 1"	6' 4"	6' 6"	20th
15th	4' 4"	4' 5"	4' 8"	5' 0"	5' 4"	5'10"	6' 1"	6' 4"	15th
10th	4' 3"	4' 2"	4' 5"	4' 9"	5' 2"	5' 7"	5'11"	6' 0"	10th
5th	4' 0"	4' 0"	4' 2"	4' 5"	4'11"	5' 4"	5' 6"	5' 8"	5th
0	2'10"	1' 8"	3' 0"	2' 9"	3' 8"	2'10"	2' 2"	3' 7"	0

    e. Do the exercise in good form with the class.

    f. Give class signal to stop and rest a few minutes before going on to next exercise.

3. The leader should not accept sloppy, half-hearted movement. Good, quick, crisp counting and explicit directions usually eliminate this.

    Specific exercises can be presented to children in an informal manner by using an indirect or problem-solving approach. The teacher may select an exercise and build a series of questions around the directions for the exercise. He must first get the children into the correct starting position, then proceed with the challenges or questions. For example: in teaching the situp he might say, "Lying flat on your back, can you curl up and touch your toes? Can you touch your right toe with your left hand? With your hands clasped behind your head, can you bend your knees then sit up and touch your right elbow to your left knee? Are your feet flat on the floor? How many times can you do this without stopping?"

    This is one way for a beginning teacher to develop the exploratory

Table 8-14. 50-yard Dash for Boys (Percentile Scores Based on Age, Test Scores in Seconds and Tenths)

Percen-tile	10	11	12	13	14	15	16	17	Percen-tile
				Age					
100th	6.0	6.0	6.0	5.8	5.8	5.6	5.6	5.6	100th
95th	7.0	7.0	6.8	6.5	6.3	6.1	6.0	6.0	95th
90th	7.1	7.2	7.0	6.7	6.4	6.2	6.1	6.0	90th
85th	7.4	7.4	7.0	6.9	6.6	6.4	6.2	6.1	85th
80th	7.5	7.5	7.2	7.0	6.7	6.5	6.3	6.2	80th
75th	7.6	7.6	7.3	7.0	6.8	6.5	6.3	6.3	75th
70th	7.8	7.7	7.5	7.1	6.9	6.6	6.4	6.3	70th
65th	8.0	7.8	7.5	7.2	7.0	6.7	6.5	6.4	65th
60th	8.0	7.8	7.6	7.3	7.0	6.7	6.5	6.5	60th
55th	8.1	8.0	7.8	7.4	7.0	6.8	6.6	6.5	55th
50th	8.2	8.0	7.8	7.5	7.1	6.9	6.7	6.6	50th
45th	8.3	8.0	7.9	7.5	7.2	7.0	6.7	6.7	45th
40th	8.5	8.1	8.0	7.6	7.2	7.0	6.8	6.7	40th
35th	8.5	8.3	8.0	7.7	7.3	7.1	6.9	6.8	35th
30th	8.7	8.4	8.2	7.9	7.5	7.1	6.9	6.9	30th
25th	8.8	8.5	8.3	8.0	7.6	7.2	7.0	7.0	25th
20th	9.0	8.7	8.4	8.0	7.8	7.3	7.1	7.0	20th
15th	9.1	9.0	8.6	8.2	8.0	7.5	7.2	7.1	15th
10th	9.5	9.1	8.9	8.4	9.1	7.7	7.5	7.3	10th
5th	10.0	9.5	9.2	8.9	8.6	8.1	7.8	7.7	5th
0	12.0	11.9	12.0	11.1	11.6	12.0	8.6	10.6	0

approach. If he works from the directions of a skill or exercise he can structure good learning experiences. With experience he can become more creative and inventive. Caution must be taken that each child does the exercise in the way it was intended to be done and vigorously enough to be of value. Too often beginning teachers do not ascertain whether each child is benefiting from exercise taught in this fashion. They concentrate on the questions and not the answers in movement.

Selecting activities to develop fitness

Activities must be selected which will provide for maintenance and development of strength in the major muscle areas, flexibility in the major joints, and general endurance. Running provides one of the best exercises or activities for the development of endurance. Since children love

Table 8-15. Softball Throw for Boys (Percentile Scores Based on Age, Test Scores in Feet)

Percen- tile	10	11	12	13	Age 14	15	16	17	Percen- tile
100th	175	205	207	245	246	250	271	291	100th
95th	138	151	165	195	208	221	238	249	95th
90th	127	141	156	183	195	210	222	235	90th
85th	122	136	150	175	187	204	213	226	85th
80th	118	129	145	168	181	198	207	218	80th
75th	114	126	141	163	176	192	201	213	75th
70th	109	121	136	157	172	189	197	207	70th
65th	105	119	133	152	168	184	194	203	65th
60th	102	115	129	147	165	180	189	198	60th
55th	98	113	124	142	160	175	185	195	55th
50th	96	111	120	140	155	171	180	190	50th
45th	93	108	119	135	150	167	175	185	45th
40th	91	105	115	131	146	165	172	180	40th
35th	89	101	112	128	141	160	168	176	35th
30th	84	98	110	125	138	156	165	171	30th
25th	81	94	106	120	133	152	160	163	25th
20th	78	90	103	115	127	147	153	155	20th
15th	73	85	97	110	122	141	147	150	15th
10th	69	78	92	101	112	135	141	141	10th
5th	60	70	76	88	102	123	127	117	5th
0	35	14	25	50	31	60	30	31	0

With permission of the American Association for Health, Physical Education and Recreation, 1201 Sixteenth St. N.W., Washington, D.C.

to run, some variation of running might be included in every lesson. Distance running may precede each lesson and serve two purposes, building endurance and releasing energy and tension. Running may be done in place, around the gym or in a prescribed area outside. Suggestions for variations of running may be found on pages 232–233.

Exercises for development of specific physical components are given in Chapter XIV. Suggestions are given for making each progressively more difficult or demanding. These may serve as a source for building an exercise program for individuals or a series for warmups, maintenance, or building fitness for the class.

Summary

It is readily apparent that a good state of fitness is vital to the health and happiness of individuals and to the vitality of a nation. Fitness and fitness activities are not reserved for children and youth; however, it is

Table 8-16. 600-Yard Run-Walk for Boys (Percentile Scores Based on Age, Test Scores in Minutes and Seconds)

Percentile	Age								Percentile
	10	11	12	13	14	15	16	17	
100th	1'30"	1'27"	1'31"	1'29"	1'25"	1'26"	1'24"	1'23"	100th
95th	1'58"	1'59"	1'52"	1'46"	1'37"	1'34"	1'32"	1'31"	95th
90th	2' 9"	2' 3"	2' 0"	1'50"	1'42"	1'38"	1'35"	1'34"	90th
85th	2'12"	2' 8"	2' 2"	1'53"	1'46"	1'40"	1'37"	1'36"	85th
80th	2'15"	2'11"	2' 5"	1'55"	1'48"	1'42"	1'39"	1'38"	80th
75th	2'18"	2'14"	2' 9"	1'59"	1'51"	1'44"	1'40"	1'40"	75th
70th	2'20"	2'16"	2'11"	2' 1"	1'53"	1'46"	1'43"	1'42"	70th
65th	2'23"	2'19"	2'13"	2' 3"	1'55"	1'47"	1'45"	1'44"	65th
60th	2'26"	2'21"	2'15"	2' 5"	1'57"	1'49"	1'47"	1'45"	60th
55th	2'30"	2'24"	2'18"	2' 7"	1'59"	1'51"	1'49"	148	55th
50th	2'33"	2'27"	2'21"	2'10"	2' 1"	1'54"	1'51"	1'50"	50th
45th	2'36"	2'30"	2'24"	2'12"	2' 3"	1'55"	1'53"	1'52"	45th
40th	2'40"	2'33"	2'26"	2'15"	2' 5"	1'58"	1'56"	1'54"	40th
35th	2'43"	2'36"	2'30"	2'17"	2' 9"	2' 0"	1'58"	1'57"	35th
30th	2'45"	2'39"	2"34"	2'22"	2'11"	2' 3"	2' 1"	2' 0"	30th
25th	2'49"	2'42"	2'39"	2'25"	2'14"	2' 7"	2' 5"	2' 4"	25th
20th	2'55"	2'48"	2'47"	2'30"	2'19"	2'13"	2' 9"	2' 9"	20th
15th	3' 1"	2'55"	2'57"	2'35"	2'25"	2'20"	2'14"	2'16"	15th
10th	3' 8"	3' 9"	3' 8	2 45	2 55	2'02"	2'22"	2'26"	10th
5th	3'23"	3'30"	3'32"	3' 3"	2'47"	2'50"	2'37"	2'40"	5th
0	4'58"	5' 6"	4'55"	5'14"	5'10"	4'10"	4' 9"	4'45"	0

With permission of the American Association for Health, Physical Education and Recreation, 1201 Sixteenth St. N.W., Washington, D.C.

the responsibility of the school to build a positive attitude toward fitness, a knowledge and understanding of the components of fitness, and the skills to maintain fitness. In order to do this, the schools must provide a comprehensive physical education program. Within this program there must be provisions for identifying children who are physically underdeveloped and opportunities provided for their improvement. A well-balanced comprehensive program of activities must be offered which provides for natural growth and development of strength and circulatory-respiratory endurance, flexibility, and other aspects of physical fitness.

The teacher should be familiar with all of the various factors and components which are involved in physical fitness and know how a child's level in each of the areas may be improved. He should recognize the interrelationship between a child's physical fitness level and his ability to move. Physical fitness level is truly one of the foundations of good movement skills.

SUGGESTED REFERENCES
FOR FURTHER STUDY

American Association for Health, Physical Education and Recreation, *Youth Fitness Test Manual* (Washington, D.C., National Education Association, 1966).

Bucher, Charles A., "What Can Parents Do? (About Their Child's Health and Fitness)," *National Education Association Journal* (February, 1962).

Espenschade, Anna, "Why Be Physically Fit?," *National Education Association Journal* (February, 1962).

Hunsicker, Paul, *Physical Fitness: What Research Says to The Teacher,* #26 (Washington, D.C., Department of Classroom Teachers, National Education Association, 1963).

Kelly, Ellen Davis, *Teaching Posture and Body Mechanics* (New York, Ronald, 1949).

President's Council on Youth Fitness, *Youth Physical Fitness* (Washington, D.C., Superintendent of Documents, 1960).

Vermes, Hal G., *The Boy's Book of Physical Fitness* (New York, Associated Press, 1961).

Vermes, Jean, *The Girl's Book of Physical Fitness* (New York, Associated Press, 1961).

Walsh, John E., *The First Book of Physical Fitness* (New York, F. Watts, 1961).

Chapter IX

ANALYSIS OF BASIC MOVEMENT

Movement education

Factors of movement study

Analysis of fundamental skills

Locomotor movements

Combinations of basic locomotor movements

Nonlocomotor movements

Basic catching, throwing, and striking patterns

In the primary grades most of the program time is directed toward the provision of many varied experiences with basic movement skills in order to have each child become aware of his body potential and develop a natural ease and confidence in general movement. At the same time he learns the mechanical principles which govern the movements of the body and the methods by which he can approach and solve new motor skill problems. In this way a foundation is laid for application of these knowledges to the learning of work skills and the various game, sport, and dance activities which are the basis of the active leisure time pursuits of the adolescent and adult.

There are several basic skill-patterns which are common to all movement activities. Specific work, sport, dance, and apparatus skills are but combinations of these basic patterns adapted and interrelated for specific purposes. It is essential that in the first three grades, children learn how to do the basic skills and understand the factors that affect the proper execution of them. In this and subsequent chapters many references to similarities between and uses of skills are made; most refer to sports, gymnastics, and dance activities, since these constitute the major content of the physical education program in the upper grades and in high school.

No matter what method or approach the teacher utilizes in facilitating the learning of the basic skills, it is imperative that he know all of the elements relative to the successful execution of them in order to analyze and correct faulty performance. As was stated previously, most children have experienced the skill before they are in a physical education class. Thus, the introduction of the skills is not as vital as is the analyzing of errors and the assistance in eliminating them at the early stages of practice and application.

There are two major aspects of all skill learning which the teacher must consider when planning and conducting lessons. One is quality of performance and the other is variety in use of skills.

Quality of performance

A primary grade child learns as the teacher presents skills in their own form, or guides the child into exploring what the body can do and helps him discover the proper execution of a particular skill. Whatever the method or the variation or the factors that are brought to bear on the execution of the skill, performance of poor quality is not acceptable, except in the experimental stages. Regardless of how imaginatively or creatively the method has led the child to perform, certain basic principles of correct fundamentals of execution or procedure must be retained in the performance. The teacher must elicit a high quality of work through the proper introduction of the skill or problem, followed by careful observation and evaluation of progress and subsequent coaching. He can do this only after he carefully studies the skill and proposes problems which, when properly solved, will lead to the correct execution of skills.

Since what is good performance for one child may not be for another, no one standard of performance can be adapted for a whole class. The standard for the class is safety. The standard for the individual is progressive improvement. Proficiency and finesse will come with practice.

Variety in use of skills

The importance of variety in use of skills lies in the fact that the primary grades are the years for laying the foundation of understanding, adaptability, and confidence for all motor skills that the child will encounter. At this time he learns what the body is capable of doing, the influences of other factors upon movement, and the joy of movement. Later, when he encounters new skill combinations, games, or other new situations which call for adaptation of the basic skills, his experiences in exploration in a variety of forms will prove invaluable. This is not to say that one will automatically learn new skills well because one does others well, for it is believed that skill learning is specific to each new skill. However, control of the body, a sense of timing, and general coordination which results from a good foundation of varied experiences with basic skill work will lend a readiness and capability to learn new skills quickly.

An example of variety of use of skills in the second grade is the development of running throughout a series of lessons. The class may be given problems in running as fast as possible, as slow as possible, fast then slow, running in a straight line, in a circle, in a zigzag pattern, with a long stride, with a short stride, with many stops and starts, with a partner, holding hands with two people, and many other variations. In these instances he is concentrating on the skill of running. A chasing and tagging game like Chinese Wall (p. 335) could be played during any one of the periods. Here the child will have to change speed, direction, and length of stride as he runs, but he must also concentrate on dodging the tagger and watching for one or more taggers as he runs. His first experiences of concentrating on running will enable him to run in the necessary patterns confidently and efficiently while he also thinks of his other tasks. Later, this same game may be played, but one must hold hands with a partner while running and fleeing; this increases the difficulty of the game.

Other games of low organization requiring more variations of running and additional tasks are played in subsequent grades. In the upper grades these same children will learn games like soccer and hockey where they must run down a field at varying speeds, change directions quickly whenever the ball does, work with ten other players, avoid opponents, and at the same time adapt to handling the ball with the foot, or in the case of hockey, a stick and a ball. In this instance the values of good running skills and confident movement gained in earlier years is apparent.

MOVEMENT EDUCATION

In recent years the physical education program in American elementary schools has been greatly influenced by programs of English physical educators. These people place a great deal of stress on studying basic movement at an early age through a developmental and an exploratory approach.

This influence reflects several factors operative in American education. There has been a trend in all subject areas in the elementary school toward a developmental approach and the use of exploration and experimentation as a method of teaching. More information on the growth and development of children is available. More state legislation calling for physical education in the elementary school curriculum has been enacted in the last few years. Due to these and other changes, physical educators became increasingly interested in elementary school methods and curriculum.

As a result of several years of study, conferences, exchange teachers, and publications dealing with movement education, or movement exploration as it is called by some, there has been a definite pattern of acceptance of the English method and content in American elementary school physical education programs. There have been many modifications, and there is much diversity in use of terminology, but there appears to be wide agreement that the movement education approach is most agreeable to the developmental concept of education in America. Movement education or movement exploration is not physical education in the elementary school but it is one approach to teaching basic skills or new skills and related aspects of movement.

The work of Rudolph Laban [1] is the basis for the modern concept of the structure and development of the importance of basic movement education. The concept of a structure for studying movement as presented in the following pages is an oversimplification of Laban's analysis of movement; however, his basic theories are utilized. This structure is a result of practical application and experience with many elementary school children.

As exploration is an approach or a method of teaching, only the content and factors affecting movement are discussed in this chapter. Methods are discussed in Chapter IV.

FACTORS OF MOVEMENT STUDY

All basic movement is studied in terms of four factors: Qualities of Movement, Space, Body Actions, Relationships.

Qualities of movement

In the performance of all movement skills the body must make adjustments to the factors of time, force, pattern, and flow—all of these being dependent upon the purpose of the movement.

Time

Time refers to the speed at which a movement takes place. The extreme degrees of time are sudden and sustained. There are many instances in games and sports when a sudden explosive movement means the differ-

[1] Rudolph Laban, *Modern Educational Dance* (London, MacDonald and Evans, 1948).

Table 9-1. Factors of Movement Study

QUALITIES OF MOVEMENT	SPACE	BODY ACTIONS	RELATIONSHIPS
Time	*Direction*	*Nonlocomotor skills*	*Partner*
Sudden Acceleration	Forward	Twist Turn	Small group
Fast Slow Deceleration	Backward	Stretch Bend	Large group
Sustained	Sideward	Swing Lift	Team or side
	Diagnona	Push Pull	
Force	Upward	Fall	*Objects*
Light	Downward	Various combinations	Small equipment
Heavy			Apparatus
	Level	*Locomotor skills*	
Body shape	High	Walk Run	
Direct	Medium	Jump Hop	
Twisted	Low	Leap Skip	
		Slide	
Flow		Various combinations	
Free		Weight bearing	
Bound		Initiating movement	
		Receiving weight	
		Transferring weight	

General — Personal

225

ence between beating an opponent on the take-off, reaching a ball that otherwise would have been just out-of-reach, or a quick dodge in running games. Sustained movement allows a person to continue moving while still in control of the body, yet capable of changing speed if necessary. There are many variations of time between these two extremes. The ability to accelerate with ease comes with an awareness of how to control the body.

Force

Force refers to the tension of the muscles of the body and the degree of strength needed for a certain movement. Experiences in moving lightly, or heavily, will help a child to control the tension of muscles only to the extent that is needed to fulfill the purpose of a task. For example, contrast the force needed to push an empty box as opposed to that needed to push a box of sand; or the amount of force needed to get up on a high bench as opposed to that needed to jump from it. In the latter the tension of the muscles has to be little, yet not completely absent in order to make the landing light but controlled.

Body shape

Body shape refers to the way in which the body moves through space, with a straight or direct path, or with a twisted or flexible path. There are many variations between direct and twisted. The direct manner is the most economical and fastest. Contrast the movement of jumping up to reach a basketball as it rebounds off the backboard with that of a fish flop (p. 526) where the feet must lead, and all parts of the body must snap into action in sequence to gain force and balance to get up on the feet.

Flow

Flow refers to the sequence of actions and the transition from one position to another. There can be a smooth, controlled series of movements joined together which give continuity to the pattern. *Free flow* describes a movement which must continue to a controlled conclusion, while a *bound flow* is movement which can be stopped and balance maintained at any time. For example, a routine on a piece of apparatus, no matter how simple or complex, calls for both free and bound flow. Each exercise on the equipment must flow together in a continuous pattern; however, each exercise may involve a movement that calls for building momentum to a point where momentum must be checked and a certain position sustained for a period of time before the movement is completed. Many experiences of work with skills and flow lead to efficient, graceful movement.

Space

All movement takes place in space which in itself may be quite varied. The amount of space available demands many adjustments in the performance of specific skills. There are two kinds of space. *Personal* space is the space about or around an individual which can be utilized when he is in a stationary position. The skills pertinent to use in this situation are nonlocomotor or axial. *General* space is that area into which a person or all people in the room can move.

Movement into space can be in different *directions:* forward, backward, sideward, diagonally, upward, downward, and any combinations of these. It can be in different *levels* of space: high, low, or medium. Becoming aware of spatial elements will help a child learn to judge heights from which balls are approaching, opportunities to evade opponents, distances and levels at which to lead passes to opponents, distances to clear apparatus, to mention but a few practical applications.

Body actions

This factor actually involves learning what movements or skills the body is capable of doing. There are movements that can be done in a stationary position. The body may move as a whole, or various parts may move independently or together. These are the nonlocomotor skills of twisting, turning, stretching, swinging, bending, shaking, bouncing, pushing, pulling, and combinations of these. The body can move in space utilizing the locomotor skills of walking, running, jumping, hopping, leaping, and various combinations of these.

Children should realize that any part of the body may initiate the movement into space. The weight of the body may be borne by different parts of the body and locomotor movements developed from many positions such as walking on the hands, hanging by the hands, and turning over a bar with the head leading down.

The body or parts of the body can receive weight in the form of outside objects or weight of other body parts; for example, in receiving the weight of the body as in landing from a jump or fall; in catching balls.

The body can transfer weight of the body itself or that of an outside object; for example, in dodging (the body weight must be transferred from one part of the body to another part as a base), in propelling the body in the air as in many gymnastic events, in throwing and/or striking objects.

Relationships

In most game, dance, and apparatus activities children do not move alone in space. They must move with someone, oppose someone, overcome obstacles, or use implements of some type. In early skill learnings children must have experiences where they adapt skills to performance with or in opposition to a partner, then in a small group and with a variety of obstacles and objects. When working with a partner one may imitate the other's movement pattern, do the movement together, oppose the other's pattern, or each may do his own pattern, but relate it to that of the other. When working in a group one may move following a leader, move with four or five other people, move in response or opposition to another group, work with a group in solving a problem or creating a pattern together, work in the group where each does his own movement but relates it to every other group member's pattern.

Skills in all the activity areas may be studied utilizing the four major factors just discussed whether the skill requires manipulation of the body in relation to other objects (balls, boxes, bars, bats, paddles, water) or in the expressive forms. Examples of ways in which skills may be studied can be found after the analysis of each skill in the next section of this chapter.

ANALYSIS OF
FUNDAMENTAL SKILLS

The remainder of this chapter is devoted to an analysis of the fundamental body actions which are common to all physical education activities and should be developed in the first three grades. As these are essential in all activities, the teacher must become familiar with their execution and their use.

The analysis of the actions is made in the form of a description which is intended to help the teacher gain a clear concept of the pattern. It is much too detailed for the elementary school student. Following the description of all but the nonlocomotor skills are the basic mechanical principles relative to the understanding of the different factors involved in the movement pattern. The principles are stated in a manner which should help the teacher gain an understanding of *why* the pattern is done in a specific way so that it is most efficient. The common faults which children often make are then related to the mechanical principles. Key words or phrases which have been found useful and meaningful to young children are suggested as aids in teaching or stimulation for correction.

The uses of fundamental skills in sports, gymnastics, dance, and utilitarian efforts are described. A recognition of the many different ways in which each fundamental skill is adapted and used serves to emphasize the importance of learning how to do each one well and in many variations at an early age. The uses should give the teacher some ideas for study of the skill through imagery or the actual actions.

Suggestions for the study of each skill are presented. These may be utilized in a variety of ways, as ideas for exploration, self-testing projects, problems, or in whatever way the teacher may wish to present the lesson. The teacher may rephrase the suggestions and use them for an indirect technique. For example, "Jump and turn around in the air"; as a challenge, "Who can jump and turn around in the air?"; a direct technique, "Stand on a line, jump and turn in the air and land on the same line facing the same direction"; or even more direct, "Put your two feet on a line, twist your arms to the left, swing them right and jump in the air turning your body. When you land, bend your knees, and pull your upper body back to regain balance, put your arms out to the side. Like this . . . (demonstration)." All of these are revisions of the original suggestion to jump and turn in the air.

The basic locomotor skills are presented first, followed by the most frequently used actions which are combinations of the basic skills. The basic nonlocomotor skills are described next with actions which are combinations of locomotor and nonlocomotor skills following. The fundamental catching, throwing, and striking patterns complete the section of analysis.

The chapter is summarized by a teacher's guide for analyzing selected fundamental skills. When a child does not reach skill goals, the teacher should look for mechanical errors in these six major areas: base of support and balance, production of force, direction of application of force, focus, follow-through and absorption of force. The chart is intended to serve as a quick reference for identifying errors or causes of errors in execution of skills.

In subsequent chapters reference is made to the basic body actions as they relate to specific sport, dance, and gymnastic skills. The reader will find it helpful to refer to Chapter VII and to this chapter for a review of elements involved in understanding and correct execution of the specific skill under consideration.

This material is intended for the improvement of the teacher's knowledge, as is evidenced by the vocabulary. How successfully he utilizes this information with children is dependent upon his application of the learning principles and teaching methods discussed in Chapters IV and V.

LOCOMOTOR
MOVEMENTS

Walk

Description
A natural walk is a movement which carries the body through space by a transference of weight from one foot to another. The movement is initiated with a push-off diagonally backward against the ground with the ball and toes of one foot. After the push-off is made, the leg swings forward as flexion is initiated at the hip joint, then the knee and the ankle lift the foot clear off the floor. The weight is transferred from the heel along the outer edge of the foot to the ball and to the toes as the next push-off is made. The feet point straight ahead and the inner borders fall along a straight line. As the arms swing freely and in opposition to the legs, they counterbalance the rotation of the trunk and help carry the upper part of the body forward. There is a brief period of time when both feet are in contact with the floor and a new base of support is established. The position of the body should be erect and easy.

The surface on which the walk is done influences the amount of force necessary in the push-off due to the amount of counter force from the surface. If walking on soft surfaces, more force must be exerted, as much of the force is lost in pushing back the sand, snow, or whatever one encounters. When walking on ice or another slippery surface, one should reduce force and shorten the stride in order to keep a larger base of support. If walking up a hill, the body must lean forward so the center of gravity is over the base of support. If walking down hill, the reverse would be true. The lean should be made from the hips. In order to increase speed of the walk, the force must be increased and the stride lengthened.

Basic mechanical principles
1. The angle of push-off must be in the desired direction. Too much vertical push results in a bouncy inefficient gait.
2. The period of double support allows a new base of support to be established for security. When feet are pointed straight ahead and the inner edges are placed along a line, the center of gravity may shift directly over the base of support.
3. The sequential transference of weight from heel, to outside edge of foot, to toes, allows the force to be absorbed over a longer period of time and thereby reduces the shock of the contact with the ground.

4. If the feet are moved straight ahead the base is too wide and the weight must be shifted a great distance from side to side. Thus there is much swaying of the body and great inefficiency. If the feet are placed one foot in front of the other, the base is too narrow and unstable. There also is a loss of efficiency when each foot has to be swung out and around the other on every step.
5. An exaggerated arm swing rotates the trunk excessively and hinders the forward movement.
6. A more forceful contraction of the extensor muscles of the leg creates greater resistance from the surface and drives the body forward at greater speed.

COMMON FAULTS:
1. Too much vertical push, resulting in bobbing or bouncing motion.
2. Walking with toes turned out, resulting in "duck walk" appearance.
3. Feet placed too far apart, resulting in "duck walk" appearance.
4. Feet placed too close together, resulting in "jerky" appearance.
5. Walking with toes turned in, resulting in "pigeon-toed" appearance and weakening of arch.
6. Excessive swing of arms from side to side.
7. Head forward.

KEY TEACHING PHRASES:
1. Push off with toes.
2. Swing leg from hip.
3. Land on heel and let weight roll along outside edge of foot to toes.
4. Point toes straight ahead.
5. Walk lightly.
6. Head up, look straight ahead.
7. Swing arms and hands forward easily.

Uses

The walk is the most basic skill, for we employ it as we move about in our daily tasks. It is learned early in life, and little heed is paid to the instruction of it. However, many children develop poor habits of walking which add stress and strain to various body parts and consume unnecessary amounts of energy through inefficient movement. Correct body alignment and mechanics of the walk add to the aesthetic values of appearance. The walking step is used in combination with other forms of movement to make up many other skills. There are very few sports which do not involve the use of the walk. Most dance steps are variations of the walk combined with other movements.

SUGGESTIONS FOR STUDY:
1. Walk freely (stress good alignment).
2. Walk in place, forward, sideward, backward, and zigzag.

3. Walk, using various combinations of the above.
4. Experiment walking with toes turned out, toes turned in, toes straight ahead. Contrast in terms of rotation, smooth flow, speed, feeling, and appearance.
5. Walk on tiptoes.
6. Walk on heels.
7. Walk, changing speeds from fast to slow, alternate with stopping, and then make a smooth transition from slow to fast and vice versa.
8. Walk with knees held high.
9. Walk as if in a slow processional.
10. Walk as if on ice.
11. Walk with legs held stiff.
12. Walk as if in a parade.
13. Walk while slowly lowering and raising the body.
14. Walk while turning, twisting, stretching, or curling the body.
15. Walk slowly with long steps, very tiny steps.
16. Walk fast with long steps, very tiny steps.
17. Walk as if walking up a hill, down a hill.
18. Walk in combination with other locomotor movements.
19. Walk beside a partner. Can you stay in step? Can you swing arms together?
20. Walk with a partner holding hands; change directions.
21. Walk with a partner holding hands; one walk forward at the same time one walks backward.
22. Make up a routine involving _____ factors (teacher or student can assign factors).

Run

Description

The run pattern is much like that of the walk; however, there is a period of no support in the run. The foot contacts the ground under the center of gravity, and the weight is first taken on the ball of the foot. The knees are bent more than in the walk and are carried upward and forward. The arms are bent at the elbows and swing in a forward backward direction alternately with the legs. In order to increase speed quickly, short driving steps are taken, and thereafter the stride is lengthened. Bending the supporting knee more as the weight is taken helps increase speed. Contrast the form of boy A in Figure 9-1 as he runs from his knees and swings his arms crosswise with the good form of boy B.

Basic mechanical principles

1. Landing on the ball of the foot first makes it possible to give with the ankle, knee, and hip which helps absorb the force gradually.

2. Bending the knee shortens the length of the lever to be moved and this allows the leg to be moved faster. This also applies to the bending of the elbows.
3. If the knee is bent more when the foot is pushing off against the ground, the leg muscles are able to extend more forcefully and, as a result, more speed is gained.

COMMON FAULTS:
1. Taking weight on the heels first.
2. Running in an erect position.
3. Swinging arms from side to side.
4. Throwing legs in and out, rather than upward and forward.
5. Failing to lift knees.
6. Carrying arms straight down at sides.

A   POOR   D   GOOD

Figure 9-1. Running Form.

KEY TEACHING PHRASES:
1. Run on balls of foot (if child tends to run on heels, exaggerate and tell him to run on toes).
2. Bend elbows and knees.
3. Swing hands and arms forward.
4. Head up.
5. Run lightly.

Uses

Running is vital to many games which children play during the elementary years, as well as to many sports. Basketball, tennis, and badminton require short runs with quick changes of direction and rapid acceleration and deceleration. The field games of soccer, hockey, lacrosse, football, and speedball all demand longer runs along with quick changes of direction and sudden stops. Track events require either short sprints or long-distance running. A short but powerful run precedes some field, apparatus, and tumbling events. The run as used in dance activities is basically the same but acquires a more expressive style.

Suggestions for study:
1. Run in place, then move running fast; move in slow motion; lift knees high; run lightly; heavily; vary speed.
2. Run straight ahead for specified distances; run as fast as you can (dashes).
3. Run around or between objects.
4. Run, making one's own pattern of direction.
5. Run and dodge objects or people.
6. Combine run and jump.
7. Run for increasingly longer distances each day.
8. Run and stop on signal, then run again.
9. Run in relay formation.
10. Run with a partner side by side, run, holding hands with partner.
11. Run following the leader.
12. Run under a rope.
13. Run over or through a turning rope.
14. Run while throwing and catching a ball to oneself, then with a partner.
15. Run in a small group following a zigzag pattern set by the leader.
16. Run in a column of five; the last person runs around the group to the head of the line, then adjusts his speed to that of the group. The last person in line then moves up to the front, continuing pattern (interval running).
17. For expressive style use imagery and imaginative movements regarding feelings, animals, objects.
18. Children love the joy of running. As running is vital to so many activities, it is wise to include some type of running in nearly every lesson. Always stress good form regardless of the variation.

Leap

Description
The leap is much the same as the run; however, in a leap the ankle and knee actions are increased so that a more upward motion is achieved. The knee leads out and then stretches forward as the foot reaches out for the landing. The rear leg extends backward in the air after a vigorous

push-off from the ground. The period of suspension in the air is greater in the leap than in the run. The arms move upward to sustain the body in the air. The take-off is from one foot and the landing is on the other foot. Usually a leap is preceded by one or more running steps in order to gain more momentum for the lift into the air.

Basic mechanical principles
1. The same principles which apply to the run also apply to the leap.
2. The greater push-off from the floor adds force and momentum for the more vertical path of the body.
3. A few preliminary running steps help gain momentum for both the distance and height desirable for the leap.
4. A forward upward motion of the arms helps produce momentum to help carry the body in the desired direction.

COMMON FAULTS:
1. Failing to push-off with enough force to elevate the body.
2. Failing to suspend body in air.
3. Failing to stretch or reach with the legs.
4. Failing to use arms.
5. Landing on two feet instead of one.

KEY TEACHING PHRASES:
1. Push up, and stretch and reach.
2. Swing arms up and forward.
3. Run, run, *leap* (accent *leap* to denote greater push or effort).

Uses
The leap is usually combined with running. The leap is utilized when a slight obstacle is to be cleared without breaking the running pattern. When catching a high pass on the run, a leap is preferable to a jump since the running pattern can be continued easily. The leap is the basic hurdling pattern without the hip rotation.

SUGGESTIONS FOR STUDY: (The leap is difficult for young children and much variation in the pattern is difficult for them to control. Practice on the leap itself with variation in the distance and height to be attained are sufficient for the primary and intermediate grades.)
1. Run several steps and leap.
2. Leap over a rope on floor (raise rope off floor gradually).
3. Leap a distance between two lines (increase the distance between lines).
4. Run and leap over a small box or other obstacle.
5. Run and leap over small hurdles, 12 inches to 20 inches high.
6. Run and leap over a series of hurdles without breaking stride.
7. Do series of leaps without running steps between; emphasize distance and height in leap.

Jump

Description

A jump is a motion which carries the body through the air from a take-off from one or both feet. The body is suspended in mid-air momentarily and then drops back to the ground to a landing where the weight is taken on both feet. The purpose of the jump may be to gain distance forward or to gain height. For both purposes the power is produced by a quick action of the extensor muscles of the legs against the ground and a strong arm swing in the direction of the desired movement. As the hips, knees, and ankles must be bent in order for the force to be produced through extension of the muscles, it is important that the take-off be from a crouched position.

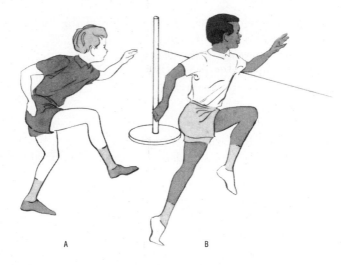

A   B

Figure 9-2. Jumping Over a Rope.

If the purpose of the jump is to gain distance, there is a forward lean of the body and the arms swing backward and then forcefully forward for the push-off. The legs are bent and swing forward under the body as it travels through the air. The angle of take-off is approximately 45 degrees.

If the purpose is to gain height, the knees are bent and the push-off is against the floor straight up and the arms are swung upward. The body extends or stretches as far as possible into the air. In Figure 9-2 contrast the vertical lift and elevation of all parts of the body of the boy in A with the forward direction and lack of elevation of the boy in B.

Basic mechanical principles

1. The initial crouching position provides for the hips, knees and ankles to be bent so that the extensors of the legs exert more force against the floor. (The crouching is necessary only if maximum height or distance is needed).
2. The swing of the arms in the direction of the jump produces greater momentum to carry the body in the desired direction.
3. The forward lean of the body carries the center of gravity beyond the base of support, thus gravity aids the forward motion of the body when distance is desired.

COMMON FAULTS:

1. Failing to bend the legs after taking off so that the feet touch the ground. This almost immediately causes distance loss.
2. Upper part of body leaning forward in the jump for height.
3. Failing to swing arms forward or upward in time with take-off.

KEY TEACHING PHRASES:

1. Swing arms back and forth, down and up.
2. Bend knees and ankles, and "blast off."
3. Stretch and reach.

Uses

The jump is utilized in a jump stop in all games requiring running with quick stops where one needs to maintain balance. One jumps from many objects. Landing from a jump is treated separately. Long jumping and high jumping are field events. The jump pattern is found in basketball as a jump-and-reach in rebounding, a tossed ball, and a lay-up shot. The jump-and-reach is also the pattern for the spike and block in volleyball. In any sport where an object is thrown or hit and must be caught, a jump often accompanies the throw and catch.

SUGGESTIONS FOR STUDY:

1. Jump in place with an emphasis on height; make light jumping movements, heavy jumps.
2. Jump and turn.
3. Jump like a bouncing ball, continuously; vary the bounce pattern; bounce high, low.
4. Jump and move.
5. Jump and reach for various objects and at various heights.
6. Jump forward, backward, sideward.
7. Jump in and out of a hoop held at various heights.
8. Jump in and out of a circle or circles drawn on the floor.
9. Jump over a rope, a bench, a box.
10. Jump for distance.

11. Jump off benches or trampolet for height, knees bent, arms out, turn in the air.
12. Jump around obstacles.
13. Change directions while jumping.
14. Jump with a rope.
15. Jump while bouncing a ball, or throwing and catching with a partner.
16. Jump over a partner.
17. Jump with a partner.

Hop

Description

The body is pushed off the floor from one foot and after a slight suspension in the air it is returned to the floor with the weight taken on the same foot. The knee of the inactive leg is bent, and the leg makes no contact with the floor. The arms move upward to help with the body lift. The landing is on the toes, and immediately the weight is shifted to the ball of the foot and then to the heel.

Basic mechanical principles

1. The upward swing of the arms adds momentum to the vertical lift.
2. The vertical lift keeps the center of gravity over the base of support.

COMMON FAULTS:

1. Taking off on one foot and landing on the other.
2. Trying to go forward more than upward.
3. Landing on the whole of the foot rather than on toes first, then ball to heel.
4. Losing balance because of body sway and lack of arm swing.

KEY TEACHING PHRASES:

1. *Up* in the air on one foot and *down* on the same one.
2. Lift arms up.
3. Head held high.
4. Bend knee.

Uses

In dance and sport activities a hop is usually used in combination with a jump or walk. It is used in the traditional steps in dance in the skip, step hop, schottische, polka, mazurka. A hop step precedes a stop in running games.

SUGGESTIONS FOR STUDY:

1. Hop in place. Hold position with weight on one foot for varying lengths of time.

2. Hop and turn; make a pattern of turning.
3. Hop forward, backward, sideward, make a pattern.
4. Hop holding free leg in various positions.
5. Hop high, low.
6. Hop covering varying distances.
7. Hop over a rope.
8. Hop with a partner.

COMBINATIONS OF BASIC LOCOMOTOR MOVEMENTS

Slide

Description

A slide is a combination of a step and a leap. The individual steps to the side and draws the other foot to the side of the supporting foot and puts the weight on it. The same foot always leads. The sliding pattern may be done in a forward or backward direction; however, then it is often called a gallop. When the direction is to be changed, a slightly higher leap is taken, and the weight is shifted in the desired direction.

Basic mechanical principles

1. The momentum generated for the step sideways is checked by the upward movement of the hop; therefore, balance is maintained easily.
2. The hop, as used in the slide for most sports activities, involves gaining little height.
3. As the body weight is always within the base of support, the sliding pattern provides a well-balanced position for quick changes of direction.

COMMON FAULTS:

1. Failure to shift weight from lead to following foot.
2. Hopping too high and not gaining distance sideways.

KEY TEACHING PHRASES:

1. Step to side.
2. Draw foot up toward other and hop.
3. Lead with the same foot.

Uses

The slide is an important element of defensive footwork in basketball. It allows one to move efficiently in a balanced manner and to be ready to move quickly in any direction. A slide movement is utilized in volleyball, tennis, badminton, softball, and baseball to gain position for subsequent play when changes in direction and actions are necessary. The slide is a basic dance step and is found in many simple folk dances.

SUGGESTIONS FOR STUDY:

1. Slide sideward to the right; reverse direction.
2. Slide sideward, then forward. Make a square by changing from sideward to forward then backward.
3. Slide slowly without much lift.
4. Slide with a big lift.
5. Slide, turning in air on hop every fourth slide step.
6. Slide ten times right, ten times left, eight times left, eight times right, six times left . . . two times left, two times right, back and forth.
7. Slide left four times, run forward ten steps, slide right four times, continue in pattern.
8. Slide with a partner, holding hands.
9. Slide facing a partner, without holding hands.
10. Slide with a partner using a mirror effect; designate one as leader, and have other follow leader's movements.
11. In a circle with other children slide a set number of times in one direction, then change direction. Stress smooth changes of directions.

Skip

Description

The skip is a combination of the walk and the hop. One steps forward on one foot and then hops on the *same* foot, then steps forward on the opposite foot and hops on it. The skip can be executed in any direction, but the pattern is always done on alternate feet with the weight shifting on each walking step. The arms should be swung in opposition to the legs to maintain balance and help gain height, if the latter is desired.

Basic mechanical principles

(The principles which apply to the walk and the hop apply to the skip.)

1. It is the propulsive force exerted by the one foot push-off of the hop which gives the upward movement of the skip.
2. The upward swing of the arms adds momentum in the desired direction, if height is desired.

COMMON FAULTS:

1. Stepping on one foot and hopping on the other foot. The weight is transferred on the hop rather than the step.

2. Gaining forward distance rather than height because the leg is not lifted upward.

KEY TEACHING PHRASES:

1. Step forward and hop UP!
2. Swing arms up. (If a child has difficulty with the pattern, take his hand and skip with him.)

Uses

The skip pattern is an important part of footwork in most games and sports where quick stops and changes of direction are needed. A skip stop is useful for a quick stop and regaining of balance and position. A skip usually precedes a lay-up shot in basketball. The skip is a traditional dance step used in many folk dances.

SUGGESTIONS FOR STUDY:

1. Skip forward, backward, in a circle, make a pattern.
2. Skip high, low.
3. Skip lightly, heavily.
4. Skip and add another movement pattern.
5. Skip around obstacles.
6. Skip with a partner.
7. Play relays with skipping as a means of locomotion.

Landing

Description

In landing or regaining balance after the body comes to the ground, all the body parts bend or give as contact with ground is made. The weight is taken on the balls of the feet, the ankles and knees bend, and the upper body and head are held erect. The feet can be in a side stride or forward stride position, depending on the direction of the movement. As soon as the weight is absorbed, a quick extension of the legs is made and a rebound action made to the standing position. The arms should be extended sideward to aid in maintaining balance.

Basic mechanical principles

1. Landing on the balls of the feet with knees and ankles bent absorbs the force and helps decelerate momentum gradually.
2. The wider the base of support the lower the center of gravity is, hence equilibrium is regained more easily. (Caution: the base should not be so wide as to put strain on joints and ligaments. It should be no more than the width of the hips sideways.)
3. Holding the upper part of the body and the head erect helps keep the center of gravity over the base of support.

COMMON FAULTS:
1. Landing with feet in flat position.
2. Keeping knees rigid.
3. Landing with feet close together.
4. Looking down at the floor.
5. Bending forward at the waist.

KEY TEACHING PHRASES:
1. Come down on balls of feet.
2. Extend arms sidewards.
3. Bend knees.
4. Keep chest and head high.
5. Look in the direction of the next movement.
6. Rebound from the floor with a little jump into a standing position.

Uses

Every jump must be accompanied by a landing, a skill used in all sports and games. In basketball one lands from a jump ball, jump shot, rebound, jump stop, and after catching high passes. Landing techniques are needed after spikes and blocks in volleyball. Catching high balls in softball, football, and lacrosse all demand that one come down to the ground and quickly regain balance before the next move is made. Whenever a jump upon, over, or from a piece of apparatus is executed, a landing must be made. The jumping events in track and field all demand the ability to land properly and safely. Any dance movement which takes the body into the air requires a landing.

SUGGESTIONS FOR STUDY:
1. Jump into the air, and land with knees bent.
2. Jump into the air, land, and immediately rebound into another jump.
3. Run, jump, and land.
4. Jump from benches, bleachers, tables, or boxes of increasingly greater heights, and land.
5. Jump over ropes and land.
6. Jump over a bench or box and land.
7. Jump over a partner who is in a hands-and-knees position.
8. Jump and land, preceded by and followed by another type of movement.
9. Jump, turn in the air, and land.

Stopping

There are two styles of stopping, the running stride stop and the skip stop. In the former the runner simply stops running with feet in a forward stride position, bends the knees, leans the body weight backward and reestablishes balance. The latter employs a step and a hop before the actual stop. The weight is carried back and taken on the balls of the feet which are in a forward stride position. The hop allows the individual to gain more forward distance on the stop. The latter is dependent on the angle of take off of the hop.

Basic mechanical principles

1. Forward momentum must be checked and balance gained in order to stop.
2. Bending the knees helps absorb the momentum gradually and also lowers and moves the center of gravity backward.
3. The upward motion of the hop checks the forward momentum to a greater extent than the sudden stride stop does.

COMMON FAULTS:

1. Failing to bend knees.
2. Letting body weight continue forward thus balance is not regained and additional steps are required before a stop is made.
3. Taking off for the hop at too small an angle, i.e., jumping forward rather than upward.

KEY TEACHING PHRASES:

1. Bend knees.
2. Lean back at waist.
3. Land with feet apart, forward and backward.
4. Head up.
5. Step, hop, and land (for skip stop).

Uses

The skill of stopping is used in all movement activities since one has to come to a stop whenever any locomotor movement is made.

SUGGESTIONS FOR STUDY:

1. Run a certain distance and stop.
2. Run and stop on signals—whistle, drum, voice, clap. Vary locomotor movement preceding stop.
3. Follow the leader, stop when the leader stops.
4. Draw a line in front of a barrier. Run and stop between line and barrier.
5. Jump down from a height, run and stop.
6. Run in a circle, stop on command.
7. Make a pattern of running a certain number of steps, then stop for a certain count, and then continue running.
8. Play relays with command stops and starts.

Pivot

Description

The pivot is used to change directions efficiently when in a stationary position. The individual uses one foot as the base of support and keeps the ball of that foot in contact with the floor as he pushes off from the floor with the other foot in the desired direction. The knees should be bent with the body weight kept low over the stationary foot. In this manner one can make a turn of any degree in all directions. The direction the turn is made is dependent on the purpose of the pivot and the proximity or position of an opponent or partner.

Another form of turning is the reverse turn. With the feet in a forward stride position the player spins to the rear on the balls of both feet while the feet remain on the floor. In this situation the turn may be made in the direction of the rear foot only. As in a pivot, the knees are bent and the body weight is low. The weight is equally distributed over both feet. The same principles are followed when other parts of the body are the base of support. One body part, such as one hand, may be the base of support.

Basic mechanical principles

1. The nearer the center of gravity to the base of support the greater will be the balance; therefore, the body weight is lowered.
2. The off-center application of force by the free foot causes the body to move in a circle about the pivot foot which is the center of rotation.
3. The rotary movement around an axis is fastest when the radius is shortest; therefore, the closer the body appendages and external objects are carried to the body and over the base of support the faster the turn will be.
4. Spinning on the ball of the foot reduces the friction that would be created in turning on the whole foot without actually moving it.
5. By keeping the body weight low over the base of support, the person is in a balanced position and ready to initiate any new movement rapidly after he assumes the desired direction.

COMMON FAULTS:
1. Moving the pivot foot.
2. Changing pivot foot.
3. Trying to spin on the whole foot.

KEY TEACHING PHRASES:
1. Spin on ball of foot.
2. Push with the free foot.

Uses

The pivot and reverse turn are utilized in all sports when a quick, efficient change of direction is desired. Many dance patterns and changes of direction in dances are initially dependent upon a pivot or reverse turn. Gymnastic activities involve many pivots with a variety of bases of support.

SUGGESTIONS FOR STUDY:

1. Using the pivot, change directions on command.
2. Facing a partner, learn to pivot away from him.
3. Run, stop, pivot or do a reverse turn, and run back to a starting point.
4. Receive a ball from a partner, pivot and pass to another point.
5. Walk and pivot.
6. Pivot around in a circle.
7. With a partner pivot around in a circle.
8. Walk forward and do a reverse turn.
9. Make a pattern of walks and reverse turns.
10. Using the hands as a base of support, pivot around in a circle.
11. Using the hips as a base of support, pivot around in a circle.

Dodge

Description

In order to execute a dodge, the individual stops running forward and changes the direction of the motion of his body by bending the knees, dropping the weight to a low point, and shifting the weight in the direction of the dodge. The latter may be described as a lean away from the original direction. The subsequent forward movement in the new direction is made by pushing off from the ground or floor with the foot which bears the body weight. One foot or both feet may be used to stop as the dodge is initiated and to push off from the ground in the new direction.

Basic mechanical principles

1. Dropping the weight lowers the center of gravity; consequently, better balance is gained. Also, the momentum of the forward or sideward movement can be absorbed over a greater period of time.
2. Since one of the principles involved in running is to put the body off balance to start, the purpose of shifting the weight in dodging is to bring the center of gravity back over the base of support in order to stop and shift into a starting position again.
3. The forward motion of the body is started by upsetting equilibrium by means of putting the body weight outside the base of support and pushing off by one or both feet.

COMMON FAULTS:

1. Failing to bend knees.
2. Failing to check forward momentum by not shifting weight far enough

back over base of support at the start of the change of direction.

3. Holding balance too long and therefore getting a slow start in the new direction.

KEY TEACHING PHRASES:
1. Bend knees.
2. Check forward movement.
3. Lean toward dodging side.
4. Push off in new direction.

Uses

A dodge is employed in all sports and games where evading an opponent is involved. The field sports of hockey, lacrosse, speedball, football, and soccer utilize the dodge pattern extensively.

SUGGESTIONS FOR STUDY:
1. Run to a certain line, change direction.
2. Run around a series of obstacles.
3. Run to a partner and go around him (it is best to designate a line which the dodger must cross before changing direction).
4. Run to a partner who reaches out to tag dodger. Dodger tries to avoid being tagged.
5. Run to a partner who moves out to tag dodger. Dodger tries to avoid being tagged.
6. Run, and dodge a ball thrown by someone else.
7. While dribbling a ball with hand or foot follow the same series (3–6).
8. While dribbling a ball with hand or foot, dodge around pins as in an obstacle course.
9. Run anywhere trying to avoid an opponent who tries to tag the dodger.

Falling

Description

There is always the possibility of losing one's balance and falling to the ground. As a safety measure in regard to all activities, it is important that children be taught to fall safely.

If balance is lost and one falls, the principles of absorption should be applied. One should relax so the joints can give, and force can be absorbed over a longer period of time. If possible, the fall should be taken on the padded parts of the body—the hips, thighs, buttocks, or back of the shoulders and on the greatest number of these as possible at one time. If a fall onto the arms or hands is impossible to avoid, the wrists and elbows must give. It should be stressed that a fall directly onto the head, elbows, or knees should be avoided. One should assume a rolling motion or curled position. Tuck the head or give a slight twist to the area of the body about to strike the floor.

Basic mechanical principles

1. Absorbing the force on the padded areas of the body reduces momentum gradually.
2. The rolling motion gives a greater amount of time for momentum to decrease.

COMMON FAULTS:

1. Falling onto outstretched rigid hands.
2. Failing to tuck head.

KEY TEACHING PHRASES:

1. Relax.
2. Bend joints.
3. Roll with the fall.
4. Tuck head.

Uses

Skills should be taught with a positive approach so that children may move confidently and safely; however, a loss of balance is encountered in many situations for many different reasons. The mechanics of the rolls in tumbling should be related to the mechanics of falling safely.

SUGGESTIONS FOR STUDY:

1. Roll in a curled position.
2. Teach mechanics of tumbling in a forward, sideward, backward position.
3. Be a ball and roll around in a circle.
4. From the end of a low box, put hands on the floor, and go into a forward roll.
5. Jump from a low box, and go into a roll.
6. Melt like an ice cream cone.
7. Collapse like a balloon.

NONLOCOMOTOR MOVEMENTS

Bend

Description

A bend is a movement around a joint where two adjacent parts of the body (bones) join together. The technical term is flexion. Very small bending movements or large bending movements can be made, such as bending the fingers or bending at the waist. Bending and stretching often go together when the bend is a preparatory movement for greater stretching power. A number of bending actions are made at one time for some actions. For example, in making the body as small as possible a great number of joint actions are made simultaneously.

TEACHING HINTS: The structure of some joints determines the range of bend. The extent of bending one can do is dependent upon flexibility, and this flexibility is specific to each joint. Children are usually quite flexible but become less so as they get older. Thus the teacher should continue to provide many opportunities for bending at all grade levels. The terms "curl" and "tuck" are often used when referring to bending movements.

Uses

Bending of some body parts is essential to the majority of dance, sports, apparatus, and aquatic skills as well as to daily tasks. The degree of bend of the knees and ankles in most locomotor skills helps regulate the amount of force built up from the subsequent extension of these parts. The rate of absorption of force upon landing or falling is also dependent upon the bending of various parts; and success in many rotary actions is related to the extent of the bending or tucking of the appendages.

SUGGESTIONS FOR STUDY:
1. With arms outstretched, bend the lower half of the arm upward and toward the body; sideward and out, in. Do it slowly, then faster.
2. Bend the arm from the shoulder, upward, downward, sideward, in all directions, and in various combinations.
3. Standing on one leg, bend the other knee upward, bend the ankle upward, then downward.
4. Standing on two feet, bend the knees forward and downward.
5. Standing, bend the trunk forward and downward, sideward and downward, backward and downward.
6. Make various combinations of knee and arm bends.
7. Standing, touch the floor in front and to the side.
8. Lying on the back, bend knees toward chest; alternate bending knees.
9. Lying on the front, bend one knee upward, then the other; alternate.
10. Bend knees, and jump up as high as possible.
11. Bend up and down as you bounce like a ball.
12. Walk while bending the knees deep, walk without bending the knees.
13. In kneeling position with weight on lower legs, bend each upper body part until head touches knees.
14. Make yourself as small as possible.

Stretch

Description

A stretch is the extension or hyperextension of the joints of the body. The stretching action may take place at any of the joints of the body in various combinations. Stretching may also be thought of as expanding any part of the body.

TEACHING HINTS: Precede tasks involving maximum stretching with gradual loosening up activities. Stress good balance before maximum stretch. Using imagery with primary grade children fosters a good concept of stretching.

Uses

The ability to stretch or extend at will helps maintain flexibility of the joints. Stretching is allied with flexing or bending where the latter is most often a preparatory movement to aid in full extension. Stretching is utilized in many daily tasks of reaching for objects. Almost all sports skills involve stretching as an aid to achieve maximum force, distance, and speed in actions. Many dance skills employ stretching in various factors of time and positions and as an expressive movement.

SUGGESTIONS FOR STUDY:
1. Stretch whole body tall.
2. Stretch fingers, arms, or other isolated body parts.
3. Stretch wide.
4. Stretch like a rubber band.
5. Reach for spots, real or imaginary, on the wall.
6. Combine bends and stretches.
7. Hang and stretch on bars of some type.
8. Jump and stretch.
9. Stretch out while running.
10. Stretch one leg while bending the other.
11. Stretch in an inverted position.
12. Lie down, and be as long as possible.
13. Jump and stretch with legs apart, legs together.
14. Leap and stretch.
15. Stretch legs high and wide while weight is on shoulders and upper back.

Pull

Description

A pull is a forceful movement made to move or draw an object toward the body. This is most often done with the arms. Initially, the arms or arm are extended. Then, as the object is drawn toward the body, the elbows and wrists bend, and the body straightens. The body leans slightly forward, and the knees are bent. According to the resistance or weight of the object, more force may need to be developed by using the strong muscles of the legs.

TEACHING HINTS: If a heavy object is to be moved, stress a wide stable stance. Stress bending at the knees and letting the muscles of the legs do the work.

Uses

The pull is a utilitarian skill needed in daily work tasks, such as pulling: a wagon, a door open, a window closed, a sweater down over the head, a drawer out, oars in a boat, and so forth. Swimming requires one to pull oneself through the water. Archery depends on a strong pull on the bow string. The body must be pulled up from the floor to various positions on different pieces of apparatus.

SUGGESTIONS FOR STUDY:
1. Pull an object toward body (use a real object or imagine one).
2. Pull an object from in front of body, from in back, from the side. Use both arms, use only one arm.
3. Walk and pull something from behind, then from in front.
4. Sit and pull an object.
5. Kneel and pull an object.
6. Pull an object while lying down.
7. Pull an object quickly, then slowly.
8. Pull a partner who is standing across a line on the floor.
9. Pull a partner who is sitting down across a line.
10. Pull a partner who is lying down up into a standing position.
11. Play tug-of-war with four or five people on each end of a rope.
12. Lying down, have a different partner hold onto each hand and pull yourself into a standing position.

Push

Description

A push is a forceful movement made to move some object away from the body or a movement made against an object to move the body away from it. A push may be made by the legs, wrists, arms, feet, hips, shoulders, or a combination of these, depending upon the amount of force needed. There is usually a preparatory bend and forceful extension as the pushing motion is made.

TEACHING HINTS: If a heavy object is to be moved, all of the mechanical principles relating to balance and the development of force and application of force must be applied, including the placement of feet in a forward stride position wide enough to maintain stability, the preparatory flexion efforts for building momentum, a summation of all the forces, and a direct application of the force in the direction the object is to be moved. Stress using muscles of the legs to push heavy objects.

Uses

A push is a utilitarian skill needed in daily tasks, such as pushing a lawn mower, saws, vacuum sweeper, moving heavy boxes and other objects. Many stunts, tumbling, and apparatus activities require one to push oneself up off the floor, away from apparatus, and off apparatus. Some contact sports require that one push the opponent out of position.

SUGGESTIONS FOR STUDY:
1. Push lightweight objects across the floor, heavy objects (use both real and imaginary objects).
2. Push with two hands, with one hand.
3. Push with feet.
4. In a kneeling position, touch forehead to floor, with hands, push body back into a straight kneeling position.
5. Lying down, push self up with hands.
6. Push partner across a line, using hands, then shoulders, then hips.
7. Lying on back, bend knees. Partners put soles of feet together and push.
8. On hands and knees, push partner across line.
9. Stand one foot away from the wall, lean forward from ankles, bend arms at elbows and place hands and head against wall. Push away from wall. Increase distance.
10. Jump up and support weight against a box or bar, hold and push away and return to standing position.

Lift

Description

A lift is a movement which raises an object or a body part from one level to another. Pushing and pulling movements are involved in lifting. Lifting is actually pushing and pulling in a vertical direction rather than in a horizontal direction. The hands and arms bend as the object is moved upward and extend as it is placed in a high position or moved to another place at a lower level. The knees bend as the object is picked up and extend as they assist in raising the object.

TEACHING HINTS: If the object to be lifted is heavy, the width of the stance should be great, and the knees bent more than usual. A stooping position should be taken to get body close to the floor. The strong muscles of the leg should be utilized. The hands should be placed under the object and it should be brought up in the air close to the body.

Uses

The lift is primarily a utilitarian skill and is used in many household and vocational tasks. In some stunt, tumbling, and apparatus activities the body must be lifted into various positions from the floor. In sports activities balls and implements must actually be lifted into positions. The arms and legs themselves are lifted in all sports and dance activities.

SUGGESTIONS FOR STUDY:
1. Lift the arm sideward to shoulder height, forward to shoulder height.
2. Lift a leg forward and upward, backward and upward.
3. Sitting, lift one leg at a time. Alternate legs, lifting and lowering slowly.
4. Lift one foot at a time.
5. Lift a basketball, a balloon, a bowling ball.
6. Lift a rock (real and imaginary).
7. Lift a box and put it on a high shelf.

Swing

Description

The swing is a movement of arms, legs, upper trunk, head, or body as a whole in a circular or pendular fashion around a stationary center. The part to be swung is dropped into space where the power from the drop will carry it upward in the opposite direction; then it will drop downward again. The swing may be continued by adding more force to the body part at the beginning of each drop. When more force is added, a faster swing will result. If enough force is added, the swing will carry over and drop back on the other side, thus making a full circle swing.

TEACHING HINTS: Help arms or other swinging body part move as they swing down. No more force should be added to downward movement if the swing is to stop gradually. When swinging movements are being done on rings, swings, or bars, one should get off or drop off at the back of the swing as the momentum is temporarily halted.

SUGGESTIONS FOR STUDY:
1. Swing one arm across the front of the body. Let it fall limp. Swing it three or four times, let it fall limp.

2. Swing one arm across the front of the body keeping it going at the same speed. Make it swing faster, slower.
3. Swing one arm across the front of the body several times, then make it go in a circle. Do the same with the leg.
4. Repeat the above sequence with both arms and legs.
5. Swing one arm backward and the arm forward in opposition to each other.
6. Standing on one foot, swing the other leg back and forth, swing it fast then slow.
7. Swing one arm and the opposite leg.
8. Lying down, swing one leg back and forth, then swing both legs.
9. Standing, swing the upper part of body, bend over and swing it. Let arms swing with body.
10. Swing head from side to side.
11. Hang by the hands from a bar and swing the lower part of body; the whole body.
12. Swing with one hand only holding the bar.
13. Hang by the knees and swing.
14. Swing on a hanging rope.
15. Swing on a rope, and get off while swinging.
16. Swing on a rope, and land on top of a box.
17. Swing arms, and jump high.
18. Swing arms, and jump for distance.
19. Standing on one leg, swing several times, then jump. Try this, and turn in the air and jump.

Turn

Description

A turn is a rotation or circular movement of the body or body parts around in space. Joint structure restricts some body joints to twisting rather than turning. The focal point of the turn is the space in which the body or body part turns.

TEACHING HINTS: When speed or force is to be gained in the turn, a preliminary twisting motion in the opposite direction of the turn will help develop momentum. Stopping after a fast turn will require regaining balance and control of weight.

SUGGESTIONS FOR STUDY:
1. See how many body parts can turn all the way around. Make big circles; then little ones.
2. Turn the whole body around.
3. Standing on one foot, turn body around quickly, then slowly.
4. Sitting down, turn body around quickly, then slowly.

5. Lying on stomach, turn around.
6. Turn while walking, running, skipping.
7. Start with a small part of the body turning, then make other parts turn until the whole body is turning.
8. Turn around a chair, a ball, another person, a wand, a rope.
9. Turn with a partner.
10. Hold hands with a partner, one turn left, the other turn right.
11. Move around the room while turning with a partner.
12. Kneel with hands on ground, make hands walk around body.
13. Support weight on part of body other than feet and turn around.
14. Jump up and turn in the air.
15. Jump off a box and turn in the air.

Twist

Description

A twist is a rotation of some body part around its own long axis. Twisting action can only take place at the spinal, neck, shoulder, hip, and wrist joints.

TEACHING HINTS: Children often confuse twisting and turning. Ask them to think of the lower arm as a rod around which the muscles twist. The focal point in the twist is the action around the body part itself. In the turn, the focal point is the space in which the body part turns.

Uses

The twist is a utilitarian skill used in many household tasks such as, twisting lids, dials, screwdrivers. Often the head must twist in order for one to see objects at various angles, the body must twist to get into and out of small cars and through small openings. Twisting movements are used in many stunt, tumbling, apparatus, dance, and sport activities.

SUGGESTIONS FOR STUDY:
1. Twist one arm around the body; both arms.
2. Standing, lift one leg and twist it as far as possible.
3. Twist one body part one direction, another in the other direction.
4. Standing on one foot twist the whole body, untwist quickly.
5. Standing with feet apart, twist right arm around the left leg and pick up an object lying between the feet.
6. Twist the head around, and determine how far you can see in the opposite direction.
7. Hold the head steady, and twist the shoulders around as far as possible.
8. Support weight on hands and knees, and twist into a position where weight is supported on the back.

9. From a standing position, twist body and place hands on floor to the right of the body, and then support weight on hands.
10. Twist trunk from right to left while walking.
11. Twist like a screwdriver.
12. Twist like a spring.
13. Put hand against wall and twist under the arm.
14. With arms out to sides, twist vigorously from side to side.

BASIC CATCHING, THROWING, AND STRIKING PATTERNS

Catching

Description

It is essential to be in line with, directly behind, or underneath the ball before attempting the actual catch. The palms face the direction from which the ball is approaching. If the ball is coming at a level below the waist, the hands are held with the fingers pointing downward (little fingers together). If it is to be received above the waist, the hands are held with the fingers pointing upward (thumbs together). The fingers are spread and slightly curved. The arms reach forward slightly to meet the ball. As soon as the ball comes into the hands, the arms pull it in toward the body. The feet should be in a forward stride position. The faster the oncoming ball approaches, the wider the stance should be.

Basic mechanical principles

1. Being in line with the ball enables the force of the oncoming ball to be taken close to the center of gravity of the body.
2. The stride position in the direction of the oncoming ball increases the stability of the body.
3. Pulling the object in toward the body decelerates the speed of the object by increasing the time and distance over which the force can be reduced. This is sometimes referred to as a cushioning effect or as "giving" with the ball.

COMMON FAULTS:

1. Reaching out to the side to catch, and therefore not being in line with the ball.
2. Failing to draw ball in toward the body.
3. Keeping fingers straight and rigid, hence the ball hits finger tips and rebounds forward and often causes injury.
4. Putting heels of hands together, thus object bounces out of hands.

5. Losing balance if the ball comes hard and fast because the feet were too close together in a side stride position.

KEY TEACHING PHRASES:
1. Get in line with ball.
2. Stand with feet in forward stride position.
3. Curve fingers. (Stand with arms hanging at side, notice that fingers are curved naturally as the arms hang loose.)
4. Pull ball in toward body.
5. "Give" with the object.

Uses

The basic catching pattern is used when catching any size or shape of ball. The cushioning effect of drawing an object in toward the body is found in blocking the ball as in soccer, bunting in softball, fielding the ball with a hockey or lacrosse stick, and the block volley in tennis. The same pattern is used when receiving another person's weight in stunts, tumbling, or dance activities, or in receiving a heavy box or object from someone.

SUGGESTIONS FOR STUDY:
1. Throw to self. Use a bean bag at first, then different sizes, shapes, and weights of balls.
2. Throw ball against the wall and catch it. Vary the speed of the throw.
3. Catch ball as it bounces off the floor.
4. Catch objects thrown by a partner. Vary speed and force of throw.
5. Catch balls that are thrown at different levels.
6. Combine study of throwing, striking, and catching.

Throwing

There are three basic throwing patterns—overhand, underhand, and side-arm. The type of object to be thrown and the purpose of the throw determine the pattern to be used. The basic principles which are essential to success in using any one of the patterns are similar. The speed, distance, and direction of the object to be thrown are the essential elements that are controlled by the correct execution of the throw.

Speed is controlled by the momentum given the object by the body. Momentum is developed by the backswing, proper stance or width of the base, body rotation, shifting of body weight forward, and follow-through. The extent of the use of these factors is dependent upon how hard or how far one needs to throw the object. A step, run, or hop taken just before the throw adds speed because the forward momentum is added to that of the object.

The distance the object will travel depends upon how fast it is moving at the time it is released and the angle at which it is released from the hand. Although it is not of great importance to the type of throwing learned and used in the elementary school, the teacher should recognize that wind and spin applied to an object do affect the distance the object will travel in the air.

The *direction* which an object takes is dependent upon the direction the hand is moving at the point of release.

Overhand throw pattern

Description

The thrower stands in a stride position with the left side toward the target. The ball is gripped by the fingers. To start the backswing, the throwing arm is brought back with the elbow bent so that the arm is at a right angle and away from the body. The ball is held about ear high, and the wrist is cocked. The trunk is rotated or twisted back in the direction of the throwing arm. The left arm is up and pointing toward the target (Figure 9-3). The ball is brought forward with the elbow leading, the wrist and hand snap forward, and the ball is released. As the forward motion is made, the trunk rotates toward the target, the body weight shifts to the forward foot. The ball is released shoulder high. The throw-

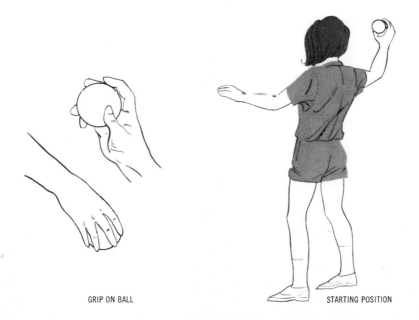

GRIP ON BALL   STARTING POSITION

Figure 9-3. Overhand Throw.

ing arm and hand follow through pointing toward the target. A step is taken with the right foot to regain balance and to get into position for the next move.

Basic mechanical principles

1. Since an object will move at the same speed that the hand is moving at the time the object is released, the teacher should recognize the factors that allow maximum speed to accrue. The wide-base stance with the left foot and left shoulder to the target allows the weight to be transferred to the rear foot and permits maximum rotation of the body. (Try twisting the trunk with the feet parallel and a short distance apart, then open the stance with the right foot back and twist the trunk. One can readily feel the greater freedom to twist in the latter instance.) All of this contributes to a longer backswing which allows more time for momentum to build. The amount of momentum is then transferred to the object.
2. As a short lever is easier to move, the elbow is bent at all times in the backswing.
3. The follow-through enables the ball to be released when the hand is moving at its fastest rate, which is at the center of the arc of the throw. Stopping the hand at the moment of release would reduce the momentum of the hand before the ball is actually released and speed would be lost. (Since a thrown object moves in a tangent to the arc the hand is traveling at the point of release, the flatter the arc which the hand travels, the greater the accuracy will be.)
4. The trunk must rotate and the weight of the body be transferred forward in order to move the shoulder forward.

COMMON FAULTS:
1. Starting the throw with the body facing square to the target.
2. Failing to rotate the trunk.
3. Holding the ball in the palm of the hand.
4. Failing to keep elbow bent and to lead the throw with the elbow. (Key to many girls' problems.)
5. Holding elbow close to the body, resulting in a pushing motion.
6. Failing to transfer weight to forward or left foot.
7. Dropping the wrist before releasing the ball.
8. Using little or no follow-through.

KEY TEACHING PHRASES:
1. Keep eyes on target.
2. Start with shoulder to target.
3. Hold left arm at shoulder level, and point to target.
4. Twist body backward.
5. Keep elbow bent and shoulder high and away from body.
6. Lead throw forward with the elbow.

7. Whip arm through to target.
8. Snap wrist.
9. Release ball off fingers.
10. Reach for the target.
11. Step onto right foot.

Uses

The overhand throw is used primarily for throwing an object which is small enough to be held by the fingers. The overhand pattern is commonly used for all throwing in baseball, softball, and football. It is the basis of the overhand serves in tennis and volleyball, and the smashes in the racket games. It is the preferred pattern for throwing in lacrosse.

SUGGESTIONS FOR STUDY:

1. Start with beanbags or darts with large suction grippers on the ends. Standing close to wall, throw at wall. Emphasis should be on having the elbow bent and held high. Pattern instead of distance should be stressed.
2. Using tennis balls or fleece balls, throw at wall at varying distances. (Children can grasp fleece balls in their fingers easily, and they will not rebound very far after hitting the wall. Tennis balls can be held with fingers but rebound with greater force.)
3. Move progressively farther back from wall, and throw. Teacher should point out the body rotation and shift of weight necessary to throw at increasingly farther distances.
4. Throw at targets on the wall.
5. Throw ball through a hoop held by a partner.
6. As catching skill improves, throw and catch with a partner.
7. Throw at a moving target, another person, a moving ball.
8. Throw a football for distance.
9. Throw a football for accuracy.
10. Throw a softball for distance. Add a preliminary run.

Underhand throw

A child's first attempt at throwing is usually that of a two-hand toss or underhand throw. As the hands get larger and when a small ball is used, the one-hand throw develops.

Description

With feet together the thrower stands facing the target. The right arm is brought straight down and back. At the same time the body rotates slightly to the right, and the weight is shifted to the right foot. The arm is swung quickly forward, and at the same time a step forward is taken onto the left foot. The ball is released when the arm is at a right angle to the target. The left arm swings backward to aid in balance.

Basic mechanical principles

1. The amount of momentum generated by the body is transferred to the ball. The rotation of the body, the backswing, and the shift of the weight to the rear foot allows the ball to be brought back farther so that there is more time to build up momentum in the forward movement.
2. The straight arm affords a greater arc through which the ball travels to build up momentum.
3. The follow-through enables the hand to be moving its fastest at the moment of release. The object moves in a tangent to the arc the hand is travelling at the time of release; consequently, the point of release is when the arc of the hand is tangent to the target.

COMMON FAULTS:
1. Using little or no rotation of the trunk.
2. Failing to use a long enough backswing.
3. Failing to shift weight backward.
4. Releasing ball too high.
5. Failing to step forward on left foot.
6. Failing to follow through.

KEY TEACHING PHRASES:
1. Face target.
2. Twist body to right as ball is brought back.
3. Bring arm down and straight back, and then swing it straight forward.
4. Step forward on left foot.
5. Reach for the target.

Uses

The underhand throw pattern is effective for throwing tasks involving accuracy because the throwing hand follows a straight path. It is used as a pitch and a short throw to basemen in softball; as a roll-in for hockey; as the delivery in bowling; it is used when a pass of short or medium distance is needed in basketball. The underhand pattern is the basis of many skills—such as volleyball serve and the badminton serve—which use the hand or other instruments as striking objects.

SUGGESTIONS FOR STUDY:
1. Using a beanbag or fleece ball, throw to wall, and increase distances.
2. Using a large ball, throw to wall. Left hand will have to support ball on backswing.
3. Roll ball at targets.

4. Throw at targets on the wall.
5. Throw to a partner.
6. Run, stop, throw a short pass to a partner.
7. Run, pivot, throw to a partner who is a short distance away.

Sidearm throw

Description
The thrower stands in a forward stride position with the right foot
back. If the object is large, the palm of the hand holds it against the
lower arm. A small object is held with the fingers. The body rotates or
twists toward the right, and the body weight is transferred to the back
foot as the arm swings back in a *horizontal* arc. When the object is
small, the forward actions are the same as in the overhand throw with
the exception of the horizontal arm pattern. That is, the arm moves
with a whiplike action with the elbow leading, the body rotates toward
the target and the object is released when the hand is at a point tangent
to the target.

If the object is large, the arm moves as one long lever, and no series
of joint actions is practical. The ball must be released at the moment
that the arc of the throwing arm is tangent to the target.

Basic mechanical principles
The long backswing, the body rotation, the follow-through, and the
movement of weight forward all contribute to the force and speed which
is transferred to the object as it leaves the hand.

COMMON ERRORS:
1. Failing to rotate the body backward.
2. Failing to shift weight back, then forward.
3. Releasing ball too early (ball goes to the right).
4. Releasing ball too late (ball goes to the left).

KEY TEACHING PHRASES:
1. Eyes on target.
2. Hold large ball against wrist.
3. Shift weight back.
4. Twist body.
5. Whip the ball forward with the elbow leading.
6. Follow through with the hand in direction of target.

Uses
The sidearm pattern is generally used to throw large objects for distance, such as the discus and basketballs. Deck tennis rings are thrown
with a sidearm pattern. It is also the basic pattern for drives in badminton, tennis, and paddle tennis.

SUGGESTIONS FOR STUDY:
1. Throw a basketball or a soccer ball for distance.
2. Throw a deck tennis ring from the right side, from the left side (forehand and backhand).
3. Throw a small ball to the wall, to a partner.
4. Throw at a target on the wall.

Striking

Description

The striking pattern is utilized in almost all sports activities. Most of the activities involve hitting an object with some part of the body or an implement which is controlled by the hand. The object to be struck may be stationary or moving. The striking pattern is much the same as that involved in any one of the three throwing patterns.

No matter what plane the implement of striking follows, the speed of the struck object is governed by the same principles as those involved in throwing. The amount of momentum developed depends on the length of the backswing, the number of muscles brought into play, and their orderly sequence of action. The object to be struck should be contacted at the instant the maximum speed of the swing has been reached. The implement must follow through in the direction of the target. The implement should be held out and away from the body and swung in a plane that is a right angle to the object to be hit.

A stance which provides a solid base is important if fast moving objects are to be struck and propelled any distance. The firmer the hitting surface of the striking implement, the greater the forward force becomes. Implements vary in their firmness; however, a strong grip is always essential. If the hand or foot is the striking tool, the broadest, firmest parts must be the striking surface, i.e., the top of the instep of the foot or the broad area of the fist. Specific striking patterns such as batting in softball, kicking in soccer, serving in volleyball, and so forth are described in Chapters Twelve and Thirteen.

Basic mechanical principles

1. As a stationary object is struck, it will move only if the force applied to it is sufficient to overcome its inertia. Therefore, it is essential to develop great speed in the striking movement. This movement is accomplished by weight shift, body rotation, length of backswing, and sequence of muscle actions.
2. The reaction of an object against a striking surface is just as great as the force which projects the object. Therefore, the striking surface should be as firm as possible and the striking tool held as firmly as possible.

3. The more nearly an object is contacted in line with its center of gravity, the greater the amount of force that is transferred to the object in the direction it should travel. Since in most striking activities encountered by elementary children, it is intended that the object go forward and slightly upward, this may be interpreted as slightly below dead center.

COMMON FAULTS:
1. Failing to use sufficient backswing.
2. Rotating body too little.
3. Keeping elbow in too close to the body (when arm action is involved).
4. Failing to grip striking implement tightly.
5. Hitting too far above center of object or "topping object."

KEY TEACHING PHRASES:
1. Eyes on object to be hit.
2. Shift weight back and through.
3. Make a big swing.
4. Hit just below center of object.
5. Make a level swing.
6. Follow through in direction of target.

Uses

The striking pattern is used with parts of the body being tools, as the hands in volleyball and in basketball; the head, shoulder, knee, or foot in soccer; the hand in handball. The same pattern is employed with implements such as the rackets in tennis and badminton, the sticks in hockey, golf, and softball.

SUGGESTIONS FOR STUDY:
1. Hit balloons with the hands, fists.
2. Hit playground balls or volleyballs with hands and fists for distance.
3. How high can volleyballs or playground balls be hit?
4. Use a large wooden paddle to hit a 5-inch playground ball thrown by someone else.
5. Throw ball in air, and hit it.
6. Use plastic fun balls, and hit them with paddles.
7. Using a batting tee, hit plastic balls with plastic bats.
8. Kick a stationary ball for distance.
9. Kick a stationary ball to a partner.
10. Stop a rolling ball with the feet and then quick-kick it to a partner.
11. Kick into a target area.
12. Walk and kick a ball, keeping it close to body.
13. Hold a ball in the hands, drop it and kick it before it touches the ground.
14. Kick a ball back and forth with a partner while running.

Table 9-2. Teacher's Guide for Analyzing Selected Fundamental Skills

Skill	Base of Support and Balance	Production of Force	Direction of Application of Force	Focus	Follow-Through	Absorption of Force
Walk	Brief period of support on both feet, weight shifted in direction and new base of single support. Feet pointed straight ahead, placed alternately along a line.	Contraction of extensor muscles of leg, ankle to push off with toes. Arms swing in opposition to the legs.	Push off horizontally and very slightly vertically. Arms swing back and forward, not across body.	Head up, eyes straight ahead.		Weight taken on heels, transferred along outside edge of foot to toes.
Run	Base: one foot. Body weight forward, lean from ankles.	Contraction of muscles of hip, knee, ankle; push off from toes.	Feet placed straight ahead; legs move upward and forward; arms swing in opposition, forward and backward. Elbows bent.	Head up, eyes straight ahead.		Land on ball of foot.
Jump A. Height	Base at take-off weight even over both feet; weight low, with knees bent, but hips must be tucked under. In flight, erect position of body. Landing, body erect, weight over both feet; use arms for counterbalance.	Hips, knees, ankles bent; force is derived from extension of these muscles. Arms swing forward and upward.	Push off directly vertical. Arms swing upward.	Head up, eyes upward.	Stretch and reach with all parts of body.	Landing, bend knees, ankles; take weight on balls of feet.

Table 9-2. Continued

Skill	Base of Support and Balance	Production of Force	Direction of Application of Force	Focus	Follow-Through	Absorption of Force
B. Distance (Standing)	Base: Take-off weight over both feet, forward lean of body. In flight, weight forward. Landing, weight low and forward on both feet.	Hips, knees, ankles bent; force derived from extension of these muscles. Arms swing first backward then forward, vigorously.	Forty-five degree angle upward. Legs swing forward under body.	Head up, eyes straight ahead.	Whole body stretches and reaches forward.	Land in a crouched position, weight on balls of feet.
C. Distance from a running start.	Preliminary run demands take-off from one foot. Same as B in flight and landing.	Greater forward momentum gathered from fast run. Push-off is from one foot. Arms swing forward vigorously.	(Same as B)	(Same as B)	(Same as B)	(Same as B)
Hop	Base: weight on one foot, brief period of no support, weight returned to same foot. Arms counterbalance.	Contraction of extensor muscles of hip, knee, ankle. Push-off from one foot. Upward swing of arms.	Upward amount of forward movement depends on use of hop.	Head up, eyes straight ahead.		Land on toes, shift weight to ball of foot.
Landing	Base: Feet in side on forward side-stride position (no more than width of hips sideways). Weight low and over base. Use arms to counterbalance.			Head up, eyes straight ahead.	As soon as weight is absorbed, legs are extended and rebound to standing position.	Hips, knees, ankles bend, land on balls of feet.

Table 9-2. Continued

Skill	Base of Support and Balance	Production of force	Direction of Application of Force	Focus	Follow Through	Absorption of Force
Leap	Longer period of nonsupport than for run. Base shifts alternately on feet which are placed along a straight line forward. Weight forward, arms counterbalance.	Greater flexion of knee and ankle than in run to increase upward movement. Vigorous push-off from rear leg. Forceful upward movement with arms adds to vertical force. This is preceded by a run to gain more momentum for height.	More vertical push off than horizontal as in run. Forward-upward direction of arms.	Head up, eyes straight ahead.	Stretch and reach with whole body.	Land on balls of feet.
Skip	Period of nonsupport on hop, weight shifts to alternate feet on step. Arms counterbalance.	Propulsive force upward from one-foot push-off of hop gives upward momentum. Arms swing upward.	Forward and upward.	Head up, eyes straight ahead.		Land on toes and transfer weight to balls of feet.
Slide	Base moves to alternate feet. Weight shifted from lead to following foot. Weight always within base of support.	Extensor muscles of leg as foot pushes vertically and horizontally.	Sideways, more vertical push-off if height is desired on hop.	Head up, eyes straight ahead.		Weight taken on ball of foot.

motor

walk

run

leap

jump

hop

slide

skip

landing

stopping

pivot

dodge

falling

non motor

bend

stretch

pull

push

lift

swing

turn

twist

basic catching
throwing & striking
patterns

Table 9-2. Continued

Skill	Base of Support and Balance	Production of Force	Direction of Application of Force	Focus	Follow-Through	Absorption of Force
Stopping	Feet in stride position. Weight brought directly over both feet.			Head up, eyes straight ahead.		Bend knees, ankles, land on balls of feet. Lean back from waist.
Dodge	Body weight drops low and is brought back over both feet to initiate dodge; the weight is then shifted outside. The base of support is the new direction of movement.	Push off with one or both feet.	Push off horizontally in new direction.	Head up, eyes straight ahead.		Bend knees, land on balls of feet.
Falling	Make broad padded areas of body new base—hips, thigh buttocks, or back of shoulders.			Tuck head, eyes on landing spot.		Relax joints and muscles, land on padded areas, go into roll so there is a greater amount of time for momentum to decrease.
Pull	Base: both feet in wide stance. Body weight low. Weight shifts in direction of pull.	Preparatory movement of extension of arms, knees bend. Object drawn to body by flexion of arms and extension of legs.	Arms toward body, legs backward at center of gravity of object to be moved.	Head up, eyes on object to be pulled.	Body straightens.	

Table 9-2. Continued

Skill	Base of Support and Balance	Production of Force	Direction of Application of Force	Focus	Follow Through	Absorption of Force
Push	Base: Both feet in wide stance. Weight low, weight shifts in direction of push.	Preparatory movement of flexion of arms, hands, knees. Summation of forces in extension of legs, arms, and hands.	Directly forward at center of gravity of object to be moved.	Head up in direction object is to be pushed.	Body Straightens.	
Lift	Base: both feet in wide stance. Weight low.	Preparatory flexion of legs, arms, hands, then a summation of forces from an extension of legs and arms as object is raised and placed somewhere else.	Upward under center of gravity of object to be lifted.	Head up, eyes on spot to where object is to be lifted.	Whole body straightens.	
Catching	Base: stride position in direction of ball. Wide stance, body weight low. Weight directly over base.			Eyes on ball.		Fingers spread, slightly curved. Reach with arms slightly forward, curl fingers around ball, pull in toward body. Whole body gives slightly.

Table 9-2. Continued

Skill	Base of Support and Balance	Production of Force	Direction of Application of Force	Focus	Follow-Through	Absorption of Force
Throw	Base: both feet in stride position. Weight shifts to rear foot on back-swing to forward foot on throw. A forward step is taken as part of follow-through to regain a stable base on both feet.	Preliminary move-ment includes backswing, trunk rotation, shift of weight to increase arc and develop greater momentum. Forward motion: trunk rotates for-ward, all leg, trunk, arm, wrist, hard muscles extend se-quentially. Ball re-leased with final snap of wrist and fingers as arm is straightened. Weight shifts to forward foot as upper arm passes; shoulder and lower arm is fully ex-tended.	All in direct line toward target.	Head turned toward target, eyes on target.	Arm and hand follow directly to the tar-get. Step onto right foot to regain balance.	

SUGGESTED REFERENCES
FOR FURTHER STUDY

Andrews, Gladys, Jeannette Sauborn, and Elsa Schneider, *Physical Education for Today's Boys and Girls* (Boston, Allyn and Bacon, 1960), Chapter 1.

Bilbrough, A., and P. Jones, *Physical Education in the Primary School* (London, University of London Press, 1965).

Inner London Education Authority, *Educational Gymnastics: A Guide for Teachers* (London, The Authority, 1965).

Murray, Ruth L., *Dance in Elementary Education* (New York, Harper & Row, 1953), Chapters 5, 8, and 10.

Part IV

MOVEMENT EXPERIENCES

Chapter X

DANCE

*Fundamentals
of dance*

Creative dance

*Structured forms
of dance*

Dance steps

*Basic dance
formations,
positions, figures,
and terms*

Teaching dances

*Suggested
progression for an
elementary school
dance program*

Dance activities have served many cultures as a form of art and recreation; they continue to play an important role in American life. Dance in the elementary school curriculum is vital to the child's development of body control, of expressiveness, and of creativity. A child learns what his body can do and how to adapt the various movements of the body to force, space, and objects through all activities, but movement affected by a time structure is learned best through dance activities.

Children usually have a sense of rhythm, a natural love for rhythmic movement, and an innate creative ability. How extensively all of these qualities are developed depends upon the opportunities a child has to express them. These opportunities are provided by a variety of dance forms.

Dance has many forms of which only four are generally studied in the elementary school—fundamentals, creative, folk, and recreational. In the primary grades the emphasis is placed on the fundamentals and the creative forms. Simple singing games and folk dances are included. The fundamentals are the foundations of a movement action vocabulary and provide an understanding of the rhythmic elements affecting movement. They also enable creative responses to be expressed, since they are the foundation on which the child may experiment, explore, and interpret.

In the intermediate and upper grades more emphasis is placed on learning the structured folk and recreational dances than in the primary grades. Creative dance is important at upper levels also, but frequently teachers spend less time on it. This is particularly true when boys and girls are separated in physical education classes. Unfortunately, due to cultural pressures, creative dance for the boys is often considered unmasculine. Teachers should try to deemphasize this concept and include a balanced portion of creative movement experiences. A good dance background in the primary grades and proper selection of themes for creative dance activities will help overcome this problem.

FUNDAMENTALS OF DANCE

The fundamentals of dance include basic locomotor and nonlocomotor skills and various combinations of them, and an understanding of rhythm, space, and force. These are the basic tools for all other dance forms and, as such, are given major emphasis in the primary grades.

Actually, the movement skills and the elements of space and force that must be considered are the same as those discussed in Chapter IX; however, in dance the expressive form of the skills is stressed. More emphasis is given to the coordination of the movements and rhythm elements. Since all movements for each individual have an internal rhythm, it is difficult to make a great distinction between dance movement and basic movement.

Frequently, people say dance experiences must have accompaniment, but this is not so. Since each person has his own internal time organization, it is difficult for young children to develop many good movement skills within an imposed external rhythm. They must learn to match their rhythm with that of another person or with an accompaniment of some kind. Whether the young child's experiences in exploration and experimentation with movement is called part of a dance unit or part of a movement exploration unit is immaterial. The significance lies in his having the experiences in using his body to make creative responses, and in acquiring the tools to learn structured dances.

Locomotor movements

Locomotor movements are those that move the body in space in any direction; the feet are the moving base. The four basic locomotor movements are the walk, run, jump, and hop. They are performed in an even rhythm.

Various combinations of basic locomotor movements performed in a specific space and time pattern are the traditional dance steps. The gallop, slide, and skip are the simplest of these to learn and are known by many children before they come to school. They are taught and used in first grade dance activities. The walk and run are also used in their natural form as dance steps.

1. The gallop is a combination of a walk and a run. The same foot is always the lead foot.
2. The slide, a combination of a walk and a leap, is much the same as a gallop, but it is usually done in a sideways direction.
3. The skip is a combination of a walk and a hop.

These steps are performed to an uneven rhythm. Even though they are actual dance steps, they are considered fundamentals because they are a vital part of children's movement vocabulary before dance steps are utilized in structured forms.

Nonlocomotor movements

Nonlocomotor or axial movements are those in which various parts of the body move in space, with one part of the body serving as an axis or base around which the other parts move. The nonlocomotor movements are the swing, sway, stretch, bend, twist, turn, rock, push, pull, and various combinations of these.

Any of the locomotor and nonlocomotor movements may be done in combinations with one another. Variations of any one should be explored after the movements are learned in their original form. All of the nonlocomotor and locomotor movements included here are analyzed in Chapter IX.

Elements of rhythm

All dance movements are affected by the elements of rhythm since they are performed within a time structure. This structure is bound by the same elements of rhythm as music is. These elements should be studied simultaneously in music and physical education. The elements of rhythm which should be learned in relation to dance are underlying beat, rhythmic pattern, measure, tempo, accent, phrasing, and intensity.

Underlying beat
The underlying beat is the steady continuous sound that is heard or felt throughout any rhythmical sequence. It is the constant unit of measure upon which rhythmic structure rests. It may be likened to the steady

beat of the heart or the pulse. Each movement is synchronized with the underlying beat. For example, a step is taken and completed within the time limit of each beat on a drum. A new step is taken on each beat of the drum. The length of the beat may vary.

Rhythmic pattern

A rhythmic pattern is a definite grouping of sounds or beats related to the underlying beat. A particular pattern of unequal sounds or beats must fit within a unit of underlying beats. For example, the uneven pattern of the skip has a rhythmic pattern fitting into units of the underlying beat as follows:

Rhythmic pattern	walk	hop	walk	hop	walk	hop	walk	hop
Underlying beat	(skip)		(skip)		(skip)		(skip)	

Measure

A measure is an identical grouping of underlying beats. The number of beats in a measure and the time value of each beat is dependent on the meter of the measure, i.e., 2/4, 4/4, 3/4, 6/8 time.

Accent

The accent is the force of emphasis in movement given to any one beat in a series of pulse beats in measure. In dance the accent is usually on the first beat of every measure.

Tempo

Tempo is the rate of speed of the movement, music, or accompaniment. It may be fast, slow, or moderate.

Phrasing

A phrase is a group of measures which completes a sequence of sounds or movements. It can be likened to a sentence or an idea in itself. It is very important that children learn to recognize and identify phrases in their rhythm experiences, as phrasing is essential to learning folk dance easily. The end of a phrase usually signifies changes in direction or movements.

Intensity

Intensity is the quality of the movement or music. It denotes the loudness or softness of music or forces of a movement.

Space elements

Whether creating a dance or following a traditional dance, an understanding of the space elements which affect movement are important.

These elements are direction, level, and floor pattern. Although these are described in detail in Chapter IX, they will be reviewed briefly here as they relate specifically to dance.

Direction
Direction is the line of movement taken. It may be forward, backward, sideward, diagonally, upward, downward, or combinations of these.

Level
Movement through space may be done at a high, low, or medium level.

Floor pattern
The design made by the body as it moves in space is called the floor pattern. It may take the form of a circle, square, straight line, or zigzag.

Teaching the fundamentals of dance

The dance fundamentals can be learned best through a progressive series of teacher-directed experiences wherein the child learns to use his body in relation to all of the factors that affect movement (Chapter IX). These must be teacher-directed to ensure the sequential, purposeful acquisition for all concerned. If the approach is hit-or-miss and poorly planned, the child's movement foundation will be deficient. The experiences should be planned by the teacher with opportunity for the class to enjoy experimentation and problem-solving. Also, refinement and development of movement skills can be enhanced by creative experiences introduced by the teacher.

The elements of rhythm should be taught along with the movement skills. Both can be taught in the classroom or the gym and can be integrated naturally. If there are specialists to teach music and physical education, they should work together in planning for dance and rhythmic experiences.

Kindergarten and first grade objectives should include: (1) recognition that one starts and stops when the accompaniment starts and stops; (2) recognition of one's own space; (3) maintenance of a general direction pattern. It is suggested that much time in the first two grades be devoted to individual work with the basic locomotor movements in their natural form. Simple variations in tempo, direction, and level should be introduced. These variations can become more complex after a year along with the teaching of additional uses of body parts in non-locomotor movements. Young children will perform large movements better than small confining movements. As soon as movements are done well alone and the pupil can respond to simple external factors that affect movement patterns, combinations of movements should be attempted.

Learning to move with the tempo of the accompaniment is also an early objective. In the beginning stages, the accompaniment should be a drum, hands, sticks, piano, or some other means by which the teacher can control the tempo. Young children are not accustomed to moving with an imposed time and rhythm. They progress from a consciousness of their own tempo to that of the groups' and finally to that of the accompaniments'.

Children should be encouraged to provide their own accompaniment, since it helps them gain a knowledge of beat, tempo, accent, and phrasing. Clapping their hands may be the first experience. Sticks, shakers, and drums can be handled easily by children. Making one's own instrument is a worthwhile project. Those of the primary grades will be crude and simple, but they will be a source of pride to the child and will serve to augment his understanding of rhythmic elements.

CREATIVE DANCE

When dance fundamentals are fairly well grasped, they should be refined and expanded through creative experiences. Acquiring dance tools and using them are interrelated, since movement skills are needed as the tools of expressive movement, and at the same time these tools are improved and expanded through creative experiences.

The development of creativity is one of the major objectives of education. Torrance states that "man seems to prefer to learn creatively, by exploring, questioning, experimenting, testing, and modifying ideas and solutions." [1] Too frequently children are not encouraged to learn in this way, and consequently they do not develop their creative ability. Creative dance experiences provide an opportunity for such development, since these skills are concerned with self-expression through the media of movement. Opportunities to solve movement problems and to relate his experiences and feelings in an outward expression enable a child to think creatively in a rather permissive, accepting environment. Young children are naturally very expressive and readily show their feelings. If the opportunities to use powers of expression are continued in all of the elementary grades, children will develop their powers of creative thinking.

Creativity reflects one's concepts and perceptions, or to generalize, one's experiences. Feelings or emotions, ideas, and interpretations may be

[1] E. Paul Torrance, "Seven Guides to Creativity," *Journal of Health, Physical Education and Recreation* (April, 1965), p. 24.

expressed through exploration, improvisation (moving freely in response to various stimuli), solving a problem (usually working out a problem posed by the teacher), composition (making a dance which has a definite form, beginning, and ending), or modifying an established step, pattern, or dance.

The experiences of primary grade children are rather limited compared to those of older children. The ability to abstract grows with age. Therefore, the main themes for creative dance lessons for young children must center on their immediate surroundings and experiences. They enjoy being "like something" or moving "like something." Their reaction to moving like something is usually dramatic. The younger the child, the more apt he is to be imitative. This changes as his experiences broaden and as he develops the tools of movement. Imitation and pantomime should be channeled. For example, if after a field trip to the fire station a story play is worked out, the trip should not be pantomimed but the children should be a fireman, a fire truck, or a fire hose.

As children grow into the middle grades, their experiences broaden as do their interests in other people and the world beyond their immediate environment. They are very curious as to the when, where, and how of things. Their intellectual powers and, of course, their classroom studies open new vistas of knowledge about science, history, and adventure. Their ability to reason and to abstract grows. They are less self-centered and more interested in sharing and working with others in small groups. More conscious of other people, they have emotional reactions to what other people think, do, and say. They are in need of a means to express emotions through movement.

As coordination and motor skills become more refined, boys become very interested in vigorous activities and the development of strength. Creative and rhythmic experiences that meet these new interests for boys must be selected carefully so that they do not appear unmasculine.

Children need avenues of expression as they enter puberty and encounter many frustrations and feelings of insecurity. Relationships between boys and girls change at this time. Good vigorous dance activities provide social settings for boys and girls where they can work and play together and feel comfortable in their interactions.

Suggestions for teaching creative dance

There are a number of approaches one may utilize for ideas for the creative efforts of children. Later, suggestions are made for approaches from songs, music, objects, poems, imagery, designs, experiences, and dance steps.

A great deal of the creative dance lesson is spent on problem-solving, improvisation, and composition work. Compositions may range from a very simple interpretation or expression to a complex dance of many parts or sequences in time and form. The process of arriving at the final composition may involve experimentation and exploration.

The teacher must lay the foundation whenever the class as a whole, as members of small groups, or as individuals are to be given problems to solve or composition work. First he may present a simple problem to the whole class so that each child must work out his own answer. The problem may be presented in stages so that children experience the format of working out a pattern for a dance, changes in direction, or partner relationships, before becoming a member of a small group.

Children should be taught how to approach a problem. If everyone is to work on the same topic, it should be discussed first. Possible answers or solutions may be presented, and ideas for format discussed. After dividing into small groups, the first step is discussion of the problem, then presentation of individual ideas, modification of ideas, use of them, further discussion, then final refinement. After the working period is over, each group should have a chance to present their answer or composition. Observation and evaluation should follow.

Children in primary grades work best alone or in partners. As they get older, small groups of three to five provide a satisfactory working number. Larger groups become difficult, since frequently the less imaginative youngsters let the more aggressive ones do all the planning. There is apt to be disagreement among group members and much time consumed in planning verbally instead of in movement. Groups should be assigned so that the most and least aggressive youngsters are scattered throughout the groups. Care should be taken that everyone is working and contributing. A chairman may be appointed.

The same problem may be assigned to each group or a different problem to each group. Only about eight to ten minutes should be allowed for planning and working on most compositions. Children are most productive in the first six minutes. If they have not reached the acting stage or refining stage by then, chances are they will not for a long time. Polished productions should not be expected. The emphasis is on the process, not necessarily the product. Some compositions may warrant further refinement. Naturally, more time should be taken for refining the pattern if a dance is designed which may be learned by all, may be used in the future, or may be taught to others. In the upper grades larger group compositions may be undertaken, possibly for presentation to another group or a parent group. This may also be a culminating activity for either a classroom unit or a dance unit.

Whenever an individual or small group presents their solution to a problem, an evaluation should be made. It might include points that were not considered in the solution, other ways to solve the problem, use of movements, quality of movements, and perhaps suggestions for refinement or further pursuance.

The teacher sets the stage, serves as a catalyst, then an audience, and finally as a mediator in evaluation and observation of the creative efforts of children. His most crucial responsibility lies in the selection of themes, problems, and activities for the creative lesson. How he presents the material to the class is also important in terms of the children being able to understand the problem clearly. As children are working on their compositions, he serves as the catalyst—asking questions, prodding, giving few suggestions but much encouragement. As children present what they have done, he serves as an audience, or at least as part of the audience, and after the performance as a mediator in the evaluation.

Suggestions for creative dance experiences

Teaching creative dance to children is as much a creative exercise for the teacher as it is for his students. Developing ideas to fit a specific group, expanding old ideas, using new media, and so forth is a constant challenge. Presented here are a few ideas to use as a springboard into teaching dance. The teacher will find that ideas come rather easily. One's ideas grow and flourish from watching and listening to children as they work.

Teaching elements of rhythm

Underlying beat

1. Using a drum, beat steadily and have the children clap on every beat, then step on every beat. Vary means of locomotion. Change to asking for axial movements as a response. Change rate of speed of beat.
2. Have children provide beat with hands, feet, sticks, or other instruments.
3. Use different instruments, and assign a different movement to each one. Children must stay with the beat as each change of instrument is made. Assign a different direction for each beat.
4. Use a march record, and step on every beat.
5. Jump rope to the beat.
6. Bounce balls to the beat.
7. Policeman: Use a drum or a record for accompaniment. Leader

stands where everyone can see him. Using his arms as a policeman does to direct traffic, he indicates different directions in which class should move. The object is to make the changes without losing the beat. Predetermined signals for various other changes may be made, such as changes in level and force, and changes to locomotor from nonlocomotor activities.

Rhythmic pattern

1. Make up a series of two speed patterns. Children clap out the pattern. Use a combination of walks and runs as next responses. Later, three speed patterns can be added; however, these are more difficult (Figure 10-1).

Figure 10-1. Rhythmic Pattern.

2. Clapping Names (Figure 10-2).
   Names are selected, and the rhythm of the name is clapped and spoken. Later, one group may select names for a designated category, and the other children must guess which name it is. Movements may be added to the pattern.

SUSAN ELLEN THOMPSON

TOM JOHNNIE JONES

Figure 10-2. Clapping Names.

3. Clapping Rhymes (Figure 10-3)
   Select a favorite nursery rhyme. Clap out the rhythmic pattern. Divide into small group. Each group selects any nursery rhyme. Each child in each group will clap one beat of the pattern. After this, movements may be substituted for claps.

Figure 10-3. Clapping Rhymes.

4. Echo

Teacher claps a rhythm pattern. Children must echo the pattern with claps. Progress to having the children echo with movement.

5. Radio Stations

Small groups of four or five children are stationed in each corner of the room and are given letters of radio stations. One station sends out a clapping message. The next station must pick it up and duplicate the message. The message should be in claps first, then in movement.

Accent

1. Select a meter and beat the drum accenting the first beat in each measure. Have children clap on accent. Change accent to different beats.
2. Clap on every beat but the accented one.
3. Vary response to accent with locomotor movements and nonlocomotor movements.
4. Combine walking on a nonaccented beat with a forceful nonlocomotor movement on accent.
5. Change direction on accent.
6. Change levels on accent.
7. Divide into groups; each group may be assigned a different beat to accent.
8. Use claps or beating instruments at first, then movements.

Tempo

1. Play drum, changing speeds. Children change speeds as drum changes. Try walking at double time, quickly, slowly.
2. Select objects or animals which usually move at a fast or slow rate. Whenever tempo of accompaniment is like that of their chosen object or animal, they move as it does.

Phrasing

1. Listen to record. Clap at the end of the phrase. Move, changing direction at end of phrase. Change level, style of movement, alternate nonlocomotor and locomotor each time the phrase changes.
2. Use various folk dance records to identify phrases. Make several

groups. Each group is assigned to move at the end of each phrase. If in a circle formation, one group may move in when the phrase changes, and the other group may move out. Try the same thing with partners.

Creative approaches for primary grades

EXPLORING MOVEMENT WITH DESCRIPTIVE WORDS AS MOTIVATION:

tall —short	tight —loose	loud —quiet
sleepy—peppy	windy —still	dark —light
happy—sad	cold —hot	elastic—spongy
big —little	crooked—straight	smoky—wispy

EXPLORING MOVEMENT AND IDENTIFYING OBJECTS AND PEOPLE FROM DAILY EXPERIENCES: animals, pets, toys, favorite play activities, story book characters, community helpers, home chores, seasons, nursery rhymes.

MUSIC: Many good records are available with selections of music which stimulate improvisation by children as a response to the mood, tempo, rhythm structure, and quality of movement suggested by the music.

SUGGESTED RECORDS

Elementary Rhythms. Phoebe James, Box 134, Pacific Pallisades, California. Four different records. Two are particularly good for work with basic movements. Two may be used for exploration and simple composition work.

Let's Play Series, #1 and #2. Ortman Recordings, 1644 West Broadway, Vancouver, British Columbia. The suggestions for activities are set in story play form. Excellent for primary grades.

Listen and Move, I, II, III, IV. McDonald and Evans Limited, 8 John St., London, England. (May be ordered from Canadian FDS, Audio-Visual Aids, 605 King St., Toronto, Canada.) These records contain interesting short pieces featuring percussion instruments, voices, and music of different moods. Excellent for use in exploration, improvisation, and compositions.

Sing and Dance. Educational Dance Recordings Inc. *Living with Rhythms.* David McKay Co. Inc., 119 West 40th St., New York, N.Y. *Rhythm and Meter Appreciation.* Helps acquaint the teacher with fundamentals of music theory emphasizing rhythms and meters. Basics of music given which are necessary to know before an understanding of rhythm and meter are understood. One side shows how rhythm and meter dictate specific physical reactions.

The Rhythm Program, E71, 72, 73, Vol. I, II, III. R.C.A. Victor Record
Division, 155 E. 24th St., New York, N.Y. Each volume contains
short pieces of work of well-known composers. The records may be
used for exploration of fundamentals, improvisation, and compositions.

SONGS: Children can make dances to the music and the words of songs
with which they are familiar or can learn easily. The type of movement and the form of the dance follows the music and spirit of the
song. The words usually suggest the nature of the dance that is
composed. Most songs used with primary grade children should be
short. They may be taken from the school music books or be songs
which are learned before attempting to make a dance to them. Since
most school music books are excellent sources of songs, and many
music teachers do encourage learning a dance to songs, no particular books will be recommended here.

POEMS: Poems afford an excellent source of dance making for children,
since most of them have a rhythmical, rhymed pattern that is ap-
pealing and almost automatically sets one off on a movement accompaniment. Poems may be used as an accompaniment, or the
poem may be read and the meaning interpreted in movement.
Whichever way the teacher chooses to use the poem, it should be
either learned or read and discussed before children begin to make
their dances. Poems which include a moving character or object are
better than those with abstract meanings or feelings.

DESIGN: Primary grade children should become aware of design and can
easily portray their own work from the art class in movement. Simple
line drawings or writing one's name in movement is challenging to
them. Before doing them in movement, they should first make their
designs on paper or on the blackboard, then work them out in movement.

STORIES: Stories serve as an excellent opportunity for children to be dramatic in their movements. Children should not be told to pantomime the story, but should be encouraged to move as if they were the
characters in the story. Stories from readers, simple story plays, or
stories that children write may be the basis for the dramatization.
The story may be read prior to the class and plans made for dramatization to be done in the gymnasium. With primary children a
story may be read as they interpret the action line by line. Stories
which involve animals or actions which are big and bold serve best.

CIRCUS IN TOWN

"We're off to the circus parade. We have to wait on the side of the street for
the parade to come. What comes first? Listen to the circus band. What kind of

an instrument is on that wagon? Look at the elephants, lions, horses, tigers, and all. A clown just came over and gave some one a balloon. What did he do as he went back into the parade? It looked as if he were upside down. What do those men and women do who are wearing long tights? There are more clowns. Look at the trained dogs. What can they all do? Look at that wagon. The sign says 'The Fattest Woman in the World.' Why do you suppose she is riding in the wagon? There is the strongest man in the world, and he is walking. Here comes the last wagon in the parade. What do you suppose is in it? Let's follow the parade to the circus grounds."

INDIAN BUFFALO HUNT

Dance around the campfire before the hunt starts. Check the bows and arrows before starting out on the plains. Ride the horses out to see where the herds are grazing. Sneak up on the herd so we can get close enough to shoot. Aim and shoot, the herd will start to run after the first shot, so be ready to ride after them.
Collect buffaloes that were shot, and prepare to take them back to camp.
Carry buffaloes back to camp.
Dance around the campfire to celebrate a successful hunt.

Creative approaches for intermediate and upper grades

The basic approaches for children in the intermediate and upper grades are similar to those for lower grades, however, the themes have to be consistent with their experiences and interests as previously described. Lessons are based on dance problems and projects developed in progressive fashion from advanced study of the dance steps, direction, accent, level, rhythmic patterns, cumulative rhythm, and tempo. Every period should culminate in small group compositions with evaluations of same contributing to future lessons. Problems and compositions can be related to classwork and interests growing from classroom subjects. At these grade levels children become more interested in the historical and theoretical background of the problems.

AREAS OF EXPERIENCES AND INTERESTS: Sports movements (as participants, as spectators), occupations, transportation, machinery, space age, favorite storybook characters, cheerleaders, television commercials, moods, and emotions

CLASSROOM UNITS: History and people of the United States; history, peoples, customs, trades of other countries

SONGS: Rounds, work chants, popular songs

DANCE STEPS

POEMS: Verse, nonsense rhymes
MUSIC
PROPS: Balls, scarves, hoops, ropes, sticks
SENSORY CUES: Colors, textures, sounds, pictures, designs

Sample problems for small groups

1. Make up a dance using the schottische step and the step-hop. Include three changes of direction and three different partner relationships.
2. Using the telephone number 351–1798, make up a dance. Either the group or an individual may do the actions for each number. Use the same movement between each number to signify a change in number. Use either locomotor or nonlocomotor movements. (Each group may be assigned a different number; then each must guess the numbers of the other groups.)
3. Make up motions for a cheer. "Fight team, fight! Fight team, fight! Fight together, now or never, fight team, fight!" Use at least three different nonlocomotor movements, two locomotor movements, two changes of level. Half of the group should do opposing movements. Use focus and use quality of movement which is indicative of the mood of the cheer.
4. Each group is given an object, such as a feather, scarf, coconut, or piece of driftwood. Each one is to show through movement how the object feels. He may describe the form or the shape of the object; he may use movements that denote surfaces that are smooth, rough, jagged, and so forth. (This problem is easily adaptable to work with individuals.)
5. Work in couples with a ball for each couple. Make a pattern of combinations of throwing, catching, and bouncing. Change levels and directions at some points in the pattern. Utilize phrasing in making the changes.
6. In groups of four make a dance which combines swinging, twisting, and turning. At some point use opposing movements with half of the group, then return to movements in unison.

STRUCTURED FORMS OF DANCE

The forms of dance which involve movements done in a specific pattern and sequence are folk dances and recreational dances. In these forms children learn to use the fundamental skills and formations of dance within a prescribed structure of pattern, time, and style. The major purposes for including these structured forms are to develop cultural understandings, to experience the moods they suggest, to control body movements in a defined relationship to other people, to promote social abilities and adjustments, and to fulfill the need for vigorous activity.

Folk dance

Folk dance is a cultural art form which communicates the customs, rituals, occupations, and beliefs of the people of a country or a nation. Since folk dances have been handed down from generation to generation, the dances we know today are not entirely authentic. Nonetheless, they provide an excellent source of information about the peoples who originated them.

America's true folk dance is considered by some to be the dance steps which originated with the jazz music of 1915–1920, developed in New Orleans. From the basic shuffle step came the lindy, the jitterbug and other dances. Because this style originated in America (although today it may be found all over the world), it is referred to as the American style of dance. The play-party dances—square, couple, and round dances— which became popular in pioneer times and days of westward expansion are sometimes called American folk dances; but they were really based on formations and steps borrowed from folk dances of other countries.

As folk dance is an art form, it is a valuable part of the school curriculum in the study of other countries and peoples. Folk dances should not be taught for the exclusive purpose of learning the steps or formations. These should be learned out of context of a dance and become a part of the child's movement vocabulary. The major focus in folk dance, then, is the dance itself and the selection of it should be an outgrowth of the study of some aspect of a people or country. The folk dance can make this aspect come to life for the student and enrich his learning in social studies, language, literature, music, and art.

Mere mention of the nationality of a folk dance or pointing out its origin on the map does not foster cultural understandings. Too often this is a common practice. Units of folk dance are often planned in which dances from various countries are selected because they are listed as appropriate for a grade level. Folk dances should be taught when the countries, peoples, and customs are being studied in other subject areas. Rather than have one or two units of folk dance a year, several short units may be planned to coincide with classroom study. Two or three dances of a country may be learned. These give the students a good background for the dance, because they may be able to put themselves in various roles of the people they are studying.

Early study of folk dance may become a foundation for a lifelong leisure time activity. Many college and adult recreation groups are formed for the preservation and study of authentic folk dances, as well as for the enjoyment of the dance activity.

Recreational dance

Recreational dance includes square, round, longways, couple, and social dances. The primary values of these types of dances are recreational and social. For the most part, the terminology of the forms is derived from the shape of the formation of the dances.

The square and longways (or contra) dances are products of America's westward expansion and provide a good opportunity for study of pioneer life. Round and couple dances are social dances usually based on combinations of walking steps, the two-step, the schottische, and polka steps. Frequently, they are of quite recent origin and are put to popular tunes played in a country style. They are usually easy to learn and often provide for many changes of partners.

Many mixers with very simple patterns based on the walking step ease the tension between boys and girls in the early pubescent years. These dances also may be used to make it less obvious that some boys are shorter than the girls. Square and longways dances have a particular appeal to boys in intermediate and upper grades because they are quite vigorous, easy to learn, and do not involve positions which require boys and girls to be close to each other for long periods of time.

Since social or ballroom dancing is one of the most popular leisure time activities of adolescents and adults, children need a good foundation in the accompanying social skills, procedures, and courtesies. Usually children have their initial contact with social dance during the seventh and eighth grades, if not earlier. Whether or not social dance is a part of physical education before this is dependent upon the community customs and the needs of the children. If there is no occasion or place where social dancing is appropriate outside of class, many boys are not interested in learning these skills before they reach high school.

DANCE STEPS

Although the walk, run, and hop are frequently steps used in structured dances, there are a number of combinations of these basic movement patterns which are called dance steps. All of these should be taught to children out of context of folk or recreational dance so that they become a part of their dance and movement vocabulary. When dances are introduced which require the use of any one of the steps, then it is only necessary to refer to the step or to review it before the pattern of the dance is taught. In this way the focus is on learning the dance and the associated cultural knowledge, rather than on the skills of the dance.

Basic format for teaching a dance step

A general format or procedure which has proved successful for teaching a new step is described here. As some step patterns present unique problems, specific suggestions are made for each step. All of the steps of the general format are not repeated but are implied, and they should be incorporated into the teaching of each dance step, especially steps 11, 12, and 13.

1. Play the music.
2. Clap the rhythm.
3. Step in place with the music.
4. Teacher performs the step.
5. When children feel ready, they should try the step. (At this point a verbal description may be necessary for some steps.)
6. Individuals work on the step, teacher helps those who are having trouble. Cue words are used.
7. Vary the direction.
8. Combine with other steps.
9. Explore the step for other variations.
10. Do the step with partner.
11. Partners try variations of the step.
12. Do a dance which uses the step.
13. Make up a dance using the step.

   Those steps which are usually called traditional dance steps are (progressing to the most complex): slide, gallop, skip, step-hop, schottische, polka, two-step, waltz, and mazurka. The first three step patterns can be learned easily in the primary grades. They have been previously described. All of the others should be taught before the end of the sixth grade. Each of the last three is analyzed, and specific suggestions are given for teaching and developing each step.

STEP-HOP (record: RCA 1957) 2/4 or 4/4

Count	1	2	3	4
Cue words	step	hop	step	hop
Foot pattern	left	left	right	right

1. Standing in place, step and hop on left foot, then on right.

2. After pattern of step-hop is established, move forward with step, hop. Sometimes children step on one foot and want to hop on the other foot.
3. Combine four walking steps, then four step-hops, repeat.
4. Do four walking steps, then four walking steps going around in a circle.
5. Vary directions of step-hops; backward, sideward.

SCHOTTISCHE (record: Imp. 1046A) 4/4

Count	1	2	3	4
Cue words	step	step	step	hop
Foot pattern	left	right	left	left

1. Standing in place, take three steps on alternate feet and on the fourth count, lift the leg and hold. Repeat. (Left-right-left-lift right, right-left-right-lift left)
2. Progress to hopping on the supporting foot on the fourth count as the leg is lifted and swing slightly forward. Stress *not* putting weight on the foot that was hopped on. Some children want to leap rather than hop.
3. Move forward around the room changing directions. Go forward, backward, sideward, in a circle.
4. Use a light run emphasizing a light spring in the air with the hop.
5. Accent the fourth count with a lift on the arms to coincide with the hop.
6. Take two schottische steps and then four step-hops in place. Continue pattern.
7. Move with a partner; make many different space relationships with partner.
8. Using a record with a faster tempo, take light running steps rather than walking.
9. Try variations while working with three people.
10. Teacher should teach a simple folk dance with schottische steps. (Danish Schottische—World of Fun, record 102A)
11. Make up a partner dance using the schottische.

POLKA (record: RCA 25–2009) 2/4

Count	and	1	and	2	and	1	and	2
Cue words	(hop)	step	close	step	hop	step	close	step
Foot pattern	(right)	left	right	left	(left)	right	right	right

Note that the hop in the polka is on the last *and* of a measure. It comes on the upbeat. Due to this, the step has a bouncy quality. The polka step can be learned easily from the slide by following this suggested progression.

APPROACH FROM A SLIDE:

1. Everyone in a circle takes eight slides to the right. This may be done in a scatter formation also.
2. Turn back to center, and take eight slides in the same direction around the circle.
3. Turn face to center, four slides in same direction around circle.
4. Turn back to center, four slides in the same direction around the circle.
5. Turn face center, two slides in the same direction around the circle.
6. Turn back to center, two slides in the same direction around the circle.
7. Continue turning on every two slides. This is the polka.
8. In the circle facing a partner, everyone has the inside hands joined. They take one polka step starting on outside foot, turn and take another step with backs to one another, continue. This is the face-to-face, back-to-back polka.

APPROACH FROM A GALLOP:

1. Starting with right foot leading, take eight gallops.
2. Left foot leading, eight gallops.
3. Right foot leading, four gallops.
4. Left foot leading, four gallops.
5. Right foot leading, two gallops.
6. Left foot leading, two gallops.
7. Repeat with left foot leading, then right, left, right, etc. This is the polka step.

APPROACH FROM A TWO-STEP:

1. Using a two-step, make the step short and bouncy, with a quick hop at the end of each measure becoming part of the first step at the beginning of the next measure.
2. Continue with variations in directions and partner relationships.

TWO-STEP (record: WD 7621) 2/4

Count	1	and	2	and	1	and	2	and
Cue words	step	close	step	(hold)	step	close	step	(hold)
Foot								
pattern	left	right	left		right	left	right	

A step forward is taken with the left foot, the right foot is brought forward and placed next to the left heel with the weight put on the right foot. Another step forward is taken with the left foot, and the weight is held on it for one count. The sequence is repeated with the first step being taken with the right foot. Frequently children do not get the idea of leading with alternate feet. The cue may be changed to: *Left,* two-three, *right,* two-three, with an accent on the alternate foot leads.

1. Standing in place, clap the rhythm. Clap, clap, clap, with no clap on the fourth count. The idea of quick, quick, slow; quick, quick, slow should be caught.
2. Step in place. Left, right, left, hold weight on left; right, left, right, hold weight on right. Continue, and then say "quick, quick, slow."
3. Move forward step, close, step; step, close, step. Alternate cue words with quick, quick, slow.
4. Move to side, changing directions as lead foot alternates.
5. Move forward four two-steps, backward four two-steps. Continue pattern.
6. Holding hands and facing a partner do pattern in #5 with one moving backward and one forward.
7. Alone. On the first step turn left shoulder to the left and step with left foot placing toes toward the left; bring right foot beside left and step and hold on left foot. Dancer has made a half turn. This may be repeated right.
8. Try various combinations of quarter turns, half turns, and sequence of steps in different directions.

WALTZ (record: MG 649) 3/4

Count	1	2	3	1	2	3
Cue words	step	step	close	step	step	close
Foot pattern	left	right	left	left	right	left

1. Clap 1, 2, 3, on each beat of the measure, accent the first beat with a loud clap.
2. Standing in place, step on alternate feet, 1, 2, 3. Accent first step of each measure with a slightly heavier step, then a deeper bend of knee; for emphasis dip the same shoulder. All notes and steps have an equal time value.
3. Step forward taking a long step on first count, a medium step on second count, and a tiny step on third. The third step should become a closing step. Move around the room with this pattern.
4. Move forward taking a long first step on left foot, a short step sideward with right foot, and bring left foot close up to the right foot ("Forward, side, together"). Step backward on the right foot, step sideward on the left foot and bring right foot close up to the left foot ("Backward, side, together"). These two movements done together comprise the box waltz.
5. Move forward four waltz steps, move backward four waltz steps.
6. Turn, using the first and long step as the move in a new direction and the second closing step to complete the turn.
7. Facing a partner and holding hands, waltz forward, backward, do a box waltz, turn, and repeat.

MAZURKA (record: FC 1130) 3/4

Count	1	2	3	1	2	3
Cue words	step	close	hop	step	close	hop
Foot						
pattern	left	right	right	left	right	right

1. Clap 1, 2, 3; 1, 2, 3, accenting the first count and the second count.
2. Standing in place, step left, right, hold left. Accent counts 1 and 2 with slightly heavier step.
3. Still in place, step left, right, and hop on right.
4. Move forward step left, step right hop, on right; left, right, hop. The same foot always leads as the weight is held on the hopping foot.
5. Lead left, right, hop-swinging the free "left, right" leg down for the next lead step.
6. Do the step with a partner.

There are several dance steps which are frequently used in folk and recreational dances which are not referred to as traditional dance steps. These too should be a part of every child's movement vocabulary and should be learned before they are encountered in folk dances. These are the stamp, draw, bleking, heel and toe, step swing, buzz, grapevine, and a basic Indian step. The fox trot, the lindy, and if desired, a contemporary dance step should be taught if social dancing is part of the upper grade curriculum.

STAMP: One foot strikes the floor forcibly but no weight is taken on the stamping foot.

DRAW: A step to the side is taken, the free foot is then drawn up close to the supporting foot, and the weight is usually shifted. The sideward step may be exaggerated by a body lean in the direction of the step.

BLEKING: A hop is taken on the left foot, and the right leg is extended forward with the heel touching the floor. A hop is taken on the right foot with the left leg extended. The position of the left heel and right heel are exchanged in a rhythmic sequence.

HEEL AND TOE: The heel of one foot is touched to the floor forward, the toe of the same foot is touched to the floor backward. Sometimes the heel of one foot is touched diagonally forward and a slight hop is taken on the other foot. The toe of the same foot is then touched to the floor across the other foot near the instep. A slight hop is taken on the other foot as the change is made.

STEP SWING: A step is taken on the left foot and the right foot is swung across in front of the left; a step is taken on the right foot and the left foot is swung across in front of the right leg. Toe of swing foot is pointed in the direction of the diagonal swing.

BUZZ: With weight kept on one foot, the other foot pushes against the floor as the weight revolves around the pivot foot. A pushing step is taken on each beat of the music. This is usually done with a partner.

GRAPEVINE: This is a sideways walking step. The right foot is crossed over in front of the left foot; another step is taken on the left foot; the right foot is brought behind the left foot, then a step is taken on to the left foot. Cue words may be right over, left, right back, left. The step may be done in either direction.

BASIC INDIAN STEP: A step is taken onto the ball of the left foot, then weight is dropped onto heel of left foot; a step is taken onto ball of right foot, then weight dropped onto heel of right foot. The knee bend should be exaggerated and the arm on the opposite side swung forward.

Social dance steps

Fox TROT (record: RCA 20–3663A) 4/4

Count	1	2	3	4
Cue words	step	hold	stcp	close
Foot pattern	left	(hold)	right	left

1. Clap the first and third beats.
2. Standing in place, walk on first and third beats.
3. Walk forward.
4. Walk backward.
5. Step forward on left foot, hold, step to right on right foot, bring left foot up to side of right putting weight on left foot. Step forward on right, hold, step to left on left foot, bring right foot up to side of left putting weight on left foot ("Slow, quick, quick").
6. Move, using step forward and backward.
7. Combine forward and backward step to make a box pattern.
8. To turn, take first step in the desired direction, complete the turn by bringing the other foot around to a square position in desired direction.
9. Combinations with a partner.
   a. Step sideward left, close with right, taking weight on right; step sideward left, close with right but do not take weight (side step).
   b. Combine two fox trot walks and one fox trot (step, hold; step, hold; side together).
   c. Combine two fox trot walks and half turn with two fox trot turn steps.
   d. Four fox trot steps forward, four backward, turn, walk four steps, repeat.

Basic fast step

LINDY (record: RCA 20–2421A) 4/4

Count	1	2	3	4
Cue words	slow	slow	quick	quick
Foot	sideward	sideward	backward	right
pattern	left	left	left	in place

1. Step in place to learn the beat of the music.
2. In closed position, lead person steps to the left side with left foot, then steps to right side with right foot, then turns away to a semi-open position by stepping backward on left foot putting it behind the other foot, then rock forward in place with right foot. The knees bend slightly on each step. The two quick steps are known as the rock step.
3. After practicing the basic step the double lindy can be learned. Lead steps sideward left onto ball of foot, then brings the heel down, steps sideward right onto ball of foot, then brings heel down, backward on left, and steps on right in place. Cue words are: toe, heel, toe, heel, backward left, and step on right. This is called the dig step.

   The lindy step is small and is usually done in one spot on the floor. The dancers move around each other, forward and back, and the girl moves under the boy's arm. Many variations and combinations of the dig step and the rock step can be done.

BASIC DANCE FORMATIONS, POSITIONS, FIGURES, AND TERMS

Directions for folk and all of the forms of recreational dances utilize a common terminology. Most frequently the terms are not explained within each set of directions, since it is assumed that the reader knows what they mean. Each of these formations, positions, and figures should be learned by children before the pattern of a dance is taught. This is termed preliminary teaching. Then, as with the dance steps, these will become a part of the children's dance vocabulary, and they can readily respond to the directions of a new dance without interruptions in the pattern to learn a new figure or position.

Dance formations

FREE: Couples or groups of three take a position anywhere in room.

CIRCLE:

1. *Single with no partners:* All dancers stand in a ring facing the center, or facing counter-clockwise in the circle.

2. *Single with a partner:* All dancers stand in a ring. If facing toward center of circle, girl is on boy's right. If partners face each other, girl's right hand is toward the inside of the circle and the boy's left hand is toward the inside.

3. *Double:* Couples stand in a ring formation. Boy is on inside of circle. Usually both face counter-clockwise if not facing each other.

GROUPS OF THREE OR TWOS: Any combination of threes; may be in circle or free formation.

LONGWAYS OR CONTRA: Any number of couples standing in a double line, usually boys on one side, girls on the other and with partners facing. Head of the set is on end nearest the music. Foot of set is at the opposite end.

SQUARE: A set of four couples arranged in a square formation. The couple with its backs to the music is called couple number 1. The couple to their right is number 2, the couple opposite them is number 3, and the couple on their left is number 4.

QUADRILLE: A set of four couples arranged in a square formation. The couples facing the music and with their backs to the music are the head couples. The other two are side couples.

Directional terms

CLOCKWISE: Direction in which a clock moves.

COUNTER-CLOCKWISE: Direction opposite clockwise, usual direction of movement in a circle.

LINE OF DIRECTION: Direction the dance takes—usually counter-clockwise.

Dance positions

OPEN: Partners stand side by side with inside hands joined. Girl is usually on boy's right.

SKATING OR PROMENADE: Partners stand side by side facing same direction, girl on boy's right. Hands are held, right in right and left in left, with the right arms above left.

VARSOVIENNE: Partners stand side by side facing forward. Boy stands slightly behind and to the left of the girl. Boy holds girl's right hand in his right, her left hand in his left just above shoulder level.

TWO-HAND: Partners stand face to face and join both hands. May be used in place of closed position or shoulder-waist position.

SHOULDER-WAIST: Partners stand face to face; boys put both hands on girl's sides. Girl puts both hands on boy's shoulders.

CLOSED (SOCIAL DANCE POSITION): Partners stand face to face; boy puts his right arm around the girl placing his hand just below her right shoulder blade; girl puts left hand on boy's right shoulder. The girl's right hand rests lightly in the boy's left palm which is held just below shoulder level. They look over each other's right shoulder.

Position terms

INSIDE FOOT OR HAND: Foot or hand nearest the partner when side by side.

OUTSIDE FOOT OR HAND: Foot or hand farthest from partner when side by side.

HOME: The original or base position in a set or circle.

CORNER: Boy's corner is the girl on his left, lady's corner is boy on her right.

Dance figures

TURNS:
1. *Elbow:* Boy and girl hook elbows and walk, skip, or step-hop around each other as directions indicate.
2. *Two-hand:* Right hands and left hands clasped and walk, skip, or step-hop around each other. (A one-hand turn may be substituted.)
3. *Hungarian:* Partners stand with right sides together; right arms on each other's waist, left hand raised above head with elbow bent. (One- or two-hand turn may be substituted.)

SWINGS:
1. *Elbow:* Partners hook elbows and swing around clockwise with either a running or walking step, usually two complete turns.
2. *Two-hand or one-hand:* Holding hands partners swing around clockwise with either a running or walking step.
3. *Buzz:* In either an elbow or two-hand or closed turn position weight is held on one foot, and the other foot pushes against the ground while pivoting on right foot. Movement is clockwise, and usually two complete turns are made.

PROMENADE: Partners walk or dance around the circle or set side by side in a counter-clockwise direction.

GRAND RIGHT AND LEFT: In a circle or square formation, partners face one another, holding right hands. All boys face counter-clockwise and all girls clockwise. All move forward passing right shoulders, reaching out for the next person's hand. When the hand of the next person is grasped, the other hand should be released and that arm extended to meet the next person. Continue around the circle in the *same* direction alternating right and left hands and right and left shoulders. The figure appears as a weaving in and out. Continue until original partners meet.

ALLEMANDE RIGHT: Partners face each other, join right hands and then walk *completely* around once in a clockwise direction, returning to their position.

ALLEMANDE LEFT: Same as allemande right, only left hands are grasped, and the walk is in a counter-clockwise direction. May be done with a partner or a corner.

DO-SI-DO: Partners face one another, cross arms over chest and move forward four steps, take one step to the side and then walk backwards back to place. May be done with corners.

REEL: (Usually found in longways dances.) Head couple goes to center of set and does an elbow turn one-and-a-half times around, the girl goes to the first boy in the boy's line and does an elbow swing, boy does same with first girl in girl's line. They both return to the center and do an elbow swing once around with each other; they then return to the third boy and girl respectively and do an elbow swing, and go back to the center for an elbow swing. They continue to proceed in like manner to the end of the line.

RIGHT-AND-LEFT-THROUGH OR PASS THROUGH: Two couples exchange places; both walk forward. They drop hands when they meet the opposite couple whom they pass through by passing right shoulders. The boy turns the girl around in the new position so that she is on his right.

LADIES' CHAIN: Girls walk across set and meet their opposite girl, grasp right hands, pass right shoulders, drop hands and reach out to take left hand of the opposite boy; he turns her around and the ladies repeat the same pattern back across the set back to their homes.

STAR: Four dancers go to the center of the set, join right hands high in center and walk around in a counter-clockwise direction. They may reverse direction and reverse hands and go once around in clockwise direction.

TEACHING DANCES

Since each dance has its own structure of formation, time, steps, positions, figures, and patterns, the teaching of dances must necessarily follow the nature of a direct method. The teacher who develops a technique of teaching a dance where children may be involved in each step of a progressive sequence of the presentation will find his students eager, cooperative, and absorbed in learning the dance. Thereafter they will enjoy dancing for the pleasureful satisfaction of doing it well.

Some preliminary teaching is necessary for each dance. This may be in the form of a long term preliminary preparation where dance steps, positions, and figures have been explored, learned, and performed in many variations. It may be done prior to the learning of the dance itself when a new figure specific to that dance must be learned. Perfection of a step must not be demanded before it is used in a dance, but certainly familiarity and confidence in doing the step must be gained before trying to adapt it to a time and pattern structure, or there will be frustration and displeasure.

When a dance has been selected for its cultural implications, much of the discussion about the dance can take place in the classroom. A brief follow-up or review may be conducted in the dance setting. Many of the recreational dances have interesting historical backgrounds or portray a colorful incident which makes the dance more meaningful for the children. The introduction should be brief. The real value of the dance to the child is the enjoyment derived from the participation in the dance and the satisfaction gained from doing it well. The name of the dance should be made clear to the children so they can identify the dance easily.

While children are in the formation of the dance, the music should be played at least once or twice through the entire dance. Most dance patterns or sequences are repeated several times so there is no need to play the entire record. While the music is playing, the children will feel the beat. If they have a good dance background, references can be made to the beat and phrases identified. They will learn to identify fast and slow movements and recognize what steps the time and rhythmic patterns suggest. They may clap the pattern or try some of the steps in place. The teacher may guide their understanding by a few cue words such as, "What does that sound like? A skip?"

After listening to the music, the children should see a demonstration of the dance. How much of the dance can be demonstrated depends on the length and complexity of the dance and the number of people in a set. Perhaps only one part of it can be performed at a time. With the music, the teacher should demonstrate as much as possible of the dance. The teacher may select an alert pupil as a partner quickly telling him the sequence, and then guiding him through the dance. The children can see how the dance looks and better understand how the various parts relate to the whole.

Verbal descriptions may then accompany the demonstration. Depending on the complexity of the dance or dance part, the children may be asked to try it with the teacher when they think they see and feel the pattern. If many children cannot follow the demonstration, the class should go through the pattern without the music. The teacher should continue doing the dance with the class and give cue words when there is a change of direction, position, or step.

Long practices without the music should be avoided. Music helps children feel the pattern and also holds their attention. Long practices at a tempo slower than the accompaniment should also be avoided. If a variable speed record player is available, the speed can be decreased while the dance is learned and then gradually increased. The transition from a slow tempo without the music to that of up-to-time with the music may be difficult, and all that was gained may be quickly lost.

When there are many parts to the dance, the dance must be broken down to be learned and then put together. The parts may have to be repeated several times. Each child will learn from repeating and from watching others. Often if the teacher can be the partner of a child who is having trouble for just a few trials, the youngster will be better prepared.

When individuals or couples have had a chance to work out the pattern, the whole dance should be done a few times. The teacher can spot those having trouble quickly. If the whole group or a large number lose the timing or get confused, the dance should be stopped immediately and started again from the beginning.

The teacher should continue to use cue words; however, he should stress listening to the music and particularly to the phrases. When children have to depend on listening to the phrases for cues, they become much more involved, and inattentiveness is avoided.

The dance should be practiced several times during subsequent periods so that children will know it well and enjoy doing it. Only after the dance pattern has been learned well should much attention be given to style. Controlled body movements, good posture, attention to neat sets and other factors can be stressed at that stage.

The sequence of teaching a dance is summarized in these points.

1. There should be preliminary teaching of new steps, positions, figures, or review of those already learned that are included in the dance to be learned.
2. Name of the dance is given, and associated learnings discussed briefly.
3. The children should listen to the music, identify phrases, beat, etc.
4. Demonstration of dance is given in its entirety.
5. Students try the dance or parts, first with music if possible, or without music if necessary.
6. Unify the parts, dance the whole dance.
7. Refine problem spots.
8. Refine whole dance in a series of practices.

Selection of partners

Since many dances require partners, the teacher must have a prearranged plan in order to set up partner relationships quickly. Boys in the intermediate grades frequently have anti-girl and anti-dance attitudes. In sixth and seventh grades some girls are taller than boys in their room. At both of these stages, problems arise in dancing and particularly in selecting partners.

The extent of these problems depends upon the teacher's selection of dance content and the atmosphere he creates. If dance of all forms has been a part of the children's physical education program in each grade, the children will have a wholesome attitude toward dance, and few problems will arise. When boys and girls are together for all activities, they usually learn to respect one another's skills, and they treat dance as naturally as anything else. When they come together only a few weeks out of the year for dance units, there may be some uneasiness. Under these circumstances, the units should begin with vigorous individual work with balls, ropes, sticks, and then gradually structured work with Indian dances, line dances, longways dances, and finally with dances which call for closer partner relationships.

The teacher should not hesitate to make changes in dances if they are too difficult, or if positions call for close proximity of boys and girls which may cause problems. For example, if the directions call for a varsovienne position, and several boys would have to stretch up to hold the girl's hands at shoulder height, it would be much more practical to ask for a two-hand open promenade position.

It would be most desirable for everyone to have a partner of his own choice, but this is not always practical. There is not always an equal number of boys and girls, some would always be asked last, some would argue over the choice. Learning to choose partners quickly is a long-term process. Children should realize that it is fun to dance with different people; it is a challenge to adjust to various people's style; it is polite to accept the first invitation; it is kind to help other people learn and improve.

Mixers, where after a certain sequence in the dance everyone automatically gets a new partner, provide an opportunity for children to focus their attention on the dance and deemphasize the importance of who one's partner is. If choices are allowed, little time should be given for choice, and an emphasis should be placed on choosing the nearest boy or girl. A few suggestions follow for arranging partners.

1. Boys form a circle facing one direction, and girls form one on the outside of it facing the opposite direction. All walk to the music, and when it stops everyone stops, turns, and faces his partner.
2. One large circle is formed with every other person a boy. Girl on boy's right is his partner.
3. Form two lines, boys on one side, girls on the other. Walk forward to the music and meet a partner.
4. In the same formation as described in number 3, each line walks around the room in opposite directions, and the two lines meet in the

middle. As they meet they pair off and walk down the center of the floor. This may be repeated, or partners may be established at this point. A grand march may be conducted in much the same manner.

5. Form a single circle with every other person a boy. Do a grand right and left around the circle. Persons who are together when the music stops are partners.

6. Move freely about the room doing whatever step the music suggests. When the music stops take the nearest person for a partner and be ready to move together when the music starts again. Do this several times before partners for dances are established.

7. Look at someone, focus on someone else's eyes. Two people should be staring at each other; they should walk toward each other and become partners.

8. When doing couple dances, have broom dances or ribbon dances where the extra person gives the object to someone and takes his partner.

When there are more boys than girls and the dance directions call for boy and girl parts, do not have boys take girls' parts (and vice versa). Extra children may operate the record player, do the steps at the side, or sit and wait their turn. There should be a definite rotation pattern for these children to be included in the dance. If the class is made up entirely of girls, color bands should be used to identify the lead parts. The term "lead" should be used rather than "boys."

Accompaniment

One of the best and least expensive types of accompaniment for dance is a percussive instrument. A percussive instrument is one which is struck to produce sound. Included in this type of instrumentation are drums, sticks, bells, cymbals, clapping hands, tapping feet, shakers of all types, and many more. A percussive instrument provides a strong, easily identifiable beat. It is especially valuable when working with young children and when teaching dance fundamentals. The beat can be adjusted to the tempo that dancers take. A good drum is an essential piece of equipment for the teacher of dance. Children can make many other percussive instruments.

A piano is most desirable for use in instruction; however, many schools cannot provide one. Also, many teachers can play the piano, but some find it difficult to give suggestions, directions, and help individuals at the same time. Ideally, an accompanist who enjoys children and who can improvise should be available.

A sturdy, reliable record player is another essential. It is desirable to have a three-speed player with a variable speed control so that the speed may be decreased for beginning work with structured dances. There are many good records available for accompaniment for all forms of dance. Most records or albums contain well-written directions for the dances or suggestions for the use of listening or rhythm records.

The school should have a file of current catalogs from major educational record companies. In larger cities some record shops carry educational records. Most shops will gladly order for schools or individuals and will usually have current record catalogs.

Selection of dances

It is difficult to assign a specific grade level at which a dance should be learned, since the background of the dancers is such an important factor. However, there are certain factors that make a dance difficult or easy. Even though a grade level is assigned to a dance, the teacher should read the directions with the following factors in mind before deciding if it is appropriate for his particular group.

1. *The dance skills and rhythm skills required in the dance:* Have the children in the class learned the steps, formations, positions, figures required in the dance? Have they done them enough that they can quickly adapt to the rhythmic factors present in the dance music? If they haven't learned them, can they learn them quickly before the dance is taught?
2. *The number and combinations of dance skills required in the dance:* Can the students handle many different steps or variations or changes of formations at the same time?
3. *The number and length of parts in the dance:* Can the whole dance be learned quickly? Are there so many parts that it will take a whole period or longer to learn the complete dance?
4. *The positions and style required in the dance:* Are the positions called for consistent with the maturity level of the group? Are the movements too confined for the maturity and interest level of the group? If so, can they be altered to fit the needs of the group?
5. *The compatibility of the cultural learnings inherent in the dance with the background of the group:* Will there be value in the associated learnings in relation to classroom units? Will the cultural meanings have any significance to the group?

Suggested dances

A variety of folk and recreational dances are suggested for the primary, intermediate, and upper grades. The name, nationality, formation, skills needed for the dance, and suitable records are listed for each dance. Complete descriptions and directions for each dance are not given because they are included with the records which are suggested. Frequently timing and sequences within the same dance are different on records of different labels. For this reason when directions are taken from a book, care should be taken that the suggested record is used. A key to the suggested records and addresses of the record companies precedes the dance list.

SUGGESTED PROGRESSION FOR AN ELEMENTARY SCHOOL DANCE PROGRAM

Kindergarten, grades one and two

MOVEMENT SKILLS: Explore and refine the basic locomotor and nonlocomotor skills in expressive style with accompaniment as they are affected by speed, intensity, level, direction, and various relationships. *Dance steps:* slide, gallop, skip, and step-hop

RHYTHM SKILLS: Learn and understand the use of underlying beat, measures, even and uneven rhythms, tempo, rhythmic pattern, and phrasing in relation to movement. *Rhythmic games:* Clapping Names, Clapping Nursery Rhymes, Policeman

Table 10-1. Key to Suggested Records

Company	Code	Company	Code
Radio Corporation of America Victor Record Division 155 E. 24th St. New York, N.Y.	RCA	Folkcraft Records 1159 Broad St. Newark, N.J.	FC
World of Fun Records Methodist Publishing House 150 Fifth Ave. New York, N.Y.	WF	Imperial Records 137 North Western Ave. Los Angeles, Calif.	IMP
Windsor Records 5528 North Rosemead Blvd. Temple City, Calif.	WD	MacGregor Records 729 South Western Ave. Hollywood, Calif.	MG
		Folk Dancer Box 201 Flushing, N.Y.	FD

Table 10-2. Singing Games for Primary Grades

Dance	Nationality	Formation	Skills	Record
Bluebird	American	Single circle	Walking and skipping, dramatization of bluebirds	FC 1180
Rig-a-Jig-Jig	English - American	Single circle	Skip	FC 1199
Loopy Loo Did You Ever See a	English	Single circle	Walk, dramatization with various body parts	FC 1184
Lassie	Scottish	Single circle	Imitation of one person's actions	FC 1183
Farmer in the Dell	English - American	Single circle	Skip	FC 1182
The Muffin Man	English	Single circle	Skip, word dramatization	FC 1188
The Big Gray Cat	American	Circle or scatter	Dramatization of cat and mice movements	RCA WE 87
How Do You Do My Partner	Swedish	Single circle	Skip	FC 1190

Table 10-3. Folk Dances

PRIMARY GRADES

Dance	Nationality	Formation	Skills	Record
Shoemaker's Dance	Danish	Double circle, partners	Skip, dramatization of shoemaker	FC 1187 RCA 1624
Danish Dance of Greeting	Danish	Single circle, partners	Run	FC 1187
Children's Polka	German	Single circle, partners	Draw, stamp	FC 1187 RCA 1625
Chimes of Dunkirk	French	Double circle, partners	Run, walk	FC 1188 RCA 1624

INTERMEDIATE GRADES

Dance	Nationality	Formation	Skills	Record
Greensleeves	English	Double circle, two couple sets	Walk	WF 106 RCA 1624
Cshebogar	Hungarian	Single circle, partners	Slide, skip, draw, turn	FC 1195 RCA 1624
Bleking	Swedish	Free, couples	Bleking step, hop	RCA 1626 FC 1188
Gustaf's Skoal	Swedish	Quadrille	Walk, skip	FC 1196 RCA 1622 WF 108
Norwegian Mountain Dance	Norwegian	Groups of threes	Running step, step-hop	RCA 6173
Circassian Circle	English	Single circle (mixer)	Walk	FC 1247 WF 104
Seven Jumps	Danish	Single circle	Step-hop, follow the leader actions	RCA 1623
Ace of Diamonds	Danish	Double circle, partners	Face to face, back to back polka, elbow swing	RCA 1622 WF 104

Table 10-3. Continued

INTERMEDIATE GRADES

Dance	Nationality	Formation	Skills	Record
Danish Schottische	Danish	Double circle, partners	Schottische, step-hop	RCA 1622
Hansel and Gretel	German	Free, couples	Heel-toe	RCA 1624

UPPER GRADES

Dance	Nationality	Formation	Skills	Record
Black Nag	English	Longways, sets of 3 couples	Running	WF 109
Waves of Tory	Irish	Longways	Walk, star, promenade, cast-off	WF 102
Mayim	Israeli	Single circle	Grapevine	FC 1108
Troika	Russian	Groups of 3	Running	WF 105
Tantoli	Swedish	Double circle	Heel-toe polka, step-hop	FC 1160
Weggis	Swiss	Free, couples	Heel-toe polka, step-hop	FC 1160
Little Man in a Fix	Danish	Groups of 4 couples	Waltz, run	RCA 20449
Road to the Isles	Scottish	Free, couples	Schottische, hop	IMP 1005 A
Horah	Israeli	Single circle	Side-step, step-swing	FC 1110
The Roberts	Scottish	Single circle, partners	Draw, heel-toe, two-step	FC 1161
Kalvelis	Lithuanian	Single circle, partners	Polka	FC 1051

Table 10-3. Continued

Dance	Nationality	Formation	Skills	Record
Hop Mor Anika	Swedish	Double circle	Walk, skip, polka	RCA 4142
Crested Hen	Danish	Groups of 3 couples	Step-hop, stamp	RCA 6176
Tinikling	Filipino		Leap, jump (over 2 poles held by 2 people)	RCA 4126
Miserlou	Greek	Single circle	Grapevine, walk	RCA 1620
Cherkassia	Israeli	Single circle	Grapevine, step-hop	RCA 1623
Ersko Kolo	Yugoslavian	Single circle, partners	Schottische, side-step	FD MA 3020 A
Korobushka	Russian	Free, couples	Schottische, balance	FC 1170

Table 10-4. American Play Party – Mixers – Round – Couple Dances

INTERMEDIATE GRADES

Dance	Type	Formation	Skills	Record
Bingo	Mixer	Single circle	Walk, grand right and left	FC 1189
Glow-Worm	Mixer	Double circle, partners	Walk	IMP 1044
Patty-Cake Polka	Mixer	Double circle, partners	Heel-toe, slide, skip	FC 1124
Oh Susannah	Play party	Single circle	Walk, grand right and left, promenade	FC 1186
Skip to My Lou	Play party	Single circle	Walk, skip	FC 1192
Heel and Toe	Couple	Free	Slide, polka	FC 1166
Virginia Reel	Play party	Longways	Walk, skip	FC 1181
Bow Bow Belinda	Play party	Longways	Walk, skip, cast-off, do-si-do, elbow swing	FC 1189
Paw Paw Patch	Play party	Longways	Walk, skip, cast-off	FC 1181 WF 111

UPPER GRADES

Dance	Type	Formation	Skills	Record
Teton Mountain Stomp	Round	Double circle, partners	Side-close-stomp, walk	WD A 753
Wrangler's Two-Step	Round	Double circle, partners	Walk, grapevine, balance turn	WD 7621
All-American Promenade	Mixer	Double circle, partners	Walk	WD 7605
Jessie Polka	Couple	Free	Two-step or polka	FC 1071
Ten Pretty Girls	Mixer	Single circle, partners	Walk, point	WF 113
Put Your Little Foot	Couple	Free	Mazurka, waltz	FC 1165
Cotton-Eyed Joe	Couple	Free	Heel-toe, polka, hop, two-step	WF 118
Rye Waltz	Couple	Free	Slide, waltz	FC 1166
Brown-Eyed Mary	Mixer	Double circle, partners	Walk, skip, promenade, allemande	FC 1186

CREATIVE DANCE:

> Move expressively with accompaniment, relating sounds to movement.
>
> Use dramatic rhythms.
>
> Relate story plays.
>
> Create own movement sequences.
>
> Make simple dances.

STRUCTURED DANCE:

1. *Singing games:* Loopy Loo, Bluebird, Did You Ever See A Lassie, Rig-a-Jig-Jig, Farmer in the Dell, Mulberry Bush, Muffin Man
2. *Folk dances:* How Do You Do My Partner, Danish Dance of Greeting, Chimes of Dunkirk, Kinder-Polka, Shoemaker's Dance

Grades three and four

MOVEMENT SKILLS: Continue working on combinations of movement with many variations, and stress quality of movement.

> *Dance steps:* schottische, step-hop, polka, draw, heel and toe, Indian step

RHYTHM SKILLS: Respond in movement to accent, phrasing, note values, and rhythmic patterns.

> *Rhythmic games:* Echo, Radio Stations, Clapping Orchestra, Lummi Sticks, ball bouncing, jumping ropes, exercises with music

CREATIVE DANCE: Move expressively with accompaniment in solving problems, improvisation, and composition.

> *Basic themes:* Work and play ideas, poems, stories, songs, occupations, transportation, pioneer days, Indian dances, machines, props

Table 10-5. American Square Dances

Dance	Record
Birdie in the Cage	FC 1261 *
Texas Star	FC 1268 *
Forward Six	FC 1279 *
Buffalo Gals	FC 1135
Dip and Dive	FC 1270 *
Red River Valley	FC 1053
Let's Square Dance (Dick Kraus, Caller)	RCA 3001 Album I, RCA Album II

* Calls on one side, instrumental on the other.

STRUCTURED DANCE:

1. *Formations:* double circle, groups of three, longways, quadrille, square
2. *Positions:* open, promenade, two-hand
3. *Figures:* honor, elbow turn, two-hand turn, reel, do-si-do, grand right and left, elbow swing, two-hand swing, promenade, allemande
4. *Dances:*

   Walk: Greensleeves, Norwegian Mountain March, Oh Susanah, Bingo
   Slide: Cshebogar, Hansel and Gretel, Patty-Cake Polka
   Bleking: Bleking
   Skip: Paw Paw Patch, Gustaf's Skoal, Virginia Reel, Bow Bow Belinda
   Step-hop: Seven Jumps
   Polka: Ace of Diamonds
   Schottische: Danish Schottische

Grades five and six

MOVEMENT SKILLS: Continue working on refinement and use of skills in creative work particularly. Use more difficult variations and combinations stressing quality of movement.
Dance steps: two-step, waltz, mazurka, grapevine

RHYTHM SKILLS: Continue work on all rhythm skills with an emphasis on tempo, accent, cumulative rhythm, double time. Solve rhythm problems.

CREATIVE DANCE: Do improvisation and composition work utilizing the following themes—conversation in movement, making dances based on traditional steps, historical subjects, poems, nonsense rhymes, cheerleading, sports, machines, current heroes, sensory cues

STRUCTURED DANCE:

1. *Figures:* swings, right and left through, chain, star, buzz step
2. *Positions:* varsovienne
3. *Dances:*

   Walk: Sicilian Circle, Brown-Eyed Mary, Glow Worm, All-American Promenade, Ten Pretty Girls
   Two-Step: Jessie Polka, Texas Schottische, Badger Gavotte, Ten Pretty Girls
   Waltz: Little Man in a Fix, Rye Waltz
   Grapevine: Cherkassia, Serbian Kolo
   Polka: Tantoli
   Run: Troika
   Schottische: Four Horse Schottische, Weggis, Road to the Isles
   Square Dances: Birdie in the Cage, Dive for the Oyster, Take a Little Peek, Buffalo Gal

Grades seven and eight

MOVEMENT SKILLS: *Dance steps:* Mazurka, fox trot, lindy

RHYTHM SKILLS: Symmetrical and assymetrical movement, accumulative rhythm, resultant rhythm, grouping

CREATIVE DANCE: Emphasis on improvisation and composition work; suggested themes for boys and girls (together) are the same as for fifth and sixth grade with expectations of compositions being more expressive and refined. Emphasis on work with themes which center on original designs, poems, mirroring, rounds, ball gymnastics, music. (If girls are alone for creative dance, beginning modern dance techniques may be started.)

STRUCTURED DANCE:
1. *Social:* fox trot with variations, lindy with variations, current fad dance
2. *Square Dances:* Birdie in the Cage, Texas Star, Forward Six, Dip and Dive, Solomon Levi
3. *Line Dances:* Mayim, Miserlou, Cherkassyia
4. *Folk and Round Dances:*
   Slide: Teton Mountain Stomp
   Jump: Tinikiling
   Two-step: Sentimental Journey, Laces and Graces, Jessie Polka, Susan's Gavotte
   Waltz: Black Hawk
   Mazurka: Put Your Little Foot
   Schottische: Highland Schottische, Korobuscha
   Polka: Cotton-Eyed Joe, Kalvelis

SUGGESTED REFERENCES
FOR FURTHER STUDY

Andrews, Gladys, "Creative Rhythmic Movement Contributes to Learning," *Journal of Health, Physical Education and Recreation* 36 (April, 1965), p. 69.

Andrews, Gladys, *Creative Rhythmic Movement for Children* (Englewood Cliffs, N.J., Prentice-Hall, 1954).

Kraus, Richard, *A Pocket Guide of Folk and Square Dances and Singing Games for the Elementary School* (Englewood Cliffs, N.J., Prentice-Hall, 1966).

Murray, Ruth L., *Dance in Elementary Education* (New York, Harper & Row, 1963).

Saffran, Rosanna, *First Book of Creative Rhythms* (New York, Holt, Rinehart, & Winston, 1963).

Chapter XI

GAMES OF LOW ORGANIZATION

Selecting games

Active games of low organization

Relays

Classroom and inactive games

Individual and dual games

Knowing how to play a variety of games is important for all children. Most games have a rich cultural heritage since they have been handed down from generation to generation with few changes in their basic structures. Active games of low organization are the sports of the primary grades and are an essential part of the physical education program, as well as comprising the child's free play activities on the playground and in his neighborhood.

Games of "low organization" are termed such because they involve few and simple rules and little or no equipment; they utilize the simple basic skills, they may be adapted to suit the space available, and they may be played by groups of various sizes. Since they can be taught and organized very quickly, they can be enjoyed by children of all ages and even by adults. However, the amount of time spent playing games of this type decreases as children reach the intermediate and upper grades, for they become interested in the more complex and more highly organized lead-up games to sports.

SELECTING GAMES

Each game that is taught or played in the physical education class should be chosen for specific reasons and goals. These may vary from practice of specific skills, social learnings, leadership opportunities, and fitness values, to pure fun, or combinations of these. Games taught at each level should reflect an ordered progression in terms of difficulty.

Each game is assigned a grade level or a span of grade levels. The grade first mentioned is usually that when the game can safely be introduced with a typical group. Often a class with a good physical education background can easily learn a game graded one or two years ahead. If a game that is too simple is introduced, children quickly lose interest in it, behavior problems may arise, and the values inherent in the game itself may be lost. If the game is too difficult, the same situation may prevail and, in addition, the children may become frustrated and discouraged. A game may be played in successive years; however, if variations are not added to challenge the increased skill and maturity from year to year, the physical education period may become a play period rather than a learning situation.

When children are encouraged to choose games, they usually will select old favorites. They like what they know how to do well and what they are comfortable in doing. If the teacher utilizes children's choices frequently, it is his responsibility to make provisions to suggest variations and to teach new and challenging games periodically so that the pupils will have a suitable repertoire from which to choose.

There are many sources and hundreds of games from which a teacher can select those to include in the lesson. Some are naturally better than others, but all have their merits. The teacher must learn how to select the best for the particular group he teaches. Discussed in order are the following four major areas of consideration which provide the criteria for selection.

1. Values to be gained from the game.
2. Opportunities for maximum participation for all class members.
3. The degree of teacher supervision needed.
4. The difficulty of the game.

Values of games

A few of the values to be gained through games of low organization and the types of game experiences which provide these are summarized in list form. One game is suggested as an example for each value. The teacher should formulate what he hopes to accomplish through game play in each lesson, and then analyze the description of selected games to see which game will most nearly fit his objectives.

Values to Be Gained	*Types of Game Experiences*
SOCIAL-EMOTIONAL	
1. Release of tensions.	1. Games played at beginning of period which involve gross body movement; everyone is active at the same time—Jet Pilot (p. 329).
2. Group spirit.	2. Games involving double line formations where one group is against another or relays—Crows and Cranes (p. 333).
3. Specific competitive experiences (individual, group).	3. Games in which individual pits his skill against another for team points—Snatch Club (p. 332), or in which whole team works together in one effort—Prisoner's Base (p. 351).
4. Self-discipline.	4. Games in which class can be broken down into small units; the games can be played without direct teacher supervision—Poison Pin (p. 346).
5. Group cooperation.	5. Games in which one group must work together and make or change strategies while game is in progress—Battleball (p. 354).
6. Recognition of individual efforts.	6. Games of tag in which the first one to cross a goal without being tagged becomes IT—Fire Engine (p. 333).
7. Leadership.	7. Games in which students are officials, callers, or organizers of the game.
PHYSICAL	
1. Use and development of basic skills.	1. Games involving running, dodging, throwing, catching, body control, and tagging—Battleball (p. 354).
2. Flexibility and agility.	2. Most chasing and fleeing games —Man from Mars (p. 334).
3. Endurance.	3. Games involving sustained running, jumping, throwing, and dodging—Busyball (p. 355).
4. Accuracy.	4. Dodgeball and target games in which size and distance of target differs—Agents and Spies (p. 353).

Values to Be Gained	*Types of Game Experiences*
5. Speed.	5. Once control is developed in skills, games and relays stressing speed in a self-competitive or team situation—Gap Ball (p. 344).
6. Relaxation.	6. Games which are semi-active, or mental and guessing games—Poor Pussy (p. 379).
INTELLECTUAL 1. Application of knowledge learned in classroom.	1. Games which can be correlated with classroom activities. Using mental games in the classroom to supplement and enhance learning of specific knowledges—Subject Baseball (p. 382).
2. Appreciation and knowledge about other lands and peoples.	2. Games from other countries—Chinese Wall (p. 335).

Maximum participation

Every class period should be planned so that the majority of the time is spent in vigorous activity; each game that is presented should provide an opportunity for as many members of the class as possible to be active. Learning results only from doing. Game descriptions should be analyzed to determine how many children may be active at one time and how large a group is necessary to make a game playable.

Unfortunately, many books contain descriptions of circle games where only one or two players are chasing each other while the rest of the group waits for turns. Circle games are valuable in that they provide a confined area for kindergarten or first grade children in their early games experiences. The circle gives the children a feeling of security and enables the teacher to see and speak to the whole group in a very controlled manner. When the class has learned how to listen carefully and has assumed responsibility, and when the teacher has confidence in his control of the class, he should avoid selecting many circle games.

One method to circumvent the inactivity of this type of game is to break the class into two or more circles. A new game may be introduced to the whole group in one circle, and after everyone appears to understand the game well, more circles may be formed. One circle may be utilized for a demonstration group while the rest of the children sit in the circle formation, watching and listening. After learning the game procedures, the other groups can begin play.

Games which call for elimination of players should be avoided. Many rules state that a child who is caught or hit should leave the game and wait until all but one is eliminated and another game is started. Usually the slowest or most poorly skilled child is eliminated first, and this is the very person who needs more practice in order to improve. Children who are always among the first to be eliminated often develop a negative attitude toward activity and become resentful and disinterested.

Most often, elimination games can be modified to provide some other activity for those who are eliminated or a system can be developed which recognizes they were hit or tagged but allows them to remain active in the game. For example, some descriptions of simple dodgeball games state that when one is hit, one must leave the game and wait until only a single player remains in the center and is declared winner. This could be changed to the rule that if one is hit, one goes into the outside circle and becomes a thrower, and the last one in the center is still declared the winner. In the same games those who are hit may be assigned a point each time they are hit, and the person with the least number of points at the end of a specified time is the winner. Another adaptation is to have the person who hit the center person exchange places with the person he hit.

Regardless of the formation, some games may not provide maximum participation. The directions must be read carefully so that they are interpreted correctly. For example, the directions may read: Divide group in two, half on one side and half on the other. The teacher may interpret this to mean that the class is divided into half, and therefore, a very inactive game may result. For example, most frequently the game Club Snatch or Steal the Bacon (p. 332) is described in the following manner: Divide players into teams, number each player, place a club in the center between the two teams. Call a number, and the player from each team with the corresponding number runs and tries to get the club and take it back to his team line before the player from the other team can tag him. This can become a boring, inactive game if more than five players are on a side. Two or three games of this can be played at the same time with only one person calling the numbers, and each child will have three times as many chances to run out to try to get the club. Most games which do not utilize the entire playing area as boundaries can be broken down into several playing units. In summary, these are the guidelines for selecting games which will provide for maximum participation.

1. Avoid circle games where only one or two people are active at one time.
2. Avoid elimination-type games unless you can change the elimination rule to an active status.
3. Break down game into the smallest logical units of play.

Student leadership of games

Since much of children's out-of-school time is spent in play, they should be taught a number of games which they can play without a teacher or another adult. Previous discussions have emphasized the values of good playing skills and knowledge of games to a child's social acceptance. Many children learn games in their neighborhoods or on playgrounds, but since some children have no opportunity to do this, provision for this type of learning must be made in school.

Emphasis has been placed on breaking down games into many units so that maximum participation is possible. This implies that children must be capable of conducting the game without direct teacher supervision. Children do not accept this responsibility or directions from student leaders automatically. They must have guided experiences in the class situation where they learn both to lead and to follow student leaders; they also learn to accept responsibility when a leader has not been designated by the teacher.

Modifications may have to be made in order to play a game with greater or fewer number of players than stated in the rules. The teacher should help children understand how this adjustment can be made so the game can be used in out-of-class situations.

A study of the social-emotional values of games reveals that much emphasis must be placed on independent decisions and recognition of sacrifices for the good of the team. A major criterion in the selection of most games should be their usefulness in unsupervised free-play situations.

Degree of difficulty of a game

Although most descriptions of games suggest a grade level at which the game can be played, the teacher must analyze the game in relation to the readiness of his particular class. Guidelines for determining the difficulty of a game are discussed in the following paragraphs. The teacher may apply these guidelines when selecting new games, when creating new games, and when making an old game more challenging.

Skills involved in the game
The teacher must look first for the skills basic to the game. If a skill vital to the conduct of the game has not been taught to the class, naturally

the game must be disregarded or the skill introduced, explored, and practiced prior to the introduction of the game. Some basic skills are harder than others; for instance, skipping is harder than running, catching is harder than throwing. Beyond checking the skills involved, one needs to analyze *how* the skills are used. First graders can run, but it is much more difficult to make many changes in direction while running. It is relatively easy for one student to evade being hit by a ball, but when holding on to another the difficulty is increased. Hitting a moving target is harder than hitting a stationary target.

Number and combination of skills involved in the game

The number of skills utilized in a game may increase the difficulty of it. Remembering how to do each skill, recovering balance from executing one skill, and immediately initiating a new and different movement is difficult for inexperienced or young children. For example, in Simple Dodgeball (p. 332) one has only to dodge one ball. In Battleball (p. 354) one has to dodge the ball, pick it up after it has bounced once, throw it at another moving target; and at the same time be alert to dodging a second ball which is also in play. Obviously, proficiency in skill and mental application to sequence of skills and rules are involved in the latter game. Each of these skills is not difficult alone, but in combination with others under the stress of speed and competition, the game becomes an advanced game.

Number and complexity of rules involved in the game

Just as the number of skills compounds the difficulty of a game so does the number of rules. Greater maturity and an increased attention span are necessary before children can remember and follow a number of direction or pattern of doing things. Using Battleball (p. 354) as an example again, one has to remember that he cannot touch the ball before it bounces; he is not out if he is hit below the waist or if the ball hit him after it bounced; he may not take steps as he holds the ball; he may not hold it more than 3 seconds; he may throw at people on the other team or to his teammates; after he is hit he goes to another area and continues to play. In Simple Dodgeball (p. 332) he rejoins the circle after being hit whenever the ball hits him below the waist. Both of these are dodge ball games where the primary skills are dodging and throwing and the object is either to hit a person with the ball or to avoid being hit, depending on the position at the time.

Naturally, the more complex the rules the longer it takes to understand and learn the game. Contrast the simple version of Squirrels in Trees (p. 331), in which the squirrels change trees upon a signal and the one who does not find an empty tree is left out, with the more advanced

version, Hounds and Rabbits (p. 333), in which two are out of the trees
and one chases the other. The one chased may enter an occupied tree,
whereupon the one in the tree must leave and becomes the chaser. The
latter version if introduced first is too complex for a first grader.

Strategy and responsibilities involved in the game

When a game requires specific responsibilities or positions for individual
players it becomes difficult. If everyone does basically the same thing, it is
easy to remember what to do, and the game pattern is learned quickly.
When position responsibility calls for unique action or rules on the part
of several different players, it takes more concentration and time to learn.
Although all games require some strategy, the more complex it becomes
the more advanced the game is. Coordinating the skills, efforts, and ideas
of several people takes more maturity and concentration than primary
children can handle. Even double line games involve more teamwork
than beginning first graders can produce. Contrast the chasing and fleeing games of Brownies and Fairies (p. 327) and Prisoner's Base (p. 351)
where running, dodging, and tagging are the skills involved. In Brownies
and Fairies one runs away from the line and toward home base trying
not to be tagged. In Prisoner's Base, the strategy is very involved and requires group planning and cooperation to get just one person from home
base to the base of another team.

Duration and continuity of game

The length of playing periods of a game may increase the difficulty of it
in terms of physical and emotional demands due to sustained concentration and excitement. If a game is played for a long time and the attention span is short, pupils become disinterested. Inattention and behavior
problems will arise.

Number of people involved in terms of
direct competition and cooperation

The greater the number of players one has to relate to on his own team
and to compete directly against, the more demanding the game becomes.
There is a definite progression of difficulty in all skill drills and games. A
certain degree of competency and confidence in a skill is necessary before
it is used in a game situation. Each opponent or teammate added to the
game makes it necessary to use a skill in a somewhat different manner.
This is obvious in the transition from the very simple games in which
most of the skills are done in an independent fashion, to the more involved team games where one plays with or against increasingly larger
numbers. For young children, cooperation with more than one person is
as great a problem as competition for young children.

Considerations when teaching games

Preliminary preparation

1. The teacher or the pupil presenting the game should know the game thoroughly. Condense the rules for presentation into the simplest and shortest terms.
2. Have all necessary equipment ready and accessible.
3. Select playing area before class time. If lines are necessary, mark them before the class period. Use chalk, poster paint, or plastic tape indoors. Lime, ropes, or pins may be used outside. Do not ask children to imagine lines.
4. Most game rules can be changed to fit the available space, amount of equipment, or number of students. Don't hesitate to modify to adapt to the needs of the group.
5. When games call for mingling of players from opposite teams, provide some type of color identification for each team.
6. Plan to play games of varied formations but neither too many nor too different. Frequently, much time is wasted in just moving groups from one location to another.
7. Play outdoors if at all possible. Directions may have to be given in the classroom if it is cold, windy, or if there are many outdoor distractions.

Method

The methods a teacher employs in the teaching of games will depend upon his objectives. An extension of a lesson involving exploration of specific movement skills may be to set a problem of developing a game in which to use the skills, or the pupils may be asked to use the skills in a variation of a known game.

If the objective is to get vigorous activity underway immediately, a more direct approach should be utilized. The teacher or a student would describe the game, state the rules, and then proceed with the game. Rules may all be presented at one time or introduced individually as they are needed in the game.

Whatever method is used, caution should be taken that activity gets underway quickly and a minimum of time is taken for talking and demonstration. It is best to have the group in formation for play so that after the directions are given, the children stand up and play immediately.

Activity

1. Select an alert pupil to start the activity.

2. Encourage children to admit having been tagged and to raise hands when they are aware that they made a foul or violation.

3. Enforce rules immediately. If the rule says: "No stepping over the line," then follow the line rule. If the progress of the game is hindered by too many stops for rule infractions, it is possible the rule is too difficult for the group and that it needs to be modified.

4. Be sure that teams are of equal size or number before play begins.

5. If it is obvious that there is a misunderstanding about the rules or procedures, stop the game and straighten out the difficulty immediately.

6. The teacher may play in the game occasionally, but he should not dominate the play. Children enjoy having the teacher play, but they usually will not notice if he withdraws gracefully as the game progresses.

7. Try to make sure that everyone has a turn and that a certain few do not dominate game play.

8. Continue teaching once the game is started. Introducing the game may be mechanical or routine, but teaching during the game is essential. Look for those who need encouragement. Look for teachable moments when the game can be stopped and a concept can be learned in light of the situation or positions of the players at the time. Watch for use of skills and space. Plan for evaluation after the game.

9. Rotate positions so that all have an opportunity to play in favored positions.

10. Once the game is apparently understood by all, regroup into smaller units, if possible.

11. When interest appears to be waning, stop the game. Do not wait until all interest has been lost.

12. Check the time remaining in the period. Do not start a new game unless there is time to play it for at least a few minutes.

13. Maintain a learning atmosphere. A certain amount of noise accompanies good hard play, but screaming or uncontrolled boisterous noise should not be allowed. Establish signals for quiet and attention.

Evaluation

1. Culminate the game with a meaningful discussion of its procedure. Have the students make suggestions for improving game play. Evaluation need not come at the end of a game; it should come when appropriate or when a rest period or change of positions are necessary. Praise good performances and sportsmanship.

2. Make plans to play the game again. Repetition will improve skills and strategy.

3. Be sure the pupils know the name of the game.

Safety factors
1. A wall must never be a goal. Lines should be eight or ten feet from the wall or from any other hazard. A permanent line should be painted around the entire gym at these distances.
2. Tennis shoes are the only suitable footwear on gym floors. If the floor is clean and free from splinters, children may play in bare feet, but never in socks alone.
3. Rules must be established as to where one may hit another person with the ball in dodgeball games. It is safest to hit another person on the legs or on the shoulder region. The use of a playground ball or volleyball is recommended for dodgeball games rather than the heavier soccer or basketballs.
4. Glasses should be removed when playing dodgeball and other games where the player is not always focusing on the ball.
5. Traffic patterns for throwing and running should be established to avoid collisions.

ACTIVE GAMES OF LOW ORGANIZATION

Most of the active games of low organization fall into two general categories: running, chasing, and fleeing games, and ball skill games. In the former, the object usually is for the player to run and avoid being tagged by a person who has been designated as IT. In some games there is only one chaser and one fleer. In others, the whole group may be fleeing from one person. Chasing and fleeing games are popular with all age groups. Younger children love the independent vigorous running the game affords. As they grow older, competition and excitement become more important.

Beginning games usually involve a circle formation which provides the initial experience of staying in a confined area. Unfortunately, in this formation there is only one chaser and one fleer (Beater Goes Round, p. 348). Games involving a single line boundary follow, in which the whole group may run from one line to the other trying to avoid the IT, who initially stands in the center (Chinese Wall, p. 335). This calls for more independent control, as the boundaries are larger and less confining. The next step is to utilize double line formations where two parallel lines are used as goals for two different groups or teams. This is the first venture into teams or two sides at play, where one's actions affect the entire team (Blue and Gold, p. 335). A whole area boundary formation may involve one goal, or many goals, or even changing goals—i.e., a player may run anywhere within the defined play area (Squirrels in Trees, p. 331). The latter calls for independent decisions and close attention to the rules.

Ball skill games provide opportunities to handle the ball with hands or feet in various ways. They also enable various locomotor skills to be combined with throwing, catching, and striking. Stationary and moving targets may be used, and many games may be modified to become skill drill games. A variety of formations may be utilized.

Game descriptions

The descriptions of active games of low organization are grouped at the grade levels most suitable for them to be introduced. Many of the games may be played at several different grade levels, but, for the most part, they should not be introduced in grades lower than those suggested. The teacher should apply the guidelines and determine the degree of difficulty of the game before making a selection.

Playing areas should be permanently marked with outside boundary and center dividing lines of a size that fits most game court dimensions, 25 by 50 feet. The size of the playing area may be altered to the available space in order to adjust to ability level of the class. Most often 8½ inch utility balls are recommended, but any ball of approximately that size may be substituted. The minimum number of players for each game is suggested. When the players recommended are few, several games can take place at the same time. The person who starts the game is identified as the leader, this may be the teacher or a student.

Kindergarten and first grade

CALL BALL (K, 1)

SKILLS: Tossing ball in the air, catching.

EQUIPMENT: 8½-inch playground ball.

FORMATION: Circles of six, one child in the center.

DESCRIPTION: The child in the center throws the ball into the air and calls out the name of one of the players who tries to catch the ball *before* it bounces. If the person called is successful, he becomes the next thrower; if not, the first thrower has another try. The name must be called as the ball is thrown, and the ball must not go outside of the circle.

VARIATIONS: Numbers may be used instead of names. More than one number may be called once skills are well developed. If children have trouble catching the ball in the air, it may be caught on the first bounce (use with kindergarten).

CHARLIE OVER THE WATER (1)

SKILLS: Selected locomotor skills, stooping, tagging.

EQUIPMENT: None.

FORMATION: Single circle, one or two children in the center.

DESCRIPTION: One or two children are chosen as Charlie, depending on the size of the group. Charlie stands in the center of the circle. The others walk, run, skip, or hop around the circle chanting:

> Charlie over the water,
> Charlie over the sea,
> Charlie catch a blackbird,
> Can't catch me!

As "me" is said the children stoop quickly. Charlie tries to tag as many as he can before they are in squatting position. Charlie is allowed three turns then chooses someone he tagged to take his place.

VARIATION: Points may be kept for those tagged; however, the initial emphasis should be on trying to avoid being tagged.

CIRCLE STRIDE BALL (K, 1)

SKILLS: Rolling ball, stopping ball with hands.

EQUIPMENT: 8½ inch or 10-inch playground ball.

FORMATION: Single circles of eight, one child in the center is it.

DESCRIPTION: Players stand with legs apart, but in a balanced position. Their feet should touch the feet of player beside them. One player is IT and stands in the center. He tries to roll the ball outside of the circle through the legs of the other players. The latter try to keep the ball in the circle by stopping it with their hands. If the ball goes out, the players between whose legs it went chases the ball and becomes the new IT.

COWBOYS AND INDIANS (OR BROWNIES AND FAIRIES) (K, 1)

SKILLS: Running, tagging, dodging.

FORMATION: Double line formation with goal lines at opposite ends of the playing area. Two teams.

DESCRIPTION: Half of the group are Cowboys and stand behind one goal line, the other half are Indians and stand behind the other goal line. The Cowboys face away from the Indians' goal line and the Indians quietly walk up behind them. The teacher or leader waits until the Indians are quite close and calls out "The Indians are here!" The Cowboys turn around and chase the Indians back to their goal line. Any Indians who are tagged before reaching the line must become Cowboys. The Cowboys then become the chasers, and the game continues with alternating chasers and fleers.

VARIATION: The game may be called Brownies and Fairies, Cats and Dogs, or any combination of enemies.

GARDENER AND SCAMP (1)

SKILLS: Selected locomotor skills, dodging, tagging.

EQUIPMENT: None.

FORMATION: Circles of eight, one child inside the circle, one outside.

DESCRIPTION: One player is selected as Scamp and stands inside of the circle made by the rest of the group. One is selected as the Gardener and walks around outside the circle, saying "Who let you in my garden." The Scamp answers, "No one," and the Gardener begins to chase him. The Gardener must use the same locomotor movements that the Scamp uses in the chase. They may cut across, in and out and around the other players. When the Scamp is caught, he and the Gardener select replacements, and the game starts again. If the Gardener does not do the same movements that Scamp does, a new Gardener is selected by Scamp.

VARIATIONS: Players in the circle may hold hands and must raise their arms to let the runners in and out. Scamp should be encouraged to change his movement patterns frequently. If the Gardener cannot catch Scamp after a short time, halt the game and select new runners.

HOT BALL (K, 1)

SKILLS: Kicking.

EQUIPMENT: One soccer ball.

FORMATION: Single circle.

DESCRIPTION: One player is chosen to "set a fire" under the ball. He dramatically "heats" the ball, then kicks it into the circle and says "the ball is hot." The players try to kick the ball away to keep from getting "burned." If the ball stops in the center of the circle or goes out of the circle, the person who kicked it last gets it and must "start the fire" again. The ball should be kicked with the side of the foot and kept close to the ground.

VARIATION: The ball may be thrown or pushed away.

JET PILOT (I)

SKILLS: Running.

EQUIPMENT: None.

FORMATION: Lines drawn across each end of the playing area. One designated as the take-off line and the other as the turning line.

DESCRIPTION: All players are considered to be Jet Pilots except for one who is the starter. The Pilots all stand behind the take-off line. The starter calls out: "Tower to Pilots—Take off! All Pilots run down to the turning line and back across the take-off line. The first Pilot back shouts "Checking In" and becomes the new Starter.

VARIATION: Pilots may be called Space Ships, the words may be: "Control center to Space Ships, blast off!"

OLD MOTHER WITCH (I)

SKILLS: Running, dodging, tagging.

EQUIPMENT: None.

FORMATION: A goal line at one end of playing area. Large box or circle drawn at other end of playing floor.

DESCRIPTION: One child is chosen to be Old Mother Witch. The Witch walks around in the box while the rest of the children walk around the outside of the box or dash across and out of the box. The children chant:

> Old Mother Witch
> Fell in a ditch,
> Picked up a penny,
> And thought she was rich!

At the end of each verse the Witch asks, "Whose children are you?" The children may answer with any name; however, when one child answers "Yours," the Witch must chase the children back to their goal line. The first child tagged becomes the new Witch.

VARIATIONS: One child may be appointed as a Leader responsible for saying, "Yours." The Witch may catch any number of children she can, and gets a point for each child caught. A new Witch may be chosen by the old one.

RED LIGHT (*1*)

SKILLS: Running, fast starts, fast stops.

EQUIPMENT: None.

FORMATION: A goal line drawn at each end of the playing area.

DESCRIPTION: All of the players stand on one goal line. One person is selected as IT. IT stands on the far goal line and faces away from the others. He counts "1, 2, 3, 4" and may say "Red Light," any time before he reaches "10." As he is counting the others advance as far as they can before "Red Light" is heard. Upon saying "Red Light," IT turns around. If he sees anyone moving, he sends them back to their goal line. The counting is repeated. The first one who reaches the other goal line becomes the new IT. Players may move anytime; however, if IT sees them, he may send them back to their goal line.

VARIATION: Instead of counting, IT may say, "Green Light," pause, and then say "Red Light" as the signal to stop.

SLAP JACK (*K, 1*)

SKILLS: Running, tagging.

EQUIPMENT: None.

FORMATION: Circles of eight, one child is IT.

DESCRIPTION: All players in a circle stand facing the center with their hands held together, palms up, behind them. One is chosen as IT, and he walks around the outside. When he slaps a player on the hands, that player chases IT around the circle and tries to tag him before he reaches the empty place in the circle. The chaser becomes the next IT.

VARIATION: IT may run, skip, or perform any kind of locomotor movement.

SQUAT TAG (*K, 1*)

SKILLS: Running, dodging, tagging.

EQUIPMENT: Colored scarf.

FORMATION: Large playing area with defined boundaries all around.

DESCRIPTION: One player is IT and tries to tag any other player. To be safe, runners assume a squat position. When one is tagged, the tagger gives the new IT the colored scarf.

VARIATIONS: More than one player may be IT, but all should carry a colored scarf so that the IT is easily identified. Other safe positions may be designated.

SQUIRRELS IN TREES (K, 1)

SKILLS: Running.

EQUIPMENT: None.

FORMATION: Groups of three scattered about the playing area.

DESCRIPTION: Two players hold hands and form a "tree" for the other person to stand in. Two players are chosen as Squirrels and have no Tree. The leader gives a signal and all the Squirrels must get out of their trees and find a new one to get into. The extra Squirrels get into a Tree, and of course two are left out again. Emphasis should be placed on finding a Tree. Rotate Trees with Squirrels until everyone has been a Squirrel.

Second grade

BOUNDARY BALL

SKILLS: Throwing, catching.

EQUIPMENT: Volleyball or 8½-inch playground ball.

FORMATION: Playing area divided into half.

DESCRIPTION: Opposing teams are scattered in each half. One ball is given to a player on each team. The purpose of the game is for a team to throw, roll, or bounce a ball across the opponent's goal line. A point is scored for a team whenever this occurs. The game continues without interruption for a set period of time or until a set number of points is reached by one team or the other. Players may stop the ball in any manner they can.

VARIATIONS: Kicking may be employed rather than throwing. Children may be prohibited from walking with the ball.

CAT AND RAT

SKILLS: Running, dodging, tagging.

EQUIPMENT: None.

FORMATION: Single circle.

DESCRIPTION: One player in center of circle is the Cat, one on the outside is chosen to be the Rat. Circle players hold hands. The Cat tries to chase and tag the Rat. The circle players let the Rat in and out of the circle but try to prevent the Cat from going in and out by not lowering or raising their hands. When the Rat is caught or after the Cat has had ample time to catch the Rat, each chooses someone else to take his place.

SIMPLE DODGEBALL

SKILLS: Throwing at a moving target, dodging.

EQUIPMENT: 8½-inch playground ball.

FORMATION: Playing group divided in half. One half makes a single circle, other half is inside the circle.

DESCRIPTION: The players in the outside circle try to hit those inside the circle somewhere between the waist and ankles. The ball may be rolling or in the air. When one is hit he joins the circle. The last one to remain in the circle is the winner. If the ball goes outside of the circle, the last one who threw it goes after it. Players may step inside the circle to get the ball, but must return to circle before throwing it. When a winner has been declared, the game is started again with the teams changing places.

VARIATIONS: When a player is hit he may exchange places with the player who hit him. As skill increases, the rule may change, i.e., the ball must be in the air when it hits the players.

CLUB SNATCH (OR STEAL THE BACON)

SKILLS: Running, tagging, dodging, reaction time.

EQUIPMENT: Club or beanbag.

FORMATION: Two groups along parallel goal lines about 30 feet apart. Mark an x in the center of the two lines, and place the club on it.

DESCRIPTION: Number players; start at opposite ends with 1. The leader calls one of the numbers. The player from each team having that number runs out and tries to snatch the club and take it back across his goal line without being tagged by the other player. The player who successfully gets the club across his goal line receives 2 points for his team. If the other player tags him before crossing the line, 1 point is awarded to his team. The club is set back in the center, and new numbers called. The team with the most points at a designated time wins. Stress deceptive movements in trying to snatch the club.

CROWS AND CRANES

SKILLS: Running, changing directions, tagging.

EQUIPMENT: None.

FORMATION: Two lines 3 feet apart are drawn across the middle of the playing area. Goal lines are drawn at either end.

DESCRIPTION: Players are divided in half, one group called Crows and the other Cranes. They line up on respective opposite center lines. The leader calls out "Cr-rr-r-ows" and the Crows turn and run toward their goal line with the Cranes in pursuit trying to tag as many as possible before they cross the goal line. When a player is caught he must join the opposite team. The leader should drag out the "Cr" and mix calling the teams so there is suspense and a need for quick reaction on the part of both runners and chasers.

VARIATIONS: Children may be challenged to find sound-alike words to vary the name of the game.

FIRE ENGINE

SKILLS: Running.

EQUIPMENT: None.

FORMATION: A starting line is drawn. A parallel goal line is drawn across the playing area at the other end.

DESCRIPTION: Everyone stands along the starting line. Each child is given a number between 1 and 5. The numbers signify an alarm number. A child chosen to be Fire Chief stands midway down the side line. He claps loudly stopping at any number between 1 and 5. When he finishes he calls "Fire!" All children having that number run down to the far goal line and then back across the starting line. If the Chief counts to more than 5 he calls "General alarm," and everyone runs. The first one to return to the starting line becomes the new Fire Chief.

VARIATIONS: The Chief may call, jump, or use any other signal to signify the alarm number. Fire Stations may be formed by groups, each player within the group having an alarm number. The first person back to the line would win a point for his team.

HOUND AND RABBIT

SKILLS: Running, tagging.

EQUIPMENT: None.

FORMATION: Groups of three.

DESCRIPTION: Two hold hands and are called the Tree, the other is a Rabbit and stands in between them. There is an extra Rabbit and Hound. The Hound tries to catch the Rabbit. The Rabbit can be safe by dodging into a tree. The Rabbit who was in that tree must get out and then becomes the Rabbit who is chased. If the Hound catches the Rabbit, they change places. Periodically, the game should stop, and Rabbits and Trees exchange places until all have had a chance to be Rabbits. This is an advanced version of Squirrel in Tree.

MAN FROM MARS

SKILLS: Running, tagging.

EQUIPMENT: None.

FORMATION: Large playing area with end lines and defined side boundaries.

DESCRIPTION: One player is chosen to be the Man from Mars. The other players stand behind one end line and call, "Man from Mars, may we chase you to the stars?" The Man from Mars says, "Yes, if you are wearing green" (or any other color he wishes to call). All those who are wearing some clothing of the color called chase the Man from Mars until he is tagged. The player who tags him first becomes the new Man from Mars.

MIDNIGHT

SKILLS: Running, tagging.

EQUIPMENT: None.

FORMATION: Large playing area with end lines, and defined side lines.

DESCRIPTION: One end is the Roost and one the Den. One player is chosen as the Fox, the remainder are Chickens. The Chickens walk slowly up to and around the Den line and ask the Fox, who is in his Den, "What time is it, Mr. Fox?" The Fox answers with various times. When he says "Midnight," the Chickens all run for the Roost. The Fox tries to catch as many as possible and then sends them to his Den where they join him in trying to catch Chickens the next game. No one may start to flee or chase until the Fox calls, "Midnight!" When a greater number of Chickens have been caught, the Fox chooses someone to replace him and the game starts again.

Third grade

BLUE AND GOLD

SKILLS: Running, dodging, quick reaction, and change of direction.

EQUIPMENT: A piece of cardboard or rubber painted blue on one side and gold on the other.

FORMATION: Playing area divided in half with goal lines and side lines marked off. A 3-foot space should separate the two halves. Players divided into two teams.

DESCRIPTION: The teams, called Blue and Gold Teams, line up along their center line. The leader throws the object up in the air between the teams. The team bearing the name of the color side of object which lands facing upward, turns and runs to its goal. The members of the other team try to tag them before they cross the goal. If tagged, a player must join the other team. The team with the most players at the end of a specified time wins.

VARIATIONS: Points may be given to a team rather than having players change teams when caught. Any two color combinations may be used.

CENTER TOUCHBALL

SKILLS: Throwing and catching.

EQUIPMENT: 8½-inch playground ball.

FORMATION: Single circle, one player in the center as IT.

DESCRIPTION: Circle players pass ball around circle and IT tries to touch the ball. If he is successful, the player who threw ball last becomes the new IT.

CHINESE WALL

SKILLS: Running, dodging, tagging.

EQUIPMENT: None.

FORMATION: Two end boundary lines with two parallel lines about 10 feet apart drawn across the middle of the playing area. This space is called the Wall.

DESCRIPTION: Two children are chosen as Defenders of the Wall. Everyone starts behind one end line. At a signal everyone tries to cross the Wall and get to the other end line without being tagged by a Defender. Everyone who is caught becomes a helper for the Defenders. New Defenders are chosen from among the last few who have not been caught and the game starts again. Defenders may not go off the Wall.

VARIATIONS: Points may be given for each time one crosses the Wall. People may cross the Wall with partners. If one gets caught the other is considered caught also. This will encourage strategy in trying to outwit the Defenders.

CIRCLE RACE

SKILLS: Running.

EQUIPMENT: 8½-inch playground ball.

FORMATION: Single circle. Children number off by threes around the circle, each set of three becomes a team and each team is given a number. (It is wise to write the team number in front of each team with chalk.)

DESCRIPTION: The space between each child must be the same. Each player sits facing the inside of the circle with his legs crossed in front of him. The ball is placed in the center of a circle. A small circle is drawn around it so as to mark the center. The leader calls number 1, 2, or 3. Each player having the called number gets up and runs counter-clockwise around the outside of the circle and runs into the circle through the spot where he was sitting. The first person to the center of the circle must pick up the ball and hold it high over his head and call out the number of his team. No one can take the ball away from anyone after it has been touched. Emphasize stooping to get ball and bringing it up high to avoid collisions in the center. The number one player on each team is charged with keeping score for his team. The team with the most points at the end of a specified amount of time is the winner.

VARIATIONS: Players may be given names of cars, animals, or planes and may win points for themselves.

CLUB GUARD

SKILLS: Throwing, blocking the ball with legs.

EQUIPMENT: 8½-inch playground ball, pin.

FORMATION: Single circle. With small circle drawn in center of circle. Place pin in center.

DESCRIPTION: One child is chosen to be the Guard, and he must stop the ball from knocking over the pin. He may not step into the small circle. He may kick ball, block it with legs, or if it comes above his thighs, he may bat it away with his hands. The players in the circle throw at the pin. They may pass it around the circle quickly to try to draw the Guard out of guarding position. Whoever knocks down the pin becomes the new Guard. If the Guard knocks over the pin, the person who last threw the ball gets to be the new guard. The Guard changes places with the successful thrower.

EXCHANGE DODGEBALL

SKILLS: Throwing, dodging.

EQUIPMENT: Playground ball.

FORMATION: Single circle, small square drawn in center. Children number off around circle by threes.

DESCRIPTION: One child is chosen as IT and stands in center of circle with ball on floor in the square. IT calls a number, and all players with that number exchange places. IT picks up ball and throws it at a player below the waist who is exchanging places. If one is hit he becomes the new IT.

VARIATIONS: Names may be called instead of numbers. Players may be given names of cars, animals, or flowers rather than numbers.

FREEZE BALL

SKILLS: Throwing, dodging, running, catching.

EQUIPMENT: One 8½-inch playground ball.

FORMATION: Single circle, one person chosen to be IT stands in the center.

DESCRIPTION: IT throws ball straight up into air and calls someone's name. As the player called runs to catch ball everyone else scatters. When the ball is caught, the player calls "Freeze," and everyone must stop where they are at that time. Then he tries to hit one of the players below the waist. If he hits the one at which he aims, he gets to be IT and throws the ball. If he misses, the person at whom he throws becomes IT. When a player is hit he receives a point. The winner is the person who has the least number of points at the end of the playing time. Limit the area into which players may scatter if the playing area is large or if players have trouble hitting anyone. The thrower may be allowed one step to get nearer to someone before he throws.

LAST COUPLE OUT (Figure 11-1)

SKILLS: Running, dodging.

EQUIPMENT: None.

FORMATION: Partners standing in a file formation. One odd person is IT, and stands on a line 15 feet from the first couple. Side lines 30 feet apart.

DESCRIPTION: IT stands with back to the file of players and calls "Last couple out." The last couple in the file separate and each runs on the outside of his respective line and tries to join hands with his partner somewhere in front of the IT player who tries to catch one of them as soon as he can see them coming. If he catches one, he takes that person's partner and the caught runner becomes IT for the next turn. If he does not catch one he is IT again. Runners may not run outside of the side boundaries.

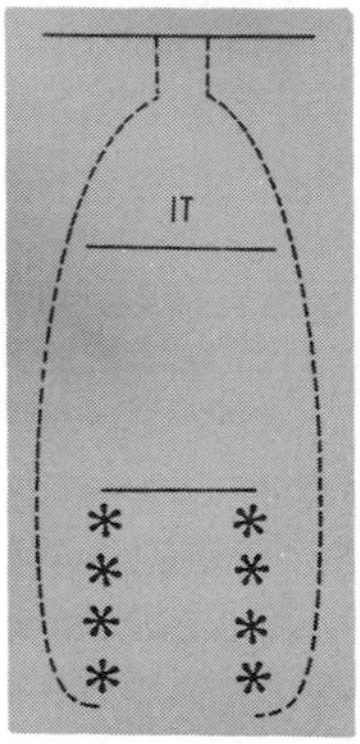

Figure 11-1. Last Couple Out.

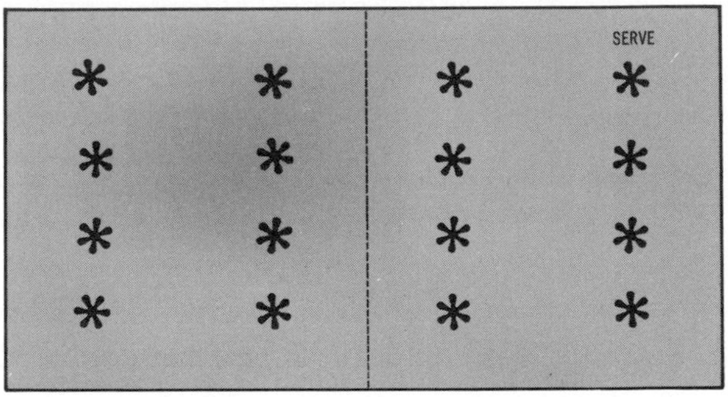

Figure 11-2. Newcomb.

LOOSE CABOOSE

SKILLS: Running, dodging, tagging.

EQUIPMENT: None.

FORMATION: Players in groups of three, holding onto waist of one in front of him. The first player is the Engine, the second the Baggage Car, and the third the Caboose, all forming a train.

DESCRIPTION: One or two players are designated as Loose Cabooses, and must find a train to latch onto. The Engine tries to avoid the Loose

Caboose and the rest of the train must try to dodge with him. The Loose Cabooses try to latch on to other Cabooses. If they do, the present Caboose becomes Loose or IT, the Engine becomes the Baggage Car, the Baggage Car the new Caboose and the former Loose Caboose the new Engine. If a train pulls apart in trying to be evasive, the Loose Caboose joins the train and the Caboose is IT.

NERVOUS WRECK

SKILLS: Throwing, catching, reaction time.

EQUIPMENT: One 8½-inch playground ball.

FORMATION: Single circle with one person chosen as IT in the center of circle.

DESCRIPTION: IT throws the ball to each person in the circle or pretends to throw it. If the catcher makes any move to catch the ball and it is not thrown he must sit down. If it is thrown, he must catch it or sit down. The thrower must be encouraged to move very fast. The last one standing is the new IT. With small circles the game should go very quickly. Catchers may not hold onto their clothing in order to avoid flinching.

NEWCOMB (Figure 11-2)

SKILLS: Throwing, catching.

EQUIPMENT: One volleyball or 8½-inch playground ball, 6-foot net. Rectangular court approximately 20 feet by 44 feet.

FORMATION: Group divided into teams of eight each. Each team forms two lines on a side of the court.

DESCRIPTION: The player in the right hand back row corner throws the ball over the net into the opponent's court area. This is called a serve. The ball is thrown back and forth over the net until one team misses the ball or one team throws it out-of-bounds. When this happens, the successful team wins a point and continues to serve or wins a point and the serve. The server remains the same until his team loses the serve. When the serve returns to the first team, the second person from the right in the back row is the server. When everyone in the back row has served, the two lines change places. A player may not walk with the ball. The ball may be thrown to a teammate before it is thrown over the net except on the serve. The team which has the greatest number of points after ten minutes wins the game.

VARIATIONS: A shorter serving line may be designated if children cannot throw ball all the way over the net. Rotation by moving in a clockwise direction in a circular fashion may be taught. A certain number of throws per side might be established to encourage team work and change of direction.

NUMBERS EXCHANGE

SKILLS: Running.

EQUIPMENT: None.

FORMATION: Single circle, players numbered off around the circle. IT chosen to be in the center of circle.

DESCRIPTION: IT calls two numbers. Players whose numbers are called try to exchange places. IT tries to get in one of the vacated positions before the other gets there. The player left without a position becomes the new IT.

PRISONER BALL

SKILLS: Throwing, catching.

EQUIPMENT: 8½-inch playground ball.

FORMATION: Parallel lines drawn about 25 feet apart, across playing area. Players divided into teams one on each side of center area.

DESCRIPTION: A leader is appointed for each team. He sees that each player has a number between one and the number on the team. This should be done so players on the other side do not know who has what number. The ball is given to one team. A player throws the ball across the center area. As he throws he must call a number. Anyone on the other team tries to catch the ball. If he misses, the player who has the number which was called becomes a prisoner of the throwing team and must stand at the side line. If the player catches the ball, he calls a number and throws the ball back to the other team. Prisoners may be released one at a time when their team throws a ball and their opponents fail to catch it. The team with the least number of prisoners at the end of the playing time wins.

STICK CATCH

SKILLS: Quick reaction time, running, catching.

EQUIPMENT: Stick or wand.

FORMATION: Small circle with players each given a number, one IT.

DESCRIPTION: IT stands in center and balances stick on end, calls a number and lets go of stick. The person whose number is called runs to center of circle and tries to catch stick before it reaches ground. If he is successful, he becomes IT. If the stick is not caught, the original IT calls a new number as he balances stick again.

VARIATION: Names may be called rather than numbers, and ball bats may be used rather than sticks.

TRADES

SKILLS: Running, dodging, pantomime.

EQUIPMENT: None.

FORMATION: Playing area divided into half with a free space of 5 feet between two center lines. Players divided into two teams, standing behind own goal lines.

DESCRIPTION: Team 1 selects some trade or occupation of which each player will pantomime the movements which characterize the trade. As they advance toward the center line, the players call out:
(Team 1) "Here we come!"
(Team 2) "Where from?"
(Team 1) "Detroit (or any city)."
(Team 2) "What's your trade?"
Following this Team 1 acts out their trade. Members of Team 2 call out what they think the trade is. If and when they do call the correct one, all members from Team 1 run for their goal line and members of Team 2 chase and try to tag them. They count the number of players caught and the score is recorded. A new game is started and Team 2 becomes the tradesmen. The winners are those who have the most number of points at the end of the playing time.

UP THE FIELD

SKILLS: Throwing, catching.

EQUIPMENT: 8½-inch playground ball.

FORMATION: Entire playing area inside, or large rectangular area approximately 100 feet long and 50 feet wide outside divided in half by center line. Divide players into two teams each scattered in their own half of playing field.

DESCRIPTION: Ball is given to a player on one team three quarters of the way back toward their goal line. The ball is thrown with intent to get it across the opponent's goal line. When the ball is caught, it must be thrown immediately with the option of taking only one step forward. Each team tries to get the ball across their opponent's end line while it is in the air and not touched by the other team. Whichever team succeeds in getting the ball across its opponent's goal line first wins a point for their team. The ball is then put into play by the opposing team at a point similar to that at the beginning of the game.

Fourth grade

BOMBARDMENT (Figure 11-3)

SKILLS: Throwing, catching, blocking ball.

EQUIPMENT: A pin for every player, ten balls.

FORMATION: Playing area divided into half. A restraining line drawn across the end of each side 4 feet from the end line. The pins are set up in this area an equal distance apart.

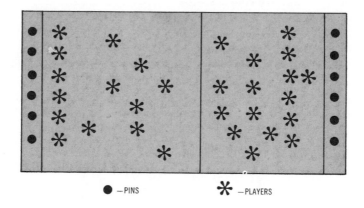

● —PINS   ✱ —PLAYERS

Figure 11-3. Bombardment.

DESCRIPTION: Five balls are given to each team. Players try to knock down the pins in their opponent's goal area and at the same time try to keep their own pins from being knocked down. No one may step over the restraining line. Each pin knocked down should be removed from the playing area. The team which knocks down all of its opponent's pins first or the team which has knocked down the most pins at the end of a specified time wins. A new game is then started.

CORNER BALL (Figure 11-4)

SKILLS: Throwing, catching, dribbling.

EQUIPMENT: Junior-size basketball.

FORMATION: Playing area divided into half. A 4-foot square is drawn in each of the rear corners. Playing group is divided into two teams which take scattered positions on their respective half of the court. Two players from each team are chosen to take positions in the squares in their opponent's end of the courts.

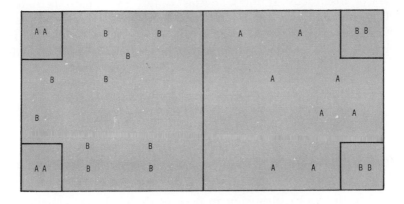

Figure 11-4. Corner Ball.

DESCRIPTION: The ball is thrown high in the air at midcourt. Whoever catches it initiates an attempt to throw the ball to one of his corner men on the other half of the court. The opponents try to intercept the ball and throw it to their own corner men. When a corner man catches the ball in the air one point is awarded to his team and the ball is started in the center again. Players may not go out of their court area, may not run or walk with the ball, may not hold the ball over five seconds, or step into or out of the corner spaces. Violation of any one of these causes the ball to be given to the opponents. Players may take three bounces with the ball. Corner men should be changed periodically. It is best to have girls in the corners at the same time and boys at the same time. The team with the greatest number of points at the end of a specified period of time is the winner.

GANGSTER AND HIS GUARD

SKILLS: Throwing, blocking ball.

EQUIPMENT: One 8½-inch playground ball.

FORMATION: Single circle with small 3-foot diameter circle in center. One player chosen as Guard and one as Gangster.

DESCRIPTION: The Gangster sits in the small circle with arms folded across head. The players in the circle throw the ball trying to hit the Gangster. The Guard tries to keep ball from hitting the Gangster by kicking or blocking the ball with his body or hands if it comes above his thighs. If the Gangster is hit, the Guard becomes the Gangster and the person who hit him becomes the Guard. The Gangster takes the new Guard's place in the circle. Encourage throwing the ball around rapidly in order to get the Guard out of position.

GAP BALL

SKILLS: Throwing, catching while standing and on the run.

EQUIPMENT: 8½-inch ball for each circle.

FORMATION: Small circles of eight are formed with a leader in the center.

DESCRIPTION: The leader throws the ball to one person who returns the ball to the leader, then runs in back of the circle to the next gap or between the next two people. The leader again throws the ball to the same person who likewise returns it and runs to the next gap, etc., until he is back in his original position. The next person does the same until each has completed his turn around the circle.

VARIATIONS: This can be used as a race between several circles. Leader in the center may be rotated.

GUARD BALL (Figure 11-5)

SKILLS: Throwing, catching, guarding.

EQUIPMENT: 8½-inch utility ball, junior-size basketball or soccer ball.

FORMATION: Two parallel lines about 20 feet apart. Two teams.

DESCRIPTION: One team is in the center of the two lines. The other team has half of its players behind either line. The players on the outside of the lines try to pass the ball back and forth to each other

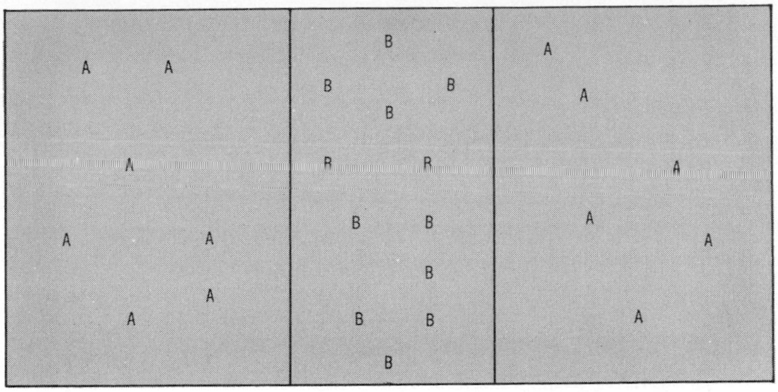

Figure 11-5. Guard Ball.

without the players in the center getting it. Balls must be passed below head level. They may use bounce passes or roll the ball. The players in the center attempt to intercept or to block the passes with their arms. If they catch the ball it is returned to the other team. One point is awarded for each successful pass. Teams change places after four minutes. Deceptive maneuvers with the head, eyes, and arms should be stressed.

JUMP THE SHOT

SKILLS: Jumping, timing of jump.

EQUIPMENT. A rope about 20 feet long with a beanbag, deck tennis ring, or tennis shoe attached to the end of it.

FORMATION: Single circle.

DESCRIPTION: One person or the teacher swings the rope around the circle so that the object is traveling no more than 1 foot from the ground. The players jump over the rope as it swings under them. If a player is hit by the rope or shot, he has one shot on him. The winner is the player who has the least number of shots at the end of the playing time. As it takes a little practice to control the swing of the rope, the teacher may start the game and then teach the students how to swing. The one with least number of shots may be the turner.

VARIATIONS: The length of the rope and the speed of the rope may be adjusted according to the number and skill of the players. The game may be made more difficult by having the circle players walk and then run around the circle and jump on the move.

POISON BALL

SKILLS: Throwing at a moving target.

EQUIPMENT: As many balls 7 inches or over that one has, and one large ball of a distinctive color which is called the Poison Ball.

FORMATION: Class divided into two groups with a goal line drawn across each end of playing area.

DESCRIPTION: Balls are divided equally between teams. The Poison Ball is placed in center of playing area. Each team's players try to hit the Poison Ball, trying to knock it across the opposite team's goal line. Players may not hold the balls or go out into the playing area to retrieve them. No one may touch the Poison Ball to keep it from crossing his line. If many balls get stuck out in the middle, someone may be appointed to go get them and throw them back to the players of each team. When the Poison Ball crosses a goal line, play ceases, a point is awarded to the team who caused it to go across, and a new game is started.

STEALING STICKS (Figure 11-6)

SKILLS: Running, dodging, strategy.

EQUIPMENT: Twelve sticks or pins, color bands.

FORMATION: Playing area divided in half. Two teams, one each side of playing area. At one end of each goal line is a 4-foot square area

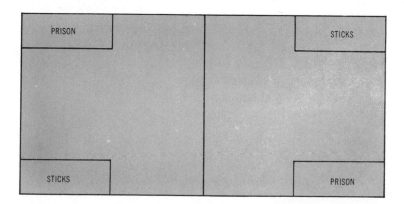

Figure 11-6. Stealing Sticks.

marked off as the Stick area and at the opposite end of it is a 4-foot square area marked off as the Prison. Six sticks are placed in each team's stick area.

DESCRIPTION: The object of the game is for one team to take one stick at a time from the opposing team without being tagged. When players cross over the center line they may be tagged by members of the other team. If tagged they are put in prison. They may be rescued by a teammate who can reach the prisoner's outstretched hand before being tagged. A rescuer and prisoner may go home free if they walk back to their side holding hands. The game ends when all the sticks have been taken from one team or, if time does not permit this arrangement, whichever team has the combination of most sticks and prisoners wins. Teams should be encouraged to plan strategy in guarding sticks and prisoners and in going in platoons to get sticks or prisoners.

TADPOLE (Figure 11-7)

SKILLS: Running, throwing, catching.

EQUIPMENT: One 8½-inch playground ball.

FORMATION: Two teams. One in single circle, other in file formation at one point behind a member of the circle.

DESCRIPTION: The ball is given to the circle team. The ball is thrown around to each member of the circle. As the ball is started, the first person in the file line runs around the circle. When he returns he tags off the next runner and goes to the end of the line. The object is to see how many trips the ball can make around the circle

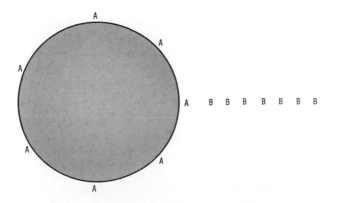

Figure 11-7. Tadpole.

before everyone on the running team has gone around the circle. The game is repeated with teams changing sides. The team which had the most round trips with the ball wins the game.

VARIATIONS: Vary the type of pass required. Vary the locomotor skill used in going around the circle.

Fifth grade

BALL STAND

SKILLS: Running, throwing.

EQUIPMENT: 8½-inch playground ball.

FORMATION: A wall with a restricted playing area marked out in front of it is utilized, the size of the area depending on the number of players. All players are given a number then line up in front of the wall.

DESCRIPTION: The leader throws a ball against the wall and calls a number. All except the person whose number was called run as far away from the ball as possible while staying within the playing area. The one whose number was called chases the ball and when he catches it he stands still and calls "Ball stand." Everyone must stop immediately and stand with their backs to the person with the ball, who tries to hit another player's back with the ball. If a player is hit he calls out "Ball hit" and retrieves the ball. After gaining possession of it he calls "Ball stand" and attempts to hit someone. After hearing the words "Ball hit" all the other players run away again. The game continues like this until someone is missed in the hit attempt. Then the player who last tried to hit someone starts the game anew by throwing the ball against the wall and calling a new number.

BEATER GOES ROUND

SKILLS: Running.

EQUIPMENT: One towel with knot tied on end.

FORMATION: Single circle. Players stand facing center, hands clasped behind their back. One player selected as IT stands outside the circle with the towel.

DESCRIPTION: The IT runs around the outside of the circle and drops the towel into someone's hands. This person becomes the Beater and immediately starts chasing his right hand neighbor who runs and tries to beat the Beater back to his place in the circle. The Beater may hit the person he is chasing with the towel whenever he is near enough. He may hit the person only across the seat. When the evader is back in place he becomes the new Beater.

CAPTURE THE FLAG (Figure 11-8)

SKILLS: Running, dodging, tagging.

EQUIPMENT: Two flags or towels.

FORMATION: Playing area divided into half. At each right hand rear corner a rectangle 3 feet by 6 feet extends into the court and is known as the Jail or Prison. The flag is placed in a small circle drawn in the center of the court behind the goal line.

DESCRIPTION: Once the game is started any one who steps over the center line into his opponents half of the court is eligible to be caught. If caught he is taken to the Prison. The major objective of the game is to capture the enemy's flag. A player must get through the enemy lines without getting tagged. Prisoners may be rescued by teammates who get through enemy lines without being tagged and touch the prisoner's outstretched hand. If rescued, both the prisoner and rescuer may walk back to their own court hand in hand down the side-line without being tagged. The last prisoner caught becomes the end man in a line formed by prisoners so that the first one caught is the first one released. Only one prisoner may be rescued at a time. When a player reaches the flag and holds it up high the game is won. A new game may be started and a point given for each game won. Students are charged with planning their own strategy in getting the flag, rescuing prisoners, guarding flag and prisoners.

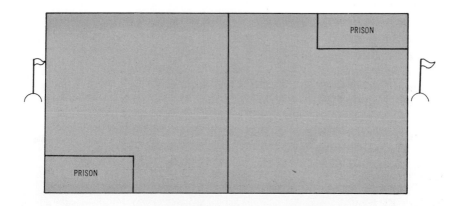

Figure 11-8. Capture the Flag.

VARIATIONS: A player may be required to bring the flag back to his team without getting caught on the way back. All prisoners must be out of Prison before flag can be captured. This game may be adapted to a large outside play area and be considered a war game in which patrols are sent out in various maneuvers.

CHAIN TAG

SKILLS: Tagging, running, dodging.

EQUIPMENT: None.

FORMATION: Scattered. If the outside area is too large, side and end boundaries should be established. One player selected as IT.

DESCRIPTION: IT tries to tag someone. As soon as he does, they join hands and work together to tag some one else. Each new person caught joins the chain. Only the head and end players may tag. If the tagging or chain line breaks, no one may be tagged until it is rejoined. If the group is large, two chains may be formed. Play may continue until all are caught or until a specified time elapses.

FOOTBALL GOAL CATCH

SKILLS: Throwing, catching.

EQUIPMENT: Junior-size football.

FORMATION: Playing area approximately 40 by 50 feet divided into half. Lines drawn parallel to each end line about 6 feet from them. This area is the goal area. Playing group divided into two teams with four players in the goal area opposite their end of the field. The rest are field players and play anywhere in their half of field.

DESCRIPTION: A ball is given to a goal line player on one team. He tries to throw it to one of his teammates at the opposite end of the playing field. The fielders then try to pass the football to a goal line player. If one catches it, the team receives 1 point. The opposing players try to intercept or knock down the pass and in turn try to throw it to one of their goal line players. The team which has the most points at the end of ten minutes is the winner. Rotate field and goal line positions periodically.

KICK-OVER

SKILLS: Kicking.

EQUIPMENT: 10-inch playground ball or cage ball.

FORMATION: Players divided into two teams which sit on parallel lines 8
feet apart and face one another.

DESCRIPTION: The ball is rolled or bounced down between the lines by
the leader. Players from both teams sit with their hands palms down
on their respective lines and try to get the soles of their feet under
the ball and kick it over the heads of their opponents. Whichever
team kicks it over the opponent's heads wins a point, and the ball
is put into play again by the leader. The team with the most points
at the end of a specified time wins.

VARIATIONS: The leader stands at the head of the line. When the ball is
kicked over, he moves back to a distance he thinks is equal to the
distance away from the line the ball travels. The end player on the
team who kicked the ball over must run and touch the leader's hand
and go to the head of his line before the other team's end player
runs out, retrieves the ball, and brings it back to the head of his line.
The first one back wins a point for his team.

MACHINE GUN RUN

SKILLS: Running, dodging, throwing at a moving target.

EQUIPMENT: Six 8½-inch playground balls.

FORMATION: Players divided into three teams. Parallel lines drawn about
25 feet apart and 40 feet long.

DESCRIPTION: Team 1 lines up behind one of the lines, Team 2 on the
other. Team 3 waits at the end of the lines. Teams 1 and 2 are each
given 3 balls. Upon a signal players on Team 3 run down between
the two lines to one end and back. Players on 2 and 3 repeatedly
throw the ball and try to hit players above the ankles or below the
waist with a ball. The number who were not hit are counted, and the
teams rotate; Team 3 takes Team 1's place, Team 2 becomes the
running team. After each team has run the line twice, scores are
compared, and the team with greatest number of people who were
not hit wins.

VARIATIONS: Distances may be varied to fit the throwing ability of the
groups. More balls may be added. More running turns may be allowed.

PRISONER'S BASE

SKILLS: Running, dodging, tagging.

EQUIPMENT: None.

FORMATION: A goal line is marked off at each end of the playing area. Prisons 3 by 9 feet are marked off at the right hand corners of the goal lines. Players are divided into two teams, each lining up along their assigned goal lines.

DESCRIPTION: The object of the game is to take as many Prisoners as possible in the time allotted for the game. Once a player steps over his goal line he is free to be caught by someone from the other team who must declare that he is "fresh on _____" before the chase begins. Therefore one may chase a specific player and be chased by a specific player. At any time that a player returns to his goal line, he erases the "fresh" for the person he was chasing and the "fresh" on him is eliminated. If a person is tagged, he is taken to Prison. Prisoners form a chain from the back of the Prison with the last one caught taking the back position each time. A Rescuer and Prisoner may come back to their line free if they clasp hands and hold them high. A leader should be appointed for each team and he is responsible for team strategy. Players should be very clear about their vows about being "fresh" on a certain person.

THREE TEAM DODGEBALL (Figure 11-9)

SKILLS: Throwing at a moving target, dodging.

EQUIPMENT: Two 8½-inch playground balls.

FORMATION: Court is divided into three equal courts longwise. Playing group is divided into three teams, with one team occupying each court.

DESCRIPTION: Play is divided into three playing periods of four minutes each. At the end of each period the teams rotate positions so that at the end of the game each team has been in every court once. A ball is given to each of the end court teams. The object is for everyone to try to hit someone on another team. The ball must hit below the waist, and be in the air when it hits. Once the ball has bounced it may be picked up and thrown. No walking, or holding the ball over five seconds. When a player is hit he goes to the sideline directly opposite his team's court and sits down until that playing period is over. The number sitting is counted each period and all players reenter the game. The team with the least number of points at the end of the three periods is the winner. The team in the center will always have the greatest number eliminated.

VARIATIONS: Add more balls if the game goes slowly. Teams may be called red, white, and blue.

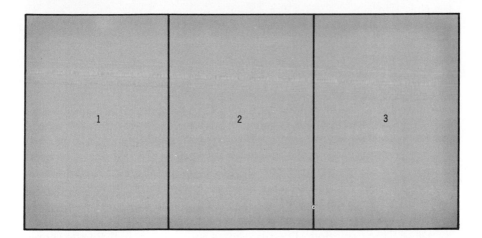

Figure 11-9. Three Team Dodgeball.

Sixth grade

AGENTS AND SPIES

SKILLS: Running, throwing, accuracy.

EQUIPMENT: A utility ball and a pin for each team.

FORMATIONS: Each team has four players. One half the teams are Agents and the other half are Spies at the start of the playing time. Teams line up in single file with a team of Agents behind a line 40 feet across from a line behind which the Spies stand. Midway between each set of Agents and Spies is placed a ball and a pin. It is wise to mark a small circle in which each is placed. Upon a signal from the leader, the first person in the Agents' line and the Spies' line, respectively, run out to the center. The Spy picks up the pin and tries to get it back to his line before the Agent can pick up the ball and throw it and hit the Spy. If the Agent hits the Spy his team gets 2 points; if the Spy gets home safely his team gets 2 points. After everyone has had a turn, the teams are reversed in their actions and titles. Play may continue for a set length of time and at the end of the period the team with the most points wins. Agents retrieve the ball and the Spies must return the pin to place each time. Any number of teams may play at the same time.

BATTLEBALL (Figure 11-10)

SKILLS: Throwing, dodging.

EQUIPMENT: One 8½-inch playground ball.

FORMATION: Players divided into two teams. Playing area is divided into two equal areas approximately 20 by 40 feet. The center line is extended three feet out to each side of the courts.

DESCRIPTION: Each team is scattered in its own court. A player from each team is stationed outside the boundary lines at the opposite end from his own team. This player is called the end guard and will be joined later by the members of his team who are legally hit by the ball. These players may throw the ball at the opposite team's players, but must stay outside the boundary lines and may not cross the center line extension. The play starts with a jump ball (in the center of the court) with a person from each team jumping and immediately returning to his own court. Players try to eliminate players from the opposite team from the center court. The team with the last player in its center court wins. The ball must be in the air when it hits a player and it must hit below the waist. A player may pick up the ball as soon as it has hit the floor or another person. A player may not walk with the ball or hold it over 3 seconds. He may bounce or dribble the ball three times. The ball may be passed from player to player. As soon as one is hit he goes to the outside court at the opposite end anywhere around the sidelines of that court and remains active in the attempt to get balls to hit his opponents.

VARIATION: Use two balls.

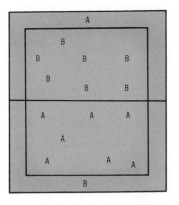

Figure 11-10. Battleball.

BRONCO DODGEBALL

SKILLS: Throwing, dodging.

EQUIPMENT: 8½-inch playground balls.

FORMATION: Single circle. Two sets of three people each are selected. The three must hold onto the waist of the player in front of them. Players in the circle try to hit the last person with the ball. If a player hits the last in the chain, he then becomes the head, and the tail player takes his place in the circle. The three players must work together to dodge the ball. The head player can hit the ball with his hands or kick it. If the three break their chain, they must stop and regroup.

VARIATIONS:
1. More broncos may be added.
2. More balls may be added.
3. Scattered formation may be used.

BUSYBALL

SKILLS: Throwing, catching.

EQUIPMENT: An odd number of volleyballs, utility balls, soccer or basketballs. At least nine balls, the more the better. Volleyball net.

FORMATION: Volleyball court, players divided into two teams. Divide the balls equally between the two teams, with the leader keeping the odd ones.

DESCRIPTION: The leader gives the signal to start and members of both teams throw the balls over the net into the other team's court. The leader tosses the odd ball into one of the courts at the signal to start. The object is for a team to have the least balls on its side of the court when the whistle blows at the end of three minutes. The game may be repeated for a set number of playing periods.

VARIATION: Players have to hit ball over net rather than throw it over.

HEMENWAY BALL (Figure 11-11)

SKILLS: Throwing, striking with hand, running, dodging.

EQUIPMENT: Base, volleyball or 8½-inch playground ball.

FORMATION: A rectangular area about 90 feet by 40 feet is designated. A line is drawn down the center lengthwise. The base is placed 8 feet

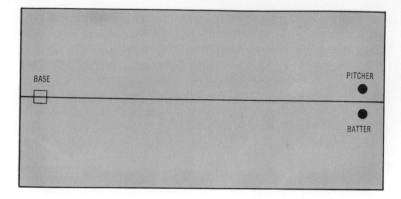

Figure 11-11. Hemenway Ball.

from the end line and on the center line. At the opposite end a batter's box is marked off on one side of the line and a pitcher's box
directly across from that. Players are divided into two teams, one
out in the field area, and one lined up behind the home line and to
the left of the center line.

DESCRIPTION: The object of the game is for the batter to hit the ball into
the field, run down the right side of the center line, touch the base,
and run back to the batter's box on the left side of the center line
without getting hit by the ball. The first person in the line tosses the
ball up so the second player can hit it with his fist out in the field.
If the ball is caught in the air by the fielders, the batter is out. The
fielders try to field the ball and then throw it at the runner. They
may not walk with the ball, hold it more than five seconds, or hit the
runner above the waist. They may pass it to other teammates. If the
runner reaches home line without getting hit, he scores a run for his
team and then goes to the end of the line. Everyone else moves up a
position until each has had a turn batting, whereupon the sides
change. After each team has had a specified number of equal bats,
the team with the most points wins. A violation of the rules gives
the opposing team a point.

POISON PIN

SKILLS: Pulling, pushing.

EQUIPMENT: A pin for every three players.

FORMATION: Divide players into groups of three, scattered about the floor.

DESCRIPTION: Players make a small circle and place pin in the center.

Holding onto hands, each tries to pull the others into the circle so they knock the pin down. When the pin is knocked down, a point is given to the one who was responsible. The pin is reset, and the game is started again. This will be tiring to the arms, but it is strength-building. The player with the least number of points at the end of a specified playing period wins.

WALL KICK-BALL (Figure 11-12)

Skills: Running, kicking.

Equipment: 10-inch playground ball or cageball.

Formation: Players are divided into two teams. A line is drawn parallel to the wall and 6 feet from it. Two parallel lines, 8 feet apart, are drawn perpendicular to this line. Players of one team sit on one line and those of the other across from them on the other line. A base is established 20 feet from the ends of the team lines.

Description: The leader throws the ball between the two lines so that it hits the wall and rebounds in between the teams. Players try to kick the ball over the heads of their opponents. When the ball is kicked over, the end players next to the wall get up, run behind their lines, to their goals and back to the other end of the line. The first one back wins a point for his team. The team which kicked the ball over the heads of the other's also receives a point. The game continues for a specified length of time, and the team with the most points at the end is declared the winner. Stress bending knees and kicking the ball up with the soles of the feet.

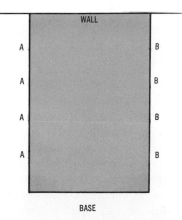

Figure 11-12. Wall Kick-Ball.

Seventh and eighth grades

BASKET BASEBALL

SKILLS: Throwing, catching, running, shooting baskets.

EQUIPMENT: Four bases, one basketball or soccerball.

FORMATION: A home base is placed at the free-throw line of the basketball court with the other three placed in positions as for a regular softball game. Players are divided into two equal teams. Boundary lines are the same as for a regular softball game.

DESCRIPTION: One team is at bat and stands along the first base line. The fielding team is scattered throughout the playing field. One player is designated as the catcher. The first batter throws the ball into the field and proceeds to run the bases in order. The fielders attempt to catch or field the ball and relay it in to the catcher, who attempts to make a basket. If he makes a basket before the runner reaches home base, he scores 2 points for his team. If the runner returns before a basket is made, he scores 2 points for his team. Once everyone has run, the teams change sides. A new catcher should be appointed or chosen each time the sides change. The distance between bases may have to be shortened if the fielding team always returns the ball to the catcher before the runner gets home. If the runner always beats the ball, the bases may be too close.

BASKET NETBALL

SKILLS: Catching, throwing, guarding, shooting baskets.

EQUIPMENT: Basketball, volleyball net, color bands.

FORMATION: Volleyball net divides the basketball court into two sides. Players are divided into two teams. One member of each team is selected to play in the keyhole area of the opposite team's court.

DESCRIPTION: The ball is given to one team which tries to pass the ball over the net into the keyhole area to a teammate. If the teammate gets the ball, he attempts a shot for a basket. One point is given for a completed pass to the keyhole, and 2 additional points if a basket is made. Once a basket is made, a new player is rotated into the keyhole. Whether the basket is made or missed, the ball is given to the opposite team at their end line to the right of the free-throw lanes. The ball may be passed among teammates. No steps may be taken with the ball, no bounces, and no player may hold the ball for more than five seconds.

BULL IN THE RING

SKILLS: Throwing, catching, guarding.

EQUIPMENT: One soccer, basketball or 8½-inch utility ball.

FORMATION: Single circle of 6 to 8 players. Players are each given a number. One player is IT. IT calls a number and tosses the ball to any player in the circle. The person whose number was called is the "Bull." He goes immediately to the center of the circle and attempts to intercept or "tie up" the ball. The circle players must pass the ball around or across the circle. They may not pass it to the player standing next to them in the circle. No player may hold the ball more than five seconds. As soon as the ball is tied up or intercepted by the Bull, he returns to the circle, calls a number, and starts the ball in play again.

VARIATIONS:
1. Points may be given for intercepting or taking the ball.
2. More than one number may be called.
3. More than one ball may be used.

CRAB SOCCER

SKILLS: Crab walk, kicking.

EQUIPMENT: Soccer ball, color bands.

FORMATION: Playing area approximately 40 by 60 feet with a goal line designated for each team. Players are divided into two teams.

DESCRIPTION: Teams line up on their own goal line. Ball is placed in the center of playing area. On signal, players from both teams advance using a crab walk (weight on hands and feet, with seat toward the floor) and try to kick the ball over the opposing team's goal line. Hands may not touch the ball. Two points are awarded to the team which gets it across the opponent's goal line. After a goal is made, the ball is placed in the center, and play starts again. The winner is the team with the most points at the end of a designated period of time.

VARIATION: If scooters are available, one may sit on them and kick the ball.

FLAK DODGEBALL (Figure 11-13)

SKILLS: Running, dodging, throwing.

EQUIPMENT: Base, 8½-inch playground ball.

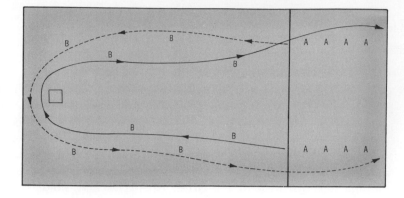

Figure 11-13. Flak Dodgeball.

FORMATION: A goal line drawn 15 feet from the end of the playing area and a base placed 10 feet from the other end and midway between the sides. A circle 3 feet in diameter drawn around the base.

DESCRIPTION: One team (fielding) is scattered anywhere in the field except in the restraining circle around the base. The other team (running) is divided in half. One group is in a line marked on the goal line 10 feet from the right side line, and the other is lined up 10 feet from the left side line. The leader throws the ball into the playing area, and the first person in each of the running team's lines runs out in the field and tries to circle the base and to go to the end of the other line. The fielding players try to hit the runners below the waist and above the ankles with the ball. Fielders may not walk with the ball nor hold the ball more than five seconds. They may pass the ball around to other teammates. If a runner is legally hit, he raises his arm high and immediately goes to the sideline and walks back to his line. The raised arm is a signal for the runner next in line to start running. If the runner reaches the goal line safely, two points are counted for the running team. This is also the signal for the next in line to run. Since the running is continuous, and no signals to run other than those mentioned are given, everyone has to be alert. There are always two runners in the field. If fielders violate the rules, one point is added to the running team's score. After everyone has run twice, the teams exchange sides. It is wise to ask one person in each line to keep score; the scores may be added as teams are changing sides.

VARIATION: Two balls may be put into play when the game is understood by all.

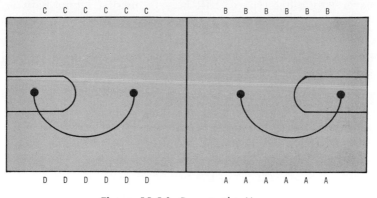

Figure 11-14. Race to the Moon.

RACE TO THE MOON (Figure 11-14)

SKILLS: Passing, catching, basket-shooting.

EQUIPMENT: Two basketballs or soccer balls, basketball goals.

FORMATION: Basketball court, or parallel lines about 40 feet apart. A large new-moon-shaped line drawn in the center of the two lines. Players are divided into two equal teams, each lined up along its respective side line. Half of a basketball court may be used thus, and two games can be played at one time. A ball is placed at each tip of the moon. Each player is given a number.

DESCRIPTION: The leader calls a number. Players having this number run out to the center, pick up the ball closest to them and start throwing the ball to each member of their teams. When they have thrown the ball to and received it from each of the players, they dribble to the basket and attempt to make a basket. They shoot until they do, then race back and place the ball on a tip of the moon. The first one back to his goal line wins 2 points for his team. The game continues, another number is called. The team with the most points at the end of the playing time wins.

VARIATIONS:

1. A player may make only one attempt for a basket.
2. Two points are given for a basket, and 1 is given for the person who replaces his ball on the moon first.

SKEET BALL

SKILLS: Throwing at a moving target.

EQUIPMENT: A large cardboard or stiff plastic disc, a tennis ball for each player (any other type of ball may be used if tennis balls are not available).

FORMATION: Two parallel lines, drawn about 30 feet apart. Players are divided into two teams. Teams line up behind their designated goal line. Players are numbered.

DESCRIPTION: Leader calls a number and at the same time throws the disc up in the air. Those bearing the number called try to hit the disc. A point is given to the team of the player who hits the disc. Each player retrieves his own ball; the leader, the disc. The game is repeated any number of times. The team with the most points at the end of a designated time or the first team to reach 20 points wins.

VARIATION: A large ball or beanbag may be used instead of a disc.

RELAYS

Relays are a form of games in which each child is on a team, and each team member in order performs a skill. Teams compete against each other in a race to see which team's members can complete their turns first. Relays may also be used as skill practice formations when no race is involved. This form of game is not recommended for first graders or second graders. Relays are actually a form of team game, and the confinement, cooperation, and excitement of the organization is too advanced for primary children.

There are a number of formations or patterns which relays may take. Several of these are described in Chapter V. The most common one is a single file formation. Children enjoy relays a great deal and are highly motivated. They very quickly see that their efforts are important to the success of the team. A great deal of self-control is required, since children must wait their turns, react quickly in starting their turns, and follow strict rules. It is important that skills are fairly well-developed, and directions are understood before the relay race is begun.

Considerations when teaching relays

1. Divide class into teams of six. Be sure teams are equal. If they are not, make provision for players on the short teams to take two turns. Put slow or handicapped players in middle of the team. When a team loses, it often appears to children that it is the last player's fault even though it may have been the second player who was too slow.

2. Select skills which are familiar to children or teach the skill before the relay.
3. While teams are seated, clearly establish goal line and starting line.
4. Be definite about when a person starts, how one must tag the next person's right hand with his right hand before he may cross the line, and what one does when he returns to the end of the line. If a ball is being kicked, dribbled, or thrown, it must be in the next player's hands (or hit his feet) before he starts across the line. It is best to have everyone sit down when finished, so that it is easy to distinguish the winning team. An object or ball which is dropped must be retrieved by the person dropping it, and play is resumed at the place where it was dropped first. These rules should be enforced by setting a definite penalty for infractions.
5. Briefly describe the purpose of relays. One group may walk through relay to demonstrate the procedure.
6. If the combination of skills or the pattern is new, everyone can have a trial without the elements of racing being involved.
7. Have an object as turning point at the far goal line. This object should be easy to see in order to maintain straight lines.
8. Use an established signal to start relay. "1, 2, 3, Go!" or "Ready, (blow whistle)."
9. Recognize winning team, and second, third and fourth places. Do each relay several times. A whole period should not be devoted to relays; however, if much of the period is concerned with this type of game, points can be kept for winners, and a final winner declared when total points are tallied. As it usually takes only a few seconds to run through a relay, there should be several races to justify the time it takes to assume the formation.

Safety factors

1. Have goal line be 8 to 10 feet from the wall.
2. Place teams far enough apart so there is room to run between lines.
3. Establish a traffic pattern. "Run back on right side, tag right hand of next partner with your right hand, and go to the end of line." Demonstrate carefully.
4. Sit with legs crossed in order that returning members do not trip over feet of the other players. Keep lines straight.

Description of relays

A number of relays are suggested. The teacher or students can create relays to fit the needs of the group; the same ones may be used for different

grade levels, but the distances may vary. The following types of activities lend themselves well to relay games.
1. Locomotor skills and combinations
2. Skills and stunts from self-testing units
3. Obstacle relays
4. Object-handling activities
5. Specific sport skill practices
6. Novelty stunts for parties and for limited spaces

FILE FORMATION RELAYS (Figure 11-15)

This is the basic relay formation for beginners to learn. The skill of walking may be utilized first to learn the format. The first player walks down to line B, goes around the object, returns to line A, touches the second

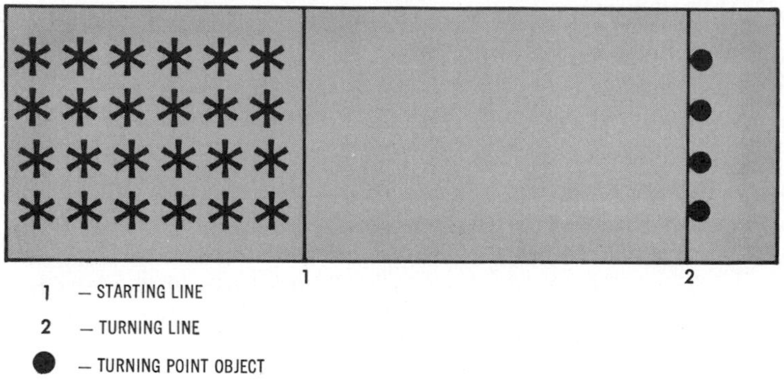

1   — STARTING LINE
2   — TURNING LINE
●   — TURNING POINT OBJECT

Figure 11-15. File Formation Relays.

player, and then sits at the end of his line. This is repeated by each person in turn. The first team in which everyone is sitting wins. The following skills may be utilized in this format:
1. Any one of the locomotor skills; variations in style may be designated
2. Animal walks: bunny hop, elephant walk, seal walk, etc.
3. Bouncing the ball while running or walking
4. Various stunts
5. Riding scooters
6. Skills combined inventively by students and teacher

ATTENTION RELAY

EQUIPMENT: None.

FORMATION: File; players are numbered in own lines. Leader is selected.

PROCEDURE: Leader calls a number. Each player who has the number called steps out of his line on the left side, runs down to the turning point and returns to his place on the right side of his line and sits down. The first player sitting wins a point for his team.

VARIATION: May be used in classroom with seats in a row.

CARRY AND FETCH RELAY *(Figure 11-16)*

EQUIPMENT: Two blocks of wood 3 inches by 5 inches, beanbags, or pins.

FORMATION: File; objects are placed in a small circle drawn approximately 20 feet out in front of the team. Another circle is drawn at the turning line.

PROCEDURE: Upon signal, the first person runs to the objects, takes one, and carries it to the circle on the turning line. He goes back to get the next object and places it in the circle on the running line, then tags off the next player. This player returns the objects one at a time to the first circle. This pattern continues until everyone has had a turn.

CIRCLE RELAY

EQUIPMENT: Ball for each circle.

FORMATION: Several small circles.

PROCEDURE: A line of direction is established. The ball is passed around the circle from each person to the player next to him. When the ball reaches the person who started the passing, the relay is over.

CORNER SPRY *(Figure 11-17)*

EQUIPMENT: Ball for each team.

FORMATION: Four teams. A square formation is used with each team forming one side of the square. A square 6 feet by 6 feet is drawn in the center. A person from each team stands in the center square and faces his team.

PROCEDURE: On the signal the ball is thrown back and forth from leader to his teammates in order down their line. When he throws to the last player in line he calls "Corner spry" and goes to the head of the line. The last player carries the ball into the center and becomes the new leader. This continues until the original leaders are in the center. The first one back sits and his team is declared winner.

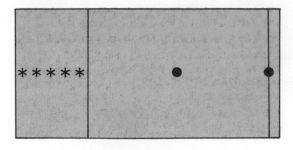

Figure 11-16. Carry and Fetch Relay.

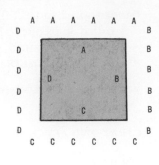

Figure 11-17. Corner Spry.

DRIBBLE UP, THROW BACK

EQUIPMENT: Ball for each team.

FORMATION: File; half the team at the starting line, other half at the turning line.

PROCEDURE: First person in line dribbles up to the turning line, pivots, and throws the ball back to the second person and stays there or goes to the end of the line. This continues until the members of the team have returned to their original places.

VARIATION: The ball may be dribbled with the foot and kicked back.

HUMAN HURDLE RELAY (Figure 11-18)

EQUIPMENT: None.

FORMATION: Circle for each team. Players are in prone position. They face the center of circle; their arms are outstretched, fingers touching. One player remains standing.

PROCEDURE: The player who is standing must run and jump over each player on his team in order. When he reaches his starting point, he exchanges places with the first person. Everyone has a turn.

VARIATIONS:
1. Players may bounce a ball over each person, do a vault over him, or whatever teacher or class decides.
2. Each player may be given a number, and when a leader calls that number, the player on each team with that number will rise, hurdle over everyone around the circle, and return to his place. The first player back in place wins a point for his team.

JUMP THE STICK RELAY

EQUIPMENT: Stick or wand for each team.

FORMATION: File; stick placed on turning line.

PROCEDURE: First person runs and picks up stick. He returns to the team, and the second person grasps one end of the stick. The two carry the stick back to the end of the team, drawing the stick under each player. Each player must jump over the stick. When they come to the

Figure 11-18. Human Hurdle Relay.

end of the team, the first player remains there. The second player takes the stick to the head of the line and the third player grasps one end of the stick. It is again taken to the end. This continues until everyone has a turn. The last player will carry the stick down and place it on the turning line and return to the line.

VARIATION: Each player may run down to the turning line and back after he brings the stick to the front.

LEADER AND CLASS

EQUIPMENT: Ball for each team.

FORMATION: Leader for each team is chosen. Teams line up, each member faces the leader who stands 15 feet in front of the center of the team. (This distance should be decided according to the passing ability of group.) Upon a signal, the leader throws ball to each person in order. After returning ball to the leader, players sit down.

VARIATIONS:
1. Various types of passes may be indicated, depending on those which have been learned.
2. Beanbags may be used.

OBSTACLE RELAY

EQUIPMENT: Chairs or pins are placed in intervals of 8 feet along the way to the turning line.

FORMATION: File.

PROCEDURE: On signal the first person must run around each obstacle on his way down to and back from the turning point. He touches off the second player, and the relay continues until the players of one team have finished.

VARIATIONS:
1. Players may dribble the ball; another form of locomotion may be used.
2. Apparatus equipment or objects to go over and under may be used as obstacles.

OVER AND UNDER RELAY

EQUIPMENT: Ball for each team.

FORMATION: File.

PROCEDURE: Ball is alternately passed back between a person's legs and over his head. When the ball reaches the last player, he brings it back to the front of the line and starts the ball moving back again by passing it between his legs. When all players have returned to their original places, the relay is over.

VARIATIONS:
1. Various objects may be passed.
2. In the classroom any objects may be passed under and over the seats.

RESCUE RELAY

EQUIPMENT: None.

FORMATION: File; one person from each team stands on the turning line and faces his team.

PROCEDURE: On signal the person on the turning line runs down to his team, takes the hand of the first person in line, and they run together to the turning line. The person who started stays there and the second person goes back to the team and brings the third player back. This continues until every player has been brought back. The first team to be sitting in order at the turning line wins.

SHUTTLE RELAY

EQUIPMENT: None.

FORMATION: File; one person standing on turning line.

PROCEDURE: On signal the first person in line runs down and tags off the person standing on the turning line and stays there. The other player runs to the team, tags off the second person, and goes to the end of the line. This exchange of places continues until everyone is back in his place.

VARIATIONS:
1. This makes a good style relay for track and field units for the intermediate grades. Distances between lines may be varied.
2. Ball may be dribbled either with foot or hand.

STAR RELAY (*Figure 11-19*)

EQUIPMENT: Ball for each team.

FORMATION: Star formation, five players on a team arranged in the fashion of a five-point star. Each player is given a number.

PROCEDURE: The number 1 player on each team throws the ball to the number 2 player and after he has thrown he runs to the number 2 position. The number 2 player throws the ball to the number 3 player and then runs to the number 3 position. This continues until everyone is back in his own position. The first team to complete their trip around the star wins.

Figure 11-19. Star Relay.

STRIDEBALL RELAY

EQUIPMENT: Ball for each team.

FORMATION: File; players standing with feet in a wide side-stride position.

PROCEDURE: Ball is rolled down between the spread legs of the team. The last player picks up the ball and runs to the head of the line and starts the ball back again. When everyone has returned to his original position the relay is over. As player is carrying ball to front, all other players should be moving back so first player will be standing behind line.

VARIATION: Ball may be passed under legs rather than rolled.

TASK RELAY

EQUIPMENT: One jump rope, one ball for each team.

FORMATION: File; three circles are drawn equidistant between the starting line and the turning line. The rope is put in the first circle, the ball in the second.

PROCEDURE: Upon signal the first person runs to the rope, jumps it five times, replaces it in the circle, and runs to the next circle. There he bounces the ball five times, replaces ball in the circle, and runs to the next. Here he must do five mule kicks, run to the turning point, and then tag off the next player in line. Objects must be placed in circles and the required tasks done properly the required number of times. When everyone has had a turn, the relay is over.

VARIATION: Any stunt or task may be utilized. Squads may be assigned the responsibility of making a relay for designated periods.

CLASSROOM AND
INACTIVE GAMES

Occasionly the teacher has a need for games which involve a restricted space and little vigorous activity. In some situations the physical education class must be conducted in the classroom whenever there is inclement weather. This may be a permanent situation when there is no gym or playroom in the physical plant, or a temporary one where the usual play space is being used for another purpose. The latter is frequently true where multi-purpose rooms are utilized for plays, community events, displays, concerts, and other events.

In addition to including inactive games in the regular physical education period, the teacher may use them for relaxation, indoor recess, and recreation. Most teachers realize that it is valuable to incorporate game ideas in learning situations in all phases of the curriculum. Quickly organized inactive games at the end of a stimulating and vigorous physical education lesson serve as a calming agent before the children return to academic work in the classroom.

When the classroom is the only indoor play space, the teacher must plan a program composed of a great deal of vigorous activity outdoors and including adaptable activities which permit a maximum of activity in the classroom. Many dance and self-testing activities are suitable for classroom space. Consideration in selecting the activities must revolve around:
1. Space available
2. Safety factors
3. Noise resulting
4. Amount of participation by all
5. Equipment needed

Space
Today most schoolrooms are equipped with movable furniture. If the desks must be moved frequently in order to clear large spaces, a plan should be devised whereby this can be done quickly, quietly, and efficiently. Some games can utilize traffic patterns created by the usual furniture placement.

Safety

Regardless of the furniture arrangement, the classroom has many safety hazards, i.e., protruding objects, windows, and waxed floors. The safest possible games (in terms of the hazards specific to the room) must be selected, and safety rules must be established and maintained.

Noise

The acoustics of the room may sometimes determine whether or not any semi-active games or dances can be utilized. Any teacher recognizes that learning is difficult when loud noises come through the ventilating systems, the walls, and ceilings. As a result, play may be restricted to seat, table, blackboard, or mental games.

Participation

As in any other activity, one of the primary goals of classroom games should be the maximum participation of all students. Coupled with the inactivity imposed by space elements, inactivity for many due to unwieldy numbers and other factors can make classroom activities boring and valueless. Modifying activities and breaking into small play groups are methods by which maximum participation may be achieved.

Equipment

Naturally, games requiring a great deal of equipment are not suitable for use in an overcrowded area. Ball games will be difficult to play in limited space, and there are many hazards such as glass, wall hangings, and desk corners. Beanbags, balloons, paper balls, and yarn balls may substitute for the bouncier, harder balls; and many table- and target-type game boards can be constructed by the children or purchased commercially.

Suggestions for games will be made in the categories of:
1. Semi-active games
2. Mental and guessing games
3. Skill games

Although most of these games need not be restricted to any one grade level, Int is used to indicate intermediate grades or above, P is used to indicate primary grades. These are the two major divisions within which the use of these games will be most effective.

Semi-active games

Games may be adapted to classroom or limited space use by modifying the means of locomotion, using beanbags, or fleece balls for the regular balls and varying as the directions suggest:

GAMES	PAGE	LEVEL
Hot Ball	328	P
Numbers Exchange	340	Int
Circle Stride Ball	332	P
Club Snatch	332	Int
Fire Engine	333	P
Stick Catch	340	Int
Trades	341	Int
Gangster and His Guard	344	Int
Nervous Wreck	339	Int

Primary

BIRDS FLY

EQUIPMENT: None.

FORMATION: Standing anywhere in room. A leader is chosen and stands where everyone can see him.

DESCRIPTION: Quickly, the leader gives the name of anything that flies. When he does, the rest of the players flap their arms vigorously like wings. If the leader gives the name of something that does not fly, no one is supposed to flap arms. If someone does he must sit down. If everyone is eliminated in quick order, the last one down becomes the new leader. Otherwise a new leader is chosen after several minutes. *Example:* "Ducks fly, . . . geese fly, . . . mosquitoes fly, . . . mules fly."

BOILER BURST

EQUIPMENT: None.

FORMATION: Everyone seated in seats or in circle. One person chosen to be the first storyteller.

DESCRIPTION: The storyteller begins to tell a story. He may end the story at any time by saying the words "and then the boiler burst." This is a signal for everyone to get up and exchange seats. The storyteller attempts to get a seat. The person left standing becomes the new storyteller.

VARIATION: This may be done in a circle, and everyone must exchange places at least two places from his original place.

FRUIT BASKET UPSET

EQUIPMENT: None.

FORMATION: Everyone sitting in own seat. Class divided into four teams. A leader of each team is appointed. An IT is appointed.

DESCRIPTION: Leaders give each player a name of a fruit. IT calls out the name of a fruit, and each player bearing the name of the fruit exchanges seats with someone else of that fruit. IT tries to get a seat for himself. The person left without a seat is the new IT. When IT calls "Fruit basket upset," everyone gets a new seat.

SEAT CHANGE

EQUIPMENT: Seats arranged in any fashion, one less seat than players.

FORMATION: Everyone seated. A leader is chosen.

DESCRIPTION: The leader calls out the direction that players are to go as he gives the signal to change seats, i.e., "Left change." "Front change." "Right change." When the leader says "Scramble," the players may change seats in any direction. At this time the leader tries to get a seat. The person who is left without a seat becomes the new leader.

SIMON SAYS

EQUIPMENT: None.

FORMATION: Everyone standing beside his seat; standing in a circle, or in a scattered formation. One chosen to be Simon.

DESCRIPTION: The person who was chosen to be "Simon" says, "Simon says, 'Stand up.'" Everyone follows his command. He continues to give commands in this fashion and the members of the group do what he says. If he omits the words "Simon says" preceding the command, they are not supposed to do the action. Those who do are eliminated or are given a point. Simon should mix commands and actions very quickly so the group must listen carefully. The one who can stay in the longest or has the fewest points becomes the next Simon.

Intermediate

BEANBAG TARGET RELAY

EQUIPMENT: Four beanbags for each team; circle 30 inches in diameter drawn on blackboard in front of each team.

FORMATION: Seats are arranged in rows, or children sit in relay file formation in front of blackboard.

DESCRIPTION: Upon signal from the leader the first person in each row throws his four beanbags and tries to hit his target. Two points are given for each target hit. After throwing the last beanbag, he gets up and retrieves his bags. Meanwhile, every other child moves up one seat. The first person places the retrieved bags on the first desk then sits in the last seat. The second person then takes his throws at the target. This process is repeated until all have had a chance to throw. The winning team is that which has the most points.

BLACKBOARD RELAY

EQUIPMENT: A piece of chalk for each row of seats; blackboard.

FORMATION: Desks or seats are arranged in rows. People may sit in rows if there is room to run.

DESCRIPTION: Each person in the row is numbered. Rows must have an even number. Upon a signal the first person in each row runs or walks (space determines type of locomotion) to the blackboard, takes the chalk out of the chalk tray, and writes his number on the board. He replaces the chalk and returns to his seat. The second person goes to the board and writes his number under the first one. This is repeated until the last person is back in his seat. The row who completes the order first is the winner. A space on the board can be marked off for each team.

VARIATION: Each player may be required to write a word on the board. The object is for a row to complete a sentence. The row with the most complete and logical sentence at the end wins.

LAST MAN OUT

EQUIPMENT: None.

FORMATION: Everyone sitting in seats, seats arranged in rows.

DESCRIPTION: One player is chosen to be the fleer, one player the chaser. Walking is the only skill permitted. The chaser tries to tag the fleer. To be safe the fleer may stop in front of any row and say "Last man out." The last player in that row becomes the fleer. Everyone moves back a seat and the old fleer sits in the first seat. If the chaser tags the fleer, the two reverse responsibilities.

MESSAGE CENTER

EQUIPMENT: Blackboard, and a piece of chalk for each team.

FORMATION: Everyone is seated in rows.

DESCRIPTION: The leader puts a series of letters (the same number as there are people in each row) on the blackboard in front of each row. Upon signal the first person goes to the blackboard and writes a word utilizing the first letter in his space. After he returns to his seat, the second person writes a word using the second letter. The object is for each row to make a message out of their five or six letters. A special topic may be chosen before the class starts. The first row with a good message wins. Each team should finish its message, since the first one finished may not be judged appropriate to the topic or it may not be grammatically correct.

MOUSE (Figure 11-20)

EQUIPMENT: Blackboard; piece of chalk for each team.

FORMATION: Seats are arranged in rows; each sits in his seat.

DESCRIPTION: Before the game starts, a picture of a mouse is drawn on the blackboard. The number of parts it has is dependent upon how many people there are in a row. Numbers are given to each part. This is a relay, and the object is to see which row can complete a picture of a mouse first. Upon signal the first person in each row goes to the blackboard and draws the head, places the chalk in the tray, and sits down. He taps the person behind him who goes up and draws the left ear, and so forth. The type of locomotion must be designated. The winner is the row with the first complete mouse drawn.

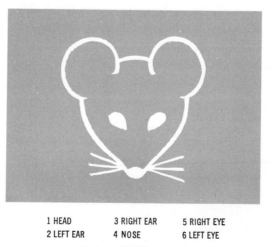

| 1 HEAD | 3 RIGHT EAR | 5 RIGHT EYE |
| 2 LEFT EAR | 4 NOSE | 6 LEFT EYE |

Figure 11-20. Mouse.

OBJECT RACE

EQUIPMENT: Eraser, beanbag (or some soft object of similar size) for each row.

FORMATION: Seats are arranged in rows. Each person is seated in his seat.

DESCRIPTION: The eraser or object is passed back over the head of the first person to the next person in order. The last person in the row gets out of his seat on the right side and runs to the head of the row. Everyone else gets out of the seats on the left side and moves back one seat. When the last person has reached the front of the row and is seated he starts the object back again. Some words may be called as a signal for everyone to change seats. The first team to have completed a full exchange of seats is the winner. The style of locomotion should be stated before the game begins.

SEAT TAG

EQUIPMENT: None.

FORMATION: Everyone is sitting in his seat. One child is chosen IT, and another the runner.

DESCRIPTION: The IT chases the runner. In order to avoid being caught or tagged, the runner may sit with someone. The latter must then get up and becomes IT and chases the old IT who is now the runner. The style of locomotion must be declared before the game begins.

Mental and guessing games

Primary

BIRD, BEAST, OR FISH

EQUIPMENT: None.

FORMATION: Children seated, class divided into two teams. One person is the leader.

DESCRIPTION: The leader points to a child and says either "bird," "beast," or "fish." Immediately he starts counting aloud to 10. The person to whom he points must say the name of a bird, beast, or fish (whichever was called). For example, if "bird" were said, the child could answer, "Sparrow." If the child cannot give a satisfactory answer before IT counts to 10, the opposite team receives a point. A member of the opposite team is selected to give the answer.

VARIATION: Any types of categories may be substituted for bird, beast, or fish.

BUTTON, BUTTON

EQUIPMENT: Large button.

FORMATION: Everyone standing in a single circle, holding hands out in front. IT is chosen, and he stands in the center.

DESCRIPTION: With his eyes closed, IT counts to 10. While he is counting, the button is passed from child to child around the circle. When IT has finished counting to ten, he opens his eyes and says "Button, button, who has my button?" Children cease passing button and keep hands clenched so IT has to guess who has it. IT has three guesses. If he guesses correctly, he remains in the center. If he fails, he changes places with the person who has the button, and the game is repeated.

DOG AND BONE

EQUIPMENT: Eraser or plastic bone, small chair.

FORMATION: Everyone is in seats or sitting in a circle on the floor. Chair is in center.

DESCRIPTION: One child is chosen to be the Dog. He sits on the chair. The bone is placed under the chair. The Dog must close his eyes and cover his face. A child is chosen to tiptoe into the center of the circle and steal the bone without letting the Dog hear him. If the Dog does hear him, he makes a barking sound and points to where the child is. The bone-stealer returns to his seat and another child is chosen to steal the bone. If the bone is stolen, the successful child changes places with the Dog, and the game resumes.

HUCKLE BUCKLE BEANSTALK

EQUIPMENT: Beanbag.

FORMATION: Players are seated with heads down and eyes closed. One child is chosen as IT.

DESCRIPTION: IT hides the beanbag somewhere in the room. The beanbag must be visible when one is near it. After hiding the beanbag, IT claps his hands, and everyone gets out of his seat and looks for the beanbag. As soon as one sees the bag, he quietly returns to his seat. When nearly everyone has seen it, the game stops, and the first one who was seated retrieves the beanbag and is the new IT.

I SAW

EQUIPMENT: None.

FORMATION: Children sitting in seats or in a circle.

DESCRIPTION: One child chosen to start the game stands in center of circle or in front of room. He says "On my way to school this morning I saw ____." He then portrays with body actions what he saw. The class has three guesses to say what he saw. The child guessing correctly becomes the next person to describe what he saw. If no one guesses and the portrayal was reasonably correct, he may do another one. If the portrayal was not true to form, he may be asked to choose someone to take his place.

POOR PUSSY

EQUIPMENT: None.

FORMATION: Everyone seated in seats or in a circle. One child chosen to be Pussy.

DESCRIPTION: The Pussy walks around and stops in front of a child. He strokes a child's face and says "Poor pussy" three times. In between each he makes funny faces. If the child laughs or smiles before this is done three times he can not become the Pussy. If he can stay sober-faced the three times, he becomes the Pussy.

TELEGRAMS

EQUIPMENT: None.

FORMATION: All seats are arranged in equal rows. Everyone is in his seat.

DESCRIPTION: Everyone places hands on desk and closes eyes. At a signal, the last player in each row taps the shoulder of the child in front of him. This child in turn taps the shoulder of the child in front of him. When the first person in the row is tapped, he stands up and the first one up indicates the winning team.

WHO HAS GONE FROM THE ROOM

EQUIPMENT: None.

FORMATION: All children are sitting in their seats. One is chosen as IT.

DESCRIPTION: IT hides his eyes. The leader indicates which child should leave the room. After he has left, IT opens his eyes and guesses who has gone. If he names the child correctly, that child is IT the next time. If he fails to name the child, he closes his eyes, the child returns to the room. IT opens his eyes and guesses who has returned to the room. If he fails to do so, he is IT again.

Intermediate

BUZZ

EQUIPMENT: None.

FORMATION: Children are seated.

DESCRIPTION: A number is selected to be the Buzz number. The object of the game is for everyone in turn to count consecutively to 100. Each time the number designated to be the Buzz number comes up, the word Buzz must be substituted. The child who fails to do this correctly is given a letter of Buzz. If he fails the first time he gets a B, the second time a U, etc. The idea is to have as few letters as possible. *Example:* If the number 5 is chosen, the counting goes: 1, 2, 3, 4, Buzz, 6 . . . 13, 14, Buzz, 16. Fifty-five would be Buzz, Buzz. When 100 is reached, counting may start over again.

CITIES

EQUIPMENT: None.

FORMATION: Players are sitting.

DESCRIPTION: The first child names a city. The next child must give the name of a city which starts with the last letter of the first city, i.e., Detroit, Toledo, Owosso, etc. No name of a city may be repeated. If no name is given within 10 seconds, that player is eliminated. The object is to stay in the game as long as possible.

VARIATION: The category may be changed to that of states, rivers, countries, or any other topic the class is studying.

CONCENTRATION

EQUIPMENT: None.

FORMATION: Children are sitting in a circle. IT is chosen to be number 1. IT sits at designated spot in circle, and rest of group is numbered off in order around the circle.

DESCRIPTION: An order and rhythm of clapping is established. Clap hands, slap thighs, and say number. IT begins by saying his number first and adding any other number. This must be done in perfect rhythm, and in the following manner: Clap thighs, slap hands, "One—four." The child numbered four must respond in rhythm with: Slap thighs, clap hands, "Four—six" (or any other number). If child does not respond in perfect rhythm or say his number first, he must go to the end of the line. Everyone who came after that number is renumbered. The object is to work up to the head of the line.

FIND THE LEADER

EQUIPMENT: None.

FORMATION: All are in circle. One player is chosen to leave the room.

DESCRIPTION: One person is chosen to make different gestures and be the leader. As this child makes various gestures, everyone else imitates him. The person who has left the room returns and tries to guess who is the leader. He gets three guesses. If he is successful, he chooses someone to take his place. If he is not, the person who was the leader gets to choose someone to go out of the room, and a new leader is chosen.

HUMAN TIT-TAT-TOE (Figure 11-21)

EQUIPMENT: Nine x's are marked on the floor about a foot apart in a square formation.

FORMATION: Nine players are assigned to a team. Two teams are waiting to the right of the block of x's.

Figure 11-21. Human Tit-Tat-Toe.

DESCRIPTION: A member from each team steps on an x, alternating turns. The first team which has three players in a row wins the game. Row may be diagonal, across, or up and down.

KIM'S GAME

EQUIPMENT: Table in front of room; fifteen or twenty objects placed on the table with a cover over them; paper and pencils on each desk.

FORMATION: Everyone gathers around the table.

DESCRIPTION: Cover is taken from the table, and everyone may look at the objects. At the end of two minutes the cover is placed on the table. Each child goes to his seat and writes down the name of as many objects as he can remember. The person who has the most objects listed correctly wins the game.

RADIO STATIONS

EQUIPMENT: None.

FORMATION: Teams of six; each group is standing or sitting together in a corner of the room.

DESCRIPTION: Each group chooses to send a message of several simple combinations of claps and practices for a few minutes. Each group in turn sends its message, and the others try to catch it and repeat the message.

SEVEN UP

EQUIPMENT: None.

FORMATION: Everyone is sitting in his own seat, heads down on desk, eyes closed. Seven people are chosen from the group.

DESCRIPTION: The chosen seven walk around the room, and each touches a person. When a person is touched he raises his hand. The seven then go to the front of the room and the leader says "Seven up." Each of those touched tries to guess who touched him. If one is successful in guessing, he gets to be one of the seven for the next game.

SUBJECT BASEBALL

EQUIPMENT: None.

FORMATION: Each player is given a position on a baseball team.

DESCRIPTION: Any subject may be chosen, such as arithmetic. The leader asks a question, and the first player on the first team at bat tries to answer it. If he is correct he gets a hit and goes to first base. (The game may be diagramed on the blackboard.) If he misses, he is out. If the second player answers his question correctly, the person on first moves to second. The object is to be moved around the bases by having people answer questions correctly. When a runner crosses home, a run is scored. After three outs the batting teams change, and the other team has a chance to bat (or answer questions).

Skill games

BALLOON VOLLEY

EQUIPMENT: Balloon or very light-weight ball.

FORMATION: A rope is strung across the room; children are standing.

PROCEDURE: This is a modification of volleyball. Children try to keep balloon going back and forth across the net. The same skills, rules, and scoring should be used as those that would be used in the regular game at this stage (p. 479).

VARIATIONS:
1. Rope might be strung between two chairs and players could sit on the floor.
2. Players may sit in seats and try to hit across a stretched rope. Extra balloons would have to be readily available.
3. No net is needed. Class may be divided into two teams with every other row being members of a different team. The object is for the team to get the balloon over to the designated side of the room which are their respective goals. Players may hit the balloon only with their fingers.

BOWLING

EQUIPMENT: Plastic bowling sets (or empty plastic bottles) and playground balls.

FORMATION: Most rooms will afford some floor space which can be used for bowling games. If the desks are arranged in rows, the aisle space would suffice.

PROCEDURE: The same procedure can be utilized as is suggested for bowling (p. 385).

FLOOR TABLE TENNIS

EQUIPMENT: Table tennis paddles, balls.

FORMATION: If no table tennis table is available, a court of similar size may be marked off on the floor. Players can stand, kneel, or sit depending on the amount of space available and consequent size of the court.

PROCEDURE: The same rules and scoring should be followed as in regular table tennis (p. 394). Some modifications may have to be made due to the change in size of equipment, etc.

FOUR SQUARE

EQUIPMENT: Small tennis or "pinkie" ball.

FORMATION: Court is laid out on floor as for Four Square (p. 387), except with modification of size to fit space. Smaller ball should require less space.

PROCEDURE: The same procedure is used as in Four Square.

VARIATION: Court may be laid out on a table, and table tennis ball used.

PASSING RELAYS

EQUIPMENT: Fleece balls, yarn balls, plastic balls, rolled-up socks, paper balls, beanbags.

FORMATION: Any type of formation that will use the space to its best advantage. Since objects may be thrown across desks, places where many small objects are kept must be avoided. A line of direction for throwing balls must be established. The best background for the balls would be the blackboard. Various relay drills could be done in this manner.

PROCEDURE: Same procedure is used as for any passing practice. Proper throwing and catching techniques should be stressed.

QUOITS OR HORSESHOES

EQUIPMENT: Stakes, made from block of wood with piece of broomstick or dowel nailed to one side; deck tennis rings, rubber horseshoes, or rings made of rope.

PROCEDURE: Distance between stakes will depend on room available. Game may proceed as suggested on p. 390. Scoring should be the same, but game score should be decreased to 25.

Target games

RING TOSS

EQUIPMENT: Boards that have holes in them for object to be thrown through, boards with hooks extending so rings may hook on to them, or chair turned over so that legs will serve as hooks; rings made out of rope, deck tennis rings, or mason jar rings.

PROCEDURE: Children can take turns throwing a certain number of rings and keep score the number of times the target is secured.

WASTEBASKET BALL

EQUIPMENT: Wastebasket for a target; playground balls, fleece balls, rolled socks. Basket may be placed on a table or on the floor.

PROCEDURE: Establish a starting line. Each child takes a certain number of turns to throw and attempt to put the object into basket. Score is kept of the times the object goes in basket, and the person with the best score at the end of a certain number of rounds wins.

INDIVIDUAL AND DUAL GAMES

Individual and dual games are those which may be played by one, two, three, or four people. They are sometimes referred to as recreational games since they need so few participants, and once learned they can be played without direct supervision. They are valuable in establishing social experiences and relationships as well as in creating opportunities for skill development. Each player is active all of the time. These games afford good co-recreation activities for older boys and girls.

BOWLING

EQUIPMENT: Plastic bowling set, regular bowling pins, or Indian clubs. One 8-inch ball. Pins should be set up in triangular fashion with five pins in the back row, three in the next, two in next, and one in the front. A space just as long as the pin should be left between the pins. It is best to mark the floor where the pins will sit, or to mark an oilcloth or paper and set pins on it. Mark a starting line 25 feet from the head pin.

PLAYERS: Two to five players.

PROCEDURE: Each person rolls the ball in turn at the pins. If he hits all of them down on the first try he marks his score 10. If not, he gets a second ball to try to hit the remaining pins. The total number of pins knocked down on the two attempts is then recorded. The winner is the player who has the highest total after ten turns. One person is appointed pinsetter, but after the first person has bowled he becomes the pinsetter, and the responsibility continues to be rotated. Children should be encouraged to place the ball on floor as it is released instead of throwing or dropping it down hard. A cardboard may be placed behind pins so they do not fly so far.

VARIATION: Any number of trials may be allowed depending on the skill level.

CROQUET (Figure 11-22)

EQUIPMENT: Croquet set; wickets set out as in diagram.

PROCEDURE: Players decide on playing order. Object of the game is for a player to hit his ball through each wicket around the course and be the first to reach the home goal or stake. Players alternate in turns. Each gets one hit in turn, and an additional hit each time his ball goes through a wicket. If he can hit his opponent's ball, he gets two bonus shots. One of these may be used to hit his opponent's ball out of the way. This is done by the hitter placing both balls side by side and then putting a foot on his ball so that it may remain in place as the mallet hits it; the resulting force drives the other ball away.

VARIATIONS: The first player returning his ball to the home goal or stake may be termed "poison" after he hits the stake. Following his regular turn he may then try to hit other player's balls and thus eliminate them from the game. If four or six are playing together, teams may

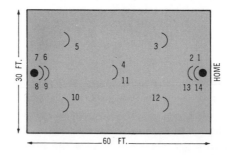

Figure 11-22. Croquet.

be formed in which all play strategically in order to get one member of the team home and "poison."

DECK TENNIS

EQUIPMENT: One deck tennis ring. Court 25 feet by 50 feet. Net 5 feet.

PLAYERS: Game may be played as singles (two players) or as doubles, (four players).

PROCEDURE: The object of the game is for one player or team to keep the ring going back and forth across the net and to try to throw the ring so the opponent will miss it. The game is started with a service by one player from behind his base line (from the right side of the court). He must deliver the ball with a forehand delivery in an upward fashion to the diagonally opposite half of the court. If the server or his teammate makes a point, the server continues to serve from the left side of the court. Server continues to alternate serving from right to left courts until his side makes an error or a foul. In doubles his partner then has a term of service, and in singles the serve goes to his opponent.

SCORING: The serving side scores a point whenever the receiving side makes an error or a foul. No point is scored if the serving side errors or fouls, the serve is won by the opponents. A game is won by the first team to win 15 points. If the score is tied at 14, one team must win two successive points to win. A time limit may be set, and the team with the most points at the end of it is the winner.

FOULS:
1. Catching the ring with two hands.
2. Changing ring from the catching hand in order to throw with the other.
3. Making a downward stroke with the ring.
4. Causing the ring to land outside the boundary lines.
5. Stepping over the line when serving.

FOUR SQUARE (Figure 11-23)

EQUIPMENT: Volleyball or 8½-inch playground ball. Court as diagramed.

PLAYERS: Four. Additional players may rotate into game and wait at points marked X on the diagram.

PROCEDURE: The object of the game is to stay in square A (or move there and remain as long as possible). The ball is put into play by the player in square A who drops the ball, then hits it underhand from

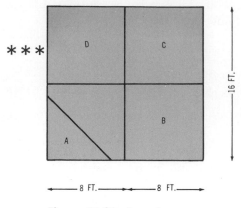

Figure 11-23. Four Square.

the bounce into one of the other courts. He must stand behind the diagonal service line. The game continues, each player hits the ball off the first bounce as it comes into his court. It may be redirected to any of the courts. The object, though, is to get the player in A to move down. If a player errors or fouls, play ceases and that player moves down to square D or to the end of the waiting line. All other players move up one square, or the first person in the waiting line moves into square D. The ball is again served by the player in square A.

FOULS:
1. Failing to return the ball to another square. Balls hitting lines are considered fouls.
2. Stepping on or over the service line when serving or the inner court lines during the game.
3. Striking ball with fist or letting ball hit anything but hands.
4. Hitting ball overhand or carrying ball in the volley.

HANDBALL (Figure 11-24)

EQUIPMENT: One tennis ball, small rubber ball, or handball.

PLAYERS: Singles, two players; doubles, four players; or three may play, each against the other.

PROCEDURE: The object of the game is for one player to hit the ball against the wall and have it rebound into the court area in order to cause the opponents to error or foul in trying to return it to the wall. The server, while standing in the front of the service line, drops the ball and hits it with the palm of his hand so that it hits the wall and rebounds into the court area behind the service line.

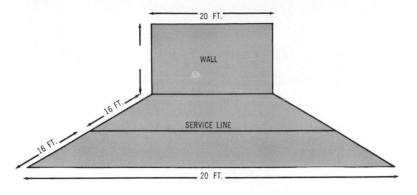

Figure 11-24. Handball.

The receiver then tries to hit the ball so it will hit the wall and rebound back anywhere in the court. The receiver may hit the ball on the fly or off the first bounce. Play continues with server and opponent alternating hits until an error or foul is made. The server receives a point if the receiving side is at fault. If the server is at fault it is called a "handout" and the serve goes to the opponent. When three are playing the server must play every other ball. When serving he alternates his serve with the opponents. After a handout the players rotate on the court counter-clockwise for the serve. In doubles the ball must be hit alternately by a member from each team. The server has two trials to make a good serve.

SCORING: The serving team scores a point when a foul or error is committed. The receiving team wins the serve when a handout is made. Twenty-one points constitute a game.

FOULS:
1. The server must have the service rebound beyond the service line or it is short. He receives a second trial if the serve is short. The ball must rebound within the lines of the court. A ball landing on a line is considered good.
2. The ball must be hit alternately by members of each team in doubles.
3. The ball may be hit with one hand only and may not touch any other part of the body.
4. The ball may be hit in the air or after the first bounce. The receiver may not stand in front of the service line when waiting for a serve.
5. If a player intentionally interferes with an opponent, a foul is called.
6. If the interference is unavoidable, the point is replayed.

TEACHING HINTS: This game may be considered a lead-up game for tennis. If it is treated as such, tennis terms and scoring may be stressed from the start.

HOPSCOTCH (Figure 11-25)

EQUIPMENT: Stone, checker, button, or penny for each player.

PROCEDURE: There are a great many forms of this game. The general
    rules are presented here along with a few variations. Just a few of the
    many styles of courts are diagramed. Players determine the playing
    order. In turn each player tosses his stone into the space numbered
    one. He then hops into the first space, picks up the stone, and hops
    back to the starting space. He repeats this going as far as he can
    until an error is made. Neither the stone nor a foot may touch a
    line. If a player loses his balance and touches any part of his body to
    the ground, an error is declared, and the turn is over. The winner is
    the one who goes through the whole sequence with the fewest misses.

VARIATIONS:
1. Some games demand that the player kick the stone back to the starting
   place rather than carry it back.
2. Certain squares may be designated where both feet may be placed.

HORSESHOES

EQUIPMENT: For outside use where there is plenty of space, regulation
    metal horseshoes may be used. For beginners where the space sur-
    rounding the pits may be small in area, hard rubber shoes should
    be used. Indoor sets of rubber stakes and shoes may be secured; four
    shoes and two stakes are required for each game. Stakes set 30 feet
    apart.

PLAYERS: Two or four.

PROCEDURE: In singles, both players alternate turns, each throwing both
    shoes at a turn. In doubles, one player from each team is at each end.
    Play starts at one end with players from opposite teams alternating
    turns. The object is to get the shoe over the stake or as near to the
    stake as possible while standing at the stake 30 feet away.

SCORING:
1. 1 point—Horseshoe nearest stake.
2. 2 points—Both shoes of one player nearer to the stake than either of his
   opponent's shoes.
3. 3 points—Ringer (the horseshoe must encircle the stake far enough
   to permit a stick or ruler to touch both ends of the shoes and still
   clear the stake).
4. Game score for singles is 21 points; for doubles, 50 points.

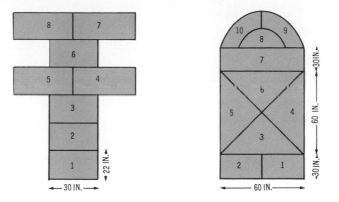

Figure 11-25. Hopscotch.

FOULS:

1. When throwing, the instep of the rear foot must not be farther forward than the stake. If it is, the position of the thrown shoe is disregarded for scoring.
2. Shoes that are hit and displaced by an opponent's shoe are scored where they finally rest. Displaced ringers are not counted as ringers.

JACKS

EQUIPMENT: A set of jacks, one small rubber ball, and a smooth surface.

PLAYERS: Two or more.

PROCEDURE: A player throws the jacks out on the playing area. He then tosses the ball into the air, and with the same hand, he reaches out, picks up one jack, and catches the ball after it has bounced once. The jack is put in the other hand. Each jack is picked up in this fashion. After picking them up successfully, two at a time are picked up, then three, and so on until all have been picked up at one time. When a player makes an error or foul he relinquishes his turn to the next player. Upon starting again, he must start at the beginning of the set where he made the error.

FOULS:

1. Touching a jack other than the one which is supposed to be picked up.
2. Dropping the jacks or ball.
3. Failing to catch ball on first bounce.
4. Switching hands to catch the ball.
5. Failing to pick up the correct number of jacks.

VARIATIONS: There are a great number of variations at local schools or playgrounds. Ball may be caught before it bounces once. Jacks must be transferred to other hand before ball is caught. Toss ball up, throw jacks down, catch ball in right hand. Throw ball up, pick up all jacks, catch ball in same hand.

MARBLES

EQUIPMENT: One marble and one shooter for each player. Ring 6 feet in diameter drawn on smooth but not too hard playing surface.

PLAYERS: Two to six.

PROCEDURE: Each player puts one or two marbles in the center of the circle. The playing order is established by all "lagging" or throwing their shooter toward a line. The players shoot in order of closest to the line first. The first player shoots his shooter or "taw" from the edge of the circle and tries to knock a marble out of the ring. If he is successful he keeps that marble and shoots again. He continues as long as he knocks marbles out of the ring and his taw stays in the ring, or until he commits a foul. The players play in order. Whoever has the most marbles at the end of the game or playing time wins. Marbles are given back to the owners of them.

FOULS:
1. Failure to have the knuckles in contact with the playing surface when the taw is shot.
2. Taw leaves ring.

SHUFFLEBOARD (Figure 11-26)

EQUIPMENT: Eight discs, two cues for singles, four for doubles. Court as diagramed.

PLAYERS: Two for singles, four for doubles. If two, each stand at the same end of the court and shoot together. If four, one from each team stands at opposite ends.

PROCEDURE: The object of the game is to push one's discs into the scor-

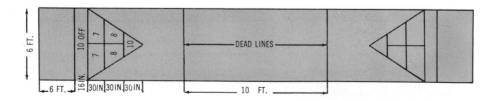

Figure 11-26. Shuffleboard.

ing areas and at the same time try to knock out opponent's discs. Once a disc is in scoring position it is wise to place another disc in front of it for protection. Discs are shot from within the 10-off area. Players shoot discs alternately until all are shot. Then they walk to the other end and count the score. Any disc touching a line is not counted. In singles, the two players then shoot the discs back to the other end. In doubles, it is not necessary for players to go to the other end to count, since partners may do this. If a disc is hit into the 10-off zone, 10 points is deducted from the score. Game score of 50, 75, or 100 should be declared before the game starts.

TEACHING HINTS: Players should be taught to place cue directly against discs and then push forward gently. There is a tendency for beginners to bring the cue back and hit the disc, thereby hindering control and accuracy.

SIDEWALK TENNIS (Figure 11-27)

EQUIPMENT: One tennis ball or other small rubber ball.

PLAYERS: Singles, two people; doubles, four people.

PROCEDURE: The object of the game is to bat the ball back and forth across the net line with the palm of the hand until someone makes an error or a foul and a score is made. Players stand where S is indicated in the diagram. Play is started by one of the players who serves the ball with the flat of the hand across the net line into the area in front of the base line. After the ball has bounced, his opponent returns the ball over the net line. On the return the ball may be hit while in the air or on the first bounce.

SCORING: A point is scored only by the server. When an error is made or a foul is committed, either a point is given the scorer or the receiver wins the serve. In doubles each side has two turns of service. A server continues to serve until he makes an error or foul. Game is 15 points. If the score is tied at 14-all, one person must make two consecutive points to win.

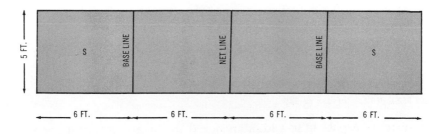

Figure 11-27. Sidewalk Tennis.

FOULS:

1. Hitting the ball with any part of hand or body but the palm.
2. Stepping over base line to serve.
3. Any ball which lands outside of the lines.

VARIATION: The game lines may be squares of a sidewalk. Lines may be painted or marked in chalk on blacktop or gym floor or drawn in sand. A larger ball may be utilized; however, in this case the court should be larger.

TABLE TENNIS

EQUIPMENT: Table tennis table, a paddle for each player, a table tennis ball.

PLAYERS: Singles, two people; doubles, four people.

PROCEDURES: In singles, play starts with a serve and continues with the opponents alternately playing ball until one player misses the ball, errors, or fouls. In doubles, the serve begins from the server's right hand court and bounces into the opponent's right-hand court. After the serve, partners alternate playing the ball until there is an error or foul committed. On the serve the ball must bounce on the server's side of the net before crossing the net.

SCORING: A point is awarded to the opponents of the player who errors or fouls. A player serves until 5 points are made. In doubles, the serve then goes to his partner or to the opponents if both partners have served. Twenty-one points constitute a game. If the score becomes 20-all, one team must then make 2 consecutive points to win.

FOULS:

1. Illegal serve—when ball does not bounce on server's side first; when a ball does not go diagonally across to opponent's service court.
2. A ball which is hit before it bounces.
3. Touching hand to table while ball is in play.
4. A ball that is hit off table or hits on receiver's side during rally.

VARIATION: A progressive game with many players may be played. Each player hits the ball then lays paddle on table and the next person must pick it up and play the next ball. Player drops out if he makes an error or foul. Players must move around table and play on both sides.

TETHER BALL (Figure 11-28)

EQUIPMENT: A pole 10 feet high anchored in the ground firmly or set in movable but stable base. A tether ball hanging from a rope attached

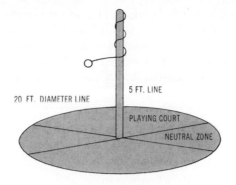

Figure 11-28. Tether Ball.

to the top of the pole and reaching down 3 feet from the ground. Mark off 20-foot circle as shown in diagram.

PLAYERS: Singles, two players; doubles, four players.

PROCEDURES: Players stand on opposite sides of pole. One player starts the game by hitting the ball in either direction all the way around the pole. The object is for either player to get the rope wound around the pole above the 5 feet mark until the ball touches the pole. The first player who succeeds in this wins the game and the winner then starts another game. If a foul is committed, the game is awarded to the opposite player. In doubles, the ball may be hit alternately by each team player or by whoever can hit it. Player who wins four games first wins match.

FOULS:
1. Hitting the ball with any part of the body except hands.
2. Stepping over the neutral zone or court lines.
3. Catching or holding the ball during play.
4. Touching the rope or pole during play.

VARIATION: A tennis ball and paddles may be substituted for the larger ball and the hands.

VOLLEY TENNIS

EQUIPMENT: One volleyball, paddle tennis court (p. 490), 3-foot net.

PLAYERS: Singles, two players; doubles, four players.

PROCEDURE: The game is started with a serve from the right-hand base line to the serving court diagonally opposite. The ball must be dropped and hit from the bounce. The fist or open palm may be used. The ball is returned anywhere in the court by the receiver. The ball may be hit while in the air or on the first bounce only after the serve is returned off the first bounce. The server continues to serve from alternate courts until he makes an error or a foul. Then the serve goes to the opponent. When the opponent errors or makes a foul the server scores a point. The first side to make 15 points wins the game. If the score is tied at 14-all, one side must make two consecutive points.

FOULS:
1. Failure to hit ball within the service court.
2. Failure to hit ball within the boundary lines.
3. Catching or carrying the ball in hand.
4. Stepping over base line when serving.
5. Allowing ball to hit any part of body but hands.
6. Touching the net or reaching over it to hit a ball.

VARIATIONS:
1. With four players the serving side has two terms of service.
2. Ball is hit by whoever is in the best position to hit.
3. The game may be played with six players; however, the court should be enlarged in this situation.

SUGGESTED REFERENCES
FOR FURTHER STUDY

American Association for Health, Physical Education and Recreation, *How We Do It Game Book* (Washington, D.C., 1959).
———, *Classroom Activities* (Washington, D.C., 1957).
Blake, O. William, and Anne Volp, *Lead-Up Games to Team Sports* (Englewood Cliffs, N.J., Prentice-Hall, 1964).
Hunt, Sarah E., and Ethel Cain, *Games the World Around* (New York, Ronald, 1950).
Latchaw, Marjorie, *A Pocket Guide of Games and Rhythms for the Elementary School* (Englewood Cliffs, N.J., Prentice-Hall, 1958).
Nagel, Charles, *Play Activities for Elementary Grades* (St. Louis, Mosby, 1964).
Richardson, Hazel A., *Games for the Elementary School Grades* (Minneapolis, Burgess, 1951).
Smith, Brian Sutton, and Paul Gump, "Games and Status Experience," *Recreation* (April, 1955), p. 173.

Chapter XII

SKILLS AND LEAD-UP GAMES FOR TEAM SPORTS

General teaching considerations

Basketball activities

Basketball skills

Football activities

Football skills

Soccer activities

Soccer skills

Softball activities

Softball skills

Volleyball activities

Volleyball skills

As children reach the third grade and have a good background of understanding and proficiency in the fundamental skills of movement, they are psychologically and physically ready to learn specific sport skill patterns. Their yearly physical education experiences should provide opportunities to combine skill patterns into specific skills demanding the use of a variety of implements and objects.

Since children become acquainted with traditional American sports at an early age, they desire to learn how to play all types of sports and games. Therefore, the school program should include sports and games appropriate to the season and suitable to the maturation level of the children involved.

This chapter presents the teacher with a comprehensive study of the skills, concepts, rules, and basic strategies of games which enable children to play the traditional American team sports. The emphasis in this chapter is on a progressive acquisition of these items. A progression chart for each sport precedes the content to be learned. It indicates the order in which skills, rules, knowledges, and focal lead-up games for the grade level should be introduced. These are accumulative, and by the seventh or eighth grade the official sport may be learned. There are usually some modifications of official rules, playing time, and size of playing areas even at the high school level.

GENERAL TEACHING CONSIDERATIONS

There are many general considerations common to the teaching of the team and individual sports. The latter are presented in the next chapter. The reader is referred to the discussion of the placement of skill drills, skill games, and lead-up games in the organization of units and lessons in Chapter V; many suggestions are given for implementing the teaching of the content presented in this chapter.

Teaching of skills

1. Most of the sport skills are similar to one another and, of course, are based on basic skill patterns. The teacher should relate characteristics of skills already known to those of the new ones.
2. Skills can be improved only through practice. Skill practice is essential in some form—whether it be drills, skill games, or individual practice.
3. Skills should not be perfected before being used in a game, but some prior practice under game conditions should be provided. Game play will indicate practice needs and may motivate additional practice.
4. The cross-reference charts of drills and skill games are designed to improve specific skills. The pages on which the drills and games are described may be found in the Index. Many of the drill formations and active low-organized games may be adapted in order to practice most skills. A chart for each sport precedes descriptions of drills and games for the sports which are not described elsewhere in the book.
5. The skills are analyzed for right-handed players.

Equipment and space

1. For the most part, junior-size equipment should be used in grades three through six.
2. Playing areas may be modified to fit the abilities of the group or the space which is available.
3. Equipment should be improvised if what is called for in the game directions is not available.

Seasonal activities

1. Units of skills and games should coincide with the traditional seasonal sports. The field games of soccer and football are played in the fall,

basketball and volleyball are usually played in the winter, softball in the summer and spring.

2. Older children should be taught (not just assigned) to officiate. This will make them aware of the rules and prevent arguing over rules when play is held without teacher supervision.
3. The rules that generally govern the official sports for girls and women are those of the Division for Girls' and Women's Sports of the American Association of Health, Physical Education and Recreation. Annual or semi-annual rule books are published and are available from The Association, 1201 Sixteenth St., N.W., Washington, D.C., 20036. Rules for boys are set by the National Federation of State High School Athletic Associations and are available from The Association, 7 South Dearborn Street, Chicago, Illinois, 60603.
4. The rules for the lead-up games are modifications of these rules, and if learned accumulatively they should lead to a knowledge of the official rules.

Class participation

1. Each child should have an opportunity to participate in game play. Suggested team sizes should be retained as much as possible.
2. Children who must wait for turns should be practicing skills at assigned areas. Specific arrangements must be made for this.
3. It is usually more efficient to divide the playing space and conduct two games instead of one if large numbers must be accommodated.

Evaluation of skills

1. Skill tests are suggested for each sport. Only skills which have been stressed should be tested.
2. Most skill tests also make good practice drills.
3. The reader is referred to the *Sports Skill Test Manual* of the American Association For Health, Physical Education and Recreation for more extensive tests, detailed instructions, and norms for boys and girls of ages ten through eighteen for each specific sport.

Terminology

1. Game terms are somewhat synonymous and should be used consistently.
2. Official terms should be used as soon as the rules and concepts are introduced. For example, the terms "violation" and "foul" should be used appropriately whenever an infringement of a rule occurs.
3. The terms "offensive" and "defensive" should be introduced early and used consistently. Offensive refers to the team which has the ball or is in the process of attempting to score. Defensive refers to the team which does not have the ball and is trying to prevent the other team from scoring.

Selecting games

1. Although games are suggested which have proven to be satisfactory for children at the grade level mentioned, each class is different and the teacher must select games carefully. The guidelines which were suggested for selecting low organized games should be utilized in the selection of skill and lead-up games.
2. The presentation of too many games within a short period of time is confusing to children and not very productive. Learning to play one game well is better than merely being familiar with three games.
3. Only one, or in some cases two, lead-up games should be played in one unit. This game is the sport for that grade. Sometimes the lead-up game which was played the year before is played at the start of a unit to refresh memories for rules and skills. Sometimes the focal game for the following year is presented at the very end of the unit as a preview.

Extraclass activities

1. Opportunities to play the games taught in class should be offered in the after-school program where children may learn to enjoy playing active sports in their leisure time. The class period is an instructional period for everyone. Those who wish it can receive additional help in the voluntary program.
2. The activities of the intramural program should be drawn from those taught in the class.
3. Students can learn to use strategies and teamwork cooperatively as they play in a more student-directed situation.

Boys and girls together

1. The activities presented here may be played by both girls and boys. However, the boys develop a greater interest in more vigorous play than girls do as they grow older. Both boys and girls will benefit from a combination of being separated at times and playing together at other times.
2. When boys and girls are separated within the class or by classes, official rules for some sports may be introduced earlier for boys than for girls, since boys frequently are playing these games outside of school.
3. The football games suggested for the upper grades are usually not taught to girls.

Rules

1. The rules of a game should always be enforced. If the game is persistently delayed for infractions and penalties, the rules are probably too difficult for the group or are not well understood.
2. Children should be taught to call their own infractions. This is not to say they should officiate and play at the same time. The game moves faster if a child holds up his hand when he touches the ball last before it goes out-of-bounds than if a teacher must call this. Calling one's

own infractions leads to good sportsmanship and a knowledge of the rules.

BASKETBALL ACTIVITIES

Basketball is one of the most popular American indoor winter sports. It is one of the few team sports which originated in the United States. The game was created by Dr. James Naismith in Springfield, Massachusetts, in 1892.

The original game varied from the game played today. Designed for men, the game consisted of teams of nine players who were allowed to throw, bat, and pass in the attempt to get the ball into peach baskets suspended from a gymnasium balcony. The object then, as now, was for one team to make more baskets than the other.

Today boys play in teams of five, and girls play in teams of six. Although the rules for each sex differ somewhat, the skills, knowledges, and strategies are similar.

Children seem to be fascinated by the challenge of putting a ball through a basket, and the values of the game are many. Most of the skills are not complex and are all based on the fundamental skill patterns of throwing, catching, running, and jumping. Thus vigorous exercise is provided for all the participants. Few players are needed to set up a game, and the equipment is inexpensive and can be improvised.

The skill games and lead-up games suggested for the intermediate grades call for repeated use of simple skills in a controlled situation. Those for the upper grades require faster action, a mingling of players from both teams, and have a greater emphasis on strategy.

Teaching considerations

1. Soccer balls, 8½-inch playground balls, and volleyballs may be used in the intermediate grades for ball-handling practice and lead-up games.
2. Junior-size basketballs should be used until seventh grade; at this time the official size ball may be used.
3. Baskets should be mounted or lowered to a height of 8 feet or less until the seventh grade.
4. Color identification bands are needed for all lead-up games.
5. Boys and girls can play the suggested lead-up games until the seventh grade when both should be playing the modified official game for their sex. If in an after-school program of the sixth grade they play separately, they should also play separately in class.

Table 12-1. Progression of Skills, Knowledges, Rules, and Lead-Up Games for Basketball

Skills	Knowledges and Rules	Lead-Up Game	Grade
Catching	Out-of-bounds ball		
Short passes	Line violations		
Chest	Holding ball more than five seconds		
One-hand underhand			
Bounce	Traveling		
Long passes	Forwards		
Shoulder or overhand	Guards	End Ball	3
Pivot	Scoring field goal		
Reverse Turn	Illegal dribble		
Dribble			
Shooting		Basket End Ball	3-4
Unguarded set shots		Six-Court Basketball	
Free throw	Scoring free throw		
Guarding technique	Use of terms		
Jump for tossed ball	Violation		
Passing on the move	Foul		
Catching on the move	Fouls		
Push shot	Snatching ball		
	Pushing		
	Tie ball	Toss-Up Basketball	4-5
Rebound	Defense		
Lay-up shot	Offense	Alley Basketball	6
Lead passes	Charging	Modified Boys Basketball	7-8
Cutting	Blocking	Modified Girls Basketball	
	Roving players (girls)		
		Sideline Basketball	7-8
		Half-Court Basketball	

BASKETBALL SKILLS

Catching

Catching is described and analyzed on page 255. The basic principles of catching should be emphasized when catching is first used in basketball games. As proficiency develops and as the need arises, the following points should be stressed.

1. Move to meet the ball to shorten the distance it has to travel and to cut off the opponent.
2. Draw the ball in toward the body and use this motion as the backswing for a subsequent pass.

Passing

There are a number of passes and each has specific uses. The distance the ball has to travel and the position in which the ball is caught often determines the choice of the pass. Accuracy is important in passing. All passes are based on the basic throwing patterns described on pages 257 through 262. The method by which they are adapted for different purposes is described here.

Chest pass

If the ball is caught at chest height, it can be passed quickly from this position with both hands. The ball is held by the fingers with the thumbs behind the ball. It is brought slightly downward then upward and pushed away from the chest and released with a snap of the wrists and fingers. Elbows should be bent and kept close to the body. The arms are pushed forward from the shoulders as the elbows straighten. More distance can be gained if the knees are bent, a step forward is taken, and the weight is transferred to the forward foot. This is a good pass to use for covering short distances.

COMMON FAULTS:

1. Holding the ball in palms of hands; prevents quick release of ball.
2. Holding elbows away from body; thus force is lost as movement is all in the forearm.
3. Using little or no wrist or finger snap.
4. Ball is released too high, causing a high looping pass.

TEACHING PHRASES:

1. Hold ball with fingers, thumb behind ball.
2. Elbows are in close to body.
3. Bring ball down, around, push upward, and then forward.

4. Snap wrist and fingers as ball is released.
5. Arms follow through toward target.

Bounce pass

This pass may utilize a one- or two-hand overhand, underhand, or chest pass. The new element in this pass is that a bounce is used with the pass so that the ball may bounce into the receiver's hands. The passer must judge the spot where the ball is to bounce according to the distance to be covered and the height at which the ball is to be received. For beginners, it is helpful to suggest that the ball should strike the floor three-fourths of the distance from the passer to the receiver if it is to be caught at waist height.

COMMON FAULT: Actually bouncing ball downward rather than throwing it forward.

KEY TEACHING PHRASES:
1. Bounce the ball at a point three-fourths of the way to the target.
2. Reach out as ball is thrown.

One-hand underhand pass

This pass utilizes the underhand throwing pattern (p. 259). Since the ball is large, the left hand is put on top of the ball to steady it when the ball is brought back by the right hand and arm; however, it is removed as the ball is brought forward. Only the right hand and arm follow through toward the target as the ball is released. This is a good pass for a short hand off-play on the move in advanced games where several opponents are in the same area.

Shoulder pass

This pass utilizes the overhand throwing pattern (p. 257). Since the ball is large, the left hand is placed on top of the ball in the backswing as a steadying agent; however, it is removed as the ball is brought forward. Although long passes are not particularly encouraged in basketball, passes of varying distances are often necessary. Scoring passes in End Ball are usually shoulder passes.

Dribbling

Dribbling is a legal way for a player to move with the ball. The ball is bounced repeatedly; impetus is given to the ball after each bounce and the ball is not allowed to rest or to be caught in one or both hands between bounces. The bounce is controlled with the fingers and wrist actions. It must be pushed so that it strikes the floor at an angle from which it will rebound up to the player the desired distance the player wishes to move. The bounces should be low. This skill can be learned prior to its use in actual basketball-type games.

COMMON FAULTS:
1. Using the flat of the hand to slap the ball rather than using fingertips to push it.
2. Bouncing ball too high so that it gets away from player as he moves.
3. Carrying ball because the hand is put underneath ball between dribbles.

KEY TEACHING PHRASES:
1. Push ball with fingertips.
2. Use wrist to control bounce.
3. Keep ball below the waist.
4. Push ball forward slightly.

Shooting

The basic patterns for basket shooting are those of throwing. According to the height of the basket, adjustments must be made in the angle of release of the ball and in the force required to send it to the basket. The various shots are described in order of difficulty.

Two-hand underhand shot
This is one of the easiest shots for children to make as the underhand motion allows for a big backswing, has the assistance of the strong leg muscles for additional force, and enables greater accuracy than any other shot. The ball is held high in front of the body; the fingers of both hands are under the ball and the thumbs are pointing upward so that the rim of the basket can be seen over the ball. The knees are bent and the ball is brought down between the legs, then upward as the knees straighten. The ball is released when the arms are fully extended in the direction of the basket. The follow-through should be high in the direction of the basket.

One-hand push shot
The ball is balanced by the fingers of the shooting hand and partially supported from underneath by the other hand (Figure 12-1). The ball is brought up to and in line with the shoulder of the shooting hand. In this position the elbows are bent. As the ball is released, the shooting arm is extended upward and toward the basket. The wrist flexes as the fingers guide the ball. The follow-through is high and toward the basket. The amount of knee bend and subsequent extension attending the shot is dependent upon the distance from the basket. A jump from the floor should be encouraged. The shot is difficult to guard since it starts high and can be released quickly. This shot can be executed after a two-foot jump into the air (jump shot) and thereby becomes even more difficult to guard.

Two-hand set or chest shot
This shot is like the chest pass, but the angle of release is different. The ball is brought upward and released when the arms are fully extended

Figure 12-1. One-Hand Push Shot.

toward a point above but in line with the basket. As the distance to the basket will be greater than that for which a chest pass is used, more flexion and extension of the body is required than in the pass.

Lay-up shot

The mechanics of the lay-up shot are similar to the one-hand push shot, but the ball is aimed at the backboard so it can rebound into the basket. Most commonly, a player approaches the basket from the side with a dribble or receives a pass from a teammate as he is running. In either event, as he jumps high in the air, the ball is brought to a position off the shoulder of the shooting hand. With the arm fully extended, the ball is pushed and guided by the fingers to a spot on the backboard. The jump is started with a take-off from the foot of the nonthrowing side. The step pattern is a *step* and a *hop* high into the air. Children should practice the shot without the jump first so they get an idea of where on the backboard the ball must hit in order to fall into the basket.

COMMON FAULTS:
1. Failure to bring ball up high off the bounce.
2. Stopping, then shooting.
3. Failure to extend arm fully and to release ball as high as possible.

KEY TEACHING PHRASES:

1. Eyes on basket.
2. Jump and reach.
3. Lay ball against backboard.
4. Guide ball with fingers.

GENERAL CONCEPTS ABOUT SHOOTING:

1. Obtain balance before attempting a shot.
2. Use fingers to hold ball and let ball roll from fingertips.
3. Bend knees and thrust body upward when more strength is needed for long shots.
4. Aim for farthest rim of basket or for the backboard.
5. Reach way up and out with arms so that the ball has an arch and will fall down into basket.
6. Do not shoot when directly under the basket. Pass out to a teammate, or pivot and dribble out.

Individual tactics

Body control

Since basketball is a very fast game with many quick stops, starts, jumps, and changes of direction, body control is essential for every player. Many of the skills and techniques are studied in the primary grades, but as children grow older and develop more control the same skills must be practiced in relation to the demands of the game being played.

Reverse turn and pivot. These skills are analyzed on pages 244, and suggestions are made for practice on page 245. These two basic skills are used in every game for changing direction. The pivot is an essential maneuver in both offensive and defensive play.

Stopping. Regaining balance without taking steps is vital to retaining possession of the ball and in gaining position in basketball. Stopping is analyzed on page 242. The skip stop, where one takes a hop and a step as he stops, puts one in the best position for subsequent action. Children can learn this easily from skipping and stopping, then running and taking one skip and stopping.

Dodging is a technique used to evade an opponent. It is analyzed on page 245.

Offensive tactics

Passing and catching on the move. Since basketball is a very fast game, and the fastest way to move the ball is to pass it, a player will frequently receive the ball and pass it while running. A moving player is much more difficult to guard than a stationary player. Any pass may be made while on the move, but the choice of pass is usually made on the basis of the position of the ball. If the ball is caught low as a result of a pass or a bounce, it would be inefficient to bring it up high to initiate a subsequent pass.

Children should be taught to catch a ball and make the absorption phase of bringing the ball in toward the body the backswing for the next pass. They should be taught to be alert and to throw to a player at chest level.

Lead passes. Passes should either be passed ahead of a player or to his nonguarded side rather than directly at him unless he is absolutely unguarded and the pass is fast and direct. Although a guard is not normally in front of a player, he can easily step in front of him by the time the ball arrives.

Cutting is an evasive technique which a player uses in order to get into position to receive a pass or to shoot. He watches his teammate who has the ball, and when this player is ready to pass, he breaks for an open spot toward the basket. The pass should reach the open spot at the same time as the person who has cut. Frequently, a player will make a short pass to a teammate and immediately cut toward the basket. Speed in moving and a quick change in direction are aids to misleading opponents as to the intended direction of the cut.

Defensive tactics

Guarding. For the simpler lead-up games where opponents do not play in the same area, guarding is a matter of jumping high and intercepting passes. Children should learn to keep their eyes on the ball. When two are in the same area, the emphasis changes. The usual rule in basketball is to stay between the person one is guarding and the basket. The guarding stance is taken with feet spread, arms outstretched to the side with one arm up and one down. A guard stays between the basket and on the inside-basket side of his opponent when he does not have the ball. The knees are slightly bent, weight slightly forward on the balls of the feet. He is ready to move in any direction. His eyes are on the ball and his opponent. If the opponent moves, the guard adjusts his position with a sliding step and tries to cut off the opponent's path to the basket.

When the opponent receives the ball, the guard moves within two or three feet of him and assumes the same ready stance and tries to deflect the ball from the opponent's hands or to deflect the pass. Frequently, beginners will want to face their opponent whether he is facing the basket or not. They also become overly concerned with chasing an opponent. They must understand that by staying between the basket and their opponent and by using a sliding step they have less distance to cover and will be in a better defensive position. Since approximately ninety percent of the goals which are made are shot from an 18-foot radius of the basket it is important for guards to cover this area rather than to be drawn out toward the center of the court.

Jump for toss-up. Many lead-up games are started with a toss-up between a player from each team. When two opposing players tie a ball or both cause a ball to go out-of-bounds at the same time, a toss-up occurs. The two opposing players stand with sides to each other facing their own basket. The ball is tossed up between the two players. Each should jump and reach to tap the ball with their fingers to a teammate. The jump should be made when the ball reaches its highest point. While waiting, eyes must be kept on the ball, weight low and on balls of feet, knees flexed, and elbows flexed. At the right moment, the arms are brought forward and upward, feet push off from the floor, and the whole body stretches and reaches to tap the ball. The jump and return to the floor must be vertical so players do not fall into each other, thereby causing a foul and possible injury.

Rebounding. This is a jumping and positioning tactic for getting possession of the ball after it has bounced off the backboard or rim of the basket. Usually the ball will rebound at the same angle it hit. It is an advanced skill to be able to time the jump and be in the right spot to get the ball. At an early stage, children should be taught to get into position for the rebound as soon as a ball is shot and to jump and reach for the ball.

General offensive and defensive team play

OFFENSIVE CONCEPTS:

1. All players must have a constant awareness of their teammates' positions.
2. All players should be alert to chances to cut into empty spaces.
3. Players should cut following their pass.
4. When the ball is secured under the other team's basket, the ball should be brought up court quickly. Passes in front of the basket should be avoided and the ball played toward the sideline.
5. Generally, the same player should always take the ball out under the basket in order to put the ball into play quickly.
6. Short passes are generally more successful than long ones.
7. Dribbling should be permitted only when a pass is a poor risk.
8. Players should *run* to become free.

DEFENSIVE CONCEPTS:

1. Most of the guarding efforts should be concentrated in a semi-circle from the free-throw line back (toward the basket) since few goals are made from a distance beyond that.

2. Each player should know whom he is guarding.
3. At least one guard should always stay back to guard the vulnerable space near the basket.
4. Guards should stay between the basket and the player they are guarding.
5. Guards should *slide* to stay with their opponent.

Skill drills and games to improve basketball skills

ODD AND EVEN

EQUIPMENT: Two balls.

FORMATION: Circle, players numbered around circle by ones and twos.

PROCEDURE: Balls are started anywhere in the circle. Ones throw in sequence to each other; twos do the same. When the ball returns to the person who started he shouts "Odds" ("evens"), and all players on that team sit down. The first team to sit down wins.

VARIATIONS:
1. Balls can be started in opposite directions.
2. Balls can be started side by side; however, this may cause confusion as to whom they belong unless different colored balls are used.

TEN TRIPS

EQUIPMENT: One ball for every three people.

FORMATION: Players are in sets of three. Number one stands midway between two and three who are about 25 feet apart.

PROCEDURE: Several sets compete against each other. A trip for the ball consists of one throwing to two, who throws a long pass to three, who throws it to one. Each time one receives the ball he counts aloud then starts the ball on another trip. When the count reaches ten, the team sits down. The first set to complete ten trips wins.

VARIATION: Vary the style of passes used for the short passes.

CENTER MISS BALL

EQUIPMENT: Two balls for each circle.

FORMATION: Single circle, leader in center.

Table 12-2. Skill Drill and Skill Game Guide for Practicing Basketball Skills

SKILL DRILLS AND SKILL GAMES	SKILLS								
	Catching	Passing	Shooting	Pivoting	Guarding	Dribbling	Dodging	Stopping	Starting
Odd and Even	x	x							
Ten Trips	x	x							
Center Miss Ball	x	x							
Tally Ball	x	x			x		x	x	x
Leader and Class	x	x							
Center Touch Ball	x	x							
Tadpole	x	x							
Gap Ball	x	x							
Boundary Ball	x	x			x				
Poison Ball	x	x							
Corner Spry	x	x							
Star Relay	x	x		x					
Maze Relay						x			
Dribble Up, Throw Back	x	x				x			
Red Light							x	x	x
Stop and Go							x	x	x
Mirror Game					x		x	x	x
Around the World			x						
Twenty-One			x						
Pig (or Horse)			x						
Guard Ball	x	x			x		x		
Keep-Away	x	x			x	x			

PROCEDURE: The leader has one ball, the person in the circle has the other. On signal, the player in the circle passes to the leader, and at the same time the leader passes to person who is standing to the right of the circle passer. If the leader misses or fumbles the ball, he exchanges places with the person who last threw the ball. If the pass was poor, the leader is allowed to remain in the center.

VARIATION: Vary the style of passes used.

TALLY BALL

EQUIPMENT: One ball. Colored pinnies.

FORMATION: Teams of six, both on one half of a basketball court.

PROCEDURE: Ball is given to one team out-of-bounds at the center line. Team in possession of the ball tries to complete six consecutive passes. Each time a pass is completed the person who catches it calls out the number of completions so far. When six consecutive passes have been made, the last person may walk to the free-throw line and try for a basket. One point is awarded for six passes, two for each successful free throw. Players from the opposite team attempt to intercept passes. After the attempt for basket is made, the ball is put in play by the opposite team at the free-throw line. The winner is the team which has the most points at the end of a specified period of time.

VIOLATIONS:
1. Walking with the ball.
2. Holding ball more than three seconds.
3. Batting ball from opponent's hand.
4. Pushing or holding an opponent.

PENALTY: Free pass in from side lines given to opponents.

VARIATIONS: The whole court may be used, and four players from each team may be on each end of the court. They are designated as forwards at one end and guards at the other. The forwards try to tally the points, the guards try to intercept passes and throw the ball down to their forwards at the opposite end of the court.

MIRROR GAME

EQUIPMENT: None.

FORMATION: Leader, everyone else scattered about room facing the leader.

PROCEDURE: Leader makes sliding movements—forward, backward, sideward, moving arms up or down. Everyone else tries to match the movements of the leader. After a specified time, the leader may select someone to take his place.

VARIATION: The same thing may be done with couples, each taking turns being the leader.

AROUND THE WORLD

EQUIPMENT: One ball for each player.

FORMATION: Mark six circles at varying spots around the basket. Put a number in each circle.

PROCEDURE: One child stands in each circle and attempts to make a basket. When he does he moves on to the next circle in order. If someone else is in that circle, they take turns shooting. The first one to go "around the world" or to have made a basket from each circle is the winner. Each successive circle should present a slightly different challenge as far as distance and angle is concerned.

TWENTY-ONE

EQUIPMENT: One ball for each playing group.

FORMATION: Small groups of four to six, each given a number for shooting order.

PROCEDURE: In turn each player shoots one ball from in back of the free-throw line. If made, the shot counts 2 points. The player retrieves his own ball and tries a second shot from wherever the ball is recovered. If made, the shot counts 1 point. The first person to reach a total of 21 points wins. The total required may be altered.

PIG (OR HORSE)

EQUIPMENT: One ball for each playing group.

FORMATION: Small groups of four to six, each given a number for shooting order.

PROCEDURE: The first player may shoot from wherever he wishes with whatever type of shot he wishes. If the shot is made, the next player must attempt the same style shot from the same place. If the shot is missed, the player receives the first letter of the name of the game, P (or H). Then the next player may choose his style of shot and place to shoot from. As long as the shot is made, the player who follows must attempt a shot of the same style and from the same place or receive a letter. When one completes the name of the game he is eliminated or the game starts over.

KEEP-AWAY

EQUIPMENT: One ball for each playing group, color bands.

FORMATION: Small teams of three or four.

PROCEDURE: The ball is given to one team which tries to keep possession of it by passing it back and forth between teammates. The other team tries to gain possession of the ball by intercepting passes. Play continues for a specified length of time.

VIOLATIONS:

1. Holding the ball for more than three seconds.

2. Pushing or holding another player.
3. Steps taken while in possession of ball.

PENALTY: Opposite team is given the ball.

VARIATIONS: A point may be awarded to a team each time they intercept a pass.

Basketball lead-up games

END BALL (Figure 12-2)

AREA: Volleyball or basketball court divided in half. A line is drawn approximately 5 feet from each end line to form two end zones. Two teams of equal size. Half the players are designated as forwards and are placed in the end zone. The other half are guards and are placed in the zone farthest from their own end zone.

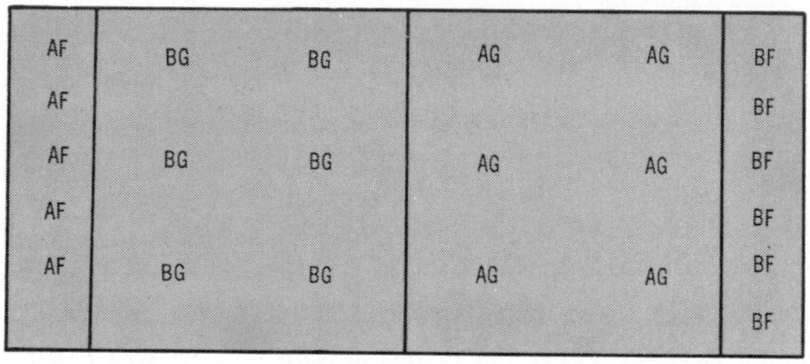

Figure 12-2. End Ball.

PROCEDURE: The ball is given to any guard on the court; he tries to pass over the heads of the opposing team to one of his own forwards. If the ball is caught by a forward, 2 points are scored. (If the opposing guards intercept, they attempt to pass to their forwards.) After the score, the ball is given to the opposing guards. The game may be played for any period of time. Forwards and guards should be rotated several times during the playing period.

VIOLATIONS:
1. Stepping out of assigned area.
2. Walking with the ball.
3. Holding the ball more than five seconds.

PENALTY: Ball is given to opposing guards.

BASKET END BALL

The rules for End Ball are followed with these exceptions:
1. All players may use the unlimited dribble within their own area.
2. After a forward catches the ball and 2 points are made, he may shoot for goal anywhere within the end zone. If the first attempt is not successful, the ball goes to the opposing guards. Two points are given for a successful field goal.

SIX COURT BASKETBALL (Figure 12-3)

The rules for Basket End Ball are followed except that:
1. Two additional lines are added to the court markings.
2. A line of guards from one team is between the two lines of guards from opposing teams. Therefore, more interceptions and quicker passes are possible.

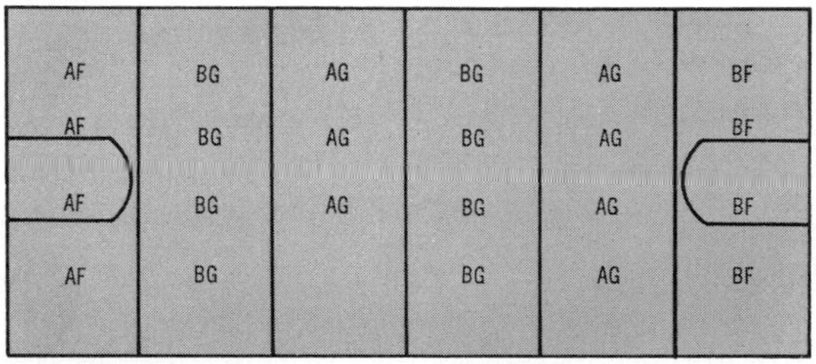

Figure 12-3. Six Court Basketball.

TOSS-UP BASKETBALL (Figure 12-4)

AREA: Half of a basketball court (allows two games on one court). Two teams of six to eight players arranged along each sideline and numbered consecutively.

PROCEDURE: The leader stands with the ball under the basket. A number is called, and the ball is rolled, bounced, or tossed up between the two teams. Players with the called number scramble for the ball. The player who gains possession of it must complete two passes with his own sideline players before shooting. After a shot for goal, the ball is dead and another number is called.

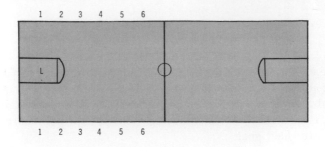

Figure 12-4. Toss-Up Basketball.

VIOLATIONS:
1. Traveling.
2. Shooting before two or more passes have been made.
3. Illegal dribble.
4. Ball out-of-bounds.

PENALTY: Ball is put in play by a sideline player of the opposing team.

FOULS:
1. Snatching ball from opponent.
2. Personal contact.

PENALTY: One free throw—distance may be modified in relation to size and ability of class. Ball is dead and play resumes with leader calling another number.

VARIATIONS:
1. Increase the number of players on the court to four, two from each team.
2. Rebounding may be added.
3. A full court may be used.
4. Alternate positions of teams on each sideline to allow for passes to either side.
5. Alternate boys and girls on each side so when numbers are called, boys will be playing opposite boys, and girls opposite girls.

ALLEY BASKETBALL (Figure 12-5)

AREA: Regulation basketball court divided into three alleys lengthwise. The center alley is narrower than the outside lanes. A player from each team is assigned to each alley. Players in the three lanes nearest their own basket are forwards; those nearest opponent's basket are guards. There should be six players on each team.

PLAYING TIME: Two halves of equal length (six to eight minutes).

PROCEDURE: Game is started with a jump ball after which the players advance ball toward their own basket by passing and use of the dribble. Only forwards may shoot. After a field goal is made and two points awarded, ball is put into play under the basket by a center forward of the team not making the score. The center forward takes the free throw when a foul occurs. Whether made or missed, the ball is put into play at the side opposite the free throw line by a side alley forward. Players of scoring team rotate clockwise one alley after each score is made.

VIOLATIONS:
1. Stepping on or over a boundary line.
2. Traveling.
3. Illegal dribble (catching ball between bounce and pushing it with two hands).
4. Holding ball in play more than three seconds.

PENALTY: Out-of-bounds at the side line for opposing team.

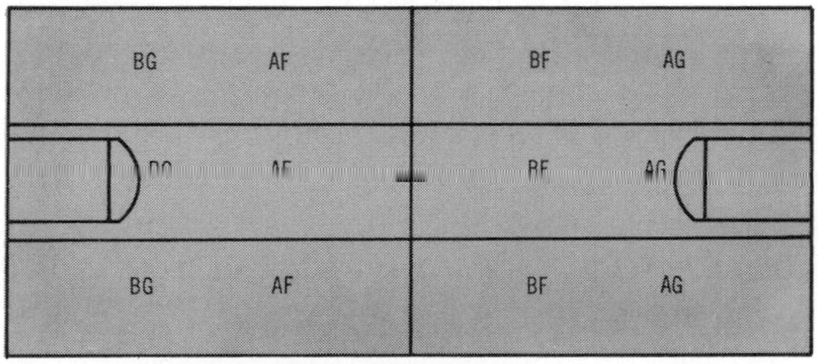

Figure 12-5. Alley Basketball.

FOULS:
1. Snatching ball from opponent.
2. Personal contact.

PENALTY: 1 free throw for opponents; 1 point if successful.

VARIATIONS:
1. Number of players may be increased by adding players on sidelines. These players take the out-of-bounds balls. Players on court may pass to side line players to advance ball towards basket.
2. Court may be divided into nine areas by making two lines width-wise, thereby increasing the number of players who may play at one time. The same rules can be followed as when using six courts.

MODIFIED BASKETBALL FOR BOYS (Figure 12-6)

AREA: Court with markings as indicated in diagram.

PLAYERS: A team consists of five players with positions designated as a center, two forwards, and two guards. All players may shoot for the basket. Guards are designated as defensive players, all others as offensive players. Each team shoots at one goal and guards the other. Players may range all over the court.

PLAYING TIME: Four quarters (six to eight minutes). Teams change ends of court at half time.

PROCEDURE: Game is started with a jump between the centers from each team in the center circle. Centers may not touch the ball again until it has touched the floor or has been touched by another player. Each team tries to either advance the ball toward its own goal or to gain possession of the ball and then advance it to the goal. The ball may be passed or dribbled in order to advance it. After a field goal is made, the ball is put in play behind the end line by one of the opponents. After a foul is made, a free throw is given the player who was fouled. The other players line up on both sides of the free-throw lane in an alternate fashion. If the free throw is made, one point is awarded, and the ball is taken out under the basket by the opponents. If the free throw is missed and rebounds into the playing area, it is once again in play. If two opposing players gain possession of the ball simultaneously, a *tie ball* is called, and a jump is taken in the nearest restraining circle.

VIOLATIONS:
1. Stepping on or over the boundary lines while in possession of the ball.
2. Traveling with the ball.
3. Double dribble.

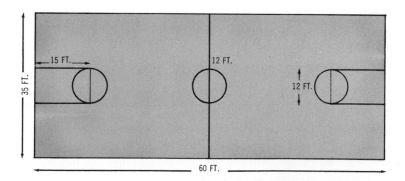

Figure 12-6. Modified Basketball for Boys.

4. Causing the ball to go out-of-bounds.
5. Kicking the ball or striking it with the fist.
6. Stepping into the restraining circle before the ball is tapped.
7. Stepping over the free-throw line and lane lines before the ball hits the rim of the basket.

PENALTY: Out-of-bounds for the other team at the sideline.

FOULS:
1. Personal fouls are those in which a player makes body contact with an opponent.
2. Technical fouls are those in which a player commits an unsportsmanlike act or delays the game.
3. If a player accumulates five fouls during the game he is disqualified from play. One technical foul for unsportsmanlike conduct may disqualify the player if the official decrees it.

PENALTY: A free throw is awarded to the player fouled or to any member of the opposing team in the case of a technical foul. A player who is fouled in the act of shooting receives two free throws if the goal is missed.

SCORING: 2 points for each field goal; 1 point for each free throw.

MODIFIED BASKETBALL FOR GIRLS

AREA: The same court is used as for the boy's game. See diagram on page 418. The center line divides the court into an offensive court and a defensive court for each team.

PLAYERS: A team consists of six players. Two are designated as forwards and play in the offensive court of their team. Two are designated as guards and play in the defensive court of their team. Two players are called roving players and may play anywhere on the court.

PLAYING TIME: Four quarters. Six-minute quarters are recommended for intramural play.

PROCEDURE: The ball is put into play by a center jump at the beginning of each quarter. The team gaining possession of the ball tries to advance the ball toward their goal by passing and by dribbling. Once the ball is caught from the dribble, it may not be dribbled again until possession is gained at another time. The roving players play offensively when their team has the ball, and defensively when their team does not have possession of the ball. When guards gain possession of the ball, they attempt to advance it down to the offensive end of the court. If a ball is caught or held by two opposing players at the same time, a *tie ball* is called, and a toss-up is taken in the nearest restraining circle. Advanced players may be taught to put two hands firmly on the ball when an opponent is holding it, thus causing a tie ball. When a score is made, the ball is put in play by a member of the opposite team at any point behind the end line. Players line up alternately along the free-throw lane when a free throw is attempted. If the free throw is made, the ball is put into play by opponents from any point behind the end line. If it is missed and touches the rim and rebounds into the court it is in play again.

VIOLATIONS:

1. Stepping on or over a boundary line while in possession of the ball.
2. Causing the ball to go out-of-bounds.
3. Stepping over the free-throw line or lane before the ball touches the rim or backboard.
4. Hitting the ball with the fist or kicking the ball.
5. Traveling with ball.
6. Illegal dribbling.
7. Holding the ball more than five seconds when closely guarded.
8. Holding the ball more than five seconds before passing it in from out-of-bounds.

PENALTY: Out-of-bounds for opponents at the side line.

FOULS:

1. Any personal contact with another player.
2. Snatching ball from opponent. (This should remain a foul until the teacher thinks it advisable to introduce it as a technique.)
3. Unsportsmanlike conduct.

PENALTY: A free throw is awarded to the player fouled. A player is disqualified from the game if she accumulates five fouls or one disqualifying foul for unsportsmanlike conduct.

A player fouled in the act of shooting receives two free throws, if the goal was missed.

SCORING: 2 points for each field goal; 1 point for each free throw.

HALF COURT BASKETBALL

AREA: One half of a basketball court is utilized for each game. Thus two games may be conducted at one time. The free-throw line is extended all the way across the court. Both teams shoot at the same basket.

PROCEDURE: The same rules are followed as in regular modified basketball with the exception that the team which gains possession of the ball must throw the ball to a team member behind the restraining line before it can be passed in for a shot at the basket. This game may be played with boys' rules or girls' rules.

SIDELINE BASKETBALL

AREA: The same areas as used in regular modified basketball. Teams are doubled in number.

PROCEDURE: The same rules are followed as in regular basketball. Half the players are stationed along the sideline. The ball may be passed to these players and they play all out-of-bounds balls. The sideline players may not shoot for the basket. After five minutes of playing time, the sideline players change positions with the court players. This is repeated several times. This game is good to use with boys and girls, particularly when only one court is available. It may also be used for a co-recreational game. A team is composed of eleven players (six girls and five boys). The two sexes alternate on the sideline and in the court. Girls play their rules and boys theirs when they are on the court. The score is accumulated to see which team has won; but the boys and girls never directly compete with each other.

Skill tests

Wall pass test
A target which is 8 feet wide, 4 feet high, and 3 feet from the floor is drawn on the wall. A restraining line 4 feet from the wall and parallel to it is drawn on the floor. The subject must throw the ball against the wall repeatedly as many times as he can in twenty seconds. The ball must go in the target area, but need not be caught to be successful. The score is the total number of passes that hit the target area when thrown from behind the restraining line. Two trials are given and the best of the two scores is recorded.

Set shot shooting
A mark is made on the floor directly in front of the basket and ten feet from it. (The distance may vary for different grade levels.) The subject shoots fifteen shots from behind this line. The score is the number of goals made from behind the line.

Dribble test
Six chairs are set in a line with a distance of eight feet between them and a line is drawn 10 feet from the first chair. The subject starts from behind the line on the signal "Go" and dribbles the ball going to the left of the first chair, to the right of the second, and continues to weave in and out down the line and back. A stopwatch is started on the signal "Go" and is stopped when the subject crosses the finish line. Two trials are given, and the fastest time is recorded.

One minute shooting test

The subject stands at the free-throw line. Upon the signal "Go," he shoots for the basket. When he retrieves the ball he may shoot from anywhere. The object is for him to make as many goals as he can in one minute. He must retrieve his own shots. Two trials are given, and the best of the two is recorded.

FOOTBALL ACTIVITIES

Football is a popular American fall sport. Official football is a contact sport and as such is strictly a male game. In the elementary school, games are played where no body contact is involved. Girls enjoy the novelty of playing with the odd-shaped ball and enjoy the first few lead-up games. Boys and girls should be separated when the more traditional game is played, even though no body contact is involved.

Some boys in the upper grades are involved with football leagues organized by groups outside of school. Tackle football is not recommended for boys of this age. It is particularly important that boys know the basic skills well and learn satisfying games which do not involve contact so that their after-school play will be safe and wholesome.

Ball-handling experiences with a football should be included in the primary grades. The skill patterns of throwing and catching are familiar to children, but much practice is required since the shape of the ball makes the performance of these skills more difficult in football than in some other sports. Since the strategy and involvement of position-responsibility can be quite complicated (even in Flag Football), prior to the sixth grade the games listed are primarily concerned with skill development.

Teaching considerations

1. Since most boys know that official football involves tackling and blocking, they should be taught that when these skills are used proper protective gear is required. They should also be helped to understand that the contact version of the game is for a later age group when the body has the ability to withstand such types of activity. It is for these reasons that Flag or Tag Football is played in school and on the playground.
2. Junior-size footballs should be used until seventh grade.
3. Some type of color identification for teams must be provided.
4. Using of flags or strips of cloth is recommended rather than tagging to signify when the runner is caught or downed. If a flag must be pulled

out of a player's belt, both the runner and his opponent learn to be more evasive and the chance of body contact is lessened. It is much more objective to see a flag that is pulled, than to judge, if and when a player has been tagged. Flags should be worn in such a way that each player has the same amount of cloth showing.

5. Girls should learn to handle the football, play some of the skill games and the first few lead-up games, and learn the terminology of football. Children may be divided by sex for all football type games, or boys may play football and girls may play soccer (or some other activity). Soccer should not be excluded from the boy's program.

6. Since the line and back positions require use of different skills, positions should be rotated frequently.

FOOTBALL SKILLS

Passing

Learning to use the proper grip (Figure 12-7) is essential to passing a football. The fingers and thumb hold the ball between one end and the middle. The fingers are spread over the laces and the thumb is around the ball. The actual pass is made using the overhand throw pattern (p. 257). The throw should be aimed about a foot in front of the runner (who is usually moving).

Figure 12-7. Correct Grip on a Football.

COMMON FAULTS:
1. Holding ball in palm rather than gripping with fingers.
2. Elbow held low and close to body.
3. Failure to snap wrist on release.

Table 12-3. Progression of Skills, Knowledges, Rules, and Lead-Up Games for Football

Skills	Knowledges and Rules	Lead-Up Game	Grade
Passing	Passers		
Catching	Receivers		
	Touchdown	Football Endball	4
Centering	Kickoff		
Carrying the ball	Linesmen		
Stance	Backs		
Field running	Line of scrimmage	One-Down Football	
	Down	Kickoff Football	5
Blocking	End zone		
Punting	Safety		
Covering or guarding	Touchback		
	Off-side		6
	Penalty	Flag Football	
Handoff	Laterals	Flag Football	7
	Plays		
	Formations	Flag Football	8

424

KEY TEACHING PHRASES:
1. Point left foot toward target.
2. Grip ball toward one end with fingers across laces.
3. Focus on target.
4. Rotate body away from target.
5. Bring ball back beyond ear.
6. Keep elbow bent, high, and away from body.
7. Cock wrist.
8. Bring ball forward past ear with elbow leading.
9. Let ball roll off fingertips after wrist snap.
10. Follow through with arm toward target.

Receiving a pass

The principles of catching any ball apply to catching a football. Most passes are caught with the little fingers together. The ball should be caught with the fingers and brought into the body. As soon as the ball is secured, it should be put into *carrying position* (see carrying the ball position). Almost all catching is done on the move.

COMMON FAULTS:
1. Failure to wrap fingers around ball.
2. Catching ball against body and arms and having it bounce off body.

KEY TEACHING PHRASES:
1. Eyes on ball.
2. Reach out for ball.
3. Wrap fingers around ball.
4. Bring ball in toward body.
5. Put ball into carrying position.

Carrying the ball

The ball is carried near the body. The hand is put under and around the end of the ball. The other end is placed in the bend of the forearm and elbow.

Centering

Centering is used to initiate play from the line of scrimmage. The ball is passed from a player on the line to a backfield player. The center takes a position with feet spread wide, knees bent. The right hand reaches down and grasps the ball as for passing. The left hand rests lightly on the opposite side of the ball to serve as a guide. The ball is tossed back through the legs with the arm and a wrist snap.

Stance

The basic stance taken before the ball is put in play has the feet shoulder-width apart (either parallel or one foot slightly ahead of the other), knees bent, the weight slightly forward and resting on the knuckles of one hand. The head is up and eyes focused straight ahead. This stance gives the player an opportunity to take a fast running start and also gives stability for linemen when they block.

Blocking

Blocking in Flag Football should only be that of getting the body in front of the opposing player to block his path or to prevent him from getting the ball. Use of the hands and pushing with the shoulders and hips should be prohibited, since body contact is illegal.

Punting

Punting in football is like that in soccer, and practice in either will improve skill in both. The football must be held out in front of the right foot at shoulder height. The right hand is under the ball at the center, the left hand is on the front end and to the side of the ball. A step forward is taken with the left foot, and the right leg is brought forward with the knee bent and toes pointing. The ball is dropped just before the foot contacts the long axis of the ball with the instep of the foot. The leg straightens as contact is made and follows through high, with toes pointing toward the target.

COMMON FAULTS:
1. Ball is tossed in air rather than dropped.
2. Toes are pointed up in the air rather than at target, so that ball goes straight up in the air.
3. Ball is kicked with toe rather than instep.

KEY TEACHING PHRASES:
1. Eyes on ball.
2. Hold ball straight out from shoulders in front of right leg.
3. Step on left foot.
4. Bring right leg forward with knee bent, toes pointing toward target.
5. Kick ball with instep.
6. Follow through with leg in direction of target.

Handoffs

When simple plays are used in Flag Football, the ball is centered to a back who has the option of passing, running with the ball, or handing it off to someone else. On the handoff the ball is actually placed in the receiver's hand, and he quickly puts the other hand down over the ball to reduce the chances of a fumble. After the handoff the ball is put into the carrying position.

Offensive and defensive team play

OFFENSIVE CONCEPTS:
1. Each player must know his offensive assignment but must not reveal his intentions as he lines up using the regular stance.
2. While running, the player should hold the ball in the carrying position.
3. Dodging, feinting, and changing pace should be used to evade a defensive player when an offensive player is to receive a pass or is running down field with the ball.
4. Both hands are always used to catch the ball.

DEFENSIVE CONCEPTS:
1. A player defending against a pass receiver should not let his man get behind him. He should play to the inside so that he can dash between the passer and the receiver and intercept the ball.
2. Defensemen should keep their eye on the ball not on a particular player unless it is a pass defense; then, of course, he must watch both.
3. Defense players should watch for "tell-tale" moves and for the direction the feet of offensive players take in the line-up so that they are able to anticipate directions of plays.

Skill drills and games to improve football skills

PASS DEFENSE DRILL

SKILLS: Passing, receiving, centering, and defending.

FORMATION: A line of pass receivers stands next to the center. A line of

Table 12-4. Skill Drill and Skill Game Guide for Practicing Football Skills

SKILL DRILLS AND SKILL GAMES	Passing	Receiving	Centering	Blocking	Ball Carrying	Evasion Techniques	Punting	Handoff	Guarding or Covering
Kickover							x		
Leader and Class	x	x							
Shuttle Relay					x			x	
Keep-Away	x	x				x			x
Obstacle Relay					x	x			
Star Relay	x	x							
Corner Ball	x	x							
Football Goal Catch	x	x							x
Corner Spry	x	x			x				
Pass Defense	x	x	x			x			x
Blocking Drill				x		x			

defenders stands opposite them about 5 yards apart. A passer waits in position to receive the ball from the center.

PROCEDURE: As the ball is centered, the first receiver runs out to receive the pass. The first defender moves out and tries to intercept the pass. Afterward, both go to the ends of the opposite lines. Specific patterns, like running straight out and cutting across center, may be stated. There may be two lines of receivers and defenders. The passer throws to whichever receiver is open.

BLOCKING DRILL

SKILLS: Blocking, evasive tactics.

FORMATION: Partners. Line marked off in 8-foot lengths. Partners take a football stance on either side of the line facing one another. One partner is designated as offense, one as defense.

PROCEDURE: Upon a signal, "hike," the offense player tries to get around the defense player. He must stay within his 8-foot area. The defense player tries to contain the other player in the area. No hands or body contact may be made. Dodging, feinting, changing of pace should bc used. The assignments should be changed periodically.

Lead-up games for football

FOOTBALL END BALL

Football End Ball is played just like End Ball (p. 414) except that a football is used.

KICK-OFF FOOTBALL

AREA: A field space 15 yards by 20 yards, goal lines at either end, line at midfield.

FORMATION: Teams of six each. At the start of the game one team lines up at midfield, the other team spreads out deep in its own half of field.

PROCEDURE: A player on the team at midfield throws the ball into the other team's area. A player there either catches or picks up the ball and tries to return it to the far goal line. He may pass the ball back (*lateral*), to a teammate or run all the way with it. Members of the other team try to tag him before he reaches the goal. If he crosses the goal untagged, his team gets 6 points. After he is tagged or makes a goal, the ball is returned to midfield, and the ball is thrown (kick-off) to the opposite team. The winner is the team with the most points at the end of a specified playing period.

VARIATIONS:
1. Once children learn to kick, this game can be used for kick-off practice.
2. When blocking is learned, blocking for teammates may be permitted.

ONE DOWN FOOTBALL (Figure 12-8)

AREA: Field 20 yards by 25 yards with goal lines and midfield line.

FORMATION: Two teams of eight. Five are linemen and line up at the line of *scrimmage* (line where ball is put in play), and three line up 6 feet behind linesmen and are called the backs. Players on each team line up across from each other.

PROCEDURE: The ball is put into play by one team at midfield. The ball is centered to a back who may either run with the ball or pass it to a

LINE OF SCRIMMAGE

LINESMEN ✳ ✳ ✳ ✳ ✳

BACKS ✳ ✳ ✳

Figure 12-8. One Down Football.

teammate. The object is to carry the ball over or pass to someone over the goal line. The ball may be passed any number of times from any place on the field, in any direction. Players from the opposite team try to tag the player with the ball with a two-handed touch above the waist. When a player with the ball is downed, the ball is given to the other team. Each team has only one down in which to make a touchdown. The defensive players play a man-to-man guarding system and try to intercept passes and/or tag runners. When the ball is downed, it is put into play at various locations depending on the following situations.

1. If an incomplete pass is made from behind the line of scrimmage, the ball is given to the other team at the original line of scrimmage.
2. If an incomplete pass is made beyond the original line of scrimmage, the ball is given to the other team from the point where the ball was thrown.
3. When a player with the ball is tagged, the ball is given to the other team at the point where he was tagged.

FLAG FOOTBALL

AREA: Field 60 yards by 30 yards, goal line at either end, lines drawn across field at 20-yard intervals. A line 10 yards behind each goal line designates the *end zone* within which passes may be caught for touchdowns.

FORMATION: Teams may consist of six to ten players each. If less than seven are playing, four are linemen and two are backfield men. Two of the linemen are ends and usually go out for passes. If eight or more play, no more than four backfield players are allowed.

PROCEDURE:

1. *Kick-off*: The game is started with a kick-off from the goal line of the team which is designated by lot or choice. If the ball is kicked out of bounds, it is brought back to the goal line and kicked again. If it goes out of bounds on the second kick, the other team starts play at their 20-yard line. The kick-off may not be recovered by the kicking team unless the other team touches and fumbles it.
2. *Line of scrimmage:* The ball is placed wherever a player is downed and this is called the line of scrimmage. If a pass was attempted and was not caught or intercepted, it is returned to the line of scrimmage.
3. *Downs:* A team is allowed four downs, or attempts to move the ball either by running with it or passing it 20 yards or into the next zone. If they can not move into the next zone in four downs, the ball is given to the other team at the line of scrimmage.

4. *Huddle:* This is the term applied when a team meets in a huddle or circle to plan their next play. After huddling the teams line up, and play is started when the ball is centered.
5. *Forward pass:* The ball may be thrown forward by a player from behind the line of scrimmage. He may lateral the ball from any point. This is a pass thrown to a man behind the passer.
6. *Blocking:* A player may block only by putting his body in the way of an opponent. No hand or body contact is permitted.
7. *Tackling:* A player may only be *downed* or tackled by having one flag pulled from his belt. Players may be required to wear two flags, one on either side; or only one flag may be required, and that is worn in the center of the back of the belt. A tackler may not grab the runner and then the flag.
8. *Punting:* All punts must be announced before the ball is centered. Neither team may cross the line of scrimmage until the ball is kicked.
9. *Fumbles:* If a ball is dropped on the center pass behind the line of scrimmage, it may be picked up by a back. When a ball is dropped anywhere on the field, no one may pick it up and advance it. The first person to touch it gains possession of it for his team.

SCORING: Touchdown—6 points. Point after touchdown—1 point. After a touchdown, one play is given the team from a spot 3 yards out from the goal to make an extra point. Safety—2 points. A safety is called when the defending team causes the ball to go back over the goal line, either by fumbling it, or a player being chased over it and caught. If a player intercepts a ball behind the goal line and does not run it out, or if the ball is kicked over the goal line, a touchback occurs and the ball is taken out to the 20-yard line and given to the team who was defending the goal.

PENALTIES: Loss of 5 yards for the following:
1. Failure to announce intention to punt.
2. Initiating a forward pass beyond line of scrimmage.
3. Off-side (player over line of scrimmage before ball is centered).
4. Delaying the game.
5. Tucking flag too deep in the belt.

Loss of 15 yards for the following:
1. Illegal blocking.
2. Illegal tackling or use of hands on either offense or defense.
3. Unsportsmanlike conduct.

VARIATIONS: The size of the football field and number of players is dependent upon the skill level of the class and the space available. The field may be divided by 10-yard zones rather than 20. Six downs rather than four may be allowed to go 20 yards.

Football skill tests

Forward pass for distance

The directions for the Throw for Distance Test (p. 203) may be followed for this test. Three trials are given, and the farthest throw is recorded.

Forward pass for accuracy

A target is painted on the wall with three concentric circles measuring 2 feet, 4 feet, and 6 feet in diameter. A point value of 3, 2, 1, respectively is allotted to each circle. A line is drawn 15 feet from the wall. A player is given ten trials to throw at the target. His score is the total points earned on the ten trials. He must pass from behind the line. If the ball strikes a line, the highest value is given.

Punt for distance

The same test directions are used for the Punt for Distance as for the Throw for Distance. The subject is given three punts, and the farthest distance is recorded.

Ball carrying zigzag run

Five pins are arranged in a straight line 10 feet apart with the first pin 10 feet from a starting line. The subject puts the ball in carrying position and on the signal "Go" runs to the right around the first pin, as he passes to the left of the second pin he changes the ball to his left arm, and continues in and around each pin. Each time he passes a pin, he must change the ball to the outside arm. When he reaches the end pin he turns and continues back to the starting line in the same manner. The Stopwatch is started on the signal "Go" and is stopped when the subject crosses the starting line again. The player is given two trials and the fastest time is recorded.

SOCCER ACTIVITIES

Soccer is a fall field sport which is extremely popular in most countries other than the United States. In this country it is played most frequently by elementary school children and women.

Young children love to play all versions of soccer since it is a fast moving, running, vigorous game. They seem to be particularly intrigued with the fact that the ball must be handled with parts of the body other than the hands. The uniqueness of using the feet to stop and propel the ball the majority of the time makes the skills difficult to learn as well as interesting. For this reason a great deal of practice is necessary to gain control and accuracy in the use of soccer skills. A ball, some type of goal posts or markers, color bands, and a level playing field is all the equipment needed to play the game.

Teaching considerations

1. Safety rules must be taught and maintained from the first lesson on to avoid hazardous playing habits.
   a. Kicking the ball with the instep and the inside of the foot prevents injury to the toes when soft rubber shoes are worn.
   b. Since play is vigorous and kicking is involved, pushing, shoving, tripping, dangerous kicking, and body blocking must be discouraged immediately through the enforcement of rules which prohibit this type of play.
   c. Children should be taught to protect the face (and girls, the chest) from high-kicked balls by folding arms across face or chest.
   d. Emphasis should be placed on keeping the ball low and avoiding dangerous high kicking when close to another player.
2. Most soccer games involve a great deal of sustained running and changes of directions. This is one of the assets of the game; however, some children are not aware when they are over-fatigued and continue to play when they should rest. Since some positions are more demanding than others, they should be rotated frequently.
3. When soccer balls are used indoors, they should be slightly deflated so that they may be controlled more easily.

SOCCER SKILLS

The basic skills of soccer are described under the general headings of advancing the ball, stopping the ball, and defensive tactics.

Advancing the ball

The ball may be advanced by kicking it or by allowing it to rebound from any part of the body except the hands and arms (volleying). As volleying is quite difficult for elementary school children to control, it will not be analyzed in detail. It should suffice to tell upper grade children that one should get in line with the ball and stiffen the part of the body against which the ball is to rebound.

Table 12-5. Progression of Skills, Knowledges, Rules, and Lead-Up Games for Soccer

Skills	Knowledges and Rules	Lead-Up Games	Grade

Kick
  Instep
  Inside of foot
  Outside of foot
Dribble
Trap
  Sole of foot
Place kick for accuracy
Dribble and drive
	Free kick
	Goal
	Rotation
	Team positions
	  Forwards
	  Sideline guards
	  Goal Line guards
		Line Soccer	3

Dribble and pass
Trap
  Knee:
  Single
  Double
	Forward positions
	Team positioning
	  Attacking team
	  Defending team
		Advanced Line Soccer
		Alley Soccer
			4

Tackle
  Straight
  Dodging
	Kick-in
	Kick-off
	Penalty kick
	Team positions
	  Backs
	  Forwards
		Alley Soccer	5

Tackle Hook	Forward line Backfield Defensive-offensive play Penalty kick	Advanced Alley Soccer	5-6
Punt	Corner kick Defense kick Goalkeeper privileges Official positions	Modified Soccer	7
Triangular passing	Marking	Official Soccer	8

Kicking: inside of foot

The ball is contacted with the inside edge of the foot. The kicking foot is turned outward, and the leg is bent at the knee diagonally backward and outward. The leg is swung across in front of the body. The knee straightens as the ball is met just in front of the body. The ball should be contacted slightly below center. The arms are used for balance, and the foot follows through toward the target. In order to increase force, a few preliminary running steps may be taken. This type of kick is used to move a stationary ball a long distance, to pass to a teammate after trapping a ball, to pass to a teammate when dribbling, or to shoot for goal.

Figure 12-9. Kicking with the Inside of the Foot.

COMMON FAULTS:
1. Kicking with toes.
2. Failure to turn foot outward.
3. Contacting ball too low, causing it to rise too high in the air.

KEY TEACHING PHRASES:
1. Turn kicking foot outward.
2. Bend knee.
3. Turn leg out, and swing it back.

4. Swing leg forward and across the body.
5. Contact ball slightly below center.
6. Foot follows ball toward target.

Kicking: outside of foot

The right leg is brought across in front of the left leg and swings to meet the ball slightly in front and near the outside of the left foot. Because of the limited force of the kick, this must be used for short passes to a teammate on the right side of a player. It may also be used when trying to dodge and avoid a tackler.

COMMON FAULT: The ball is pushed rather than kicked when it is contacted too far to the right of the left foot.

TEACHING PHRASES:
1. Swing right leg across and through.
2. Contact ball in front of left foot.

Kicking: instep of foot

The kicking leg is swung straight back, with the knee bent and the toe pointing toward the ground. As the leg is swung forward with the toe pointed, the ball is contacted below its center with the instep of the foot. The foot follows through in the desired direction. This kick is used for a long pass to a teammate, place kicking, or long kick for goal. A few preliminary steps adds more force to the kick.

COMMON FAULTS:
1. Ball is met too high above the center, and ball does not get off the ground or gain much speed.
2. Failing to meet ball squarely on instep.
3. Losing balance as ball is met due to lack of forward lean into the kick.

KEY TEACHING PHRASES:
1. Swing leg straight back and forward.
2. Lean into kick.
3. Point toe, and contact ball slightly below center squarely on instep.
4. Follow ball with leg pointed at the target.

Punt

This skill is more advanced and should be taught later than the instep kick; however, the mechanics of the punt are much the same as those of the instep kick. The ball is held out in front of the right leg slightly above the waist. A step forward is taken on the left foot, and the right leg is brought back. The ball is dropped and the leg swings forward and upward. The leg follows through toward the sky. Only the goalie may punt the ball out of the goal area. The punt is used to clear the ball over the heads of the opponents and down the field.

COMMON FAULTS:
1. Dropping ball too early, thereby missing ball.
2. Extending knee too much and kicking ball too high.
3. Kicking with toes instead of instep.

KEY TEACHING PHRASES:
1. Hold ball arm's length in front of right leg.
2. Eyes on ball.
3. Step on left foot, swing right leg back from hip, drop ball, swing leg through and kick.
4. Contact ball squarely on instep.
5. Follow through toward the sky.

Dribbling

Dribbling is a means of moving the ball and keeping it under control. The ball is tapped gently with the inside edge of the foot. As the player runs, he should tap the ball with alternate feet. The ball should never be more than a foot ahead of the runner. The dribble is a vital but a difficult skill. The dribbling pattern should be stressed first, then speed and control in moving with the ball. The dribble should be learned and practiced in a ball handling unit before a soccer game is introduced.

COMMON FAULTS:
1. The ball is kicked with the toe.
2. The ball is kicked too hard and consequently moves too far ahead of runner.

KEY TEACHING PHRASES:
1. Tap ball lightly with instep of foot.
2. Tap ball with right foot then left foot when running.

Stopping the ball

Blocking

Blocking is a means of stopping the ball with the body in such a way that the ball will fall to the ground in a spot near the player where he can quickly kick the ball. The major action of blocking is absorbing the force of the ball so it will not rebound away from the body. The player should get in line with the ball and let it hit the body. The ball may be blocked with any part of the body. Just as the ball contacts the body, the player should give with it and take a slight jump backward. Children should be taught to fold their arms across their chest and hold their sides with hands to prevent reaching out to hit ball with arms and hands.

COMMON FAULTS:
1. Failure to get in line with ball.
2. Reaching to meet ball.
3. Failure to give with ball or to jump back.

KEY TEACHING PHRASES:
1. Get in line with ball.
2. Fold arms across chest (if ball is high) and hold onto sides of body.
3. Let ball hit your body.
4. Give with ball.
5. Jump back from ball.

Trapping: sole of foot

Trapping may be described as catching the ball with the feet. To use the sole of the foot in trapping, the player must first get in line with the ball. As the ball reaches the player, he raises the sole of the trapping foot with the toes upward. He quickly brings the sole down over the top of the ball and traps it between the ground and the foot. He immediately removes the foot so he can kick the ball. The weight is on the opposite foot all the time. It is best to use this trap with a slow moving ball. Every ball should be trapped before it is kicked so direction of the kick can be controlled.

COMMON FAULTS:
1. Meeting the ball too soon so that it hits the sole and rebounds off the foot.
2. Meeting ball too late so that foot slides off the ball and presents the possibility of a fall.
3. Failing to bring foot down quickly and release it quickly so that ball is in a position for a kick.

KEY TEACHING PHRASES:
1. Eyes on ball.
2. Get in line with ball.
3. Bend knee, raise toes.
4. Put sole down over ball, and trap it between the ground and foot.
5. Release it quickly.

Single leg trap

The player must first get in line with the ball. The foot of the trapping leg is brought diagonally back of the other foot. The foot flexes so that only the toes are contacting the ground. Both knees are bent. As the ball reaches the leg, the lower leg presses against the ball and traps it. The weight is held on the other foot. The ball is released immediately, and the player is ready to kick the ball. Upper torso should be erect so that balance is kept. The leg traps make it more difficult for an opponent to get at the ball than if a sole trap is used. However, it takes longer to get into kicking position than if sole trap is used.

COMMON FAULTS:
1. Failure to get in line with the ball.
2. Failure to time trap properly so that ball hits leg and bounces away.
3. Leaning upper trunk forward as knees bend, and falling forward.

KEY TEACHING PHRASES:
1. Eyes on ball.
2. Get in line with ball.
3. Bring foot diagonally back.
4. Bend knees.
5. Press lower leg against center of ball.
6. Keep weight on nontrapping foot.
7. Release ball immediately and get ready for a kick.

Double leg trap

The player gets in line with the ball. As it approaches the feet are slightly apart and pointed outward. The knees bend deeply and quickly and trap the ball against the ground with the shins. Weight is held on the balls of both feet. Arms are used for balance. The body is quickly extended into a vertical position as ball is released from the shins. This is an effective but difficult trap because of the balance problem.

COMMON FAULTS:
1. Meeting the ball off center.
2. Bending too early so the ball is actually hit rather than trapped.
3. Leaning forward at waist and losing balance.

KEY TEACHING PHRASES:
1. Eyes on ball.
2. Get in line with ball.
3. Weight on balls of feet.
4. Bend both knees quickly and deeply, trapping ball between ground and shins.
5. Keep upper trunk erect.
6. Use arms to side to keep balance.
7. Release ball quickly and get into position for a kick.

Defensive tactics

Taking the ball away from another player or causing him to make a poor pass or overrun the ball is accomplished by tackling the ball.

Straight tackle

The tackler comes to a position directly in front of a person who is dribbling and attempts to put his foot on the ball. He then either quickly kicks it away from the dribbler or holds it until the dribbler overruns it.

Hook tackle

The tackler approaches the dribbler from the front but quickly steps to one side and reaches with one leg and, using it as a hook, attempts to draw the ball out to one side. The supporting leg must be bent at the knee so that a longer reach may be made with the hooking leg. When using either tackle, the forward momentum of the body must be checked in order to avoid body contact with the opponent.

COMMON FAULTS:
1. Failure to reach for ball with tackling foot and therefore running into opponent.
2. Failure to quickly clear the ball away from opponent.
3. Poor timing on the reach.
4. Failure to maintain weight on supporting leg, thereby falling into the opponent.
5. Failure to excute a dodge to avoid opponent.

KEY TEACHING PHRASES:
1. Check forward movement.
2. Reach for ball with one foot.
3. Pull ball to one side.
4. Quickly clear ball to teammate.
5. Step out of the way of opponent.

Marking

In games where there are backfield players and forward line players, there is a responsibility for guarding a specific player. The term "marking" should be used as soon as guarding an individual is necessary. The goal line is defended, not guarded.

General offensive and
defensive team play

There are a few basic concepts of defensive and offensive play which should be stressed in the first soccer experience. Additions to these are made as the games become more complex.

OFFENSIVE CONCEPTS:
1. Use short, quick, controlled kicks.
2. Have ball under control before kicking it.

3. Pass diagonally ahead to a teammate.
4. Change direction of pass frequently to keep opponents off guard.
5. Clear ball out to sidelines until ball must be centered near the goal area.
6. Stay in own position area.
7. Only one player from a team should attempt to kick the ball at one time.
8. Forwards should let their own backfield players get the ball from opponents if possible, so they can run ahead to receive a pass.

DEFENSIVE CONCEPTS:
1. Backs should stay behind their own forwards to pick up missed or intercepted balls.
2. Backs should attempt to intercept ball before it reaches opponent.
3. As soon as an opponent gets control of the ball, backs should prepare to tackle the ball.
4. When backs gain possession of ball, they should pass it ahead to their teammate immediately.
5. The ball should be cleared from in front of goal with a hard kick toward sideline.

Skill drills and games to improve soccer skills

CIRCLE SOCCER

SKILLS: Kicking, trapping, blocking.

EQUIPMENT: One soccer ball for each circle.

FORMATION: Single circle with a line drawn across the center. One team fills in the circle on each side. It is best if a circle is drawn on the floor or ground.

PROCEDURE: The ball is put in play with the leader rolling the ball across the circle. The object of the game is for each team to try to kick the ball out of the circle on the opponent's half of the playing area. The ball must go below waist level and out of the circle to count 1 point. If a player touches the ball, goes into the center while kicking, or kicks the ball above waist level, 1 point is awarded to the opposing team. If the ball comes to rest in the center of the circle, a player from the team on whose half of the circle it rests may go in and kick it out to his teammates.

Table 12-6. Skill Drill and Skill Game Guide for Practicing Soccer Skills

SKILL DRILLS AND SKILL GAMES	Kicking	Trapping	Blocking	Dribbling	Passing	Goal kicking	Punt
Circle Soccer	x	x	x				
Mickey Soccer				x			
Soccer Goal Kick	x	x	x	x		x	
Diamond Soccer	x	x	x		x		
Circle Trap		x			x		
Kick Over		x					x
Dribble Maze Relay				x			
Dribble Up and Kick Back	x			x			
Shuttle Relay	x			x			

CIRCLE TRAP

SKILLS: Passing, trapping.

EQUIPMENT: One soccer ball for each circle.

FORMATION: Single circle with one player in the center.

PROCEDURE: The leader puts the ball into play by rolling it across the circle. Circle players keep the ball moving by passing it to one another. The person in the center tries to trap the ball. If he does, he takes the place in the circle of the person who kicked it last. If someone lets the ball go out of the circle, he must exchange places with the person in the center.

SOCCER KICKOVER

Same rules as Kickover on p. 350 except that a soccer ball is used instead of a football.

DRIBBLE MAZE RELAY

SKILLS: Dribbling.

EQUIPMENT: One soccer ball, some type of obstacles set up 15 feet apart from the starting line to the far end line. Number of obstacles varies with the skill of the children, as does the distance between obstacles.

FORMATION: File relay, with maze set up for each line.

PROCEDURE: Each player in turn dribbles the ball in and out of the obstacles down the line and back. Team which has everyone complete the maze first wins. This may become a timed event and may also be used as a skill test.

DIAMOND SOCCER (Figure 12-10)

SKILLS: Kicking, trapping, blocking, passing.

EQUIPMENT: One soccer ball for each diamond.

FORMATION: Two teams line up as indicated in the diagram.

PROCEDURE: The players nearest the middle line from each team come out to the center of their playing area. The Leader rolls the ball into the center. The two players from each side try to kick the ball out of the diamond of their opponent's half of the court below waist level. The players on the outside lines try to block the ball and kick it back to their inside players. When the ball goes over the outside lines below waist level, a point is awarded the team kicking it out. Inside players take a position on either side of the far end of their half of the diamond. All others rotate one position. The team which was scored against puts the ball in play again. One point is awarded the opposite team which a player touches the ball or kicks it above waist level.

MICKEY SOCCER

SKILL: Dribbling.

EQUIPMENT: One soccer ball for each team placed in a small circle in the center of the circle.

FORMATION: Class divided into circles with even number of players, six or more.

PROCEDURE: Each player in each circle is numbered. The ball is placed in the center of the circle. The leader calls a number. Everyone having that number runs into the center of his circle, dribbles the ball out through his place in the circle and goes to the right around the circle, back through his place, and puts the ball in the center of the circle. The player who returns to his place in the circle first wins a point for his team.

SOCCER GOAL KICK (Figure 12-11)

SKILLS: Kicking, trapping, blocking, dribbling, goal kicking, goal keeping.

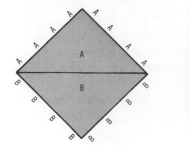

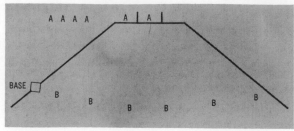

Figure 12-10. Diamond
Soccer.

Figure 12-11. Soccer Goal Kick.

EQUIPMENT: One soccer ball, two lines or posts forming a goal 9 feet wide, one base placed approximately 45 feet at about a 60 degree angle from the right goal post. Lines should run out into the field in front of the goal at 45 degree angles from each goal post.

FORMATION: Two teams of six each. One team spread in semi-circular fashion in front of goal posts. The other team waits for kicking turns to the right of the goal posts. One player is first kicker, one is first goal-keeper.

PROCEDURE: The kicker kicks the ball and runs to base. He tries to get back to the goal posts before the fielding team can kick the ball between the goal posts. The fielders should be encouraged to trap the ball, then kick for goal, dribble closer before kicking, or pass to a team-mate who is closer to the goal. A point is awarded to the kicking team if the player gets back to the goal before the ball crosses the goal line. The fielding team gets a point if the ball beats the kicker across the goal line. After a point is made, the kicker goes to the end of his line, the goalie becomes the kicker and the next person in line becomes goalie.

VARIATIONS: Players may play for their own points. The procedure would be the same as for work-up softball, where each player rotates one position into the kicking spot, and no one waits in line for a turn to kick. A point would be awarded to the goalie if he blocked a goal, to the fielder if he kicked the ball through the goal, and to the kicker if he beat the ball back.

Soccer lead-up games

LINE SOCCER

AREA: Playing field 25 feet wide and 60 feet long divided in half by a centerline with a small circle in the center of it. A restraining line drawn 5 feet in from each end or goal line, a penalty mark centered 15 feet from each goal line.

PLAYERS: There are two teams of equal size. Two players from each team stand along opposite sidelines on their respective half of the field. Their responsibility is to put all out-of-bounds balls into play. The other players line up between the goal line and the restraining line and are called goal line guards. Their responsibility is to prevent the ball from crossing the goal line.

PROCEDURE: The ball is placed in the center circle. Upon a signal, the right corner player from each team becomes a forward and runs out to the center. The forwards try to draw the ball sideward then attempt to kick it across their opponent's goal line. The ball must pass below the shoulders of the guards to count as a goal. After a goal is made, the forward takes the place of the right sideline guard who crosses over and becomes the left sideline guard. All of the other players move one position to the right. The ball is returned to the center circle and play continues with the new right corner player becoming the forward.

FOULS: Touching the ball with the hands, pushing another player, kicking ball above shoulder level. Penalty is a free kick at the point where the foul occurred. If a goal-line guard steps out over the restraining line, a penalty kick is awarded to the forward of the opposite team. This is an unguarded kick from the penalty mark.

SCORING: Field goal—2 points; penalty kick—1 point.

ALLEY SOCCER (Figure 12-12)

AREA: Playing field 100 feet long, 75 feet wide divided lengthwise into five alleys 15 feet wide. A restraining line 10 feet in front of each goal-line. A center line. Two teams of ten players each. One player stands between goal line and restraining line of each lane and is the goal line guard of that lane. One player stands in each lane on his team's side of the center line and is the forward line player of that lane for his team.

PROCEDURE: The object is for the forwards to dribble the ball down the field and kick the ball over the opponent's goal line. The opposite forwards try to get the ball to go toward the other goal. The team with the ball is known as the attacking team, the team without the ball as the defending team. Play is started in the center alley at the center line with the official giving the ball to one team. Forward line players should pass the ball across alleys and down field to other forwards. After a goal the ball is given to the nonscoring team at the center line. Players rotate one lane from left to right starting at the

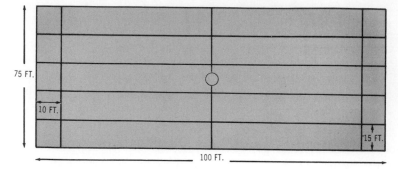

Figure 12-12. Alley Soccer.

left forward position. If there are more than ten players on a team, the extra players become sideline guards. In that case the right forward moves into the right sideline guard position rather than moving directly to the right goal line position. Sideline players put all balls in play on their side of the field.

FOULS:
1. Touching the ball with the hands.
2. Stepping over alley lines.
3. Pushing an opponent.
4. Goal-line guards stepping over restraining line to defend goal.
5. Forwards stepping over restraining line to kick or retrieve ball.
6. Kicking ball for goal above shoulder height.

PENALTY: Free kick from spot where foul was made (unguarded kick).

SCORING: 2 points for each field goal.

ADVANCED ALLEY SOCCER

The rules for Alley Soccer are used with the following exceptions. An additional restraining line is added midway between the goal line and center line of each half of the field. A line of backfield players is added. They take a starting position just behind the new restraining line. Sideline guards are omitted (if possible) and the ball is taken out by the outside alley player from the team opposite that which last touched the ball before it went out of bounds. There is only one goalkeeper, and the goal is restricted to the center alley. This alley should be marked by goal posts or pins of some type. Backfield players do not cross the center line. Fouls which occur between the 25-yard restraining line and the goal restraining line are penalized with a penalty kick from a line marked 15 feet from the goal line. Rotation must change with the left backfield player becoming the goalie and the goalie becoming the left forward. The goalkeeper may catch and throw the ball out to his teammates. He should be encouraged to throw it toward the outside lane players.

MODIFIED OFFICIAL SOCCER (Figure 12-13)

AREA: The lane lines are removed and the field is enlarged to 70 yards long and 40 yards wide. A center line and restraining lines 5 feet on either side are drawn. A semicircle with a radius 15 feet from the goal line is called the penalty area.

PLAYERS: Players have definite positions and responsibilities and are placed on the field as is shown in the diagram.

1. *Forward line players:* Right wing, right inner, center forward, left inner, left wing. *Responsibilities:* To advance the ball into opponent's half of field and score. Players should stay in their respective positions across the field and play the ball between them as they move forward down the field. Forward line players should go only about three-quarters of the way down into their own defensive half of the field.

2. *Halfbacks:* Right half, center half, left half. *Responsibilities:* Play as both offensive and defensive players. They back up the forward line when on offense and mark or guard the right wing, center forward, left wing respectively on defense. They put the ball in play from out-of-bounds balls with a kick-in.

3. *Fullbacks:* Right full, left full. *Responsibilities:* Primarily defensive. They stay in own half of field and mark or guard the inners. They drop back toward the goal line and are the last line of defense before the ball must be stopped by the goalkeeper. They should clear the ball out toward the side lines, preferably to their wings.

4. *Goalkeeper:* Guards the goal. He may use his hands to stop ball and to clear it out and away from the goal. He may punt the ball down field.

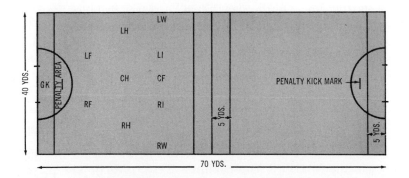

Figure 12-13. Modified Official Soccer.

He never leaves the penalty area. He takes balls which go out over the end line with a kick-in (defense kick).

PROCEDURE: The ball is started at the center circle with a kick-off by one team. The ball must roll over the distance of its circumference at least once before it may be touched by another player. No one may cross the center line before the ball is kicked by the center forward. The forwards try to advance the ball down toward the goal area. When a field goal or a penalty kick is made, the ball is returned to the center and the kick-off is given to the nonscoring team.

FOULS:
1. Pushing, tripping, holding.
2. Touching ball with hands.

PENALTY: Free kick on spot. If foul is made in the penalty circle by the defending team, a penalty kick is awarded. This is an unguarded kick 12 feet from the goal line. Only the goalkeeper and the kicker may be in the penalty area until after the ball is kicked.

OUT OF BOUNDS: Balls which cross the side line are taken by a kick-in at the spot where they went out. A ball crossing the end line and last touched by the offense is taken by a fullback at the point where it went out. If it were last touched by a defense player, it is taken by a wing at the corner of the field.

SCORING: Field goal—2 points. Ball must cross line between goal posts and under them (below shoulder height of goalie, if no goal posts are available). Penalty kick—1 point.

Skill tests

Dribbling

Four pins are set 15 feet apart in a straight line, the first being 15 feet from a starting line. On the signal "Go" a player dribbles the ball from the starting line weaving around the pins. When he gets to the last pin he starts back. A timer starts a stopwatch on the signal "Go" and stops the clock when the ball passes over the finish line. If the dribbler loses control of the ball or does not go around the pins in order, he must regain control or position and continue the course. Two trials are given and the best of the two is recorded as the score for the test.

Punt for distance

The same field markings and procedure can be used as for the throw for distance in the AAHPER Youth Fitness Test (p. 203). The player must kick the ball from behind the starting line. He has three trials, and the best of the three is recorded as the score for the test.

Place kick for distance

The Place Kick Test for Distance can be conducted the same as the Punt for Distance. The distance measured is where the ball rolls dead. Three trials are given, and the best of three is recorded as the score.

Kick for goal (*Figure 12-13*)

A line is drawn 5 yards across in front of the goal posts, and another 8 yards in front of them. Another line is drawn out from the goal line from a point 10 feet to the side of the right post (facing the goal posts), and is extended into the field 18 yards. The player must dribble the ball into area A and kick for goal from this area without stopping the ball. One point is given if the ball is kicked from the correct area and goes between the goal posts. No point is given if the player kicks from outside the area or stops the ball before kicking it. Five trials are given, and the sum of points earned in the five trials constitutes the score for the test.

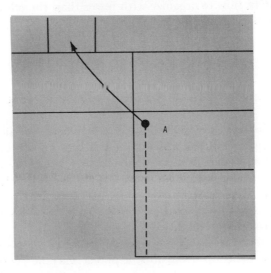

Figure 12-14. Kick for Goal.

Trapping

Two parallel lines are drawn 20 feet apart. The instructor stands on one and kicks the ball hard to the player who is behind the other line. The player tries to trap the ball successfully. Ten trials are given. One point is given for each successful trap. The score for the test is the sum of the points from the ten trials.

SOFTBALL ACTIVITIES

Historically, softball is an outgrowth of the sport of baseball. Softball has been developed as a playground and recreational game as it takes less room to play, less protective equipment, and it is a safer game than baseball. The rules and format of the two games are quite similar. Children, particularly boys, desire to learn and play softball at an early age and continue playing the game into adulthood. The game involves the skills of running, throwing, catching, and batting. It is not classified as a very active game.

Due to the nature of the skills involved and the early acquaintance with the format and rules of the game through neighborhood play, television, and organized baseball leagues for young boys, instruction in the skills and very simple lead-up games should begin in the third grade. As children play softball in their leisure hours, it is important that they learn how to play safely, how to organize with fewer than the official number of players, how to officiate the game, and how to use the skills properly.

Teaching considerations

1. Safety considerations are paramount whenever the first lesson is conducted.
   a. Waiting batters must wait along the first base line in a designated area. Going out of this area may constitute an out or loss of bats. Reasons for this rule should be given. A few are described here. If a player throws a bat, it will probably go down the third base line. More foul balls are hit off to the left than to the right. Batters crowding around the home plate can easily be in the way when the ball is thrown to home base.
   b. Players should be taught not to let go of or throw the bat after hitting. In order to avoid this, a player may be required to carry the bat to first base, or lay it down at a certain mark on the way to first. Failure to do this may constitute an out.
   c. Face masks should be provided for the catcher whenever bats are used, not necessarily because they will be hit by the bat, but the ball may be fouled off the bat into the catcher's face.
   d. Care should be taken that soft bases are used. Children should be taught the dangers of using sticks, stones, or cans for bases.
2. Games with a pitcher should be avoided until accuracy in pitching has been gained. A batting tee should be used instead. The game becomes too inactive if a ball can not be thrown into the strike area consistently.

3. Umpires should be used in each game. This may be a rotating assignment for members of the team at bat so that no one must be inactive for a whole game. Plans to use rotating umpires should be discussed so that children will use them in their playground games and learn to accept the umpire's decision without arguing. The latter proves to be a problem since children often get a poor impression from watching adults do this.

4. Since softball positions require specific actions and responsibilities, and some positions are more active than others, they should be rotated often.

5. Very soft softballs should be used in the intermediate grades and with girls.

6. The game will go faster and more people will be active if everyone on the team hits before sides are changed. If the three-outs and the change-of-sides rules are followed, one team may be up to bat all period or out in the field all period if the fielding team can get no outs.

Table 12-7. Progression of Skills, Knowledges, Rules, and Lead-Up Games for Softball

Skills	Knowledges and Rules	Lead-Up Games	Grade
Catching	Outs:		
Overhand throw	Fly caught		
Underhand throw	Touch base		
	Positions:		
	Fielders		
	Baseman		
	Catcher		
	Maintain batting order		
	Foul ball	Long Base	3
Fielding:	Positions:		
Flies	Infielders		
Grounders	Outfielders		
Batting off tee	Outs:		
	Tag runner or base	Throw It and Run	
	Throw ball ahead of runner	Tee Ball	4
Pitching	Position play		
Batting a pitched ball	Outs:		
	Runner off base on a caught fly		
	Balls	Modified Softball	
	Strikes	Work Up	5-6
Base running	Backing up	Modified Softball	7
Stealing	Third strike rule		
	Infield fly rule	Official Softball	8

SOFTBALL SKILLS

Throwing

Overhand throw

The overhand throw is described on pages 257–9. It is used almost exclusively in throwing to bases and returning the ball from the outfield. Balls thrown to a base from the infield or between bases should be fast and travel in as straight a line as possible.

Underhand throw

The underhand throw is described on pages 259–61. In softball it is used more as a toss than a throw with the exception of the pitch. The ball is usually tossed to a baseman when the ball is fielded close to the base.

Catching

Catching is done in the same manner as described on pages 255–6. However, the teacher must remember that the softball is smaller and harder than most balls.

Practice with catching thrown balls will help build confidence and skill before batted balls must be caught. Gloves will help absorb some of the force; they are, however, too expensive for some schools.

Fielding

Catching or stopping the ball after it is propelled by the batter is spoken of as fielding. If the ball is in the air, it is called a fly ball. If rolling or bouncing on the ground, it is called a ground ball.

Fielding fly balls

Basic catching mechanics are employed. The player should keep his eyes on the ball from the time it leaves the bat, watch the pattern of its flight, and then move into position to catch it. Since a batted ball comes with great force, it is essential to get in line with the ball. Beginners should be taught to catch high balls just above the chin by keeping the thumbs together. Balls which are dropping low should be caught between the waist and shoulders. The little fingers should be together. The stride should be forward and backward with feet spread. This helps maintain balance and also allows a good stance for the return throw to the infield.

COMMON FAULTS:
1. Failing to get in line with ball.

2. Moving up too quickly to meet ball and frequently running too far under it.
3. Holding outstretched fingers rigidly to meet ball.
4. Trying to catch ball in front of eyes and face.
5. Trying to catch ball with one hand under and one hand over the ball rather than hands side by side.
6. Failing to give with fingers and elbows immediately upon grasping ball.

KEY TEACHING PHRASES:
1. Watch flight of ball as it leaves bat.
2. Move into position.
3. Catch high ball with palms out, thumbs together (just above chin).
4. Catch low balls with palms up, little fingers together (between waist and shoulders).
5. As soon as fingers contact ball, squeeze it, and "give" with whole body.

Fielding ground balls

The player should move to meet the ball and get in line with it. With the left foot forward, the player bends at the ankles, knees, and hips and gets into a semi-crouched position keeping the upper part of the body almost erect. With the fingers pointing toward the ground, the hands are placed opposite the left foot. As the ball is met, it is picked up and brought back into a position to start the next throw.

COMMON FAULTS:
1. Failing to get in line with the ball.
2. Bending from the waist and losing balance.
3. Putting hands out with fingers up, thereby letting the ball bounce off the heels of the hands.
4. Feet spread in a side stride position (balls roll between them).

KEY TEACHING PHRASES:
1. Left foot forward, move to meet the ball, and get in line with the ball.
2. Bend at the ankles, knees, and waist, with fingers pointing down; place hands opposite left foot.
3. Clasp fingers around ball.
4. Bring ball in toward body and back for the throw to infield.

Pitching

Pitching utilizes the underhand throw pattern (p. 259). At the start of the pitch, both feet must be parallel, and both hands are on the ball. The right arm is brought back as the body rotates. The ball is released

off the ends of the fingers about hip level. The left foot is brought forward as the ball is brought forward. The right foot is brought up parallel
to the left foot so the pitcher is in ready position to field the ball. Pitching arm follows ball straight toward plate.

COMMON FAULTS:

1. Failing to use enough rotation and backswing to get force and speed
   on the ball.
2. Bringing arm across the body before releasing the ball and causing it
   to go from right to left.
3. Releasing ball too high or too late.

KEY TEACHING PHRASES:

1. Feet together.
2. Ball held in both hands.
3. Bring arm straight back.
4. Rotate trunk to right.
5. Step on to left foot as arm is brought straight forward.
6. Let ball roll off fingertips at a point directly in line with target.
7. Follow ball with hand and arm pointing at target.
8. Bring right foot up beside left foot.

Batting

The bat is held with the left hand wrapped around the handle of the
bat about 2 inches from the end, and the right hand wrapped around
just above the left hand. If the bat is heavy or long, it may be held or
"choked" further up on the handle. The batter stands facing home
plate with feet shoulder width apart, feet pointing straight ahead toward
the plate and parallel to it. (It helps to draw a line parallel to the plate
about 18 inches from it so the player has a guideline.) The player reaches
out with his bat and touches the far side of the plate with the bat. This
helps him judge how far away he needs to stand. (If a batting tee is used
the thick part of the bat may be placed on the tee.) He holds the bat
away from the body with right elbow bent and out. The bat is held at
shoulder height and points diagonally upward. The knees are bent,
weight is on the back foot, but hips and shoulders remain level. The
batter looks over his left shoulder at the pitcher and watches the ball
as it approaches the plate. The forward swing is initiated by the hips
rolling forward and a short step is taken toward the pitcher. The bat is
swung forward level with the ground. The wrists are snapped as the bat
contacts the ball and continue to roll over as the follow through is
taken. The weight is shifted to the forward foot. The bat is dropped as
the first step toward first base is taken. The trademark of the bat should
be facing the pitcher.

Figure 12-15. Batting Stance.

COMMON FAULTS:
1. Putting wrong hand on bottom of bat handle.
2. Resting bat on shoulder.
3. Facing the pitcher.
4 Elbows and arms in close to body, causing a punchy, choppy swing.
5. Swinging upward and under the ball instead of level with ground.

KEY TEACHING PHRASES:
1. Place left hand below right hand (right-handed batter).
2. Choke bat if necessary.
3. Face home plate.
4. Feet parallel to plate.
5. Hold bat back and up just over right shoulder.
6. Arms and elbows out and away from body.
7. Eyes on ball.
8. Weight on right foot.
9. Twist back.
10. Swing big and level with ground.
11. Shift weight to left foot.
12. Snap wrists.
13. Meet ball squarely.

14. Roll wrists over.
15. Follow through.
16. Drop bat.

Baserunning

Initially, children need only be taught to run beyond first base. When games use four bases and all of the game skills become more refined, emphasis can be placed on proper base-running techniques. The runner should touch the inside of the bases and not run wide at each base. A runner waiting on base should assume a forward lean position with the left foot on the base and the right foot ready to push off as soon as the ball is released by the pitcher. Until the majority of the class can hit the ball far enough to run farther than first base on the hit, work on base running is a poor use of time.

Position play

PITCHER:
1. Fields balls hit near him.
2. Covers first base when first baseman must field a hit ball.
3. Backs up third baseman when a runner is on first.
4. Backs up catcher when a runner is on second.
5. Covers home on a passed ball or wild pitch.

CATCHER:
1. Fields balls hit or bunted near the plate.
2. Backs up first baseman when no runner is on first.

FIRST BASEMAN:
1. Plays 10 feet to his left of base when no one is on first.
2. Fields all balls coming toward the first base area.
3. Backs up second baseman on throws from left and center fields when no one is on first.

SECOND BASEMAN:
1. Plays between second and first base about 10 feet behind baseline and 12 feet from second base.
2. Fields balls hit to the left of second base.
3. Covers second base when hits are to the left side of the base.
4. Covers second base on throws from catcher.
5. Relays throws from center fielder and right fielder to infield.

SHORTSTOP:
1. Plays about 10 feet behind the baseline and halfway between third and second base.

2. Fields balls going between second and third base.
3. Covers second base on balls hit to the first base side of second base.
4. Backs up second baseman on balls thrown from catcher.
5. Relays throws from left fielder to infield.

THIRD BASEMAN:
1. Plays about 8 feet to his left of third base and about 4 or 5 feet behind baseline.
2. Fields balls hit to left side of field.

LEFT FIELDER:
1. Backs up the center fielder on hit balls.
2. Backs up third baseman.

CENTER FIELDER:
1. Backs up left and right fielders on hit balls.
2. Backs up shortstop and second baseman on ground balls.
3. Backs up second baseman on all plays.

RIGHT FIELDER:
1. Backs up center fielder, second baseman and first baseman on hit balls.
2. Backs up plays at first and second base.

Basic offensive and defensive concepts

From the very first lead-up game, simple offensive and defensive concepts can be stressed once the format of the game is grasped. A few basic concepts are listed in order of presentation. The nature of the lead-up game determines whether or not these are plausible.

OFFENSIVE CONCEPTS:
1. Batter runs out all hits.
2. Overrun first base.
3. Baserunners know how many outs there have been and are aware of the bases occupied.
4. Hit to empty spaces.

DEFENSIVE CONCEPTS:
1. Fielders assume a ready position as soon as ball is pitched.
2. They know how many outs there are, check which bases are occupied, and plan where to throw ball.
3. After ball is fielded they throw it to a baseman or a relay man immediately; they should not hold it or run with it.
4. They throw to the base to which the runner is going.
5. They try to put out the player who is nearest to scoring a run.

Table 12-8. Skill Drill and Skill Game Guide for Practicing Softball Skills

SKILL DRILLS AND SKILL GAMES	Base throwing	Catching	Fielding	Overhand throw	Batting	Pitching	Base running	General rules and format of game
Beat Ball	x	x					x	
Flies and Grounders			x	x	x			
Throw Over	x		x					
Around the Bases							x	
Pepper			x	x	x			
Target Pitch						x		
Kick Ball								x
Leader and Class		x		x				
Star Relay		x		x				
Hit Pin								x

6. When there are two outs, they play to the nearest base for a force out.
7. They keep eyes on ball and either get into position to catch it, or move to a covering or backing-up position.

Skill drills and games to improve softball skills

BEAT BALL

SKILLS: Throwing, base throwing, running, catching.

EQUIPMENT: Four bases, softball diamond, one ball.

FORMATION: One team at bat, one in field.

PROCEDURE: Rules for Throw It and Run or Modified Softball are followed (as far as positions and outs are concerned). A player may bat or throw the ball into the outfield. He runs all around the bases and tries to reach home before the ball does. The fielders must start the ball at second base and try to get it from second to third to home before the runner reaches home. The baseman must have one foot touching the base when he throws. Teams change sides after everyone has had a batting turn. The team who scores the most runs after a specified equal number of turns at bat wins.

FLIES AND GROUNDERS

SKILLS: Batting, fielding, overhand throw.

EQUIPMENT: Bat, six balls, batting tee, for each group.

FORMATION: One batter; five other players scattered out in field.

PROCEDURE: Batter hits balls into the field. Each time a player is in position to field a ball, he must yell "Mine" and attempt the play. If he catches a fly ball, he receives 5 points. If he catches a fly on the first bounce, he gets 3 points. If he catches a grounder, he receives 1 point. The first person who reaches a total of 15 points takes the place of the batter who goes into the field.

VARIATION: This same game may be played with throwing rather than batting.

THROWOVER

Throwover is just like Kickover on page 341. Instead of kicking the ball the players on one team use an overhand throw. The length of a football field may be used.

AROUND THE BASES

SKILL: Base running.

EQUIPMENT: Four bases, 45 feet apart.

FORMATION: One squad lines up behind each base.

PROCEDURE: The first person in each squad runs around touching the inside corner of every base. The second player steps up on the base as his player is coming toward the base. The runner touches off the next runner by hitting his outstretched hand. The team whose members first complete their trip around the bases wins.

KICK BALL

SKILLS: Kicking, throwing, catching, general format and rules of softball.

EQUIPMENT: Four bases, softball diamond, one soccer ball.

FORMATION: Same playing positions as for Throw It and Run, page 462.

PROCEDURE: The same rules as Throw It and Run are followed. Instead of hitting the ball, the batter kicks the ball. The pitcher rolls the ball on the ground for the pitch.

HIT PIN

The basic rules for Beat Ball apply to Hit Pin. Instead of flat bases, pins are set in the middle of 1 foot circles. The home base circle is 3 feet in diameter. The pitcher must roll a soccer ball within the circle to make a strike. The batter must kick the ball while standing in the circle. The runner must run outside and around each base in order and try to reach home before the catcher receives the ball and knocks over the home pin. The ball must be started at first base. Whenever the ball beats the runner to a base the baseman may knock down the pin and the batter is declared out at that point.

PEPPER

SKILL: Batting, fielding, throwing.

EQUIPMENT: One softball and bat for each team or squad.

FORMATION: Members of a squad line up in a single line with about 9 feet between them. They are facing the leader. The leader stands 20 feet in front of the others.

PROCEDURE: The first person in line throws the ball or pitches it to the leader who tries to hit a ground ball to the next player in the line. This person then pitches it back to the batter and the process is repeated. If a line player misses a ground ball, he goes to the end of the line. The first person in line takes his place, and everyone moves up one place. If the pitch is wild, the person who threw it must go to the end of the line. The object is to be batter as long as possible.

VARIATIONS: The game may be played by having someone throw grounders or flies instead of batting.

TARGET PITCH

SKILL: Pitching.

EQUIPMENT: Four softballs per target.

FORMATION: Targets drawn on the wall which approximate the strike zone of children the age of those playing the game, approximately 36 inches by 18 inches and 20 inches above floor. Pitching line drawn 35 feet away from wall. Two children play against one another; each represents the pitcher for a team.

PROCEDURE: Each player in turn pitches no more than a total of seven balls. He tries to get a combination of three strikes or hits within the target to make an out. If he gets four balls or misses before he gets three strikes within the seven pitches, the other player gets a run. Players take turns. When each has had an equal number of specified turns, the player with the most runs is declared the winner.

Softball lead-up games

LONG BASE (Figure 12-16)

AREA: Small softball field with only one base off to the right of home plate about 30 feet away. Two teams of six. One team is at bat and stands in batter's area to the right of homeplate. One team in the field, with a pitcher, a catcher, and four fielders spread over the field.

PROCEDURE: The pitcher throws the ball to the batter using an underhand throw. The batter catches the ball and throws it anywhere within the playing field and then runs to the long base and back trying to reach home before the fielders can field the ball and get it to the catcher, who must step on home plate when he has the ball in his hand. One run is scored if the batter gets home before the ball does. Everyone on the batting team has a turn to bat, then sides change. The distance from home to long base will have to be adjusted to fit the skills of the group. If the fielding team always gets the ball back

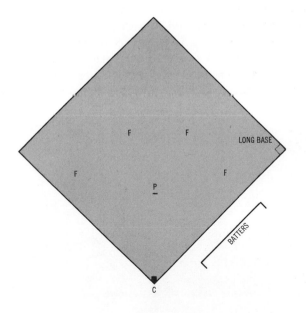

Figure 12-16. Long Base.

before the runner does, the base is too far. If the runner always wins, the base is too close.

OUTS: An out or no point is called if:
1. Fly ball is caught.
2. Catcher touches home with ball in hand before runner reaches home.

VARIATION: The runner may be allowed to stay at first base and come home on the next hit. In this case a first baseman is needed. Players can also be put out at first if the ball reaches the first baseman before the runner gets there.

HINTS: Several games of Long Base may be going on at one time, since it requires so few players and a small amount of space for third grade children. Insist that fielders return ball to catcher with an overhand throw and that they do not run with the ball.

THROW IT AND RUN (Figure 12-17)

AREA: Small softball diamond as diagramed. Two teams of nine players each. One team is at bat, one team takes regular softball positions in the field.

PROCEDURE: The pitcher throws to the batter and the batter throws the ball overhand to the field within the foul lines. He then runs to first base. If he sees that the ball will probably not beat him to second base, he goes onto second and continues around to home, if possible. He stops where he must in order to prevent being put out. The fielder throws the ball to the base where the runner is going. The ball is returned to the pitcher, and another batter throws the ball. The base runner advances, if possible. The team bats around once,

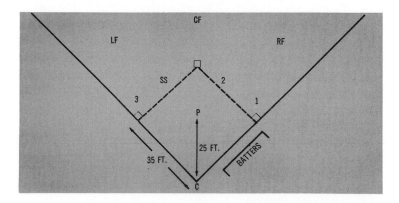

Figure 12-17. Throw It and Run.

then the teams change places. An inning is a division of the game during which each team has a turn at bat.

SCORING: When a batter completes the circle of bases without being put out, he scores a run. The team with the most runs after an equal number of turns at bat wins.

OUTS:
1. A batter is out if he misses three well-pitched balls.
2. The batter is out if the baseman steps on base with the ball in hand before the runner can get there. A "force out" takes place when the runner cannot go back to a base because a teammate is occupying it.
3. The batter is out if a fielder tags him with the ball before he reaches a base.
4. The batter is out if a fly ball is caught.

STRATEGIES:
1. Baseman should learn to cover their base where they are not involved in fielding the ball that has been hit.
2. Fielders should throw to the base to which the runner is running.
3. Batters should throw to an open area.

TEE BALL

This is the same game as Throw It and Run, however, a batting tee is used, and the ball is hit rather than thrown. Batting should be learned and practiced before the game is played. It will be easier for children to learn the format of the game if they throw first rather than bat. The inning may last until the team has made three outs rather than until everyone has been at bat.

MODIFIED SOFTBALL

AREA: Softball diamond with bases 45 feet apart, pitcher's box 35 feet from homeplate. These distances may be altered according to the ability of the groups playing. One team takes the fielding positions and one becomes the batting team.

PROCEDURE: The game starts with the pitcher pitching to the first batter who attempts to hit the ball into the field and get on base. If he is successful, subsequent batters try to get hits and advance the runner around to home to score a run. Fielders attempt to put batters and runners out. When three outs have been made, the teams change places. A definite batting order must be maintained. A set number of innings may be specified, the usual number being seven. The team with the most runs at the end of the seven innings wins. If there is a tie, the game is extended until one team gets more points than the other after an equal number of turns at bat.

INNING: The period of time in which both teams have been at bat and have made three outs.

STRIKE: A pitched ball which goes over the home plate in the strike zone and which the batter fails to strike at, or strikes at and misses. A foul ball which is not caught is considered a strike if the batter has less than two strikes. The strike zone is the area over the plate between the batter's knees and shoulders. Three strikes constitute an out.

BALL: A ball is a pitched ball that does not go in the strike zone and is not struck at or hit by the batter.

WALK: Four balls constitute a free pass or walk to first base. If there is a runner on first base, he moves on to second. If the batter is hit by a pitched ball he is awarded a walk.

FOUL BALL: A ball which is hit and settles (or is touched by a fielder) outside the base line between first and third, and between home and first base; one which lands outside of the baselines beyond first or third base. It is called a fair ball when it settles (or lands) inside these areas.

OUTS: The batter is out when:
1. Three strikes are called. If the catcher drops the ball on the third strike and first base is not occupied, the runner may run for first and must be played on as usual to be put out.
2. A fly ball is caught, whether it is fair or foul.
3. The baseman at first touches the base with ball in hand before the batter reaches first.
4. There is an infield fly hit and there are runners on first and second bases with less than two outs.

A runner is out when:
1. He is tagged with a ball whenever he is off the base.
2. When he is forced out at a base. This occurs when he cannot go back to the base he was on since someone else must occupy it.
3. He advances to the next base before a fly ball is caught and does not return and tag the base he left.

OVERTHROW: When a ball is overthrown at a base, the runner may advance as many bases as he can. If the ball is blocked or hits an obstruction behind first or third base, he may advance only one base.

STEALING BASE: A player may leave the base as soon as the ball leaves the pitcher's hands. If a foul was hit, he must return to base. If there is no backstop, it is not recommended that stealing be allowed on a passed ball. Stealing bases should not be allowed if the throwing and catching skills do not permit defensive plays to be made with any success.

WORK UP

AREA: A small softball diamond such as that diagramed on page 462 is used. Seven to fifteen players may play.

PROCEDURE: The value of Work Up is that two games may be played at the same time in a class of average size, or as few players as seven may play in a pick-up game. Rather than having two teams, each player is assigned a fielding position and three batters are designated. If twelve players are available, all fielding positions can be covered. The rules are the same as for modified softball. When a batter is out he goes to right field or some other predetermined position, and everyone rotates to a new position working their way up to be a batter. Usually the order is: batter to right field, right to center, center to left, left to third, third to shortstop, shortstop to second base, second to first base, first to pitcher, pitcher to catcher, catcher to umpire, umpire to batter. This game has value when there are not enough players to man two teams, but it has more value in a regular class because everyone is more active, has a chance to play different positions and to bat more often. This game is recommended for all grade levels above fifth at some time during the unit. There is a need to play by sides and to learn to work as a team; however, better skills can be developed first by an exposure to different positions and when there is more opportunity for action. Work Up may be played using a batting tee or a pitcher.

Skill tests

Throw for distance
The directions and norms that are given in the AAHPER Youth Fitness test on page 203 may be used to test this skill.

Overhand throw for accuracy
A target consisting of three concentric circles with 3 diameters of 24 inches, 36 inches, and 48 inches is drawn on the wall 3 feet above the floor. Each circle is labeled 3, 2, 1 points respectively. The target may be painted on oilcloth or paper and hung on wall. A line is drawn on the floor 50 feet from the wall. (This may vary in respect to age level.) Each player is given ten consecutive throws from behind the throwing line.

Points are counted for the scoring area which each ball hits. Balls hitting on a line count the higher value. The score is the sum of points recorded for each hit.

Pitching

A target 17 inches wide and 36 inches high is drawn on the wall 16 inches off the floor. A line is drawn 35 feet from the wall in front of the target. This distance should be the same as that of the usual distance from the plate to the pitcher's box. The pitcher is given fifteen consecutive trials. He must use a legal underhand pitch and must keep one foot on the pitching line before the ball is released. One point is scored for each ball which goes in the target area or touches a line.

Baserunning

Upon a signal the batter swings the bat at an imaginary pitched ball, puts the bat down, and circles the bases which are set at the distance the class is used to playing in the game. A timer starts the stopwatch when the signal to hit is given. The bat must not be thrown or carried more than 12 feet. Each base must be touched in order. The watch is stopped when the runner touches home plate. Two trials are given and the best trial is recorded as the score.

Fielding

Fielding is more difficult to test objectively since projecting the ball for the student to field can not be done with any great consistency. Only a test for ground balls is recommended.

Fielding ground balls

A rectangular area is marked out on the field which is 25 feet by 60 feet with a restraining line marked 10 feet in from one end. The player stands in this 10-foot restraining area. From the opposite end the test administrator throws a hard rolling ball within the side boundary lines. The player being tested moves to meet the ball somewhere in front of the restraining line. The ball must be fielded without a bobble and returned to an assistant who is feeding the balls to the administrator. If the ground ball is outside the testing area or is a poorly thrown ball, the trial is repeated. Fifteen trials are given. Each ball successfully fielded scores one point. The final score is the total of points scored on the fifteen trials.

VOLLEYBALL ACTIVITIES

In 1895 volleyball originated at a Y.M.C.A. in Holyoke, Massachusetts. Since that time it has gained great popularity as a sport that is played by men and women of all ages. It is a good recreational game as it takes very little equipment and a small amount of space, it can be learned quickly, and it can be either a highly competitive fast-moving game or be enjoyed by those who are not highly skilled. With few modifications it can be played by boys and girls together and by just a few players; it may be played on the beach, on the playground, or in the gym.

Since the skills of volleyball are few in number and the most basic ones can be learned at an early age, there is little need for teaching many lead-up games. It is more important to modify the size and weight of the ball, the size of the court, the height of the net, and the game rules than to modify the skills and the format of the game. The game is unique in that players from opposing teams are separated by a net and are not in the same playing area. This eliminates one of the needs for modification that is necessary in all of the other team games.

The official game calls for two teams of six players. Each team occupies half of a rectangular court which is divided by a net. The object of the game is to hit a ball back and forth across the net with each team trying to earn points by placing the ball so that their opponents cannot return it.

Teaching considerations

1. Since the overhand volley is the most frequently used skill in the game, it should be practiced extensively. It can be taught first in a basic skill lesson unrelated to volleyball, but stress must be put on correct execution and upon hitting the ball high in order to avoid forming poor habits even before the game is started. The serve can also be learned out of context of the game.
2. Nets should be adjusted to the height of the players. It can be very frustrating and discouraging to young children who can actually perform the skill, but cannot be successful in the game because the net is too high for them.
3. Lightweight balls or heavy-weight balloons can be used first since young children can learn the skill pattern, but may lack the arm and wrist strength to hit a heavy ball.
4. Smaller balls (7-inch) should be used at first, since children's fingers are short, and they are apt to hit a large ball off-center.
5. Although volleyball is often advertised as a game which can accommodate large numbers of children enabling everyone to play, this is not always true. When more than six or eight are on a team, children experience little action. Most of them are standing and seldom have a chance to touch the ball. It is far better to make two courts out of one and have two games with six on each team in a smaller space than twelve on a team in a larger area. Control and placement of the ball should be emphasized rather than the ability to send it a long

distance. Therefore, small courts with a few players will allow for more practice and participation by all. If playing space is limited, some players may practice skills against the wall or even work on different kinds of activities at various stations around the room. When there are seven players, one may stand on the sidelines opposite the left front-line player. When the team rotates, he becomes the left front player and the left back becomes the sideline player. This system may be adjusted for a larger number of extra players.

6. Ropes with ribbons dangling from them may be substituted for a net.
7. Teams should be responsible for keeping their own scores in class games; the server announces the score before each serve.
8. The ball should be rolled under the net to the server. This saves a great deal of time.
9. The wall should be utilized extensively for skill practices, since the ball rebounds with more regularity than if two beginning players were returning it to each other.
10. Newcomb, Net Ball, and Deck Tennis are good active games which can be utilized to teach scoring, rotation, and format of the game in the third grade. When the latter are taught in volleyball, reference to their use in these games should be made; however, the games themselves should not be played during a volleyball unit since they all involve throwing and catching the ball (fouls in volleyball). They are not volleyball lead-up games.

VOLLEYBALL SKILLS

Overhead volley

The overhead volley is used whenever the ball is received at chest level or higher. The hands are held at eye level with the fingers spread and thumbs and index fingers almost touching. This gives the appearance of a triangle or window to look through as the ball is hit. The wrists are hyperextended, elbows are flexed and out at shoulder height, the knees bent. As the ball is hit, the knees and arms extend forcibly upward and forward with a complete follow-through high in the air in the direction the ball is to go. The ball is contacted by all the fingers and the thumb simultaneously, as the wrists flex and have a flicking motion. The emphasis should be on hitting the ball high, about 15 to 20 feet off the floor, and finishing with the whole body in a fully extended position. A jump off the floor as the ball is hit should also be encouraged. The overhead volley is used (when the ball is received from the serve) to pass the ball to a teammate who then uses the volley as a set to a teammate who sends the ball over the net.

Table 12-9. Progression of Skills, Knowledges, Rules, and Lead-Up Games for Volleyball

Skills	Knowledges and Rules	Lead-Up Games	Grade
Overhead volley Serve	Service Court positions Rotation Official scoring Side out Point One hit per person Unlimited hits per side Touching net foul	One Line Volleyball 5-foot net Court 15 by 30 feet	4
Dig Passing	Line violations Unlimited hits per side One, two, three attack (simple) Ready position	Modified Volleyball 6-foot net Court 20 by 40 feet	5
High set	Backing-up Fouls: Catching Holding Pushing Body Game strategy	Modified Volleyball 6½-foot net Court 25 by 50 feet	6
Recovery from net Spike Block	3 hits per side One, two, three, attack	Modified Volleyball 7-foot net Court 25 by 50 feet	7
	Official rules	Official Volleyball 7½-foot net Court 25 by 50 feet	8

469

COMMON FAULTS:
1. Fingers are pointed straight up, no hyperextension of wrists.
2. Ball is slapped by the palm of the hand.
3. Ball is contacted in front of the chest and pushed forward rather than upward.
4. Body is straight when ball is hit.
5. Knees, arms, and wrists do not extend; therefore little power is gained.
6. One hand is used instead of two.
7. Player reaches off to side to hit the ball.
8. Ball goes over head because of poor positioning.

KEY TEACHING PHRASES:
1. Eyes on ball.
2. Make window with hands, thumbs and index fingers nearly touching.
3. Knees bent.
4. Elbows bent and held shoulder high.
5. Look through "window" and hit ball.
6. Hit ball high and forward, and reach high with whole body.

Underhand serve

The player stands with the left foot slightly ahead of the right, knees bent. The ball is held on the left hand directly in front of and at the same level of the right hand as it hangs down at the side. The serving motion is like that of an underhand throw. The right hand forms a fist. The right arm swings straight back and forth in a pendular motion. The ball is contacted slightly below center and hit off the hand. The right arm follows through above the shoulder in the direction of the target.

COMMON FAULTS:
1. Eyes are taken off ball.
2. Ball held too high.
3. Ball held too far to left of body.
4. Ball is tossed in air.
5. Left shoulder is lifted as right arm is swung forward, and ball is above the right fist at contact.
6. Elbow of serving arm is bent in forward swing.
7. Ball is contacted too low, therefore it goes too high in the air.
8. Backswing is too short, resulting in lack of force.
9. Arm is brought across in front of body causing ball to go to left.

KEY TEACHING PHRASES:
1. Eyes on ball.
2. Left shoulder toward net.

HAND POSITION

CONTACTING THE BALL

Figure 12-18. The Overhead Volley.

3. Measure where ball should be held by swinging right arm straight back and forth.
4. Swing arm backward and forward.
5. Hit ball off hand.
6. Follow through in direction of target.

Two-hand dig

When a ball must be received below waist level, the ball must be hit with an underhand motion. One hand is placed in the palm of the other; the thumbs are on top (Figure 12-19). The forearms are close together and parallel, elbows touching. The body must be in line with the ball, knees bent. As the ball is hit, the knees extend and the body rises upward. The ball actually rebounds off the flat side of the forearm and wrist. Little follow-through is necessary. It is essential that the body be directly behind the ball if direction is to be controlled. The ball should be sent high. The dig is used to receive most serves, to take all low balls, and to recover the ball from the net. In an emergency when the player cannot get into position for a two-hand dig, a one-hand dig may be used. In this case the ball rebounds off the flat side of one forearm.

COMMON FAULTS:
1. Body not in line with ball.
2. Failure to keep forearms close together.
3. Failure to bend knees and extend them as ball is hit.
4. Elbows bend as arms swing up to contact ball.
5. Too much follow-through.

KEY TEACHING PHRASES:
1. Get directly in line with ball.
2. Grasp one hand tight in other hand.
3. Keep forearms together.
4. Bend knees.
5. Extend knees as ball is contacted.
6. Contact ball at wrist area.

Figure 12-19. Body Position and Hand Position for the Two-Hand Dig.

The set

The set is usually the second hit in the series of three allowed. The ball is hit to a teammate so it is in position for a spike. The overhead volley is used; however, the set must be about fifteen feet high and about one foot from the net in a position where a teammate can spike it over the net. Even before children can spike the ball, they should be taught to set the second ball high. A ball which is high and soft is much easier to redirect no matter what kind of a hit is used.

Spike

The spike is a ball that is sent smashing downward into the opponent's court so that it is very difficult to return. The spiker stands close to the net facing the direction from which the ball is coming. As the ball starts to come down, the spiker jumps high in the air, swings his right arm upward. The ball is hit downward when it is still above the net. The body turns in the air and the spiker lands facing the net. The ball must be set up high enough so a hit can be downward on top of the ball. The net may be lowered when the spike is first taught. Weight must be controlled so the body does not fall forward into the net.

COMMON FAULTS:
1. Jumping too late.
2. Hitting ball underneath and causing it to go upward.
3. Falling forward on the jump.
4. Standing too close to the net.

KEY TEACHING PHRASES:
1. Eyes on ball.
2. Jump high just as ball starts down.
3. Reach and hit downward on ball.
4. Turn and land facing the net.
5. Keep upper body erect.

Block

The block is the defense against the spike. The blocker faces the net and jumps at the same time the spiker does. He swings both arms upward so hands are about 6 inches above the net. The fingers are spread and the ball actually rebounds from the hands. This is a difficult skill because of the timing of the jump, but it can be learned by seventh and eighth graders.

COMMON FAULTS:
1. Poor timing; jump is made too early or too late.
2. Hands are apart.
3. Hands push or hit at ball.

KEY TEACHING PHRASES:
1. Eyes on ball.
2. Jump with spiker.
3. Hands outstretched, thumbs close together.
4. Let ball rebound from hands.
5. Do not follow through.

Net recovery

When the ball hits the net it will rebound in different ways depending upon how hard it hits and on what part of the net. The class should study this before attempting net recoveries. If there have been two hits or less, a player may hit the ball as it bounces off the net. He faces the net, watches where the ball hits the net, quickly gets into position, bends the knees, and uses a two-hand dig to send the ball directly upward. In desperation a one hand-dig may be tried. This is a difficult skill, as again the timing is crucial.

COMMON FAULTS:
1. Failing to anticipate the rebound correctly.
2. Failure to bend and get under ball.
3. Ball is held momentarily.
4. Ball swept backwards over shoulders.

KEY TEACHING PHRASES:
1. Watch where ball hits net.
2. Bend knees.
3. Get under ball.
4. Hit ball upward.

General offensive and defensive team play

OFFENSIVE CONCEPTS:
1. The serve should be placed into open areas and preferably deep in the court and near the side lines.
2. The three hits allowed before the ball is sent over the net should always be used. The basic 1, 2, 3, attack should be followed in the modified games as well as in the official games, even though a spike cannot be executed.
   One is the initial *pass* made to a front line player when the ball is received.
   Two is the *set* to a front line player.
   Three is the *spike* or the volley over the net.
3. Forward line players never play with backs to net.
4. High passes are essential.

DEFENSIVE CONCEPTS:
1. All players should be in a position of readiness. Eyes on ball, weight evenly placed over both feet which are in a forward stride position.

2. Most serves are received by backline players. Front line players should be ready to receive a pass.
3. A ball that goes above a forward line player's shoulders should always be taken by a back.
4. The backs always back up certain players on the serve. The right back backs up the right forward and the left back; the left back backs up the left forward, the center back and the left back; the center back backs up the center forward.
5. A player should call out "Mine" when he intends to take a ball and when there may be some doubt as to who is going to take it.

Skill drills and games to improve volleyball skills

CIRCLE KEEP IT UP

SKILLS: Overhead pass.

EQUIPMENT: One ball per circle.

FORMATION: Small circles of six. The object of the game is to see which circle can get the most consecutive hits.

PROCEDURE: One player throws the ball up to himself, then volleys the ball to anyone in the circle. The ball is volleyed until it falls to the floor or is caught, pushed, or thrown. A leader calls out the number of hits. When a team makes a foul or the ball hits the floor, they drop out of the game. The game moves quickly, so a number of games should be played to see which team can win the most times.

VARIATIONS: The game may be played to see which team can make the most completed volleys in thirty seconds. The number may be accumulative not necessarily continuous. If the ball hits the floor or a foul is made, the ball is put into play again with a set. It can be specified that only overhead passes may be made or that only digs can be used, although the latter are harder to control.

WALL VOLLEYBALL

SKILLS: Overhead pass, two-hand dig.

EQUIPMENT: One ball, a wall space 10 feet wide and 5 feet high.

FORMATION: This game may be played by two, three, or four people.

PROCEDURE: The object of this game is to keep the ball bouncing against the wall above the line. Two people oppose one another. One puts

Table 12-10. Skill Drill and Skill Game Guide for Practicing Volleyball

SKILL DRILLS AND SKILL GAMES	Volley pass	Set	Dig	Serve	Spike	Block	Net recovery
Call Ball				x			
Circle Keep-It-Up	x						
Zigzag Volley	x		x				
Wall Volleyball	x		x	x			
Shuttle Volley	x						
Volley by Two	x	x					
Volley by Four	x	x					
Serve to Wall				x			
Toss and Dig			x				
Wall Dig			x				
Toss and Spike					x		
Set and Spike		x			x		
Spike and Block		x			x	x	
Toss and Recover							x

it into play with a serve against the wall. It must be returned by the next person, and play continues with alternate hits. When one fails to hit it above the net line or fails to return it, the other player receives a point or the serve. Only the server may win points. If three are playing, the same rules apply only players must hit the ball in order. If four play it is a game of doubles, and partners alternate hits and serves. The first to win 15 points wins the game.

ZIGZAG VOLLEY

SKILLS: Overhead pass, set.

EQUIPMENT: One ball per team.

FORMATION: Groups of ten line up in two staggered lines so each person faces an empty space. The lines are 9 feet apart.

PROCEDURE: The ball is started at one end. Upon a signal the first player tosses the ball up and hits it to the first player in the opposite line. The ball zigzags back and forth between the two lines to the end and back to the first player who catches it. Everyone sits down. The first team sitting wins. The overhead pass must be used. If the ball is dropped or missed it is set up by the person who missed it, and play continues.

VARIATIONS: Lines may be moved closer together and the ball hit to the other side as if it were a set.

SHUTTLE VOLLEY

SKILLS: Overhead volley.

EQUIPMENT: One ball for each group, a rope stretched between two posts at a height of 15 feet.

FORMATION: Groups of eight. Lines drawn parallel to both sides of the rope and 4 feet from it. Four players stand behind one line, four behind the other.

PROCEDURE: The ball must be volleyed by the first person in one line above the rope, dropping so that the first person in the other line can volley it back across the rope to the second person in line. After a player has volleyed he runs to the end of the opposite line. When everyone is in his original position, the team sits down. The first team finished wins the game.

Since there are few really good skill drill games for volleyball, a few practice drills for the skills are suggested.

Volley drill

VOLLEY BY TWOS: Partners volley ball back and forth across the net.

VOLLEY BY FOURS: Two line up on both sides of the net. The two nearest the net are front line players, the two in the back are the backs. The first back sets the ball up to himself then passes it to the front player who hits it over the net over the head of the opposite front line player to the back, who in turn passes it to his front line player. Play continues with players rotating frequently.

Serve drill

SERVE TO WALL: Individual player repeatedly serves to a point on wall 5 feet high from varying distances from the wall.

SERVE TO PARTNERS: Partners serve back and forth to one another from a distance of 20 feet, then 30, depending on skill level. If there is not a ball for every two people, single-line formations on each side of the court may be used.

Dig drill

TOSS AND DIG: Working in partners, one tosses the ball for two to dig. They alternate toss and dig responsibilities.

WALL DIG: A player tosses the ball against the wall and uses a dig to hit the ball back against the wall, continuing this until he has to set the ball up with another toss.

Spike drill

JUMP AND REACH: Players should practice the jump and reach against the wall. Chalk lines can be used to mark how high they jump each time. This should be done at the net, so players see how high above the net they can reach.

TOSS AND SPIKE: Players are in two lines facing the net about 2 feet beside it. One person is on the opposite side of net to retrieve balls. The right hand line is the tossing line, the left the spiking line. The ball is tossed 15 feet high and about 1 foot from the net. The spiker attempts to spike it across the net. The spiker takes the retriever's place, the retriever moves to the end of the tossing line, and the tosser to the end of the spiking line. The net may be lowered 6 inches below its usual height.

SET AND SPIKE: The same drill may be used with the tosser setting the ball to himself with a toss, then setting it for the spiker.

Block drill

SPIKE AND BLOCK: The same drill formation as for Toss and Spike may be used, only the retriever becomes a blocker.

Net recovery drill

TOSS AND RECOVER: Working in partners, one tosses ball into the net, the other tries to recover it. Two lines may be formed, and turns taken, playing with partners.

Lead-up games for volleyball

ONE LINE VOLLEYBALL (Figure 12-20)

AREA: A court area 15 feet by 15 feet marked as in the diagram. Two teams of four. All members stand on one line near net.

PROCEDURE: The ball is served by the player in the right hand corner position. The ball is returned by a member of the other team. The ball is hit back and forth until it goes out of bounds, or until a team fails to return it across net or makes a foul. The ball may be hit any number of times on a side before it is returned, but not twice in succession by the same player. Players rotate to the left when the team wins the serve. The end person goes to the head of the line and

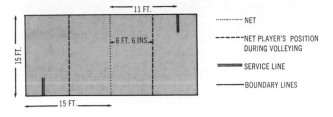

Figure **12-20.** One Line Volleyball.

becomes the server. The serve must go over on the first try. The serving line may be adjusted to the needs of individuals or the team.

SCORING: A point is scored by the serving team if the ball is not returned over net or if it goes out of bounds on return. A team either wins a point or the serve. Ten points constitute a game. The server must announce the score before serving, stating the score of his team first.

FOULS: A player may not touch the net or step over the center line. These rules may not be necessary the first few times the game is played. The ball must be clearly batted, not caught and thrown. The teacher can introduce these rules depending on the skill level of the class.

VOLLEY BALL (Figure 12-21)

AREAS: Court 25 feet by 50 feet as marked in diagram.

PLAYERS: Six players on each team. Positions are called: left forward, center forward, right forward, right back, center back, left back.

PROCEDURE: The ball is put into play by the right back player from anywhere behind the end line. He must remain behind the line until he

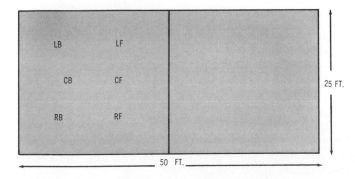

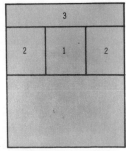

Figure **12-21.** Volleyball.

Figure **12-22.** Serving Test.

hits the ball. The ball must clear the net. The opponents try to return the serve and, if they are successful, the game continues with the ball being hit back and forth across the net until a player misses or makes a foul. If the receiving team misses, the serving team is awarded a point and the server serves again. He continues to serve until the serving team misses at which time "side out" is called, and the receiving team wins the serve. Only the serving team may score. When "Side out" is called, the team winning the serve rotates. Each player moves one place in a clockwise direction with the RF becoming the server.

GENERAL RULES:
1. Any ball (except on the serve) which touches the net and continues over the net is legal, and play continues.
2. The ball may be hit only with the hands and the forearms.
3. The ball may be hit three times by each team before it is sent over the net. No player may strike it twice in succession.
4. A ball touching a boundary line is considered good.
5. Balls may be hit by a player who is standing outside of the boundary lines.
6. A player must let a ball hit the floor if he thinks it is out of bounds; he may not catch it and call it out of bounds.

FOULS:
1. Hitting the ball twice in succession.
2. Hitting the ball with any part of the body but the forearms and hands.
3. Not clearly hitting the ball, catching it momentarily, pushing it, and lifting it are all illegal.
4. Stepping over end line when serving.
5. Stepping over center line.
6. Touching net.
7. Reaching over net to hit a ball.

PENALTY:
1. If the foul is committed by the serving team, "Side out" is called and the other team wins the serve.
2. If the foul is committed by the receiving team, point is won by the serving team.

GAME SCORE:
1. The team which wins 15 points first wins.
2. A team must be 2 points ahead to win.
3. A time limit may be set for the game, perhaps eight minutes, and the team who is 2 or more points ahead wins.

FURTHER MODIFICATIONS: The most common modifications are: unlimited hits per side, shorter service line, lower net, smaller courts, and shorter games.

The progression chart (p. 469) indicates the modifications used at different grade levels. Rules are introduced in the order they are needed and can be handled by the players.

Skill tests

Wall volley test

A line is drawn on the wall 6 feet from the floor. This line represents the net and may be altered to coincide with the net height that is used in the game. A restraining line is drawn on the floor 3 feet from the wall. The child stands behind this line and tosses the ball into the air, then volleys it against the wall. He continues to volley the ball back and forth against the wall from behind the restraining line. If the ball does not hit above the line, no score is counted. Whenever the ball hits the floor it may be started with a toss up to self again. Another child counts the successful volleys. A timer gives the signal "Go" and starts a stopwatch. At the end of twenty seconds he signals "Stop." Two trials are given, and the highest score is recorded.

Serving test

A volleyball court is marked as in the diagram. The numbers are the point value for each area. The child serves the ball from behind the end line attempting to put the ball into the highest scoring area. He is given ten trials. His score is the total of the ten trials. It is wise to make a diagram of the court on cards and have one child record where each hit landed on a separate card for each child. Later a tally of the scores can be made.

SUGGESTED REFERENCES
FOR FURTHER STUDY

American Association for Health, Physical Education, and Recreation, *Skills Test Manual* (Washington, D.C. The Association). Manual available for each sport.

Barnes, Mildred, Margaret Fox, Pauline Loeffler, and M. Gladys Scott, *Sports Activities for Girls and Women* (New York, Appleton-Century-Crofts, 1966).

Blake, O. William, and Anne M. Volp, *Lead-up Games to Team Sports* (Englewood Cliffs, N.J., Prentice-Hall, 1964).

American Association for Health, Physical Education, and Recreation, Division for Girls' and Women's Sports, *Basketball Guide* (Washington, D.C., current year).

————, *Soccer-Speedball Guide* (Washington, D.C., current year).

————, *Softball Guide* (Washington, D.C., current year).

————, *Volleyball Guide* (Washington, D.C., current year).

Gromback, John V., *Touch Football* (New York, Ronald, 1958).

Lavega, Robert, *Volleyball* (New York, Ronald, 1960).

Miller, Kenneth, ed., *Physical Education Activities* (Dubuque, Iowa, Wm. C. Brown, 1966).

National Federation of State High School Athletic Associations, *Basketball Rules* (Chicago, current year).

————, *Football Rules* (Chicago, current year).

Porter, Lorena, "Volleyball for Classroom Teachers," *Volleyball Guide 1963–1965* (Washington, D.C., American Association for Health, Physical Education, and Recreation, D.G.W.S.), p. 36.

Schurr, Evelyn L., "Developing Basketball Skills in Elementary Grades," *Basketball Guide 1964–1965* (Washington, D.C., American Association for Health, Physical Education, and Recreation, D.G.W.S.), p. 19.

————, "A Suggested Volleyball Unit for the Fourth Grade," *Volleyball Guide, 1965–1967* (Washington, D.C., American Association for Health, Physical Education and Recreation, D.G.W.S.), p. 48.

Trotter, Betty Jane, *Volleyball for Girls and Women* (New York, Ronald, 1965).

Chapter XIII

SKILLS AND LEAD-UP GAMES FOR INDIVIDUAL SPORTS

Badminton activities

Badminton skills

Tennis activities

Tennis skills

Track and field activities

As children grow older their interest in individual and dual sports increases. Most leisure activities of youth and adults are those in which only a few people participate at one time. Some of the individual and dual games suggested in Chapter II continue to be favorites at all ages. There are a few individual sports which children can learn progressively through lead-up games which modify equipment and size of court, but utilize skill patterns of the official game in the same manner as those of the parent sport. Those which do not require extensive space and expensive equipment are the racket games of badminton and tennis. The skills and lead-up games for these two sports should be taught in class and offered as activities in the intramural program starting in the sixth grade.

Track and field is categorized as an individual sport because all of the events, with the exception of relays, are individual in nature. Track and field is fast becoming a popular sport in America; due in part to the success of the United States team in the Olympic Games.

BADMINTON ACTIVITIES

Badminton is becoming a very popular recreational sport. It is a demanding, fast, vigorous sport for the experts, yet beginners can learn the basic
skills quickly. Many families own badminton equipment and set up courts
inexpensively in their backyards and driveways. Boys and girls enjoy
playing this game together.

The long-handled badminton racket is difficult for some young players to control. The game of paddle badminton (or aerial darts) utilizes
wooden paddles and the same size court and the same rules as badminton. The handles of the paddles are shorter than in badminton and therefore easier for beginners to control.

There are commercially marketed aerial dart paddles and aerial
darts. The latter are shuttlecocks made with a sponge-rubber base and
heavier feathers than a regular shuttlecock. The heavier dart or outdoor

Table 13-1. Progression of Skills, Knowledges, Rules, and Lead-Up Games
for Badminton

Skills	*Knowledges and Rules*	*Lead-Up Games*	*Grade*
Grip	Ready position		
Footwork	Home position		
Long serve	Service		
Underhand clear	Court areas		
Overhead clear	Scoring *		
Smash	Faults		
	Singles		
	Doubles	Modified Paddle Badminton	6
Short serve	In side		
Overhead drop	Out side		
	One hand down		
	Inning		
	Setting		
	Strategy	Paddle Badminton	7-8

* See variations in Paddle Badminton

shuttlecocks are best to use with the paddle. Paddles may be constructed
from three-ply plywood.

The basic strokes, rules, and knowledges of badminton can be learned
as early as sixth grade. These strokes can be refined and more advanced
strokes learned in the seventh and eighth grades or until regulation badminton equipment is available. The skills are described as they are performed with a paddle.

BADMINTON SKILLS

Forehand grip

This grip is used for all strokes that are received on the right hand side of the body and for the serves. The paddle is taken with the small edge upward and grasped as if shaking hands. The fingers and thumb are wrapped around the handle with a V being formed by them along the handle. The handle is gripped by the fingers and not allowed to rest in the palm of the hand.

Backhand grip

This grip is used for all strokes that are received on the left side of the body. From the forehand grip position the hand is moved one quarter of a turn to the left so that the palm is directly over the handle as one looks down on the edge of the paddle. The thumb is placed along the back of the handle in a slightly diagonal direction.

Ready position

When waiting to receive the shuttle, a player should always assume a stance facing the net, the left foot slightly ahead of right. The weight is evenly distributed and slightly forward. The paddle is held up in front of the body and pointed at the opponent. From this position one can move quickly in any direction and have the paddle ready for overhead returns.

Footwork

In badminton, quick changes of direction, a balanced position for stroking, and a return to ready position for the next shot are essential fundamentals at any learning stage. When a shuttle is received on the paddle side of the player, he must face the right sideline and, conversely for shuttles on the nonpaddle side, he must face the left sideline.

After a shot, the player should always return to the "home position," which is slightly behind and to the left of the intersection of the service court line in the center of the court. Moving into position for a stroke should be done by taking short diagonal sliding steps.

Serve

The badminton serve pattern is much like the underhand serve in volley-ball. The serve must be an underhand stroke. As it hits the shuttle, the top edge of the paddle must be at the level of the wrist, and contact with the shuttle made below the waist.

The shuttle is held by the feathers with the thumb and forefinger well out in front of the body and slightly above knee height. The wrist is cocked, and the paddle is held against the shuttle. The arm is swung back so that the paddle extends backward at hip height. It is then brought forward forcibly, with the wrist uncocked and whipped into the shuttle just as it is contacted. The shuttle is dropped as the forward swing is started. The weight is shifted to the back foot with the start of the back-swing and forward as the body leans into the hit. The follow-through is high and toward the desired line of flight.

Whether it is intended for the serve to be long or short, the stance and backswing are the same. For a short serve the speed of the paddle is checked on the forward swing just before contact with the shuttle is made. The wrist is not uncocked with great force but the shuttle is stroked gently with the uncocking wrist stopping at the point of contact. Very little follow-through is employed.

COMMON FAULTS:
1. Dropping shuttle too soon.
2. Dropping shuttle too close to the body.
3. Full arm-swing with paddle brought too high in back of body.
4. Failing to cock wrist fully on backswing.
5. Failing to use whip action of wrist.
6. Using too much body rotation which results in pushing shuttle rather than hitting it.
7. Using too much upward follow-through on the short serve which causes shuttle to go too high.

KEY TEACHING PHRASES:
1. Hold shuttle by feathers.
2. Eyes on shuttle.
3. Take a semi-crouched position, knees bent, upper body forward, shuttle and paddle well below waist level.
4. Swing back, drop shuttle, swing forward, whip, and hit.
5. Follow shuttle with paddle.

Underhand clear

This is a defensive shot to hit shuttles that cannot be hit with a downward stroke. The bird should be hit high and deep into the court so that the player has a chance to return to home position. The mechanics of the stroke are the same as those of the serve, the only exception being that the bird is often hit when it is at a point above the waist, and the stroke may be taken on either the forehand or backhand side.

Overhand clear

The pattern for all of the overhand strokes is much like that of the overhand throw. This similarity should be pointed out to the students. The overhand clear may be taken on either the forehand or backhand side. The paddle is brought back behind the head with the wrist cocked and the elbow bent and well away from the body. The forward, upward swing starts with the elbow leading. The arm whips through with a full extension of the elbow, and the wrist is whipped forward as the bird is contacted at a point high above the head. The weight is carried forward and the follow-through is forward and upward toward a point on the ceiling beyond midway back in the opponent's court. The overhand clear drives the opponent deep into his court to return the shuttle.

COMMON FAULTS:
1. Failing to turn side toward the net.
2. Failing to cock wrist fully on backswing so that wrist may whip the paddle into the shuttle.
3. Contacting shuttle too low with paddle face closed too far. Shuttle flies short and low and often becomes a setup for a smash.

KEY TEACHING PHRASES:
1. Eyes on shuttle.
2. Swing back and hit all in one motion.
3. Elbow leads forward swing.
4. Reach for shuttle.
5. Follow through toward the ceiling.

Smash

The mechanics of the smash are the same as those of the overhand clear, but the shuttle is contacted high and well in front of the body with the paddle face downward. The follow-through is downward and diagonally across the body. The path of the shuttle is sharply downward, and it should just clear the net. The smash is used as an offensive stroke since it is very difficult to return due to the speed of the shuttle and the sharp angle of flight.

COMMON FAULTS:
1. Contacting shuttle too close to body with paddle face open causing too much height in return shot.
2. Contacting shuttle too low with elbow bent causing shuttle to go into net.

KEY TEACHING PHRASES:
1. Eyes on shuttle.
2. Reach high and contact shuttle in front of body.
3. Bring paddle down on shuttle.

Overhead drop

The mechanics of the overhead drop are the same as those for the smash except that the speed of the forward swing is checked just before the shuttle is contacted and the wrist uncocks slowly and stops when it is in line with the arm. There is little or no follow-through. The drop shot is used to catch off guard the player who is deep in the rear court. It is a good change-of-pace stroke mixed with clears and smashes. Since all of the preparatory motions and the start of the forward swing are the same for all three strokes, the use of the drop can be very deceptive.

General concepts students should learn about badminton play

1. Fingers should be used to hold paddle, not palm of hand.
2. Use wrist action with all strokes.
3. Turn side toward net for all forehand and backhand shots.
4. Use sliding steps to get into position to hit shuttle.
5. Always return to "home position" after a stroke and assume "ready position."
6. Any stroke hit in a downward manner is an offensive stroke. Any stroke hit in an upward manner is a defensive stroke.
7. Reach for the shuttle and step into the hit.
8. Keep opponent on the defensive by using various shots and by placing shots up, back, and to one side or the other in different order.
9. Vary use of long and short serves to keep opponent off guard.

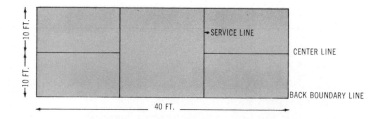

Figure 13-1. Paddle Badminton.

PADDLE BADMINTON (Figure 13-1)

AREA: Court 20 feet by 44 feet marked as in diagram. Net 5 feet high.

PLAYERS: Singles—two players, one on each side of court; doubles—four, two on each side of court. The side having the right to serve is the "in side," and the receiving side is the "out side."

PROCEDURE:
1. The game is started by a serve from the right side of the court.
2. The serve must go diagonally into the opponent's serving court.
3. The shuttle must be hit before it touches the ground.
4. Play continues with the shuttle being hit back and forth over the net until a fault is committed.

SINGLES PLAY: The serve starts from the right court when the server's score is 0 or an even number of points, and from the left court when the server's score is an odd number. A person alternates courts after each point is scored and continues to serve until the in side makes a fault at which time "service over" is called, no points are scored, and the receiver becomes the server.

DOUBLES PLAY: When a fault is committed by the in side when the first server is serving, "second service" is called, and no point is scored. The partner of the first server becomes the server. When one of the partners has served it is called "one hand down." When both partners have served or both hands are down, an inning is declared, and the serve changes sides. Whenever a side becomes a serving side, the partner on the right-hand side serves first. The side serving first in the game has only one hand or turn of service in the first inning.

COMMON FAULTS:
1. On the serve the shuttle must not be contacted above the server's waist. Paddle head must not be above server's hand when shuttle is contacted.
2. Shuttle must fall into proper service court.
3. Feet of server and receiver must be in respective service courts until shuttle is delivered.
4. During play the shuttle must fall within or on a boundary line and go over net.
5. Shuttle may not be carried with paddle.
6. If a shuttle hits the net and falls into the proper boundary area, it is fair.
7. The shuttle may only be contacted once by a player and only once on each side.
8. A player must not touch net or reach over the net to hit a shuttle.
9. If player completely misses a shuttle when attempting to serve, it is not a fault.

SCORING: A point may be scored only by the player on side which is serving.

GAME: Singles—11 points; doubles—15 points.
> *Setting:* If the score is tied at 9-all in singles play, the game may be set at 3 points by the player reaching 9 first. When it is tied up at 10, it may be set at 2 points. Then whoever gets 3 or 2 points respectively wins the game. If the option to set is turned down, whoever reaches 11 first wins. In a tie at 13 in a doubles game, whoever reaches 13 first may set the game at 5 points, or if it is tied at 14, the game may be set at 3 points.

VARIATIONS: The official scoring and terminology for doubles may not be advisable to introduce early in a unit. Short games of 6 or 8 points with no provision for setting are desirable in the first unit.

TENNIS ACTIVITIES

The modern game of tennis originated from the early game of handball as played by the Greeks and Romans. In the process of development of today's game several different instruments, among them a wooden paddle, were used until the racket was adopted in the early 1500's. Tennis may be played by two or four people and is enjoyed by both men and women as a recreational sport. Boys and girls can learn a modified game in which wooden paddles and a small court are used.

The long handle of the tennis racket extends the lever beyond the arm itself; consequently, more force and speed can be developed when stroking the ball with a racket. However, the longer lever is difficult to control. Short-handled wooden paddles may be used as a substitute for rackets when children and adults are learning the fundamentals of the game and when they are acquiring the strength and timing to control the longer lever. Some companies sell a short racket which is desirable because it is lighter, but it is also more expensive than the paddle.

Handball provides a beginning game where no racket at all is needed. Players learn the timing of the bounce of the ball as it rebounds off the floor and at the same time learn the basic ground stroke patterns. Ground strokes involve hitting the ball after it has bounced once. Hitting the ball against the wall provides a faster and surer method of getting the ball back to a player to hit than if a large court area were used and beginners had to rely on equally weak players to return the ball. When a beginner is hitting with his hand rather than with a racket, it seems easier for him to adjust to turning his side to the wall or the net in order to hit with greater force.

Wall paddle tennis capitalizes on the small space and the rebound from the wall to give beginners chances to hit the ball and gain confidence in their strokes before the use of the net and full court play. The same rules and strokes, with the exception of the volley, are used for this game as for paddle tennis.

The game of paddle tennis utilizes a court half the size of the tennis court. Actually, it is the same size as the paddle badminton court, page 488. The net is only 2½ feet high. The rules are the same as those for official tennis. For adults the overhand service is outlawed because of the low net. Many experienced tennis players play paddle tennis inside in the winter as a means of maintaining physical condition and a familiarity with tennis skills. Many outstanding tennis coaches advocate using wooden paddles in the teaching of elementary strokes to people of all ages.

Paddle tennis courts can easily be set up on blacktop play areas, parking lots, and in gymnasiums. The same net which is used for all beginning net games (or a rope with strips of cloth hanging from it) may be used. Ground sleeves with removable caps can be set in the blacktop or portable weighted standards may be utilized for securing the net. Regular paddles may be purchased or made from four-ply plywood. Old tennis balls or sponge-rubber balls are suitable. Paddle tennis provides an inexpensive and fascinating game for upper grade children.

TENNIS SKILLS

Ready position

While waiting for the ball, the player always assumes a position in which he faces the net, has weight evenly distributed over both feet, knees slightly bent, and weight slightly forward so he can move quickly in any direction. The racket is held with the left hand slightly below the head and the right in a forehand grip with the racket pointing at the net.

Forehand strokes

The paddle is held with the small edge of the paddle facing upward, then gripped with a handshake. There should be a V between the thumb and first finger. The fingers and thumb should be firmly wrapped around the handle and slightly separated. From the ready position the body must turn sideways to the net. The left foot steps across, and the left shoulder is then toward the net. The weight is shifted to the back foot. At the same time, the paddle is brought back horizontal to the ground. The arm should be fully extended without bending at the wrist. The paddle should be pointing to the back line of the court. All of these movements should be started as the ball crosses the net. The paddle is brought forward so the ball can be hit squarely at waist height. The ball should be out in front of the left foot toward the net so one has to reach and swing into it. The body twists, and as the right shoulder comes around, the weight is shifted forward. The wrist must be firm as the paddle contacts the ball. The stroke should be continued as though the paddle is pointing to the spot where the ball is intended to go. After the stroke is completed the player should return to ready position. The forehand stroke is used to return balls which are received on the paddle side of the body. It is the most frequently needed stroke in tennis. The flight of a forehand drive should be low, long, and hard.

COMMON FAULTS:

1. Failure to turn side toward net.
2. Getting body too close to ball so elbow must be bent and full extension of the arm is prevented.
3. Turning paddle and the wrist as ball is hit.
4. Too short a backswing and/or follow-through.
5. Opening paddle face, whereupon ball travels in an upward path over net rather than in a horizontal path.

KEY TEACHING PHRASES:

1. Shake hands with the paddle.
2. Eyes on ball.
3. Side to net.
4. Swing big!
5. Step into ball.
6. Wrist firm.
7. Twist and reach for target.
8. Back to ready position.

Backhand drive

The backhand drive is used to return balls which come to the nonpaddle side of the body. The grip changes as soon as the player realizes that the ball must be hit from the nonpaddle side. The right hand is shifted to

Table 13-2. Progression of Skills, Knowledges, Rules, and Lead-Up Games for Tennis

Skills	Knowledges and Rules	Lead-Up Games	Grade
Using hand:	Server		
Forehand stroke	Receiver		
Backhand stroke	Rally		
Serve from bounce	Scoring		
Footwork	Faults	Handball	5-6
Using paddle:	Ready position		
Forehand stroke	Ground strokes		
Backhand stroke	Faults		
Serve from bounce		Wall Paddle Tennis	6
Overhand serve	Set		
Volley	Serving rules		
	Official scoring	Paddle Tennis	7-8

the left so the V points straight down the left side of the handle. The thumb is held behind the handle to give added support when the paddle contacts the ball. The turn and footwork are the reverse of those in the forehand stroke. The player is watching the ball over the right shoulder with right side to the net. The backswing, forward swing, and follow-through are the same as in the forehand drive. Failing to turn the side squarely to the net is one of the most common faults of beginners.

The backhand appears to be a difficult shot for many players; hence many try to avoid using it and will run around the ball so they can use their forehand. The teacher should see that each player has many chances to use and practice the backhand drive.

Serve

Initially, a serve where the ball is bounced and a forehand drive stroke is employed may be used in game play. This permits use of the forehand and backhand strokes in game play and confidence and familiarity with the game before the more difficult overhand serve is introduced. The regular serve pattern is much like that of an overhand throw and should be introduced as such.

The paddle is held with the same grip as that used for the forehand drive. The left foot is placed at a 45 degree angle to the base line. The right foot is parallel to the base line. The left side is to the net with the shoulder pointing directly toward the intended path of the ball. The paddle is swung down and around and makes a loop behind the right shoulder. Then the paddle swings up until the arm is fully extended and the wrist is cocked. The wrist snaps, and the paddle smashes quickly down on the ball as it is met slightly forward of the body. The follow-through is made with the paddle continuing downward and across the left side of the body. The weight is shifted to the back foot when the ball is tossed. All of the weight is thrown into the downward stroke with the right foot being brought forward taking the weight on the follow-through.

The key to good serving is the timing of the toss-up of the ball. This should be practiced before the serve is attempted. The ball should be tossed straight up with the left hand in front of the left foot. The arm should reach high and the fingers guide the ball upward. The ball should go at least a foot higher than the height of the outstretched arm and paddle. The left arm initiates the throwing motion upward at the same time that the right arm brings the paddle downward in a continuous rhythmical pattern.

COMMON FAULTS:
1. Hitting the ball with elbow bent rather than arm fully extended.
2. Meeting ball with paddle face open due to lack of wrist action or insufficient height of toss.
3. Tossing ball too low, behind head, or too far forward.

KEY TEACHING PHRASES:
1. Stand in a forward stride position.
2. Toss ball, bring paddle down.
3. Bring paddle up fast and "crash" down on ball.
4. "Throw" paddle toward target.
5. Step forward onto right foot.

Volley

When the volley is used, the ball is hit before it touches the ground. The grip, body position, and action in the volley are similar to that of the forehand and the backhand. The major difference is in the amount of backswing and follow-through employed. A punching motion is used, with the ball being hit at a point in front of the body and directly downward if the ball is received above and near the net. Less body rotation is needed. When the ball comes directly at the player's body, he can use a backhand volley more quickly than a forehand drive. The volley is used near the net where the ball can be driven deep and/or angled so that the opponent is put on the defensive. The volley is also used when one is caught mid-court, and the ball is received above the waist and below the shoulders.

COMMON FAULTS:
1. Too much backswing, ball is hit too hard.
2. Weak grip.
3. Paddle face is open, ball gets too much loft.

KEY TEACHING PHRASES:
1. Eyes on ball.
2. Punch ball.
3. Pivot from hips.
4. Keep firm grip.

General concepts children should learn about tennis play

1. Hold paddle firmly when the ball is contacted.
2. Keep a firm wrist in all strokes except the serve where the wrist is flexed.
3. Turn side toward net for all strokes taken on either side of the body.
4. Use short sliding steps to get into position to hit the ball.
5. Reach for the ball, and hit it when it is at full reach and slightly ahead of the body.
6. Keep eyes on ball.

7. Try to place shots deep and into the corners of the opponent's court.
8. Vary placement of shots from side to side.
9. Assume ready position between shots.

Lead-up games for tennis

HANDBALL

Handball is described on pages 388–389. The principles involved in the forehand and backhand drives and footwork should be stressed when the hand is used as the implement to hit the ball.

WALL PADDLE TENNIS (Figure 13-2)

AREA: A wall space 20 feet wide and 20 feet high, and a hard surface area in front of the wall 20 feet wide and 26 feet deep is marked off. A net line is drawn on the wall 2 feet above the floor and parallel to it. A service line is drawn on the floor 13 feet from the wall and parallel to it.

PLAYERS: Two people.

PROCEDURE: Singles play Play is started by the first server standing behind the base line. He bounces the ball once and hits it at the wall within the boundary lines above the net line. The ball must rebound off the wall beyond the service line within the court boundaries. The op-

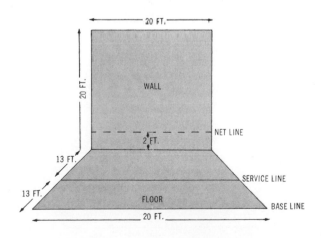

Figure 13-2. Wall Paddle Tennis.

ponent must return the ball to the wall above the net line after it
has bounced. The ball may rebound anywhere within the court
boundaries. Play continues until the ball is hit out of bounds or
fault is made. The server continues to serve until he loses it by making a fault. Only the server may score one point when the opponent
makes a fault. Game is 10 points.

VARIATION: Game may be played as doubles with four people. The serve
alternates between teams with each team having the two terms of
service.

PADDLE TENNIS (Figure 13-3)

AREA: The paddle tennis court dimensions and markings are diagramed
below. Net 2½ feet high.

PLAYERS: Singles—two people; doubles—four people.

PROCEDURE: The game is started with a serve from the right-hand court.
The ball must go into the opposite service court and be returned
after it has bounced once. It may be returned anywhere within the
court boundaries and be hit before it strikes the playing surface.
Play continues until the ball goes out-of-bounds or a fault is made. A
point is awarded to the person who did not make the fault or hit the
ball out-of-bounds. The same person continues to serve for a whole
game.

RULES:

1. *Serve:* The ball is served from behind the baseline beginning from the
right court. The serve must pass over the net and hit the ground
within the service court diagonally opposite the server. When the total
number of points is 0 or even, the serve is from the right court. When
the total number of points is odd, the serve is from the left court.

2. *Foot fault:* Server steps over the base line while serving.

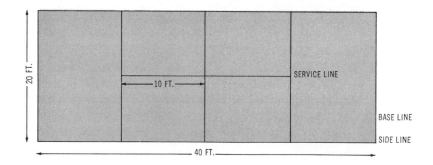

Figure 13-3. Paddle Tennis.

3. *Let service:* Ball hits the net and continues over into the service court. Another serve is allowed.
4. *Serve fault:* If ball does not land in opposite service court, and if there is a foot fault. The server is allowed two consecutive faults before a point is declared and service changes to opposite service court.
5. *Order of serve:* In singles, the serve changes sides at the end of each game. In doubles, partners alternate games when their side is to serve.
6. *Changing sides:* Players change sides of the court at the end of the first, third, and all odd games.

SCORING:
1. *Game:* Points made: 0, 1, 2, 3, 4. Terms used: love, 15, 30, 40, game.
2. *Deuce game:* Game must be won by two points; therefore, 40–40 would be deuce game.
3. *Advantage in:* Server makes first point after deuce.
4. *Advantage out:* Receiver makes the first point after deuce.
5. *Set:* Six games comprise a set. The set must be won by two games. Same principles as apply for the deuce game.

POINT AWARDED:
1. If the server makes two consecutive service faults.
2. If ball, when returned, does not land within the court or on a line.
3. If ball hits surface of court twice before it is returned.
4. If player reaches across net to return ball.

TRACK AND FIELD ACTIVITIES

Track and field activities involve the basic skills of running, jumping, and throwing. Most children love to do these activities and are excited when track and field is in season, which is usually in the spring. This is sometimes considered a team sport, since individuals usually belong to a team, and the individual wins are recorded for a team. With the exception of the relays, all the events are individual and self-testing in nature and demand that a child have ample opportunity to practice them in order to improve.

Men have competed in running, throwing, and jumping events for centuries. The relation of track and field with Greek history and the Olympic Games makes an interesting classroom study along with the unit in physical education. A meet between classes or squads may culminate a unit and be patterned after the Olympic Games.

In recent years there has been a revival of interest in track and field for both boys and girls across the United States. Many children have an opportunity to participate in track clubs and meets outside of the school.

Teaching considerations

1. Since most of the events are the basic skills of running and jumping, they are learned and performed in the primary grades but on a more informal basis. For example, the running broad jump is called Jump the Brook. Children run and jump across two lines which are moved progressively farther apart. High jumping is called High Waters. A rope is held at increasingly higher levels, and more than one child jumps over it at a time. Jumping is performed in the grass, and no pits are used.
2. Organization is important for the conduct of a track and field class. Since practice is indispensable for improvement, each child must have many opportunities to practice skills. Therefore, many stations have to be set up for small-group and individual practice. A rotation plan for squad work should be devised at the start of the unit and posted in the classroom or gym. Squads will know where they are to start work each day and where they may take out the equipment they need. The teacher may wish to introduce new skills or emphasize important coaching points to the whole class before it is split into working groups. A great deal of the teacher's time is spent moving from station to station coaching individuals.
3. Warm-up activities should precede jumping and sprint work. Light jogging, slow bending and stretching activities should be done.
4. Younger children should run on a grassy surface free from stones, sticks, and broken glass. Older boys and girls may run on a cinder or all-weather track if it is in good condition.
5. Pits filled with loose sand, sawdust, or tanbark are necessary for jumping events.
6. Good form in all events should always be stressed.
7. Times and distances should be recorded two or three times during the unit. A child can visually and mentally record his progress during daily practice.
8. No skill tests are needed because the activities are self-testing. If a meet is conducted at the end of the unit, scores recorded then may serve as an evaluation of status and, if compared with earlier scores, of progress.
9. Two wooden paddles or blocks of wood clapped together make a good starting signal.

Track events

The basic mechanics of the run are described on page 232. The modifications necessary for the various events are described in the following paragraphs.

Table 13-3. Progression for Track and Field Events

	Primary	Grade 4	Grade 5	Grade 6	Grade 7	Grade 8
Track Events						
Dashes	Informal Racing	G: 30-yd. B: 30-yd.	40-yd. 50-yd.	60-yd. 75-yd.	75-yd. 100-yd.	75-yd. 100-yd.
Distance Runs	200-yd.	G: 300-yd. B: 300-yd.	400-yc. 400-yc.	500-yd. 500-yd.	600-yd. 600-yd.	600-yd. 600-yd.
Hurdles	12-in.	G: 18-in. B: 18-in.	20-in. 20-in.	24-in. 36-in.	24-in. 36-in.	24-in. 36-in.
Field Events						
Long Jump	Standing Jump the Brook	Standing Running	Standing Running	Standing Running	Standing Running	Standing Running
High Jump	High Waters	G: Scissors B: Scissors	Scissors Roll	Roll Roll	Roll Roll	Roll Roll
Throws	Softball	G: Softball B: Softball	Softball 4-lb. shot	4-lb. shot 6-lb. shot	6-lb. shot 8-lb. shot	6-lb. shot 8-lb. shot

Dashes or sprints

The crouch start is the best method for a fast get-away in the sprints. At the signal, "Take your mark," the left or front foot is placed about ten to twelve inches behind the starting line. The right or rear foot is placed approximately next to the heel of the left foot. A comfortable position is taken with hands shoulder-width apart, fingers extended and together behind the starting line. On "Get set," the hips are raised so that the back is parallel to the ground. The body weight is balanced mostly on the hands. Caution beginners to hold still until the signal "Go!" Upon the words "Go" or the sound of the whistle, the run is started by a push off from the toes to overbalance the body weight forward. The runner keeps the body low and uses short, hard, driving steps and a powerful swing of both arms to regain balance and pick up speed. When the 30-yard mark is reached, the runner should be moving full speed. In full stride, the knees should be lifted high and brought down forcefully, the toes pointed straight forward, and the arms bent at the elbow and moved back and forth forcefully. About ten yards from the finish line the runner should lean forward slightly to initiate a final burst of speed. He should cross the finish line at top speed and run about ten yards beyond the line.

Pursuit relay

In a pursuit relay, runners run in the same direction on the straight or oval track. Teams consist of four runners each running an equal distance. It is recommended that from two to four teams compete at the same time. The first member stands at the starting line. All others are stationed at intervals of 30 or more yards around the track. Lead-off runner starts from a crouch position. The race is started in the manner as the dash. Runners run to the next position where they pass batons to respective teammates. The batons are passed within a 10- to 20-yard zone, and these zones should be on straightways rather than on the curve of the track. The receiver of the baton assumes a stance near the back line of the passing zone. On a signal from the passer, the receiver starts to run. He receives the baton with the right hand cupped with fingers spread to side of the body. He grips the baton tightly as it touches the hand. The baton is shifted to the left hand as quickly as possible after receiving it. The passer of the baton extends the left arm and reaches as far forward as possible. He holds the baton near the end. A cue is "Give the receiver the big end of the stick." The baton must be extended at the proper height for the exchange, and some pressure exerted on the hand of the receiver so that he will know the baton is there. The passer runs near the receiver and continues to run several yards beyond the place of exchange.

Shuttle relay

In a shuttle relay, runners go back and forth across the same space. The lead-off runners start from a crouch position. All the others start from a standing position with right arm extended forward at shoulder height. They must stay behind the line until touched by a runner or given a baton. Runners always pass right shoulders.

Hurdling

In the primary and intermediate grades, hurdling can be taught as a leap over the hurdle while running and not breaking the run. Emphasis should be placed on bringing the lead leg high and straight out in front of the body. Very short hurdles which fall off their supports easily should be used. They may be as simple as a thin dowel laid between two cardboard boxes, or even thin cardboard boxes.

The regular hurdle is done in the following manner. The take-off begins about three to four feet in front of the hurdle, with the lead leg kicking straight up in front of the body. At the same time the leg is kicked up, the arms are thrust forward to give more lift to the body. The lead leg stretches forward as far as possible. As the lead leg crosses the hurdle, the trailing leg is bent with the knee pointing directly to the side. The toe of the trailing leg must be raised high enough to clear the hurdle. The lead leg is brought down and touches the ground as close to the hurdle as possible. As the lead leg starts down, the trailing leg comes around and takes the first step toward the next hurdle. The faster the foot touches the ground the quicker the move toward the next hurdle. An uneven number of steps should be taken between hurdles. The first few lessons in hurdling should be conducted on the grass.

COMMON FAULTS:
1. Failure to raise lead leg high enough and keep it straight.
2. Failure to use arms to add lift.
3. Failure to bring lead leg down fast once it has crossed bar.
4. Failure to keep knee of trailing leg pointed to the side.
5. Letting foot of trailing leg drop and catch bar.
6. Failure to bring trailing leg around in order to take the first step toward the next hurdle or finish line.

Field events

The field events include jumping for distance and for height, and throwing for distance. Jumping is described in detail on p. 236. The overhand throw is described in detail on p. 257. The only new skill pattern is the shot put which is analyzed later.

Standing long jump

The jumper achieves balance and gains momentum before the jump by rocking from heel to toe. This motion serves as a preliminary wind up for the jump. A sitting position is assumed in the air with the arms and upper body reaching forward. On landing the jumper should reach forward with the hands. The measurement is taken perpendicularly from the first break in the pit (body, feet, hands) to toe mark on the take-off board.

Running long jump

A preliminary run is taken starting sixteen full strides from the take-off board. The run is fast, and the last stride is shortened to enable the jumper to adjust his center of gravity and to step flat-footed on the take-off board. A hard and flat-footed step on the take-off board should be made to gain drive and spring for the forward lift. The jump is made by pushing off vigorously and extending one or both legs, depending upon the type of jump. The arms as well as the legs should be swung upward and/or forward to gain power. When the top of the jump is reached, the jumper is in a sitting, running, or layout position in the air. Upon landing the arms are snapped back to insure forward motion. The runner should reach forward on landing.

Running high jump

The scissors jump. An approach of six to eight steps is taken from a 45-degree angle to the jumping bar. The run is easy, and the last stride is usually lengthened to give more room for an upward swing of the leg. The take-off is made from the outside foot. The inside leg is kicked up in front of the body and forward over the bar. The spring is achieved from the take-off foot, the lift of the arms, and the vigorous upward swing of the inside foot. The landing is made on the lead leg. The take-off must be made very close to the bar. Practice may be initiated by jumping over a pole or line on the floor.

The modified western roll or straddle roll. The approach is slower than that for a scissors jump. The take-off is begun about an arm's length from the bar by kicking the outside leg high and toward the bar. The push-off is made from the foot nearest the bar (inside foot) when the center of gravity is directly over the take-off foot. The swing of the outside leg should turn the body so that the abdomen and chest face the bar at the height of the jump. The take-off leg is rolled over the bar. The landing is made on the lead leg and both hands.

Throw for distance

Most often a softball throw for distance is included in an elementary school track and field unit. An overhand throw pattern is used. A running approach is taken from behind the restraining line. The approach adds more momentum to the throw.

Shot put

Four- to eight-pound shots may be used from the fifth grade on. The shot is pushed rather than thrown. The shot is held in the right hand at the base of the three middle fingers and is balanced on the side by the thumb and little finger. The elbow is bent and away from the body. The shot is rested against the neck and collar bone and is nestled into the side of the chin. The thrower stands with his left side to the intended target. The feet are spread about shoulder width apart with the weight on the right foot. The left leg is swung across the body and then forward. A short hop is taken with the right foot and as the left foot hits the ground, the body rotates forward. The right arm pushes the shot forward with the body until the body weight is over the left foot. The elbow is straightened, and wrist and fingers extend to propel the shot forward and upward. The left leg and arm swing on around, and all of the body weight is taken on the left foot.

COMMON FAULTS:
1. Throwing the shot rather than pushing it.
2. Failure to keep sustained movement of the whole body until shot has been released.

KEY TEACHING PHRASES:
1. Rest shot in hand at base of fingers. Balance it with the thumb.
2. Tuck shot into neck.
3. Elbow bent and away from the body.
4. Swing left leg across body then forward.
5. Hop on right foot.
6. As left foot hits ground twist body.
7. Push shot forward and upward.
8. Follow around with left leg and arm. Take weight on left foot.

Track and field meets

A basic format is followed whether a track meet is organized within a class, between classes, or for the whole school. There are several factors that must be considered.
1. *Events:* The events for the class meet should be those which the class has practiced throughout the unit. If several classes are participating it is wise to include dashes, a relay event, running long jump, high jump, and a throw for distance.

2. *Teams:* A class may be divided by squads, color teams or teams named for various countries if it is called an Olympic Games meet.

3. *Competition:* Boys compete against boys, and girls against girls, except in the relays where teams are mixed. A boy from one team runs at the same position as boys from other teams. For each event there will be places for winners for boys and for girls with the exception of in the relays.

4. *Participation:* A limit is usually set on how many events one person may enter. Everyone may be in the relays and in two individual events. Each team may be required to enter two contestants in each event. The number in the meet sometimes dictates how this must be done. A child may enter the events he choses, or the teams as a whole may decide who will be best in what events.

5. *Scoring:*

   First place—5 points—blue ribbon
   Second place—4 points—red ribbon
   Third place—3 points—white ribbon
   Fourth place—2 points—yellow ribbon
   Fifth place—1 point—green ribbon

   Color of ribbons have been designated if one wishes to award cloth or paper ribbons to winners. A card describing the event and place won may also be given as recognition of achievement.

6. *Planning the meet:* Plans must be made for participants to sign for events ahead of the meet. Once they have signed, the children can practice in earnest. Score sheets can be drawn up, and a time schedule with names of participants can be made and posted ahead of the meet. Judges must be secured to time running events and conduct and measure the jumping events. One starter starts all running events.

7. *Conducting the meet:* The referee is in charge of the meet. This may be the teacher in the class. He should read the events and the names of students who compete in them. The students also should know where they go for each event, and what to do when they have finished. The relays usually climax the meet. If a child is to be in a running event and a field event at the same time, he goes to the running event first. Field events usually take longer to conclude than running events. If there are fewer running lanes than there are people entered in the dash, there will have to be several heats. Only winners and runners-up of each heat participate in the final dash events.

   Jumping events take a long time to complete. A minimum jumping height based on class records may be set as a qualification for entering a jumping event. In the high jump each participant is allowed three trials at each height. Should a tie occur, the person with the least number of misses for all trials is declared the winner. In all other jumping events three trials are given, and the one with the longest jump wins.

Scores should be reported to a master scorer as soon as events are completed so that a running score may be kept and the results of the meet announced immediately after the last event. Scores and winners should be posted on the bulletin board as soon after the meet as possible.

SUGGESTED REFERENCES
FOR FURTHER STUDY

Ainsworth, Dorothy, ed., *Individual Sports for Women* (Philadelphia, Saunders, 1963).

Athletic Institute, *Track and Field for Elementary School Children and Junior High Girls* (Chicago, The Institute).

Bresnahan, George, W. W. Tuttle, and Francis Cretzmeyer, *Track and Field Athletics* (St. Louis, Mosby, 1960).

Davidson, Kenneth, and L. R. Gustafson, *Winning Badminton* (New York, Ronald, 1953).

Division for Girls' and Women's Athletics, *Tennis and Badminton Guide* (Washington, D.C., American Association for Health, Physical Education and Recreation, current year).

Division for Girls' and Women's Athletics, *Track and Field Guide* (Washington, D.C., American Association for Health, Physical Education and Recreation, current year).

Murphy, Bill, and Chet Murphy, *Tennis Handbook* (New York, Ronald, 1962).

Chapter XIV
GYMNASTICS

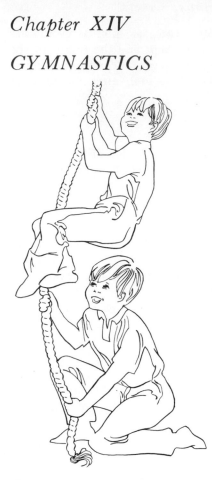

Suggestions for teaching gymnastic activities

Developmental stunts and exercises

Tumbling

Apparatus

Small equipment

Suggested progression for an elementary school program

Developmental exercises, stunts, tumbling, and activities utilizing small equipment and large apparatus are the activities in the gymnastic area. These types of activities provide a setting for basic body actions where the elements of strength, flexibility, agility, power, muscle endurance, and balance can be developed in a specific manner. The highly individualized learning situation also helps to develop determination, perseverance, courage, and self-confidence.

Children enjoy these activities since they involve the natural movements of jumping, climbing, hanging, rolling, twisting, and turning that figure in the young child's play. A youngster, motivated to master a particular exercise or stunt, must rely on his own powers and efforts to overcome specific obstacles, such as height, time, force, or space. Although he may have to work hard to succeed, the satisfaction gained will motivate him to approach problems of even greater difficulty.

Gymnastics affords the best medium of all physical education activities by which to develop the muscles of the thorax, shoulder girdle, and arms, and flexibility in specific joint areas. Most other activities are performed with the feet as the base supporting the body weight. Isolated muscle groups or joints can be given special work loads and tasks to perform in order to correct weaknesses or deficiencies.

As in all of the activity areas, the emphasis in the primary grades is on children exploring, experimenting, learning, and adapting to a wide variety of challenges, problems, and different types of equipment. Experiences have to be planned which present progressively difficult situations. The experiences provide the child with a chance to become familiar with many new positions and new pieces of small and large apparatus. Perfection and style in performance should not be demanded, but encouragement to do things well is always important. A knowledge of the wide variety of individual differences and stages of maturity of primary grade children gives the teacher a basis for his expectations of performance.

While still in the primary grades, children should be learning the body movements fundamental to all aspects of gymnastics; in addition they should enjoy the physical and social values of the exercise. Basic to almost all gymnastics work are the fundamentals of jumping, landing, supporting weight on hands, transferring weight, hanging, curling, flight, rolling, and extension. All of these can be first learned and practiced on the floor or in relation to apparatus that fits the size of the youngsters.

In the intermediate grades more specific tasks are set, and greater demands made for control and quality of performance according to each child's abilities. More time must be devoted to the perfecting of skills in order to master the fundamentals necessary for more complex tumbling and apparatus work which is undertaken at the junior and senior high school level.

One vital phase of both floor and apparatus work is the development of a coordinated sequence of movements or routines. Gymnastics routines may be compared to compositions in dance which challenge both creative and physical efforts.

In the upper grades, exploration and experimentation give way to acquisition and practice of definite movement patterns needed for safe and skilled performance in specific gymnastic activities. Exploration and experimentation have built confidence, understanding, and control in the various basic movements.

SUGGESTIONS FOR TEACHING GYMNASTIC ACTIVITIES

Method

An exploratory approach provides the most stimulating learning process for a primary child. When teaching fundamentals, the teacher provides a variety of situations in which he sets a task to be done in the form of responsibility for or a challenge to a personal spontaneous solution. He may need to give leading suggestions, pose pertinent questions, and/or ask for changes in execution. Basic principles necessary to fundamental learning may be isolated before class activity starts and then implemented in experimentation and in practice.

In this chapter (p. 544) suggestions for problems and challenges for ball-handling skills are given as an example of an indirect approach to individual work in the primary grades. When specific patterns are to be learned and practiced, observation must be made of correct procedure gained through guided experimentation. All answers or solutions to a teacher-set problem may not be correct. If a sequential progression to a specific stunt is being developed, proper procedure must be learned. Consequently, a problem-solving or a direct approach is most often more productive and efficient in intermediate or upper grade activities. The teacher can select those whose solution to the problem was correct to demonstrate for others. Discussion and evaluation of the problem are followed by further practice and refinement.

The lesson

Each lesson should allow for light warmup work for the individual or for the group. Generally, the first part of the lesson should be teacher-directed; new skills are introduced and problems are solved by the group. The last part should be devoted to individual practice, problem-solving, or work on routines. During this time the teacher should give individual help. The period may end with a "show off" time. Perhaps one or two children at each station (if small-group work is being done) may be selected by their group or by the teacher to demonstrate whatever was studied during the period. If routines were to be developed, these are presented.

Achievement charts

Young children are interested in performing and competing with others, but only for a short period. They enjoy instant challenges. Older children usually respond to achievement charts (individual or group) when a definite series of skills or patterns are to be learned. The child may check off his own skill when it is completed, or the teacher may do it in the process of evaluation. In every case, the standard and procedure for checking should be clearly established at the onset of the unit. The chart should contain some stunts which are easy enough for everyone to complete and

Table 14-1. Squad Achievement Chart for Apparatus

SQUAD_____	PARALLEL BARS					HORIZONTAL BARS					BALANCE BEAM				VAULTING BOX			
Names	Straight-arm support	Support swing	Hand walk	Riding seat	Routine	Double knee hang	Single knee hang	Pull over	Number of chins	Front scale	Knee scale	Straddle mount	Routine	Knee mount	Courage dismount	Squat vault	Flank vault

some that are a challenge to the most highly skilled. Adequate time should be allowed to practice and to check off patterns listed on the achievement chart (Table 14-1).

Development of skills

Floor work

In the primary grades, work with the basic movement skills in relation to the factors that affect movement (space, time, form, pattern, flow of movement, and the various body actions) establishes the foundation of gymnastics. It is difficult to say when one is working in the area of basic movement or gymnastics. At the same time that skills and control of the body are being developed, so are the physical elements of strength, flexibility, agility, and balance which are basic to future gymnastic work.

A tumbling skill is traced here as it developed from early basic movement work.

BASIC MOVEMENT SEQUENCE:

1. Walk about the room, stop and take your body weight on your hands; walk and stop, take weight on hands. Run and take weight on hands.
2. Skip and take weight on hands (hoops may be scattered on floor and hands put in hoops when weight is taken).
3. Skip and take weight on your hands, flutter your feet in the air. Repeat. Flutter higher.
4. Skip about room; change weight from feet to one hand, then the other (but not both at the same time).
5. Move about the room changing weight from hands to feet stretching your body as you change.
6. Move about the room changing weight from hands to feet; twist as you go so that feet come down in a different place.
7. (Rope is stretched about 8 inches off floor.) Run alongside rope; take weight on hands on other side of rope, and land on feet on other side.
8. Run on and change to other side in same manner.
9. Take weight on one hand, then the other; land on one foot, then the other.
10. Turn body as you go over rope. Repeat, stretching leg out high above you.
11. Repeat this action down the length of the rope. Do this without the rope and it is a cartwheel.

(This all would not be done in one day but over a length of time; these are only the major tasks around which the teacher can develop the sequences.) Shoulder strength will be built from the support. Placement of whole hand flat on the floor with fingers pointing in line with the shoulders should be stressed. This series develops the cartwheel, the round off, and the other more advanced tumbling skills where weight must be taken on hands, body turned in air, where there is a return to floor, and an immediate movement into another pattern undertaken.

A series of activities which develop agility and leads to future vaulting techniques and stunts while in the air is traced.

1. Run and take off with two feet, and land on two feet. (Emphasize good landing techniques.)
2. Run, jump from two feet, land on two feet, take another jump.
3. Run, jump from two feet, land on two feet, do a roll (encourage performing different types of rolls), and stand up.
4. Run, take off from one foot, land on two feet.
5. Run, take off on one foot, land on two feet, and jump again onto two feet.
6. Run, jump, curl body while in air, and land with a double jump.
7. Run, stretch body in air, land with double jump.
8. Run, twist in the air, land with a double jump.
9. Run, jump, make a different shape in the air, land with a two-foot jump.

(These can be done over a period of time. Jumps can be made free or over an outstretched rope which is laying on the floor or held at various heights from floor.)

From here the child is ready to jump on or over or off apparatus and be able to make various body shapes while in the air. If hand support work has been done on the floor at the same time, enough strength and feeling for vaulting will have been developed. Vaulting is going over or onto an object by a run, a jump, and use of the hands on the object as a support to push off and over the object.

Many stunts done on the apparatus are done in similar fashion on the floor in order to learn the pattern and to obtain body control while the body is close to the ground and in a stable position. For example: the V sit (p. 525), single leg circles (p. 525), front scale (p. 525), upspring (p. 525) on the floor which becomes the courage vault (p. 542) off a box.

Small equipment

Working with all types of small equipment develops the child's manipulative abilities, his creativity and ingenuity, and his ability to use his body in relation to other objects. As the child works with various sizes of balls, paddles, and other objects, he becomes familiar with them and learns to adjust his movements according to the length and weight of the tools. He is laying a foundation for acquisition of skills requiring specific sport and work tools.

The pattern of work with small equipment should be as follows:

1. Orientation to the equipment and exploratory activities.
2. Development of specific skills through problems and challenges.
3. Self-testing activities designed for practice and refinement of skills.
4. Creative routines or sequences of activity.

As children grow older and become more skilled, their interests change, and work with small apparatus becomes more specific to particular sports. Objectives in ball-handling units become more specific as to acquisition of skills related to sports and precede or accompany work with lead-up games. The majority of work with small equipment is done in the first four grades.

Apparatus

Children should work with large apparatus which has been scaled to their size. Many manufacturers have developed pieces of apparatus for the elementary student, and they have safe, stable, relatively inexpensive, and easily stored models of regular apparatus. Many of these pieces can be made by workers in school shops, maintenance men, or parents. The first approach to the apparatus should be exploratory; children will find many ways in which to use different pieces. Then the teacher should emphasize the various safe ways to get on and off each piece (mounting and dismounting). Concurrently, each lesson should involve going over the equipment, going under, through, along, above, across, and various combinations of these. Work such as this should produce safe, and satisfying activity for each youngster, since no specific patterns are demanded, and each can work at his own level of skill and strength. Gradually, more tasks are set up which require body actions to be modified by the factors of space, force, time, flow, and shape. Later, more specific actions are required in which proper execution and form require personal adjustments and practice.

Routines

Assignments are then made to develop a routine or a sequence in which specific movement pattern are used. The teacher sets up the general requirements of the routine allowing each child to choose a variety of movements and positions to be performed with continuity. The movement patterns must first be learned and practiced, then put together in a creative effort by the child. The child should start all routines, no matter how simple, in a good, erect, standing position, and end them in a good, erect, balanced, standing position. Intermediate and upper grade children should be taught to perform in good form, which means they must have good body control throughout the routine. They should strive for good posture and head position, point toes, hold arms and legs in position (rather than let them dangle loosely), and control the body in an easy landing position. Neither the pattern nor the routine need be complex when the children are first encouraged to become conscious of good form.

The values of individual routines are numerous, since the child has a specific goal. Individual work and practice is necessary and creative thinking and movement are encouraged. Every youngster likes to perform when he has mastered something and knows that he is demonstrating his skill in a warm, permissive, and accepting atmosphere. From observation of performances of others, children become critical thinkers and discover ideas which can be applied to their own problems. While children are doing their routines, the teacher has an opportunity to evaluate his own planning and teaching methods, as well as the students' achievements.

Suggested routine requirements

FLOOR WORK

REQUIREMENTS	POSSIBLE CHOICE OF MOVEMENTS
A. 1. Forward locomotor movement	1. Run
2. Rotary movement	2. Forward roll to 2 feet
3. A jump turn	3. Jump and make 180 degree turn in air to
4. Low landing	4. a squat landing.
B. 1. Balance in a 2-point contact position	1. Frog stand
2. Show strength of shoulder girdle while moving	2. Seal walk
3. Balance low on a one point contact position	3. V sit
C. 1. An inverted sideward movement	1. Cartwheel
2. Two rolls	2. Forward rolls
3. Flight	3. Straddle leap
4. Inverted hand support	4. Handstand
5. One leg balance	5. Scale
6. Flexibility-movement (spine)	6. Twist into a
7. Roll	7. backward roll
8. Feet locomotor movement	8. Run
9. Flight	9. Leap
10. High landing	10. Extended jump to land.
D. 1. Fast movement to a position for shoulder strength movement	1. (Fill in the blanks after reading further)

2. 2 rolls followed	2. _____
3. by inverted position, hold	3. _____
4. fast full extended position to	4. _____
5. a low passive position	5. _____
6. Movements requiring abdominal strength	6. _____
7. Spring up into a	7. _____
8. rotary motion sideward	8. _____
9. Balanced landing	9. _____

E. Balance Beam

1. Mount from standing position	1. Crotch seat
2. Travel with uneven movement on beam	2. Skip
3. One foot balance position	3. Front scale
4. Dismount with a turn	4. Jump, half turn in air.

Organization

Since one of the greatest values of gymnastic activities is that they require individual efforts, the class and equipment must be organized so that each person has an opportunity to be active throughout the class period. Unless mats and apparatus are used and unless there is not enough small equipment for each child, everyone can be working in his own space and at the same time. Whenever small groups are doing different things, the class will have to be evenly distributed in groups and assigned to work at stations. Children may be divided into squads or groups by size, ability, or at random. Regular squads facilitate handling equipment and moving from station to station.

Directions on problems should be given verbally to each squad or written on a card which is left at each station. The directions should be very simply stated, for instance:

1. Balance beam: Move across beam, changing levels as you go.
2. Vaulting box: Mount, change body shape, dismount.
3. Low bar: Hang from four points of support, change to two and back to four, dismount.

If the directions are the same for all stations, they could more easily be given verbally. In this case, children would try to do the same type of activity at each station to which they rotate; for example, the teacher might direct, "Stretch and curl on the apparatus then make a light landing."

If there are only one or two mats, other stations should be set up where activities are performed which do not require mats. Mats are needed for activities which involve inverted positions where the weight is taken on the head, hands, or feet; they are needed for a landing with great force or with forward momentum; and they are required under and around apparatus pieces where one does inverted activities or other activities at heights. For example, although a mat is not needed for a 6-inch balance beam, it is needed for a 30-inch beam. When the teacher feels he must supervise work at a specific piece of large apparatus because the activity is new or requires his help, he should plan other stations at which the children can work without supervision.

If mats alone are being used, they should be arranged so that the teacher is able to see everyone with one glance. If the room is small and mats must be close together, traffic patterns should be established so that a child coming off the end of one mat does not collide with one coming off an adjacent mat. Primary and intermediate children can usually use the width of the mat rather than the length; therefore, everyone is able to have a greater number of turns rather than having to wait in line for a long period of time.

Vary the type of activity children perform on either the apparatus or in floor work. Use an interval method of working or change the pace often. After a supportive exercise, change to running. From work in an inverted position change to an erect position; from flowing to a sustained movement; from work in prone position change to an erect moving position. Squads should be allowed to work at each station long enough so that each person has several opportunities to improve his skill. There is no value in rotating each squad to each station every day gymnastics is scheduled. It is better to be at half the stations one day and at half the next session. A rotation chart can be made and put on the board so children know exactly where they are to go and can begin work immediately. In this way they will also realize that everyone has an equal amount of time to work at each station.

A layout for activity stations and an organization plan for rotation of squads is presented for small-group work both with large apparatus and small equipment. Since each squad works at two stations during each period, it takes three lessons to complete the circuit. Then the order is repeated.

Safety considerations

Common sense and logical procedures should eliminate the major safety hazards in tumbling work and work on apparatus. Too often one of the greatest dangers results from the attitude of the teacher. If the teacher

1. ZIGZAG FOOT DRIBBLE
2. HOOPS
3. LONG JUMP

4. BALLS (TARGET PRACTICE)
5. LONG JUMP ROPES
6. WANDS

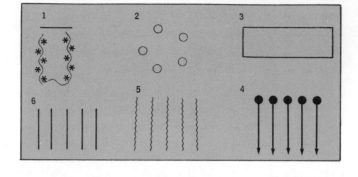

APPARATUS STATIONS

1. MAT WORK
2. HORIZONTAL BAR
3. VAULTING BOX

4. PARALLEL BARS
5. BALANCE BEAM
6. HANGING ROPES

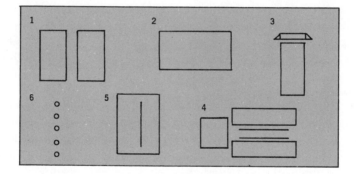

ROTATION PLAN

SQUAD	LESSON 1 STATION	LESSON 2 STATION	LESSON 3 STATION
1	1 & 2	3 & 4	5 & 6
2	3 & 4	5 & 6	1 & 2
3	5 & 6	1 & 2	3 & 4
4	2 & 1	4 & 3	6 & 5
5	4 & 3	6 & 5	2 & 1
6	6 & 5	2 & 1	4 & 3

Figure 14-1. Layout of Activity Stations and Organizational Plan for Small Group Work.

had little experience in his own school years or is not sure of what he is doing, he tends to be apprehensive and overcautious. Care must be taken so that his anxiety is not transferred to the children. Proper planning and observance of the following procedures can eliminate this situation.

1. Equipment should be of good quality and inspected regularly for faulty mechanics or broken parts.
2. Equipment should be placed so that adequate space surrounds each piece so that collisions may be avoided.
3. A traffic-flow plan should be established so that no one will accidentally swing or walk into the path of another performer.
4. Use mats where performer will be landing with great force from high places or will be performing in inverted positions on high pieces.
5. Set limits of how many people can work safely on the apparatus at one time for the specific types of activities.
6. Organize class so that the working groups are small enough for children to be involved in doing, assisting, or watching the stunt. If children must stand in long lines and await turns, they become restless. Frequently they become boisterous, and distract the performer.
7. Follow a careful plan of progression from simple to complex activities so that children are not required to perform skills which are too difficult for them to do well. Individual differences must be observed; consequently flexibility in the plan of progression is necessary.
8. Select activities according to the class member's strength, flexibility, and endurance. If a student cannot support his weight on the parallel bars, he can hardly be expected to walk on his hands across the bars.
9. Allow time for light warm-up activities at the start of class. A brief period of time should be spent warming-up whenever exercises or stunts that call for intensive muscular effort are to be undertaken. In the primary grades, there is little need for warm-ups, since the beginning activities themselves can serve as the warm-ups. Activities or exercises selected should be done rhythmically, slowly, and should include stretching, swinging, and light endurance movements. Warm-ups may be done as a group, or each child may do his own series as soon as he comes in the gym. Practice of previously learned stunts may suffice, if these stunts do not make excessive physical demands. The teacher may ask to see various body movements with no set formal pattern; however, careful observation needs to be made so that each child is doing something that fulfills the intended purpose of the warm-up period.
10. Avoid activities requiring hyperextension of and excessive strains on the ligaments and muscles surrounding the knee joints such as, knee walking, knee dips, sudden full-knee bends.
11. If activities at one station are new or are very demanding at the initial stages, the teacher should plan to work with children at that par-

ticular station. He should plan activities at other stations so that little supervision is needed.

12. Place pieces of apparatus in positions so that the rotation plan may operate in such a manner that children will not be required to do stunts requiring use of the same body parts at subsequent stations. Note in Figure 14-2, the order is such that demands are made on various muscle groups in a balanced fashion.

13. Children should not be forced to do things when they are obviously frightened and display tension. Instead, they should be given alternate assignments which will increase their readiness and bolster their confidence. This does not mean they should be excused when they show disinterest. It should be made clear that their alternate assignment will help prepare them for what they are hesitant to do. Most children will operate in a conscientious manner and not overextend themselves until they are quite confident.

14. Teach children to "spot" or assist others in work on apparatus or in some tumbling stunts. "Spotting" means knowing what the other person is going to do, watching him, and being ready to assist him by helping him catch his balance, break a fall, or giving momentary support while he catches himself. It does not mean lifting or catching. Children should not be expected to catch or lift a weight greater than their own. In regard to spotting, the following should be kept in mind:

a. *Activities in which there is potential danger to the head, such as rolls and dives.* Place hand between head and the surface it may touch. Just the motion of putting the hand there in the early stages of learning will sometimes cause the performer to tuck the head closer to the chest.

b. *Activities on balance beam.* Walk alongside the beam with one hand upraised so performer *may* reach out and grasp hand in order to steady himself. If a child is particularly tense, just the pressure of the fingertips will be assuring to him and will relieve tension somewhat.

c. *Activities where weight is supported on hands.* Grasp the wrist with one hand and just above the elbow with the other. This prevents the arm from collapsing and prevents a possible hard fall.

d. *Activities in inverted position where legs may overswing, such as a headstand or handstand.* Extend arms straight out so forward swing of legs will be checked. Legs may be pushed and child told to bend knees and go down.

These are just a few suggestions and by no means the only spotting methods that may be employed. However, they should be sufficient for most beginning activities.

15. Teach children how to land properly and how to break a fall in case

of an error. The principles of absorption of force should be reemphasized.

    a. Land on large padded areas of body. Avoid landing on outstretched hands. Tuck head.

    b. Absorb weight over a longer period of time by rolling upon contact with floor.

16. When hanging on bars, a grip should be used whereby the fingers are wrapped around the bar in one direction, and the thumb in the other (Figure 14-2). This offers a check if hands momentarily slip.

17. Children should wear clothing which will not inhibit their movements or distract their attention. Girls should wear shorts for gymnastic activities. All objects should be removed from pockets and left in the classroom.

Mechanical principles basic to gymnastic activities

There are a few mechanical principles operative in gymnastic activities which the teacher should recognize as essential to safe and efficient performance. Since most stunts, tumbling, and apparatus are dependent upon the proper control of balance, rotary motion, and force, a few generalizations about the principles as applied to selected activities is described.

1. The successful execution of most balance stunts depends upon a wide base of support and adjustments to keep the center of weight over the base of support.

    a. Whenever the weight is borne on the hands, care should be taken that the hands are far enough apart, that they are flat with fingers slightly spread. When supporting and hanging, the hands should be placed in line with the shoulders.

    b. Compensatory movements of arms or legs must be made in opposition to stabilize balance when body weight is shifted. Movement or weight added to one side of the body changes the body alignment,

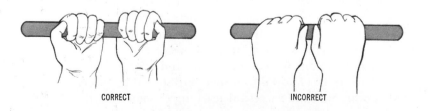

CORRECT   INCORRECT

Figure 14-2. Finger and Thumb Position When Hanging on Bars.

and imbalance results. When in an inverted position, the slightest movement of the feet or legs may cause instability, and a quick shift of weight is necessary for realignment. The pelvis must be stabilized over the base before the child is able to recognize automatically the need for proper compensatory movements.

c. Whenever a roll is to be made on the floor or over a bar, balance must be lost. For example, when turning over a bar from a front rest position, the top of the body must be made heavy so that the body will go forward. Whenever an inverted position on the ropes or bars is desired, the head must be dropped in the desired direction and legs and hips lifted. Many children have trouble doing an inverted hang because it is unnatural for them to drop their head backward.

2. In rotary movements the shorter the radius of rotation is, the faster the movement becomes. The body will move faster in a tuck position (feet and knees tucked to chest) than in a layout position (body extended). The body should be lengthened to decrease the speed of rotation, and shortened to increase speed of rotation.

3. The principle of absorption of force must be applied when landing from a jump. Bending the ankles and knees provides greater time and distance over which to absorb force.

4. Force should be applied equally in the intended line of direction. A push-off in the backward or forward roll must be given equally from both hands or the performer will roll to the side. A take-off from both feet will give a greater lift for a vault.

5. The angle of take-off in vaulting should be great enough so that a vertical flight results rather than a low angle and horizontal flight. The take-off should be near enough to the bar so that the body reaches its highest point in flight over the bar, rather than descending as it reaches the bar.

Activities

Suggestions are made for activities for each type of gymnastic work. They are presented in order of difficulty. Generally, they suggest a main theme or task from which the teacher may construct his lesson plan. Many are activities which children will discover naturally when they are asked to give movement answers to specific questions.

Specific directions for certain stunts and exercises are given for the teacher's knowledge of how the finished skill should be executed and how it should appear. Safe and successful learning of some activities depends on prescribed movements and proper execution and leaves no room for variations. The teacher must know what is to be learned and present it to students by a method which will be stimulating, challenging, and motivating. A suggested progression for an elementary school gymnastic program can be found after the descriptions of the activities.

DEVELOPMENTAL
STUNTS AND EXERCISES

No specific activities other than traditional stunts and exercises are suggested here for the primary grades. Exploration of basic movement skills in respect to the factors which affect them (described in Chapter IX) is the basic content of gymnastics for younger children. Suggested movement variations and combinations are also given in Chapter IX.

Particular emphasis should be placed on activities which develop shoulder girdle strength, flexibility, balance, and agility. The body actions of curling, twisting, turning, rolling, extension, and the fundamentals of jumping, landing, transferring weight, supporting weight on various body parts, and flight should be studied and practiced in many variations and combinations.

Exercises for development of specific physical elements

STRENGTH OF SHOULDER GIRDLE AND ARMS:

1. *Push-ups:* Weight on knees and hands, which are placed directly under shoulders. Bend elbows and touch chest to ground, keep back straight. Straighten elbows, pushing body up. Repeat. To make more difficult, extend whole body, put weight on balls of feet and on hands. Raise and lower body, keeping body straight.
2. *Straddle chins:* With partner. One lying on back, between legs of other who stands with elbows straight, arms down in front of body. Clasp hands of partner, pull body up, keeping body straight, until elbows are bent; lower body to floor.
3. *Upper back:*
    a. Prone position. Arms extending in front of head. Raise and lower arms alternately keeping knees straight; raise and lower arms together. Alternate raising opposite arms and legs at same time.
    b. Prone position with hands locked behind neck. Raise head and arms slowly off floor. Continue to repeat.
    c. Same position as b, lift legs alternately.

ABDOMINAL STRENGTH:

1. *Curl-ups or sit-ups:*
   a. Lie on back, knees slightly bent, arms at side. With head leading, curl body up into a sitting position, roll down into lying position. Exhale when going up, inhale when returning to lying position. Partner may hold feet.
   b. Vary with hands held behind head.
   c. Vary rate of speed and number of exercises to be done. Test how many can be done in a specified amount of time.
2. *Leg lifts:* Lying on back, hands at side, knees slightly bent.
   a. Raise one leg, straighten it and return it to former position. Repeat with other leg. Continue.
   b. Sit on floor leaning on elbows, knees slightly bent. Raise legs, straighten and lower to floor slowly.
   c. Vary by moving legs sideward and back as they are extended in air; describe a circle with them.

LEG STRENGTH:

1. *Half squats:* Stand erect, hands on hips. Feet flat on floor.
   a. Bend knees slightly, hold, straighten knees.
   b. Increase depth of knee bend.
   c. Bend and raise heels off floor. (Avoid sudden deep knee bend)
   d. Spread feet sideways and repeat.
2. *Lunge:*
   a. Assume same position as 1. Shift weight to side, slide leg sideways to a side stride position bending knee. Keep other leg straight, alternate legs.
   b. Lunge forward.
   c. Lunge backward.
3. *One leg squat:*
   a. Erect position. Lift one leg, squat on other. Return to position. Alternate legs.
   b. Hop onto foot on which squat is made.

FLEXIBILITY:

1. *Rocker:* Prone position. With arms back, grasp ankles and make body rock forward and backward.
2. *Ostrich walk:* Bend at hips, grasp ankles. Walk forward keeping legs fully extended, head held high.
3. *Wing flings:* Body erect, feet slightly apart, arms extended at side at shoulder level.
   a. Bring hands together in front of chest.
   b. Fling arms back as far as possible, keeping them at shoulder level.
   c. Repeat, keeping head and trunk straight and still.
4. *Arm circles:* Body erect, feet slightly apart, arms extended at sides, slightly above shoulder level.

   a. Circle arms backward, alternate forward.
   b. Vary levels at which arms are held.
5. *Trunk twist:* Body erect, feet slightly apart, arms extended out to sides.
   a. Twist at the waist from side to side, look at some object behind body.
6. *Bobbing forward:* Erect position, feet slightly apart.
   a. With knees straight bob several times trying to touch floor.
   b. Try to touch floor in back of legs.
   c. Move feet closer together to make exercise more difficult.
7. *Bend sideways:* Erect position feet slightly spread, hands at side.
   a. Bend or bob to side, alternate sides.
   b. With elbows bent, hands on shoulder bend to side.
   c. With one hand held high and the other at side, bend to side.
8. *Pick up:* Place beanbag on floor 8 inches in front of toes. With feet just a few inches apart and knees straight, lean over and pick up beanbag. Repeat placing beanbag farther away each time.

GENERAL ENDURANCE:
1. *Running in place:* Erect position. Arms at side.
   a. Start running in place, use arms (with elbows bent) in opposition with legs.
   b. Raise knees high, and use arms vigorously.
   c. Use interval pacing, run slowly, then vigorously, slowly, vigorously, etc
2. *Jumping jacks:* Erect position, feet together, arms at sides, jump to wide stride position, fling arms up sideward and touch hands overhead, jump to starting position. Feet together, arms at side. Continue for specified number or amount of time.
3. *Grasshopper:* Assume a squat sitting position; bend forward, and place hands under shoulders just in front of knees; extend right leg backward; chest resting on forward knee. Exchange positions of the legs and continue as long as possible.

Developmental stunts

1. *Dog walk:* Walk on hands and feet: Vary directions, vary speeds.
2. Run and stop, taking weight on hands momentarily. Run and stop and repeat weight-bearing.
3. *Mule kick:* Same as 2, only kick legs up behind high in the air.
4. *Rocker:* Jump from hands to feet several times in a row without stopping.
5. *Lame dog (three-legged walk):* Weight on hands, lift one leg behind, and walk on hands and one leg.
6. *Seal walk:* Weight on hands, prone position, walk on hands, drag feet behind.

7. *Coffee grinder:* Place one hand on floor, other on hip. Straighten arm and extend body so that it is on a straight plane. Walk around a circle, hand as a pivot. Keep head back, body straight. Change hands and repeat.

8. *Crab walk:* Sitting position. Hands on floor behind hips. Take weight on hands and feet, raise weight and walk on hands and feet. Body should be straight from knee to head. Change direction of walk.

9. *Turk stand:* Sit cross-legged on the floor. Stand without using hands to help get up.

10. *Top:* Erect position. Jump into air and turn around landing facing opposite direction. Also, jump into air and turn all the way around landing in take-off spot.

11. *Heel click:* Stand with feet about 12 inches apart, leap into air, and click heels together before landing. Try to click heels together several times.

12. *Heel slap:* Erect position. Jump up bringing heels up behind and slap heels with hands one or more times before landing.

13. *Thread the needle:* Erect position, hands clasped in front of body. Bend over, step over clasped hands with right foot and then with left foot. Clasped hands should be in back of body at finish. Reverse order so that clasped hands are in starting position.

14. *One-foot balance:*
    a. Standing on one foot, close eyes and balance as long as possible. Arms may be used.
    b. Hands on hips, rest left leg against right knee and maintain balance on right leg.

15. *Walk a straight line on floor.*
    a. Walk on a line 15 feet long painted on the floor.
    b. Close eyes and walk straight line.

16. *Russian bear dance:* Start in semi-squat position, arms folded across chest. Jump and extend one leg out in front. Exchange position of feet as quickly as possible. Try to get close to floor. Arms may have to be extended to help maintain balance. Weight should be to the side of the supporting leg.

17. *Corkscrew:* Erect position, feet slightly apart. Place beanbag outside of heel of right foot. Pick it up with left hand by passing left hand in front of body, around outside of right leg, forward between legs, and around in front of right foot. Do same with beanbag on opposite side and use opposite hand.

18. *Human ball:* Start in sitting position, knees bent close to chest. Put arms down inside legs, around outside of shins and clasp hands in front of ankles. Roll to right side, over on back, to left side and up to sitting position.

19. *Jump over foot:* Face wall, place one foot on wall about 12 inches

above floor. Keeping foot on wall, jump over that leg with other foot, executing a half turn in the process.

20. *Up-swing:* Sit on balls of feet in a kneeling position. Swing arms back and forward, and bring body up into a standing position.

21. *Up-spring:* Kneeling position, feet extended behind, toes flat on floor. Swing arms back forcibly and then forward, and jump to a standing position.

22. *V sit:* Sitting position. Raise legs straight up and reach out with arms and grasp ankles. Try to maintain balance in this position.

23. *Knee scale:* Kneeling position, hands on floor in front of body. Raise left leg, extend behind in air. Raise arms diagonally sidewards and balance on one knee.

24. *Front scale:* Erect position. Bend forward at hips, lift and extend right leg up behind until right leg and trunk are parallel to floor; arch back. Arms extended diagonally backward and sideward to help maintain balance; head help up, eyes focused directly forward.

25. *Side scale:* Erect position. Left leg and foot pointing diagonally forward; slide left arm down left leg to point just above ankle; raise right leg upward and sideward; right arm extends over the head and to the right. The right arm, trunk and right leg form one line parallel to the ground. Support may be needed at first so position may be assumed. Right leg may rest on chair or beam.

26. *Single leg circles:* Squat position with both hands flat on floor. Left knee is between arms, right leg extended sideward. Swing right leg forward, and when it meets right arm, lift right hand and place it to right of right leg. Shift weight to right arm as right leg circles under left leg and left hand back to starting position. Make a few circles. Back should be held as vertical as possible, left knee bent.

27. *Jump and touch toes:* Jump into air, extend legs forward and upward with feet apart. Touch toes, keeping back vertical throughout jump. Extend legs downward and return to floor with two-foot landing.

28. *Jump and tuck:* Jump into air, bring knees to chest, grasp shins with hands; release, extend legs down, and return to floor with far foot landing. Keep back vertical.

29. *Jump and jackknife:* Jump into air, lift extended legs forward and upward with feet together to touch toes. Extend legs downward and return to two-foot landing.

30. *Jump and swan:* Jump into air, pull arms high over head, and pull body into an arched position. Hips forward, head and shoulders pulled back hard, legs extended to rear. Return body to vertical position for two-foot landing.

31. *Jump and turn:* As opposed to the *top,* arms should be held close to body as body turns in air. Body should be fully extended, toes pointed. Children should be encouraged to make other changes of

shapes while in the air. (All jump styles should be done on the floor before they are used off various pieces of apparatus.)

32. *Arabesque:* Erect position. Raise both arms forward and upward. Lift one leg backward; bend forward at hips; arch back and maintain balanced position.

33. *Front break fall:* Erect position. Keep knees and hips fully extended and fall forward catching self on hands. Arms flex slightly on contact with floor or mat.

34. *Forward drop:* Same as *front break fall,* only one leg is lifted off floor during fall.

35. *Fish flop:* On back, arms at side. Right foot is kicked up hard enough to bring body up on right shoulder. Turn over face downward with head pointing in opposite direction. This can be done so that body will be in almost the same place on the mat at the end of the stunt.

PARTNER STUNTS:

1. *Bouncing ball:* One person squats and bounces up and down like a ball. The other person exerts pressure on the "ball's" back to make it bounce. The amount of pressure exerted determines the amount of bounce.

2. *Wring the dishrag:* Partners face one another and join hands. Arms are raised as the partners turn away from each other under the raised arms and then return to face each other as the opposite arms are raised.

3. *Sawing wood:* Partners face one another standing with one foot slightly forward of the other. Hands are placed in each other's palms. Opposite arms are pushed back and forward as if sawing wood.

4. *Rocker:* Partners sit facing each other legs extended; each child sits on other's feet. Grasp each other's arms and rock back and forth. One leans backward and lifts other child up. Until momentum is built up, the other will have to lean forward some.

5. *Chinese get-up:* Partners of equal heights stand back to back with elbows locked. Both lower bodies to floor then rise to a standing position by pushing against each other's backs.

6. *Leapfrog:* One person bends over with knees slightly bent and places hands on knees. Other one runs forward, jumps with legs in straddle position, places hands on partner's shoulders, and pushes self up and over partner, landing with controlled landing on both feet.

COMBATIVES:

1. *Bulldozer:* Hands and feet (not knees) facing partner, with right shoulders touching. Each tries to push (not bump) his partner backwards. Change shoulders and repeat.

2. *Back to back:* Sit down, back to back. Using hands and feet, each tries to move partner without lifting his seat from floor. Keep head down.

3. *Toe boxing:* Hands on hips, facing partner. Each tries to tap partner's

toes *lightly* with foot. Keep feet moving so that each cannot tap the other's toes.

4. *Bottoms up:* Sit facing partner, hands joined, legs slightly apart with feet touching. Each tries to pull partner so that his hips come up off floor.

5. *Hand push:* Stand, face to face, feet together and exactly the length of one foot away from partner's feet. Place palms against the palms of partner and try to make him lose his balance (move one of his feet) or touch any place but on palms. Hands may be pulled away quickly or pushed, as long as balance is not lost.

6. *Indian leg wrestle:* Two performers of equal size lie on the mat side by side, facing in opposite directions. Place hips at opponent's waist line. Grasp opponent's inside shoulder with inside hand. On signal "one, two, three," raise inside legs simultaneously three times. On count "three" hook inside knees and try to force opponent over into a backward roll.

7. *Indian club fight:* Opponents face each other, arm's distance apart. Join hands. Place an Indian club an equal distance between opponents. On signal "go," force opponent to knock over the club by pulling, pushing, or jerking him into the club.

8. *Pulldown:* One partner on hands and knees. Other partner on knees, beside first partner. On signal, try to get partner off his hands and knees by pulling his arms or legs out from under him or by turning him over. Partner on hands and knees does not fight back, but simply tries to stay on hands and knees. Change and repeat.

9. *Rope pull:* Four inside a circle of rope—square off and see who can pull who away from his corner.

10. *Cock fight:* Partners facing, hold one foot behind you with the *opposite* hand. Try to make your partner let go of his raised foot, lose his balance, or both by pushing or pulling.

11. *Elbow wrestle:* Lie on your stomach with head facing partner; legs are spread wide apart. Hold right hands together, elbows touching, with other hand behind back. Try to force partner's hand to the floor, without moving elbow off floor. (Partner will have to roll over as his hand is pressed toward the floor.)

TUMBLING

Tumbling activities fall into two general categories: stands and balances, and rolls and turns. A mat should be used for most of the following activities. The activities are arranged in order of difficulty. Regardless of grade at which one starts tumbling activities, he should start with the first mentioned.

Stands and balances

In all balances and stands, there should be a good base with hands under shoulders, elbows body-width apart not pointing out, hands flat, fingers slightly spread.

1. *Frog stand:* Squat position; both hands flat on floor with elbows inside and bent to press against knees; lean forward, slowly take weight on the elbows and hands until feet are clear off floor; keep head up. Hold as long as possible.

2. *Tripod:* Squat position; place hands flat on mat; crown of head about one foot in front of hands so the three points form a triangular base; lift body weight, resting knees on bent elbows. Maintain this position.

3. *Head stand:* Take tripod position and extend legs up over head, arch back, keep legs straight and toes pointed. Maintain balance. To come down, bend knees and let body weight come down into squat position. A partner may stand beside and hold arm across behind other person so legs can be stopped from flying over too far. (Partner should not lift legs.)

4. *Handstand:* Erect position. Push off with one leg, place hands directly under shoulders, take weight on hands and at the same time swing legs above head. Keep push-off leg slightly bent until balance can be held for more than 3 seconds, arch back, head up. Partner should stand in front to catch thighs if legs overswing. Bend knees, drop feet, and return to erect position.

5. *Shoulder balance:* Lying down, raise legs straight above hips, and balance on back of head, neck and shoulders; arms extended up the sides.

6. *Forearm balance:* Kneeling position with forearms on mat. Palms down, index fingers and thumbs touching, head is placed between them; extend right leg and swing it up overhead; at the same time spring off the left leg and bring both legs into straight balanced position.

PARTNER STUNTS:

1. *Standing balance on thighs:* The base stands directly behind the top, facing the same direction. Base squats, places head between top's legs, and grasps the top's thighs just above the knees and stands up with top sitting on his shoulders. He keeps his knees bent and body erect so leg muscles are doing most of the work. The top places his toes on base's knees with rest of feet on thighs. Base holds top's thighs just above the knees, and the top stands erect as the base moves his head from between the top's legs. Stunt is complete then as the top is in a fully extended, erect position. On signal the top jumps down, and base lets go of his legs.

2. *Knee shoulder balance:* Base lies on back with knees bent and feet flat on floor, hands stretched up and forward ready to support top's shoulders. Base stands in front of top's bent knees and places his hands on base's knees. He leans forward so shoulders are supported by base's hands. He springs to a balance, legs extended over head, head up, body arched to maintain balance. (Caution base to keep arms perpendicular to body and not to reach forward with them.) On signal from base, top should bend knees and drop feet back to floor.

3. *Horizontal stand:* Base lies on back, knees bent. Top stands with feet just behind base's head, hands on base's knees. Base grasps knees of top. As top springs up and shifts weight to hands, base raises arms perpendicular to floor.

4. *Angel balance:* Base lies on back with legs raised, knees slightly bent with feet placed diagonally alongside of top's pelvic bones. He takes top's hands in his and slowly raises top into a balanced position. Hands are let go, and top balances with arms out to side. On signal base bends knees and lowers top to floor where top returns to standing position.

5. *Sitting balance:* Base lies on mat with legs raised and knees slightly bent. Top sits on base's feet and extends arms back, grasping base's hands. Base straightens legs and releases top's hands who extends arms to sides to help maintain balance.

6. *Three man mount:* Two people get down on hands and knees beside one another. Third person gets on top of the other two and places one hand and one knee on the back of each of the bases. Care should be taken that weight is not placed in the small of base's back. On signal everyone "squashes" by extending their legs and extending weight on the hands.

PYRAMIDS:

Children enjoy designing, working out, and especially "squashing" at the end of a pyramid. Making pyramids gives a group a chance to create a design and to make up new stunts or perfect known ones to use in their design. Man mounts of three, five or more are usually, but not necessarily, the focal point of a pyramid. Partner and single stunts form a design around the center. Some stunts which are frequently used in pyramids are: headstands, handstands, arches, tip-ups, bridges, shoulder rest, knee shoulder stand, horizontal stand, angel balance, sitting mount, standing knee mount, front rest, front scale.

Rolls and turns

1. *Log roll:* Lie across the end of the mat, arms stretched overhead. Roll over and over evenly in one direction, twisting shoulders and hips and keeping legs and arms straight.

2. *Front roll:*
   a. Stand, squat at edge of mat; place hands on mat, shoulder width apart, fingers pointing straight ahead, lean forward; touch chin on chest; push off with feet and roll forward, hips high; take body weight on hands and carry it forward until shoulders, back, and hips touch mat. Hands may shift from mat to shins as one rolls to a squat then a stand.
   b. Start from a standing position.
   c. Do two or three continuous rolls.
   d. Take several steps, jump, and spring into a roll.
   e. Dive over a mat and into a roll (Figure 14-3).

It is best if the roll is first learned as one comes off the end of a box or a bench by placing hands on mat, tucking head, and hitting shoulder area first, then rolling to a stand.

3. *Egg roll:*
   a. Stand, heels touching edge of mat; squat, rock back, placing hands beside head, fingers pointing toward shoulders. Rock forward with hand push.
   b. From squat position, roll back a little farther; place hands beside head; touch toes to floor beyond head, and rock forward to squat.
4. *Backward roll:* Start as for an egg roll, but tuck head and turn all the way over as hands push hard against the mat. Return to standing position.
5. *Backward extension roll:* Start as for a regular roll, but when hands push against mat the feet are extended and a momentary handstand position is held before feet are snapped down into standing position.
6. *Eskimo roll (partners):* Base lies on back, second person stands strad-

Figure 14-3. Dive Over an Object into a Forward Roll.

dling partner's head facing his feet. Base lifts feet; each grasps the other's ankles. Top does a forward roll pulling base upright, then base does a forward roll through top's legs pulling him up. They continue this to the end of the mat.

7. *Cartwheel:* Place both hands in center of mat, while keeping feet just off one edge. Jump from one foot to opposite edge of mat onto other foot, keeping hands in center. Repeat movement but begin with one foot swinging over, followed by second foot. Continue, working for height of leg swing. Shift to standing position and place one hand down, as first leg swings up, then second hand and second leg. The rhythm is hand, hand, foot, foot, with no two points touching mat at the same time.

8. *Round off:* Start as for a cartwheel but when both feet are overhead, bring feet together in mid-air, twist and land on both feet simultaneously, facing direction from which one came.

APPARATUS

Activities done on the various pieces of apparatus are very much alike; however, each piece provides some particular height, size, and shape to which the movements must be adjusted. Many opportunities for exploration and experimentation with different ways to climb, hang, turn over, travel, swing, jump on, jump over, jump off, and balance should be provided in the primary grades. At the same time principles of landing and proper grip should be stressed.

Figure 14-4. An All-Purpose Developmental Piece of Equipment for Traditional and Creative Activities. *Photograph:* courtesy of Lind Climber Company, Evanston, Illinois.

Suggestions are given here for tasks for experimentation and for specific stunts and exercises which may form the basis of creative routines on various pieces of apparatus. Most pieces of equipment are rather versatile and can be utilized for many informal and exploratory activities.

A few terms and positions common to work on many pieces are explained first.

1. *Starting position:* Performer assumes an erect position, focuses both his eyes and thoughts on what his first movement is to be. He then takes a couple of steps forward and initiates the first movement related to his task.
2. *Finish position:* Performer ends the movements related to his tasks and returns to a balanced, erect position. He pauses a few seconds before walking away from the apparatus or mat.
3. *Mount:* The process of getting onto a piece of equipment or another person who will be the supporting base.
4. *Dismount:* The process of getting off a piece of equipment or another person who was the supporting base.
5. *Vault:* Going over a piece of equipment and using the hands as supportive assistance.
6. *Pike position:* Body is bent at the hips, and legs extend at right angles to body.
7. *Tuck position:* Knees are flexed, and thighs are held up and in toward chest.
8. *Layout position:* Body is fully extended.
9. *Straddle position:* Legs are each extended outward from the body.
10. *Squat position:* Legs are bent, and seat is close to feet.
11. *Front support or front rest:* Weight is taken on hands, body rests on bar at a point where body is balanced. Legs are extended, toes are pointed. Hands may be taken off bar and arms extended to sides.
12. *Flank:* Both legs and body move to the same side of a piece of equipment, either in vaulting, mounting, or dismounting.
13. *Inverted position:* Body is upside down.
14. *Quarter turn:* Body makes a quarter turn to right or left.
15. *Half turn:* Body ends facing opposite direction.
16. *Full turn:* A complete turn is made in the air and body ends facing same direction in which it started.
17. *Scale:* Any stunt where one foot serves as the base.
18. *Overgrip:* Grasp on bar with fingers pointing away from body.
19. *Undergrip:* Grasp on bar with fingers pointed in direction of body.

Horizontal bars

Most of these activities may be done also on doorway gym bars, chinning bars, between the parallel bars, or on a medium or high balance beam.

Some require various heights, and some more room under the bar and behind the bar than others.

1. *Passive hanging:* Jump and grasp bar; hold body weight as long as possible; drop and land safely.
2. *Active hanging:* As above, but contract muscles into firm position, point toes, hold head high.
3. *Flexed arm hang:* Grasp bar, pull body up, chin resting on bar, arms flexed. Hold position as long as possible. Dismount.
4. *Hang and swing:*
   a. Swing legs from hips slowly; keep body straight.
   b. Swing from side to side.
   c. Swing and dismount at back of swing.
   d. Swing and dismount at front of swing.
5. *Hang and raise legs:*
   a. Raise legs to tuck position.
   b. Raise legs from hips, lower slowly.
6. *Front rest:* Grasp bar and balance with bar just above hips. Extend legs behind, head is up and reaching (Figure 14-5)
7. *Double knee hanging:* Lift legs up and over bar, press feet down hard,

Figure 14-5. Front Rest on the Horizontal Bar.

and let the body hang from the back of the knees. Pull up to bar, disengage knees, and dismount.

8. *Skin the cat:* Grasp bar, flex knees and hips, and pull legs up between the arms and under the bar. Slowly roll over until hips are higher than head or feet touch floor. Reverse roll back to original position and dismount.

9. Grasp bar, swing and run, back and forth, back and forth, swing out and up on third run onto a box or bench.

10. Vary position of the body while inverted, from pike to lay out, tuck, etc.

11. *Single knee hang:* Grasp bar, body hanging below bar with legs elevated. Pull hips up, and hook one knee over bar between hands. Unlock knee, dismount.

12. *Pull over:* Grasp bar, swing right leg forward up, hard, both legs swing around and over bar, while pulling self toward bar to finish in a front support position on the bar. (In order to get to the other side of the bar, the head must be dropped backward so center of body weight will go to the other side as the arms pull the body around.) Push away from bar from front rest position and dismount.

13. *Single knee mount:* Assume a single knee hang position; swing extended knee downward and backward, pull bar toward hips (with straight arms), and turn up into a position on top of the bar with back of one knee on bar and other leg extended.

14. *Single knee circle:* From the straddle position assumed from the swing knee mount, swing extended leg forward, then backward, slide other leg back so bar is in crook of knee, then swing extended leg forward, drop head and shoulders backward. Completely circle the bar, and assume straddle position. Dismount. (Leg must be straight and swung forcibly forward as head and shoulders are dropped or there will not be enough momentum to get around and on top of the bar again.)

15. *Chinning:* Grip bar in undergrip (hands toward body). Pull body up, touch chin on bar, lower body, pull up, touch chin on bar, repeat as long as possible.

Balance beam

Initial experiences should be exploratory so confidence is gained. If the beam is too high for children to mount, a chair or stool should be provided. Most children will climb up onto a high beam from an underhang hand foot grasp. Medium or high beams may be used for hanging, climbing, and vaulting activities as well as for balance stunts. Most balance activities can be started using a line painted on the floor or a narrow flat board on the floor and as the child progresses, the beams will be a progressively higher distance off the floor. Arms should be used to help maintain balance, and eyes should be focused forward rather than downward at feet. Balance should be attained before changes in position are made. When one wavers excessively on the beam, he should step or jump off and start again.

1. Walk forward.
2. Walk backward placing toe of foot directly behind heel of other foot.
3. Walk on toes (Figure 14-6).
4. Slide sideward.
5. Walk sideward crossing one foot over the other.
6. Hop forward, backward.
7. Vary positions of hands and arms in all of these so adjustments in weight to keep balance must be in other parts of body.
8. Hold objects of varying weights in one hand, on the head.
9. Step over and around a wand extended across beam. Go under a wand.
10. Step through a hoop held over beam.
11. Throw and catch a ball with a partner who is on the floor some distance away.
12. Change levels—sit, lie down, stoop, stretch.

Figure 14-6. Walking on the Low Balance Beam.

13. Crawl on hands and knees across beam.
14. Squat on one foot, extending nonsupporting leg.
15. Do a half turn.
16. Do a full turn.
17. Do a half turn with one foot, full turn on one foot.
18. Jump up and down.
19. Jump and turn.
20. Walk on hands and feet forward, backward, sideward.
21. Skip across beam. (With musical accompaniment try other dance steps.)
22. Walk and dip nonsupporting leg down beside leg.
23. Knee scale (page 525), Figure 14-7.
24. Front scale (page 525).
25. Side scale (page 525).
26. V Sit (page 525).
27. *Straddle stand:* Stand facing sideward on beam, with legs in straddle position. Bend trunk parallel to floor, arms extended sideward.
28. *Backward roll:* Lie on back on beam; reach over head, grasp underside of beams with both hands, place head to one side of beam, pull with arms, bend hips and roll over backwards; when coming out of roll, take weight on knee. (This should be done first on a low beam with a spotter.)

Figure 14-7. Knee Scale on the Balance Beam.

MOUNTING MEDIUM OR HIGH BEAM:

1. *Straddle seat:* Front support on side of beam, raise one foot to beam, put one leg over and straddle beam, push down on beam, raise body to a standing position.
2. *Side seat:* Sitting on edge of beam, push down on inside hand on beam pull inside foot on beam, swing outside leg up and onto beam.
3. *One knee:* From end of medium height beam, push down on beam as hands swing back and forward and land on beam on one knee.

DISMOUNTING:

1. Jump off side, off end.
2. Jump and quarter turn placing one hand on beam.
3. Straddle jump to stand, from side, from end.
4. From hand support on beam, push up and away, landing with one hand on beam.
5. Squat jump.

SAMPLE SEQUENCES:

1. Straddle mount.
   Push up into front scale.
   Push off with hands to landing position on floor.
2. Cross seat mount.
   Series of movements along beam from high to low.
   Quarter turn dismount.
3. Mount.
   Hop into a full turn, two deep knee bends, half turn into a scale, change to another scale, slide into a dismount from end of beam.

Stall bars

Many schools have stall bars. The top bar which extends out farther than the others can be used for chinning bars or free hanging. Stall bars afford opportunities for hanging and lifting body parts while hanging, yet they take little space in a room or gym.

FACING BARS:

1. Climb up a few rungs. Hands grasp bar. Walk up until feet are as close as possible to hands, walk down.
2. With arms straight, legs at angle, bend arms, and pull body up.
3. Hang with one hand.
4. Hang with two hands, swing from side to side.

BACK TO BARS:

1. Hang, and pull up to flexed-arm position.
2. Hang lift legs into tucked position.

3. Hang lift legs into straight position.
4. Hang lift legs and arch, jump away from bars, jump and turn in air.
5. Hang, and raise feet all the way above head.

Parallel bars

The height and width of adult parallel bars makes it very difficult for small children to do stunts while supporting their weight on their hands. Unless elementary-size bars are available, only exploratory movements and stunts under or between the bars can be done safely. One bar can be used much like a horizontal bar. Both boys and girls can do the stunts suggested here. Girls seldom do more advanced stunts than those on the even parallel bars because of the great shoulder strength which is required.

UNDER AND BETWEEN BARS:
1. *Inverted hang* (p. 534)
   a. Tuck position
   b. Layout position
   c. Pike position
2. *Skin the cat* (p. 534)
3. *Bird's nest:* Standing at center between bars, grasp bars with an outside grip. Lift legs to pass through the inverted hand position and backward to hook feet on bars. Extend legs, body, and arms along bars; hold head high. Bring legs back, tuck, and return to inverted position and dismount.

AT END OR MIDDLE OF BARS:
1. *Straight arm support:* Place hands on bars with outside grip directly under shoulders, jump off floor, extend arms fully and support weight (Figure 14-8).
2. *Hand walk:* From straight arm support position, walk the length of the bars by shifting body weight from one hand to another.
3. *Straight armswing:* From a straight arm support, swing the body back and forth in an extended position, push off and back and dismount.
4. *Back foot leaning rest:* At center of bars, assume straight arm support position, bring legs up and rest feet on bars in front of body. Extend body fully. Bring legs down and dismount.
5. *Front leaning rest:* From straight arm support position brings legs behind arms and rest feet on bar. Extend body fully. Swing legs forward and dismount.
6. *Support swing to inside cross riding seat:* From straight arm support position bring body to a sitting position on right bar with legs between bars. Maintain an erect position, extend left leg, and bend right leg and hip. Return to straight arm support and dismount.

Figure 14-8. Straight Arm Support on the Parallel Bars.

7. *Support swing to outside cross riding seat:* Same as 6, but legs are on outside of bars.
8. *Support swing to straddle seat:* From straight arm support swing both legs up and over bars resting thighs on bars in straddle position. Push up, swing legs down, and dismount (Figure 14-9).
9. *Straddle travel:* Same as 8, only rather than dismounting, another swing is made and a straddle position taken. These movements should be done in a flowing continuous motion the length of the bars.

DISMOUNTS:
1. *Rear vault:* Straight arm support swing. As feet rise above bar on swing, lean to right and bring both legs over right bar flexing at hips as legs pass over bar. At the same time, grasp right bar with left hand and release right hand. Land alongside bar facing original direction. Later variations of quarter and half turns may be added to rear vault.
2. *Front vault:* From support swing, feet rise above bar on *backward* swing, lean to the left shifting weight to left arm and bring both legs over left bar. At same time, grasp left bar with right hand and release left hand. Land alongside bar facing original direction. Later add variations of landing with different degrees of turns. (Older and stronger children can learn to do rolls and balances on top of the bar as they are able to lift and control body weight above the bar.) (Figure 14-10).

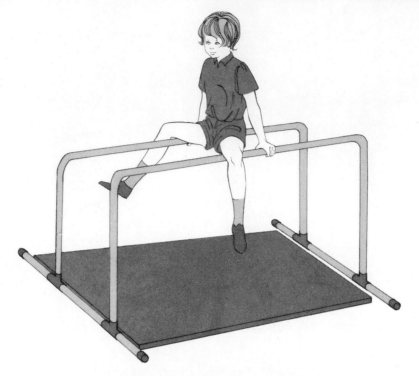

Figure 14-9. Straddle Seat on the Parallel Bars.

Swedish boxes or benches (vaulting and jumping)

Initial work on jumping and vaulting can be taught using improvised equipment. A low sturdy table, a strong wooden box, a sturdy gym bench, a sturdy stool, or springboard may be used if a Swedish box is not available.

USING A LOW BOX:
1. Walk up to box, step onto it, jump off. (Stress good landing techniques, extended body.)
2. Run, jump on box, jump off.
3. Run, jump on box, vary body positions in air on jump. (Tuck, pike, straddle, twist, etc.)
4. Run, jump, land on box on two feet, jump off.
5. Run, vary take-off foot.
6. Run, jump over box, changing body position in air.
7. Jump off box, and do a forward roll.
8. Jump on box, try a balance stunt, dismount.

Figure 14-10. Shoulder Balance on the Parallel Bars.

Be sure children can recognize and perform with both symmetrical and asymmetrical patterns.

USING A LONG BENCH:
1. Run, jump on bench, run along it, jump off.
2. Run, jump on bench, hop along bench, jump off.
3. Crab walk along bench, dismount.
4. Jump on and off alternate sides of bench.
5. Jump over and back along length of bench.
6. At end of bench, crouch vault onto knees (take weight on hands), push back and off.*
7. At side of bench, face it, vault over it with bent knees.*
8. Taking weight on one end, fence vault (one-hand support) across bench.*
9. Go length of bench fence vaulting back and forth across it.*
10. Face vault (extending legs).*

Vaulting box

A higher padded box, bench, or buck may be used. Repeat many of the previous activities off higher box.
1. Climb up on box, dismount.
2. Jump up on box using hands to help dismount.

* Low box may be used.

3. *Basic vault:* Approach the box, take-off on one foot, bring other foot up alongside so both may land at the same spot for a double foot take-off in a vertical direction. The hands are placed on the box and the push of them against the box helps the body gain height. The feet, hips, and knees are pulled upward to clear the box. Push-off with hands, but the hands are removed from the box as the feet clear the box (Figure 14-11).

4. Vault atop box landing on knees. Upswing dismount (courage dismount) (p. 525).

5. Vault to a crouch position, stand erect, jump off. Vary shape of body in air.

6. Vault to a standing position on box, jump off, varying style.

7. Vault to a standing position, turn, jump landing.

8. *Squat vault:* Basic vault approach with knees bent and brought up to chest.

9. *Flank vault:* Basic vault approach with weight taken on one arm only, legs pass extended to one side of the box, side of body passes over box. Legs swing down over other side of box (Figure 14-12).

10. *Rear vault:* Basic vault approach, hips turn so body achieves a V position facing the side (seat passes over box). The right hand (if vault is executed to left) is removed from box and placed on the box again after body has passed over it. Right hand leaves box and swings to the side as landing is made.

11. *Straddle vault:* Basic vault approach with both legs spread wide outside arms, push off with hands, land with feet together.

Figure 14-11. Assisting with a Basic Vault.

Hanging ropes

1. Grasp rope, pull up from lying position to sitting position and return. (Hand movements—hand over hand.)
2. Pull up from sitting position to ropes and hang—arms bent.
3. Pull up from lying position to standing position and return—legs straight.
4. Climb rope:
   a. Stand with rope between legs, wrap rope around back of calf of right leg, and over instep of right foot. Place left foot on top of rope where it crosses instep.
   b. Grasp rope in right hand above left hand and above head.
   c. Bring knees up toward chest. (Flex knees.)
   d. Straighten legs. Hands should now be in front of chest.
   e. Now reach up as high as possible with hands.
   f. Repeat knee action. Continue up rope.
   g. Come down in the same manner. Do not slide.
5. Bicycling: Jump and grasp rope above height of head. Flex knees alternately, as though riding a bicycle. Count number of times you can do this before letting go of the rope.

Figure 14-12. A Side or Flank Vault.

6. Reverse hang.
7. Chin on rope, pulling self up to bent arm position until chin is even with hands. Lower body until arms are completely extended; without touching floor, pull up again.
8. If two ropes hang side by side, various stunts can be performed.
    a. If one rope is held in each hand: tuck position, pike position, skin the cat, reverse hang.
    b. Move from one rope to another.
9. Climb rope using arms only; feet are hanging free.

Swinging on ropes

Children must be taught to dismount or get off of the rope at the back of the swing. At this point, momentum is halted temporarily, and one can drop straight down onto the balls of the feet.
1. Swing on the rope by taking a few approach steps, jump and grasp rope so feet are free of floor. Swing and dismount.
2. Stand on box, swing off and out, and dismount.
3. Swing up and land on box, dismount from box.
4. Swing over box. (Legs must be tucked.)
5. Run and swing over cross bar on jump standards. Raise bar at intervals.

SMALL EQUIPMENT

Suggestions are given here for activities using the most common types of small equipment. A creative teacher will undoubtedly include other pieces of equipment in his program. For the most part major ideas or themes for work are suggested to give the teacher a springboard for planning lessons.

The suggestions for ball-handling activities are stated in a manner which includes both method and content and follows the pattern of work suggested for activities with small apparatus. Lead questions are given which would necessarily be expanded in the lesson on the basis of the children's answers and performance. The suggestions should serve as an example for the teacher to follow in implementing other activities.

Ball handling skills

PROBLEMS AND CHALLENGES FOR THROWING AND CATCHING:
1. Throw the ball to yourself. How many different ways can you throw it to yourself?

2. How straight can you throw the ball over your head?
3. How high can you throw the ball and still catch it? How did you make it go higher? Where should you be standing in order to catch the ball easily when it comes down?
4. Starting in a sitting position, throw the ball up and catch it while you are standing.
5. How do you catch the ball most easily? With arms bent or arms straight? Do you bring the ball in toward your body?
6. At how many different levels can you catch the ball?
7. Can you stoop down to catch it and jump up and throw it while you are still in the air?
8. Can you throw the ball up in the air, take four steps, and catch it?
9. How many times can you throw the ball against the wall and catch it before you miss it?
10. Step back farther from the wall and throw. Do you have to throw harder so it comes back to you? How did you do this? Which direction was your body facing when you threw? If you twisted away from the wall as you brought the ball back, then twisted toward the wall as you threw the ball, did the ball go farther?
11. Move back. Throw again. This time try taking a step forward as you release the ball. Does this help the ball go faster or farther?
12. Pick a spot on the wall. When you throw this time, make your arm follow the ball and point to the spot. Did your ball hit that spot? How many times can you hit your target?
13. Can you throw with your left hand?
14. Who can run and throw and catch at the same time without slowing down?
15. With a partner, count the number of levels at which each can throw and catch the ball. Where do you look when you throw to your partner?
16. Throw and catch the ball with a partner while you are both running. Can you trade places without stopping the ball-throwing?
17. Can you bounce the ball back and forth to a partner while you are both running?

SELF-TESTING ACTIVITIES FOR THROWING AND CATCHING:
1. Throw the ball against the wall and catch it at increasingly wider distances. The general throwing pattern may be varied.
2. Throw at a stationary target on the wall or into a box, barrel, or basket.
3. Throw through a large hoop suspended from the ceiling.
4. Throw and catch the ball off the the wall for 20 seconds. (Similar to wall pass test, page 421.)
5. Throw the ball over a rope, a bar, or a net; run under and catch it on the other side.

6. Throw to a moving person. Specify that the ball must reach the runner as he reaches a certain mark on the floor.
7. Set up a maze which involves going under, over, and around objects in the interim between throwing the ball into the air and catching it.

PROBLEMS AND CHALLENGES FOR BOUNCING AND DRIBBLING:
  1. How many times can you bounce the ball in succession?
  2. Which way can you bounce it the most times before losing control of it—by catching it every time or by pushing it down each time with your fingers? Why?
  3. How do you use your wrist when you bounce the ball? Is it stiff or does it bounce with the ball? Which way can you bounce the ball the fastest?
  4. Can you bounce the ball best with your right hand? Left hand? Both hands? Can you switch from right to left without losing control of the ball?
  5. Who can bounce the ball once and turn around before catching it again? Who can turn around twice?
  6. How low can you bounce the ball? How high can you bounce it? Who can bounce it low, then high, then low, etc.? Which way do you have the best control? Why?
  7. At how many different levels can you be while bouncing the ball? Who can sit on the floor while bouncing the ball? Who can be on his stomach? On his back? Can you get up while still bouncing it?
  8. Can you move forward while bouncing the ball? How do you make the ball go forward? We call this dribbling.
  9. Who can skip forward while dribbling the ball? In a circle?
 10. Staying in your own space, how many different directions can you dribble the ball?
 11. When you move in different directions and dribble, where do you look or focus your eyes?
 12. Try to "write" your initials on the floor with the ball by dribbling in the shape of letters rather than in a straight line.

SELF-TESTING ACTIVITIES FOR BOUNCING AND DRIBBLING:
 1. Count the number of continuous bounces in fifteen seconds. Alternate hands and vary the levels for this. Length of time may be changed.
 2. Bounce with rhythm of music.
 3. Dribble with rhythm of music.
 4. Move while dribbling, and change directions each time the whistle sounds.
 5. Dribble through a maze made of Indian clubs. Dribble through the maze for time.
 6. Dribble through a series of hoops.
 7. Dribble through a maze which involves going under and over objects while dribbling.

Problems and challenges for kicking:
1. Kick the ball so it travels along the ground.
2. Can you kick the ball so it travels in the air? Did you kick it differently than you did when it traveled on the ground? How?
3. Kick the ball as far as you can.
4. Can you kick it even farther? What did you do differently? Did your arms help? What did your other leg do? What did your kicking leg do after it hit the ball?
5. Can you kick the ball very gently, first with one foot then the other? Can you touch it with either foot each time you take a step? Why not? Don't let it get away from you.
6. Can you kick the ball up in the air so you can catch it? What part of the foot did you use to kick it?

Self-testing activities for throwing and catching:
1. Place-kicking the ball for greater distances.
2. Place-kicking the ball at a target.
3. Kicking the ball over an obstacle.
4. Dribbling the ball in zigzag fashion through a maze of chairs or pins.
5. Time the maze dribble.

Problems and challenges for striking ball with hand:
1. Hit the ball with some part of your hands.
2. Hit it with another part of your hands.
3. Can you hit it overhand?
4. Can you hit it underhand?
5. Can you hit it very high against the wall? How high are your hands when you touch the ball? Does it help to bend your knees and stretch high as you hit it?
6. Can you hit the ball underhand with your fist?
7. How far from the wall can you get and still hit the wall? What helps you to hit it harder?
8. Hit the ball back and forth to a partner.

Self-testing activities for hitting ball with hand:
1. Draw lines on wall and floor and progressively move back and hit higher on the wall.
2. Count how many continuous hits can be made on the wall.
3. Count how many times couples can keep ball going between them.

Problems and challenges for hitting the ball with a paddle:
1. Can you drop the ball and then hit it against the wall? How did you swing the paddle? Try it another way? In which direction was the paddle facing?
2. Can you hit the ball as it rebounds from the wall? Which way were you facing? What did your legs do? What did your paddle do after it hit the ball?
3. Can you hit the ball high, low, straight ahead?

SELF-TESTING ACTIVITIES FOR HITTING THE BALL WITH PADDLE:
1. Count how many times the ball can be hit against the wall continuously.
2. Set up a large target area. Hit the ball into target.

Jumping ropes

Rope jumping contributes greatly to the development of leg muscles, endurance, and rhythmic coordination. Young girls particularly enjoy rope jumping, but boys normally do not choose it for one of their play activities. However, older boys and men do employ rope-jumping as a training and conditioning device. There are a great many rope-jumping activities which can be challenging to complete at any age. Generally, short ropes are used for jumping by individuals and longer ropes by several people with two needed to turn the ropes.

Individual activities with short ropes

Beginners have to learn to turn the rope as well as to jump correctly. The following means of teaching this activity is suggested. First, the student should practice turning the rope over his head (from back to front), letting the rope touch the ground in front of him. (Hands should be held out to sides and not over shoulders.) Then, the jumper should swing rope over head, let it touch ground, and jump over it with both feet. On the jump the heels are lifted first, then the push-off is from the toes. In landing the knees and ankles bend, the weight is taken on the balls of the feet first. With practice the pause between each jump can be eliminated, and jumping will be continuous. Once a child can swing the rope successfully, teach the double jump, a little jump for balance while the rope is overhead and a bigger jump over the rope as it touches the ground.
1. Jump while turning rope forward.
2. Jump while turning rope backward.
3. *Cross elbows:* cross arms at elbows and turn rope with hands far out at sides.
4. *Rock* one foot in front of the other. Hop on front foot, then on back foot and continue rocking motion—change feet and repeat.
5. *Heel, heel:* hop, placing alternate heels forward on ground.
6. *Feet together and apart:* alternate jumping with feet together and feet spread apart.
7. *Toe tap:* hop with free leg and ankle extended forward with little toe of forward foot tapping ground.
8. *Leg swing:* hop on one foot, swing the other foot forward.
9. *Toe tap in back:* hop on one foot, tapping in back with the toe of the free foot.

10. *Legs crossed:* jump on both feet with one ankle crossed over the other.
11. *Single hop:* hop on either right or left foot, other foot is raised and held high with knee bent.
12. *Skip:* skip in place and skip while traveling.
13. *Partners jump:* one turns rope, partner runs in and jumps with him.

OTHER USES FOR SHORT ROPES:
1. Holding ropes at both ends in one hand, swing the rope in various patterns around, over, and under the body.
2. Stretch and land, holding rope tautly between the two hands.
3. Use rope for jumping marker.
4. Lying on floor, use the positions of ropes as a basis for body shapes.
5. Jumping in time with music; develop creative rhythm patterns.

Activities with long rope

To teach beginners, have them first stand next to the rope and jump over it. Then swing the rope slightly from side to side and have them jump it each time it touches the ground. Increase the arc of the swinging rope. Then have them stand next to the rope, swing it overhead, and have them jump over it as it touches the ground on the other side of them. Jumping off both feet should be taught first, with emphasis on jumping on toes and landing on toes and balls of feet with knees slightly bent to absorb the jar. The double jump as the rope touches the ground should be taught next. To help children get the rhythm of the double jump, call "And jump, and jump," or "Jump, JUMP, jump, JUMP."

1. *Run in the front door:* Child runs in as the rope is turned toward him and is at its highest point, jumps, and runs out other side.
2. *Run in back door:* Child runs in as the rope is turned away from him.
3. a. Swing the rope over and toward the jumper and he runs through.
   b. Then two runners run through.
   c. Time it so that each turn of the rope a new couple runs through.
4. *Follow the leader:* Leader is selected, players follow leader doing whatever jump rope stunt he chooses to do. One who misses is out.
5. For groups of four—two swing the rope, the other two jump.
   a. Join hands, turn around.
   b. Skip around each other.
6. Jump to rhymes.
7. Bounce a ball while jumping.
8. While jumping, play catch with someone who is not jumping.
9. Two ropes with two partners, each turn the ropes in opposite direction (double dutch).
10. Two ropes, two sets of partners turning ropes so they cross in the center (egg beater).

11. *Pepper:* As a player jumps, the other players say "Salt, vinegar, mustard, pepper." On the word "pepper" the turners gradually turn the rope faster and faster until the jumper misses.

12. *Hot Pepper—H-O-T spells red hot pepper:* On word "pepper" turners turn rope faster and faster. Jumper jumps until he misses.

13. *High Water:* The turners swing the rope on a low arc while a player jumps over it each time it goes by. The rope is gradually raised higher and higher from the ground until the jumper misses.

In jump rope activities, verses or rhymes are used. The *italicized* word or syllable indicates when the jump should be made.

Teddy Bear:

Teddy Bear, *Teddy* Bear, *turn a-round* (jumper turns while jumping),
Teddy Bear, *Teddy* Bear, *touch* the *ground* (jumper touches the ground),
Teddy Bear, *Teddy* Bear, *show* your *shoe* (jumper sticks one foot out to side while jumping),
Teddy Bear, *Teddy* Bear, *please skiddoo* (jumper runs out).

Around I Go:

Oh *in* I run and *around* I go (run in, turn around),
Clap my *hands* and *nod* just *so* (clap hands, nod head up and down),
I *lift* my *knee* and *slap* my *shin* (lift knee, holding it up while jumping until shin is slapped),
When *I* go *out* let _____ come in (call name of next jumper and run out).

Candle Stick:

_____ be nimble and _____ be quick (substitute jumper's name),
_____ jump *over* the *candle* stick,
Oh *jump,* and *jump,* and *jump* so *high,*
But you'd *better* jump *out* or _____ will *cry* (name next jumper and run out, next jumper comes in, and verse begins again).

OTHER USES FOR LONG ROPES:

1. Long ropes can be held stationary between two people and used for leaping over, going under, or various combinations.

2. Lay two long ropes parallel on ground for long jump markers.

3. Elastic ropes can be held very firmly and at an even height where the whole class can be running over or going under at the same time. One rope can be held high, one low, and children must pass between.

Wands

Wands 36 inches long may be purchased, or broomsticks may be cut down to the required size. One-and-a-half-inch doweling may also be purchased in desired lengths. Bamboo poles and long broom handles may be used for some partner work.

1. In a sitting position grasp the wand with both hands. Put legs over it, now back again, and lower legs quietly to the floor. Extend legs over the wand without touching it.
2. Stand the wand upright in front of you. Turn around quickly and regrasp the wand before it falls to the floor.
3. Grasp the upright standing wand with one hand and twist around, ducking under your arm without letting go of wand.
4. Jump over the stick. (Hold it by yourself.)
5. Hold wand in two hands at waist level, put right foot between right hand and wand, bring wand over back, twisting so that left foot can be placed back over wand and it is returned to starting position without the hands ever leaving the wand.
6. Balance wand on open palm.
7. Lie on back, pass bent legs under wand (both at the same time), stretch the legs between wand and body, pass legs back under wand.
8. Hold wand in two hands at chest height, drop wand, bend knees and catch it coming to an erect position.
9. Set wand on floor, use it to jump over. Set a series of wands in a design on the floor, and jump over with two feet. Hop over.
10. Place a wand on two boxes or chairs:
    a. Jump over wand
    b. Crawl under wand
    c. Vary height of wand

PARTNER STUNTS:

1. Standing opposite partner, one person holds wand on floor vertically with fingertip. When wand is balanced, the person lets go of it and the partner tries to catch wand before it touches floor.
   a. Increase distance between partners.
   b. Each lets go of a wand at the same time, and then tries to catch his partner's.
2. *Wand wrestle:* Each holds onto one wand with an overhand grip, and tries to wrestle the stick away from his partner.
3. Face each other, hold one end of the wand in both hands; step over and turn under the stick until returned to starting position.
4. Face each other, hold wand in both hands at arms length, lean back, pull, and make circle with small sideward steps around circle.

IN GROUPS OF THREE:

1. Two hold wand between them, third jumps over wand.
2. Two hold wand between them, third uses wand as a horizontal bar.
3. Partners are facing each other with wands held between them. One is held down at thigh height, the other above head. Third person runs and jumps through "window" made by wands.

Long poles can be used also; partners hold the end of two poles. The two move the poles up and down, or in and out, in a pattern, and a third person jumps or hops over them. The dance Tininkling (Table 10-1) is a Filipíno dance in which this is done in a rhythmic fashion.

Hoops

Bicycle tires and automobile tires may be utilized for some of these activities, as well as regular wooden or metal hoops.
1. Roll the hoop straight forward, around in a circle, and backward.
2. Run faster alongside of the hoop.
3. Swing the hoop like a skipping rope, and jump through it each time it comes around.
4. Roll hoop, run and cross over in front of it, let it pass on other side and catch it.
5. Roll the hoop, and run through it. Try again, and again, and again. (This may be difficult depending on size of person and size of hoop.)
6. Twirl hoop around wrist, arm, neck, waist, ankle.
    a. Change direction of twirl.
    b. Twirl one hoop on wrist, one on leg.
7. Spin hoop around its vertical axis, run around it one or more times, and catch it before it stops spinning.
8. Place hoop on floor.
    a. Jump into it and out.
    b. Go around hoop stopping on signal to support weight on hands inside of hoop.
9. All hoops on floor arranged in pairs side by side. Run down line of hoops placing one foot in each hoop.

PARTNERS:
1. Each holds one side of a hoop, pulls and leans back, taking small quick steps around a circle.
2. Using only one hoop, throw it over head of partner (who also may assume a sitting position and lift legs for target). Vary distance from target.
3. One holds hoop vertical and off floor, while the other tries to jump through it.

Beanbags

Beanbags may be used much like small balls with young children. They can be grasped easily with the fingers and will not bounce or roll far away if missed or thrown at a target. Their use with older children is most valuable when working space is small.

1. Throw beanbag at various targets, up in the air, for distance.
2. Place beanbag on head and hop, run or jump trying to keep it in place.
   a. Vary movements.
   b. Vary position of beanbag from head to shoulder, knee, foot, etc.
3. Place beanbag on foot, kick it up, and catch it with hands.
   a. Try to catch it on head.
   b. Catch it on opposite foot.
4. Pass beanbag back and forth from one hand to another.
   a. Clap between passes.
   b. Turn between passes.

SUGGESTED PROGRESSION FOR AN ELEMENTARY SCHOOL GYMNASTICS PROGRAM

Kindergarten, grades one and two

FLOOR WORK:

A. Exploration of basic movement skills, emphasis on development of:
   1. Elements of strength, flexibility, agility, and balance
   2. Movements of curling, twisting, turning, rolling, and extension
   3. Fundamentals of jumping, landing, transferring weight, supporting weight on various parts of the body, and flight
B. Stunts: Imitative animal walks, curls, top, rocker, seal walk, lame dog, heel clap, mule kick, human ball, jumping jack, bouncing ball, sawing wood
C. Tumbling: Forward roll, rocking chair, egg roll, frog stand
D. Exploration of basic movement skills in relationship to small equipment
   1. Hoops, beanbags, wands
   2. Jumping ropes
      a. Short ropes: Turning, big jumps, little jumps, forward, backward, jump on both feet, alternate feet
      b. Long ropes: Turning, sequence of run in back door and in front door, jump a number of times and run out, jump on alternate feet, combine jumping and turning
   3. Balls
      a. Throwing with large balls and small balls. Using overhand pattern with small balls, rolling at target, throwing underhand vertically and horizontally for distance

  b. Catching thrown ball from self, from wall, and from partner
  c. Bouncing to self with control, to wall, and to a partner at various levels and in various combinations
  d. Striking with flat of hand and fist against wall, kicking to wall and to partner for distance and control

APPARATUS:
A. Exploration and free use of all pieces of apparatus available
B. Freestyle mounting and dismounting
C. Problems and tasks involved in going over, under, through, along, above, across (and various combinations of these) all pieces of apparatus
D. Routines
E. Good understanding and use of correct grip; understanding and use of landing techniques from high places

Grades three and four

FLOOR WORK:
A. Continued exploration of basic skills
  1. Emphasis on development of shoulder girdle strength, flexibility, and balance
  2. Refinement of movements of curling, twisting, turning, rolling, extension
  3. Routines involving movements in continuity and variations in jumping, landing, transferring weight, supporting weight on various parts of the body, and flight
B. Exercises and stunts
  1. General: Sit-ups, modified pushups, bobbing, running in place, jump and touch toes, jump and tuck, leg lifts, half squats, lunge, rocker, heel click, thread the needle, one-foot balance, corkscrew, wring the dishrag, chinese get up, leapfrog
  2. Combatives: Bulldozer, back to back, toe boxing, hand push, bottoms up
C. Tumbling: Tripod, headstand, handstand, forward roll, continuous roll, backward roll, three man mount, simple pyramids
D. Exploration of basic movement skills in relationship to small equipment
  1. Hoops, beanbags, wands
  2. Jumping ropes
    a. Short ropes: Turn and jump with elbows crossed; rock; feet together; feet apart; feet crossed; skip in place, travel and skip; swing rope holding ends in one hand and make patterns; jump with a partner; create original patterns

      b. Long ropes: partners jump, bounce ball and jump, pepper, jump the shot, helicopter, high water
3. Balls (using tennis balls, softballs, soccerballs, volleyballs, basketballs, footballs, and playground balls of all diameters)
      a. Throwing: For distance, for accuracy, at a moving target
      b. Catching: Ball thrown by partner from various distances and at various heights; grounders
      c. Bouncing: Continuous dribble with either hand
      d. Striking: Kick for accuracy, kick for distance, dribble for control, strike a volleyball with two-hand overhand pattern, serve a volleyball or 8-inch playground ball, bat a softball off a tee, bat a tennis ball against wall with paddle

APPARATUS:
A. Problems and tasks involved in going over, under, through, along, above, across (and various combinations of these) all pieces of apparatus
B. Routines
C. Specific stunts
    1. Balance beam (6-inch, 24-inch): Various locomotor patterns across beam, turns, balance stands, front rest
    2. Climbing rope: Bent arm hang, inverted hang (lay out), sitting hang, swing and drop, climbing
    3. Hanging bars:
      a. Bar at maximum reach: knee hang, passive hang, active hang, flexed arm hang
      b. Bar at low level: front rest, front rest somersault, skin the cat
    4. Vaulting box: Knee mount, dismounts, jump with quarter turn, straddle jump, tuck jump, fence vault

Grades five and six

FLOOR WORK:
A. Free exercises
    1. Various combinations of basic movement skills
    2. Use of stunts and stands in combinations for creative free exercise routines
B. Exercises and Stunts:
    1. General: Straddle chins, leg lifts, sit-ups, lunge forward, backward, shoulder twist, arm circles, trunk twist, pickup, grasshopper, coffee grinder, crab walk, leap frog, jump over foot, up-spring, knee scale, front scale, jump and jackknife, jump and straddle, jump and turn, arabesque, routines

 2. Combatives: Indian leg wrestle, rope pull, Indian club fight, pull-down
C. Tumbling: Handstand, shoulder balance, standing balance on thighs, horizontal stand, Eskimo roll, cartwheel, routines
D. Small equipment: Skills related to sports and games units
E. Apparatus:
 1. Horizontal bar: Chinning, hang and raise hips, double knee hang, single knee hang, pull over, routines
 2. Parallel bars:
 a. Under bars: Inverted hang (tuck, pike, layout), skin the cat, bird's nest
 b. Between bars: Straight arm support, support swing, hand walk, inside cross riding seat, outside cross riding seat, riding seat to seat quarter turn dismount, routines
 3. Climbing ropes: Climb using legs, climb using hands only, swing and drop over an obstacle, travel between ropes
 4. Vaulting box: Knee mount, courage dismount, squat vault, flank vault
 5. Balance beam:
 a. Mounts: Front rest, front rest to straddle seat, side seat
 b. Balances: Knee scale, front scale, routines
 c. Dismounts: Jump with quarter turn, jump with half turn, straddle jump

Grades seven and eight

A. Free exercise: Various combinations of basic movement skills, stunts, balances into free exercise routines
B. Exercises and stunts:
 1. General: Push-ups, sit-ups, trunk twister, grasshopper, arm circles, V sit, front scale, side scale, single leg circle, front break-fall, forward drop
 2. Combatives: Cock fight, elbow wrestle, rope pull
C. Tumbling: Forearm balance, knee shoulder balance, angel balance, sitting balance, pyramids, backward roll with extension, roundoff, routines
D. Small Equipment: Skills related to specific uses in sports and games units
E. Apparatus:
 1. Horizontal bar: Chinning, one knee mount, single knee circle.
 2. Vaulting box: flank vault, rear vault, straddle vault
 3. Parallel bars: Back foot leaning rest, front foot leaning rest, straddle travel, rear vault dismount, front vault dismount, routines

4. Balance beam:
   a. Mounts: Straddle seat, side mount, side seat, one knee (at end of beam)
   b. Balances: V sit, side scale, forward roll, shoulder stand, routines
5. Climbing ropes: Climb, swing over an obstacle

SUGGESTED REFERENCES FOR FURTHER STUDY

Baley, James, *Gymnastics in the Schools* (Boston, Allyn and Bacon, 1965).

Bilbrough, A., and P. Jones, *Physical Education in the Primary School* (London, University of London Press, 1963).

Diem, Liselott, *Who Can* (Frankfort, Germany. Wm. Lippert, 1957). Available from George Williams College, Chicago.

Edmundson, Joseph, and Jack Garstang, *Activities on Physical Education Apparatus* (London, Oldbourne, 1962).

Fisher, Hugo, and Dean Shawhold, *Individual and Dual Stunts* (Minneapolis, Burgess, 1950).

Johnson, Barry L., *A Beginner's Book of Gymnastics* (New York, Appleton-Century-Crofts, 1966).

Mosston, Muska, *Developmental Movement* (Columbus, Ohio, Merrill, 1965).

Provaznik, Marie, and Norma B. Zabka, *Gymnastic Activities with Hand Apparatus for Boys and Girls* (Minneapolis, Burgess, 1965).

Willee, A. W., *Small Apparatus for Primary School Physical Education* (Melbourne, University Press, 1955).

INDEX TO
SPECIFIC MOVEMENT
EXPERIENCES

DANCE

GAMES AND SPORTS

GYMNASTICS

INDEX